P9-DHH-109

PRAISE FOR ALISTAIR HORNE AND *La Belle France*

"How much happier life would be if one could read books as riveting as Alistair Horne's . . . every week of the year. Horne has a masterful way of infusing grand historical themes with rich narrative detail."
—Francine du Plessix Gray

"Horne [is] one of the most graceful and satisfying of historians."
—*Milwaukee Journal Sentinel* .

"The writing is sharp, the pace terrific and hardly a page turns without leaving a memorable detail or telling phrase to savour. Horne in top form is not to be missed. A full-throated wonderfully readable chronicle."
—*The Independent* (London)

"A fluid, graceful, deliberate prose stylist. . . . Horne's purpose is not to be encyclopedic but to paint a portrait, and this he does surpassingly well." —*The Washington Post Book World*

"This is the history of France one has always wanted—erudite, affectionate, vastly entertaining and carried along with Tolstoyan sweep as all the characters leap to life." —*The Daily Telegraph* (London)

"Horne [possesses] broad erudition and [an] intense feel for French history." —*The Washington Times*

ALISTAIR HORNE

# La Belle France

Alistair Horne is the author of eighteen previous books, including *A Savage War of Peace: Algeria 1954–1962*, *The Price of Glory: Verdun 1916*, *How Far from Austerlitz?: Napoleon 1805–1815*, and the official biography of British prime minister Harold Macmillan. He is a fellow at St. Anthony's College, Oxford, and lives in Oxfordshire. He was awarded the French Légion d'Honneur in 1993 and received a knighthood in 2003 for his work on French history.

# La Belle France

# La Belle France

## A SHORT HISTORY

# ALISTAIR HORNE

VINTAGE BOOKS

*A Division of Random House, Inc.*

*New York*

FIRST VINTAGE BOOKS EDITION, JUNE 2006

*Copyright © 2004 by Alistair Horne*

All rights reserved. Published in the United States by Vintage Books,
a division of Random House, Inc., New York. Originally published in Great
Britain under the title *Friend or Foe* by Weidenfeld and Nicolson, London,
in 2004. Subsequently published in hardcover in the United States by
Alfred A. Knopf, a division of Random House, Inc., New York, in 2005.

Vintage and colophon are registered trademarks of Random House, Inc.

The author and publishers are indebted to the Bridgeman Art Library
for the majority of the illustrations.

The Library of Congress has cataloged the Knopf edition as follows:
Horne, Alistair.
[Friend or foe]
La belle France / Alistair Horne. —1st ed.
p. cm.
Originally published under the title: Friend or Foe : An Anglo-Saxon
History of France.
London : Weidenfeld & Nicolson, 2004.
Includes bibliographical references and index.
1. France—History. I. Title.
DC38.H67 2005
944—dc22
2004042329

**Vintage ISBN-10: 1-4000-3487-6**
**Vintage ISBN-13: 978-1-4000-3487-1**

*Author photograph © Jerry Bauer*
*Book design by Virginia Tan*

www.vintagebooks.com

Printed in the United States of America
10   9   8

*For Bobbie Richards—without whose unstinting support,
over many years, nothing would ever be written*

# CONTENTS

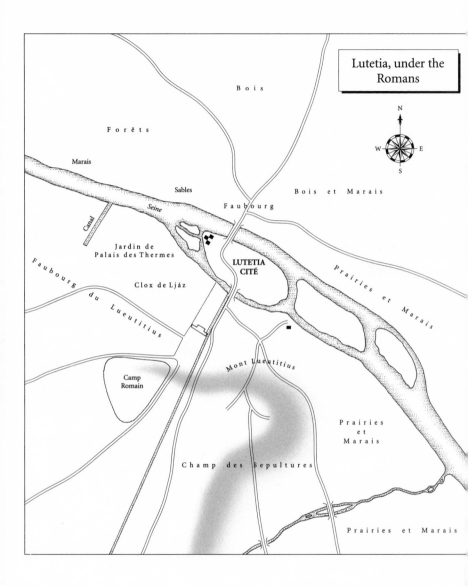

Lutetia, under the
Romans

N
W E
S

Bois

Forêts

Marais

Bois et Marais

Sables

Seine

Faubourg

Canal

Jardin de
Palais des Thermes

LUTETIA
CITÉ

Prairies et Marais

Clox de Ljáz

Faubourg du Lueutitius

Mont Lueutitius

Camp
Romain

Prairies
et
Marais

Champ des Sepultures

Prairies et Marais

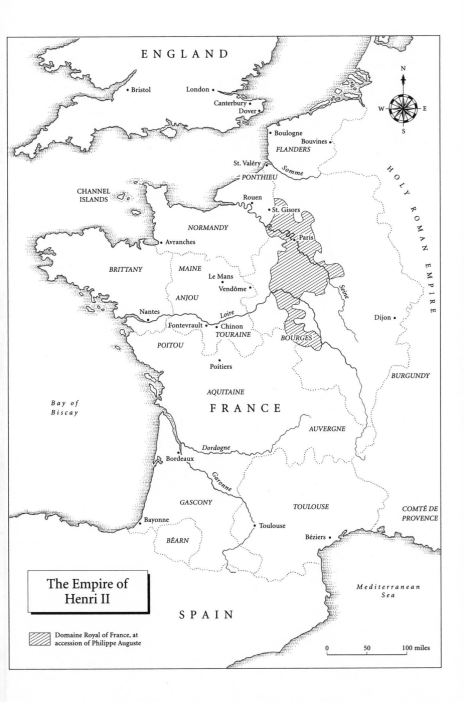

# The Empire of Henri II

N Domaine Royal of France, at accession of Philippe Auguste

0    50    100 miles

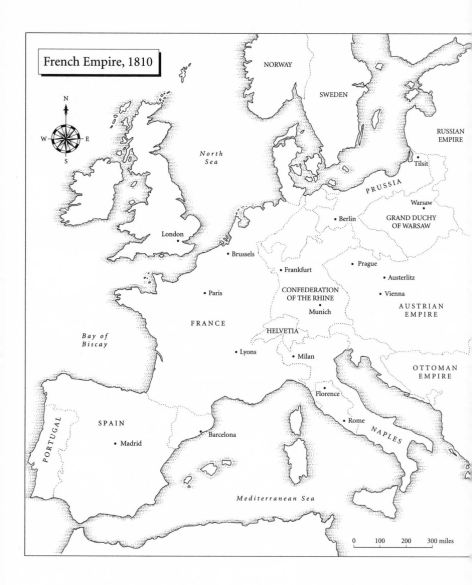

French Empire, 1810

NORWAY

SWEDEN

RUSSIAN
EMPIRE

*North
Sea*

Tilsit

PRUSSIA

Warsaw

• Berlin    GRAND DUCHY
OF WARSAW

London •

• Brussels

• Prague

• Frankfurt

• Austerlitz

CONFEDERATION
OF THE RHINE    • Vienna

• Paris    •
Munich    AUSTRIAN
EMPIRE

FRANCE    HELVETIA

*Bay of
Biscay*    • Lyons

• Milan    OTTOMAN
EMPIRE

• Florence

SPAIN    • Rome    NAPLES

• Barcelona

PORTUGAL    • Madrid

*Mediterranean Sea*

0    100    200    300 miles

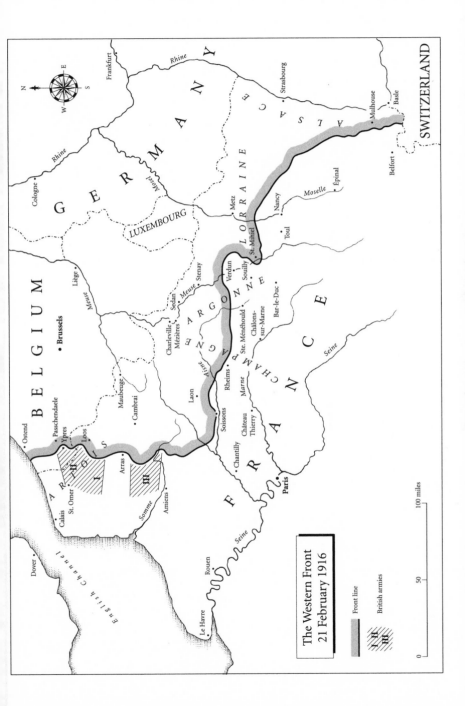

The Western Front
21 February 1916

Front line

British armies

# ACKNOWLEDGEMENTS

THIS JOURNEY through two thousand years of French history represents, for me, the culmination of some four decades of a love affair with France, of study—and of enjoyment. In the first instance I owe an unquantifiable debt of gratitude to France herself, and to very many French people. In particular I would just like to repeat once again my thanks to all, in both Britain and France, who are listed in my recent sister work of *Seven Ages of Paris*. Without their continuing support I could never have persisted with the present work. In addition, I am especially beholden to Ash Green, and my publishers, Knopf, of New York, for their outstanding marketing success of *Seven Ages* in the US, and also to Macmillan, London, for kind permission to use sections of their edition of *Seven Ages*; and to them in addition as publisher of no less than eight of my titles on French history, over a period of more than forty years. On all of these (listed among the bibliography) I have been able to draw for the present work. As the great English historian Namier Lewis once acidly remarked: History doesn't repeat itself—only historians repeat each other. But we do try hard not to repeat ourselves too often. In this context, I am above all indebted to my editor at Weidenfeld & Nicolson, Ion Trewin, and his assistant editor, Anna Hervé—and, for his dedicated long hours of work in cutting, polishing and serving up a thoroughly messy MS, to Jon Jackson. A vast work was also done on collating and selecting from a whole museum-load of pictures by Tom Graves of Weidenfeld & Nicolson, and thanks to John Gilkes for his work on the maps. Much meticulous work was put in at proof stage by Ilsa Yardley and Chris Bessant. To all I remain deeply beholden.

I had the great good fortune to be able to persuade my old friend, Professor Douglas Johnson—one of the English-speaking world's most distinguished historians of France—to read through what I have written and check for howlers. At various stages in the work he gave me invaluable help and encouragement; as did (once more) that stalwart defender of the *langue française,* Maurice Druon, KBE, of the Académie Française. It goes without saying that any surviving solecisms, or repetitions, have to be the fault of the jaded author alone.

Once again, Janet Robjohn slaved uncomplainingly on research, filing and secretarial work; while Douglas Matthews coped nobly with a complicated index.

For help on contemporary cultural themes, I am beholden to Monsieur Olivier Chambard, Cultural Attaché in the French Embassy, London; and, lastly, I owe a special and most agreeable debt to France's much-loved ambassadorial team in London, Gérard and Virginie Erréra.

Finally, I cannot go without mentioning once again my old college at Cambridge, Jesus, for providing occasional solace and facilities for research at the University Library, far beyond the due of a Hon. Fellow—and, again, that willing and most long-suffering treasury, indispensable to all historians, the London Library.

# INTRODUCTION

E VER SINCE, back in the 1960s, I wrote the *Price of Glory* trilogy about Franco-German wars, I have been enticed by the dangerously ambitious project of attempting a full-scale History of that complex, sometimes exasperating, but always fascinating country—France. At last, the year 2004 provided a kind of launching pad. It was the hundredth anniversary of the signature of the Entente Cordiale, the Treaty which ended centuries of war and enmity between Britain and her neighbour. Friend or Foe? Over the centuries more often the latter than the former. (2004 also happened to be the bicentenary of the Coronation as Emperor of Britain's deadly enemy, Napoleon Bonaparte; he who came within several inches that same year of repeating the success of William the Conqueror, failing where a later despot, Adolf Hitler, also failed.)

The Entente Cordiale conveys rather different things in British and American history—and for France. For France it meant, quite simply, the certainty at last of an ally who would counter-balance the dread power of Kaiser Wilhelm II's vast and menacing Reich on her doorstep; and regain the lost provinces of Alsace-Lorraine so brutally torn from her thirty-three years previously. At terrible, unacceptable cost for France, it would bring victory in 1918, but predictable defeat in 1940.

For Britain the Entente, if it signified the end of all those centuries of conflict with France, it also meant inevitable involvement in a major European war, for the first time since 1815—and against a new enemy. (There are today, however, still a revisionist minority of British scholars who think that maybe the Entente was a thoroughly bad thing for Britain, and that somehow we should have kept out, and made friends with the Kaiser with his glaring eyes and aggressive moustaches, and hang-ups derived from that shrivelled arm.)

For the USA, the Entente, which was still to leave an unbalanced alliance not sufficiently powerful enough to defeat Germany by itself in 1914–17, would make inevitable involvement in two world wars, and (to date) a permanent departure from the exhortations of Washington's Farewell Address. So, inescapably, perceptions of French history and its message differ radically from one side of the Atlantic to the other.

While writing *Seven Ages of Paris,* I was constantly reminded of the unique centralism of Paris throughout the history of France. In Maurice Druon's generous preface [p. xiv], he remarks ". . . he offers us, in effect, a new history of France herself—a personalised history . . ." I am proud to think this might be so. In reading Druon's words, I too came to realise how impossible it is to write a history of Paris without it in some way being a history of France—and vice versa. And this new book is also, unashamedly a highly personalised, idiosyncratic view of France through the ages, written by a Briton, a *cher ennemi.*

I should perhaps explain the title. When I was researching my first book about France, *The Price of Glory: Verdun 1916,* in the early sixties, every morning the head of the *Service Historique de l'Armée* out at Vincennes, a splendid central-casting for a French Army officer of the epoch, [General] de Cossé-Brissac, would greet me with a warm handshake, and the words "*Mon cher ennemi!*" It echoed the sentiment of that sixteenth-century warrior-poet, Sir Philip Sidney

"That sweet enemy, France!"

and he explained this superlative oxymoron as follows: though we've been at war almost all our histories, we do really quite like you. In the context of the recent rift with France, the oxymoron may be somewhat less comprehensible to US readers. As one New York publisher remarked: "Americans today have some difficulty in seeing the adjective 'dear' in relation to those French people!" But, I repeat, this is, as *Seven Ages* was, a highly *idiosyncratic* book, written by a twentieth-century Briton, partially educated in the US of A.

This leads one to those different *perceptions* of French history in UK and USA. For the best part of a thousand years England was at war with France, with brief (and often rather artificial) intervals of peace in between. There was, for instance, the Peace of Amiens, 1802, which lasted three months. It dates back, obviously, to the Norman Conquest (though the French really couldn't be blamed, as the Normans of 1066 were not in effect French); it runs through the Hundred Years War (two of them), the wars of Louis XIV, and of Napoleon. Even in July 1940 Britain's killing of 1300 French sailors at Oran, out of the necessity of fighting Hitler, struck a terrible blow at the soul of France—and brought Churchill, that great Francophile, to tears in the Commons. The following year British troops were killing the French of Vichy in Syria.

Hence the 2003 rift over Iraq came perhaps as less of a shock to the British system than to the American. For America, there were the French-Indian wars of the 1750s; but they were long ago, peripheral, and fought against what was shortly to become a common foe—the British Redcoat. Then came Lafayette and Yorktown, the Louisiana Purchase and the Napoleonic Wars; in all of which France to America was a benevolent item. In the War of 1812, surely that most foolish of all conflicts, it was against Britain—not France—that Americans fought their sole engagement of the Napoleonic Wars. So 1904 signifies America's reluctant, but decisive involvement in two European wars. "Lafayette, we are here!"—was it France the doughboys of 1917 came to save? Then came the wild 1920s, with the proper slogan "good Americans die in Paris." In 1944, many did die on Omaha and Utah beaches (whence William once sailed to conquer England), to save France yet a second time over.

In such a reading of history the terrible shock to post-9/11 USA of the perceived "ingratitude" of 2003 becomes comprehensible. "Enemies," to some—but not very "dear." France, however, with her two thousand years of history behind her, goes on immortally, pursuing her own unique path—sometimes inspiring, sometimes infuriating, but *never* boring, to her friends and neighbours. Charles de Gaulle perhaps judged it well when he once wrote of the country, whose virtues and faults he often personified:

> In the classical French garden, no tree seeks to stifle the others by overshadowing them; the plants accommodate themselves to being geometrically arranged; the pond does not aspire to be a waterfall; the statues do not vie to obtrude themselves upon the admiring spectator. *A noble melancholy comes over us,** from time to time. Perhaps it comes from our feeling that each element, in isolation, might have been more radiantly brilliant. But that would be to the detriment of the whole; and the observer takes delight in the rule that impresses on the garden its magnificent harmony.

The pursuit of harmony, though by no means always attainable, is what France is about.

---

*Author's italics.

# La Belle France

# ONE

# Beginnings: Caesar to the Capetians

A barbarous country where the houses were gloomy,
the churches ugly and the customs revolting.

—*Anne of Kiev, 1051*

WHEN OCCUPIED VICHY's Admiral Darlan was assassinated by a young French zealot in Algiers in December 1942, Winston Churchill observed to the House of Commons—in exasperation moderated with great sympathy—that the "Good Lord in his infinite wisdom did not choose to make Frenchmen in the image of the English." Some, on both sides of the Channel, may shout "Bravo!" or "Hear Hear!" but the fact is incontrovertible. With even less likelihood of challenge, the same could be said of the two nations. Geography, as much as history, though hand in hand, is what creates a nation. Over the centuries, while England lay protected from the invader (often, indeed, from outside influence) by the Channel, the North Sea and the Atlantic, France had nothing to guard her from the "barbarian at the gates." As Guderian and Rommel proved in May 1940, not even her great but sleepy rivers like the Meuse, the Oise, the Somme and the Marne could prevent an invader from sweeping across the boundless flat plains of northern France to threaten her capital city, Paris—any more than the Vistula and the Niemen could preserve Poland, with a geography that was so similar. (And see what a deal history dealt to the Poles!) West of the Rhine, all through her history, France had no topographical boundaries on which she could rely.

Thus much of her first two millennia encompasses an eternal hunt for security, on the one hand through strengthening herself at home; on the other, by aggressively pursuing expansionism abroad—often under the slogan of *la gloire*. In the pursuit of security, opposing instincts of the libertarian versus the authoritarian would repeatedly vie against each other.

In the beginning, France consisted of little more than an embattled island in the middle of the River Seine, surrounded by bristling palisades, in what is now Paris's Île de la Cité. The Romans founded "Lutetia," as they called it, at a time when, as readers of *Asterix* know, Gaul was divided into three parts under Julius Caesar. (The word "Lutetia," romantic as it sounds, in fact derived from the Latin for "mud" —appropriately enough, as its long-suffering denizens would discover over many successive centuries.)

Fortunately, Emperor Julian (AD 358) found Lutetia, with its vineyards, figs and gentle climate, so thoroughly agreeable that he refused a summons to lead legions to the Middle East. Surprisingly, he even found the Seine "pleasant to drink, for it is very pure and agreeable to the eye." Already in Roman times Lutetia became prosperous and alluring enough for it to be worth assault, and burning, by marauders from across the Rhine. About the same time as Nero watched Rome burn, the whole of the wooden settlements on the left bank were razed by fire. The city contracted, the Parisians withdrawing, once again, into the highly defensible fastness of the Île de la Cité. One of the first of many Germanic invasions was seen off by Emperor Julian, after the Alamanni had come to within only twenty-five leagues away—roughly the same spot as their grey-clad kinsmen reached under the Kaiser in 1914. The prayers of Sainte Geneviève, patron saint of Paris, reputedly caused Attila the Hun to swing away from the city in 451, and over the ages intercessions to her were to be made to save Paris from latter-day Huns—with varying degrees of success.

Rome gave Paris her first revolutionary martyr, Saint Denis, decapitated at what became the "Mons Martyrum"—or Montmartre. The fields around his place of execution were said to have "displayed a wonderful fertility." Ever after, the Roman tradition would run like a vital chord all through French history, summoned up and referred back to at crucial moments. In his godlike splendour, the "Roi Soleil" tapped into it, content to see himself portrayed as Hercules on the Porte Saint-Martin. The Great Revolution and its heirs reinvented such artefacts as consuls and senators, tribunes and togas. Napoleon I had himself crowned Emperor, then emulated Trajan's Column to vaunt his victories over his foes at Austerlitz in the Place Vendôme; Napoleon III, also assuming the title of Emperor, reverently clad the statue of his great uncle atop it in a toga, and when things were going badly for him in 1869, went to seek inspiration at the Roman ruins of Lutetia.

Equally, the Seine was, and is, and always will be, Paris. From earliest days the navigable river and the north-south axis that intersected it at the Île de la Cité formed one of Europe's most important crossroads. The island itself constituted a natural fortress, all but unassailable. In marked contrast to the estuarial, shallow and narrow Thames, the Seine's waters were not too swift and were capable of carrying heavy loads, ideal for commerce in wine, wheat and timber. It enabled Paris to dominate trade in the north as Lyons on the Rhône did in the centre, and Bordeaux on the Garonne and Nantes on the Loire in the west— thus making Paris a natural commercial capital early in the Middle Ages; never to lose this primacy. Resting on the river like a great ship, Paris appropriately adopted the motto of *Fluctuat Nec Mergitur* ("She Floats But Does Not Sink"), retaining it as city burst far beyond its island bounds.

A DYNASTY OF FRANKISH RULERS, mostly yobbish louts whose name appropriately derived from the Latin word for "ferocious," now pushed in from the east and devastated the Gaul lands as they went. Once established in France, having moved to Paris from the temporary capital of Rheims they came to be known as the Merovingians.* Over two-and-a-half dark centuries they wrangled and split among themselves, beginning with the first Merovingian king, Clovis, who killed off most of his family; "after each murder," writes Maurice Druon,[1] with some acidity: "Clovis built a church." They were not gentle, or nice people, these Frankish forebears of the modern-day Parisian—especially the women, who were strong, dominating, often ferocious, and who lived to great ages. There was Queen Fredegonda (545–97), described as glowing "like the eye of a nocturnal carnivore," who had women burned alive on flimsy allegations of being responsible for the deaths of her children, and for whose fierce pleasures her lover, King Chilperic, had his first two wives murdered within the same week. Even after Fredegonda's death, her bitter rival, Brunhilda (543–613), now a venerable septuagenarian, was brutally put to death. Tortured for three days, her last descendants

---

*On account of their Frankish origins, Aldous Huxley once claimed the modern French to be "Germans that have gone partially Latin."

slain before her eyes, chroniclers have it that she was then hoisted onto a camel (possibly a somewhat rare spectacle in contemporary France) and paraded in front of her deriding army. Finally she was "tied, by one arm, one leg and her white hair, to the tail of an unbroken horse,"[2] allegedly along what is now the Rue des Petits-Champs, stronghold of bankers in the 2nd *arrondissement.*

During the ascendancy of these formidable early Frenchwomen, precursors of Reine Margot and Madame Defarge, convents were burned to the ground with their inmates inside, leaders assassinated in conjugal beds, children abducted and murdered, hands severed, eyes gouged, lovers defenestrated, and cunning poisons developed in the name of statecraft. Byzantium had nothing more deplorable to show than the Merovingians. But at least, under Clovis, the notion of Paris as a capital city first became accepted, from which—in the brief three last years of his grisly life—Clovis administered a kingdom even larger than modern France. His descendant, Dagobert, died of dysentery, aged only thirty-six, but his interment at Saint-Denis established the principle for the burial of subsequent kings of France. In a curiously progressive fashion, none of the Merovingian rulers was ever crowned, they were all elected.

The throne of France would have fallen into Muslim hands if, a hundred years later, the usurping strong-man and bastard, Charles Martel, had not halted the Saracens at Poitiers. As it was, the closing years of the century saw the last of the Merovingians and the arrival of Charlemagne, a rather less attractive character than his portraits and subsequent canonisation would suggest. He was more German than French (and looked it), and an absentee ruler who did little for France, or Paris; it has mystified many that a statue was erected to him in front of Notre-Dame. It was more for his greatness than his goodness: crowned Holy Roman Emperor on Christmas day in the year 800, Charlemagne fought forty-seven campaigns in as many years; he married four times (he divorced his first wife, and then three died—to be replaced by four concubines). He forbade his daughters to marry, preferring them to live at home and populate the court with bastards. Charlemagne's Carolingian dynasty would last another 200 years. His empire extended from the Pyrenees to the Elbe—but he ran it all from Aix-la-Chapelle (Aachen), rather than Paris.

THE GREAT EMPIRE was short-lived. Under Charlemagne's son, the first of eighteen named Louis (nicknamed "the Pious"), it was dismembered into seven parts. As the Carolingians wrangled, and all Europe sank into a kind of lethargy, in the ninth century a new and unknown warrior race emerged to the north—Norsemen, surging out of Scandinavia to invade the British Isles and Russia as far as Kiev, and even reaching Constantinople. In 843, Nantes was sacked, the bishop killed on the steps of his altar. Only two years later, 120 long-boats, terrifyingly decorated and with thirty pairs of oars, attacked Paris unexpectedly from upstream. Once again the population fled; the Norsemen departed, carrying off tons of booty—including the magnificent bronze roof of Saint-Germain-le-Doré. They appeared everywhere, like some terrible plague of locusts, even sailing up the Rhône to pillage Valence, and striking at Pisa in Italy. Defenceless Paris was sacked—and more churches lost their roofs—another five times over the next twenty years. How these dauntless seaborne marauders were able to strike, with such impunity and effect, so far inland remains something of a mystery. Meanwhile the useless Charles the Bald occupied himself by putting out the eyes of his son, suspected of plotting against him.

As in the time of Attila, Paris shrank back into the original twenty-five acres of the Île de la Cité. In 885, with Charlemagne's legacy disintegrating and the throne of France to all intents vacant, there came the first siege of Paris. Setting forth from England, a force of Norsemen captured Rouen and headed on up the Seine. Fourteen hundred boats, said to have "covered two leagues of the river" and bearing a formidable force of some 30,000 hirsute warriors, reached Paris. To have woken up and seen this terrifying array on the Seine must have been shattering for the Parisians. These Norsemen constituted a besieging force comparable only to the Prussians who were to invest the city almost exactly a thousand years later.

Led by a heroic Comte de Paris, Eudes, son of Robert the Strong, Paris refused to surrender—the first time that any city had resisted the terrible Norsemen. Eudes was to prove himself France's *homme fort,* but the siege lasted ten grim months. Natural forces even allied themselves with the attackers; on 6 February a flood swept away the Petit Pont, enabling the Norsemen to capture one of the *châtelet* fortresses. Next famine broke out. In despair, Eudes slipped out of the city and galloped to Germany to demand assistance from the Emperor, Charles the Fat. Charles set out unwillingly, but the size of his ponderous army moving down from Montmartre caused the fatigued Norsemen to hesitate. Dubious negotiations were entered into, in which the Parisians bribed the Norsemen with 700 livres of silver and a free passage of the Seine, both ways—encouraging them to carry the war upstream to Burgundy, and leave Paris in peace. It was a deal which, subjecting the unhappy Burgundians to the worst winter they had ever known, would lead to centuries of instinctive mistrust and hatred between the principality of Burgundy and France, culminating during the Hundred Years War in an alliance with the English.

As a result of his brave defiance towards the Norsemen, two years later Count Eudes found himself elected as king by the nobles in preference to a German princeling: just to pile chaos on chaos, for a while there were in fact two Kings of France of East and West—but in Paris it was Eudes who mattered. In 911, he bought off the Norsemen by giving them the duchy of Normandy. From then on their eyes were encouraged to turn northwards, with cheerful projects of conquering Saxon England.

NOW A GREAT-NEPHEW OF EUDES, Hugues Capet, saw off the Germanic Emperor Otto II on the slopes of Montmartre (close to where Saint Denis was separated from his head). In 987, in the city of Senlis, he was elected king by assembled French barons, and a month later Capet was crowned in Rheims Cathedral, thereby establishing a fresh precedent, like Dagobert's interment at Saint-Denis. He ruled for only nine years (987–96), but for the first time Paris had a French, not Frankish, king and a new French dynasty. Forced to give up title to Lorraine and concede the already historic fortress of Verdun to the Germans, however, the domain of France inherited by Hugues Capet looked like a tiny kernel surrounded by a mass of hostile pulp comprising Burgundy, Flanders, Normandy, Aquitaine and Lorraine. As the energetic Norsemen, now Normans, swarmed across the English Channel and began to reorganise the sleepy and backward Saxon England they had conquered, Capetian France remained poor, its vassals powerful, its rulers in thrall to the Church and inhibited by the lack of a common language. But by 1328, when the Capetian dynasty had run its course, the kingdom of France had become the most united and potent in western Europe.*

---

*It is also an interesting mathematical fact, perhaps illustrative of just how dark the preceding centuries had been, that Capet, founder of the first true French dynasty, stands chronologically almost exactly midway between Julius Caesar and de Gaulle.

THERE ARE NO PORTRAITS of Hugues Capet (although the surname came as a sobriquet because of the abbeys whose "cappa" he wore). He died young of smallpox, but he had arranged a dynastic marriage for his eldest son, Robert, and assured his succession as *rex designatus*. The only text attributed to him was his coronation oath:

> I, who am about to become king of the Franks, by divine favour, on this day of my coronation, in the presence of God and the saints, . . . promise to distribute justice to the people who are in my care, according to their rights.

It was to be repeated by all his successors down to the revolution. Although he seems to have been a timid and anomalous character, herein lies Hugues Capet's claim to fame; from him would be descended nearly forty kings who would succeed each other over a period of more than 800 years.

Hugues' heir was accorded the nickname of "Robert the Pious" (996–1031), which he did little enough to earn. Almost his first act was to repudiate the wife his father had found him, Rosala of Italy, while hanging on to her dowry. He promptly contracted a love-match with an older woman, his widowed cousin Berthe of Burgundy, who already had five children. He was excommunicated. After resisting papal pressure for five years, Robert capitulated. He dismissed the queen he loved, and married Constance of Provence—a terrible shrew who punished him by filling his days with nagging tantrums, and his court with plotters, thieves and debauchees from the Midi. Later Robert tried, unsuccessfully, to re-wed his true love, Berthe. To ingratiate himself with a disapproving Pope, he burned alive fourteen "heretics" in Orléans, drawn "from among the best priests and leading laymen of that town"— thereby establishing himself as a precursor of the Inquisition. Robert the Pious also set about rebuilding the Paris abbeys of Saint-Germain-des-Prés and Saint-Germain-l'Auxerrois, which had lain in ruins ever since the Norse raids. In an otherwise unspectacular reign of thirty-five years, he became the first ruler in centuries to embark seriously upon the reconstruction of Paris. But much of France as Robert the Pious left it must have been in a parlous state. When his successor Henri I (1031–60) married Anne of Kiev from supposedly backward Russia in 1051, she was not impressed by her husband's domain; nose in the air, she wrote to her father, Yaroslav the Great, complaining that it was "a barbarous country where the houses were gloomy, the churches ugly and the customs revolting."[3]

Philippe I (1060–1108) was a venal glutton who—following in the steps of his grandfather—was excommunicated following a doubly adulterous marriage; but he never let it worry him. His reign was uneventful at home, but eventful abroad. After conquering England, William of Normandy turned towards Paris. Killed in front of Mantes in 1087, the Conqueror's death may have been a cause of relief for the fun-loving Philippe; but the Anglo-Norman menace had been born which was to shake France for another seven centuries, and more.

Under the first four, rather undistinguished, Capetian kings, the realm of France expanded to almost double its size. Then, in 1108, there arrived the first of the significant rulers of the dynasty, Louis VI, "le Gros."

THE THREE DECADES spanned by Louis VI's reign (1108–37) stake out an important turning point, not just for France, but for the cultural history of the West as a whole. It was a true window of bright light in the Middle Ages, over a century before Giotto and Dante were even thought of. In France its landmarks and symbols were the soaring Gothic glories of Chartres, Sens, Laon, Bourges, Notre-Dame and Saint-Denis cathedrals, not to mention Canterbury (whose technical secrets were imported by William of Sens in 1174). Inspired by Eastern influences brought home by the early Crusaders, it was in France (and especially in the nuclear Île de France) that the innovation of Gothic religious architecture found its most fertile ground. Close to the heart of it was a most remarkable Frenchman—Abbot Suger of Saint-Denis born in 1081.

"The Twelfth-Century Renaissance," which took root in the reign of Louis VI, would thrive in France under the later reigns of Louis VII and Philippe-Auguste. Louis VI himself was a remarkable figure about whom we know more through Abbé Suger, than we know about his duller Capetian predecessors. Abbot of Saint-Denis for thirty years (1122–51) until his death, Suger was the first in a long line of able and enlightened ministers to the kings of France that was to produce statesmen like Henri IV's Sully, Louis XIII's Richelieu and Louis XIV's Colbert. He was a diplomat, statesman and businessman, outstanding for his architectural good taste, as well as being a churchman who built (or, rather, rebuilt) the magnificent basilica of Saint-Denis. But Suger was also an author, taking it upon himself to write a chronicle of his sovereign.

OUT OF SUGER's *Life of Louis VI* emerges an energetic, conscientious and chivalrous ruler. He was the first of the dynasty not to be crowned during his father's lifetime. As a young man, Suger records him as being "an incomparable athlete and an eminent gladiator" who, before he became "le Gros" had merited the nicknames of "the Warrior" and "the Alert." As his definitive nickname suggests, he was a huge eater and drinker (it was impossible to lift the King into his saddle towards the end of his life as a result of obesity and illness), but he was also profoundly religious. Beneath his gross exterior he was a sensitive man, capable of forgiving his multiplicity of enemies (these included his stepmother, Bertrade, who even tried to have him poisoned).

In the first of the long-running contests against the new foe, the Norman English, Louis challenged England's Henry I to a duel on a bridge in front of both armies. Prudently, Henry refused. Later, in 1124, the French and their allies under Louis fought and beat a coalition of Henry I of England and his namesake (and son-in-law) the Holy Roman Emperor, at Rheims. Even more important for France was his successful struggle against the feudal lords, which lasted through most of his reign.

Late in life, Louis le Gros married an admirable and extremely plain woman who bore him nine children, thus assuring the future of the dynasty. Skilfully he arranged—just before his death—the marriage of his infant son, Louis, to Eleanor of Aquitaine. It was to be an unhappy alliance that stored up trouble, but it achieved a bloodless reunification with the great duchy to the south-west—and a spell of tranquillity for the still small country that was France.

THE ABBOT SUGER, whose power survived the death of the King, was to prove of considerably greater historical importance than either of the monarchs he served. Having travelled four times to Rome, he "knew about everything and had a hand in everything." He was blessed with a prodigious memory, being able to recite twenty or thirty lines of profane Horace at the drop of a hat. He was incorruptible, and had a very clear-cut view of how a king should behave. He should have "long hands," thought Suger, and it was "shameful for a king to transgress the law, because king and law draw their authority from the same source."[4]

Suger could be described as an early peace-monger, espousing the spirit of compromise and conciliation. Nevertheless, and for all his love of beautiful things, he could also find beauty in war; provided that it was fought on behalf of his master—and was therefore a *just* war. With considerably less than distress, indeed some relish, he describes Louis' knights "piously cutting up the impious [i.e., the English enemy] by mutilating their members (that is, blinding and castrating them) and disembowelling the others with delight [*dulcissime/avec délices*]." At young Louis' siege of La Roche Guyon in 1109, both living and dead were hurled out of the castle windows onto lance-points below; while the heart of the enemy leader, "swollen with deceit and iniquity," was paraded on a stake, and mutilated bodies floated down the Seine on hurdles as a warning to the King's foes in downstream Normandy.

In this Suger was also no more than a man of his times, although the Dark Ages and the grimly Germanic Carolingian era had certainly passed. The early Crusades had opened new trade routes as well as new mental horizons, with an awareness—*inter alia*—of Arab culture and contributions to mathematics and philosophy. This was further enhanced by the great pilgrimages to Santiago de Compostela of the Romanesque world. There were the tender sprouts of a new humanism: by comparison with what had passed, social order and the supply of food and clothing seemed assured, so that the best minds could now be liberated for speculative and productive thought. The word "dialectic," meaning a true exchange of ideas, began to appear in the vocabulary of the teaching fraternity. Social structures were evolving from feudalism towards the organisation of the guild, so that now the genius of man the engineer as well as man the aesthete could make the soaring glories of Gothic realisable.*

Between the Dark Ages and the purging of heresy in the later Middle Ages, the best and brightest arbiters of Church thought had little difficulty in squaring love of God with love of worldly beauty. As Umberto Eco points out in a slender but excellent book, to view it as "puritanical, in the sense of rejecting the sensuous world, ignores the documentation of the period and shows a basic misunderstanding of the medieval mentality."[5] In Suger's delight in the sensous world, Eco rightly sees a "mystical *joie de vivre*," an essential ingenuous innocence not yet corrupted by the sins of monastic simony and greed.

---

*Perhaps also indicative of the relative lack of stress of the epoch is the longevity of men like Suger himself, and three women of such different backgrounds as Queen Eleanor of Aquitaine (eighty-two), Hildegard of Bingen (eighty-one) and Héloïse (sixty-three) (d. 1165), all far in excess of the average life-span of the Middle Ages as a whole.

Nevertheless, such an outlook would draw forth angry invective from the ascetic Saint Bernard of Clairvaux: "for us all bodily delights are nothing but dung," while of the new Gothic church ornamentation, he would question with caustic wit:

> why do the studious monks have to face such ridiculous monstrosities? . . . this elegant deformity? Those loutish apes? The savage lions? The monstrous centaurs? The half-men? The spotted tigers? The soldiers fighting? . . . one could spend the whole day marvelling at one such representation rather than in meditating on the law of God . . . why at least are we not angry at the expense?[6]

To Suger, however, there was yet another pragmatic excuse for church embellishment; it was that if the common people (that is, the illiterate) could not grasp the Scriptures, then it could best be taught them through the medium of pictures—or stories carved in stone. Here was a big divergence between medieval Christianity and the fundamental Muslim approach, which allowed of no representation of the human figure. It was all part of a Christian campaign to educate by appealing to the public's "delight in image and allegory," with the moral and the aesthetic being integrated in a visual and straightforward form of appeal.

Above all, there was Paris' own mighty Notre-Dame. Begun in 1163 under the genius of Maurice de Sully—who started life (in 1120) as the son of a peasant from the Loire—construction work in the narrow streets of medieval Paris proved an immense undertaking.* In the early Middle Ages, a church was likened to a ship steering for harbour, and what could be more appropriate than Notre-Dame's extraordinarily dominant position on the Seine, athwart the stern of the Île de la Cité— and so appropriate to the city's coat of arms, *Fluctuat Nec Mergitur*? The Pope blessed the foundation stone of Notre-Dame, while Thomas à Becket was among those to watch its building.

Four centuries later Henri IV would come on his knees to the cathedral to affirm his belief that Paris was "worth a mass"; earlier, in the latter stages of the Hundred Years' War, England's ten-year-old Henry VI

---

*Originally access from the *parvis* of Notre-Dame was via a flight of thirteen steps, but, with the accumulated detritus of the ensuing ages, the level of the whole Île de la Cité has been raised up to four metres from the earliest days of Lutetia so that you now enter on the same level. Fascinating to visit is the recently created museum beneath the actual *parvis,* which shows the ancient foundations of the Île back to Roman days.

would, provocatively, be crowned King of France before its altar; Mary Queen of Scots would be married there to Catherine de Medici's short-lived son, François II; Louis XIV would hang out the flags of his military victories in the nave, victories that would be paid for in the revolution. Then the revolutionaries of 1789 in their wild orgy of republicanism, not content with the vandalising of the great portico and ritual decapitation of all sovereigns depicted, threatened to raze it, or put it up for private sale. Fortunately they settled for transmuting the empty, desecrated building into a Temple to Reason in a bizarrely blasphemous ceremony headed by a heavily made-up ballerina from the Opéra, who was carried in state as the "Goddess of Reason." Even the bells were melted down for cannon; only the mighty 13-ton "Jacqueline" survived—to be rung only on special days.

Napoleon Bonaparte restored the cathedral so that he could be crowned Emperor there, and de Gaulle would celebrate Paris' liberation from the Nazi occupation with a *Te Deum* in Notre-Dame in 1944. Most of what one sees today, however, at Notre-Dame is the legacy of the renowned nineteenth-century restorer—or vandal, depending on the point of view—Viollet-le-Duc, creator of the walled city of Carcassonne that is so romantically exciting when seen from a distance, so phoney an empty stage-set close up.

If Notre-Dame is a prime historical symbol for France, it was Suger and his king in the twelfth century who brought the new vitality which created it, and allowed the capital to grow like its King—fat and prosperous. There grew up a whole district of Paris dedicated to commerce and provisions with street names like the Rue de la Grande Boucherie, Rue de la Poulaillerie, Rue Pied de Boeuf, etc. Along the Quai de Grève, the strand of sand that afforded a landing-stage and which was later to assume sinister associations in Parisian history as a place of public execution and horrendous torture, a major port grew up. For the next eight centuries, until de Gaulle relocated Les Halles, this area—based on the foundations of an old Roman market—was to be the city's main source of foodstuffs. Now France had both physical and spiritual nourishment.

# T W O

# A Golden Age:
# Abelard to Philippe-Auguste

'Tis sure the hardest science to forget!
How shall I lose the sin, yet keep the sense,
And love th' offender, yet detest th' offence?

—Eloisa to Abelard, *Alexander Pope*

IN THIS EARLY GOLDEN AGE of France there was played out one of history's great love stories, an intense personal tragedy—from which there emerged a new word in the French vocabulary, *Abélardiser*—the story of Héloïse and Abelard. Both were true products of the twelfth century; both, had they lived a century later, would in all probability have ended at the stake. Born around 1079, Abelard is one of those rare philosophers remembered by posterity, mistakenly, more for his life than for his thinking. The poignancy of his love affair with the incomparable Héloïse, handed down through the generations from Jean de Meung's *Roman de la Rose* to Diana Rigg (nude on stage for the first time in British theatre history) tends to obscure the fact that he was the greatest teacher of his age—as well as the inspiration and founder of the university that became the Sorbonne.

Son of a minor noble and from near Nantes, Abelard faced being disinherited by his knight father so as to pursue the studious life, but wandered from one school to another until he was drawn to the Cathedral School of Paris by the fame of the much-respected William of Champeaux (1070–1122).* Here he shocked his fellows by presuming to question the principles of his teacher. This scholarly arrogance predicated a controversial career. Finally, in 1117, he came to lodge in the house of one Canon Fulbert, as tutor to Fulbert's teenage niece, Héloïse—she aged seventeen, he now thirty-nine.

The spiral of passion and tragedy began: Abelard, handsome, brilliant and articulate, versed in poetry and music, and self-assured to excess, must surely have been a risky choice as a tutor. Today's received view is that, a quarrelsome wencher, he may have been guilty of rape, or at least of harassment. Héloïse (already a young woman of considerable learning, and who always comes across as by far the greater human being of the two) would certainly have been the first to refute it. But Abelard was not discreet, and—in his passion—neglected his students. Héloïse had a baby, given the egregious name of Astralabe.

Despite their marrying, her uncle Fulbert—outraged by this slight on his house, and possibly with a jealous passion for his niece—sought a hideous vengeance on Abelard. In the dark of night, treacherously he had Abelard castrated. The men responsible were subsequently blinded in punishment—in many ways a worse fate, in that the blind, receiving no charity, would usually be condemned to a protracted death by starvation.

HÉLOÏSE, DISTRAUGHT, TOOK THE VEIL. Bitterly, but futilely, in her letters she would incessantly lament: "I am still young and full of life; I love you more than ever and suffer bitterly from living a life for which I have no vocation . . ." Abelard, in the fury of his impotent misery, would reply, with brutality: "let us not call it love but concupiscence. In you I cloyed a wretched appetite, which was all I really loved."

Her penance was done, clearly, for the sake of Abelard—not for God; "People who call me chaste do not know what a hypocrite I am."[1] Nevertheless, as Abbess she was accorded the highest respect, and papal protection; while her religious house, the Paraclete, grew to become one of the most distinguished in France.

FOREVER TORMENTED by what he had suffered, Abelard thrashed around in his misery, like John Donne, *mutatis mutandis,* abandoning

---

*The *History of My Calamities,* as he described it (written in Latin), remains one of the great works of literature—as do the *Letters of Abelard and Heloise* (tr. B. Radice, 1974).

the pleasures of the flesh that had been forcibly removed from him for the total glorification of God (which he pressed upon a reluctant Héloïse). In contrast to Héloïse, Abelard at once accepted, unreservedly, his disaster as due punishment requiring total expiation. Through impotence Abelard flowered mightily in intellectual output—albeit in unorthodox thinking. He began by becoming a monk at Saint-Denis, though he swiftly fell into disfavour with the all-powerful Abbot Suger; as abbot in Brittany, the coarse and ungodly bawdiness of the monks made him miserable. In 1121, he was condemned for heresy for his *Theologia.* Around 1133, he returned to Paris as master at Mont Sainte-Geneviève. It was here that he began the most brilliant phase of his life as a teacher. Seven years later he was again accused of heresy by Saint Bernard of Clairvaux,* and he died at Saint-Marcel while on his way to make a personal appeal in Rome to Pope Innocent II. During his last years, Abelard would—supposedly—sit in reverie every day with his eyes turned in the direction of the Paraclete, and Héloïse.

After "forty years of the severest penance, with little faith in its religious efficacy," Héloïse died at the age of sixty-three, outliving Abelard by two decades.

The two were laid in the same coffin; legend has it that, as Abelard's tomb was opened, he raised his arms to receive her and closed them fast about her. There they remained together for over two centuries, until their remains were transferred and separated once more—by a prudish nun.

In 1792, revolutionary busybodies reinterred them in a single coffin, but with a lead partition between them. Finally, in a romantically inclined nineteenth-century France, the two lovers were reunited at fashionable Père Lachaise Cemetery under a Gothic canopy of stone, side by side, their hands raised in prayer.

ABELARD WAS LIVING in an era when Plato and Aristotle were just being rediscovered, and his intellectual fame rests on his introduction of logic and rationalism into theology, dispelling some of the mystical tenets that had held sway. By employing dialectics as a means to this end, Abelard's methods made him as controversial as the body of his

---

*Saint Bernard, like a Soviet inquisitor of the 1930s, led the prosecution, accusing Abelard of heading an international conspiracy, bent on destroying ecclesiastical authority. It has a modern ring about it.

thought, for it was unheard of for a teacher to encourage his students to argue with him: "by doubting we come to inquiry, and by inquiring we pursue the truth"[2] was his famous credo. It stood sharply at odds with the accepted norm of the times, as characterised in the credo of the Archbishop of Canterbury, the illustrious Saint Anselm of Bec: "nor do I seek to know that I believe, but I believe that I know."

While Abelard's dialectics greatly endeared him to his students, and to Saint Thomas Aquinas a century later, it further alienated rigid conservatives like his enemy, Saint Bernard, who was not unknown to flog his students. His *Theology*, snorted Saint Bernard, was not "*the*-ology" but "*stupid*-ology;" "God's secrets," he claimed, were "eviscerated" by Abelard.

Abelard's *Sic et Non*,* in which he presented hundreds of apparently contradictory statements by Church elders for evaluation by his "scholars," became a seminal work; while his *Dialectica* raised, challengingly, the whole issue of free will. If God, in his omniscience, asked Abelard, knows that we are going to perform a given act, is it not preordained that we perform it, in which case how can the act be *free*? Abelard's answer was that God's foreknowledge of our actions carried "no implication that we are not free to avoid performing them." This smacked of apostasy—and was sheer anathema to Saint Bernard, who detected "a very source of heresy," predicting that the Church would be shaken when students attempted to form an opinion. In 1121, the Synod of Soissons found Abelard guilty of heresy and condemned him to burn his own book, *Theologia*; he was perhaps fortunate that this was the only conflagration.

Acting under such pressures, Abelard and his small band of "scholars" migrated from the Île de la Cité to the Left Bank, to an area ever since known as the Latin Quarter—because of the prevalence of scholarly Latin spoken there. From then on it came to be said that Paris "learned to think" on the Left Bank.

In an age where the high costs of manuscripts and time involved in copying them tediously by hand made books scarce items, the capabilities of a teacher were of first importance. Abelard's charm and his appeal as the continent's best lecturer were immense. Students came from all over France, and Europe, just for the privilege of sitting at the feet of this brilliant but unhappy man. Through Abelard, the twelfth century became the age of dialectics; and, through the focal point his teaching

---

*It has to be remembered that all learning in France was still expressed in Latin.

provided, inevitably Paris' first university grew around it. Though modelling itself on northern Italy's Bologna, Europe's oldest university, during the reign of Philippe-Auguste this forerunner of the Sorbonne started off life as a guild*—or, in effect, and which was to be of considerable consequence in the later, stormy eras of the Sorbonne such as 1968—a trade union.

AMIDST THE CONSTRUCTION of Notre-Dame and the birth of a university, and for all the administrative reforms Suger achieved in Paris, in many aspects France's capital remained a collection of villages, with pigs roaming muddy streets. One such "diabolic boar" caused the death of Louis' first-born heir, Prince Philippe, when his horse shied and threw him near Saint-Gervais. Louis then had his second son crowned—nicknamed "Louis the Young" because he was only eleven at the time—and in that great political coup married him to Eleanor of Aquitaine. But immediately on his return from Bordeaux, Louis VI was stricken with dysentery, dying in his Palais Cité—on a carpet over which he supposedly had had ashes laid in the form of a cross. He was only fifty-six, but his final achievement had profoundly affected the destiny of France.

In 1137, just as the English Plantagenets were wreaking their revenge for the Norman invasion on the mainland of France, Louis VII, "the Young," took over the throne of France, beginning a reign of forty-three years (1137–80). From his father he inherited a united kingdom, at peace with itself and abroad, sound finances and, above all, Abbé Suger. But he inherited little of his father's strength of character. Jealously in love, he immediately fell under the spell of his bride, Eleanor, a formidable modern-age woman, intelligent and well read, coquettish and highly sexed—married at fifteen, divorced at twenty-eight, died at eighty-two, and perhaps the most outstanding personality of her age. Louis' religious policy, led by Eleanor, created a falling out with the Pope, and led to excommunication. To gain reconciliation with Rome, the King set forth on a crusade—the conventional wisdom of those days. Fearful of leaving her alone in Paris, because of her amorous propensities, he took Eleanor with him. It proved a huge mistake. During a dangerous journey plagued with heat and hunger, Eleanor came to detest her weak

---

*The Latin word *Universitas* originally meant a corporation of any kind; it was not until later in the Middle Ages that it came to denote a place of higher learning.

husband. In Syria she fell into the arms of a youthful uncle, Raymond of Aquitaine, Prince of Antioch. Pressing on to besiege Jerusalem, there Eleanor was rumoured to have bestowed her favours on a handsome Moorish slave, while Louis suffered a serious military defeat.

At home Suger ruled as regent but he had to dispense some of his own considerable wealth—as well as ransacking the coffers of Saint-Denis—to maintain political loyalties. He managed to stifle the threat of revolt by the King's younger brother, the Comte de Dreux; but, now a frail old man, he wrote urging Louis to return post-haste. "The disturbers of the kingdom have returned," he wrote:

> and you, who should be here to defend it, remain like a prisoner in exile . . . You have handed over the lamb to the wolf . . . As for the Queen, your wife, we counsel you, if you will, to conceal your resentment until, having come home by God's grace, you can settle that matter with all others . . .[3]

Louis returned with Eleanor, pregnant with another man's child. Suger was able to report, "we have seen to it that your houses and palaces are in good order."

Suger gave Louis one conclusive piece of advice: that he should not divorce Eleanor, but put the interests of the kingdom above his personal grievances. Two years after the royal couple's return, Suger died, and without his counsel, in 1152 Louis obtained an annulment from the Pope—on the grounds that he and Eleanor were too closely related. Only another two years later, a free Eleanor married Henry Plantagenet, the future Henry II of England, a potent and ruthless warlord. Although he was many years her junior, she was to give Henry a row of troublesome sons—as well as Aquitaine, representing over half of the territory that Louis the Fat had bequeathed his inadequate son. From this personal and national humiliation came a cause for what French historians call the "first" Hundred Years' War.

All the political achievements of Louis VI began to fall apart. Within ten years of Suger's death, Louis the Young had been defeated in battle by Eleanor's new husband, and had been supplanted in Brittany and Toulouse as well. By the end of his long reign France was reduced geographically to what it had been in the time of the first Capetians, and Louis had let his father's bequest—the beauty of Aquitaine, her rich dowry and all his gains—slip away.

LOUIS HAD TWO DAUGHTERS, supposedly, by Eleanor—but no heir. He remarried, but his second wife died childless. His third wife, Alix of Champagne, in 1165 finally produced a son who—fifteen years later—was to become Philippe II, named Augustus like a Roman emperor, because he had been born in August. After his death, his sobriquet in France would be "Philip the Conqueror."

The day which determined his reputation and the direction of his reign was 27 July 1214. The battle of Bouvines was to set the future shape not only of France but of Britain, too. Less than ten miles equidistant from the present-day cities of Tournai (in Belgium) and Lille, Bouvines lies in soggy Flanders, site of the terrible battlefields where the destiny of France was to be played out exactly 700 years later. Bouvines was won by Philippe-Auguste's France against a powerful coalition of foes headed by King John of England, on a Sunday—controversially, for in those days of rigid religious observance, knights and kings observed the Sabbath as far as battle was concerned.

But France's King Philippe-Auguste needed to exploit every advantage, fair or foul. When he arrived on the throne in 1180, aged fifteen, he inherited a tiny state, a fraction the size of Plantagenet England and its European dependencies, once again land-locked, and surrounded by powerful rivals. How then did he come to find himself fighting—and winning—such a key battle in so unpromising a corner of Europe? At the time of his succession, the odds against him, and France, would have seemed hopeless.

THE RULER OF ENGLAND, Henry II, was an imposing figure, particularly in the early stages of his rule: of medium height but strongly built, arm muscles like a professional wrestler, and legs bowed from being constantly on horseback. His face was leonine (in fact, a movie once epitomised him as "The Lion in Winter" in his stormy old age); there were no concessions to culture either in his unkingly and often neglected garb (he never wore gloves over his large, calloused hands) or in his way of life. Travelling ceaselessly between his English and French realms, he was seldom known to sit down—except at table, or on a horse. He was the quintessential man of action, of tireless energy. A contemporary wrote of him:

If the King has decided to spend the day anywhere, especially if his royal will to do so has been publicly proclaimed by herald, you may be certain that he will get off early in the morning, and this sudden change will throw everyone's plans into confusion . . . His pleasure, if I may dare say so, is increased by the straits to which his courtiers are put . . .[4]

A nightmare for officialdom.

We have no clear physical portrait of his fellow monarch, Louis VII, whose powerful wife he had acquired, but we know that, in contrast, Louis was an educated man, gentle and pious, compassionate to the poor—and even conspicuously tolerant (for those days) towards the Jews. He lived simply, without pomp, mingling freely and unescorted with the citizens of Paris. Once, comparing himself with Henry, he observed wryly, "He has everything in abundance—men, horses, gold, silk, diamonds, game and fruit. We in France, we have only bread, wine—and gaiety." Louis was a man of moral scruples; on good terms with the Church, he would never have countenanced the liquidation of his Archbishop. As a statesman, however, decisiveness and good judgement were not his middle names; nor was good luck.

Henry's French father, Plantagenet Duke of Anjou, had brought him the rich territories of Anjou and Normandy; and England, through his marriage to the unhappy Matilda, heiress to William the Conqueror's son, Henry I. Between Matilda and her cousin, King Stephen, England had been reduced to anarchy and was, by the time Henry Plantagenet came to the throne in 1154 at the age of twenty-one, urgently in need of strong rule. Swiftly Henry quenched the civil war that racked the country, establishing the "King's Peace," maintained through a native common law—a feature novel to European monarchies. With equal speed he defeated the unruly Scots and Welsh, bringing even the Irish to heel. He gave peace to the islands for the first time in generations, crushing the last of the barons' revolts in 1173. In short order, he found himself reigning unchallenged from the Cheviots to the Pyrenees, his short-lived Angevin Empire looming over the tiny plot centred round Paris that was France.

With little of the pre-Conquest Anglo-Saxon influences still extant, Henry's England was indeed like a kind of alternative France. French was his mother tongue; the "English Establishment" followed suit—and continued to do so well into the reign of Edward III nearly two centuries later—while for the priesthood in both countries Latin was the *lingua franca.* The refined French words for food, such as "beef," "mutton" and porc," had already replaced in English their cruder Anglo-Saxon originals like "ox," "sheep" and "swine." Trans-Channel fancies were carried away by the lilt and swing of French songs, as imported by the troubadours, by the verve of French story-telling, and by a great wave of French poetry that swept over England (and, indeed, most of Europe), threatening to obliterate the unsophisticated native *Beowulf.* During Henry's years of peace, a new English yeoman figure grew up where the agriculturalist and the huntsman tended to replace the warrior knight—the birth of the English country gentleman. Gradually the dour fortified stone castles of Stephen's turbulent times became replaced by manor houses similar in style to the early colleges that were to grow up later in Oxford and Cambridge. At the lower end of the social scale, the "villein" (in itself a French word), though in fee to his lord and in no sense a "free man," and whose lot was to be little improved by *Magna Carta,* was probably beginning to enjoy marginally more beneficial rights than his French opposite number.

With Bismarckian cunning, Henry, expanding in all directions, set about the encirclement of Louis' France by a network of alliances; at times in his reign it looked as if the Franco-English Capetians were to become vassals of the empire controlled from Westminster and Rouen. Yet there was something artificial, vulnerably ephemeral about the Angevin Empire. The unattended pendulum swings between triumph and disaster could be particularly sudden and dramatic in twelfth-century Europe—with the fate of a country so closely tied to the life and fortunes of its leader. One such swing, just in time for Louis, occurred on 29 December 1170, with the murder of Archbishop Thomas à Becket—apparently invoked, if not actually ordered, by the King. Undoubtedly a thorn in the side of the King, and a stormy petrel within the Church, dead the "turbulent priest" became an instant international martyr, and a saint. Henry could wear a horse-hair shirt and have himself flogged in Avranches Cathedral by way of atonement—yet his image, and his power, would never quite recover from this particular bloodstain.

THE INCREASINGLY UNPOPULAR HENRY now enacted a Lear-like break-up of his territories among his sons, Henry the Young (aged fifteen in 1270), Richard, the future "Coeur de Lion" (aged twelve), and Geoffrey (aged eleven); John, born only in 1167, was left out of the carve-up, and was thus to be known henceforth for ever in France as "Jean sans Terre." As Lear discovered, this was to prove folly in the extreme. Prince Henry, already crowned in 1170 and strategically married to the daughter of Louis VII, was treated by his father-in-law as if he were already king, but in fact was never to succeed.

In 1173, there was popular insurrection in France. Henry crushed, one by one, all the coalitions mounted against him. Most humiliating was the defeat of Louis at Verneuil, taking flight even as Henry approached with his army. The following year Louis was routed again at Rouen, deplorably destroying all his heavy weaponry. Once again Paris seemed directly menaced; and it became more vulnerable when, in 1176, the worst flooding of the Seine in memory swept away both bridges, carried off mills, houses and livestock on the crumbling banks, and came close to engulfing the city. Attempting a form of flood control untried in modern times, Louis and his entire court and every undrowned monk and priest, headed by the bishop of Paris, went in procession to the edge of the swirling waters. Holding aloft a nail from the True Cross, the bishop prayed: "In this sign of the Holy Passion, may the waters return to their bed and this miserable people be protected!" The rain stopped, and the waters ebbed just in time. Paris appeared to be saved once more by divine intervention.

The following year the Pope, threatening an interdict on all the provinces of the Angevin Empire, intervened to impose peace between Henry and Louis—just as Henry was about to mount the decisive assault on Paris. Considering the debility of Louis, the terms were generous. The uprising demonstrated Henry's power but also the inherent weakness in his empire—the divisiveness of his quarrelsome sons, greedy for territory and glory. Their future adversary, Philippe-Auguste, heir to the ageing Louis, saw it; aged only nine, standing before Henry's seemingly unassailable fortress at Gisors, and showing his future mettle, he is said to have remarked to his entourage: "I only wish this pile of stones could be silver, gold or diamonds . . . the more precious the materials of this castle, the greater pleasure I would have in possessing it when it will have fallen into my hands."[5] He would have to wait the best part of a generation.

In 1180 Louis the Young died. Philippe-Auguste (1180–1223) succeeded him, aged fifteen, although he had virtually taken over already the previous year during Louis' last illness, from what appears to have been a stroke that paralysed his right side. By the end of his reign of forty-three years, Philippe-Auguste would have increased the original fiefdom of Hugues Capet more than forty-fold. He nearly did not accede to the throne at all, however; while out hunting with his father the previous year, Philippe-Auguste, having been lost for two days in the Forest of Compiègne, was taken gravely ill. The King prayed for his recovery on the tomb of the martyred Thomas à Becket; Philippe-Auguste recovered, and—supposedly appearing in a vision to a French holy man—Becket declared that the young heir had been chosen to avenge his murder. To the superstitious, it was an encouraging prelude to the new reign.

Philippe-Auguste properly earned the reputation of being *rusé comme un renard* ("cunning as a fox"). The only existing contemporary pen-portrait of him[6] describes him as

> a handsome, strapping fellow, bald but with a cheerful face of ruddy complexion, and a temperament much inclined towards good-living, wine and women. He was generous to his friends, stingy towards those who displeased him, well-versed in the art of stratagem, orthodox in belief, prudent and stubborn in his resolves. He made judgements with great speed and exactitude. Fortune's favourite, fearful for his life, easily excited and easily placated, he was very tough with powerful men who resisted him, and took pleasure in provoking discord among them. Never, however, did he cause an adversary to die in prison. He liked to employ humble men [*petits gens*], to be the subduer of the proud, the defender of the Church and feeder of the poor.

Above all, Philippe-Auguste developed as a diplomat and tactician supreme; more than a knight, he was a skilful and crafty politician beyond his times. He had an aptitude for seeking the counsel of intelligent men of humble birth, notably Brother Guérin, Bishop of Senlis and Barthélemy de Roye, and he restricted his advisers at court to a very small circle. He was to give the French monarchy "the three instruments of rule which it lacked: tractable officials, money and soldiers."

BISHOP GUÉRIN WAS A MEMBER of the crusading order of the Knights Hospitallers of Jerusalem, where he was probably discovered by Philippe-Auguste. He was rich in property, principally south of Paris, through royal favour. Just before Bouvines, he was elected bishop of Senlis, close to Paris. After his election to this see, he and his church received important benefactions from the King, as was to be expected. Presiding over the exchequer, he also acted as judge, held inquests, issued commands and served on frequent special missions. As a cleric and a bishop, Guérin attended to purely ecclesiastical affairs, for example the investigation of heresy at Paris in 1209, but his position in the Church did not prevent him from also playing a key military role.

France was soon at war again. By the fifth year of his reign, the young Philippe-Auguste had managed to expand his kingdom northwards and southwards—including the key city of Amiens. Almost immediately, he found himself at war with the mighty Henry.

Henry was already old beyond his years and Philippe-Auguste was cunning in forming alliances with his ambitious sons, first Geoffrey, then Richard. By the beginning of 1188 Philippe-Auguste had doubled his forces through alliance with Richard and was poised to move into Henry's Normandy. Then suddenly came news from the Middle East that the Saracen, Saladin, had taken Jerusalem. The Pope summoned the Christian kings to cease fighting each other, and embark on a fresh crusade (the third). Before they could embark, Henry had died, on 7 July 1189, in the chapel of his French château of Chinon. It was a sad end for the old lion, his valets pillaging him of every last belonging, leaving the King "naked, as he had come into the world, save for his shirt and breeches."[7] On the 20th, Richard was crowned Duke of Normandy in Rouen, then King of England in London on 3 September. He and Philippe-Auguste then departed, as allies and close friends, for the Holy Land.

RICHARD "COEUR DE LION" was not the quintessence of the romantic, chivalrous crusading knight that posterity has made him seem. As a young prince he cruelly suppressed revolts in Aquitaine, and according to French chronicles, he indulged in debauchery, "abducting the wives and daughters of his subjects to make them his concubines, and then to hand them over to his soldiers." He was arrogant, with a habit of sowing rancour around him. At home in England (which he rashly left in the disloyal and incompetent hands of his brother John "Lackland") he was accepted as a neglectful, popular absentee ruler, as befitting the repute of a knight errant. But he also possessed the external glitter and generosity lacking in his father; was even more energetic, bolder, and possibly more ambitious, too. The glamour obscured deceptively the able military tactician and tough politician. He was not a man to be antagonised.

In contrast, Philippe-Auguste made provision for the sound governance of France in his absence. In a famous document, the *Testament of 1190,* he ordered the construction of a continuous fortified wall girdling Paris, making it impregnable for the first time. It was just as well, insofar as he and his close friend, Richard,* were soon to become bitterest enemies. Reaching Genoa together, the two leaders first fell out over the number of ships each was to provide for crossing the Mediterranean. Finally arriving in the Holy Land, the two Kings managed to tip the balance in the terrible siege of Acre, already under attack for two years. But by the time of its capitulation in July 1191, intrigues and the stresses of a grim campaign had undermined the Anglo-French entente; to the enduring rage of Richard, Philippe-Auguste now decided to break off his part in the Third Crusade and head for home.

By the end of 1191, Philippe-Auguste was celebrating Christmas at Fontainebleau, "boasting with impudence of soon being able to invade the domains of the King of England."[8] Richard, on the other hand, during his journey home was locked up by the Holy Roman Emperor, Henry VI, for months in the Danube fortress of Dürrenstein—pending payment of ransom. In deplorably bad faith, Philippe-Auguste and Richard's brother John endeavoured to bribe the Emperor to continue to detain him but Emperor Henry thoughtfully revealed all to Richard. He finally reached London in March 1194, and immediately he launched a fresh war. It was to last five years, with an unremitting ferocity rare in the twelfth century.

No quarter was given, with both sides issuing orders to blind or drown prisoners of war. On 3 July 1194, Philippe-Auguste suffered his greatest humiliation, at Fréteval in the Vendôme, losing his baggage train, his treasury and the national archives. To prevent Philippe-Auguste ever again threatening Normandy and to bottle him up in Paris, Richard constructed an unassailable fortress at Château Gaillard, on a key bend in the Seine—still a most imposing castle commanding the approaches to Paris. Defeat followed defeat for Philippe-Auguste.

By the end of 1198, it looked as if France would become a fiefdom of either Richard or the Emperor. Once again, intervention came from

---

*Their intimacy had evidently extended, in the innocent way of the Middle Ages, to once sharing a bed in Paris.

afar. News from Spain that the Moors were threatening a new invasion led Pope Innocent III to ordain a truce between the combatants. The results were extremely tough on Philippe-Auguste, forfeiting all of Normandy save the citadel of Gisors; and with it France lost all the winnings of the past ten years. Had Philippe-Auguste died at this point, he would have been remembered with scorn, for it seemed only a matter of time before Richard renewed the war, with a final drive on Paris.

Then, in the miraculous manner in which fortune could be reversed in the Middle Ages, while besieging a rebel fortress in Limousin on 26 March 1199, Richard was wounded in the left shoulder by a bolt from a crossbow. Gangrene set in. Just before he died, the warrior-king with a last chivalrous gesture requested that his assailant be spared, and given a sum of money. The moment he was dead, however, the bowman was flayed alive and impaled. "King Richard is dead, and a thousand years have passed since there died a man whose loss was so great. Never has there been his equal . . . throughout the world he made himself dreaded by some and cherished by others,"[9] sang the troubadours. In Paris, Philippe-Auguste could now look to deal with the weak, evil and hated "Jean sans Terre."


ALL THROUGH CAPETIAN FRANCE's struggles against the Plantagenets, Louis VII and his son had to contend with another powerful, and often unpredictable, player: at the wave of his crucifix the Pope could summon up armies and nations to bring to bear on a miscreant ruler. In the Middle Ages, the issue of death and eternal damnation was uppermost in all people's minds. Every man and woman hoped to die with Christ's words on their lips; to die "unshriven" was the worst fate imaginable. Life was indeed a preparation for death, and though by the later Middle Ages views on the after-life had lost some of their certainty, in the twelfth century, notions of Purgatory were little considered; it was a straight choice between the Bosom of Abraham and the Cauldron of Hell. Such was the dread of eternal damnation, of excommunication or an "interdict" upon a nation, that the mere threat could reverse policies and upturn thrones. Perhaps never again would the influence of the Pope be greater.

Pope at the time of the accession of Philippe-Auguste was Alexander III (1159–81), who had strongly supported Becket's stand against royal encroachment on Church matters. His successor was Innocent III (1198–1216)—there was a certain irony in the name, since he had his tentacles everywhere in the Christian world. Even so, his authority was challenged by the Holy Roman Emperors and an array of four imperial Anti-Popes. Like other rulers, these medieval Popes found themselves constrained to juggle alliances with often bewildering rapidity.

Innocent had been much impressed by his pilgrimage to the shrine of Becket in Canterbury. An inveterate Crusader, only the intervention of death prevented him from leading himself the Fifth Crusade in 1217. He was described as "strong, stable, magnanimous and very sharp," with no doubts whatsoever that the Pope was invested with the ultimate authority over the secular world as well as the Church. Christ, he declared, had left to Peter "the Government not only of the Church but of the whole world." Within the Church he stood for reform (which it badly needed), and orthodoxy; beyond it, secular rulers (not to mention infidels) crossed him at their peril. It was a standpoint that, eventually, was to bring into being Protestantism, but under Innocent Rome probably reached its political apogee.

PHILIPPE-AUGUSTE'S FATHER had fallen into (temporary) papal displeasure through divorcing Eleanor, but this was nothing compared with the trouble that overtook Philippe-Auguste, reverberating at various times to shake the course of his military and political successes. His first wife, Isabelle of Hainault, who had brought him Artois, died aged only nineteen. In 1193, he entered into another politically adroit union with Ingeborg of Denmark, a very pretty girl of eighteen. Usefully, her brother the King still maintained claims on England dating back to pre-Conquest days—and a considerable fleet. But the unfortunate Ingeborg arrived in France only for Philippe-Auguste to be mysteriously seized by irremediable aversion to her on their wedding night. He tried to persuade King Knut to have her back; the King refused, and complained to the Vatican. Philippe-Auguste divorced Ingeborg, who—after a spell in prison—was placed in a French convent, and three years later he married bigamously a Bavarian princess, Agnes of Merano.

One of the first acts of the succession by Innocent III was for the Pope to declare: "The Holy See cannot abandon persecuted women without defending them." He ordered the divorce annulled, and the remarriage, under threat of personal excommunication of the King. An interdict on the whole kingdom was enforced in 1198—to the deep distress of Philippe-Auguste's subjects. Finally, after nine months of resistance, he formally submitted on all counts.

Philippe-Auguste, however, was being less than honest. He sequestered Ingeborg, first in a château in the Forest of Rambouillet, then in a state of house-arrest at Étampes, while Agnes remained in France, set up in a château closer to Paris. Despite the death of Agnes in 1201, Ingeborg continued to besiege the Pope:

> I am persecuted by my Lord and husband, Philip, who not only does not treat me as his wife, but causes to be showered on me outrages and calumnies by his servants. In this prison, . . . no one dares to come to visit me, no priest is allowed in to comfort my soul in bringing me the Holy Gospel . . . I do not even have enough clothes, and those that I wear are not worthy of a queen . . . Finally, I am locked up in a house from which I am forbidden to leave.[10]

France and the Vatican were close to rupture; but, politically, they needed each other. After a decade, suddenly, in 1212, Philippe-Auguste announced that he was going to take Ingeborg back as his queen—if not his wife. But, as usual with Philippe-Auguste, the considerations were purely political, rather than sentimental. He had decided to administer the *coup de grâce* to King John, and to invade England; for which he needed the support of Ingeborg's brother, the King of Denmark, and—above all—of the Pope.

The distasteful story of Ingeborg showed the new power of the Capetian monarchy under Philippe-Auguste. He had openly defied and outmanoeuvred that most powerful pontiff over a period of twenty years when all the faults were manifestly on his side. It also demonstrated an undeflectable determination to act for himself and for France.

BY 1213, King John had alienated his subjects in France; in particular, the murder of his young nephew, Arthur, in Rouen during the winter of 1203–4, caused even greater revulsion than the murder of Archbishop Becket under his father's reign. His treatment of rebels went before him; on one occasion he had flung into a dungeon the wife of a rebel knight and her child, with only a bundle of oats and a piece of raw bacon for sustenance. Eleven days later both were found dead, the mother having eaten the cheeks of her child. In April 1204, after an eight-month siege, Philippe-Auguste had captured Coeur de Lion's imposing fortress of Château Gaillard, his intended jumping-off point for the capture of

Paris. He entered Rennes in Brittany, where no Capet had set foot since the beginning of the dynasty. From there Philippe-Auguste proceeded to the capture of Rouen, the Angevin capital in France, followed by the whole of Normandy within a matter of two months (a shorter time than it took Anglo-American might to wrest it from the Germans in 1944). The fall of Normandy meant the end of Henry II's short-lived Angevin Empire. Philippe-Auguste now sat down seriously to plan the invasion of Jean-sans-Terre's England and the creation of a new Angevin Empire, in reverse, with its capital in Paris.

Momentarily, it looked as if Philippe-Auguste had all the chips—the Pope, the Danish fleet and the Emperor—and he had already seized Brittany, Maine and Anjou. In 1213, John fell foul of Innocent III for rejecting Stephen Langton as Archbishop of Canterbury, and was placed under an interdict, with Philippe-Auguste openly invited to invade, remove John's crown and place it on the head "of someone who would be worthy." He had a candidate—his son and heir, Louis—and had already been at work subverting the Welsh and Irish against John as well as some of his own English barons. According to a French chronicler, he awoke one morning exclaiming, "God, what am I waiting for to go and conquer the English?"[11] His preparations, however, had been carefully laid. In the first serious attempt at invasion between William the Conqueror and Napoleon, a fleet of 1500 sails and an immense army was poised in the Channel ports. Like Napoleon in 1804–5 it was ready and waiting at Boulogne, on 8 May 1213.

Then, just two weeks later, as Philippe-Auguste was about to embark, came the shattering news that Innocent—perhaps still mistrusting the wayward King, and showing his claws—had reversed his policy yet again. He had become reconciled to a humbled John, prepared to meet all the Pope's demands. Philippe-Auguste was ordered to stand off.

A menacing Anglo-German-Flemish coalition against France was patched together by King John and his nephew, Otto IV of Brunswick, the Holy Roman Emperor across the Rhine—resentful of Philippe-Auguste's opposing his candidacy to the imperial throne. They were supported by French counts Ferrand and Renaud, holding domains that were vitally strategic to France and regarded by Philippe-Auguste as arch-traitors for their switching of allegiances.

Bent on revenge, in 1214 John embarked on a two-prong strategy. At the beginning of July, John himself attacked in Aquitaine, where the future Louis VIII, aged twenty-six, managed to defeat John and an army three times the size at the key position of Roche-au-Moine, close to Angers—but it was a demoralised army that hated him.

Philippe-Auguste was delighted with his heir's success, but the main threat to France lay on the other front. On the plain of Flanders, Otto and his allies had concentrated a force of 80,000 men—a truly immense army for those days—intent on moving southwards on Paris.

THE WEAPONRY, if not the tactics, of the forthcoming battle reminded one a little of the first engagement of the tank in the First World War. The cannon was not to make its appearance on the European battlefield till Crécy in 1346, where—cumbersome and unreliable—it was still hardly a serious weapon. The deadly English longbow, lethal at 240 yards, was to win battles of the Hundred Years' War for England, but would not come into its own for nearly another hundred years. Thus the master of the battlefield in 1214 was the mounted knight, heavily armoured in chain mail and equipped with either a long lance or a heavy slashing—rather than a piercing—sword. But his huge helm severely limited his vision and so heavy was his armour that, if dismounted, he could not remount—or even rise to his feet unaided. He was a prey to the lesser soldier, the infantry foot sergeants who unhorsed the knights with long hooks, harpooning them by the links of their armour, and throwing them down into the dust; or who got underneath the horses to disembowel them with poignards.

At the lowest level were the murderous villeins of low birth who roamed the battlefield, opening the visors of wounded knights to dispatch them with a blow through the eye, then rob them (no true knight would besmirch his honour with such handiwork). The knight's long-suffering steed demanded a huge lumbering beast, originating from Byzantium and bred on his feudal domains, which formed the base of medieval society.

As far as the mercilessness of the battlefield went, one famous description of King Harold, after being wounded by the fatal arrow at Hastings, was still relevant:

> Harold, though disabled, still breathed; four knights rushed upon him and despatched him with various wounds . . . One thrust pierced through the shield of the dying King and stabbed him in the breast; another assailant finished the work by striking off his head with his sword. But even this vengeance was not enough. A

third pierced the dead body and scattered about the entrails; the fourth, coming, it would seem, too late for any more efficient share in the deed, cut off the King's leg as he lay dead.[12]

Wounds delivered in battle by hacking blows were in general likely to prove mutilating rather than fatal. Those who survived them were then at the hands of the crude surgeons; where pain was certain, recovery was a great deal less so.

Actual fatalities on the twelfth-century European battlefield tended to be moderate—at least compared with the butcheries to be seen in later epochs, let alone the massacres perpetrated in the East by Philippe-Auguste's exact contemporary, Genghis Khan. The spirit of the tournament single-combat reigned, with noble knights seeking *la gloire* in confrontation with their peers, rather than the wholesale slaughter of the lower orders. A prisoner alive was worth far more, in terms of ransom, than a dead enemy.

AS THE TWO MASSIVE FORCES approached each other in Flanders, Philippe-Auguste was about to celebrate his forty-ninth birthday (thus no longer young by the standards of the day). He could muster no more than 25,000 men, of which 500 were *chevaliers,* to the Allies' 80,000 and 1500 knights.* On Philippe-Auguste's side the infantry consisted, for the first time, of a substantial body of bourgeois *Communes,* regarded as "a great novelty"[13] and which were to play a role of historic significance. (Like rival claims during the Battle of Britain air war, figures vary however with nationality; one French expert, Georges Duby, put Philippe-Auguste's knights at 1300 and infantry at 4000–6000, while Otto was never able to concentrate more than a portion of his unwieldy great force.)

The news reaching Otto's camp of John's defeat at Roche-au-Moine must have been demoralising. There were other reports reaching the Allies that Philippe-Auguste was falling back in retreat, but the French King appreciated that it was in his interest to strike fast, and boldly, before Otto could bring up his rearguard from Lorraine and Germany. Therefore, instead of attacking frontally, Philippe-Auguste decided to engage Otto by a turning movement, via Tournai and Lille.

---

*To be an accomplished tournament knight provided a source of income on a par with that of the professional football or soccer star of the twentieth century.

Otto's intention was to strike for Paris and the royal domain, which had already been apportioned to his main allies and numerous German barons, as the putative spoils of war. But on hearing of Philippe-Auguste's presence at Tournai, Otto moved north to meet him. Only Count Renaud counselled caution: "I know the French and their daring," he warned: "it would be rash to fight them in open country." But "hawks" like Hugues de Boves urged immediate pursuit to catch the French divided as they crossed the River Marcq, at Bouvines. The bridge at Marcq lay in a position of prime importance, the only crossing point in a swampy area, and the meeting point of French, Flemish and imperial territories. The high ground on either side offered good hard-going for cavalry. A consideration caused both kings to hesitate, however, before facing battle; it was then 27 July, a Sunday.

When the French rearguard spotted the Allies in full battle array, Brother Guérin, Bishop-elect of Senlis, proposed that the King draw up his lines to meet the enemy. The other counsellors thought that the Allies would never fight on the sabbath, but Guérin's judgement was confirmed when the French rearguard reported fierce attacks. The final decision to engage the imperial forces was supposedly taken while Philippe-Auguste was resting, exhausted and with his armour off, under the shade of an ash tree.

NOW, IN SHORT ORDER, the King performed rituals to consecrate the forthcoming battle, in which it was believed God's judgement would be revealed. Philippe-Auguste entered a nearby chapel to pray briefly, armed himself, and mounted his horse "as if summoned to a wedding feast."[14] To his troops, he made a stirring proclamation:

> You are my men and I am your king. I wear the crown but I am a man like you. But since I am your king you are well-loved by me. And for this reason, I pray you, on this day keep my honour and yours. And if the crown should be worn more appropriately by one of you, I will take it off and give it to him with a good heart. You may all be king and, are you not already, since without you I cannot govern?*

---

*Modern French historians are sceptical that an absolute monarch of the Middle Ages would have made such a speech with its appeal to populist emotions.

Mindful of the defection of his old allies Renaud and Ferrand, he warned his barons: "Protect me, and you will do well. For, with me, you will lose nothing. But double-cross me, and I will pursue you—wherever you may go."[15] While the royal chaplain chanted psalms of victory on the battlefield, the King then blessed his troops with outstretched hands.

To the blare of trumpets and chanting of psalms the battle formations were drawn up, in three groups facing the field and extending across the road from Tournai. In the centre was the King. The French right wing was commanded by Guérin and the Duke of Burgundy, facing an array of Flemish knights led by Count Ferrand. The left wing was entrusted to Count Robert and Bishop Philippe of Beauvais, both royal cousins. The infantry of the *Communes* participated with contingents of sergeants stationed at the centre and on the left.

The French rearguard was hit five times by forces under Ferrand and Renaud, but they were surprised to find that it was well organised. "Who ever told me," the Emperor exclaimed, "that the King of France was in flight?" Strung out in a long line, unprepared for a major battle, the Allied army was forced to regroup quickly before those in the rear could come up. It was now about 12:00 hours.

It was the *canicule,* or "dog-days" of summer, and 27 July was a day of intense heat, appalling for knights in heavy armour, fighting half-blinded by the sweat pouring down inside their helmets. In the heavy dust churned up by thousands of horses, it would have been almost as hard to obtain an overall picture as for Stendhal's Fabrice at Waterloo, so that our account of the battle is largely limited to that of an eye-witness standing close to King Philippe-Auguste, Guillaume le Breton. Guillaume's account rings of the *Iliad* of Troy with its emphasis on heroic single combats, but is informative on tactical movement—and the best we have.

As seen by Guillaume, the course of the battle evolved in three scenes, with the French right wing being the first to engage, then the centre, and finally the left. Bishop Guérin began the action on the right with a sally by mounted sergeants from the Abbey of Saint-Médard, but the Flemish nobles, "disdainful of this plebeian cavalry, received them on their lances without moving, disembowelling their horses."[16] Then three Flemish *chevaliers* rode out of the lines, challenging their French peers to combat. In a first exchange, two were taken prisoner; the third—Eustache de Macheleu—barely had time to shout "Mort aux Français!" when he was knocked off his horse and his throat slit.

This initial success gave Guérin's men encouragement, and a solid phalanx of their cavalry 200 strong smashed through the Flemish line, causing it to reel back in disarray. The French leader, Eudes Duke of Burgundy, fell under his mount but his guard managed to put him back in the saddle and "furious, he killed all who got in his way."

In the centre, the imperial sergeants were able to break through the lines of the *Communes* foot-soldiers drawn up in formation in front of the King. Striking back at them, Philippe-Auguste became briefly separated from his bodyguard. The King was surrounded by the enemy infantry, who unhorsed him with their long hooks. Pouncing on the fallen King, Otto's men tried in vain to find a chink in his coat-of-mail in which to thrust a fatal dagger.

In these brief seconds the whole history of France lay in the balance. However, the King's heavy armour and a quick response from the knights of his household, who threw themselves down protectively on his fallen body, saved Philippe-Auguste's life. They offered him a fresh horse and conducted him to safety.

The imperial attack was matched by a French counter-attack that equally imperilled Emperor Otto's life. Two French knights and Guillaume des Barres got close enough to unhorse him, but four imperial knights succeeded in conveying the Emperor to safety, although they themselves were captured. Otto galloped off the battlefield alone, hardly stopping until he had reached his base camp at Valenciennes, 30 kilometres away.

Observing the flight of the Emperor, Philippe-Auguste remarked: "We will not see his face any more today!" The battered imperial insignia, with Otto's fear-inducing great eagle mounted above a dragon, was brought triumphantly to the French King on a four-wheeled chariot, and then transported to the capital along with the captives and booty.

French attentions on the left flank now focused on the "arch-traitor" Renaud, Count of Boulogne. During the battle Renaud declared to his old friend, the hawkish Hugues de Boves: "Here's the battle you wanted, and which I didn't. Now you can flee, panicking like the rest of them. As for me, I shall continue fighting and be captured or killed."[17] Renaud continued to fight, with the courage of despair, all through the afternoon surrounded by a double line of protective infantry.

Above the confusion of battle, Renaud's imposingly tall figure could be seen with its enormous lance and double black plumes attached to his helmet, a magnetically enticing target. Eventually, a French foot-sergeant, Pierre de la Tournelle, managed to creep under Renaud's horse, and Renaud fell. A lively dispute ensued among the French knights as to who would have the honour of capturing the traitor alive, before the battered and bleeding Renaud finally surrendered to Guérin.

By five o'clock, the fighting was all but over, having lasted no more than five hours. Philippe-Auguste's victory was complete, while the main enemy army had not been engaged. Had Otto listened earlier to Count Renaud's cunctatory advice, the outcome might have been different.

As night approached, up on the plateau overlooking Bouvines, there remained a troop of 700 Brabant infantrymen, abandoned debris of Otto's vast army, who bravely refused to surrender. In an act of savagery such as sometimes marred the chivalry of medieval warfare, Philippe-Auguste had them massacred to the last man.

Finally, at the call of trumpets the French troops returned to their camp with great rejoicing. There was no accurate count of the casualties at Bouvines, but—on the French side—they were light, possibly not more than 300 knights killed. The list of captured chieftains was impressive. One hundred and thirty of them were assigned to prisons and custodians, and their names recorded—as an insult to the Emperor—in the French Royal Archives. The military leadership of the coalition were incarcerated at the Louvre and Péronne, thus effectively dissolving John's coalition against his French rival.

Renaud of Boulogne was kept cruelly shackled to a wall by a chain only half a metre long. He would die in incarceration thirteen years later. Ferrand of Flanders was assigned to Philippe-Auguste's newly built tower of the Louvre, which stood outside the defensive city walls of Paris that he had constructed, and the other captives to the two *châtelets* guarding the bridges linking the Île de la Cité with both banks of the Seine. Apart from the fate of these two, Philippe-Auguste was generous in the clemency he showed to the others, though the ransoms that accompanied the liberation enormously enriched the French exchequer.

Philippe-Auguste's victory at Bouvines evoked waves of spontaneous rejoicing; the populace danced, the clergy chanted and bells were rung. Flowers and branches festooned churches and houses, and carpeted the streets of towns and villages. Regardless of estate, family or

sex, everyone converged on the route of the triumphant army. Workers
in the fields rushed to see Count Ferrand led to Paris in chains. There,
the townsmen and grandees alike greeted the King with such enthusiasm that—so Guillaume le Breton recorded:

> one day was not long enough to satisfy their celebrations. For an
> entire week the populace feasted, danced, sang and illuminated
> the nights with torches, so that one could see as clearly as in broad
> daylight. The students particularly didn't stop rejoicing in numer-
> ous banquets, dancing and singing without cease . . .[18]

Bishop Guérin headed the procession into Paris, singing canticles and
hymns, as the King walked behind.

At various crises in French history, propagandists would dust off the
victory of Bouvines and recycle it as a touchstone of national faith: at the
time of Louis-Philippe's bourgeois monarchy in 1840, in the run-up to
the First World War and post-1945, on occasion, as a victory over *les
anglo-saxons.* On any account Bouvines was a remarkable victory. Like
Napoleon in his finest victories of 1805 and 1806, Philippe-Auguste had
succeeded in destroying his foes in detail, isolating first one (John) then
the other (Otto). It was also a victory where superior morale triumphed.

Philippe-Auguste would reign for another nine years. For him, victory meant a remarkable reconciliation between the three orders of king,
church and nobles. Never before had a French king been so secure on his
throne, or France so secure in Europe. He had fought, and won, the first
truly *national* war in French history; but, as the Duke of Wellington
observed on another battlefield not all that far from Bouvines, it had
been a close-run thing.


DISTINGUISHED HISTORIANS, both British and French, are generally agreed that Bouvines was a turning point for both countries. Says
G. M. Trevelyan:

> The poetry-loving French Court, and the University and archi-
> tectural schools of Paris, were the cultural centre of chivalric and
> crusading Europe. It was but natural that the Court should
> become, after Bouvines, the political centre of the French feudal
> provinces. But it failed to develop administrative institutions like
> those with which the Plantagenets strengthened the English

throne, and the French monarchy was therefore destined, in the days of Crécy and Agincourt, to go down once more before renewed English attack from without and feudal treason within.[19]

England, as so often in her history, withdrew to concentrate on insular priorities, while France first became conscious of being a nation, and Paris of being a capital, more and more the centre of power. As Ernest Lavisse comments: "The two nations set off in different directions. England headed towards liberty, France towards absolutism."[20]

IN FRANCE, under the benevolence of Philippe-Auguste's father, Louis VII, the Jews had been comparatively well treated. But to his shame, the reign of Philippe-Auguste was a particularly bad period: in French-Jewish lore, he came to be known as "that wicked King." Still barely fifteen, he issued orders for the Jews under royal protection in Paris to be arrested in their synagogues, imprisoned and condemned to purchase their freedom through surrender of all their gold and silver, and precious vestments. This ploy granted Philippe-Auguste the immense sum of money of 31,500 livres, one and a half times a normal year's revenue, for building the walls of Paris, and for equipping his army to defeat the Plantagenets. Two years later, he expelled the Jews from France, confiscating the totality of their wealth. Not only the Christian Church, but the great mass of wealthy French were delighted. Debts were wiped out—except for a fifth which the royal coffers appropriated.

Philippe-Auguste's expulsions brought to an end the ancient *juiverie* on the Île de la Cité, their synagogue converted by Bishop Sully, creator of Notre-Dame, into the church of the Madeleine.

This harshness was mirrored in the dispensation of justice, accompanied with the most brutal punishments, devilish tortures and frequent executions. But, on the whole, it was even handed and in many ways his era must have seemed like something of a Golden Age for Frenchmen; a huge surge of prosperity and well-being flowed over Paris. Whereas John's successor in England, Henry III, had to give up a campaign against the refractory Welsh in 1232 because of lack of funds, in 1221 Philippe-Auguste's budget showed his government saving about one-third of its revenues. The King was able to pass to his heir a bequest of ten times the estimated annual ordinary income of the monarchy, or a daily revenue equivalent to over twenty times as much as his father had left him. Fortune had tilted in France's favour.

# THREE

# Middle Ages:
# "Saint-Louis" to Philippe le Bel

> Good King Louis, you held the land under yoke
> To the profit of barons and of the little folk . . .
> To whom may poor men cry now in their woe
> Since the good king is dead who loved them so?

> —*Unknown contemporary poet*

I N PARIS a powerful new body had been founded, and had grown up over the years from Suger to Philippe-Auguste, which was to become a significant force in the land, along with the monarchy, the nobility and the Church. Better known later as the Sorbonne, the University of Paris in the centuries ahead would be a source of immense kudos for France—but also a source of controversy and, indeed, tumult. From the earliest days, its students had keenly and liberally involved themselves in city life, outside the walls of academe. In the south transept of Notre-Dame, for instance, a series of reliefs show scenes from student life, as well as a medieval seminar in progress (although listening closely, the participants appear to be taking no notes!). They also show students revenging themselves on a harlot outside Notre-Dame. She is strung up on a "bishop's ladder," while her tormentors hurl mud and filth at her; two law enforcement officers stand by watching.

In 1200, the new century began with a first major *bagarre* between town and gown in Paris, grave enough for the King, Philippe-Auguste, himself to get involved. An account given by the English chronicler Roger of Howden[1] describes how a band of German students became involved in a pre-Lenten tavern brawl in which they wrecked the place and severely beat the owner. In a punitive raid, the royal *prévôt* of Paris attacked the Germans' hostel with urban militia, during the course of which some Parisian students from the university were killed.

Outraged by this incident, and joining the students to demand redress, their professors suspended teaching and threatened to leave Paris in a body. Here, as in later centuries, the most potent weapon in the armoury of both students and masters was "a cessation of lectures." It caused Philippe-Auguste to fear that the students might boycott his city; in addition, while his dispute with the Pope was still running, he was keen to win over Paris churchmen (under whose aegis the university existed) for their support in the royal cause. In July 1200, Philippe-Auguste issued a charter, the university's first. If a townsman saw any layman assaulting a student in Paris, except in self-defence, he was required to arrest the offender, hand him over to royal justice, and give evidence against him. Particular care was to be exercised to avoid physical injury to members of the university unless they resisted arrest. All complaints of violence were to be investigated by inquest. Both the *prévôt* and the people of Paris were required to observe these measures under oath.

Here was a remarkable display of liberalism for such an authoritarian ruler, and especially when recalling his treatment of the Jewish minority. The statute gave to the university vital concessions and privileges that it would strive to safeguard over the ages.

To quote the weighty and considered judgement of Hastings Rashdall, the English authority on medieval universities:

> It is hardly too much to say that the descendants of Hugh Capet eventually succeeded in making themselves the real masters of France, just because, when their power was at its lowest, they were still masters of Paris. The political position of Paris gave the university its place in the political and ecclesiastical world which no other university has ever occupied.

In common with later rulers of France, even fearless Philippe-Auguste seems to have been daunted by the Paris students. Constituting a substantial segment of the city's population by the end of the century, these scholars enjoyed the same set of privileges that the ecclesiastical courts had formulated to protect the clergy. The first was termed the *privilegium canonis,* under which the clergy were considered sacred personages. Any violence against them was therefore sacrilege and punishable by immediate excommunication, for which absolution could be obtained only by arduous penance. Under the second, the *privilegium fori,* the clergy were exempt from the secular courts and subject exclusively to ecclesiastical jurisdiction. Since clerics enjoyed the *privilegium canonis,* the Church courts were restricted to spiritual sanctions. The *privilegium fori* posed evident problems for the secular authorities, since murder, rape, robbery and other of the most heinous crimes committed by the clergy went unpunished. At Paris, because of the concentration of scholars, the problem of repressing clerical crime was more acute than elsewhere, such as in England. Philippe-Auguste himself was reported to have observed gloomily that clerics exhibited greater rashness than knights, for whereas knights fought only in armour, clerics and students sprang into the fray brandishing knives, without helmets to protect their clean-shaven pates. Youthful students, as well as their masters and mentors, became renowned for their brawling and rioting, as well as for committing more heinous crimes, such as fornication, abduction of married women, robbery and even murder.

By 1223, there was such animosity that the Paris citizenry fought a pitched battle against the students during which 320 were killed, their bodies thrown into the Seine.

Shortly after the death of Philippe-Auguste, under the reign of his saintly grandson, Louis IX, the university reaped more of the whirlwind already sown. During the carnival of 1228–29, students entered a tavern in the suburb of Bourg Saint-Marcel, where "by chance they found good and sweet wine." A row began with the landlord; the disputants rapidly proceeded to blows, and "the pulling of ears and tearing of hair." The innkeeper called in his neighbours, who fiercely beat off the students; but the next day they returned with reinforcements, armed with swords and sticks. They attacked the host and set the taps running. Then, "filled with insolence and wine," they "sallied forth into the streets to amuse themselves at the expense of peaceable citizens and women alike." The tables were turned once more when "the savage police of a savage city"[2] killed several innocent students. The masters once more suspended their lectures, while the episode aroused strong feelings against the university—the murder of a number of students by a brutal soldiery being "welcomed by their official superiors as tending to the humiliation of the upstart university."

There followed the dissolution of the university for six years—with the consequences Philippe-Auguste had so greatly feared: the great mass of masters and scholars left Paris, many of them accepting the pressing invitation of Henry III of England, to reinforce the rising universities of Oxford and Cambridge. About the only power retained by the English universities was that of excommunicating "vagabond, truant and incorrigible scholars."

DESPITE THIS TURBULENT EARLY HISTORY of dissolution and scandal, the institution of the university had grown in size and repute since 1180, the year Philippe-Auguste was crowned, when the Collège des Dix-Huit was formed by the heirs of Abelard's handful of students— its first hall of residence opened by an Englishman called Josse. Through its distinction, the Paris of Philippe-Auguste established herself as the recognised intellectual centre of Europe; even his holy adversary, Pope Innocent III, was educated there and subsequently lent it his powerful support; after him there followed three of the nephews of Pope Alexander IV. In 1210, the royal chronicler, Guillaume le Bretonne, lauded how

> letters flourished in Paris. Never before at any time, or in any part of the world, whether in Athens or Egypt, had there been such a multitude of students. The reason for this must be sought not only in the beauty of Paris itself, but also in the special privileges which King Philippe and his father before him had conferred upon the students.[3]

In 1257, under St. Louis' confessor, Robert de Sorbon, the University of Paris gained its definitive name of the "Sorbonne." It started then as a small college with accommodation limited to only seven priests, with originally sixteen students of theology, four from each European nation, swiftly increased to thirty-six. Theology and the arts were its main disciplines; later a medical school would be added beneath its umbrella. By the end of the thirteenth century, the Sorbonne had attained the constitutional form that would carry it through the rest of the Middle Ages; by the year 1400, forty colleges would exist, while three centuries later the number would have grown to sixty-five, though most would disappear under the present Sorbonne. As of 1231, Pope Gregory IX could praise Paris as "the town of books"; Robert de Sorbon would start off the university library with a bequest of his own personal library of sixty-seven volumes; thirty years later the collection numbered 1017 titles, all painstakingly written on parchment, often exquisitely illuminated. Of these only four were in French, the remainder still in Latin.

By the fourteenth century, interest in Abelard's dialectics had begun to decline within the university, replaced by a trend towards the pragmatic; in the words of Robert de Sorbon, "is not the labourer mad who is forever sharpening his plough without ever ploughing the field?"[4] Bankrupted during the Hundred Years' War, the Sorbonne's pristine quality waned. It was to become "an annexe of Oxford" after taking sides with the English against the King of France and Joan of Arc— honour was restored as, in 1437, the university submitted to Charles VII. In 1470, the first printing press to reach Paris from Germany was set up in the Sorbonne. Under the influence of the great printer Robert Estienne (1503–59), the Sorbonne once more regained its position of eminence in Europe, but with the Wars of Religion, Estienne (a supporter of the Reformation) was proscribed for "blasphemy, sedition, and the selling of prohibited books," and he migrated—with his precious press—to Geneva, where he died.

During these retrograde days, the medical fraternity also suffered. Under the aegis of the Church, doctors had to undertake on oath not to practise surgery which cut the skin; that was left to the barbers— regardless of the requirements of the patient. In 1442, they were even summoned to refrain, on oath, from prescribing all digestive, laxative or soothing remedies; they revolted, and by the end of the fifteenth century the quarrel between medical progress and religious doctrine had become acute. To bring air into the ailing university, and impressed by the intellectual and artistic achievements he had seen in Italy, François I in 1529 founded the Collège de France, right next door to the Sorbonne. Known at first as the Collège des Trois Langues, as Hebrew and Greek were taught there as well as Latin, it adopted the revolutionary procedure of giving lectures in French.

In 1624, Cardinal Richelieu, elected Grand Master of the Sorbonne, commissioned Lemercier to reconstruct its derelict building, taking upon himself the restoration of its former glories. It would revive only to be suppressed by the revolution in 1792, remaining empty until 1806 when Napoleon enters the story. Nevertheless, its massive quarters still sitting astride the hump of the Mont de Sainte-Geneviève, for 850 years the Sorbonne has survived as the sanctuary of French intelligence; as John Russell notes, there is no institution in England that quite corresponds to it: "It is as if Eton, Harrow, Oxford, Cambridge, Manchester

Grammar School, the London School of Economics, and the Royal Institute of International Affairs were all bundled into an area less than a mile square."

THE STUDENTS OF MEDIEVAL PARIS, aged between fifteen and thirty, had a pitiably hard life. Often their backs bore the signs of heavy beating, inflicted by less amiable masters. Bitterly cold in winter, with only one much-patched garment to their name, they would lodge

> in a poor house with an old woman who cooks only vegetables and never prepares a sheep except on feast days. A dirty fellow waits on the table and just such a person buys the wine in the city . . . After the meal, a student sits on a rickety chair and uses a light, doubtless a candle, which goes out continually and disturbs the ideas.[5]

He "sits all night long and learns the seven liberal arts. Often he falls asleep at his work and is troubled by bad dreams." The next day's lectures would begin again at 5 a.m. Receiving no stipend, he would often have to pay extortionate rents for these meagre lodgings himself—as well as his master's wages; receiving no regular salaries, each had the right to teach for whatever fees he could extract from other students. When an English student, Abbot Samson of Bury St. Edmunds, was studying in Paris, he recalled how he had been subsidised by a chaplain back home, who merchandised holy water for this purpose.

Official, ecclesiastical entertainments were few, and simple; in December and January, as well as at Easter time, there were the *Ludi Theatrales,* plays which were put on at a monastery. Otherwise, in a world adorned by those perennial students, François Villon and François Rabelais, they would amuse themselves with such harmless pursuits as stealing shop signs and placing fried turds in the hoods of graduates. Pranks like this, however, could of course escalate into more serious outbreaks of violence. As a warning, *pour épater les étudiants,* in the middle of the Latin Quarter a gibbet was set up in the Place Maubert, the grim focus of a squalid area stigmatised by the philosopher Erasmus as "a cesspit." But even public executions, in heartless medieval Paris, could be a major source of entertainment.

THOUGH THE STUDENTS were clearly at the lower end of the social spectrum, life for the remainder of the populace of Paris during the twelfth and thirteenth centuries was no sinecure either, in a brutally competitive, bustling city. We know something about it from the jottings of a young English schoolmaster, Alexander Neckam, who in his early twenties went to teach in Paris around 1177. The London he left behind, he recorded, was a city much afflicted by drunkenness and fire; Paris measured up better in these respects. Reaching Montmartre, Neckam noted how it seemed to rise in three tiers of vineyards out of open fields, with the ruins of an old temple near the top. From Montmartre there was a unique view of Paris, of "a turreted city surrounded by great walls."[6] In another view of Paris, dating from 1210, members of a travelling Chanson de Geste group saw an "admirable city with many a church, many high church towers, and abbeys of great nobility. They saw the Seine, with deep fords and the mills, of which there were many; they saw the ships which bring wheat, wine, salt and great wealth."[7]

The river would have been in a state of constant movement and hubbub, with ships plodding up heavy with stone from Normandy, meeting barges coming down from Burgundy laden with wine and grain. There was a rumble of mill wheels everywhere; water mills for grinding grain run by the power of the life-giving Seine, as the windmill had not yet been invented. There were even mills mounted on floating hulls which could be shifted to allow traffic to pass under the bridges. Neckam found quarters off the Seine on the Rue de la Boucherie, where the waters of the Bièvre stream, not yet become a sewer, ran clear and pleasant through unpolluted fields. But the water of the Seine gave dysentery to all who were not natives of Paris.

Neckam's house would almost certainly have been of timber construction, and if his walls had any drapes at all, they would have been crude fabrics dyed a solid colour. His bed was put together at night fall, then dismantled in the morning; clothing and books were kept in chests ranged round the wall, and candles were the only source of light for study. If it was a more affluent Parisian household, there might be biblical scenes in coloured worsted around the walls, and a raised floor, or dais, at the fireplace end, where those of the higher rank sat and ate; but Neckam as a poor clerk would not have been permitted to sit at the fire, "nor sit at a table, but rather eat on his lap, with the household dogs flocking around to take the bread from his hand." For food, if he was lucky, on special days he would have been treated to roast pork; but mostly the fare would have been vegetables—beans, beets and peas.

There was honey for sweetening. To drink there was cider, beer and unfermented wine, from the slopes of Montmartre. By the fireplace was to be found a disgusting and evil-smelling *garde-robe* pit, into which all kitchen waste (and probably human waste, too) was thrown.

In Paris, chronically overcrowded within its protective walls, personal sanitation was ever a problem—worse than in London. When space permitted, the *garde-robe* pit would be dug outside the house, and a shed and a wooden platform placed over it. Otherwise, contributing to the endemic lack of hygiene in medieval Paris, there was always difficulty in locating a latrine—hence known as the *longaigne,* or "far-off place." In the *Life of St. Gregory,* the latrine is spoken of as a "retiring place where tablets can be read without interruption." It was the custom for kitchen pots and washbasins as well as chamber pots to be emptied by pitching the contents from the window. Hence the reason why the better-off Parisian rode through the streets on horseback, while others wore heavy shoes, with high, thick soles, plus a *chape* as a protection from ordure thrown from above. Most of the houses had a *perron* (a word used today for a railway platform) in the form of a large block of stone raised above the vile mud to serve as a doorstep, where the lady of the house would sit and gossip and watch the *va-et-vient.*

Compared with the terrible fourteenth century that lay ahead, and even the days of Louis XIV, life for peasants and city-dwellers alike was tolerable. Social degree showed itself to a large extent in apparel. In bed at night, all wore nothing. By day, a baron could be spotted in cold weather by his fur-lined *pellice.* Men of all ranks wore *braies,* the full, pleated breeches favoured by the Gauls, while the affluent also wore long stockings, or *chauces,* often in brilliant colours and of rich materials like silk or cotton (imported from Africa, and therefore of even greater rarity). Above would be worn a pleated *cote* or *bliaut* doublet with full but short sleeves, revealing the tight-fitting *chainse* shirt (handsomely embroidered in the case of the wealthy). Instead of *braies* women of the time—those who could afford it—wore a long linen *chainse* trailing to the ground. According to the early thirteenth-century *Roman de la Rose,* it was important to have a good tailor:

> you should give your garment to someone who knows how to cut [*taillier*], who can place the stitches properly and make the sleeves fit. Shoes and boots you should have fresh and new, and see that they fit so close that the low-class fellows will argue how you got into them—and how you will get out.[8]

Elegant women wore clothes of brilliant hue—possibly a purple mantle fastened by a gold pin at the breast.

To palliate the hardship of medieval life, for rich man or poor, music and verse were of the highest priority. The principal instrument of the visiting *jongleur* would be a *viele*—a flat-bottomed fiddle, slightly triangular, with three strings, tuned in fourths or fifths. The bow, concave, was a little awkward to handle. Then there was the *gigue,* a tenor *viele* and ancestor of the viola da gamba; it seems to have been set on the left knee, played like a cello. There were the *rote,* a zitherlike instrument with five strings; the *mandore,* a kind of mandolin, played on the lap; a *monicorde* or *organistrum,* played by two people, a long guitar-shaped instrument with a single string; the horn, on which, with no valves, they could only blow fundamental notes; and, of course, a rustic form of *cornemuse,* bagpipe. Finally there was the organ—played by two men, with two to four men at the bellows.

The much-loved, heroic *Chanson de Roland* could take as long as five hours to perform. With his wide knowledge of Jerusalem, of Arabs and Babylonians, drawn from the Crusades, and his tales of heroes who would give up all for the Faith, the well-travelled *jongleur* was much sought-after. Though the *chansons de geste,* like "Roland" with their attachment to chivalry that was heroic to the point of suicide, were to lead France to defeat at Crécy in the next century, they kindled for the first time a patriotic feeling of intense love for *la douce France*—principally identified with the immediately surrounding Île de France.

Out of these *chansons* grew another form of literature of great importance, centred around women and dealing with courtly love. In this early development of feminism in France, the Crusades—where, because of lengthy absence by the lord, the "lady" gained more power—played a significant role. Here Eleanor of Aquitaine was perhaps a role-model, as well as importing to rude Paris the "courtly" manners of the south. "Great ladies," says André Maurois, "had a lover when at the same time they had a husband; here were the beginnings of a long tradition."[9] Whereas in the more northerly clime of England the courtly lover of Malory and the Round Table tended to platonic adoration from afar, the Parisian woman already expected—and received—more earthy devotion. Nevertheless, as Maurois points out, such *chansons* and poems like the *Roman de la Rose* contribute to a "discipline of customs and manners which was a great step forward to civilisation." With it came the ascendant influence of the city woman, and hence the importance attached to love—as well as its close concomitant, satire.

BUT AT THE FEAST the spectre was never absent—even before the horrendous Black Death which wiped out a third of the population of France in the fourteenth century. Infant mortality was inordinate; if a man survived childhood, he could expect to live into his thirties; if he survived his thirties, the late fifties was the best he could expect. (Women such as Eleanor and Héloïse were notable exceptions.) If he reached a height of 5 foot 10 inches he would be considered a giant. Apart from war, apoplexy and heart problems like angina carried off most; the Paris drains helped with an occasional epidemic of cholera. Good teeth and sweet breath were greatly prized, but extremely rare; right up to and beyond Napoleonic times a healthy set of teeth seldom lasted into three decades.

Repairs to an ailing physique were, to say the least, primitive and rudimentary; any deep wound, such as made by an arrow, would be kept open with paraffin while (with good luck) the poison drained out. Otherwise, physicians attempted to cure illness by keeping the "humours" balanced, using herbal remedies such as

> wild spikenard, which gently brings forth, through the upper orifice, the disturbed content of the "father of the family" by which I mean stomach. Colewort and ragwort excite love, but the marvellous frigidity of psyllium seeds offers a remedy for that affliction. Myrtle too is a friend of temperance . . .[10]

When available—which was infrequently—rough toilet soap would be used for the application of an enema; and there was always the physician's centuries-old remedy of bleeding. By contemporary standards, Paris hospitals—in the shape of the Hôtel Dieu (founded in AD 660, next to Notre-Dame, as a hospital for the poor, and open to all regardless of sex, race, creed, age or nationality)—had the remarkably low mortality rate of only one in five patients, even though at times it housed up to six in a bed.

When the Reaper called, the corpse would be handed over to a religious order and sewn up in a deerskin. That of a prominent person, lay or clerical, would be laid to rest in a stone sarcophagus sealed with lead. There was no embalming; after a few years, bones would be lifted out of a grave and stacked with others in an ossuary, making further use of limited space.

IN 1216, Philippe-Auguste's old foe across the Channel, the hapless John "Lackland," died and was replaced by a child-king, Henry III. Philippe-Auguste's heir, Prince Louis, had already been elected king by a junta of disaffected English barons. Now, however, a new wave of national resurgence carried the demoralised English with it, and Louis was swept out of the country after a crushing naval defeat off Calais in August 1217, in a first display of British ascendancy at sea. Philippe-Auguste and his son now turned their eyes towards south-west France, where the last years of his reign were marred by a campaign of appalling savagery against fellow Christians: the "Albigensian Crusade." The actual heresy, labelled Manichaeism, of the unfortunate Albigensians, or "Cathars," was obscured by the propaganda of Pope Innocent III: they were charged with enormous outrages such as institutionalised sodomy. Over the distance of time the religious differences seem little greater than those of contemporary Northern Ireland may appear to future historians, but the tolerance that had enveloped Abelard's twelfth century was fast evaporating. Whole areas of Languedoc were laid waste by the ruthless Simon de Montfort in an orgy of "ethnic cleansing." Whipped on by the papal legate, Arnaud Amalric, with the alleged exhortation of "Kill them all. God will recognise his own," the brutal massacre of the inhabitants of Béziers, where 7000 men, women and children were herded into the Église de la Madeleine alone and slaughtered, is remembered to this day. The war in Languedoc was to drag on wretchedly for decades.

In September 1222, at one of the lowest points of the Albigensian affair, Philippe-Auguste went down with a fever, which he could not shake off. In July 1223, heading for a conference in Paris to discuss the latest papal agenda for a crusade, his illness worsened. On the 11th he was duly bled; the following day he insisted that he was to die in Paris. He was never to reach it, but passed on a request to his heir to "offer justice to his people, and above all to protect the poor and humble from the insolence of the proud [*orgueilleux*]."[11] With Philippe-Auguste's death France mourned a great ruler, the virtual founder of the nation.

LOUIS VIII, nicknamed "the Lion" (1223–26), kept on his father's ministers, like Guérin the hero of Bouvines, and maintained all his policies; thus Louis the Lion's short reign was but a continuation of Philippe's. At his death—the year before Genghis Khan's—his son, Louis IX (1226–70), was only twelve years old. So authority remained vested in his mother, Blanche of Castile, the regent.

Louis IX—Saint Louis, as he was canonised in 1297—was to consolidate much of the work of Philippe-Auguste. He took over the reins aged twenty-one, and for seven centuries God-fearing French mothers have held him up to their children as an example, the model king who, in the words of Maurice Druon, "was so careful to say his prayers, the good son who, even when he came of age and became glorious and all powerful, invited his mother to preside over his councils and made her sit beside him to receive ambassadors."[12]

In fact, Louis seems to have been a strange, complex man, terrified by his dominant mother, Blanche. Her threats of the Devil drove him into living by day in a hair-shirt—a garment he would hand round to his family and friends as the best possible present he could give them. At night, he would perform fifty genuflections, reciting as many Ave Marias before going to bed. His passion was for crusading—the hobby of the age for the remission of sins and acquisition of limitless loot—but he also brought to the Capetian dynasty a morality which would, alas, die with him.

In geopolitical terms, he routed Henry III's English at Saintes in 1242, the unfortunate Albigensians were finished off in 1244, and Languedoc became assimilated into France. Through his marriage in 1234 to Margaret of Provence, France acquired a claim to one of the richest and largest of his neighbours to the south, and by the Treaty of Paris of 1259 Normandy, Anjou, Maine and Poitou were attached definitively to the French crown. These gains bestowed on Louis considerable prestige throughout Europe.

Louis was very tall, thin and finely chiselled, his figure described as being "bowed by fasting and mortification." He wore the humblest of apparels—but white peacock feathers in his hat. Some of Saint Louis' earthy contemporaries were not impressed by his excessive piety—which extended to washing the feet of his nobles, and which seemed inappropriate to a king—and on occasion they jeered at him as being a "king of priests" rather than of France. Inflexible in his beliefs, he installed the Inquisition in France, with all the misery which that was to bring. He loved God and France in the abstract, but not Frenchmen in the particular. He was chillingly formal, never addressing anyone as *tu*—which is said to have contributed to the increased use of the formal address, *vous*, in French society down the years. Though remote and harsh with his entourage, he abhorred the spilling of blood; yet was proud of slaughtering infidels on a crusade. His reactions were unpredictable, and often irrational; it was one of his dreams to convert Islam to Christianity.

In 1248, in thanksgiving for recovery from a serious illness, Louis embarked on the Seventh Crusade—against the wishes of the Pope and the judgement of his counsellors. In a remarkable display of the solidity now of the French monarchy, he also took with him Queen Margaret and two of his brothers, leaving his mother, Blanche of Castile, once more in charge. The aim of the Crusade this time was to liberate the Holy Land from the Sultan of Egypt, but—as usual—things went wrong and by 1250 Louis, stricken with typhus, was a prisoner of the Sultan at El Mansura after a massacre of his forces. While Louis was a prisoner, Margaret gave birth to a son. Before the delivery, she made an octogenarian attendant swear that, if the Saracens arrived, he would behead her rather than let her fall into their hands; the old man replied, "Madam, I was intending to!"[13] The Queen was saved by the Genoese, but at a considerable financial cost. With great difficulty the King raised his own heavy ransom with recourse to the affluent Knights Templar. At first, though, they refused; one of the King's first acts on being freed was to impose public penance on them. He then opened negotiations with the Muslims for the delivery of Jerusalem—which might well have succeeded, but for news of the death of his mother.

Louis hastened home to find a sea of internal troubles arisen in his absence, including a bizarre peasant revolt known as the *Pastoureaux*. Their origins obscure, they wandered in bedraggled bands from village to village in the northern provinces, finally descending on Paris as a horde incremented by thieves, vagabonds, gypsies and tarts. Estimated at 60,000 strong, they killed several priests and indulged in various acts of apostasy. Eventually their assaults extended to the propertied nobility—and the Jews. On the King's return, the *Pastoureaux* were mercilessly hunted down as far away as Aigues Mortes, at the mouth of the Rhône—and left behind no legacy.

Reinstated in Paris, Louis was the first to realise that the complex organism that his grandfather had created could not be administered like private family property. Under him, the various organs of state began to specialise with the Grand Conseil, in charge of political matters, the Chambre des Comptes and the Parlement. (The last filled the role of the supreme court of appeal in the kingdom.) Saint Louis out-lawed private wars, such as hitherto had plagued the poor, respecting feudal legitimacy but attacking its abuses, pitying the poor and the weak—at least in principle. To his heir, he instructed: "If a poor man has a quarrel with a rich man, support the poor rather than the rich—at least until the truth can be ascertained."[14]

He created the National Archives (the first records of which had been destroyed at the lost battle of Fréteval), in which were preserved all royal acts, treaties, title deeds and judgements. It also first housed the priceless collection of illuminated manuscripts, such as those of Denis the Are-opagite, which show in marvellous detail life in medieval Paris, eventu-ally to find their way into the Bibliothèque Nationale. Louis also founded Paris' first hospital for the blind, the Vingt-Quinze, which could offer shelter to 300 people, and a home for prostitutes—the Filles-Dieu. He organised for food to be dispatched to any part of the country that was famine-stricken. The burden of taxation was alleviated (perhaps one good reason for Louis' beatification), a new middle class came into being in Paris and, by the end of his reign, the country as a whole had never known such material prosperity.

In 1259, Louis signed a conclusive peace, the Treaty of Paris, with Henry III, designed to bring to a definitive end the age-old struggle with England. National-minded Frenchmen found it hard to comprehend why Louis gave so much away to the defeated, in the shape of territories like Gascony and Guienne in the south-west. "For we have two sisters to wife," he explained, "and our children are first cousins, wherefore it is surely fitting that peace be between us." By this largesse he reckoned that Henry would "entre en mon hommage." It did not, in retrospect, pre-vent the (second) Hundred Years' War; nevertheless, by standards of the day, it was an act of astonishing, modern-minded moderation, and gave the King a reputation as a mediator to whom all Europe would resort in his lifetime—including even Henry III when in dispute with his own barons. "Never had a united Christendom come closer to realisation," comments André Maurois.


THE PIETY OF SAINT LOUIS, rigidly inflexible as it was, was to bequeath to France one of its greatest jewels, the Île de la Cité's Sainte-Chapelle (without the Crusades and all their attendant evils and brutal-ity it would almost certainly never have been built). In 1239, Louis

acquired the purported "Crown of Thorns" from the Emperor of Constantinople (Baudouin II). To house it, three years later Louis began
building the Sainte-Chapelle, completed in the record time of six years.

Against the counsel of the Pope and his own family, in the high summer of 1270, Louis rashly set off from Aigues Mortes on a new crusade,
the eighth. In Tunisia, his army was decimated by sun and plague at
Carthage, and Louis, aged only fifty-six, succumbed—his arms crossed
like a true crusader. There was widespread mourning across France. For
the next two centuries the landed gentry clamoured for a return to "the
good customs of Saint Louis." Louis' rule of moral standards was to lead
the kingdom definitively towards an absolute monarchy, with all its
attendant strengths and weaknesses, a form of rule that would remain
alien to the English. In his memory, the poets wrote—with perhaps just
a hint of ambivalence:

> Good King Louis, you held the land under yoke
> To the profit of barons and of the little folk . . .
> To whom may poor men cry now in their woe
> Since the good king is dead who loved them so?[15]

By the end of his reign, medieval France had created an image for herself
which carried inestimable weight in the Christian world, and a civilisation that was identifiably her own.

LOUIS' HEIR, Philippe III—otherwise known as "the Bold"—ruled by
contrast for only fifteen years (1270–85). He spent most of his years away
from the capital, campaigning—notably in the disastrous war with
Aragon. When at home, he suffered from succeeding under the vast
shadow of his father, and proved a spiritless ruler, who left little imprint.
His greatest, dynastic, success was to marry his second son to Joan of
Navarre, the independent kingdom down on the Pyrenees. It was
Navarre which, several centuries later, was to provide France with perhaps the greatest of all her kings—Henri IV. Philippe's first son died,
possibly of poisoning; so, in 1285, his second son succeeded him, as
Philippe IV.

MYSTERY AND CONTROVERSY surround Philippe IV (1285–1314),
except that he was swiftly to prove one of France's most unpleasant,

indeed disastrous kings. His reign and its catastrophic consequences provided the rich tissue for a great series of novels evocative of Shake-speare's history plays, *Les Rois Maudits,* by Maurice Druon. Under Philippe a new depth of savagery manifested itself in public life, a dark retreat from the enlightenment of Suger and Philippe-Auguste, his great-great-grandfather. Called "le Bel" on account of his blond, fair, but icy good looks, few reliable personal descriptions of Philippe IV sur-vive.[16] Guillaume de Nogaret, one of his chief counsellors, who owed both his swift ascent and his miserable demise to Philippe, obsequiously describes him as having been:

> before, during and after his marriage, chaste, humble, modest of countenance and of speech, never put in a rage; he hated no one; he envied no one; he loved the whole world. Full of grace and charity, pious, merciful . . . fair of face and charming in aspect, agreeable to all, even to his enemies when they are in his presence, God granted manifest miracles to the sick through the medium of his hands.[17]

This may be treated with appropriate scepticism—except perhaps for the piety; like his saintly grandfather, Philippe wore a hair-shirt much of his life. But it was a remorseless kind of piety, and under Philippe le Bel—fair of face, but most unfair by character—the Inquisition that Saint Louis had introduced into France was exploited to horrifying ends. Other, discreetly anonymous, contemporary sources describe Philippe as having been lazy, and blindly led by those bad counsellors who had gained his confidence. Perhaps more fittingly, he was also nick-named the "Iron King."

Philippe further cemented the fundamental institutions of France, and extended its territories, but all his revisions of the body politic only increased the power of the throne, heading France closer towards absolute monarchy and away from the democratic trends slowly taking root across the Channel. In Paris, in contrast to England where the Lords and the Commons were willing to sit together in legislation, the three Estates remained separate, making impossible any joint, national representation—a failing that would plague democracy in France right through to the revolution of 1789.

Systematically, Philippe applied himself to the destruction of all external, and internal, rivalry. To achieve all this he brought in hard-faced, wily lawyers from the provinces. The periodic "Consultations" held by him tended only to confirm acts and legislation already promulgated. A contemporary miniature of about 1322 portrays a saintly looking Philippe, clad from head to foot in a robe of fleur-de-lys, presiding over a Paris Parlement with bishops gossiping to his left, laity on the right; though, revealingly, it looks suspiciously as if one of the laity is handing into the King's outstretched hand a severed head.

Following Philippe le Bel would come *le déluge*; the Capetian line ends, the Valois begins. With it would follow all the misery of the Hundred Years' War as a direct consequence of his thirty-year reign. It all began with Philippe's wildly extravagant plans, in 1298, to sumptuously rebuild the Palais de la Cité to be "the most beautiful that anyone in France ever saw." It would house all the functions of administration, treasury and justice of the kingdom, with even the sinister vaults of the Conciergerie beneath being of great beauty.

In the Great Hall of the Palais, divided by two massive naves under whose columns statues of past kings surveyed the scene, his Parlements and Consultations would convene. Skins of slaughtered animals were hung from the ceiling, and extravagant meals served on a vast marble-topped table—which also sometimes served as a stage for morality plays. One of the biggest in the contemporary world, Philippe's sombre chamber, with its Salle des Pas Perdus above, still survives today, close to his grandfather's ethereal Sainte-Chapelle. Even closer was one the four great defensive towers which was known as Tour Bonbec, or "Blabbing Tower," so called because it was there that torture loosened prisoners' tongues.

PHILIPPE LE BEL was never to complete his awe-inspiring Palais-Royal—or enjoy it. Deservedly he became known as France's most spendthrift king. France stumbled under the burden of Philippe's taxes; whereas Philippe-Auguste had raised heavy taxes for its greater glory, Philippe le Bel despoiled it. He introduced rampant inflation by adulterating the currency, shamelessly reducing its weight in gold at the Mint—the first French king to do so. Private counterfeiters were subject to the hideous penalty of being boiled alive—but, as counterfeiter-supreme, the King of course remained untouchable. Riots against inflation by the impoverished *commerçants* of Paris in 1307 were ruthlessly crushed, with twenty-eight offenders publicly hanged on the eve of Epiphany from elms at the four entries to the city. Such was the grip of the "Iron King" that there would be no wider revolt.

None of this was enough to stem the outflow from the royal exchequer. In succession he turned his eyes towards the money-lenders—the Lombards, who had settled from their native northern Italy and made themselves extremely wealthy (and, consequently, unpopular) not least in funding the Crown. He also targeted the Jews. After their expulsion by Philippe-Auguste, Jewish communities had gradually trickled back to re-establish themselves in France, flourishing particularly in the south. Saint Louis hated the Jews as "enemies of Christ" and had talked of a new pogrom, but had done nothing about it.*

In 1288, three years after Philippe IV's accession, thirteen Jews of both sexes were burned at the stake in Troyes—a foretaste of what was to follow. Beginning in the summer of 1306, all Jews were condemned as usurers (though, like other Christian monarchs, Philippe had been a principal beneficiary of their usury). Declared the King: "Every Jew must leave *my* land, taking none of his possessions with him; or, let him choose a new god for himself, and we will become *One People*."[18] By 1322, there were virtually no Jews left in France. As one contemporary Christian novelist, Geoffroi, admitted, the Jewish exodus greatly impoverished the country at large, while their wealth escaped the clutches of the King.

PHILIPPE LE BEL now turned his avaricious gaze in a direction where none of his forebears had dared: the vast funds of papal wealth. Since 1294, the fiercely ambitious Pope Boniface VIII had pursued a policy of worldly intervention in the affairs of states. In his view, every human being was subject to the Pope. For the centenary of 1300, Boniface threw a gigantic party, drawing some two million pilgrims to Italy. Those from Flanders flattered him by declaring him to be the "universal judge of matters spiritual and temporal" and "heir to the rights on earth of Christ." Boniface appeared clad in the insignia of the Roman Empire, and exclaiming, "I am Caesar!"

In fact, he was heralding a century of near catastrophic turmoil for the Papacy. Boniface's ambitions brought him at once into conflict with Philippe who, ignoring the financial crisis, nourished grandiose schemes

---

*He was not alone among Jew-persecuting Christian monarchs of the time; Edward I—also in financial straits—is recorded as having hanged 200 Jews in 1278, accusing them of habitual "coin-clipping," subjected them to ransom ten years later, and finally expelled them from both England and Aquitaine.

for a new Christian empire stretching from the North Sea to the Mediterranean (run from Paris) into which the papal state would be assimilated. Philippe undermined the Pope by imposing his own tax on the clergy. Boniface riposted by preparing a bull excommunicating Philippe, a formidable document that could have resulted in the complete dismemberment of France.

Before Boniface's *Unum Sanctum* bull, the ultimate blow in his propaganda war against Philippe, could be applied, French forces invaded the papal palace at Anagni in 1303. They mobbed the pontiff in a scene of unprecedented violence with a view to forcing his abdication. Boniface declared he would rather die: "Here is my neck, here is my head!" But he never recovered, dying a month later. All Europe was shocked by this affront; Dante, though he hated Boniface, regarded it as a recrucifixion of Christ.

Confronted simultaneously with serious military defeat at Courtrai in Flanders at the hands of Edward I, "the Iron King" refused to back down. He banned the export of all currency to the Vatican, which drained its resources, leading to a battle of attrition that was to last the best part of two decades. It was a battle he was to win. Boniface's elderly successor, Benedict XI, survived only nine months; poison in a dish of fresh figs was suggested. There now followed one of the most grotesque and comic—if it were not so humiliating—episodes in all the history of the Popes. It came to be known as the Babylonian Captivity of the Popes, at Avignon. For eleven months the Conclave sat in deadlock, divided between pro- and anti-French factions and constantly harassed by Philippe. Finally, a split in the anti-French front enabled Philippe to triumph with the election of Bernard le Got, the Archbishop of Bordeaux, as Clement V. Trained as a lawyer, not even a cardinal, Clement was a shameless nepotist who made cardinals of five members of his family, and was easily manipulated by Philippe. Using the chaos in Italy as an excuse, he agreed to be crowned in Lyons and to settle in the bishop's palace in Avignon, transforming it into the magnificent Popes' Palace and beginning the seventy-year exile, presaging the Great Schism, that was an unmitigated disaster for the Church. Never again was the Papacy to know the power of an Innocent III, or a Boniface, and a French king was the cause.

THE ELECTION of a malleable French pontiff opened the door to Philippe's most fateful act—the dissolution of the Knights Templar.

Here Philippe found his ultimate hope of solvency. In Paris the Knights Templar resided in the Temple, a vast *donjon* flanked by four towers just outside the city walls.[19] The order had been founded after the First Crusade under the edict of Louis the Young, with the noble function of defending the Holy Land as "poor chevaliers of Christ." They and their rival military order, the Hospitallers, left magnificent castles across the Levant, and became recognised all over Europe by their robes of white with a red cross on the front. In 1128, the Templars had acquired a rule, supposedly dictated by the ascetic Saint Bernard himself, of dedicated austerity as monk-soldiers. But over the next two centuries loot derived from the Crusades, coupled with skilful husbandry, had enabled the Templars to amass immense riches—to become almost a sovereign power in their own right.

During the thirteenth century, they had become *de facto* bankers to the Capetian crown (Philippe-Auguste actually deposited his Treasury in the Temple), but Philippe remembered how they had incurred Saint Louis' displeasure when they had refused to raise funds to ransom him from Egypt. Now they lived in a splendour rivalling that of the Palais-Royal. The Templars' reputation for avidity and for the simpler vices of the flesh was widespread. (For centuries after their demise the expression "Boire comme un templier" was common currency in France, while the old German word *Tempelhaus* became synonymous with a house of ill repute.) Efforts at reform had been made, but the secrecy with which the Templars surrounded their activities was their worst enemy. Exploiting their unpopularity among the public, in October 1307, Philippe declared war on the Templars, based on trumped-up charges of heresy, necromancy and sodomy—like the Albigensian "Cathars" before them. In the preamble to his proclamation, Philippe spoke of "a bitter thing, a deplorable thing, a thing terrible to think about, terrible to hear, detestable, execrable, abominable, inhuman, which had already echoed in our ears, not without making us shudder with a violent horror. An immense pain developed in us. . . ."[20] The Templars were accused of "sacrificing to idols, . . . infecting the purity of the air" and of "torturing Christ a second time."

With a nod from an acquiescent Pope Clement, the Inquisition (which Saint Louis in his excess of piety had inflicted on France) now moved swiftly. In a well-orchestrated night-time raid, the Templars were arrested and their property declared forfeit. One after the other they appeared before inquisitors, counsellors of the King, and torturers, in the cellars of their own fortress and in the presence of a vast crowd of eager spectators. The tortures were so appalling that one Templar saw twenty-five *frères* die "under the question." Public burning at the stake, the modern form of pre-Christian human sacrifice from which the early Church had freed itself, was now the favoured ritual of the Inquisition. In one deplorable episode, 138 Templars were burned at the stake. As the flames rose, most of them retracted the "confessions" they had made under torture. "They suffered with a fortitude," wrote a contemporary chronicler, "that put their souls in great peril of damnation, for it induced ignorant people to consider them innocent."[21]

By 1314, the Grand-Master of the order himself, Jacques de Molay, refusing to answer charges, had been tortured and in prison for seven years, together with his chief assistant, Geoffroy de Charnay. In March they were brought out on to the *parvis* Notre-Dame to hear their sentence, anticipating life imprisonment, which had been promised them several times. But Pope Clement had abandoned them. The Templar leaders vigorously declared their innocence, protesting: "the Order is pure; it is saintly; the accusations are absurd, the confessions lie. . . ."[22] With the mob stirring against them, Philippe, enraged at their protestations of innocence, ordered them to be immolated that same evening on a special scaffold set up on the Île des Juifs. As the flames licked around him, Jacques de Molay is reputed to have uttered a terrible curse:

> Pope Clement, iniquitous judge and cruel executioner, I adjure you to appear in forty days' time before God's tribunal. And you, King of France, will not live to see the end of this year, and Heaven's retribution will strike down your accomplices and destroy your posterity.

Within forty days, Pope Clement V fell ill of an agonisingly painful disease and died on 20 April; Chancellor de Nogaret died of mysterious causes a short while later; Philippe le Bel died after a hunting accident that same year, on 29 November, aged only forty-six. Over the next few years, his three sons would equally be struck down, bringing to an end the Capetian dynasty.

The "Iron King" died a well-hated man; it may well be that Louis IX would have obtained the same effects without causing the same degree of suffering.

Under Philippe, Paris had become a harsh place of brutal punishments. Human ingenuity had introduced refinements virtually unknown in the twelfth century and the days of Philippe-Auguste, of which burning at the stake was by no means the most unpleasant. There were the rack and the wheel, hanging-and-drawing, quartering, boiling alive, and the gibbet at Montfaucon at the entrance of Paris, where malefactors died by slow strangulation, their swinging bodies left to rot as a warning to passers-by.

THAT SAME *ANNUS HORRIBILIS* of 1314, before Philippe le Bel reaped his just rewards, the royal family was rocked by a searing scandal, followed by retribution that indicated just how far since the days of Philippe-Auguste public life and social mores had become debased, the worst appetites for cruelty nourished.

On the left bank, just opposite the Louvre, stood the medieval Hôtel de Nesle. Originally a defence tower erected by the provost of Paris under Philippe-Auguste, it had grown to be a sumptuous palace after Philippe le Bel converted it into apartments for his sons and their families—not unlike present-day Kensington Palace. The three princes, all future kings as a consequence of the curse that Philippe brought down on the family—Louis X ("the Quarrelsome"), Philippe V ("the Tall") and Charles IV ("the Simple")—lived there with their wives, respectively Marguerite (a granddaughter of Saint Louis on her mother's side), and her cousins Jeanne and Blanche. Two were in their twenties, Blanche was a mere eighteen. The course of history following the Iron King's death proved their princes to be somewhat sub-standard, while the three wives were normal lusty *Parisiennes*. Jeanne was later proclaimed innocent, but Marguerite and Blanche used the old medieval tower as a place of assignation for their lovers, two dashing brothers, Philippe and Gautier d'Aulnay, who were their gentlemen-in-waiting. The two courtiers would sneak into the tower by dark of night, via a boat landing them up the Seine on the Quai de Conti. Unfortunately for the adulterous princesses, they were betrayed by their sister-in-law, Isabella—the bitter and frustrated wife of Edward II of England, a dedicated homosexual. One day she noticed the courtier-lovers carrying two purses that she had given the princesses as gifts. Spies were set to check on their nocturnal movements, then—well named the "She-Wolf of France"—she grassed on them. (The "She-Wolf of France" was also to provide one of the prime causes for the Hundred Years' War, in consequence of the territorial claims to France which she passed on to her son, Edward III—the marriage being yet another misjudgement to be laid at the door of her father, Philippe.)

It was an unimaginable scandal—a granddaughter of Saint Louis, no less! Fearful of bastardy introducing a taint into the Capetian line (which, through the Templars' curse was to be doomed anyway), the King was merciless. All five were arrested, and Princesses Marguerite and Blanche found guilty of adultery. Put to hideous torture, the d'Aulnays admitted that their liaisons had been going on for three years. They were skinned alive in front of an enthusiastic crowd, castrated and then disembowelled, decapitated and their trunks hung by the armpits on a gibbet to be devoured by birds of prey. The crowd cheered itself hoarse as the *bourreau* held aloft the severed genitals of the lovers. All who had abetted the lovers were drowned or secretly dispatched. Of the guilty princesses, Marguerite and Blanche were forced to witness the execution of their lovers. Their heads shaven like *collabos* after the Liberation of 1944, they were then condemned to solitary confinement for many months in miserable, icy conditions in Richard Coeur de Lion's old fortress of Château Gaillard. When Louis X decided he wanted to remarry, rather than spend time seeking an annulment, he had Marguerite suffocated between two mattresses. Blanche, divorced by her husband, was permitted to take the veil in the convent of Maubuisson, where she lived until her death in 1326. Mysteriously, while in Château Gaillard—incorrigible to the end—she gave birth to a child, whether by her husband, Charles, or a gaoler was never clear.

The innocent Jeanne, who remained highly suspect of participating in the tower orgies, was spirited out of Paris until the scandal died down, then reunited to a forgiving husband, King Philippe V. Rather insensitively, it would seem, he gave her the Hôtel de Nesle as her residence, where—for all the sinister ghosts that must have haunted it—she lived for ten years, seven of them as a merry widow, until she died there in 1329. Legends continued to surround the tower and its orgies, to which writers through the ages from François Villon (*Ballade des dames du temps jadis,* 1461) to Pierre Brantôme in the sixteenth century to Dumas *père* as late as 1832 would add their own contributions. The stories persisted that Jeanne, watching from her window in the 90-foot tower, would send for likely passing students and, having exhausted their virility, would have them tied in sacks and thrown from the top of the tower to drown in the Seine below. Central to the theme was Jean Buridan (the philosopher whose famous ass, unable to choose between water on one side and hay on the other, died of malnutrition).* After three days of ravenous sex, so the story goes, the wicked Queen had Buridan bundled off from the top of the tower, like his predecessors. But the wily professor had arranged with his loyal students to have a barge filled with hay moored underneath, while they dropped a large stone in the water to sound like a corpse.

Buridan survived to become an illustrious rector of the Sorbonne, outliving Queen Jeanne by thirty years; while the names of the three princesses of the Hôtel de Nesle remained almost as well known to Parisian *étudiants* through the ages as Héloïse and Abelard. After Jeanne's death, the ill-starred palace was sold to the university for the benefit of the students whom, allegedly, she had been so disposed towards, and good at disposing of. In later years, the dissolute Italian friend of François I, Benvenuto Cellini, appropriately used it as his Paris residence. François' son, Henri II, sold it to make way for the Mint. Eventually Mazarin acquired the site, ironically, for Richelieu's erudite Institut de France and the Académie Française itself.

And so the new century began, opening for France on a setting as brutal and ominously menacing as the previous one, under Philippe-Auguste, had begun brightly and full of hope. At the time of Philippe le Bel, France was the most populous and powerful country in Europe, counting 22 million to England's 2 million, while Paris—now bulging out beyond Philippe-Auguste's city wall—numbered 300,000 to London's 40,000. After the famines, wars, plague and weakness at the top which were to succeed him, it would take four centuries for France to recover that level of population. Meanwhile, as the fruits of the reigns of Philippe-Auguste and Saint Louis were scattered to the winds, across the Channel in the domain of her natural rival, under Edward III's strong rule and fifty years of domestic peace, England was being dragged out of the Middle Ages. There chivalry and literature, Chaucer and Wycliffe, were being encouraged; French was finally being replaced by English as the language of government, and Parliament consolidated as the only maker of laws. France's natural enemy was vigorous, and expansive. The road was leading towards the Hundred Years' War—on the worst of terms for France.[23]

---

*The sophism was that the unfortunate donkey lacked any determining motive to direct him to one or the other.

# FOUR

# The Second "100 Years' War":
# France Survives and Joins the Renaissance

> I have chased the English out of France more easily than ever my father
> did; for my father drove them out by force of arms whereas I have
> driven them out by force of venison pies and good wines.
>
> —*Louis XI*

> Madame, of everything there remain to me only honour and life,
> which are unscathed.
>
> —*François I, after the Battle of Pavia*

WHEN PHILIPPE LE BEL DIED in 1314, following the terrible curse of the Templars, he had "so dominated his period" that it seemed as if "the heart of the kingdom had ceased to beat."[1] But all his good works, his institutional reforms, would soon be forgotten. In the 327 years since the election of Hugues Capet, only eleven kings had reigned over France—a prodigious dynasty. Now, over the turbulent fourteen years that followed Philippe's death, there would be no fewer than four kings, all of them his sons, and none of them producing heirs to survive. Their short-lived reigns, at one point presided over by three rival regents, were to bring chaos and catastrophe. In the background there conspired two powerful and conniving women—the one, Isabella, only daughter of Philippe and mother of the future Edward III of England, the "She-Wolf of France," who had exposed royal adultery and was held responsible for the murder of her homosexual husband, Edward II; the other, Mahaut of Artois, mother of the adulterous Blanche, and supposed poisoner of two heirs to the throne—the second a five-day-old infant.

The cuckolded Louis X (1314–16), "le Hutin"—"the Headstrong," or "the Quarrelsome"—was unable even to remember his lines at his coronation; surviving just eighteen months after the death of his father in 1314, about the only notable achievement of his short rule was the execution of Enguerrand de Marigny, Philippe's all-powerful Coadjutor, deemed responsible for his financial disasters. (Marigny, in his defence, claimed that the empty exchequer was due to his having to settle the late King's huge debts. Indeed, he was regarded by subsequent generations as one of France's better superintendents of finance.) In May 1316, Louis X died after a swift bout of pneumonia, though rumours of his poisoning by Mahaut were never allayed; and his posthumous son, Jean, died mysteriously six months later. The succession would have gone to Jeanne, questionable daughter of Louis and the adulterous Marguerite, but Louis' lanky younger brother, Philippe, evoked the ancient Salic Law whereby the female line was precluded from the succession—an act of importance in the succession of future kings of France—and mounted a *coup d'état*. As Philippe V ("the Long"), husband of the now pardoned Queen Jeanne, he ruled for another brief period of six years, dying of tuberculosis in 1322. Then came Charles IV, for another six years (1322–28). Having divorced the hapless Blanche, he married again but produced only three daughters. Early in 1328, Charles was struck down by a mysterious illness, and died suddenly at Vincennes.

Thus, by 1328, three centuries of Capetian rule were over. The French throne now passed to a cousin, Philippe of Valois, who would begin a new dynasty as Philippe VI (1328–50). "Kings by chance," the first Valois were scornfully dubbed by contemporaries. But as he was already acting as regent, as well as being great-grandson of Saint Louis, Philippe's claim to the throne of France was sound. This was, however, not how it was seen by Queen Isabelle or her aggressive son, Edward III, who was about to rule England successfully for fifty years that were as good for the English as they were trying for their neighbours.

IN FRANCE IN 1315, there was a disastrous harvest, and famine settled on an unprepared Paris. Two years later, from the provinces, a new wave of half-crazed *Pastoureaux* flooded the capital. Unemployed youths, brigands, unfrocked priests, beggars and whores this time seized the Châtelet, assaulted the provost and pillaged the abbey of St. Germain-des-Prés. They swept through the country, provoking new outrages against Jewish ghettoes that had survived Philippe IV's expulsion orders. At Chinon all the Jews were rounded up and thrown into one huge fiery pit; in Paris they were burned—on the same site where the immolation of Jacques de Molay had taken place. Seized by crisis, Louis le Hutin, apparently seeking forgiveness of his sins (notably the murder of Queen Marguerite) and to curry favour with the populace, decided to empty the prisons—and crime took off.

To bring order to the chaos left by Louis, his successors had the gallows and scaffolds working overtime; in 1325, the famous wooden gibbet at Monfaucon was replaced by one of sixteen stone pillars over thirty feet high, and joined together by heavy beams. The corpses hung there until they disintegrated. That year a gentle spring and a brief period of prosperity under Charles IV, the last of the Capetians, lulled the people into false hopes of happy times ahead. Then came the bitterest of harsh winters; wells froze, trees cracked in the gardens, food prices rocketed, and so did the death toll. Nevertheless, at the royal court modish men took to adorning themselves with more jewellery than their women, wearing narrow-waisted tunics so saucily short that they revealed the buttocks, and such pointed shoes that they made walking a problem. The net impact (as well illustrated by Shakespeare's *Henry V*) was perhaps one of *déraciné* foppishness, at least compared with the comportment of their more martial and virile neighbours across the Channel.

I N  1340, Edward III of tiny England arbitrarily assumed the title of King of France. He had dynastic motives, reckoning that—since Charles IV had died without heir—he had a legitimate claim, and one (in modern terminology) of straightforward commercial imperialism, based on the complementary factors of the British wool trade and the weavers of Flanders. This alone guaranteed that the war would be a popular one. Domestic chaos in France invited an invasion aimed at "regime change." It began with the destruction of the French fleet at Sluys (Écluse) together with 20,000 French, off the Belgian coast. Edward's expeditionary force then landed virtually unopposed in the Cotentin Peninsula of Normandy, just where Eisenhower's Americans were to land almost exactly 600 years later. In 1346, the English longbowmen—possessing the most modern war weapon in all Europe of the time—won a decisive battle against the ponderous French cavalry at Crécy on the Somme. It was not far from Bouvines, but what had been gained for France in that great victory now seemed in jeopardy. In a historic scene, recorded not least by Rodin, the burghers of Calais surrendered to Edward with halters round their necks. England was to keep the port as a vital foothold for two centuries.

Despite the relative size of the English population, Edward's small armies were highly efficient, and bursting with nationalistic spirit. Proudly the English heralded

> Our King go forth to Normandy
> With grace and might of chivalry, . . .[2]

His marauding bands continually laid waste and plundered northern France. Ten years after Crécy, the Black Prince was confronted at Poitiers by a French army that had not troubled to study the lessons of the earlier debacle. There ended another shattering defeat in which the King himself, Jean II (John the Good, 1350–64), was even taken prisoner.

AS IF THIS BLACK PRINCE WERE NOT ENOUGH, now the Black Death descended, killing an estimated one-third of the world's population living between Iceland and India. In France perhaps half the population was wiped out by the combination of war and plague. Preceded—so legend had it—by a portentous ball of fire in the skies over the city, the Black Death reached Paris in the summer of 1348, two years after the disaster at Crécy. It then moved slowly on towards Flanders and Germany. Believing cats to be the source of plague, the populace killed off their most effective instruments for dealing with the plague-bearing rat population. By the Inquisition, the Black Death was utilised as a new pretext for tightening up the laws against heresy and, inevitably, against those Jews who had, after expulsion under Philippe the Fair, begun to return. They were blamed for poisoning Christian wells, and even the air, providing an excuse for fresh pogroms from Narbonne and Carcassonne in the south to Strasbourg in the north. Only in Avignon were the Jews safe. In Paris alone, the death rate among the population reached 800 a day, with the archives of Saint-Denis placing the death toll at about 50,000.*

---

*Something like one in four of the population, and this may well have been an underestimate.

In the countryside at large the Black Death gave birth to a new popular phenomenon—the Flagellants. Flagellating themselves in a zeal of religious penitence for the plague, they roamed across Europe, and France, uprooting Jewish communities as they went. Then, like the *Pastoureaux* before them, they disappeared as suddenly as they had appeared.

The auguries for Charles V ("the Wise," 1364–80), a small and deceptively frail man, were not encouraging upon his succession. While he was still Dauphin, his father, the ill-starred Jean II, and his brother, Philippe, were both imprisoned in London. Taking advantage of the King's defeat, Étienne Marcel, the headstrong provost who represented the merchants of Paris, urged reforms to tame the monarchy. Marcel was harbinger of the new coming power in France, the bourgeoisie that was neither of the nobility nor of the Church, but was based on mercantile wealth—the "Third Estate." He founded a party, to which he presented a hood dyed in the city's colours of red and blue (if added to the white of the royal standard it would already have given birth to the *tricolore*). The monarchy reached one of its most perilous moments when, at a cabinet meeting, two of the Dauphin's principal counsellors, the marshals of Champagne and Normandy, were killed before his eyes by the supporters of Marcel.

Charles decided to pull out of Paris and regroup with a view to seizing the capital by force. Around Paris the peasants, pushed over the brink by the deprivations and misery of war, rose and made common cause with Marcel. When this *Jacquerie* revolt was put down, Marcel over-reached himself by committing the unthinkable and allying himself with the English, at that time the occupying power in Paris. "Hooted at and censured," he was assassinated by his own followers in July 1358. From Compiègne Charles then re-entered Paris, showing clemency and, pushing aside Marcel's constitutional reforms, ruling as an absolute but restrained king following the death of his father in relaxed English captivity.

But France, still enfeebled, now found herself additionally menaced by the hostility of her residual enemy to the south, Burgundy. While the Burgundians made common cause with the invading English, France was torn asunder by civil strife. With no shred of legitimacy, England's dashing Henry V now renewed the claims of Edward III. Defeats like Crécy and Poitiers were followed by Agincourt, where—at the cost of a few hundred English dead—10,000 Frenchmen under Charles VI ("the Mad," 1380–1422) perished at the hands of Henry's longbowmen, in one of the bloodiest battles of the Middle Ages. As the Hundred Years' War dragged on, the new fifteenth century brought little encouragement with it for France. It was, in the words of that distinguished American historian Barbara Tuchman, "a violent, tormented, bewildered, suffering and disintegrating age, a time, as many thought, of Satan triumphant."

Indeed, it was "a bad time for humanity" as a whole. In a time of bitter cold, wolves came into Paris to keep warm. Fleeing the barren countryside, peasants sought shelter inside the girdle of walls that Charles V had built around Paris, where they occupied a tangle of reeking streets, establishing their own laws and terrorising the populace. In daytime they spilled out into the streets, transmogrifying themselves into blind or limbless beggars; by night they miraculously recovered their faculties, giving the unsavoury area the name of the Cour des Miracles.

DURING THE OCCUPATION of *les goddams,* as the English soldiery were called, from his palace in the Marais (on the present site of the resplendent Hôtel de Soubise), the Duke of Bedford, brother of Henry V and self-proclaimed Regent of France (1420–35), governed Paris—and not badly, though few Frenchmen would admit it. King without a capital, Charles VII ruled from Bourges over a divided rump of France—comparable to the area of non-occupied Vichy France post-1940. He was pious but irresolute. Then, in March 1429, out of nowhere appeared the *pucelle,* the "Maid of Orléans," Joan of Arc. With her extraordinary god-sent "voices" the simple shepherd girl managed to restore a sense of national cause and self-confidence to the French. She created an army and "liberated" Orléans, then Troyes, then Rheims. But that September she was wounded in the thigh during the assault on Paris, captured by the Burgundians, and handed over to their English allies. With support from notable lawyers of the Sorbonne, they tried and condemned her as a witch, on account of those preternatural voices—and burned her at the stake. Nevertheless, she had achieved her purpose. The fire of her funeral pyre lit a flame throughout France. The country was united as it had never been over the previous century. *La pucelle* had proved that, in the words of Napoleon, "there is no miracle which the French genius cannot perform given circumstances in which the national independence is threatened."[3]

Down through the ages Joan of Arc was to become, for France, as Anatole France put it, "the symbol of the Fatherland '*la patrie*' in arms."[4]

National leaders down to de Gaulle, adopting her emotive "Cross of Lorraine," would turn to her as a touchstone of faith.

In England a child-king, Henry VI, who was to become a gentle, scholarly figure—distinguished largely for founding Eton College—had succeeded his bellicose father, Henry V. Though Henry VI still bore the title of King of France, England had lost its instinct for foreign adventure.

As Bismarck once remarked of subsequent European affairs, "one generation that receives a beating is often followed by another which deals it out." In 1435, Philippe, Duke of Burgundy, nicknamed "the Good," switched sides to join up with the King of France, and the following year Charles VII reoccupied his capital. Normandy was regained, then Aquitaine three years later. By 1453 *les goddams,* now riven by a combination of weak leadership and their own civil conflict—the Wars of the Roses—departed. With them also went the wolves, French historians would note. Only Calais remained in English hands.

The Hundred Years' War might be at an end, terminating more or less on lines of mutual exhaustion, nevertheless France had been bankrupted by it; and there came more wars, internecine civil disputes and threats of invasion. Yet, for all the depredation and misery, it was to demonstrate one miraculous truth that would remain valid over many centuries of French history: France's extraordinary capacity to recuperate following a string of disasters. Within a few years of the departure of the last English troops, France under Louis XI recovered with astonishing rapidity. It was partly owing to the fertility of her soil, coupled with the industry of her peasants; but also to what de Gaulle later mystically identified as "une certaine idée de la France," a very distinct brand of self-assurance about being French. Hand in hand with this went a fundamental, unshakeable belief in France's universal *mission civilatrice.*

CHARLES VII (1422–61), under whose reign the Hundred Years' War petered out, was a slight man of a sallow complexion, no outstanding personality but appropriately dubbed "the Well-Served." In his château on the Loire, he lived openly with his beautiful mistress, Agnès Sorel of the legendary and much-painted breasts, known as *la dame de beauté* from the domain of Beauté-sur-Marne which the King had given her. He had four daughters by her. Bold and vivacious, Agnès surrounded Charles with bright young people, while his administrators successfully reorganised the treasury, and provided France with an efficient standing army. Copying the English system, it effectively restored order to a countryside which, in the aftermath of war, was terrorised by roaming bands of brigands and pillaging free-booters. Though a powerful and troublesome Burgundy, under its independent-minded and somewhat eccentric* duke, Philippe le Bon, continued to present a worry on his flank, Charles established a reputation outside the borders of France. "You are the pillar of Christendom!" the King of Hungary once apostrophised him. The fleur-de-lys was suddenly to be found flying from the masts of vessels all over the Mediterranean.

CHARLES' SON LOUIS XI (1461–83) is sometimes described as the "strangest of all the Valois," or the "Spider King." There was something distinctly sinister about him. He had had an unsettling childhood. His "whorish" grandmother, Isabeau of Bavaria, wife of mad Charles VI, had Louis' father, Charles VII, proclaimed a bastard; while Charles VII accused Louis of having poisoned his beloved Agnès and endeavoured to disinherit him. As a result Louis while Dauphin spent much of his early life sequestered from his father's court in his distant and backward lands of the Dauphiné. He grew up to dress like the humblest of his subjects, while cladding his greyhounds (whom he greatly preferred to humans) with jewel-encrusted collars of Lombardy leather. Louis XI is described as "a man of no great height and with black hair, brownish countenance, eyes deep in his head, long nose, and small legs"[5] and his queen, Charlotte (to whom he was unusually—for those days—faithful), was "not one of those women in whom a man would take great pleasure but in all a very good lady."[6] When his unfriendly father died, Louis forbade any mourning, put on a red and white hat (the national colours) and went off hunting.

The most restless of the Valois to date, Louis spent half of his twenty-two-year reign wandering, or at war—much as he tried to avoid it. This meant neglecting the court. Visiting Italians were amazed at the "plainness of his establishment," while the Milanese ambassador described him as "a man without a place," and complained of being unable to keep up with him, "either on horseback or in vile lodgings." Lacking in any sense of pomp and circumstance, like Philippe-Auguste, Louis surrounded himself with the bourgeois and "lesser folk"—such as the suc-

---

*He was reported to have received an English emissary whilst lying naked on a bed and caressing two Barbary goats.

cessful merchant Jacques Coeur. History has recorded his unpleasant habit of putting his enemies in cages within what Louis called his "orchard," where they were left to starve; but he deserves a better epitaph. It was he who definitively put an end to the Hundred Years' War, triumphantly making his *joyeuse entrée* into Paris in 1461.

France had been brought a long way from the spiritual authority of Saint Louis to the wily manoeuvring of Louis XI. The contemporary chronicler Philippe de Commynes claimed that he never saw Louis "when he was not preoccupied and worried,"[6] habitually suspicious and in a rage against someone. But Louis XI had inherited a France everywhere outflanked and encircled, with the powerful Duke of Burgundy both to the north and east, in Picardy and Flanders—the prize that Charles VII had unwisely given him in a vain attempt to wean him away from the English. In the west there was the Duke of Brittany and the independent provinces of Maine and Anjou. Domestically, well-intended tax reforms brought an uprising of the "League of Public Weal" and saw Louis besieged in his capital, and forced—temporarily—to abandon Normandy.

The "Spider King," however, was a Machiavelli before his time, and in the brutal fifteenth century what others sought to obtain by force he achieved through guile and stratagem. He issued probably more edicts than any French king since Charlemagne, and wove around France an elaborate web of diplomacy. First of all he was able to gain control of Roussillon and Cerdagne—for the payment of 200,000 crowns. Then, for 50,000 crowns, he bought off England's feeble Edward IV, who was threatening to renew the Hundred Years' War (once more in alliance with the Burgundians—who planned to have him crowned King of France). Cunningly Louis arrived in Amiens, where Edward had assembled a huge army, with a baggage train stuffed with presents, jewels and coin; as a result, for days on end Commynes found the taverns of Amiens filled with singing, snoring and drunk hostile soldiery. Louis was thus able to boast: "I have chased the English out of France more easily than ever my father did; for my father drove them out by force of arms whereas I have driven them out by force of venison pies and good wines."[7] With the advantageous Treaty of Picquigny in 1475 he drew a final line under the Hundred Years' War.

Louis' greatest enemy remained the rich and powerful Burgundy, which stretched from Switzerland to wealthy Flanders. Duke Charles the Bold was far more menacing than his father, Philippe, whom he succeeded in 1467. The following year, Louis rashly allowed himself to be taken prisoner by Charles at Péronne; talking his way out, it was as the "bedraggled fox makes his escape from the wolf's den." But the wily Louis struck back, first severing Charles' commerce with the Low Countries, then luring him into war with the Swiss. Terrified by the blasting away of the Swiss battle horns, the Burgundian cavalry were impaled on the pikes of the sturdy Swiss infantry—in two disasters, first at Grandson, then at Morat in 1476–77. The fearsome duke was found dead, half eaten by wolves, face down on a frozen pond. For France, it was the epitome of a Cold War, fought by proxy and with minimal casualties, and resulting in the end of the state of Burgundy; a threat that had begun when Paris had rashly unleashed the Norsemen on her in the ninth century. Louis also moved into Picardy and Artois, with its prosperous capital Arras; on top of this, in 1480 another bloodless victory through marriage brought him Provence (with its magnificent port of Marseilles), Maine and Anjou, upon the deaths respectively of King René and his nephew Charles of Anjou. He also regained Normandy, and established France's great silk industry at Lyons.

Despite his bad reputation (to some extent acquired from the novels of Walter Scott), Louis XI broke the power of feudalism to become the master of France, and his achievements during his twenty-two-year reign truly live up to his motto of "He who has success likewise has honour."

LOUIS' DEATH IN 1483 (the same year that Richard III seized power in England) marked the passing of medieval, feudal France, replaced by a centralised monarchy with absolutist tendencies. By now France had almost doubled its area, acquiring much of the geographical shape of the "hexagon" that it inhabits today. With Provence came also a foothold in Naples; and with Naples there opened the window that would bring great cultural wealth, but also lead to the undoing of many a subsequent French ruler—down to Napoleon III—seduced by the allure of sun and riches. For the first glimmer of a new light was beginning to illuminate France from the south-east, from Italy. Already during the reign of Charles VI contemporary paintings depict the mad King lying on his bed richly caparisoned in garments, the fabrics of which had made the wealth of Renaissance Florence. Liberated from the scourge north of the Channel, the Valois began to turn eager, and greedy, eyes towards Italy. There a complexity of rival states and petty tyrannies had sprung up. Skilfully, without becoming embroiled in war there, Louis had managed to maintain a balance of power, establishing himself as patron of the Renaissance.

The pull of Rome was hardly surprising. Its legacy had continued in France centuries after it had waned in Britain, particularly in the meridional regions where the roads, buildings and great amphitheatres—but above all the pervasive culture and literature, customs and laws—of Ancient Rome had survived its fall and the succeeding Dark Ages. To Rome, France owed her tendency to centralisation, which would grow as her monarchs accrued more power, her notions of justice. Between neighbouring territories that had once shared the same language, religion and, at times, the same ruler would spring a sense of continental unity. Under the aegis of that *mission civilatrice* of France, it would almost always be opposed to Anglo-Saxon interests. And of course there was the Catholic Church, binding king, state and parishioners of France to Rome itself. Here, as the fifteenth century unfolded, was to be one more major source of divergence between France and the Islanders. After Bouvines, King John's reluctant signature of the *Magna Carta* reduced the political power of the English king in favour of new liberties, while a strengthened French monarchy facing the menace of external threats pointed the way towards increasing absolutism: so now in terms of religious faith—as Britain veered towards the northern influences of Martin Luther—France looked southwards.

LOUIS' SON, CHARLES VIII (1483–98), was physically under-privileged, with an enormous head, thin, ugly to the point of being deformed, not very bright, but deeply in love with his Breton queen, Anne—who, fortunately, shared his homeliness. He inherited the throne at the age of thirteen, and with it some tiresome domestic problems. Opposing the feudal barons, in 1484 the *vox populi* called for a meeting of the semi-moribund Estates-General to hear their grievances. At it a delegate from Burgundy, Philip Pot, made a telling speech, revolutionary before its time, in which he declared, "The State is the thing of the people . . . the sovereign people created kings by its suffrage. . . ." The Estates-General were requested to meet every two years. They did not; and indeed few were the times when they would be convened before the fateful year of 1789.

In post-Norman England, the successors of William the Conqueror had opposed the holding of single large territories by great feudal vassals, who thus came to exercise quasi-regal prerogatives; instead they were assigned properties scattered through many counties. In contrast, France's great lords held their lands from the king, in return for which they were only obligated for certain services, like forty days of military duty a year. Beneath them came the mass of serfs and peasants, living on a level of mere subsistence, unrepresented and all but invisible on the social landscape.

During the Hundred Years' War, the Second Estate, the nobility— free from taxation, judged by its peers, its chief responsibility to die in battle at the side of the monarch—had become somewhat effete. It was more concerned with the chivalry of the tournament than with the reality of war, or politics. The game of courtly love was still a ritual. The father of Bayard, the legendary "Chevalier sans peur et sans reproche," instructed his sons in the code inherent to their status: "Serve God. Be kindly and courteous to all men of gentle breeding. Be humble and serviceable to all people. Be neither a flatterer nor a teller of tales. Be faithful in deed and in speech. Keep your word. . . ." These fine precepts, however, waning in the reign of Louis XI, would shortly be cast aside in the brutal wars of religion that were about to engulf France, and the rest of Europe. In the semi-feudal system that still existed in provincial France, the lord also had few responsibilities towards those dependent on him. On the other hand, the archaic *droit de seigneur* continued to give him the right of the first night with the bride of any of his peasantry (otherwise known as the *droit de jambage*; the right to put a leg into the marital bed), which, in theory, guaranteed at least a genetic continuation of the line.

Then there came the clergy, the First Estate. It still lived in some feudal splendour, and wielded great powers—despite the damage done to the Church during the Great Schism, when the currency of God had been debased for the seventy years of a rival Pope at Avignon. Finally, there was the Third Estate, representing the city bourgeois (notably, in the first instance, of Paris), the wealthy merchants who had put down a marker at the time of Étienne Marcel's brief uprising. Many bourgeois had already purchased grand seignorial domains, but they were rarely socially acceptable to the nobility, who despised anything smacking of commerce. When the Estates-General met, the Third sat in a separate section clearly apart from the others. (The system would even be visible under Napoleon's First Empire, despite its calculated appeal to populism, when—at a great imperial ball—the bourgeois would be rigidly directed to dine in salons separate from the court and the Napoleonic nobility.) Compared with England, for all her native snobbery, barriers between classes and the importance attached to protocol always remained more imposing in France. The convocation of 1484 helped define the function of these bodies which governed the destiny of France, and which, through their implacable divisiveness, were to lead ultimately to the revolution of 1789.

MOTIVATED AT LEAST IN PART by the age-old French instinct to seek distractions abroad when the going gets rough at home, Charles VIII soon became seduced "by the phantoms and glories of Italy." A blitzkrieg that was almost a "promenade" brought him to the very gates of Rome in 1494. Initially, the Italians seemed to welcome the French; in return Charles came home enthralled by Italian art. Alas, in 1498, the poor gangly fellow died after bashing his head on the low lintel of a door at Amboise on the Loire, the château to which he was so passionately attached, aged only twenty-eight. There had been time, though, through marriage, for Charles to add Brittany to the realm of France.

On his death, the succession went sideways, to the Orléans branch of the House of Valois. The new King, Louis XII (1498–1515), great-grandson of Charles V, was yet another enticed into the maze of Italian politics and intrigue, by a conniving Pope inspired by Machiavelli— Julius II, the builder of St. Peter's and the Sistine Chapel. This warrior-Pope wanted the weight of French arms as a counter-balance to his enemy, the Venetians. But the moment that Louis, occupying Milan, was too successful Julius II switched sides to be rid of the French. In 1513, Louis' army was crushed at Novara, Milan fell and the French had to beat a desperate retreat back over the Alps. Italy was lost, but certainly not forgotten.

Aged fifty-three without an heir, Louis married a third time, to Mary, the sixteen-year-old sister of Henry VIII. Apparently trying to please his lusty young English bride, he was said to have greatly exceeded his strength and died suddenly in the middle of the night on New Year's Day, 1515.

In France as a whole, enjoying a period of prosperity, and peace at home, the reign of Louis XII had been successful enough, though Paris virtually stagnated. When they were not away at the wars, the Valois monarchs concentrated their wealth and energies on the joys of *la chasse,* and on translating the marvels of the Italian Renaissance to the glorious châteaux they were building on the Loire—Amboise, Blois, Chenon-ceaux, Chaumont and Azay. These culminated finally in the "hunting lodge" of François I at Chambord—containing an entire village atop the roof, together with its two great interweaving circular staircases, large enough to ride a horse up and designed, supposedly, so that the Queen and François' current mistress could pass without either encountering the other.

Anything to be away from smelly, pestilential, surly and unruly Paris! From these delightful châteaux on the gentle Loire, the absentee rulers ran France; but it was a habit that would lead the French monarchy into gravest danger in the two centuries that were to come.

DURING HIS REIGN, Charles V—despite the raging Hundred Years' War—managed to construct a new wall round Paris, and within it transform the grim old fortress of Philippe-Auguste, the Louvre, into a handsome palace, to become the royal residence. Apart from this, there was little new building in the capital; there was just no money. But when it did start again in earnest, French architecture reflected most generously the Italian, Renaissance influence. Styles as seen, for example, in the Cour Carrée of the Louvre, or in Azay-le-Rideau floating magically on its lake in the Loire, would come to England anything up to a hundred years after reaching France from her southern neighbour. In figurative art, representation was moving from the religious to the profane; where else but France, for example, could a monarch have his mistress, Agnès Sorel, painted *aux seins nus,* and an exquisite bust at that? French miniaturists learned their trade from Italy, and in turn passed it back. The joys of the earthly paradise, as opposed to the heavenly, were wonderfully portrayed in the *Très Riches Heures du Duc de Berry,* while Angers tapestries depicted the excitement of the chase. From being an anonymous decorator of cathedrals, the individual artist became famous, and relatively rich. Historians and chroniclers such as Froissart and Commynes earned distinction.

The impassioned "Mystery Plays" of the Middle Ages began to give way to a theatre of farce, presaging Molière. The printing presses of Gutenberg reached Paris by 1470. With them, as well as a new political awareness, came a replacement of the verbally inherited *chanson de geste* composed by nameless authors; individual poets like Villon—constantly in trouble with the police—now brought a deep pessimism about the transitory nature of life, perhaps exacerbated by an excessive intake of alcohol. From Italy, via Provence, the idyllic odes of Petrarch were rediscovered. The era of courtly love of Ronsard, the troubadours and the

*jongleurs* moved on towards the uninhibited earthiness, spiced with serious learning, of Rabelais. With it the arts tended to move away from
performances in the public square, towards the more select audience of
the Renaissance, and reflected a more liberal Christian ethic that was
truly Renaissance.

IN HIS VERY PHYSICAL APPEARANCE, the robust, rumbustious
François I (1515–47) reflected the new-found self-confidence of France.
It would be hard to imagine a greater contrast, physically, than between
the sickly and delicate Louis XII and his successor. Closing the door on
the Middle Ages, François opened the vigorous century. Just twenty-one
when he succeeded in 1515 (sideways, a cousin like the heirless Louis),*
François was a giant of over two metres tall, with long legs and arms, and
huge hands and feet. Portraits show his face dominated by a large hook
nose, a low forehead, a wispy moustache and a pointed beard. In his vast
energies, appetites and tastes, he was every inch the Renaissance king; so
too in the magnificence of his clothes (where he closely resembled his
contemporary, England's Henry VIII)—the close-fitting doublets with
the slashed sleeves, the extravagant Italian shoes and feathered hats. He
brought Benvenuto Cellini to France, and Leonardo died in his arms.

In terms of statecraft, however, there were omens that the melancholy prediction of Louis XII might come true: "We busy ourselves in
vain . . . that big young fellow will spoil everything." Like his two predecessors', François' "map of Europe" lay in Italy—so did his fate. Inheriting a country once more threatened on three sides, by Henry VIII
across the Channel, Emperor Maximilian beyond the Rhine, and Ferdinand of Aragon over the Pyrenees, he lived in fear of geographic "encirclement"—a term that was to obsess latter-day German rulers from
Kaiser Wilhelm II to Hitler. Almost immediately François decided to
seize the initiative, by crossing the Alps to recapture Milan, lost by Louis
XII. It was almost an act of frivolity. At first things went well, with
François winning a glittering victory at Marignano in the same year as
his accession. On the field of battle, the chivalric hero Bayard conferred
a knighthood upon his sovereign for the panache he had displayed.

---

*The lineage now had to go obliquely to the Valois-Angoulême branch, with a
common ancestry back to Saint Louis, as did the Bourbon line which was also to produce Henri IV. François was both cousin once removed and—via his Queen, Claude—
son-in-law to Louis.

These were heady days for a young king of François' temperament. In fact, early success gained with minimum effort instilled in him a kind of rash optimism. From the Pope, Leo X, nicknamed "His Cautiousness," he was able to wring concessions which assured liberty for the French Church to nominate its own bishops—as well as providing the King with vast additional revenues at its expense. Thus it could be said that, while England's Henry VIII broke with Rome to get his hands on Church moneys, François I did the same through agreement. In Paris conservatives in the Sorbonne protested that the Concordat was "offensive to God."

At the resplendent Field of the Cloth of Gold, a forerunner of lavish state visits subsequently, François managed to entice Henry VIII into watchful neutrality—temporarily. To the east, however, the death of Maximilian I brought a far more redoubtable foe—Emperor Charles V ("Charles Quint," to differentiate him from the Valois King), Holy Roman Emperor,* Emperor of Habsburg Austria *and,* by succession, also King of Spain (1500–1558). He had a mouth which was always open and a weak chin, but the weakness of his features belied his outstanding intelligence and determination. He persuaded the rich bankers of Augsburg to back him in his ambitions.

In 1519, following the death of Ferdinand II of Spain (of the *reyes catholicos*), François rashly confronted Charles by standing himself for election as Emperor. Thereby he made a mortal enemy. Henry VIII, having at first dreamt of the empire for himself, defaulted from the tenuous alliance established at the Field of the Cloth of Gold, to give his backing to Charles. The balance of power in Europe was seriously upset; isolated, François played with outrageous schemes to gain support of the Protestant princes of Germany, even seeking common cause with Suleiman the Magnificent, the Turk threatening Vienna in the east. In various complex permutations, four more wars followed.

Thus hardly had France recovered from the Hundred Years' War against England than this new challenge appeared; Spain, released from Moorish bondage, growing rich from her discoveries in the New World and, now, united with Habsburg power, confronted her on both sides. Here too were the beginnings of France's ensuing four centuries of strife with the Germanic world. By the time of the death of François I in 1547, it should have been clear that the enduring problem for France was no longer Italy.

---

*Though it had already largely become, in the words of one famous Frenchman, Voltaire, neither Holy, nor Roman—nor an Empire.

TEN YEARS INTO HIS REIGN, a grave disaster struck the hubristic François. His cousin, Charles de Bourbon, *connétable* (constable) of the kingdom of France and its most powerful military leader, defected to the enemy. Suddenly it looked as if the humiliations of the fifteenth century might be repeated, with enemy troops advancing to within 50 kilometres of Paris. With extraordinary rashness, François was committed to leading his army across the Alps once again. This time he met with total defeat at Pavia in 1525, crushed by the Spanish infantry. The *tercios,* hardened by the wars against the Moors, and armed with Toledo steel, for a brief while were the most formidable soldiery in Europe.

François himself was wounded and taken prisoner—the last French ruler to be imprisoned by a foreign power until Napoleon on Elba. Charles' imperial forces pressed on through Provence as far as Marseilles. Paris was left all but undefended. To his mother François wrote the famous words: "Madame, of everything there remain to me only honour and life, which are unscathed." During a harsh captivity in Madrid, he wrote some verses including the moving line: "The body conquered, the heart remains the victor."[8] Meanwhile, in Paris, the Parlement—by virtue of François' absence in captivity—began to transform its judicial power. François' fearlessly devoted, and beautiful, sister Marguerite rushed to Spain and attempted to free him, even to the extent—apparently—of making a pass at the Emperor. She was unsuccessful. François was forced, under duress, to conclude a shameful treaty with Charles, which, on his release, he and the Pope promptly declared null and void.

It looked as though a resurgent, fiercely reactionary Catholic Spain was becoming master of Christendom. Meanwhile, across the Rhine at Wittenberg, an event that was soon to shake Christendom, and particularly France, went by almost unnoticed. In 1517, a little-known German monk called Martin Luther nailed his ninety-five theses to the door of the local church, in protest against the sale of "indulgences" to finance the building of St. Peter's, and the harshness of Madrid-orientated Catholicism. There followed his excommunication and his courageous appearance before the dread Charles Quint at the Diet of Worms in 1521, where he made his famous utterance: "Here I stand. I can do no other. So help me God."

Though beset by enemies, at home and abroad, François finally defeated Charles in what was to be almost the last of France's Italian wars—often taken as a starting point of modern history for the way it shaped Europe. François abandoned any claims to Italy, to Savoy, Piedmont and Naples, and within France to Flanders and Artois. In return Charles ceded definitively all claims to crucial Burgundy. In his wars François had at least succeeded miraculously in preserving the national integrity of France. But his breach between France and the Holy Roman Empire in effect marked an end to unity in the Catholic Church and, as François' foreign wars ended, so the wars of religion of the sixteenth century began, leading to an epoch of appalling civil conflicts.

While in captivity in Spain, François dreamed up a "grand design" for France. Studying his captors' success in the New World, on his release he founded the port of Le Havre for exploration and dispatched Jacques Cartier on the first of his voyages to find and found Canada. On top of his unrelenting military expenditures, François' finances were constantly in a tangle. To meet some of his burden of debt, François introduced the principle of bonds on the Hôtel de Ville, while money moved into the hands of a bourgeoisie seeking to merge with the nobility. At the same time, by the "Ordonnance of Villers Cotterets" in 1539, he substituted French for Latin as the language of law.

DESPITE HIS MANY DISTRACTIONS AND INNOVATIONS, François I was the first king since his great-great-grandfather, Charles V, nearly two centuries previously, to undertake serious works in Paris. Bringing the Renaissance firmly to establish its ineffaceable imprint there, he razed Charles' Louvre fortress as well as the last traces of Philippe-Auguste. Displaying its new sense of security at the heart of the nation, no longer was the Louvre to be a bastion (after his incarceration in Madrid, François had a horror of fortresses), but an elegant and majestic palace. Designed by the geniuses of Pierre Lescot and the sculptor Jean Goujon—"the French Phidias"—it was to possess an enchanting Renaissance grace, borrowed from Greece and Rome, but with an unmistakable Frenchness. By 1540, François' Louvre would out-dazzle the works of his former gaoler, Emperor Charles Quint. He established the Imprimerie Nationale (national printing house), and founded the Collège de France, to compete with the Sorbonne next door, and act as a corrective to its unruliness. One of the Collège's specific aims was to propagate the humanistic ideals of the Italian Renaissance, and for the first time lectures were given in an enriched French language.

Among François' most portentous introductions from Italy was a daughter of the wealthy Florentine banking family, Catherine de

Medici, as a bride for his heir. With her came Italian culture of the high Renaissance, intrigue—and the art of poison. In 1547, François died, worn out by war, hunting and sex. France mourned a colourful and much-loved King, who—despite all his hunting or military distractions, and a bad beginning—lent a distinction to the French crown unknown since Saint Louis; and who, truly and ineradicably, established the Renaissance in his native country. The fashion and style of the times in François' France sprang from the top, from the court that followed the King wherever he went—a train of 12,000 horses, tents, baggage, tapestries, gold and silver plate—and women, sisters and mistresses. "A court without ladies is a springtime without roses," he proclaimed, and later French monarchs were to follow his lead. Poetry, music, games, gallantry and revels were the order of the day in this new France, suddenly prosperous in his last years through trade with Florence and a gold-laden Spain. Whereas Louis XI (perhaps like the later sovereigns of Britain) thought that "knowledge makes for melancholy," François was genuinely a "lover of good literature and learned men." He was as adept in conversation about painting as war.

From Alexander Borgia's Italy, François' outrageous friend Benvenuto Cellini brought not only art but a new morality; in his world, *la vie sexuelle* was free and even murder was forgiven—if the offender was an artist. "Virtuous young people," he boasted, "are those who give the most thrusts with the knife." In Paris, protected by "this wonderful king," he lived a charmed life, driving François' tenants out of the Petit-Nesle where he had his workshop, chastising naked girls there who served both as his models and his mistresses, and insulting the distinguished judges of the Châtelet. In the world of Philippe-Auguste, let alone Philippe le Bel, Cellini would have rated the gallows and Hell; but in the sixteenth century he was befriended by princes amused by his antics. If the ideal of Frenchmen of the Middle Ages had been Philippe-Auguste's grandson, Saint Louis, among the Valois of the sixteenth century it was Machiavelli. To quote André Maurois, the men and women of the Renaissance, in France as in Italy, "had so much animal violence that the scruples of their minds never put a check on the motions of their bodies. They were good Catholics, but they did not go abroad without a dagger in their belts."[9]

WITH THE DEATH OF FRANÇOIS in 1547, one strong king followed another. Lacking his father's charisma, Henri II (1547–59) had been a melancholy child (marked by four years' imprisonment in Spain). He seemed cold (except to his mistress, Diane de Poitiers), not overloaded with brains, but clear-witted and ambitious. He was greatly taken to physical exercise, such as the jousting which was, so disastrously for France, to kill him. His father wedded him to Catherine de' Medici when she was fourteen. Though an immensely strong personality, outshining her husband, she was given little opportunity to display her powers during his lifetime, for, since his teens, Henri had been madly in love with and dominated by Diane de Poitiers—a woman nearly twenty years older than he, and married to the Grand Sénéchal of France. With her motto, appropriately, of *omnium victorem vici* ("I have conquered the conqueror of them all"), she was painted as the Goddess of the Chase trampling Eros underfoot, and sculpted with her stag by the great Jean Goujon. She was as beautiful as Catherine was plain—and just about as ambitious. Henri gave the exquisite Château d'Anet to her, spending a fortune on it, and handing her Chenonceaux* as well. She knew how to make the most of her long legs and high breasts, which were the delight of her portraitists. Till her death she could boast the whitest of white skins—the result, so it was rumoured, of some special drug potion. Diane was the epitome of the French mistress, wielding great influence over her lord in all his counsels. Henri consulted and took her everywhere, and wrote frequent and passionate love letters when separated:

> I beg you always to keep in memory him who has never loved, nor shall love, other than you; I beg you, my darling, to wear this ring for love of me . . .

> I cannot live without you . . . I beg you to have in remembrance him who has served but one God and one love . . .

Some may think this an excessive protestation, but Henri's dedication to his god would influence years of religious strife, while his attachment to Diane de Poitiers would last the rest of his life.

Two years after his succession, in 1549, Henri II staged his triumphal entry into Paris. The leading poets and artists were hired to decorate the

---

*To cover her living costs there, her lover imposed a tax of 2 livres on every church bell, about which Rabelais commented: "The King has hung all the bells of the kingdom around the neck of his mare."

route of the procession from the Porte Saint-Denis to Notre-Dame, under triumphal arches inscribed with verses in praise of the King. Jean Goujon and Philibert de l'Orme were among those employed, and their sculptural extravaganza included a Hercules with the features of François I atop a triumphal arch at the Porte Saint-Denis. Three Fortunes, in gold, silver and lead, representing the King, the nobility and the people, topped the Ponceau fountain in the Rue Saint-Denis. A tall obelisk on the back of a rhinoceros, symbolising a France triumphant over the monsters that threatened her, stood before the church of Saint-Sepulcre. The parade included representatives of all the city's corporations—among the hordes of artisans were fifty pastry chefs, forty barrel makers, 250 printers and 200 tailors. They were followed by all of the city's officers. It was an imposing display of optimism about France's future, and of the royal powers that would direct it.

It was not only the institution of the Valois monarchy, but the person of the King that inspired confidence and loyalty. Despite his infidelities, Catherine adored Henri, and—through her and her Medici love of the beautiful—she continued the Italianate traditions of François I, further advancing François' work on the Louvre; Catherine, as his widow, would commission de l'Orme to build a great new Renaissance Palace of the Tuileries, abutting the Louvre further west and perpendicular to the Seine. Under her influence French artisans simplified Florentine ornamentation, while introducing the typically Italian exterior staircase. But under Catherine there also intensified an altogether more sombre aspect of the Renaissance in France—the Wars of Religion. A special court was set up to prosecute heretics, and restrictive laws were passed against the Lutherans.

Ever mindful of the humiliating terms imposed on his father during his imprisonment in Madrid, not to mention his own miserable four years of acute deprivation in Spain, Henri hated Charles Quint with a deadly passion. Exhausted by gout, so ill that he was unable even to open a letter, having abdicated in 1556 Charles retired to a monastery to die. He handed over the Empire to his brother Ferdinand; but the throne of Spain went to an even greater threat to France, and Europe at large—Philip II. Taking advantage of Charles' decline and death, in 1559 Henri signed the important Treaty of Cateau-Cambrésis: under it France resolutely turned her back on Italy—at least until Napoleon. The military were furious, and it required considerable courage for the King to sign. Yet Queen Mary Tudor was forced to renounce for ever England's last foothold on the French mainland—Calais—which, in English hands for over two centuries, had remained a permanent threat. The unhappy Mary Tudor (who died within days of Charles Quint) declared, "When I die you will find Calais engraved on my heart."

It meant that England was shut out of the continent for the foreseeable future. As a consolation prize, Henri arranged the marriage of his considerably impaired heir, François, to Scotland's Mary Stuart. At the same time, Henri, conspiring with the Protestants of Germany, secured three fortresses on her eastern marches that would play a key role in wars against a new enemy. The fortresses were the bishoprics in Lorraine of Metz, Toul and Verdun; the enemy, Germany; the wars would take place in 1870 and 1914. Towards his neighbours to the east, Henri's policy was one that would be followed by various successors: it was, while appearing to strive in the defence of "Germanic liberties" in fact to "keep the affairs of the German in hand, and cause them as much difficulty as possible,"[10] which, in effect, meant the maintenance of a divided Germany.

Henri was warmly greeted in Lorraine, where Charles had made himself unloved, and his Treaty of Cateau-Cambrésis was regarded as a good deal for France. Extensive festivities were organised in Paris that summer of 1559 to celebrate both the treaty and the weddings of two royal princesses.* Participating, the athletic Henri entered a tournament at Les Tournelles palace, where once the Duke of Bedford had held sway—now the Place des Vosges in the Marais area of Paris. But the lance of his adversary, Gabriel de Montgomery (a distant forebear of the British Field Marshal), splintered on his helmet and put out the eye of the King. After ten days of agony Henri died, aged forty, having reigned barely twelve years. Though he was wearing the colours of his mistress, sixty-year-old Diane de Poitiers, his bereaved widow, Catherine, ordered the palace to be razed to the ground. Montgomery was pardoned, then executed disgracefully, fifteen years later, on the widowed Catherine's instructions. Denying a bereft mistress access to the King's bedside, with the words "The dying King belongs to the Queen," Catherine then promptly packed Diane out of her beloved Chenonceaux to her sombre fortress of Chaumont, supposedly for ever. Diane managed to escape, however, to her beloved Anet, where she spent the remaining seven years of her life under virtual house arrest.

Catherine took over, in a France that was left teetering on the brink of a crisis from which she seemed almost certain to succumb.

---

*Henri's sister to the Duke of Savoy and his daughter to Philip II of Spain.

# FIVE

# Henri II's Succession: The Wars of Religion

Rally around my white plume—
you'll find it on the road to victory and glory.

—*Henri IV*

ENRI'S PHYSICAL TORMENTS after his mortal wounding were nothing compared with what occurred as a consequence— a violent turning point in the history of both the Valois dynasty and France herself. Now began the grim period of European struggles between Catholics and Protestants known as the Wars of Religion. "There is nothing so much to fear in a Republic as civil war, nor among civil wars, as that which is fought in the name of religion," wrote Étienne Pasquier in 1562. Charles V, then Philip II of Spain, equipped with the sixteenth century's most powerful military force, gave the Inquisition full reign. Under Charles the most zealous Catholicism, hardened and sharpened by centuries of struggle against the Moors, and subsidised by looted gold from the New World, flowed into the Spanish Netherlands. Then, when indebtedness to his German financiers brought Charles to the brink of bankruptcy, Spain progressively plundered the Netherlands, one of the richest mercantile territories of Europe, a great banking centre as well as the heartland of the Renaissance in northern Europe. By the time of Philip II, Spain was deriving four times as much revenue from the Netherlands as from all the melted-down bullion of the Indies. Her hand rested with the utmost brutality on the people of the Low Countries, who in turn found in the

Reformation a kind of "Resistance." In the words of the nineteenth-century American historian J. L. Motley, "The splendid empire of Charles the Fifth was erected upon the grave of liberty."[1] In his attempts to stamp out Protestantism, in 1535 Charles had ordered that all unrepentant males were to be burned, and even repentant females buried alive. By the time he abdicated, between 50,000 and 100,000 inhabitants of the Netherlands had been put to death one way or another by the Inquisition.

Under Philip worse was to come. Horrendous massacres were perpetrated by the Spanish soldiery in Antwerp, endeavouring either to extort gold from the citizenry or to maintain order; Protestant mobs responded by comprehensively sacking its superlative medieval cathedral. In return the city was brutally sacked in the "Spanish Fury" of 1576. The Duke of Alba and the Inquisition jointly drove many of its leading citizens—like the fathers of Franz Hals and Rembrandt—out to the safety of Amsterdam and Rotterdam. Hunger and misery reigned in these once prosperous territories; roadside gallows were to be seen everywhere. By 1572, under Protestant William ("the Silent") of Orange, the burghers of the Netherlands were in full revolt against a cruel occupying force.

Inevitably, France, with Spain on one side and the Netherlands and Lutheran Germany on the other, was drawn into the religious mayhem and caught between the factions. French fear of political disintegration fanned the flames of religious zeal.

For years François I had vacillated between indulgence and harshness, finally coming down in favour of the latter, and on the side of the Catholics. Yet, for all their martyrs roasted cruelly over slow fires, the Protestants of France probably were less repressed under his stern rule than under the weak kings that were to follow him. His son, Henri II, did succeed—with a heavy hand—in maintaining a degree of interreligious peace in France. But under his widow, Catherine de' Medici, *le déluge*. The three decades from 1559 to 1590 were like a Gallic version of William Shakespeare's History Plays—the disorder which follows when strong rulers give way to weak ones. Only it was infinitely more savage.

Of notable Italian lineage, Catherine de Medici was well versed in the art of Machiavelli and unyielding in her ambition. Apparently barren for the first nine years of her marriage, Catherine then went on to produce ten children, three of whom became the next kings of France. Coming to the throne aged fifteen, her eldest son, François II, married to Mary Queen of Scots, had one of the shortest and most wretched reigns in French history (1559–60). Into the vacuum created by the

sequence of three feeble kings moved the powerful and formidable
Guise family. A branch of the princely house of Lorraine, tough men
from the borderlands of France and fanatical Catholics, the Guises
emerged as nobles in the early fourteenth century and, for military
prowess, were promoted dukes under François I. The current duke,
François, was judged a hero for his recapture of Calais from the English,
and—as a Councillor—had the ear of Henri II. He was later assassinated, in 1563, by a Protestant Huguenot,* Poltrot de Méré—the murder was a significant landmark in France's Wars of Religion. His younger
brother, Charles (1524–74), became the influential Cardinal of Lorraine,
while his sister married King James V of Scotland and was the mother of
Mary Stuart. This made the Guises uncles to the fifteen-year-old King of
France—they were the real force behind the throne, and leaders of the
campaign against the Protestants. Henri (1549–88), the eldest son of
François, would be assassinated by the King for amassing too much
power. His younger brother, Louis, was killed at the same time.

During these turbulent and bloody times, oppression of the French
Protestants, or Huguenots, reached new heights. As an excuse for the
excesses to follow, the fear provoked by their threat to established
Catholic orthodoxy must have resembled something like that of the
West to Soviet Marxism from 1917 onwards. In 1560, after summary trials, a number of their leaders were hanged from the battlements of the
beautiful Château d'Amboise—with François and Mary, reputedly,
gloating over the hanged men by torchlight.† A few months later,
François died of meningitis; Mary Stuart returned to Britain, and her
own tragic end. The next king, Charles IX (1560–74), was only ten.
Under Catherine as regent, a confused series of civil wars broke out
between Protestants—now becoming numerically threatening—and
Catholics. Multiple murders of the rival leaders, and massacres of their
supporters, exhibited a gruesomeness that seemed incomprehensible to
foreigners of the time such as Lord Burghley. It compares with the
Balkan "ethnic cleansing" of our own times, and was every bit as nasty.

Seldom was there heard any plea for toleration, on either side. Fear,
hatred, suspicion and counter-suspicion stalked and rent the country,

---

*The Huguenots originated from Geneva, the name supposedly derived from the
opprobrious German *Eidgenossen*, or "fellow oath-taker."

†As they passed by the hangings at Amboise, a French nobleman (Jean d'Aubigny)
remarked to his eight-year-old son, prophetically: "They have beheaded France, those
hangmen . . . after mine, your head must not be spared in avenging those honourable
heads."

like a snake writhing through the land, setting Frenchman against Frenchman.

ABROAD, Philip II of Spain spurred on the Catholics; Elizabeth of England the Protestants. "Everyone has his gang" was the cynical saying of the time. After a deceptive respite, the killings in France culminated with the infamous "Saint Bartholomew's Eve" massacre of 24 August 1572. In the atmosphere of confusion and mutual denunciation that prevailed in Paris, who was actually responsible for the massacres is regarded as unproven by modern historians.[2] The view long held was that Charles IX, acting on the advice of his mother, Catherine, to resolve France's dilemma by a mass purge of Protestants, gave the terrible order: "Kill them all, so that not one will be left to reproach me for it." Possibly the court only intended the liquidation of a few ringleaders, gathered in Paris for the wedding that day of Protestant Henri of Navarre to Catherine's daughter, Marguerite (Margot)—a marriage supposedly of reconciliation, but the mob then ran amok. The Protestant leader, Admiral Coligny, an elderly man of high character, was butchered and flung out of his window in the Rue Béthizy, near the present-day Rue de Rivoli—his corpse disembowelled and castrated by ghoulish children.

Some 15,000 were slaughtered that night, most of them in Paris; which, according to witnesses "looked like a conquered city." Surviving Huguenots began to leave France in legions. Over the next century, culminating with Louis XIV, the loss of their talents was to result in something akin to what Hitler achieved for Germany in his twentieth-century persecution of the Jews. Another religious war ensued, then a fourth and a fifth, and a sixth; but shortly after "Saint Bartholomew's Eve" Charles, too, died of a mysterious illness. Tuberculosis was suspected, but it has been suggested that he was poisoned by his ruthless mother.

Charles' younger brother, another son of Catherine de' Medici, now became king as Henri III (1574–89). On account of his effeminacy and occasional habit of appearing at ceremonies in drag, he earned the nickname of "The King of Sodom." Surrounded by a mincing entourage known as his *mignons,* it was clear that Henri—though married—would produce no heir, and a serious dynastic crisis ensued. The end of the Valois dynasty loomed. The obvious, and most promising, successor was his distant cousin and brother-in-law by marriage to Margot, Henri of Navarre. The only trouble was that Henri was a Protestant. The forceful reigning Pope, Sixtus V, promptly proclaimed a virulent bull nullifying his rights to the throne of France, and gaining the support of Philip II's Spain. Exploiting Elizabeth's execution of Mary Queen of Scots, François' widow, as a pretext, an eighth war of religion now engulfed France—and Europe. It was only the weather and Sir Francis Drake that saved Elizabeth's England from the Spanish Armada in 1588.

BY THE 1570S, the Guises had come to control the army, much of the Church and whole provinces of France. Paris itself lay under the power of the Catholic League, directed by the second all-powerful Henri Duc de Guise. More dangerous than anything preceding it in mobilising fanaticism, in 1588 the League organised a "Day of Barricades," virtually taking over the city. Henri III fled his capital but ordered the assassination of Henri de Guise in Catherine's bloody Château de Blois. The terrible Catherine herself died the following January. "It is not a woman," observed a contemporary, "it is Royalty which has just expired."[3]

In August of that same year, 1589, Henri III, still fleeing from his enemies, was stabbed in the stomach (while sitting on his commode at Saint-Cloud) by a fanatical monk, Jacques Clément.* It was a killing in revenge for the Duc de Guise, carried out on behalf of the League. (Clément was promptly killed, so his precise motives were never known.) At the news, in some ultra-Catholic strongholds tables were set up in the street to celebrate. With his dying breath, Henri sent for the other Henri (of Navarre) to be his successor: "*Mon frère,* I can feel clearly that it is for you to possess the right which I have worked for, to preserve for you what God has given you." He urged his successor to embrace Catholicism. The powerful Ligue in Paris, however, declared the murder of Henri III to be "legitimate," and insisted that the excommunicated King of Navarre should be barred from the throne of France.

OVER THE COURSE of her long history, Paris has been occupied by the English during the Hundred Years' War, and by the Germans in

---

*In fact, Henri III had had another option which (foolishly, as things turned out) he let slip. In the sixteenth century the Poles, progressively democratic for those days, elected their kings. Henri let his name go forward but couldn't quite make up his mind. The Polish offer was withdrawn; he returned to Paris, to be murdered a short while later. He would have done better to settle for Poland!

1940; and besieged at least four times. In the year 885, those terrifying Norsemen had sailed up the Seine in 1400 longboats, to submit Paris to a merciless siege lasting ten months. In 1870, Paris was to be besieged by Bismarck's Prussians, bringing the city to its knees the following January, after nearly four bitter months. Within weeks, Paris was besieged again—this time by fellow Frenchmen. Between the Norsemen and the Prussians a thousand years later, Paris was in fact besieged once more—also by her own countrymen—in 1590, under Henry of Navarre (Henri IV, 1589–1610). As with Philippe-Auguste before him, the fate of the capital during his reign was prefaced by a great battle outside the city—this time at its very portals, but it was a battle the King did not win.

FOR THIS SECOND SIEGE of Paris, Henri of Navarre set out from Tours with a motley force of 10,000 men, to claim his right to the throne bestowed on him by the dying Henri III. Though Nostradamus had predicted his accession to Catherine de' Medici with remarkable accuracy back in 1564,* it was a fairly distant right in that Henri was the nearest blood descendant along the line from thirteenth-century Louis IX, "Saint Louis." Nevertheless, he was enormously popular, especially down in Navarre, where he already ruled. Aged thirty-five, of average height, wiry and nervous, Henri was at the peak of his physical and mental powers. Though miserably married to the highly sexed and unfaithful "Reine Margot," daughter of Catherine de' Medici and sister to the last three kings, he was an immensely attractive figure, both to women and to men—despite it being said that he was economic with bathing and smelled strongly of goat! Tastes vary. A warm-hearted Gascon from the south-west of France, he was always in love (usually inconstant), sending his current mistress(es) passionate—and indiscreet—letters full of details of his military and political operations. As, in all probability, they had meanwhile been dumped, the scorned women tended to hand over valuable intelligence about his intentions to his enemies.

This may be one good reason why, eventually, unable to win on the battlefield, he was forced to change his religion to obtain the crown of France. Nevertheless, he was personally fearless in battle. "I rule with my arse in the saddle and my gun in my fist" was his fighting motto. He had already revealed his qualities as a soldier in 1580, at the siege of Cahors,

---

*Courting dangerous unpopularity, Nostradamus also told Catherine that her sons would not perpetuate the Valois line. He prophesied, too, the death of Henri IV.

and again in 1587 at Coutras, the first major Protestant victory against the Catholic League, which gained for him the south-west of France.

Perceptively Henri noted how, in this murderous age, "All men want me to string the bow of my business with the cord of their passion." But it was not a game he was prepared to play. Repeatedly he appealed to the French for unity, and union, declaring: "We are all Frenchmen and fellow-citizens of the same fatherland; therefore we must be brought to agreement by reason and kindness, and not by strictness and cruelty, which serve only to arouse men." His instincts were, for the times, surprisingly liberal, but assertive. "I have leaped upon the ramparts of cities," he challenged the Leaguers in Paris, and "surely I shall gladly leap upon your barricades" he warned them.

RANGED AGAINST HIM was the fanatical League of Sixteen in Paris, purging not only Protestants and those loyal to the late Henri III, but in addition those aspiring only to remain neutral. In command of the Catholic forces was Cardinal Charles de Lorraine, Duc de Mayenne, avenging brother of the assassinated Henri of Guise. Mayenne had an eye on the throne himself, while supporting him were Philip II of Spain and the Italian Duke of Savoy—both sworn enemies of France—and the Vatican, all-powerful in those days. Arbitrarily Mayenne proclaimed the aged Cardinal de Bourbon (uncle of Henri of Navarre) to be King under the title of "Charles X"*—though in fact the Cardinal had already fallen into the hands of his nephew.

Chaos ensued, with France virtually ceasing to be a state, and threatening to splinter into territories loyal to one or other armed party. The Parisian bourgeois middle class, weary of conflict, were reluctant in their support of Mayenne: "The merchants," he wrote, "think only of their business, will have nothing to do with war, and advise peace."

WITH MOST OF THE BIG CITIES SUPPORTING THE LEAGUE, Henri of Navarre decided, in August 1589, to move with his force of 10,000 into the friendly lands of Normandy. From Paris Mayenne pursued him, boasting that he would bring Henri back in a cage, like a bear; which, at the time, looked highly probable. In a confused fight in the

---

*The title was annulled on his death, Henri coming to the throne; otherwise, in the nineteenth century, the last Bourbon king would have been Charles XI.

mist, Henri narrowly escaped capture but Mayenne threw away his numerical superiority. A triumphant Henri dispatched a message, immortal in French history, chiding his favourite commander who had failed to arrive on the scene of battle: "Go hang yourself, brave Crillon, we fought at Arques—and you weren't there!"* He then headed back towards the capital, instructing Harambure, one of his more colourful captains, nicknamed "Borgne" or "One Eye": "Borgne, take forty or fifty musketeers (*maîtres*) and go right to the gates of Paris."[4] His forces attacked the suburb of Saint-Jacques, on the Left Bank, but at the same time troops under Mayenne managed to enter the city by the Right Bank.

Henri himself reached the ancient abbey of Saint-Germain-des-Prés. But surveying the vast city from its belfry, he realised that the four-centuries-old walls built by King Philippe-Auguste were too strong for him to contemplate a frontal assault. His royalists were forced to abandon their attempt to encircle Mayenne, not having the numbers to "make a city and an army succumb at the same time." On 11 November 1589, Henri of Navarre's troops disengaged from Paris, retiring anew to Normandy for the winter, and preparing to lay siege to the city. To a friend, Geoffroy de Vivans, he wrote:

> If Fortune will only smile at us, I guarantee you that neither poor weather nor bad roads will prevent me from pursuing her in whatever place she appears, without begrudging the Duke of Mayenne his rest for the moment in Paris, where I hope to rest myself in turn one of these days.

Henri lost time by deploying his limited forces to mop up behind him, and as was his wont, rashly communicated full and glowing details of his strategic movements to his mistress of the moment—a lively widow nicknamed "Corisande." He wrote boasting:

> I've taken the cities of Sens, Argentan, and Falaise. Tomorrow I'm leaving to go and attack Lisieux. Certainly, I'm covering a lot of ground, and I go wherever God leads me, since I never know

---

*"Pends-toi, brave Crillon, nous avons combattu à Arques, et tu n'y étais pas là!" (Voltaire's version of Henri IV's somewhat lengthier original). This was unfair; Crillon was one of the outstanding French military leaders of the sixteenth century; after the next battle—at Ivry—Henri IV dubbed him "le brave des braves." The famous hotel in Paris was named after him.

exactly what I must do in the end; nonetheless, my accomplishments are miraculous; also, they must be in the hands of the Great Master himself.[5]

Such careless talk ended in enemy hands.

By the spring, both sides were ready for a new campaign, in which the first engagement was fought on 14 March at Ivry, just four days' march due westwards from Paris. Mayenne had received substantial reinforcements from Spain: many of them mercenaries paid for by Philip II. The Spanish King justified this first military intervention in French affairs by declaring that there was "an imminent danger to the Holy Catholic Church." It was his intention to extirpate all heresy from France and to install the Catholics' favoured king, "Charles X," on the throne.

At Ivry, Henri de Navarre, turning towards his men, uttered words of a consummate knight:

> *Mes compagnons,* God is for us. Before us are his enemies and ours; before you, you see your king. Get at them! If you lose your coronets, rally around my white plume—you'll find it on the road to victory and glory.

Though the royalists were outnumbered by 8000 cavalry and 12,000 infantry to 2000 and 8000 respectively, after some ferocious hand-to-hand mounted combat, the day again ended in clear-cut victory for Henri. Following the battle, he showed the less pleasant side of the Renaissance warrior; mercenaries accused of past treachery at Arques had their throats cut without mercy, together with many French foot-soldiers. Mayenne fled with his cavalry towards Mantes.

Henri made sure he played up this victory, sending an official communiqué to bring the happy news to friendly countries: "It has pleased God to grant me that which I so ardently desired: to be given the means to engage my enemies in battle." Verses were composed by his supporters on the theme: "You have justly put my enemies to rout."

By 7 May 1590, the King's army was divided into separate corps to commence a blockade of the capital. Writing to Corisande, from Chelles, on 14 May, he boasted:

> I am before Paris, where God will assist me. Taking the city, I will finally begin to exercise the attributes of the Crown. I've taken the

Charenton bridge and the bridge of Saint-Maur with cannon, and hanged all who were hiding there. Yesterday, I took the outskirts of Paris, by force; the enemy lost many and we only a few; although it is true that M. de La Noue was injured, but he will survive.

He had burned all the windmills, essential to producing bread, that lay outside the city walls so that "it must happen that within twelve days, they are either rescued or they surrender." Henri was convinced that the divided Parisians would capitulate, but he had given them ample time to bolster up the city's defences and fill the stores with food.

The ancient city walls, however, had become seriously dilapidated; one stretch had been in such a state during the time of Rabelais that, as described in his habitually earthy words, "a cow farting has knocked down *plus de 6 brasses!*" (a *brasse* equals 6 feet). Little had been done to improve it since. It was at this weakest point where Henri launched one of his first assaults, but the scaling-ladders failed to reach to the top of the walls. Another effort came on 12 May, when Henri tried to take the Faubourg Saint-Martin on the Right Bank; the League's *arquebusiers* defended it so well that the assault had to be called off. Following this repulse, the League spin-doctors assured Paris that "God would never permit a heretic king to walk their streets." The siege extended to three months, as Paris held on like a mad person. Henri now sat down to starve it into submission.

BESIEGING ARMIES generally require a large numerical advantage over the defending force, but to besiege this large walled city of 220,000, the biggest in Europe, Henri IV had only some 12,000 to 13,000 men.* Against this the Leaguers could muster a 50,000-strong international garrison of French *arquebusiers,* Swiss foot-soldiers and elderly German *Landsknecht* (national guard), while men from each of the sixteen *quartiers* formed a well-armed but unreliable militia "National Guard." Pigaffetta, a veteran Italian captain in the Vatican's entourage, scornfully viewed this force on the ramparts as resembling "dogs that bark furiously on the threshold of a house, but never venture outside."[6] In addi-

---

*By comparison, in 1576, as a reprisal for the Saint Bartholomew's massacre, the Protestants had mounted 25,000 to threaten Paris with siege; it never took place. In 1870, the Prussians were to invest Paris with an initial force of approximately 150,000.

tion, however, there lurked in the background the potential relieving force of Mayenne (defeated at Ivry), and in the Spanish Netherlands the formidable Spanish infantry and Italians of the redoubtable Duke of Parma.

Henri's royal army, spread around Paris, possessed only a handful of heavy siege cannon and lighter culverins, or field pieces; the heaviest guns of the period, muzzle-loaded, fired round balls of 50 lb and 32 lb, and had an effective range against fortifications of not more than 340 paces, with no great accuracy or penetrating power against thick city walls. Moreover, as of 1590, the Huguenots were not renowned either for their weaponry or for the art of their gunnery. Therefore Henri was faced with winning Paris by attrition. Inside Paris news of the defeat at Ivry had provoked much "annoyance and astonishment" among Mayenne's supporters. As Henri tightened his grip outside, a mood of violent defiance prevailed in Catholic circles, with priests taking to the streets with cries of "Au meurtre! Au feu! Au sang! À la vengeance!" ("Murder! Fire! Blood! Vengeance!") against the King. Other factors, though, gave rise to a strong sense of foreboding, and depression. Poor peasants whose stores had been consumed by the besiegers flooded into the city. It was reckoned that there was just enough food within the city for one to one-and-a-half months of siege, and there were fears at Henri's ability to infiltrate and stir up an insurrection.

Orders were taken to expel refugees and the sick, and other "useless mouths" in order to save food—but then, mistakenly, the orders were rescinded. In a kind of "scorched earth" strategy, houses on the perimeter that might prove useful to the besiegers were demolished, while, because of the shortage of soldiers, it was decided to make little attempt to defend the *faubourgs,* or outlying suburbs.

The Paris defenders were placed under command of the twenty-two-year-old half-brother of Mayenne, the Duc de Nemours—described as being full of zeal and energy, but inexperienced. Then, upon the scene there suddenly arrived their *deus ex machina*—in the shape of Enrico Caetani, the Papal Legate, sent by Pope Sixtus, perhaps the most determined of all the Counter-Reformation Popes.* Caetani's journey was dogged with misfortune; all his baggage was lost, and at Sens the ceiling

---

*It was said of this formidable Pope that, during his first year in office, more heads were displayed on spikes along the Ponte Sant'Angelo than there were melons for sale in the markets of Rome. Perhaps fortunately for France, Sixtus died while the siege was under way.

of the Archbishopric had collapsed on top of him. Nevertheless, for the next four months—and with considerable personal courage—Legate Caetani was to provide an inestimable boost to Parisian fighting morale, acting as the Pope's personal representative.[7] Furnished with a papal credit note expressly for negotiating the release of the Cardinal, he promptly spent it on providing the besieged with arms and foodstuffs. He established his spiritual leadership with a sermon before the Sorbonne, declaring that, "whether Catholic or not," Henri was to be excluded for ever from the throne of France. The Cardinal in fact died during the siege, never to be recognised in the history of France as Charles X.

The fierily Catholic Sorbonne promised a "Martyr's Palm" to any who died in combat against the "heretics," while—a little comparable to the Red Army's political commissars in the Second World War—priests and monks bearing a miscellany of arms were attached to each civilian militia unit, to bolster its valour. As the siege began in May, bread was already rationed to 1 lb a day. In June, prices at the bakers began to soar. Several suspects, accused of planning to open the city gates, were executed *pour encourager les autres.* The defenders attempted a sortie but were repulsed, and Henri retaliated by burning all the fields round the city. Without cavalry, Nemours' forces found it virtually impossible to mount foraging expeditions.

To weaken their morale further, Henri set up two batteries of cannon on the heights of Montmartre, bombarding Paris indiscriminately. The Parisians, according to contemporary accounts, "just laughed."[8] But hunger began to bite, harder and harder. "At nightfall there were only to be seen men and women displaying their misery in words and actions, demanding bread with loud cries, and often refusing money that was offered them, because many had one and lacked the other." Plate from the churches was melted to fund provisions. Legate Caetani set up great cauldrons of soup, bran and oats in the streets, while the Spanish Ambassador, Bernadino de Mendoza, distributed 120 écus of bread daily—to be acclaimed with grateful shouts of "Vive Le Roi d'Espagne!"* There were religious processions, of barefoot penitents, with preachers promising relief within days.

It did not come; with July, there was a minor miracle in that an early hot summer produced a premature ripening of the wheat harvest within

---

*To maintain his claim to the throne of France, Philip II is estimated to have spent 30 million ducats, or more than 600 million francs.

the walls of the city, but this was not enough to avert starvation. Donkeys, then (as would happen in 1870) cats and dogs, and rats began to disappear. Rations were reduced to 4 ounces per day of repugnant bread baked from bran. One man was reported eating candle tallow; there were, reputedly, experiments in milling bones out of the graveyards for flour, and there was more than one account of cannibalism—"little children disguised as meat."[9] A mother was discovered to have eaten her two deceased children, both ostensibly interred according to due Catholic rites; but a thigh was found in an *armoire* and her maid confessed all, after the mother's own death. Thus "everyone universally, and each according to his burden, faded away in the worst extremities of famine." Suffering brought with it more brutal murders of those suspected of sympathising with Henri, while by the end of July some of the League troops began to desert.

At first Henri showed himself hard-hearted, determined to punish citizens who had prevented him from "enjoying the benefits of the Crown." His soldiers, however, were not beyond selling food to the Parisians, at grossly inflated prices, while officers with grandee relatives in the city (and, indeed, Henri himself) managed to breach the blockade to succour the rich. As always, it was the poor who suffered most, while, so it was claimed, religious establishments maintained provisions to last a year. According to Captain Pigaffetta, in the affluent quarters there were shops offering game and a wide choice of foods—at astronomic prices. On 9 July, still battering away at the walls with his inadequate cannon, Henri captured the Right Bank *faubourg* of Saint-Denis. To improve his image with the Parisians, his future subjects, on 24 July Henri allowed 3000 "useless mouths" to quit the city, and on 6 August—once privation had become all but intolerable—he accepted a parley with a deputation from the League. (Before they could even engage in talks members of the deputation had to receive special absolution from the Papal Legate, Caetani, since Pope Sixtus V had decreed that any Catholic negotiating with heretic Henri would be excommunicated.) In the meantime, Henri's force, now increased by reinforcements to 25,000 men, had taken in one day all the remaining suburbs and brought their guns up to the ramparts.

The fall of Paris seemed but a matter of time. Pacifist sentiments gathered strength. The ultra-Catholic leaders of the League braced themselves for a terrible night-of-long-knives, in revenge for Saint Bartholomew's Eve. But Henri, with his usual acumen, realised that clemency was in his interest. On 6 August, Henri declared to the Archbishop of Lyons and Bishop Gondi of Paris, sent to negotiate with him at the Abbey of Saint-Antoine:

> I speak straightforwardly, without any hesitation, what it is I have in my heart. I would be in the wrong to say to you that I do not want a general peace; I *do* want such a peace . . . I love my city of Paris, and as if she were my eldest daughter . . . I want to do her more good, grant her more grace and mercy than she would ask of me; but I want that she should show gratitude and that she should know my clemency, and not express her gratitude to the Duc de Mayenne or the King of Spain.

He told the envoys that if they were to accept his terms, within eight days there would be peace. But, if the League leaders planned to hold out to the last, "I will be constrained by my duty, as their king and their judge, to have some hundred or more of them hanged who by their malice have made many innocents and persons of quality die from hunger." Subsequently he promised that he would impose no changes on the Roman Catholic religion, "except by the determination of a legitimately assembled council," to which he undertook to conform his personal beliefs.

The League rejected Henri's terms. The siege continued. A conspiracy broke out to facilitate Henri's entry into the city. As they seized the gates of Paris, they yelled: "Either peace or bread!" and "Vive le Roi" while they waited for reinforcements. De Nemours, however, was warned in time. One of the National Guard *colonnelz de la ville,* named Le Gois, supposedly an *honneste marchand,* was killed by a conspirator—a merchant jeweller, who was executed. German *Landsknecht* mercenaries were reported to have inaugurated a hunt in pursuit of small children—of whom three were eaten. It seemed as if capitulation had to be but a matter of days away.

THEN TWO THINGS HAPPENED far away from Paris which determined events there. First, on 27 August, the uncompromising Pope Sixtus died. During his last months his enthusiasm for the League had already grown tepid. He was followed by more liberal pontiffs, three in just over a year; then came Clement VIII (1592–1605), described as "saintly but realist," who was to alter radically Vatican policy towards France, and come to terms with Henri of Navarre. In contrast and with far more immediate consequences for the starving Parisians was the news, reaching the city on 30 August, of the approach of a powerful liberating army commanded by Alexander Farnese, Italy's Duke of Parma. Commander of Philip II's northern forces and one of Europe's ablest generals, Parma had received orders from Madrid to abandon his current campaign against the Dutch and to march south with all speed to save Paris. At Meaux, some 25 miles east of Paris, close to the Marne, Parma linked up with Mayenne.

Henri made one final attempt on the southern ramparts, but a defence was mounted by four Jesuits, a librarian and a lawyer, who ran to the threatened sector with pickaxes. He was now forced to lift the siege and defend himself against Parma and Mayenne combined. To a new lover, he confided (on 31 August), ever the romantic fatalist:

> Mistress, I am writing this to you the day before a battle. The issue is in the hand of God, who has already decided what will come of it and what he deems to be expedient for his glory and for the salvation of my people. If I lose the battle, you will never see me, because I am not the kind of man to flee or to retreat. I can assure you, however, that if I die, my penultimate thought will be of you and that my last will be of God.[10]

It suggested the closeness of priorities in Henri's mind. But, manoeuvering more skilfully, Parma denied him either battle or a glorious death, instead seizing and consolidating the approaches to Paris. On 1 September a first convoy of foodstuffs reached the desperate city. By the 7th, Parma was in possession of both banks of the Marne at Lagny—close to where the French would try to break out from Bismarck's siege in 1870, and only a few hundred metres east of where the Boulevard Péripherique now runs. He was now able to rush provisions down the Seine, the age-long lifeline of Paris. In the last days of fighting, it was reported that Henri "risked that charmed life of his a hundred times"; but it was now clear that he was not going to win Paris by military means.

Proud Paris was liberated amid frenzied rejoicings. Henri had failed, at massive cost to himself and the people. Out of its pre-siege population of 220,000, as many as 40,000 to 50,000—or one in five—are estimated to have died of starvation or disease. (By comparison, during the siege of 1870–1 by the Prussians, which also lasted four months, deaths from all causes—including military casualties, disease and starvation—are reckoned to have totalled little more than 6000, out of a population roughly seven times as large.) Economic life had been damaged by the most crippling siege of any major city since that of Constantinople by the Turks in the previous century. After all their suffering and with their habitual impatience, Parisians became disenchanted with the League and dismissive of its leaders. Of the discredited Mayenne it was crudely said that he "chose to reside in the city suburbs rather than endure the preachers' hostility" and that "he was only a big pig who slept with his whore [and] could only fight a war with flagons [of wine]."[11]

After four months of privation while he had organised the beleaguered city, the Papal Legate, Enrico Caetani, could not wait to get back to his native city, Rome. One of his entourage, the Bishop of Asti, Monsignor Panigarole, was to recall the horrors of 1590: "there was no meat, no fish, no milk, no fruit, no vegetables. I would almost say there was no sun, no sky, no air . . . One thinks of the Siege of Jerusalem, one thinks of Titus and Sennacherib! It was a miracle. . . ." It was indeed, as was remarked by one eminent French historian of the early twentieth century, Jean Mariéjol, "a miracle of fanaticism."

# SIX

# *Henri IV:*
# *Good Sense and Good Taste*

France is so populous and fertile that what war damaged in a year is
restored in two.

—Discours, *F. de la Noue, 1586*

THE SIEGE OF PARIS was raised in the autumn of 1590, yet
outside the city the war continued fitfully, with Henri striving
to isolate the city from the rest of France. In January 1591, he
made another attempt on Paris, a Trojan-horse guile with soldiers disguised as peasants carrying sacks of flour, but this too was driven off.
France had arrived at a kind of stand-off; it was plain that neither
Counter-Reformation Catholicism, nor Protestantism, would be acceptable to the country, or offer it a stable future. After all the killings of the
thirty-year-long sequence of religious wars, the moral and physical
exhaustion imposed by the grim siege, the unforgiving orthodoxy of the
Leaguers and the deadly tit-for-tat of political factions, the people
longed for peaceful compromise. Unable to win a clear-cut military victory, sensing the mood in the capital and taking advantage of the new,
emollient position of the Vatican, Henri prepared to play his supreme
card.

He had come to realise that he must abjure his Calvinist faith if he
wished to become King of France. His personal salvation preoccupied
him little, but he appreciated that, if he were to move too quickly, his
Catholic subjects would doubt his sincerity. Since 1589 he had accepted
the principle of conversion, but had—wisely—refused to proceed until

the Catholic League recognised him. In the spring of 1592, there were negotiations between representatives of Henri and Mayenne, the Ultra Cardinal of Lorraine and titular head of the League, who embodied the spirit of Catholic resistance in France. These talks led nowhere. Then, in January 1593, the Estates-General of the League assembled in Paris. Mayenne manipulated to have himself made king, but fresh compromises were in the air, it being put forward by both Catholic and Protestant supporters of Henri that "the difference between the two religions was only great as a result of the animosity of the preachers [and] by his own authority, one day he [Henri] would be able to reconcile them."[1] On 17 May it was reiterated first, that no one had ever denied the legitimate rights of the first Bourbon to the Crown of France, and secondly, like a bombshell, Henri announced that he had resolved to convert, "having recognised and judged that it was good to do so." He entered negotiations with the League at La Villette, while continuing to press for a military advantage round the capital.

On Sunday, 25 July 1593, at Saint-Denis, the resting place of past kings of France, the vigorous forty-year-old Henri of Navarre solemnly abjured Protestantism to become a Catholic. The appalled Leaguers ordered requiem masses to be held to mark the dark day. Parish priests declared the excommunication of anyone who dared to take part in the "comedy of the conversion," while Mayenne ordered the guards along the walls to shoot anyone leaving the city during the next twenty-four hours. The Church's sanctions did not prevent several hundred Parisians escaping under cover of darkness to witness the ceremony at Saint-Denis. Crowds of thousands lined the streets and the square as the King progressed upon a thick carpet of flowers thrown by well-wishers who cried "Vive le Roi!" with his every step. Henri was dressed in the white he favoured, a simple doublet with gold brocade and white stockings set off by black cape and black plumed hat—symbols of purity and innocence, chosen by the King to reflect his readiness as a penitent to receive God with an open heart. He bore none of the grand insignia of office—such as fleurs-de-lys or a crown. Even his sword, a sign of justice testifying to the righteousness of his conversion, he relinquished on the church steps.

In many respects this royal procession resembled other triumphant royal entries of the Renaissance. The Prévôt de l'Hôtel du Roi led the way as master of ceremonies, his baton raised. Then 200 archers, each wearing green jerkins trimmed in gold, marched by, followed in turn by nearly 500 royal guardsmen. Ahead of the King, twelve trumpeters signalled his arrival. The King walked along among princes, grandees and knights of the Orders of Saint Michel and of the Holy Spirit, lords and other noblemen and officers. He stopped in front of Archbishop Beaune, and there knelt to the ground.

The prelate would not cede this throne to Henry IV until he had received absolution—an unprecedented expression of the Church's supremacy over the Crown. Henry IV remained kneeling before the enthroned Beaune, who asked him, "Who are you?"

Henri IV, although bereft of all the outward signs of royalty, responded, "I am the King."

"What do you want?" the Archbishop asked.

"I wish to be received into the bosom of the Roman Catholic Church," Henri solemnly replied.

"Do you wish to do so freely?"

"Yes, I desire it freely."

Following this brief interview, Henri delivered into the Archbishop's hands the texts of the abjuration and profession of faith he had signed the previous day. With tears reportedly in his eyes, either a sure sign of contrition or a testimony to his abilities as an actor, he turned to the crowd in the square and, with his hand on a Bible, recited a short version of his abjuration and profession of faith:

> I, Henri, King of France and Navarre by the grace of God, do hereby recognise the Roman Catholic Church to be the true Church of God, holder of all truth and without error. I promise before God to observe and uphold all decrees established by its saintly Councils and all canons of the Church, following the advice given to me by prelates and doctors as contained in statements earlier agreed to by me wherein I swear to obey the ordinances and commands of the Church. I also hereby disavow all opinions and errors contrary to the holy doctrines of the Church. I promise as well to obey the Apostolic See of Rome and our Holy Father, the Pope, as have all my predecessors. I will never again depart from Catholicism, but instead persevere in its profession with the grace of God until I die. For this I implore his assistance.[2]

Inside the church, Henri knelt before the altar and reaffirmed his pledges, then walked behind the altar to the confessional that had been moved there especially for the occasion. He confessed his sins to Beaune,

which reportedly took about twenty minutes. Beaune imposed peniten-
tial exercises and then absolved him for his past offences against God.

Henri's soul "cleansed" following communion, a flock of white doves
flew from the abbey's belfry, a "miracle" planned to coincide with the
King's reception of the Host. As the doves still circled, Henri IV and all
his dignitaries returned to the King's lodgings at the Hôtel de Ville. He
took up his sword again, exchanged his plain black cape for a crimson
one emblazoned with fleurs-de-lys, and distributed some 400 silver écus
as alms to the crowd. At five o'clock, after attending vespers, Henri IV
left Saint-Denis and went by horse with an escort up to Montmartre,
where he rendered thanks to God among the martyrs' tombs. From the
hill overlooking Paris he surveyed the rebellious capital which still defied
him, only a quarter of a mile away, as cannonades and fireworks lit up
the sky in his honour. Paris, Henri is famously said to have observed that
day, was "well worth a mass."*

It could be said that such spiritual flexibility was dictated by Henri's
lack of military success before Paris—exacerbated by that total inability
to keep a secret. But for all his earthy cynicism Henri IV, founder of the
Bourbon dynasty, might have proved one of France's greatest monarchs—had he but lived. The fervent cheers that day at Saint-Denis
drowned out the preachers in Paris who were fulminating from the pul-
pits that Henri's abjuration was null and void, and the Papal Legate's
vain attempt to declare that the prelates at Saint-Denis had no power to
release him from the ban of excommunication. (Papal absolution was
finally granted by Pope Clement VIII on 17 November 1595.) Their
cause was crumbling, the ground cut out from under it by Henri's conversion. There now began a steady stream of desertions to Henri's camp,
and in August 1593 a general truce was concluded with Mayenne. Henri
was set for his final progress towards the throne of France.

ON 22 MARCH of the following year, having already been formally
crowned in Chartres, he entered his turbulent and problematic capital
in triumph as Henri IV, the first of a 250-year sequence of Bourbon
kings. He did so thanks to a coup, organised secretly the previous night

---

*Popularly believed to have been said to his current mistress, Gabrielle d'Estrées, at
Saint-Denis, 1 March 1593, though some historians question its authenticity, preferring to
ascribe it to an invention of his enemies who were endeavouring to cast doubts on the sincerity of his conversion.

by the Duc de Cossé Brissac, the newly appointed Governor of Paris—eager for a marshal's baton from a grateful ruler—with two representatives of the Paris bourgeois *échevins*. It was typical of the deep distrusts still manifest in Paris that the occupying Spanish commander attached two Spanish captains to Governor Brissac in his quarters outside the city gates, with orders to kill him at the least indication of treason. But in the small hours of the 22nd, the officers, discovering nothing untoward, took themselves off to bed. Then, with a small posse of troops, Brissac seized the Porte Saint-Denis, to enter the city via the Rue Saint-Honoré. Reaching the Louvre, they were halted by a guard of some twenty German *Landsknecht*; but these were dispersed, killed or thrown into the Seine.

That was the sum of resistance. The Grand Châtelet was taken without a shot, and at 6 a.m. Brissac opened the gates of Paris to Henri. It was cold and raining, but the King nonetheless removed his ornate headdress ("la salade de la tête") as he headed, diplomatically, to Notre-Dame to sing a *Te Deum*. The pealing of the cathedral bells was the first warning the sleepy Leaguers received that the enemy they had so resolutely held at bay three years previously was now in their midst. Henri's champions ran through the city, proclaiming a general amnesty and instructing all to wear a white scarf as a sign of loyalty.

In the past, *joyeuses entrées* into Paris of kings newly anointed, or at their marriage, had been lavish affairs. Marked was the contrast with the simple spontaneity that now greeted this far more historic entry of Henri of Navarre as he left Notre-Dame for the palace of the Louvre. With some courage the King took himself on a walkabout through the streets, jostled and greeted by the curious who poured out to see him. Many were surprised to find Henry quite human, physically normal and friendly; the League preachers had never portrayed him that way.

That afternoon Philip II's Spanish garrison left the city in good order. They filed past, saluting the King. To their leaders he responded, "Recommend me to your master, but *never* come back."[3] The party attached to the Papal Legate had already decamped. The standing corporations of the city and individuals who had collaborated with the League sought an audience so as to be forgiven. Only 120 to 140 people were banished from the city; allowed to rejoin Mayenne in Meaux, should they so desire. There were no executions, no confiscations of property. On the other hand, Henri erected a gallows near the Porte Saint-Antoine, "to hang any person who should be found so bold as to attempt anything against the public peace."

RIGHT: Charlemagne. Equestrian statuette, ninth century.

BELOW: Saint Louis IX, with the Louvre and Tour de Nesle (of ill repute) in the background. Detail from the *Parliament of Paris Altarpiece*, French School, fifteenth century.

TOP: A lecture in Rhetoric at the Sorbonne. French School, thirteenth century.
ABOVE: Off to the Crusades: the French king and knights, backed up by monks. *Chronicle of France or Saint Denis*, fourteenth century.

TOP LEFT: Charles VII, with his court and Joan of Arc. French School, fifteenth century.
TOP MIDDLE: Agincourt, 1415. A very English view of triumph across the Channel. *St. Alban's Chronicle*, late fifteenth century.
TOP RIGHT: Henri II. French School, c. 1550.
ABOVE: *Venus at her Toilet*. Oil painting presumed to depict Diane de Poitiers, mistress of Henri II. Fontainbleau School, sixteenth century.

TOP: Engraving of Henri II being fatally wounded at a joust. French School, sixteenth century.
ABOVE: The assassination of Henri III and the execution of his killer, Jacques Clement. Coloured engraving by Franz Hogenberg, sixteenth century.

LEFT: Benvenuto Cellini's salt cellar, designed for François I, 1540–43.

BELOW: Louis XIV. Still life with portrait of the king by Jean Garnier, 1672.

High life at Louis XIV's Versailles. Perspective view of the chateau, as seen from the Neptune Fountain, by Jean Baptiste Martin, 1696.

RIGHT: Feeding the Sun King's veterans. Engraving of the dining room at the Hotel Royal des Invalides, Paris, built in 1674 by Louis XIV. French School, eighteenth century.

BELOW: How the other half lived: a peasant family during the reign of Louis XIV. Louis Le Nain, c. 1643.

RIGHT: Distribution of bread at the Tuileries Kiosk, during the winter food shortage in 1709. Engraving from the French School, eighteenth century.

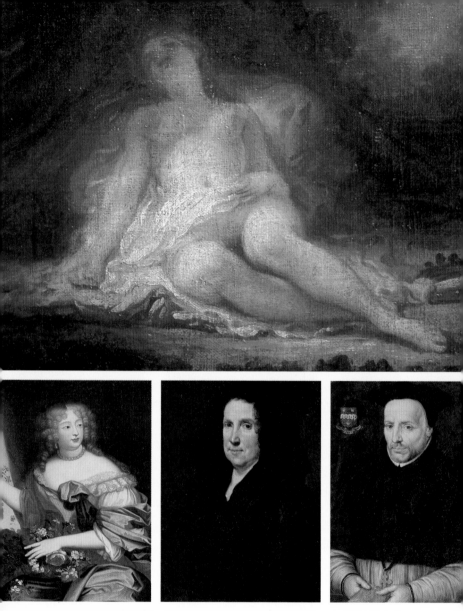

TOP: The spirit of pre-revolutionary France? *Bacchante Endormie* by Jean-Honore Fragonard, eighteenth century.

ABOVE LEFT: Madame de Montespan. Portrait of Françoise-Athénaïse Rochechouart de Mortemart, Marquise de Montespan, French School, seventeenth century.

ABOVE MIDDLE: A new wind of change at Versailles: Madame de Maintenon. Portrait of Francoise d'Aubigné, Marquise de Maintenon, French School, eighteenth century.

ABOVE RIGHT: And austerity in the Church. Portrait of Cornelius Jansen, Bishop of Ypres, Dutch School, seventeenth century.

In these days when victory seemed secure, the King at home in his capital was a gracious victor. When his council tried to bring him back to reality and obtain his opinion on political matters he reportedly said, "I have to admit that I am so drunk with ease to see myself where I am that I do not know what you are saying to me, nor what I am supposed to say in reply." Given the bitterness of recent history, Henri's clemency was supremely wise, for, as France saw that the King desired no reprisals, it followed Paris' suit in acceptance.*

THE COUNTRY COULD HARDLY AFFORD otherwise—it was in a terrible state. "Destruction everywhere," reported the Venetian Ambassador: "A great part of the cattle has disappeared, so that ploughing is no longer possible." Peasants were to be seen pulling the plough themselves, serving "as animals, with ropes over their shoulders." In the towns, populations had decreased sometimes by as much as two-thirds. Looms had stopped weaving. "All my shirts are torn," even the King himself admitted: "my doublet is worn through at the elbow; I often can entertain no one, and for the last two days I have taken my meals now with one, now with another."[4]

After all the years of bitter internecine fighting, followed by the deprivations of the 1590 siege, the capital that Henri IV inherited was indeed a sad city. Mob violence and the continual guard duty imposed on many citizens had caused shopkeepers to shut their doors, and workers to cease producing even the necessities of life. Commerce had ceased when the siege made land and river traffic impossible. One of Henri's first acts had been to order that trade should be resumed.

Still, the uncobbled thoroughfares became impassable during rains, and even on the paved streets the holes were so deep and full of mud that horses risked breaking their legs in them. If the paving originated by Philippe-Auguste was in a terrible state, so were the bridges; in December 1596, one of the wooden bridges spanning the Seine, the Pont-au-Meunier, collapsed. Lack of funds blocked even essential projects. Sanitation in this overcrowded city of already 220,000 was worse than it had ever been. The streets were covered with a thick slime of decayed garbage, ashes, urine and faeces, animal and human. Over the course of a decade and a half there were no fewer than three plague epidemics;

*Sporadic fighting in the provinces was to continue over the next four years until Brittany, almost totally pro-League, finally gave in.

30,000 had died in 1580, and two years after his *entrée,* in 1596, Henri was forced to retire to Rouen to flee *la peste.* To the multiplicity of street cries was added that of a much sought-after vendor of patent rat-traps:

> La mort aux ratz aux souriz
> C'est une invention nouvelle!

There were only eighty doctors in all Paris; yet the King was enraged to find, in 1594, one noble marquis who was sick of urine retention being tended by sixteen doctors.

To KEEP THE HORDES of militant beggars at bay, householders were allowed to have only one street door, and never to leave their homes uninhabited. Many of the beggars joined murderous bands such as the "Tire-Laine" and "Mauvais Garçons." Punishments were draconian; the Italian Ambassador recorded, in 1577, hangings every day, "at every point." Paris, still fundamentally the city Charles V had created 200 years previously, remained essentially medieval, with the Île de la Cité still at its heart. At the western end of the island stood the Palais, a chaotic maze of chiefly Gothic buildings. Since the King and court had departed, it now housed the Parlement, Chambre des Comptes, Cour des Aides, and Cour des Monnaies, together constituting the highest functions of government. Saint Louis' Sainte-Chapelle still remained at its heart, its delicate spire rising sublimely, much as now, over a bustling and scurrying population of some 4000–5000 magistrates, clerks, copyists and minor officials. Merchants, book-sellers, paper and ink sellers, prostitutes, singers, letter writers and beggars daily set up shop or frequented the dozens of stalls tacked on to the buildings. The focus of all this maze was the *grande salle,* a universal meeting place between its marble floor, heavy columns lined with statues of French kings, and gold ceiling.

Connecting the Île with the Left and Right Banks were bridges crowded with overhanging wooden buildings. In December 1596 the Pont-au-Meunier, having been swept away by currents before, collapsed and deposited its 160 or more inhabitants into the Seine. On the Right Bank, the Hôtel de Ville was an unfinished palace in the French Renaissance style, but it served as the meeting place for elected officials and visiting dignitaries. The registers and the seals of Paris, and its official

weights and measures, were kept there. Outside, the Place
then much lower than the present square and was frequentl
the Seine. Residents profitably rented out their windows on
lic execution. Eastwards, the Marais, despite its insalubric
remained the most fashionable *quartier.*

On the western fringe of the Right Bank stood the Louvre. After demolition of the *donjon* under François I, access to it was gained from the east side. After crossing the drawbridge over the moat and passing under the east wing, one entered a public courtyard crowded with carriages and the less well-to-do—drawn either by curiosity or to beg, steal or otherwise seek their fortunes. Beyond the city walls, in the *faubourgs,* monasteries had sprung up to gird Paris with a belt of cloisters, refectories, churches and gardens. On the Left Bank at the abbey of Saint-Germain-des-Prés, the richest and largest of these, a fair was held beginning a fortnight after Easter and lasting for three weeks or more. It was a fashionable and "very wild place to go." Parisians showed off their new clothes, while young noblemen would gallop through the fair on horseback, upsetting carts and picking up girls. It was a favourite haunt for pickpockets and prostitutes to prey on Parisians and hapless provincials alike.

HENRI OF NAVARRE was to prove one of the most important and attractive (a rare combination) of France's rulers, able to combine elements of both England's Henry VII and Elizabeth I. He brought unification after the bloody civil wars, and his unified country into the modern world. Not always a successful soldier, as seen, it was always the statesman and planner that was uppermost. With his characteristic energy, Henri began a deluge of orders for the capital's physical repair and reconstruction: "As soon as he was master of Paris, one saw nothing but stone-masons at work," recorded the *Mercure Française* in the year of his death. To new ambassadors returned since the days of the League, "When the master is absent, all the house is in disorder. But when he returns, it is adorned by his presence, and everything is the better for it." But building was also a personal passion for Henri: "I love my city of Paris, she is my eldest daughter. I'm jealous of her. I want to do her more good, grant her more grace and mercy than she would ask of me . . ."[5]

Within a year of his arrival, sweeping aside all obstacles and objections, Henri was extending the Louvre with the magnificent Galerie de ɔord de l'Eau, stretching for 500 yards along the Seine, and the Pavillon de Flore to link up with the Tuileries Palace laid down by Catherine de' Medici.* On its ground floor Henri set up his own school of fine and applied arts. Three years later, he was ordering completion of the Pont Neuf, the wonderfully elegant structure that still spans the Seine across the western tip of the Île. It was to be Paris's first stone structure, unencumbered by houses and able to withstand the unruly river. Funded by a new tax on every barrel of wine brought into the city, the Pont Neuf was an immense hubbub, permeated by music, where a permanent carnival seemed to take place and where you could purchase a parasol, or a tart.

Ô rendez-vous de charlatans

wrote a contemporary poet:

> Of master crooks and lowly gangsters.
> Of quacks with the newest drug sensation,
> And specialists curing constipation,
> Of musicians whose tinkling quickens,
> And of people selling chickens . . . [6]

Mirroring the love of life and bawdy tone set by the "Vert Galant" himself, it was a microcosm of a city at last released from anxiety, fear and deprivation.

Next followed an attack on the city's historically atrocious water supplies and in 1607, Henri launched a visionary scheme to develop the area between the Pont Neuf and the old Palais of Philippe le Bel. Named the Place Dauphine—after his infant son—its houses were of red brick with festoons of stonework (the style was borrowed from provincial architecture, and then recopied in the ensuing years in the many charming Louis XIII châteaux of the Île de France). All of a pattern, they were to form a great symmetrical triangle, open at the top by the Pont and framing a vista of the Palais at its base, in the first unified piazza to be constructed in Paris. Houses in the Place Dauphine swiftly filled with diplomats and

---

*An ill-starred building, running at right angles to the river, west of the earlier Louvre buildings and Napoleon's later Arc du Carrousel, it saw the downfall of Louis XVI, Napoleon I, Louis-Philippe and Napoleon III before it was finally burned down by the Communards in 1871 and was removed altogether by the Third Republic; almost certainly a benefit, architecturally, in that its removal displays the Louvre in all its true, uncluttered grandeur.

provincials pursuing lawsuits in the courts, and the arcades below with shops, workshops and restaurants.

Henri was delighted by his handiworks; to a cardinal he wrote in May 1607:

> at Paris, you will see my large gallery which runs to the Tuileries now finished . . . at the end of the Pont Neuf a beautiful new street runs to the Porte de Bussy . . . more than two or three thousand workshops are employed here and there for the embellishment of the city, so it is impossible that you will not notice a change.

The same year he launched an even grander scheme for the Marais, on the site of the razed Hôtel des Tournelles, scene of the tragic joust that killed Henri II. It was to be known as Place Royale—and finally, the Place des Vosges.* However, Henri's original intent for his Place Royale was, rather than the *quartier chic* into which it evolved, to create a low-rent development that would "house the workers whom we would attract here in the greatest possible numbers, and to serve as a promenade for those citizens of the town who were most crowded in their houses."[7] As the Place des Vosges, it remains perhaps the most lasting tribute to his reign, with its symmetrical perfection. Its construction now confirmed the Marais, until Louis XIV, as the fashionable residential area of Paris.

Grander still was Henri's plan of 1609 to build nearby a vast semicircular piazza to be called the Place de France, of the most modern design, to outdo Rome's Piazza del Popolo in splendour. It would radiate outwards into the city eight ramrod-straight thoroughfares, each bearing the name of a French province. Thus visitors entering through its gate would be instantly impressed by the unity of the capital and the country beyond under Henri's flag of reconciliation. Alas, Henri's death the following year aborted his Place de France, and his Place Royale was not completed till two years later, in 1612. Nevertheless, as one modern writer[8] comments,

> had he lived, Henri IV would be known today as the greatest early town planner. As it was, Henri gave Paris the pattern for three

---

*The name was given it under the First Empire, as a reward from a competition organised by Lucien Bonaparte, as to which *département* could raise the greatest amount of tax.

centuries of urban design. At last, the city had left the Middle Ages, and the way to a French urban classicism was open.

On top of all these vast building schemes, Henri had to find time—and money—to house his ex-Queen, the demanding Margot, and a new Queen, Marie de' Medici, not to mention the regiments of mistresses and their royal bastards he continued to accumulate. "La Reine Margot," meticulous in her personal habits and sensitive to smells, had swiftly become disenchanted by Henri's slovenliness and goatlike attributes. Almost immediately after their wedding night, each had found a plethora of lovers. Nevertheless, Henri and Margot remained curiously devoted to each other, but by the time of his coronation, the marriage had in practice broken down, and Henri was living with Gabrielle d'Estrées. Beautiful and intelligent, she represented probably the most serious attachment in the philandering life of the "Vert Galant"; Gabrielle, however, was not universally loved in Paris. Malicious pamphlets were circulating on the street as early as 1598, blaming her for the heavy burden of taxes and the political uncertainty. She was nicknamed, uncharitably, "la Duchesse d'Ordure."

In 1599, Henri had decided to ask Pope Clement VIII for an annulment from Margot in order to marry Gabrielle. This would have made their illegitimate son, the Duc de Vendôme, heir to the throne—not a step likely to please the powerful Medicis. Preparations for the wedding were already under way that spring; Henri had placed a conspicuously large diamond ring on her finger, provoking Gabrielle to remark publicly: "Only God or the King's death can put an end to my good luck!"

One evening in April, while Henri was at Fontainebleau, Gabrielle was awaiting his return in one of their favourite trysting places, a little palace in the Marais in the romantically named Street of the Cherry Orchard (which still exists). It belonged to a rather sinister figure called Sebastiano Zametti, alias Zamet, an Italian banker who also served as a kind of court jester—and probably *procureur*—to the King. A gambling companion, he was owed vast sums of money by the King and many of the French nobility. Zamet was even said to have been a lover of Gabrielle. Renowned for his table, that night he treated her to one of his famous dinners. Almost immediately Gabrielle suffered nervous convulsions, gave birth to a stillborn son and, aged only twenty-six, died in terrible pain before Henri could reach her side the following day, 10 April 1599. It was widely believed that Zamet had slipped her one of the notorious Medici poisons.

Henri was inconsolable, but the worldly Baron de Rosny (later Sully), though a life-long Protestant, urged him to consider another of those rich Medicis, Marie. His country, impoverished by war, his building projects, gambling and amours, badly needed Florentine money. Annulment papers were dispatched. But in the meantime the King's amorous instincts had been aroused by a dangerous twenty-year-old brunette, Henriette de Balzac d'Entragues. Her mother had been mistress of a former king, Charles IX, and she was reputed to be "beautiful enough to bring damnation to men." (Spurned, she was later implicated in various plots to assassinate the King, and was exiled.) Henriette gave herself to Henri for 100,000 écus, managing to acquire in exchange the title of Marquise de Verneuil—plus a written promise of marriage if she bore him a son. Sully promptly tore it up; Henri rewrote it. In fact she produced a stillborn infant, which gave Henri and Sully an excuse to consider the deal void.

Marie arrived in Lyons (with a dowry wiping out France's debts to her banking family, plus 600,000 écus) to be met by the King—and Henriette who, having just given birth to his dead child, refused to leave him. Marie was enraged when Henri insisted on bedding her in advance of the marriage ceremony on 17 December 1600. (Napoleon I was to follow the example of Henri in his second nuptials, to Marie-Louise in 1810.) Unkindly called "the fat banker," twenty-eight-year-old Marie was no beauty—but she produced an heir, the future Louis XIII, whose birth solved the problem of succession, and then settled down to an annual pregnancy. She also added to the architectural inheritance of Paris—most notably in the shape of the superlative Palais du Luxembourg, built in her widowhood in the style of her native Florence. Meanwhile, Henriette, Marquise de Verneuil, remained in the wings, producing more royal bastards, returning as Henri's mistress from time to time, and finally—in the anticipation that, with Henri dead and his marriage to Marie annulled, her own son (born just a month later) could replace the Dauphin—becoming implicated in the assassination plot that killed him.[9]

All these royal families, legitimate and not, had to be housed or financed to build sumptuous quarters. Above all, there was ex-Queen Margot, of whom her mother, Catherine de Medici, once remarked that "heaven had given her Margot to atone for her sins." Exiled for eighteen long years to Provence, where she occupied herself with numerous lovers, at fifty-two, Margot was obese and balding. Still entitled to call herself queen (part of the annulment deal with Henri), she was—so the

royal family thought—safe to allow back into Paris. With typical generosity, Henri gave her a stretch of land along the Seine on the Left
Bank, with an unrivalled view over her childhood home in the Louvre,
where she built a magnificent mansion; long since disappeared, it would
have stood roughly where the Beaux Arts is today, with an entrance on
the corner of the present Rue de Seine and the Quai Malaquais. While
work was in progress, the Archbishop of Sens let her have as a temporary
lodging his handsome Hôtel in the Marais, whose pointed turrets and
Gothic windows are still a reminder of medieval Paris today.* Coarse
Parisian wags nailed cruel verses to the door:

> Commes reine tu devois estre
> Dedans ta royale maison;
> Comme putain, c'est bien raison
> Que tu log' au logis d'un prebstre!
> (As Queen, you ought to be
> In your royal palace;
> But as a whore, it's quite right
> That you lodge in the lodgings of a preacher!)

Here in the Hôtel de Sens there ensued a grim tragedy, suggesting that
old Margot was by no means past it. She had two young lovers among
her pages—Comte de Vermond, aged eighteen, and Dal de Saint-Julien,
aged twenty. In a fit of jealousy Vermond shot his rival just as he was
handing Queen Margot down from her carriage in front of the present
gateway. Saint-Julien was the current favourite, and the murder drove
Margot insane with rage, vowing that she would neither eat nor drink
until the murderer was executed. Henri gave his assent, and two days
later she watched from a window in the Hôtel as Vermond mounted the
scaffold, unrepentant. Margot is said to have "roared like a lioness": "Kill
him, kill him! If you have no arms, take my garter and strangle him with
it." Depleted, *d'un seul coup,* of two young lovers, Margot left the Hôtel
de Sens for ever that same night of 1606.

---

*Over the centuries it fell on hard times, serving (before the First World War) as a coal
depot, a jam factory and an enterprise dealing in rabbit skins. Damaged in the fighting of
1944, it was rescued by André Malraux and—after restoration work that took longer than
the original construction—today houses a small library. Sadly, little or nothing of the
original interior remains, save the courtyard and a magnificent open chimney.

Across the river, one would like to think that she declined into a happier old age in the last decade of her turbulent life. But her gardens, on which she lavished almost equal passion, soon aroused the jealousy of her successor, Queen Marie, gazing at them from the Right Bank. To trump Margot, she laid out the superb Cours la Reine, the tree-lined *quai* a mile long, reaching to the present-day Place de l'Alma. Her son, Louis XIII, later had to sell off the property to pay off Margot's debts.

INDEBTEDNESS WAS A CONSTANT PROBLEM for Henri throughout his reign. Henri had incurred massive costs in putting an end to strife, within and without the kingdom—but this was something only he, with his immense moral stature, could achieve. In 1595, Henri persuaded Pope Clement VIII to lift the ban of excommunication, which had been placed during the 1590 Siege of Paris. At a stroke the main weapon of the Catholic extremists of the Paris Leagues was removed. In the spring of 1598, the Peace of Vervins ended the debilitating war with Spain, and the historic Edict of Nantes granted France an armistice in the Wars of Religion that had paralysed her over the past half-century. Until Henri's grandson, Louis XIV, misguidedly revoked it in 1685, the Edict bestowed on France's one million Protestants freedom of worship, rights to all state offices, and concessions such as special *Chambres de l'Édit* to hear cases involving Protestants.

By the standards of the time, it was a visionary act of reconciliation and liberalism for France. It was not to be emulated by the other European nations in the Thirty Years' War that was about to engulf them; and, as with other historic attempts to find a formula to end sectarian violence, Nantes was unpopular with Catholics and Protestants alike. Only Henri's authority could swing it, and enforce it. Meanwhile, open-handedly and despite considerable opposition, the King summoned back into France the Jesuits who had been banished as his enemies in 1594. "I hold them necessary to my state," he declared. "If they have not been such under tolerance, I want them to be such by edict." Both a dreamer and a doer, Henri proved that—once the day was won—he was also a man of outstanding compassion.

Many, possibly the majority of both sides, wished for the annihilation of their adversaries; but, at least on the surface, there was peace in which to reconstruct France. Henri went unchallenged—but for one major conspiracy by an old comrade-in-arms (in fact, his best general) and gambling partner, whom he had made *maréchal de France,* Duc de Biron and Governor of Burgundy. These honours were evidently not enough for the ambitious Biron, and (offered the hand of a sister of the King of Spain) he fell for Spanish designs on the King. Acting with ruthless speed and deaf this time to pleas from all sides for clemency, Henri had his old friend decapitated after a rushed trial, in July 1602. The execution caused the country's leading nobles to kneel in fealty, trembling before the King. Henri's absolutism was now complete.

To be considered truly great, a leader of men needs to be able to attract the best of talents to his side. If it was true of Napoleon, it was certainly true of Henri IV in his choice of Maximilien de Béthune, Baron de Rosny, Duc de Sully (1559–1641), to run his affairs. One of the most remarkable administrators ever produced by France, Sully was a friend of long standing, who had followed Henri since the age of sixteen. Being a dedicated Protestant, it was not until the settlements of 1598 that he could be brought forward as Henri's *grand voyer*\*—to become, in effect, his finance minister at the age of thirty-nine. That rare combination, a soldier-financier, Sully was a man of ruthless zeal and, crucially, was found trustworthy by Catholics and Protestants alike. Henri was possessed of rather more than genius; he also had good sense and a vast capacity for work. "Here I am," he wrote, "locked up in my office, where I examine minutely and with the greatest attention all the abuses which remain to be rooted out." He got up at 4 a.m. and worked through the day till 10 at night. Like Napoleon, he thrived on the reading of intelligence reports, observing: "I shall always maintain that without this guide, you can act only as a blind man or a rascal."

There was no time to worry about the state of the exchequer. When Sully took over, so he told the British Ambassador (Sir George Carew), he found "all things out of order, full of robbery of officers, full of confusion, no treasure, no munition, no furniture for the King's houses." France had a debt of over 300 million livres (£3 million at the prevailing rate), and only 23 million in annual income, which only supplied 7 million as the King's net revenue—all of which went on to warfare, pensions and gifts (not least to his legion of women). By 1608, ten years later, Sully had redeemed 130 millions of the debt, and had accumulated a reserve of cash in hand of 15 million livres.

*A post created in the thirteenth century.

Sully's most famed saying was "Le labourage et le pastourage, voilà les deux mamelles de la France, les vraies mines et trésors du Pérou" ("Tilling the soil and keeping flocks—these are France's paps, the real mines and treasures of Peru"). These words were to resound down through the history of agricultural France. They were to be echoed in Henri's equally famed, populist utterance about his ambition for the poorest peasant to have "a chicken in his pot every Sunday."

It was the time of the scramble for colonies in the New World—for the *trésors du Pérou*—by Spain in Peru and Mexico, and England in North America; but Sully was little interested in the heroic voyages to Canada of Cartier and Champlain. He would have echoed Voltaire's dismissive scorn when Canada was lost to Wolfe—"a few acres of snow"; like Bismarck (and like de Gaulle, many years later) he saw France's map of the world lying entirely in Europe. "Things which remain separated from our body by foreign lands or seas will only be ours at great expense and to little purpose" was Sully's view, while he invested prodigiously to repair the damages of war, repairing bridges, improving roads (and lining them with trees), laying out a network of canals, draining marshes and reorganising afforestation. Modern France is indebted to him for the ordered beauty of her countryside, as well as the conception of industries making carpets, tapestry and glass.

To finance all this, Sully without hesitation devalued the currency so that it lost a third of its value, reduced payment of interest on government bonds (a highly unpopular measure), and introduced an innovative range of indirect taxes. One of these was the *paulette*; introduced in 1604 and named after a provincial financier called Charles Paulet, it was a kind of hereditary tax whereby, in order to ensure their heirs should continue to enjoy royal office, holders had to pay the Crown an annual tax of one-sixtieth of the capital value of each office. Though it helped the monarchy out of its cash crisis, the *paulette* did little to tackle the root corruption of the "tax-farmer" system, which was to become one of the most insidious and wasteful institutions of the *ancien régime*—"the great destroyers of the kingdom's revenue," so Sully described them. In fact, the administration of Sully and Henri IV may be criticised for not tackling basic reform; but, given the delicate balances the King had inherited, there was a haunting fear that anything too radical could return France to the nightmare anarchy from which it had only so recently escaped.

Sully was something of a puritan, opposed to the idle and pleasure-loving ways of court life, and Henri's wanton extravagances. The King's favourite form of gambling was a card game called "Reversin" in which the Jack of Hearts took all. He gambled nearly every day; and almost always lost. In the early days, losing to influential subjects made a good bond of friendship, and it has been said that he may have won more Leaguers to his cause this way than on the battlefield. Unfortunately, the court imitated the King, with the Duc de Biron losing 500,000 écus in a single day. Many were the letters to Sully from Henri, begging for help to pay his debts. He was a source of despair to the frugal minister, who would write back fearlessly, chiding: "I beg his Majesty most humbly . . . to avoid all expenses on luxuries, not to waste money destined to advance his glory and to divert all expenditures on pleasures and distractions, of whatever sort, to purely military expenditures."[10]

With his hot and lusty Pyrenean blood, the Vert Galant is said to have collected at least fifty-six mistresses identified by name in the course of his career. Many, like the Marquise de Verneuil, were extremely expensive, but if stuck without Verneuil or some other regular, any girl would do: genteel daughters, bourgeois girls, barmaids or simple peasant girls all might be requested to share the King's bed. His need for women knew no bounds, with neither age nor political crisis, nor a new wife diminishing his earthy sensuality. Perhaps he had carried it too far; "They will do me to death," he grumbled. Parisians even complained openly to the Queen, Marie de' Medici, about her husband's philandering. What might have been alluring in a young hero became offensive in a beard that was turning white. His subjects now tended to see instead the cost of it all—the women, the gambling and the vast national debt accrued by all the monumental building schemes. By 1610, Henri's popularity was distinctly waning, Catholics chafed under the terms of Nantes, and the League began again to raise its head.

SINCE 1601 France had prospered in the peace that had been maintained on her borders. Now Sully began to talk ominously about "the grand design" whereby a kind of EU would rule the continent via a council of sixty elected members, which might even contemplate a joint invasion of India. More specifically, the "design" looked to Flanders and the Rhineland. There the death of the Duke of Jülich-Cleves had left control of this important principality in a vacuum, enticing to Spain. But, in the eyes of Parisians, there was far more to it than mere power politics. Aged fifty-six, Henri had unbecomingly fallen in love with a fifteen-year-old girl, Charlotte, daughter of the Constable of France, no less, from the powerful house of Montmorency. She had captured his imagination, dancing before him in a fête as one of the nymphs of Goddess Diana. Suspicious (rightly) of the King's intentions, her fiancé, the Prince de Condé, fled with Charlotte across the border to Brussels, in November 1609, escaping the King's men by only a few hours.

Stricken, the lovelorn King wrote that "I am now nothing more than skin and bone. Everything displeases me; I run away from company and if I permit myself to be brought into any gathering, instead of cheering me up, it succeeds in killing me . . ."[11] Shocking to the French body politic, it looked as if Henri was prepared to go to war to get Charlotte back. A war threatened completely to redraw the map of Europe, placing France squarely in the camp of the Protestant nations. By May 1610 a powerful (and costly) French army 50,000 strong, backed by English and Dutch troops, was indeed poised to invade. On the 14th, on the eve of Henri's departure for the front, something unimaginable occurred.

AT 4 P.M. ON 14 MAY 1610, Henri was travelling from the Louvre to meet Sully at the Arsenal when his coach was stuck in congested traffic in the narrow Rue de la Ferronnerie. Between his accession in 1593 and then there had already been twenty-four known plots to assassinate him, but Henri by now had become dismissive of the danger. Nevertheless, already in recent months, he had had several premonitions of his death. After going to mass at the Church of Saint Roch that morning, he had met with Maréchal de Bassompierre, who had found him morbid and "strange in his manner." Bassompierre chided him for his uncharacteristic gloom, remarking that he was just in the prime of life; "had he not the finest kingdom in the world, a beautiful wife, a beautiful *maîtresse* and two lovely children?" It was to no avail. "*Mon ami*," said the King, "I've got to leave it all!"

Bassompierre had just received from Italy a remarkable invention: a heavy coach enclosed by glass windows, the equivalent of an armoured limousine of its day. But on account of the cramped Paris streets, Henri was travelling that day in a small, light phaeton with its sides open to the street. Irony it was that the king who had improved the city so much should now be a vulnerable target because of its remaining imperfections.

Just like Gavrilo Princip in the Sarajevo of July 1914, a thirty-two-year-old with red hair, François Ravaillac, was awaiting his opportunity. Ravaillac was a rejected monk and failed schoolteacher from Angoulême who had done time in a debtors' prison—and a fanatical Catholic, given to hallucinations and delusions about his role as a deliverer of France. Wishing to see all heretics subjected to fire and brimstone, he had come to Paris in December 1609 seeking, in vain, an audience with the King in order to tell him to banish the Protestants, or else force conversion upon them. Returning to Paris in April 1610, Ravaillac was appalled to learn of the preparations for war, which was a war against the Pope and against God. He stole a short kitchen knife from an inn, deciding to kill the King, but changing his mind at least once.

In Rue de la Ferronnerie, Henri's coach was blocked by a broken-down haycart in collision with a waggon laden with provisions, while another cart had collapsed under the weight of barrels. The King's attendants rallied around to help. Ravaillac, having stalked the King all morning, now saw his chance, leaped on to the running-board of the coach and stabbed the King violently three times, just as he was reading a letter. Heroically Henri murmured "Ce n'est rien," but Ravaillac's second blow had severed the King's aorta. Ravaillac made no attempt to flee, and was seized by Henri's travelling companion, the Duc d'Épernon. Henri was rushed to a neighbouring apothecary, but there was no hope. His body was taken back to the Louvre, while overnight Paris was reassured that he had only been wounded.

When the truth finally got out on the 15th, misery and vengeance took over the city. For a moment the weight of taxation and sexual scandal was forgotten; the ill-conceived expedition to Jülich swiftly put on hold. But who was to blame? Who, apart from the madman Ravaillac, could be rooted out and punished? It seemed inconceivable that he had acted alone. Ravaillac, under the most appalling torture ever suffered, remained insistent that he had. Most of Paris refused to believe this; there was proof that there were several plots in hand, Henri having earned the hatred of extremists on both sides for his efforts of religious reconciliation. Heavily under suspicion was the Marquise de Verneuil, known to hope that, upon Henri's death, their bastard son would succeed. (After a lengthy, and incriminating, examination and after a principal informant had been found strangled in prison, the ambitious schemer, Henriette, was absolved—for *raison d'état*.) And there was always the sinister hand of Spain. Paralysing fear spread that, after two decades of peace, there would be a return to civil war. The Jesuits, for one, fearful that they would be blamed, hastened to praise the King and acquired his heart to bury in their chapel at La Flèche, on the Île de la

Cité; while the Huguenot leaders rushed forward to acclaim him the best king Providence had granted.

On 27 May, still protesting that he had acted as a free agent on a divinely inspired mission, Ravaillac was put to death. Before being drawn and quartered, the lot of the regicide, on the Place de Grève scaffold he was scalded with burning sulphur, molten lead and boiling oil and resin, his flesh then torn by pincers. Then his arms and legs were attached to horses which pulled in opposite directions. One of the horses "foundered," so a zealous *chevalier* offered his mount; "the animal was full of vigour and pulled away a thigh." After an hour and a half of this horrendous cruelty, Ravaillac died, as the mob tried to prevent him receiving last rites. When he finally expired,

> the entire populace, no matter what their rank, hurled themselves on the body with their swords, knives, sticks or anything else to hand and began beating, hacking and tearing at it. They snatched the limbs from the executioner, savagely chopping them up and dragging the pieces through the streets.

Children made a bonfire and flung remnants of Ravaillac's body on it. According to one witness, Nicholas Pasquier, one woman actually ate some of the flesh. The executioner, supposed to have the body of the regicide reduced into ashes to complete the ritual demanded by the law, could find nothing but his shirt. Seldom, even at the height of the Terror, was the Paris mob to be seen acting with greater ferocity, born as much of fear as of grief. If nothing else it attested to the powerful loyalty to the Crown that Henri in his person had rekindled in France.

The King's embalmed corpse was placed on open display in the Louvre up until 29 June, then conducted solemnly to Saint-Denis, where he had first made his vows as a Catholic monarch just seventeen years before.

Of Henri's all-too-brief reign, it would be hard to improve on André Maurois' assessment. The results may have been "less astonishing than legend would have them," he wrote:

> but at least Henri IV and Sully gave France ten years' truce, and the country remembered it as a golden age . . . "You cannot be a Frenchman," said Henri de Rohan, "without regretting the loss to its well-being France has suffered." Ten generations have con-

firmed this judgement, and Henri IV remains, together with Charlemagne, Joan of Arc and Saint Louis, one of France's heroes. He typifies not France's mystical aspect, but its aspects of courage, good sense and gaiety.

Henri of Navarre was the second in a row of French kings to die by the knife of a religious zealot. What would have happened in Paris if Ravaillac had proved to be Huguenot, or the tool of a Protestant conspiracy, instead of a lone, deranged Catholic fanatic, is frightening to contemplate. As it was, throughout the country renewed civil war was widely predicted. Waiting in Milan, fêted by the Spanish envoys there, was the self-exiled Prince de Condé, the last would-be cuckold of the murdered King, short on both charm and resolve, and a prince of the blood.

But Henri had at least planned a legitimate succession. For all the rival claims of the mistresses, he had left an heir by Queen Marie de' Medici, Louis XIII.

# SEVEN

# Louis XIII: Richelieu to the Fronde

My first goal was the majesty of the King;
the second was the greatness of the realm.

—*Cardinal Richelieu*

L OUIS XIII (1610–43) CAME TO THE THRONE as a child
not quite nine years old. Here was a dangerous situation for
France, whereby the ruler of a mighty country surrounded by
watchful enemies, both inside and outside, was a regent—and a
woman—governing in the name of an infant. Over the next 100 years,
there would be three child-kings in a row on the throne of France, ruling
through three regents. In the case of both Louis XIII and his son, Louis
XIV, aged four when he came to the throne, the Regent would be the
Queen Mother. In Milan was the self-exiled Prince de Condé, and in
eastern France, the powerful Duc de Bouillon, who threatened a
Huguenot uprising if the young King were to marry the Spanish
infanta—a match arranged when he was just ten years old. But Henri
had shown foresight; some six months before his death he had declared
to Maréchal de Lesdiguières that he "well knew that the foundation of
everything in France is the prince's authority."[1] For that reason, he
intended to establish the Dauphin "as absolute king and to give him all
the true, essential marks of royalty, to the end that there might be no one
in the realm who would not have to obey him." Here, *de facto,* was
enunciated the principle of absolutism by which, for better or worse,
France would be governed until the Great Revolution 180 years later—
and again, revived under Emperor Napoleon I.

On the eve of setting off for the wars, Henri had taken the wise precaution of designating his queen, Marie, to act as Regent in his absence, supported by a Regent's Council fifteen strong. She had neither the authoritarian will nor the expertise in statecraft of her predecessor and kinswoman, Catherine. Marie, fat, blonde—though comely enough when Rubens glorified her—also suffered the disadvantage of being a foreigner, and was of limited intelligence. But sensibly she stuck with all Henri's ministers. Only the ageing Sully resigned, his stewardship finally fulfilled. Acting judiciously to calm Protestant fears of another Saint Bartholomew's Eve, one of her first acts was to confirm, on 22 May, the Edict of Nantes. However, Henri had not ruled long enough for the stability he achieved to survive the assassination. "Rule in the interest of the public good, or for the good of all Frenchmen," claims one historian, "had proved too radical."[2]

When Marie was declared Regent shortly after the announcement of the regicide, the citizens were shocked and frightened. But instead of running to arms, as they might have done before Henri's death, they ran to pray and make votive offerings for the health and prosperity of his son. Thus Marie was able to lay a foundation sufficiently sound for the young Louis XIII to survive campaigns against the princes in 1619–20, and in 1627–28 against the Huguenots—as well as to resist the external pressures of the Thirty Years' War which had scourged central Europe in the 1630s. The Queen Mother contented herself with purchasing and completing her sumptuous Luxembourg Palace, summoning Rubens from his native Antwerp in 1621 to decorate its galleries with twenty-four vast canvases that celebrated, with magnificent flattery, the main events of her marriage, and the benefits to her adopted country of the Regency.

In 1612, the engagement of the ten-year-old Dauphin to Anne of Austria, daughter of King Philip III of Spain, a thoroughly dynastic arrangement, was announced. At the same time, Louis' sister, Élisabeth, was betrothed to Anne's brother, the future Philip IV of Spain. That April saw one of the most extravagant celebrations ever mounted in Paris to dignify the double engagement and inaugurate the Palace. A mock *carrousel,* called the Château de Félicité, complete with turrets and battlements, was erected in its centre. The Queen and court, with an estimated 200,000 Parisians, watched a *défilé* of 150 musicians, "twenty-four trumpets, twelve horse-mounted drums, five giants with bows and arrows," and a gigantic equestrian ballet, punctuated by the sound of cannon fired from the Bastille.

The noble *Chevaliers de la Gloire,* dressed in embroidered gold and silver, carrying bright red standards walked in front of ten companies of *assaillants* led by the late King's bastard, the Duc de Vendôme, and "a troop of many-coloured chevaliers on armour-clad horses, bandsmen, *rois captifs*, two elephants, two reinocerots [*sic*], and a chariot pulled by deer." Sibyls made their appearance, chanting eulogies specially written by the poet Malherbe. When the cavalcade ended, the "defenders" of the *carrousel* charged the *assaillants* in a mock battle. As night fell, accompanied by the firing of 4000 rockets from the towers of the nearby Bastille, the whole Château de Félicité was set alight, its defenders seen consumed by fire.

The following day there was a new, brilliant cavalcade. On the third day, Saturday, there was a salute of 200 cannon and a *grand feu de joie* outside the Hôtel de Ville where only so recently the unfortunate Ravaillac had been ritually torn apart.

TOGETHER WITH A LIBERAL HAND-OUT of graces-and-favours to the nobles, and an increase in their pensions, the great festival temporarily assured the popularity of Reine Marie—but only temporarily. Two years later the Estates-General met, to hand in a formidable list of grievances. War with both Habsburgs and Huguenots threatened, and with it financial bankruptcy; it seemed as if the age of conspiracy and rebellion might be about to return. Already suspect on account of her Italian background, Marie rashly handed great powers to her Florentine favourite, a woman widely held to be "a swarthy and greedy sorceress," called Leonora Galigai. Leonora was married to an affected fop, Carlo Concini, whom the Queen made Marquis d'Ancre, and a marshal of France—though he never fought a battle. The Concinis exerted a curious influence over the Queen Regent, enriching and foolishly flaunting themselves in front of both the "Great Ones" and the young King. They soon became the scapegoat for all the real or imagined shortcomings of the regime. Louis reached his majority, aged thirteen, in October 1614, and—dressed in white, elegant and frail—appeared before the Estates-General where the young Bishop of Luçon (which appointment he had received from Henri IV, at the tender age of twenty-one), one Richelieu, first made his mark with his forceful eloquence. The boy-King thanked his mother profusely for "all the trouble" she had taken on his behalf, and said he wished her to continue to govern and to be obeyed.

Nonetheless, the young King was but a glum shadow of his father, lacking his panache—and fearful of women. As a lonely child, sulky, morose and shy, he grew up to be secretive, cold and capable of great cruelty. He was unsociable and a dreamer, who seemed consistently bored. When asked to pardon a condemned peer (and personal friend), he is said to have remarked icily: "A king should not have the same feelings as a private man." Like his mother he made a poor choice of favourites. Left to be brought up by court servants, his choice was Charles d'Albert de Luynes, Grand Falconer at the court, whose name sounded grander than in fact he was. Luynes, who was all of twenty-three years older than Louis, was a fairly humble *petit gentilhomme* from near Aix-en-Provence, born—according to Richelieu's acid comment—of a cannon and a chambermaid. He was good looking and expert at riding and hunting, which seems to have been what most interested the King.

In November 1615, aged fourteen, Louis married his Anne of Austria (though she was, in fact, a Spanish princess), then a beautiful young woman. Anne was to become, in Dumas' *Les Trois Mousquetaires* (1844), a Queen Guinevere–like heroine of d'Artagnan and his chivalrous comrades-in-arms, protecting her honour from the machinations of Richelieu. During the marital festivities, Louis had made a show, unusual for him, of being *joyeux et galant*. He may well have been a bisexual. In total contrast to either his father or his son, Louis XIV, he was in all probability simply frigid. Deeply attached to Luynes, Louis is said not to have entered his wife's bed until five years after their marriage, and then only when he was led to it by Luynes. There was to be no issue of the marriage for twenty-two years—following a chance encounter when Louis was sheltering from a storm in 1637. But for the advent of one of history's greatest politicians, Cardinal Richelieu, Louis XIII's reign might have been a calamity for France.

The Concinis, arrogant *parvenus,* came increasingly to annoy Louis by cheekily parading outside his windows in the Louvre, with an escort of between 200 and 300. With Louis on a tight string financially, Concini added to the humiliation by offering to help him out. It was an intolerable situation. Condé had already made a failed attempt at eliminating Concini, but he had escaped and Condé had ended in the Bastille. Then, in April 1617, Louis, almost certainly egged on by his favourite, ordered the elimination of Concini, his mother's favourite. On the morning of the 24th, as the puffed-up Maréchal d'Ancre and his retinue of fifty entered the Louvre, a courtier supported by a few men sprang out and took the right arm of Concini, announcing: "The King has commanded me to seize your person." Concini cried out for help, but was immediately shot down with a volley of pistol shots. His retinue did nothing, although Louis and Luynes were waiting anxiously inside, ready to flee if the plot failed.

The city rejoiced ferociously at the death, in the courtyard of the Louvre itself, of the hated Concini, who was suspected of complicity in the death of Henri IV and even blamed for the failure to place his statue on the Pont Neuf. Buried at Saint-Germain-l'Auxerrois, Concini's body was later dug up, torn apart, and cannibalised: "having torn out the heart, one mob roasted it on a charcoal brazier, and ate it with relish."[3] At sixteen the unpleasant Louis had truly come of age; "Yes, now I am King!" he declared. Marie de' Medici, realising that her innings was over, said resignedly, "I've reigned for years, and now I expect nothing more than a crown in Heaven!" She was exiled (briefly) to Blois. Her Italian best friend, Leonora Galigai, Concini's widow, was seized while trying to conceal her jewellery in a mattress, and then burned on the Place de Grève as a witch. "What a lot of people to see a poor woman die!" she is said to have exclaimed.

WITH THE DOUBLE SPANISH MARRIAGE in 1615, the Spanish threat to France, which had so exercised Henri IV, was now approaching its end as Spanish power began its long descent following the death of Philip II. Once again the dangers were internal. With Louis and his favourite, the skein of religious reconciliation, so courageously woven by his father, began to unravel. Luynes was a Catholic zealot, although Louis, by upbringing and the influence of his Medici mother, hardly needed much encouragement. He soon found himself entangled in a campaign against the Protestants in the south-west of France, in his father's old bailiwick and against Henri's former supporters. Luynes, now appointed Constable of France (amid much derision), was put in charge of operations. Lacking both political and military experience, he had swiftly made himself almost as detested as Concini, exploiting his relationship with the King to amass wealth and titles. In 1621, he so mishandled the siege of Montauban that it had to be abandoned after three months. Among the heavy casualties was Luynes, dead of camp fever.

Louis shed no tears; they were not part of the King's make-up. Writing to Richelieu, Cardinal Bérulle described the death of Luynes as a "coup de justice et de miséricorde." Unmistakably, it was a stroke of pure good fortune for France, though it left a serious power vacuum in Paris. Into it, and out of his temporary disgrace, moved Richelieu—invited by Louis, disorientated by the loss of his favourite.

LOUIS BECAME RECONCILED to his mother and abetted the rise of her favourite Richelieu. He was made cardinal in 1622. Two years later Louis, repressing in his memory Richelieu's involvement with the Concinis, called him to take over the government. Previously Louis had viewed him as a dangerous prelate, but for France, this was to prove a marriage almost made in heaven. For the monarchy, it was to transform an unattractive and accident-prone princeling into a great king. If Louis had greatness, it lay primarily in his entrusting of the country almost entirely to his brilliant prime minister, creating a virtual dictatorship of a *premier ministre* with the acceptance of the monarch. Richelieu declared that "my first goal was the majesty of the King; the second was the greatness of his realm." Historians like Montesquieu, however, saw it differently: Richelieu had assigned the King the role of playing "second fiddle in the realm, and first in Europe."

Armand Jean Du Plessis de Richelieu was born in Paris in 1585, five years before Henri IV began his siege of Paris, younger son of a provincial family of nobles from Poitou. Obliged by them to enter into Holy Orders, he was ever a convinced Christian and strict priest, and had greatly impressed the Sorbonne with his theological theses. At the Estates-General convocation of 1614 his arched nose and thin lips, his goatee and military moustache, his pale complexion and slender figure, already lent him a distinguished bearing. Beneath the cool, reasoned exterior which was to dominate the portraits of the epoch was a man of passion, occasionally capable of violent rages. France, Richelieu saw, was dangerously caught in a power play between Spain, Habsburg Austria and Protestant Germany, menaced not only by the Catholic-Protestant split, but also by the ambitions of "Great Lords" like Condé grown too rich and too powerful under the Regency. Richelieu found himself under great pressure, on the one hand, from the *parti dévot,* successors to the sixteenth-century Catholic League, which urged him to concentrate on suppressing the Huguenots and to favour Spain; and, on the other hand, from the nobles who wanted to assert their authority. Always the pragmatist rather than a reformer, Richelieu eschewed grand designs in favour of a method—a method of making things work, avoiding confrontation. "In politics," he was fond of saying, "one is impelled far more by the necessity of things than by a preestablished will."[4]

In simplest terms, Richelieu's early programme operated on three prongs: to crush Huguenot power, to humble France's "Great Lords" and to thwart Austrian designs. In the first of these, he was greatly aided by the folly of James I's favourite, George Villiers, Duke of Buckingham. Villiers handed him an Anglo-French war into which the key Huguenot stronghold of La Rochelle on the Bay of Biscay was unwillingly drawn. Having suffered terrible privations on a par with Paris in 1590, La Rochelle was starved out after a fourteen-month siege in 1627–28. In what subsequently, to French eyes, was a scuttle comparable to Dunkirk in 1940, Buckingham pulled out, abandoning his Huguenot allies to their fate—a disastrous episode which, in England, lowered the prestige of the monarchy and contributed to the causes of the Civil War. John Felton, the assassin, removed Buckingham*—but too late to avert the damage already done.

Acting with great moderation towards the defeated Protestants, Richelieu coaxed Louis into a humane settlement, depriving the Huguenots of their fortresses and armies, but guaranteeing them liberty of conscience. As a result of this "Peace of Grace," the Huguenots caused no real trouble for the government over the next few decades.

To humble the nobles, Richelieu began by purging from the Council any ministers who opposed him, executing some. For many years without an heir, Louis was a natural object for conspiracy, particularly among his half-brothers, the Vendômes (the illegitimates of Henri IV) and his younger brother, Gaston of Orléans. Gaston (1608–60)—until 1638 the presumptive heir to the throne—an odd-looking man with thick black eyebrows, was an attractive but irresponsibly feckless libertine of no great intelligence. In 1626, he became seriously embroiled in a plot to assassinate Richelieu, led by the Marquis de Chalais. Tortured and having confessed, after a dismally botched execution Chalais was put to death. His friends swore to get Richelieu. The Cardinal doubled his personal bodyguard, while Gaston, because of his proximity to the King, remained untouchable. The episode embittered personal relations between Louis and Queen Anne, whom he accused of desiring his death so that she could marry Gaston, despite her protestations.

It was not a situation exactly favourable to producing an heir for the throne of France. But the throne was at last made secure when, seemingly

---

*In Dumas' story, Buckingham is the favourite of Queen Anne, on whom she bestows controversial diamonds; Richelieu endeavours to expose her to the King, but d'Artagnan and Co. rescue the diamonds in the nick of time. The dashing Buckingham's assassination is set up by the villainess of the novel, the mysterious "Milady," in the pay of Richelieu.

almost in a fit of absent-mindedness during that storm of 1637, Louis caused Anne to conceive an heir, born on 5 September 1638, twenty-three years after their marriage. Two years later another similar miracle produced a second son; Gaston, Richelieu's bitter enemy, lost all hope—at least temporarily—of succeeding to the throne.

IN HIS THIRD AIM of humbling the Habsburgs, now grown powerful through the aggrandisements of "Charles Quint," Richelieu was largely successful. By encouraging the armies of others to accomplish the policies of France, he kept out of the grisly Thirty Years' War that ravaged Germany and the countries east of the Rhine. It was a risky policy, however, bringing war with Spain again. At one point, in 1636, her armies invading from Holland once more reached Pontoise, almost at the gates of Paris. Though subsequently this was to be seen as virtually the last effort of waning Spanish power, in scenes similar to those of 1940 the roads to the south became crammed with fleeing coaches. For one grim moment there seemed to be nothing between Paris and the Spanish infantry. Richelieu even contemplated having to abandon the capital and flee southwards. But from Paris Louis and Richelieu dispatched a *levée en masse* of hastily conscripted soldiery. Merchants were forbidden to keep more than one apprentice; all the rest had to join up. Out of these complicated hostilities, France managed to survive intact.

BUILDING ASTUTELY, AND RUTHLESSLY, on the absolutist foundations laid by Henri and Sully, Louis XIII and Richelieu steadily tightened the monarchy's grip. It was a tendency that would continue on through the reigns of the next three Louis, to the Revolution, and beyond to the Consulate and First Empire of Napoleon I; and would then, briefly, be reanimated under the last of the Bourbons, Charles X, and the ill-fated Second Empire of Louis-Napoleon. In the mother country of liberty, the instinct for authoritarianism also lies never far below the surface. Almost never before had the charge of *lèse-majesté* been made so frequently throughout the country, although the capital remained curiously tranquil throughout the time of Richelieu. In 1630, many provincial centres erupted in violence against his massive tax increases, under chieftains attaining brief moments of glory with such sobriquets as "Jean Va-nu-Pieds" and "Bras-Nus." Typically, it was

Louis' rule of thumb that "The more considerate you are with such people, the more they take advantage."

Now Richelieu too showed himself ruthlessly determined to stamp
out what, to him, was a particularly heinous sin. Duelling had become
all the rage among *galants*. In the one year of 1607 alone, 4000 members
of the gentry are recorded to have perished in duels. *Pour encourager les
autres,* in June 1627 a well-known noble, the Comte de Montmorency-
Bouteville, was arrested for duelling, refused a pardon and beheaded.
Henceforth it was to be said that the aristocracy "tourna au galant, faute
de pouvoir tourner au tragique."* Led on by the skilful guile of Richelieu, the nobles ended weakened by division among themselves, while
loyalty was encouraged among the six *pays d'État* (the outer ring of
recent acquisitions that comprised Languedoc, Brittany, Burgundy,
Provence, Normandy and the Dauphiné) through their entitlement to
pay lower taxes.

MORE LIKE HIS VALOIS ANTECEDENTS than his father Henri IV,
when not at the wars or involved in acts of repression in the provinces,
Louis was addicted to *la chasse*. Richelieu, on the other hand, spent as
much time in Paris as he could—because that was where lay the sources
of power, the ultimate aphrodisiac. During the two Richelieu decades,
the geographical centre of gravity of Paris moved westwards, away from
the smells and congestion of the Marais. Exceedingly shrewd in matters
of real estate for a man of God, Richelieu amassed a vast property that
stretched from the back door of the Louvre to the city wall to the
north. There, between 1633 and 1639, Richelieu built a princely palace
of stone with eight elegant and classically regular courtyards, which he
bequeathed to the King.

Known initially as the Palais-Cardinal, when the royal family moved
in after Richelieu's death it gained the name it has held ever since—the
Palais-Royal. "An entire city, built with pomp, seems to have arisen
miraculously from an old ditch," extolled Corneille, his praise possibly
conditioned by the fact that he found there both a patron and a stage for
his plays. After Louis XIV died in 1715, the light-hearted and hard-living

---

*Which, contemplating Byron's famous verse from *Don Juan,* "What men call gallantry, and the Gods adultery" might well be translated "turned to adultery instead of
tragedy."

regent, Philippe d'Orléans, moved in and with his notorious *soupers* gave it the reputation which clung to it for many years. It was his grandson, who was to become "Philippe-Égalité," the turncoat regicide, who—deeply in debt—built the arcades and shops which he rented out most profitably, and laid out the delightful gardens of what remains one of the most tranquil oases amid the hubbub of Paris.

During the Terror, it was from a cutlery shop at No. 177 Galerie de Valois that Charlotte Corday bought the knife with which she stabbed Marat in his bath in July 1793. Equally profitable gambling houses and brothels made the arcades of the Palais-Royal a famous pick-up place over both the eighteenth and nineteenth centuries. It also became a centre for intellectuals like Diderot to meet for a game of chess and, in one corner, saw the birth of France's oldest three-star restaurant, the Grand Véfour. Napoleon and Josephine dined here, Fragonard is said to have died here eating a sorbet; while in 1983 it was targeted for a *plastique* by a left-wing terrorist—possibly outraged by the food and its cost. Following the post-1815 Restoration, the Palais became a favoured duelling ground, with residents complaining at being woken by the groans of the vanquished opponents.

The shift of religious balance following the death of Henri had resulted in a powerful Catholic renaissance, in which Richelieu made his ascent to power. The clergy had regained respect, and influence; and so had the Jesuits, expanding everywhere in their role of educators. There was even rash talk about a new crusade, against the infidel Turks who were threatening Austro-Hungary in the east of Europe. There was a flurry of church building, encouraged by the King as displays of thanksgiving. Louis built Notre-Dame des Victoires to celebrate the fall of La Rochelle, although the outstanding monument to his reign is not a church and lies in the middle of the Seine—the Île Saint-Louis. Just upstream from the age-old Île de la Cité were two small muddy islets, used over the centuries for grazing cattle. Henri IV had it in mind to join them together, build a dyke round them to keep the Seine out, and then develop the resulting island. His assassination brought a halt to the project, but Louis carried it forward, laying out the buildings on a grid system (which would preserve them from the attentions of Préfet Haussmann subsequently). Within a space of thirty years, the two mudbanks had been transformed into a beautiful city in miniature, a seventeenth-century jewel encapsulating in its streets of pot-bellied houses both uniformity and individualism. Many of the houses were designed by Louis XIV's famous architect Le Vau, who—understandably—kept one of the best for himself. From its inception, prostitutes from the Marais were banned from the Île. Compared with Henri's clamorous Place des Vosges, the Île Saint-Louis' straight streets were a model of sober rectitude and planned tranquillity. But the other great project envisaged by Henri IV, the grandiose scheme for the Place de France, was abandoned by Richelieu as simply too ambitious.

Richelieu's greatest cultural legacy to France lay not in bricks and mortar, however, but in the creation of the Académie Française, designed to defend and enhance the purity of the French language. Founded in 1635, initially of a group of nine men of letters, with an average age of thirty-six, under the patronage of Richelieu it was then followed, in 1648, by the Académie Royale de Peinture et de Sculpture. In 1671 came the all-powerful Académie Royale d'Architecture, designed similarly to establish and maintain standards in building.*

THE CIVIL WAR IN FRANCE had brought the arts to a new low. The League attacked Renaissance art as heretical, so few young artists of talent were attracted to Paris in those days. Henri IV was no connoisseur, and had no time to become one; Marie de' Medici lacked the necessary taste. However, to quote Douglas Johnson in his excellent short survey, "In terms of culture, as in politics, it is possible to talk of a sense of discipline replacing the restless ambition of the sixteenth century."[5] This was certainly true of French architecture and, fortunately, Richelieu possessed both taste and the political power to indulge it. He bought paintings and sculpture from Italy, and brought the portrait painter Philippe de Champaigne from Brussels. In 1635, he commissioned Nicolas Poussin to paint more of the light-hearted bacchanals and landscapes which had made his early reputation; Poussin, of Norman peasant stock, found money and fame, but in 1642 he abandoned his rich but pretentious Paris patrons for the inspiration of Rome.

His fellow Norman, the great dramatist equally capable of writing both comedy and tragedy, Pierre Corneille (1606–84), was set to work by Richelieu as one of his *cinq auteurs,* writing plays under his careful direction, sometimes performed before the King. In January

---

*Originally organisations without a home, the Académies had to wait for Mazarin to build the superb Institut de France complex. With its glistening cupola, its two arms seem to reach out to embrace the very heart of Paris from its eminence on the Left Bank of the Seine.

1637, he produced the heroic tragedy by which his reputation stands, *Le Cid*, dealing with the conflict between passion and honour. It marked a major milestone in the history of French drama, in the same year that Descartes (1596–1650) published his world-shaking *Discours de la Méthode*—"Cogito ergo sum." Corneille, too, was outstanding for his belief in freedom of will—in marked contrast to the theme of impotence conveyed in Greek classical tragedy, the tradition that was to be inherited by Racine.

Another Norman was the poet François de Malherbe (1555–1628). Renowned for his slowness in composition, he once spent three years writing stanzas on the death of a noble lady, so that when it was presented the bereaved husband had already remarried—and died! Thus Malherbe left few verses to posterity, but he possessed a rigorous purity of style and his diction eschewed all Latinisms and foreign usage, in preference for common speech. This set him aside from the more ornate style of his Renaissance predecessors, making him an important precursor of the Académie. Though Henri had not been a great patron, his reign laid the groundwork on which his widow, son, grandson—and Richelieu—were all to build a kind of "nationalisation" of the French arts. Henri's own letters, passionate and forthright as they were, broke new ground as classics of their kind. So too did the *Économies Royales* of Sully—reading as a new, more genuine form of autobiography than the ghosted and stiff *Mémoires* of Richelieu.

Finally there was the great essayist Montaigne (1533–92), much admired down through posterity for the vigour and gaiety of his language. An incorrigible digresser, he brought fresh insight to bear on contemporary mores and philosophy, on public calamities, education, virtue and prevailing attitudes towards death. He had little difficulty in supporting the legitimacy of Henri of Navarre and his descendants. The succession had been secure since the surprise birth of the future Louis XIV to the semi-detached royal couple, Louis and Anne. There followed one last conspiracy on behalf of the absentee princeling, Gaston d'Orléans—that of a courtier with the unusual name of Cinq-Mars, arrested while planning to assassinate Richelieu during a visit to Lyons in the spring of 1642. Cinq-Mars was duly beheaded, but Richelieu—his body eaten away with ulcers—was already a dying man.

The end of the Louis XIII–Richelieu era arrived with extraordinary suddenness. On 4 December 1642, Richelieu died; on being administered the last rites, when asked by the curé of Saint Eustache whether he forgave his enemies, he replied that he had none—except for those of the King and of the state. Meanwhile Louis XIII was also failing. In his youth he had suffered from persistent fevers, and in adulthood from an excess of doctors—who had once bled him fifty times in a year, and prescribed him 200 different medications and as many enemas. In 1630, he had nearly died of an internal abscess, and in December 1641 he suffered a swelling which made it hard to swallow, or to sleep, and caused such discomfort that he could not stand the shaking of a coach. At the last meeting between the King and the Cardinal, in Tarascon, both were so debilitated that Louis ordered his bed to be placed next to his Prime Minister's. It was a tearful leave-taking. Five months after Richelieu, Louis was also carried away, on 14 May 1643—apparently by tuberculosis, and amid no great mourning. Yet the Cardinal had created in the person of the King what could not unreasonably be claimed as *le plus grand roi du monde.*

By the death of Louis, the shape of France's modern geography was confirmed in the familiar "hexagon" of today. Under the Treaty of Westphalia of 1648, a large part of German-speaking Alsace would be added—and French possession of the key fortresses of Metz, Toul and Verdun recognised. Expanding also abroad, the city of Quebec was founded by Champlain, then, on a deserted island in the Saint Lawrence, Montreal as Ville-Marie, dedicated to the Virgin. Footholds were also gained in West Africa, Madagascar and Saint Lucia in the Caribbean.

Once again, France found herself ruled by a woman regent, the Queen Mother, Anne. Louis XIV (1643–1715) was not yet five years old, his coming of age perilously far away. Yet, as both an augury of what was to come and a "hands-off" warning to her foes, within a week of the child-King's accession a renewed Spanish advance upon Paris from the Low Countries was defeated, at Rocroi in the Ardennes, by the twenty-two-year-old Duc d'Enghien, "with the profile of an eagle" (he was soon to be known as "le grand Condé," son of the troublesome but ineffectual would-be cuckold of Henri IV). One of the great military victories of French history, Rocroi may also have marked the definitive end of Spain's military pre-eminence.

A new era lay ahead, but none of it would have been possible had it not been for the solid foundations laid by Louis' grandfather, Henri IV, whose short but glorious reign was the rock on which would be built the France of the "Sun King," and "the Great Nation" of the next century.

ON HIS ACCESSION, four-year-old Louis went to live in the Louvre with his mother and his younger brother, Philippe d'Orléans, then moving into the Palais-Royal which had been vacated by Richelieu, a modern, comfortable abode. From the earliest days Louis loved playing there with his silver toy soldiers, complete with miniature gold cannon drawn by fleas. As he grew older, he would march through the Palais-Royal deafening bystanders with his drum, and later still take to target practice on unfortunate sparrows in the gardens with a specially made small arquebus—already in childhood showing perhaps something of the instincts of the bully. To replace Richelieu, Anne called in his far less austere, Italian-born secretary, Jules Mazarin, "Tall, of good appearance, a handsome man, with chestnut hair, lively and amused eyes, and a great sweetness in his face."[6] There were unsubstantiated rumours that he also became the Queen Mother's lover. Aged forty, Mazarin was a highly cultivated man (though, according to Voltaire, he never learned to pronounce French properly);[7] loving the opera and drama, he seemed gentle and unassuming, flexible where Richelieu had been ruthless. But he was to follow in much the same pattern; another churchman unhesitant at resorting to the sword. Mazarin's reputation for avarice made him few friends, and he was heavy-handed with taxation. In 1648, Sully's little-loved tax on bonds came up for renewal. The Paris Parlement protested vigorously. But, with Condé's brilliant victory at Rocroi, several generals and 6000 troops captured, the war with Spain was ended in triumph for France through the Peace of Westphalia, which drew a line under the Thirty Years' War, and left Anne with forces available to reinforce her position at home.

Acting against the advice of Mazarin, however, and given to fits of rage that turned her voice into a shrill falsetto, Anne in her capacity as regent ordered the arrest of three of the leading troublemakers in Parlement. One was an elder called Pierre Broussel. Unfortunately, Broussel enjoyed singular popularity with the Parisians, who hailed him as a "Father of the People." On learning of his arrest, angry demonstrators forced Anne and Louis to take refuge in the Palais-Royal, which was not nearly so formidable a bastion as the Louvre. The next morning over a thousand barricades of chains, barrels, and paving stones were thrown up across the capital. Mazarin prevailed on Anne to give way, and Broussel was released. But the situation continued. The coach of the Chancellor, Segnier, was overturned and the barricades thrust forward to within a hundred yards of the vulnerable Palais. On 13 September 1648, the royal family fled Paris. It was an intolerable humiliation to fall on an impressionable young king. Meanwhile, his head swollen by his triumph at Rocroi, Condé was moving on Paris; and, in England, where Charles I was about to lose his, a dangerous example in rebellion had been set.

Poor France: it was roughly a hundred years since the country had been torn apart by the Wars of Religion; two centuries back she was being ravaged by the Hundred Years' War. Only one century ahead she would be approaching the chaos of revolution; two centuries on and Paris would be plunged in the bloody insurrection of 1848; three centuries, and the country would barely be recovering from Occupation and Vichy. Now it was the time of the "Frondes." In the words of Voltaire: "The civil wars started in Paris just as they did in London, over a little money."[8] And what was beginning was indeed a civil war, the first since the early days of Henri of Navarre. The rebels now called themselves *frondeurs*—or "slingshots"—because of pebbles that were flung through Mazarin's windows, and perhaps thinking in self-flattery of David versus Goliath. But the Frondes were an exercise in infantile futility.

At the end of October 1648, Anne deemed it safe to return to Paris, to await the arrival of the twenty-seven-year-old hero, Condé. But with only 15,000 men, as Henri IV had discovered, Condé was not strong enough to besiege the city. Inside the rebels won a first success with the capture of the Bastille, where Broussel's son was made governor. Once again, Anne and the child-King left Paris—reduced to penury by the exigencies of war. The crown jewels were in pawn, and the upholstery in Louis XIII's old coach hung in tatters. Often young Louis and his brother went hungry. In 1649, shocked by how matters had got out of hand in London with the execution of the King of England, the moderates of Parlement produced an agreement to withdraw from the Bastille, in return for an amnesty. But it was only a truce.

Now France's other great—and ambitious—soldier entered the list against the King. The choleric-looking Maréchal Vicomte de Turenne was egged on by his mistress, a troublesome beauty called Geneviève de Longueville (once heard to admit "I don't enjoy innocent pleasures!"), into collusion with the Spaniards. To Turenne is attributed the somewhat cynical saying "Dieu est toujours pour les gros bataillons," a tenet that would also inspire Napoleon. Together with Spanish battalions of Archduke Leopold, Turenne marched to within 30 miles of Paris.

Meanwhile, Grand Condé had proved himself a close ally of the monarchy. On 18 January 1650, Mazarin had him arrested, to which

Condé snorted: "So this is what I get for my services!" Now, as Voltaire observed, "all parties came into collision with each other, made treaties and betrayed each other in turn."[9] Upon his release from prison, Condé joined forces with the Parisians; Turenne, outraged by Condé's arrogance, switched sides to support Anne and the King. Out of favour with all sides, Mazarin slipped out of Paris into temporary self-exile. It was a moment of highest danger for the monarchy; there were rumours that the old troublemaker Gaston d'Orléans was planning to seize Louis and proclaim himself regent. At the same time, his daughter, Louis' mannish twenty-three-year-old cousin, the "Grande Mademoiselle" who had designs on the throne via the King's bed, dressed herself up in armour like Joan of Arc—then took charge of an army to march off to join Condé.

By February 1651, Paris was in a ferment; blood flowed and the Hôtel de Ville was set on fire. Anne resolved to flee yet again, but Louis' laying out of his boots and travelling suit the night before sparked off murmurs in the city of what was afoot. The mob burst through the gates of the Palais-Royal, demanding to see the infant-King. It was a potentially ugly scene, but Regent Anne played a cool hand, instructing Louis to feign sleep. An emissary of the mob, the captain of "Monsieur's" guard, was taken into the royal bedchamber, where he was greatly discountenanced to find a sleeping child.

> As they gathered round the bed . . . their old feelings of love returned and they showered a thousand blessings on the King . . . The mere sight gave them respect for him . . . Their anger disappeared: and having stormed in like furies they left like gentle subjects . . .

recorded Mme. de Motteville, Anne's lady-in-waiting.

Momentarily safe, Anne and the King remained precariously in their quarters under the threat of *frondeurs*. Mazarin continued to direct Anne by letter from exile in the Rhineland as Condé, "Monsieur" and the "Grande Mademoiselle" joined their forces in Paris. Writing to Mazarin from the sequestered Palais-Royal, Anne urged him to return: "I am having a difficult time . . . Adieu, I can't go on . . ." But she did. Though belittled by unkind Parisians as being placid "like a fat Swiss woman" (except, of course, she was Spanish), Anne of Austria proved herself to be outstandingly courageous and resourceful, foiling one plot after another by Condé and "Monsieur," while civil war incited by

Condé ripped through the countryside. Skilfully Anne fostered the loyalty of Turenne, the only general who could match Condé, and who led the royal forces to a series of victories through the provinces. Facing defeat there, the Grand Condé then decided to stake all on one last throw: he would seize Paris. In the wings Mazarin played a waiting game, assured that "there was one man on whom he could always rely against Condé, namely Condé himself."

In September 1651, at thirteen, Louis came of age. Riding in state to Parlement, which was sitting at the Palais de Justice, he declared in resolute tones:

> *Messieurs,* I have come to my Parlement to tell you that, following the law of the land, I intend to take over the government myself; and I hope by the goodness of God that it will be with piety and justice.

Writing to Mazarin, a courtier praised the young King as having displayed "the bearing and intelligence of a man of twenty-five." Louis appointed Anne as his chief counsellor, but made it plain that henceforth he in person would rule France and exact loyalty. In August he suspended Parlement and transferred it to Pontoise, whence it might operate in greater tranquillity than inside turbulent Paris. Louis was learning rapidly the art of governing.

Paris had been reduced to a miserable state of disorder. Intermittently besieged by Condé and his squabbling fellow princes, cut off from outside supplies, starvation was constantly in attendance, with fears of a repetition of the horrors of 1590. Murder, destruction of crops and pillage were the order of the day, with the troops on both sides plundering and living off the land as if it were conquered enemy territory. The death rate doubled, while births plummeted. Even five years after the end of the Frondes the main Paris hospitals had only space for a few thousand of the 40,000 beggars and vagrants put on the streets; many turned to robbery. Both Parlement and the Hôtel de Ville proved impotent to master the situation. The people, commented Voltaire sadly, "were like a stormy sea, whose waves are driven hither and thither by a hundred contrary winds."[10]

ANNE AND LOUIS had also been driven from Paris four times in four years, which had devalued the monarchy. When Mazarin finally returned from Germany he marched at the head of a small army of 7000 men, wearing green ribbons to distinguish them from the yellowy-grey of Condé's men, "not so much like a minister coming to resume his duties, as a sovereign retaking possession of his estates." Condé remained just outside Paris, daily exercising less control over his army, but with his own arrogance undiminished. Louis, aged thirteen in early July 1652, watched from the heights of Charonne during the decisive battle of Saint-Antoine—fought on the edge of the present-day 4th and 12th *arrondissements*.

As Condé moved his hard-pressed troops behind the city walls, the Grande Mademoiselle—proving herself to be one more of those formidable *Parisiennes*—assumed a crucial role. Hurrying towards the fighting, past dead and dying *frondeurs,* and undeterred by the grisly sight of a dead man still astride his horse, she set up her HQ next to the Bastille. She found Condé in tears, weeping that "All my friends have been killed." Defeat was staring him in the face; nevertheless, assuming command, the Grand Mademoiselle mounted the Bastille ramparts and herself ordered a battery of royalist heavy guns, currently pointing towards Paris, to be trained on the approaching cavalry of Turenne. Without hesitation, she ordered the cannon to be fired on the royal forces.

Later, attempting to minimise her role, "Mademoiselle" claimed that the cannon only fired "three or four salvoes," but the damage to the royal forces as the heavy balls from their own guns crashed through the advancing cavalry had a definitive effect, for among the casualties was the nephew and heir of Mazarin, Paul Mancini. "Elle a toué son mari," declared Mazarin in his fractured French; meaning that the Grande Mademoiselle had with her cannonade destroyed any hope she might have had of marrying Louis. Pulling up the Saint-Antoine drawbridge behind him, Condé retreated into the relative safety of the city walls. On 4 July a meeting of bourgeois and clergy gathered in the Hôtel de Ville to discuss the restoration of order. But it ended in massacre by Condé's rag-tag supporters. A messenger reaching Gaston d'Orléans at the Luxembourg reported, "The Hôtel de Ville is on fire; they're shooting and killing people, it's the ghastliest sight in the world." Mounting her coach with four other women and a strong escort, "Mademoiselle" sped to the Hôtel de Ville in the middle of the night, where she found much of the superb medieval building a heap of smouldering rafters. It was deserted; no one seemed in charge, save a revolutionary rabble.

Condé's cause was thoroughly discredited. The Parisians never forgave him for bringing back the detested Spanish troops whom Henri IV had expelled. Though the battle of Saint-Antoine ended in a stand-off, on 14 October, Condé crept out of the city. A week later Louis re-entered. Parlement renounced its claims to have a voice in political and financial affairs; in return Louis undertook to ensure that office-holders would be paid off. The rebellious grandees were guaranteed pensions and lands—provided they never tried to force their way into the King's council.

THE FRONDES WERE FINISHED. There was no unconditional surrender, and no savage reprisals. "Mademoiselle" and "Monsieur" were "invited" to disappear to their country estates, where, at Blois, according to Voltaire, tiresome Uncle Gaston "passed the remainder of his life in repentance . . . the second son of Henri-Quatre to die with but little glory." Condé was sentenced to death, *in absentia,* but amnestied in 1660;* though, if ever a warlord deserved to lose his head, or be locked up for ever in the Bastille, it was he. This would have been his certain fate under earlier, less forgiving, French monarchs. Later, back in favour, Condé was to win important battles against Louis' foreign enemies; he conquered the Franche Comté in 1668, defeated William of Orange in 1674, and died peacefully in his bed at Fontainebleau in 1686, aged sixty-five. To nobody's astonishment more than his own, in February 1653 Cardinal Mazarin was invited back, received by Louis "as a father and by the people as a master," and entertained at what remained of the Hôtel de Ville "amid the acclamations of the citizens."[11] The appreciative Italian flung money to the populace, but was said to have commented on their fickleness.

Thus ended the last great revolutionary struggle in France, until the year of reckoning, 1789. Though Louis had had to grant generous terms to the rebels, in return he expected total loyalty and obedience. All authority would now reside in the King alone.

---

*A fate not dissimilar to the rebel generals of Algiers who revolted against de Gaulle, in the 1960s.

# EIGHT

# The Age of Louis XIV

My dominant pattern is certainly love of glory.

*—Louis XIV*

His name cannot be uttered without respect, without linking it to an
eternally memorable century.

*—Voltaire on Louis XIV*

Louis XIV MADE HIS TRIUMPHAL ENTRY into Paris in
1652. The diarist John Evelyn, over from Commonwealth England to watch it, remarked, with possibly a touch of envy: "The
French are the only nation in Europe to idolise their sovereign." Louis
had won a notable victory, and would waste no time capitalising upon
it. As Voltaire put it, the King "found himself absolute master of a kingdom still shaken from the blows it had received, every branch of administration in disorder, but full of resources."[1]

The country he inherited had seldom been in worse straits. Fields
were covered in weeds and brambles, livestock slaughtered by marauding bands. Food had to be imported to the countryside from the royal
granaries. Paris was in a shambles, with murder and theft rampant.
The royal coffers were empty, and the national debt (in 1661)
amounted to double the King's revenues. Yet the country, blessed with
its wealth based as ever on Sully's *deux mamelles,* its prodigious combination of climate and incredibly fertile land, remained innately rich.
As another visiting London author, Heylyn, observed of the Île de
France, it was

A Country generally so fruitfull and delectable (except in *Gastinois*) that the very hills thereof are equally to the vallies in most places of *Europe*; but the Vale of *Monmorencie* (wherein *Paris* standeth) scarcely to be fellowed in the World . . .

On the first anniversary of July 1652, the now subservient Hôtel de Ville launched a grand festival celebrating the re-establishment of royal authority. But, henceforth, Louis watched it like a hawk. In June 1654, he was crowned at Rheims. While out hunting in April 1655, he had word that Parlement was meeting without his knowledge. Riding 4 miles at a gallop, he entered the Palais de Justice in his riding boots to dissolve the meeting. Legend has it that, cracking his whip, he uttered the famous words: "L'État, c'est moi." The next day he was granted the taxes he sought. For much of the rest of his reign, however, Louis would be assiduous in avoiding both Parlement and the Hôtel de Ville—which he would always remember as the focus of the Paris Fronde.

FOUR YEARS LATER, in 1659, Louis signed the Treaty of the Pyrenees, bringing an end to the wars with Spain—France's principal enemy ever since the days of François I and Charles V. He sealed it with a bond of marriage to his cousin, Infanta Maria-Theresa. For an extravagant dowry of half-a-million gold écus, his bride renounced her rights to the throne of Spain. Militarily Spain was no longer a problem. At the same time, France's other hereditary enemy, England, had ceased to menace her; Cromwell was dead, and Charles II, indebted to France for her hospitality during his exile, was about to be restored as a monarch without real power—just as Louis took over in France as her absolute ruler. The future held out the promise of exceptional stability and prosperity for France.

FOLLOWING HIS MARRIAGE on the frontier at Saint-Jean-de-Luz, Louis returned to Paris amid fanfares in August 1660. There had been something like a dummy-run for this two Septembers previously when the renowned ex-Queen of Sweden, Christina, converted to Catholicism by Descartes, had stunned Paris by riding on horseback into the city, clad in a scarlet jerkin. The royal guard, 300 archers and 15,000 citizens in arms had turned out to welcome this mannish daughter of

France's northern ally, Gustavus Adolphus. After surprising Queen Anne by her demand for a stiff drink at the Louvre, Christina hastened off to the Place Royale (des Vosges) to meet the famed courtesan Ninon de Lenclos; lodged at Fontainebleau during her two-year stay, she executed—almost with her own hands—an unreliable Italian favourite, much to the dismay of Louis, who, regretting his hospitality, would regularly take flight from her loud voice.

But, as pure *spectacle* Parisians had never seen anything quite like Louis' own entry; nor would ensuing centuries bring them anything to compare with the successive *spectacles* he laid on in evocation of Ancient Rome. At the end of the Faubourg Saint-Antoine, near where the *frondeurs* had fought their last battle, a huge throne was set up on a site henceforth known as the Place du Trône. Here Louis received all the official bodies of Paris, filing past to pay homage. Then an immense procession escorted the young couple to the Louvre. From glittering balconies they could see looking down on them Queen Mother Anne and the ageing Mazarin, the victorious Marshal Turenne—and a Mme. Scarron, who, as Marquise de Maintenon, would eventually become Louis' last wife. An estimated 100,000 Parisians saw their King that day in all his reassuring splendour; they would never be so close to him again, or to any other French monarch.

Two years later, to celebrate the birth of his first-born, Louis would mount another great *spectacle,* in which sumptuously attired horsemen vied against each other in a cross between a medieval tournament and a ballet. Louis XIV offered his unruly people circuses instead of revolt and riots—all designed to further the magnificence of his personal *gloire.* It worked. Here lay the beginnings of the myth of the Age of the Sun King. In the words of Vincent Cronin, "handsome, gifted, popular, self assured, hard working, majestic in all he did," he stood in sharp contrast to his rivals, Charles II of England, Leopold of Austria and Philip IV of Spain.


IN MARCH 1661, Mazarin died at Vincennes, aged only fifty-nine, but prematurely exhausted. A grief-stricken Louis burst into tears; "he loved me and I loved him," he later admitted about this discreet and sagacious "stepfather"—an admission he would make of no other human being. For two hours he shut himself up alone; then he called in his first Council. But possibly he was also relieved. As he wrote in his memoirs, "I felt my mind and courage soar . . . I felt quite another man.

I discovered in myself qualities I had never suspected." Later he was heard to remark: "La face du théâtre change" and, as he made explicitly plain to his entourage, "in future I shall be my own Prime Minister." Five years later his mother, Anne, also died. Louis was now alone, and the sole ruler of France. With a population of 18 million, compared with England's 5½, Spain's 6, Austria's 6½ and Russia's 14 million, it was substantially the largest country in Europe.

WOE BETIDE ANY LESSER MORTAL who might seem to try to upstage Louis, or even compete with him. Nicolas Fouquet was a vain upwardly mobile *parvenu* whose father had helped colonise the West Indies. Aged forty-five, he had just built himself a magnificent mansion at Vaux-le-Vicomte, some 30 miles south of Paris. His crest, still visible on that great unfinished pile, was a squirrel with the challenging motto *Quo non ascendet* ("How far will he not climb"). Since 1653, Fouquet also happened to be Louis' Minister Superintendent of Finances. There was some talk even that he would eventually succeed Mazarin as prime minister. He had many friends in high places; it was reckoned that some 116 people owed their wealth, or position, to him. He had spent lavishly— and not unwisely—on the arts; in fact, between 1655 and 1660 Fouquet had virtually replaced the King as the nation's leading patron, employing a galaxy of the greatest and the best of French artists and writers.

On the day after the Cardinal's death, however, Louis had appointed Mazarin's astute and incorruptible secretary, called Jean-Baptiste Colbert, as Fouquet's assistant. Five months later, on 17 August 1661, Fouquet audaciously invited the King to a sumptuous gala at Vaux-le-Vicomte. The massive iron gates gleamed golden with freshly applied gilt; in the vast gardens 200 *jets d'eau* and 50 fountains lined a half-mile-long main allée. Nothing like it had been seen before, even in the great gardens of Italy, Tivoli and Frascati. Certainly it trumped the modest royal hunting-lodge out at Versailles, which Louis was currently doing up. Was it hardly surprising that a monarch so addicted to *spectacle* should be given ideas?

The royal party dined off a magnificent gold service; by contrast, the King had had to sell off his plate to meet military expenditure. Following this feast, in an outdoor theatre lit with torches, the current toast of the Paris theatre, a Monsieur Molière, introduced a new play written for the occasion. The whole episode outraged Louis. How could his own Superintendent of Finances legitimately afford such conspicuous expense, well in excess of anything the King could mount at any of his palaces? The Queen Mother, Anne, had to restrain him from arresting Fouquet on the spot, prudently cautioning Louis: "No, not in his house, not at an entertainment he is giving for you."

Less than three weeks later, however, as he was arriving at a meeting of the Council in Nantes, Fouquet was arrested by the legendary d'Artagnan of *Three Musketeers* fame. He was heard to murmur, with supreme hubris: "I thought I stood higher with the King than anyone in France."

Fouquet's fall from the dizzy height to which the over-ambitious squirrel had risen was terrible to behold. Louis, abetted by a Colbert only too happy to spy on his boss, had in fact been planning to move on Fouquet already for several months prior to the extravaganza at Vaux. The trial—before twenty-two judges—dragged on for the best part of three years. With France's economy in a terrible mess, savage inflation and rumours of deeply entrenched corruption abounding, the spectacle of the mighty and arrogant Superintendent of Finances on trial for his life was highly popular to the mob. But most of the charges against Fouquet were disgracefully trumped up at the King's instigation, and a fair trial was hardly possible. Charges that Fouquet had "taken to confusing the credit of the state with his own" could equally have been levied against the mighty Mazarin. It was noted how the King's personal debt just about equalled the sums which Fouquet was accused of having salted away to his personal account. In subsequent ages, pungent comparisons were made between the trial of Fouquet and the Dreyfus case; certainly it did neither the regime, Colbert nor Louis, much honour. One of the judges, Olivier d'Ormesson, was sympathetic to the defendant and was ruined by the King as a result; the articulate and influential Mme. de Sévigné expressed open admiration for Fouquet, for his calmness during the protracted trial.

Had it not been for such support, the death sentence would almost certainly have been pronounced. As it was, his doctor and personal valet broke down and wept aloud in court, and insisted on following him into prison. As he was led away, Fouquet addressed the King (as recorded by Mme. de Sévigné[2]): "Sire, you know full well that one can be overtaken by events!" These were words that might well have been inscribed on the epitaphs of many a modern-day minister of finance. Though Fouquet's fate was not quite so severe as that which had overtaken Philippe le Bel's Superintendent of Finances, de Marigny, for seventeen years he suffered appalling privations in prison, then exile at Pignerol. Stories proliferated that Fouquet was the famous unknown prisoner in the black velvet mask. Never completed, his dream at Vaux was to pass through many hands until the present day, where a certain flash vulgarity in the great mansion, with its busily ascending squirrels, still shines through.

The fall of Fouquet had important consequences. Louis' ruthlessness towards Fouquet was motivated by an obsessive fear of plots against his person—by no means irrational, given the only recently ended Frondes. But, shamelessly, like a re-enactment of the story of Naboth's Vineyard, Louis also grabbed the fallen man's architect, Le Vau, his garden-designer, Le Nôtre, his muralist, Le Brun, and his skilled artisans to set them to work for the greater glory of Versailles. Moreover, as was made definitively clear after the trial, Louis would now rule supreme without any checks or hindrances. Colbert, the bourgeois son of a modest draper from Rheims, would take over Fouquet's coveted position, having so assiduously engineered his fall. Brilliant administrator though he turned out to be, Colbert would always be Louis' man. Under the "Roi Soleil," government according to the three qualities of order, regularity and unity would, for better and for worse, characterise what Louis was to achieve for his people.


THE TRIAL OF NICOLAS FOUQUET was barely over than gossip in Paris shifted to focus upon the King's mistresses. His virginity having been removed obligingly by his mother's faithful servant, Catherine Bellier,* Louis had swiftly become sexually disenchanted with his plain Spanish bride, once she had produced him an heir, and—in the way of French monarchs—had energetically set to acquiring beautiful young women from the court. First there came Louise de la Vallière, with whom Louis fell passionately in love almost simultaneously with the beginnings of his obsession with Versailles. Then there arrived the extraordinary, tall blonde beauty, Marie-Angélique de Fontanges (described by the arch-gossip, Mme. de Sévigné, as being "belle comme une ange, sotte comme un panier").

Poor Louise was forced to take flight to a convent. She was succeeded by the infinitely wilier, sexually adept and more conniving Athénaïs de Montespan. In 1677, the perceptive Mme. de Sévigné saw this mistress "covered with diamonds, the other day, such a brilliant divinity that

---

*For her services, Catherine was rewarded with the sumptuous Hôtel de Beauvais, which still graces the Marais, on Rue François Miron.

one's eyes dazzled. The attachment [to the King] seems stronger than it has ever been; they're at the stage when people can't stop looking at each other." Between them the mistresses bore Louis a regiment of illegitimates (Montespan alone provided eight, while most of the Queen's died). The most intense jealousies and rivalries would culminate in the *Affaire des Poisons*.

IN THE 1670s, a series of mysterious deaths hit Paris with a hysteria about rumours of poisoning. Allegedly, sorceresses and midwives had been practising abortion, and easily procured poison for whomever they wished. Contemporaries had come to attribute all sudden deaths to poison, including those of such eminent figures as "Madame," Princess Henrietta of England, the sad youngest daughter of Charles I. She was the first wife of the King's homosexual brother, Philippe d'Orléans, "Monsieur," who died suddenly in 1670 (now thought to have been a natural death from acute peritonitis, though a glass of chicory water was blamed at the time). There were the deaths of Mlle. de Fontanges, mistress to the King, and rival to Athénaïs de Montespan—and even of both Colbert and his successor, Louvois, and many others. The greatest public inquest of the reign now took place.

Poisoning, fashionable ever since the Medicis first introduced the art to France, was once more blamed on them as new and undetectable substances were imported from Italy. Dark rumours began to circulate in Paris of how the "Black Mass" was being celebrated at night, in caves or isolated places in the suburbs, by lapsed priests, often in cooperation with fortune-tellers. Rumours turned into fact with the trial before the Paris law courts in 1676 of a noblewoman, Marie-Madeleine d'Aubray, la Marquise de Brinvilliers. The high society trial made the city buzz with speculation. It transpired that the Marquise had poisoned both her own father and two brothers, and attempted to kill her husband, in order to marry her lover, Captain Sainte-Croix. But the lover, "who did not want a wife as malicious as himself," administered an antidote to the Marquis—or so claimed the ubiquitous and omniscient Mme. de Sévigné.

It was only with the death of Sainte-Croix, in 1672, that the police investigation began, when incriminating papers and vials of poison were found. The civil lieutenant at the Châtelet tested the arsenic solutions on animals, which promptly died. The Marquise's accomplice, her valet, was broken on the wheel. Upon her arrest Mme. de Brinvilliers made a complete confession to her judges; nevertheless she was put to *la question ordinaire et extraordinaire à l'eau*. This was a most unpleasant form of torture—not dissimilar to that practised by the modern-day French Army during the Algerian War some three centuries later—which involved filling the stomach full to bursting with water, but which left no external marks.

On 17 July 1676, facing her public execution with considerable courage, the little Marquise declared her contrition once again to a priest and received absolution. The executioner cut off her head with a single blow of the axe—the merciful treatment accorded a noblewoman. Her body was then burned.

Swiftly, public attentions moved on to other matters, such as Louis' war in the Netherlands, rumbling away distantly in the siege of Maastricht. But the *Affaire des Poisons* was far from over, with the trial and death of "la Brinvilliers" no more than a prologue to sentences passed over the next four years from 1679 onwards.

THE REVELATORY BRINVILLIERS CASE set in motion a chain of investigations led by the industrious Chief of Police in Paris, Nicolas de La Reynie, who established a *chambre ardente* especially to deal with poisoning charges. On 13 March 1679, a Mme. de la Voisin was arrested, disclosing that she had been approached by the Duchesse de Bouillon "for a little poison to kill off an old husband who is killing her with boredom"[3] (a fairly commonplace Parisian complaint!). Here there opened a whole new and even more dangerous ball-game—the supply of love philtres, Cantharides or "Spanish fly" (the Viagra of the age). It was noted that Athénaïs de Montespan, Louis' reigning favourite, had "precipitately left the court." Between 7 April 1679 and 8 April 1682, 319 people were arrested. Evidence was produced, under torture, of black masses performed by unsavoury priests. During one such black mass, incantations had been made for the death of the King, where a white wax figurine was burned.

A long procession of women of lesser rank than the Marquise de Brinvilliers went to the stake to be burned alive as witches. The list included a priest named Tournet, accused of sorcery and sacrilege, burned alive in 1677; Mme. Bosse, burned alive in 1679, less than a month into the investigation; her son François Bosse, strangled and hanged. Moreau, a shepherd, was broken on the wheel. An *écuyer* of the Marquis de Termes was accused of having delivered six poisoned bottles to Mlle. de Fontanges, but she was already confined in the Abbey of Chelles; he had the good grace to die under torture, thus avoiding the need to bring the charges to light. Accusations ran wild; even prepared was an order for the arrest of Jean Racine, the famous playwright, after Voisin had claimed that the *comedienne*, Mlle. du Parc, had died of poisoning and blamed Racine.

There were rumours that the King wanted to clean up morals, with a specific attack on sodomy; but this would have brought him into difficulties with his brother, "Monsieur." Equally, there were constant whisperings of a plot to poison the King. Finally, there arrived the day of execution of "la Voisin" herself, burned alive on 22 February 1680, at the Place de Grève. Among a vast range of confessions, she had admitted to having incinerated more than 2500 aborted children. "So much for the death of Mme. Voisin, notorious for her crimes and her impiety," commented Sévigné, hinting, ominously: "People believe that there will be greater episodes to follow which will take us by surprise . . ."[4]

La Reynie's investigation crept closer and closer to the King's inner circle. Most dangerous of all was the increasing mention of the name of Athénaïs de Montespan. Now thirty-eight, Montespan had come to feel she was losing way in the King's affections. To hold him, she had—so it appeared—liberally fed him with aphrodisiacs. The result had been to give the King terrible headaches which gravely worried his doctors. Following interrogation of Montespan's sister-in-law, Mme. de Vivonne, four clear charges now stood against Montespan, including the attempted murder of the King. But how could Louis allow a lover to whom he had been publicly attached for thirteen years, and who had been the mother of many of his children, to be subjected to the methods of the *chambre ardente*?

With stunning abruptness, further prosecutions were suspended and the work of the *chambre ardente* terminated. The doggedly persistent La Reynie was now compelled to make, for his own safety, a lame admission that he had been "unable to get to the bottom of the *affaire*," and "I must hold my judgement in suspension." The last of the "poisoners" died in 1717, surviving the King and thirty-seven years of grim incarceration. The lesser *canailles* were spirited off to exile in Canada. Louis had the trial proceedings burned; yet, the scandal would not die. When Louvois, Colbert's dour successor, died in July 1691, his son claimed that he too had been poisoned.

Although the King's intervention had saved her from the possible horrors of "examination," the reign of the powerful, Machiavellian

Athénaïs de Montespan was over. For appearances' sake—and to the "Sun King" appearances were all important—she was allowed to linger on under the eyes of the court for another ten years; then she was bundled off to Saint-Joseph, the convent she had founded, for sixteen more years expiating her sins. Worse, the prim and devout ex-governess to her own children, Françoise Scarron, otherwise known as Mme. de Maintenon, now moved in—and for the rest of the King's reign. Her takeover from Montespan occurred at almost the same time as Louis removed the court to Versailles. Given the degree of embarrassment that an abandoned Mme. de Montespan might have caused the King in Paris, and given the suspicions bandied about in the capital, could it be that Louis XIV's escape to Versailles had an added immediacy directly linked to the scandal? He had every good reason to wash his hands of the whole affair, and move his entourage out to purer air.

THE FRONDES, the trial of Fouquet and the various *affaires des poisons* had all been significant milestones on the route to Versailles of Louis XIV. But what had his considerable civil accomplishments contributed, during the first half of the reign, which ended with his decampment for Versailles in 1682?

During ten years of personal rule, Louis XIV had launched a virtually bankrupt country upon a course of remarkable prosperity. It was predicated on three factors: the avoidance of major conflict; the brilliant policies of the man who succeeded the disgraced Fouquet, Jean-Baptiste Colbert; and the extraordinary inherited and inherent wealth of the country at large. Colbert was already forty-one when appointed assistant to Fouquet in 1661. He was a teetaller, icily cold and humourless, earning the nickname of the "Man of Marble," or "le Nord." The venerable Mazarin, in whose employ Colbert's career had started, was alleged to have said to the King shortly before his death: "Sire, I owe you everything, but I believe I can repay some of my debt by giving you Colbert." It was a debt more than repaid.

A worthy successor to Sully, and in contrast to Fouquet, Colbert was immaculately honest. Uniquely among Louis' sycophantic entourage, he was able to confront the King over his extravagances and the use, or abuse, of royal power. After Mazarin and the demise of Fouquet, Louis would permit no one near him with the prerogatives of a prime minister; yet Colbert's influence came to extend far beyond that of a Superintendent of Finances, not least in the centralisation of the nation upon the capital. And the success of his financial reforms is revealed by the balance sheets for 1661—when expenditure was £18 million, leaving a deficit of £8 million—and for 1667, by which time net receipts had doubled, resulting in a surplus of £9 million. A large share of state revenue still came via such archaic and corruptible practices as the sale of offices and the tax-farmers who continued to take their cut of the revenue they gleaned. Under Colbert's regime, however, a kind of industrial revolution swept the country. Shipbuilding multiplied, the army was modernised and expanded; mines, foundries, mills and refineries thrived; so did the wool trade on the back of such prestige industries as Savonnerie carpets and France's superlative Gobelin tapestries. Overseas investments like her colony in Canada expanded vigorously. Colbert's regime put France seriously to work, emulating the serious side of its pleasure-loving King, who advised: "Never forget that it is by work that a King rules."[5]

AS IN PREVIOUS ERAS, it was the immense fecundity of rural France that produced the wealth for Colbert's treasury. Yet under the increasing burdens of his taxation, rural society remained relatively impoverished throughout much of the reign of the Roi Soleil; while Paris grew and expanded markedly to a city of 400,000, the rural population if anything declined. In the seventeenth century the French peasantry was often hit by shortages and recession; the weather was capricious, producing years of terrible harvests. In a bad year a village could easily lose between 10 and 20 per cent of its population, while agriculture had not matched the advancements being achieved in England. The price of land was such that the purchase of a holding large enough to support one family might cost a labourer the equivalent of a century's wages.

Despite occasional periods of prosperity, for the majority of Frenchmen it was, notes Robin Briggs, "an epoch of hardship, often of despair and untimely death." Moreover, the peasantry found itself exploited, parasitically, by the state, the Church, landlords and bureaucrats alike. There were sometimes popular revolts against taxation, and regular bread riots in provincial towns, yet because of the centralised power of the absolute monarchy they were never permitted to amount to anything—not for another hundred years. Paris and the provinces would continue to look at each other with mutual dislike, disdain and distrust, but what was remarkable was that the *ancien régime* forged by Louis XIV would face no coordinated uprising until the reign of his great-great-grandson, Louis XVI.

"LET NO ONE SPEAK TO ME of anything small!" Louis' Italian architect, Bernini, had declared when redesigning the Louvre for him in 1665. It was a view with which the Roi Soleil was distinctly in accord. On 6 May 1682, slightly less than a century after his grandfather, Henri IV, had gained mastery of his capital, Louis announced that the seat of the French government would be out at his former hunting-lodge, Versailles. It was 20 kilometres removed from the Louvre, or less than half-a-day's coach journey. Even so, "The Court of France forever in the country! The fashionable world was filled with dismay." But not all the criticism was frivolous. For years Colbert had beseeched his master to abandon the Versailles project, for sound economic reasons.

The house was still far from ready, but the King thought he would never get the workmen out unless he moved in himself. Jules Hardouin-Mansart was still at work finishing the Galerie des Glaces:

> Seen at night soon after its completion, the painting and the gilding fresh and new; lit by thousands of candles in silver chandeliers and candelabra, furnished with solid silver consoles and tubs of orange trees; crowded with beauties of both sexes, dressed in satin and lace, embroidered, re-embroidered, over-embroidered with real gold thread and covered with jewels, it must have been like Aladdin's cave or some other fable of the Orient.

The rest of the accommodation, designed to provide lodgings for between 2000 and 5000 people, was austere, to say the least. According to Saint-Simon, the royal apartments were "the last word in inconvenience, with back views over the privies and other dark and evil-smelling places."[6] But at least the King and his descendants could feel safe there; although they were virtually unguarded, over the coming century there would be only one half-hearted attempt at assassination.

AGED FORTY-FOUR IN 1682, Louis was at the peak of his powers. In 1661, his Queen, Maria-Theresa, had presented him with a son and heir, the Grand Dauphin (or Monseigneur), who showed promise of becoming a sound ruler and who in turn, later that same year of the move to Versailles, produced an heir, the Duc de Bourgogne. The succession of the throne of France, only recently so shaky, seemed assured. Louis' own health was excellent (in fact, he would live for another three decades), the territory of France was secure from a Spain and a Holy Roman Empire in decline, while Restoration England's pleasure-loving Charles II even drew his pay from France. France seemed to have little or nothing to fear in the world from her neighbours.

Thanks most of all to the incorruptible Colbert (though now all but worn out from his labours), the economy was as sound as it had ever been. France enjoyed nearly four times the revenue of her neighbour and rival, Stuart England, and ten times that of opulent Venice. In the arts, too, France had achieved a peak of excellence seldom surpassed—either before or after. Racine had just written *Phèdre*, the last of his dark tragedies, and had now accepted the role of Royal Historiographer—at Versailles. In Paris the magnificent Cour Carrée of the Louvre was virtually complete. More practically, order had been imposed, with crime in abeyance and hygiene immeasurably improved. With the Frondes crushed, the city was tranquil—and well lit, by the installation of 6500 lanterns. The theatre critic Chappuzeau could claim with just pride: "regardless of where one turns, Paris was never so fine nor so stately as it is today."

The nation seemed, rarely and miraculously, at peace with herself. The King could now, with some justification, call himself "Louis le Grand" (the title which the municipality of Paris had unctuously bestowed on him in 1678) and the "Roi Soleil." He could surely afford a little personal extravagance in building a new country seat; and, like many of his Valois forebears, François I for instance, Louis preferred country to town. Yet it was not so much *la chasse* that drew him as the space, but his love of order in all things, as well as the nature of Paris, discovered in his early years. He disliked and distrusted the city; he would return there only twenty-five times from 1670 to the end of his reign. There were good reasons for his dislike that were rooted in the past, and it was not just the malodorous stench that continued to reach out from the Seine to the Louvre.

AT THIS TURNING POINT in his life, Louis' outward appearance could scarcely have been more regal. By the standards of the day he looked tall, though it was an impression partly enhanced by resort to high-heeled shoes and imposing wigs. He had dark hair, an excellent and well-formed figure, was broad of shoulder and muscular, with the shapeliest legs in the kingdom. He was not startlingly good-looking, but his was a face that instantly dominated all around him. His eyes were small, often half-closed, but they missed nothing. An Italian traveller seeing him one day at mass in Saint-Germain-l'Auxerrois, recorded:

> My eyes met his only once. The moment I began to look at him I felt the secret power of the King's majesty and an insatiable curiosity to study it; but I found that I had to drop my eyes. Afterwards I dared to look at him only when I was sure he could not see me.[7]

Apart from the eyes, and the sensual lips, Louis' most striking feature was his long, beaked and powerful nose. Some historians reckoned that, through his Aragon ancestors, he had both Jewish and Moorish blood. But what was most important was the all-imposing presence. He had perfect manners, never passing a woman without lifting his hat, even down to the humblest chambermaid. The style was catching. Well could Voltaire remark in retrospect that Europe "owed her manners and her feeling for social life to the court of Louis XIV." He was instinctively kind—unlike his father—but pity anyone who should cross him; to wit the fate of his unfortunate Superintendent of Finances, Nicolas Fouquet.

If Louis had a major flaw, it was love of flattery, even the most clumsy praise, and—coupled with this—a passion for the trappings of *la gloire* that eventually was to prove his undoing, and all but fatal for France. His majesty was immense. Yet, even apart from the inevitable aphrodisiac of power, and the *droit de seigneur* (to which Louis resorted more frequently than any other), he would have been overpoweringly attractive to women. As well as his unflagging energy as a lover, Louis' legendary capacity for work made his position as absolute ruler that much harder to challenge. He would work six hours a day in his Council, assuming responsibility for signing vouchers for the least state expenditure, while keeping his own personal memorandum book that amounted to the nation's journal and ledger. On top of this, until his middle years, there was nothing Louis liked better than leading his armies in quest of *la gloire* in the field, and being painted or sculpted mounted atop a rampant charger.

All this vitality was fuelled by a vast consumption of food; he was particularly partial to game and highly spiced sauces—much to the concern of his physicians, who would have to purge and bleed him with distressful regularity for the attendant disorders. Though, by the 1680s, the *Diary of the King's Health* already ran to several hundred pages, it was fortunate that Louis was blessed with a constitution of iron. By reputation he had been born, like a camel, with two stomachs (on his autopsy, his bowels were discovered to be twice the normal length); the productivity of the royal alimentary canal was a regular source of scatological marvel to sycophantic courtiers attendant at the King's highly public daily *levé*.

ALTHOUGH LOUIS was progressively to neglect building and development in Paris in favour of Versailles, in the early period under Colbert (who from 1664 had also become Superintendent of Buildings) much of distinction was achieved. He built the Collège des Quatre Nations—for which purpose Mazarin had left in his will 2 million livres, earmarked to provide a Parisian education for sixty boys from the provinces. The old Tour de Nesle, notorious since the time of Philippe le Bel, was demolished, and in its place rose the superb piece of baroque designed by Le Vau, which was later to become the home of the Académie Française. Next came the completion of the Louvre, inviting from Rome Gian-Lorenzo Bernini whose piazza of St. Peter's had established him as the most famous architect of his day. Bernini flattered Louis indecently, producing a bust that was probably the best likeness of the Roi Soleil ever achieved, which now graces Versailles. But, architecturally, they soon fell out and with Louis' departure for Versailles the Louvre fell on hard times, which would last until its definitive salvation by Napoleon.

In the confident expectation of future peace, Louis now decreed the levelling of the existing Parisian ramparts. In their place, he laid out long and straight promenades which came to be known as the *grands boulevards* (a corruption of the German word *Bollwerk,* meaning a "bulwark" or rampart). Agreeably lined with shady trees, they immediately became places to promenade, while wealthy Parisians built stately houses looking out on to them. The greatest of these boulevards was the new Champs-Élysées, laid out by Le Nôtre. Then, on the Left Bank came the monumental edifice of the Invalides to house the veterans of Louis' wars (and one day, Napoleon).

François Blondel, first director of the new Académie Royale d'Architecture, drew on the King's patronage and vision to promote a style of unprecedented classical harmony which embraced *la gloire* and *spectacle* in the grander Parisian buildings. Imposing straight lines became the norm. In a foretaste of modern city planning, strict rules were laid down; private dwellings had to be built of stone, not timber and plaster (the catastrophic Fire of London in 1667 had left a message well heeded by Colbert and Louis' town planners), and were forbidden by law to have their first floors bulge out over the street. In the grand *hôtels particuliers* of the epoch, extensive gardens and conspicuous consumption within would be concealed from public gaze behind a sombre *porte-cochère* giving on to the street.

The *Grande Siècle* saw the emancipation of the French bourgeoisie; but perhaps as a hangover from the days of the Frondes, or of their own shady dealings, the Paris *financiers* had become obsessed by their own security. Affluent Paris was to become, and remain, a city as secret as any North African casbah. Truly, Louis XIV inherited a city of brick and left it marble. But, with the disappearance of the warm brickwork panels of Henri IV and Louis XIII, the tasteful Place Royale gave way to the bourgeois vulgarity of Vaux-le-Vicomte; and, if one seeks a monument to the taste of the Roi Soleil one only has to contemplate the florid excesses of *Boule* furniture.

The new money moved steadily westwards, up the new Champs-Élysées and away from the compressed and smelly confines of the Marais. Main thoroughfares were paved; streets were widened, and overhanging medieval houses that might have damaged passing carriages were removed. Colbert was to go down in the history of Paris as the city's "greatest urbanist"[8]—second only to Louis-Napoleon's Baron Haussmann. He dreamed of creating "a new Rome"; but his works were never completed. As recorded by the marvellously detailed paintings of Hubert Robert, far more change was to be carried out under the reigns of Louis XV and XVI than by Colbert; certainly most of the depredations to the churches of Paris occurred in the years of 1790 to 1860. Colbert regarded Versailles as "an isolated, rural château," in no way fit to be the headquarters of Europe's greatest king. But one year after the move to Versailles, in 1683, Colbert died (possibly with his heart broken, too, like Le Vau). Among so much else he had cleaned up the city and the streets of Paris—although a perceptive visiting English doctor, Martin Lister, found how water from the Seine was "very pernicious to all strangers, not the French excepted . . . causing Looseness and sometimes Dysenteries."

MORE PERNICIOUS STILL were "no-go" areas left in the aftermath of the Frondes, which the guard did not dare to enter. For the year 1642 alone, 342 murders took place at night hours on the streets of Paris. Under the threesome of Louis, Colbert and La Reynie—prosecutor of the *Affaire des Poisons*—and under his equally fearsome successor, d'Argenson, there was to be a nation-wide codification of criminal and civil law the like of which would not be seen again until Napoleon. Highly modern-sounding techniques were deployed to apprehend criminals, such as hand-writing analysis. In one case, the King personally intervened to have the police send out "identikit" sketches to prevent a fugitive skipping the frontier; in another, a murderer had shaved off his beard and donned a blond wig—but La Reynie warned Colbert to look out for him in disguise among the crowd at Versailles. The man was duly caught and executed. Another of La Reynie's first tasks was to provide Paris with a system of street lighting, so that by the end of the seventeenth century there were 6500 lamps on public streets—a marked improvement over contemporary London. Parisians enjoyed a sense of security the like of which had not existed since the all-too-brief days of Henri IV. Nevertheless, a situation was created in which lawyers thrived and became men of substance and importance.

By comparison with the draconian punishments inflicted under the regime of Philippe le Bel, or even when one recalls the grisly fate of the assassin of Henri IV, Ravaillac, penalties imposed under Louis XIV seem positively enlightened. Miscarriages of justice were redressed, with capital punishment for wrongful death sentences. Hanging was the norm—except for nobles, who were entitled to the privilege of being beheaded. As witnessed by the fates of the wretched Brinvilliers and Voisin, torture and burning at the stake were still reserved for the poisoner. From the time of Henri IV onward, distaste for the more extreme forms of torture had grown; though, even in the years of the Enlightenment of the eighteenth century, some would receive the hideous fate of being broken on the wheel.

For less serious offences, there were the galleys—an archaic form of punishment that also provided the backbone of the French Navy well after Louis XIV. The much-feared Bastille, where the average stay was short, was in Louis' reign more like a comfortable hotel for the rich in trouble. Many of the residents were there through a member of the family obtaining one of the infamous *lettres de cachet,* or "sealed warrants." Almost a thousand of these a year were issued by Louis, providing for "detention" rather than imprisonment. They were a convenient way of applying to get rid of an inconvenient relative, or of wives seeking to discipline a wayward husband (it was a punishment meted out to the Marquis de Sade in the following century). The worst fate for courtiers, in the event of royal disfavour, was the terrible sentence of exile to the miscreant's country estates, there to die of lingering boredom—a condemnation worse than hell for any Frenchman. Prostitutes, given the choice, preferred the option of becoming nuns,* but would often be transhipped to the colonies, to Canada or Louisiana, to expiate their sins by incrementing the settlers' birth rate. Such was the immortalised end of Manon Lescaut.

As with most societies, crime was closely linked with poverty—which remained appalling, despite all measures to ameliorate it. The nation, and the cities in particular, were vulnerable to crises in the countryside, such as that in the early 1660s when Colbert found himself forced to import food from as far off as Poland. As always, it was the poor who came off worst; hunger was never far removed for the urban under-privileged, as the price of bread rose constantly.

BY CONTRAST, affluent Frenchmen found themselves able to indulge in the pursuit of leisure—and pleasure. Apart from the periodic grand *spectacles* that were guaranteed to engage and distract, there were games such as the *jeu de paume*—predecessor of our modern tennis, and greatly favoured by the King. It became immensely popular, with no fewer than 114 courts springing up in Paris alone. Under Louis, gambling (largely banned) became all the rage—notably at Versailles. Recorded Mme. de Sévigné, "one plays here for terrifying sums, and the gamblers are like madmen. One howls, another strikes the table with such a blow that it resounds round the whole room." On Christmas Day 1678, Mme. de Montespan lost 700,000 écus, but, possibly with the connivance of the banker, the King's mistress was permitted to win it all back. Louis was all for gambling of every kind; the opiate of the nobles, it afforded one very simple means of domesticating them.

Under the reign of the Roi Soleil, the theatre and the opera prospered—though naturally it was Paris, centre of all the arts, that was the focus. Like a pearl, a flourishing of the arts usually requires a set of special conditions in which to be seeded. Could Shakespeare have produced

---

*In earlier ages, girls who had lost their virtue would occasionally be taken jeeringly to be "married" at the church of Sainte-Marine—the "wedding ring" made of straw.

what he did without the immense self-assurance of Elizabeth's England?* In France the sombre tragedies of Racine might have flourished in the times of Henri IV and Louis XIII, but almost certainly it required the sureties of the reign of the Louis XIV for a Molière to make such mock of human frailties. Could there have been such hilarious farces as those which so effectively flayed social affectations, performed in any previous age? Would the *Fables* of La Fontaine, with all their taunting scepticism, have fallen on such fertile ground? And what about the biting wit of La Rochefoucauld and his cynical *Maxims*? They would not have appealed without the worldly pragmatism that swept a France disenchanted by the religious wars of the previous century—and which would form an important part of the philosophical backdrop to 1789.

The taste for the theatre, as in many things, came from the King down, his passion for the stage rivalled only by his love for building. By the end of the seventeenth century, it was reckoned that the Comédie Française could count between 10,000 and 17,000 regular patrons. The educated upper classes and the rowdy, turbulent denizens of the pit alike would pay for the privilege of performances ten to twelve times a year. In the Paris theatre violence was never far off. The great Molière always had the adroitness to address his shafts to the standing room—the *parterre*. Even at his theatre in 1668, some soldiers killed the unfortunate doorkeeper for refusing them free entry. This was despite Molière's royal protection and his company's title of the Troupe de Roi.

LOUIS WAS THE FIRST of France's monarchs to offer consistent support for artists and writers. Molière was also protected by the King from the wrath of the Establishment *dévots* in the fierce row that broke out over his semi-sacrilegious *Tartuffe*. Born Jean-Baptiste Poquelin, the son of a court upholsterer, in 1622, Molière perhaps typified as well as anyone else the triumph of the bourgeoisie under Louis. (Racine, an orphan brought up by the Jansenist school at Port Royal, came of a middle-class family from the Aisne; Lully was the son of an Italian miller; François Couperin, the greatest of five generations of eminent musicians, came of a family of simple organists; Boileau, the poet and critic, stemmed from the legal bourgeoisie.) Molière first managed to catch the eye of the King

---

*Dispiriting, by parallel, is that in post–Cold War Britain the first decade of real security in the twentieth century seems to have produced little more by way of artistic creativity than a very grubby bed, displayed in the Tate Modern with all the fanfares of a *Mona Lisa*!

in 1658, through fairly outrageous forwardness, and adopted the name of *de* Molière—thereby revealing himself to be prone to the very *faiblesses* he later mocked. His immense reputation was grounded in a thorough training of years as both actor and manager/director. But it was his plays, with their invariable theme of the study of man—and contemporary man at that—his foibles and his pretensions, that made Molière's reputation, and drew him frequently into sharp controversy, including barrages of onslaught inside the Académie.

For thirteen years Molière's company took root in Richelieu's old quarters of the Palais-Royal. Here Paris witnessed the flowering of Molière's rapier wit: in *L'Avare,* excoriating the destructive consequences of the pursuit of riches; *The Misanthrope,* with its confrontation between coquetry and sincerity taken to excess; *Le Bourgeois Gentilhomme,* with its attack on bourgeois pretensions, *Le Malade Imaginaire,* with its attack on hypochondria and medical quackery; and his daring *Tartuffe,* with its attack on religious hypocrisy. For all the King's backing, Molière may well have been fortunate not to be around after the accession of Mme. de Maintenon and the Revocation of the Edict of Nantes. It was said by one of his contemporaries that, rather than provoking belly-laughs, Molière had the unique knack of making his audience "rire dans l'âme," which probably explains his timeless appeal. He died in harness, aged only fifty-one, ironically during the fourth performance of *Le Malade Imaginaire.* Collapsing on the stage, he was reported to have said, apologetically: "Sirs, I have played le Malade Imaginaire; but in truth I have a grave malady." Two hours later he was dead.*

ANOTHER LITERARY FIGURE to receive the King's favour and patronage was Boileau, the poet, satirist and critic renowned for his acid wit, who with Racine was appointed Historiographer Royal. On hearing that a cannon ball had narrowly missed Louis on one of his campaigns, Boileau remarked to him: "Sire, I beg you as your historian not to finish my history too soon." The King liked this kind of cheek, and Boileau went unreproved. Then there was Jean-Baptiste Lully (1632–87), the ugly Italian—dirty, untidy, coarse, and a heavy drinker who later became totally debauched. But he was the father of French opera's first golden age. A typical Lully production, in 1672, would open with the inevitable

---

*It appears, however, that Molière had been suffering from tuberculosis long before this final appearance on the stage, and that his friends had begged him to stay away.

prologue depicting the Sun (Louis, of course) defeating Envy and the Serpent (Holland, the current enemy). Lully was a dictator in his realm, but everywhere was the guiding hand of the King. It was Louis himself who selected the dramatist Philippe Quinault (also of humble birth, the son of a Paris baker) to produce the libretti for Lully's operas.

The King's patronage could be subject to whim. The great Corneille, for instance, was allowed to die a pauper in 1684, embittered by neglect and the success of his young rival, Racine. In 1701, after the Comédie Italienne had lampooned Mme. de Maintenon, the heavy hand of censorship descended on the theatre of Paris. Though honoured by the public, for many a long year the acting profession was repudiated by the Church, its members—however respectable—excommunicated. Molière's widow had the utmost difficulty in obtaining for him a decent, Catholic burial in consecrated ground. Even in the eighteenth century, the Age of Reason, the great tragic actress, Adrienne Lecouvreur, was refused proper burial and her remains were interred under a Paris street corner—to the rage of her friend Voltaire, who stigmatised it as a disgraceful act of intolerance.

BETWEEN 1660 AND 1700, over 600 novels appeared in Paris—and many of them were written by Mme. (Madeleine) de Scudéry, who ran an influential and gossipy salon, the salon itself being very much an invention of the epoch. Employing a style of fiction that would today be designated *roman héroïque,* the length of her novels were only exceeded by her conspicuous longevity.* Her novels, running to 15,000 pages, unashamedly praised aristocratic privileges and manners, and extolled the relentless virtue of her heroines. The naughty Ninon de Lenclos, the most famous courtesan of her time, dubbed the members of her salon *les Jansenistes de l'Amour* (after the austere religious sect) "because they speak a lot about love, but never make it!" Nevertheless, several of her fans in the Académie (where she won a prize for eloquence) tried to have the ban on women lifted so that she could join the *Immortels.*

Here one might perhaps append a note on just how relatively liberated, at least compared with other ages, were Parisian women under Louis XIV. Such a shamelessly free-living libertine spirit as Ninon de Lenclos, with her repartee of "je me fais homme" (I behave like a man),

---

*She lived to be ninety-three (1608–1701); Ninon de Lenclos to be eighty-five—yet another testimony to the vigour of some *Parisiennes.*

was widely accepted in Parisian society. The virtuous Anne of Austria had tried to have her locked up in a convent, but she protested that she was "neither a whore nor repentant," and eventually she arose triumphant: "the triumph of vice conducted with wit," as Saint-Simon put it with grudging admiration. Once the flame of vice had dimmed, Ninon was to be seen regularly receiving the Archbishop and other worthy dignitaries in her salon—and indeed declining an invitation from her old friend, Mme. de Maintenon, to move to gloomy Versailles to cheer up the increasingly morose monarch.

IF ONLY LOUIS HAD STUCK to the pursuit of *la gloire* in the boudoir, or in his insatiable urge to build, all might have been well. But he was obsessed by the great military exploits of the Caesars, of Charlemagne and his grandfather, Henri IV. After defeating the Fronde, aged only thirty, he admitted, unashamed: "My dominant passion is certainly love of glory." On the most slender of pretexts, he had already fought a hugely successful campaign against his wife's country, Spain. Almost without battle he acquired in 1668 the key cities of Lille, Douai and Tournai in Spanish Flanders. A cheap victory, signed at Aix-la-Chapelle, gave him a taste for more.

In 1683, Louis' prudent counsellor, Colbert, died. For the last decade he had been in a losing battle against the Marquis de Louvois, whom Louis made his Minister of War. An arrogant, unscrupulous genius, as the ageing Colbert declined, Louvois became virtually Minister of Foreign Affairs. From a disorganised mob at the time of Louis' coronation he had turned the French Army into the most formidable in Europe, and increased the number of galleys in the navy from six to forty, each containing 200 wretches. Originally they were manned by criminals and Turks taken in the Barbary Wars. When the Turks were worn out, they were sold into slavery and replaced by French Protestants caught attempting to emigrate illegally. Worst of all, Louvois was responsible for the worst crimes against humanity committed in the reign of the Roi Soleil: the assault on the Spanish Netherlands (1672), the laying waste of Heidelberg and the German Palatinate (1689), and the *dragonnades* massacres of Protestants in south-west France.

By 1670 France was the strongest power in Europe; she had no need of a vast army. As would have been the preference of Vauban, Europe's greatest builder of fortresses—exquisite works of art in themselves—France could have defended her frontiers without resort to war. Vauban hated the bombardments of open cities in which Louvois revelled, but Louvois pushed towards war for the satisfaction of a monarch already bent upon *la gloire.*

Instead of pursuing the follies of his forebears in Italy, Louis turned his gaze north-eastwards, to a richer prey. Having proclaimed their independence from Spain, the United Provinces of Holland were the economic success story of the century. They had driven out the sea by their network of dykes and acquired immense wealth from their trading colonies in southeast Asia. Even the great French philosopher Descartes had selected Holland for its liberalism in preference to Paris. But in 1672 Louis launched a carefully planned war of unprovoked aggression against this prosperous tiny neighbour. Typical of the brutality in which the campaign was carried out was the following instruction from Louvois: "His Majesty commanded me to inform you that he wishes you to burn twenty villages as close as possible to Charleroi . . . so that not a single house in these twenty villages remains standing."

Louis was more motivated by greed than by his dislike for staunch Dutch Protestantism. The proud Dutch flooded their dykes and the war dragged on for seven years. Holland was ruined financially, but managed to keep its frontiers intact. All the war achieved for France, through the Treaty of Nijmegen, was the (temporary) acquisition of Lorraine and the definitive cession of the Franche-Comté—plus some magnificent paintings and tapestries of the Roi Soleil, astride a prancing horse crossing the Rhine or besieging Maastricht. For Louis it was the apogee of *la gloire,* and dangerously inspired his ambitions towards the rest of Europe— particularly England, where Holland's champion, William of Orange, was about to assume the throne.

Louis' new swagger brought all his neighbours (bar Switzerland) to unite against him in the League of Augsburg. To pre-empt them, Louis marched across the Rhine, took Cologne and devastated the Palatinate. It was an excess that would poison the perception of France by Germans for decades, if not centuries. After nine more years of war, which undid many of Colbert's domestic advances, Louis was forced to renounce virtually all his gains.

The glorious reign ended, ingloriously, in yet another war—the War of the Spanish Succession. This time it was one which Louis had not sought but had blundered into. It was a war in which, for the first time since the Hundred Years' War, England had been stirred—to send a major force deep into the heart of the continent. Under Marlborough, humiliating defeat was inflicted on France: Blenheim, where Louis lost 30,000 out of an army of 50,000, and Gibraltar (both in 1704); Ramillies in 1706 and Oudenarde in 1708, and bloody Malplaquet where 11,000 French died in 1709. "God seems to have forgotten all I have done for him," grumbled Louis. In 1708, Lille was lost. The following year Nature entered the war on the side of the Alliance, inflicting on France the harshest winter on record. France lost half her livestock; at Versailles even Louis lost both his confessor and a former mistress. To continue to finance the war, Louis was forced to melt down his gold plate. Finally, as if in further punishment for his hubris, a terrible sequence of illnesses would decimate his family and menace the succession.

In 1712, the victorious allies were mustering to advance on Paris and it looked as if the country was facing total defeat. Then Marshal Villars turned the tide with a brilliant sequence of victories which, within six weeks, had driven the invaders out of France. An ailing Louis was able— just—to conclude an honourable peace at Utrecht in 1713. France, and the monarchy, was saved. But Marlborough's successful intervention on the continent had opened the prospect of a British Empire, and the economic ruin of all that Colbert had built up—with the value of the livre depreciated 25 per cent between 1683 and the Treaty of Utrecht.

ABOUT THE TIME of the move to Versailles, a fundamental change in the love-life of the hedonistic king had taken place. From the early 1660s, more or less synchronous with the beginning of his passion for Versailles, there had followed a series of mistresses coupled with casual affairs. Husbands were encouraged to sacrifice their wives to the pleasure of the Roi Soleil; "to share with Jupiter involves no slightest dishonour" was the accepted, if not altogether popular prescription. Out of all these liaisons came a whole raft of illegitimates.

By 1676 there were whispered worries around the court at the King having become excessively, indeed startlingly, promiscuous. It also seems that the prodigious sexual energy of the King, though only in his mid-forties, was showing signs of decline. Following the *Affaire des Poisons,* when La Montespan was dispatched and Mme. de Maintenon moved into the vacuum, Louis' sexual urges were to be kept closely in check, his Catholic conscience more rigorously activated. Born Françoise d'Aubigné, Mme. de Maintenon had married a (very) minor poetaster called Paul Scarron, much older than herself and a cripple—allegedly— shaped like the letter Z. She had no children by Scarron and, after eight years' marriage, he had died—leaving his widow still with her virginity intact, but little money. After she became governess to the delicate little son of Louis and Athénaïs de Montespan, she gradually assumed more and more influence with the King; until one day she swapped places with the fallen Montespan, passing her—so it was recorded—on the staircase with the dry observation: "You are going down, *Madame*? I am going up." And so it was.

The Marquise de Maintenon, as she became, was three years older than him, beyond the age of childbearing, and with some of the traditional qualities of the governess—handsome, but certainly no beauty, and pious to a fault. Late in life she would speak about her "long struggle for the King's soul." In return, the King referred to her as "Your Solidity." There remained a mystery as to whether they were ever married, morganatically. Certainly with her a sharp change of mood became apparent. In 1683, the year after the move to Versailles, the Queen—Spanish Infanta to the end, dividing her time between her Spanish confessor and Spanish maid—died, in the arms of Mme. de Maintenon. "Poor woman" was the King's immortal epitaph: "It's the only time she has ever given me any trouble." The Widow Scarron's power at court was now total.

UNDER HER INFLUENCE, and with Louvois at the King's ear, Louis embarked on his choice of war not love. Worst of all for the future of France, although her grandfather had been a Protestant, and a friend of Henri IV, Scarron egged Louis on to take the fateful step of the Revocation of the Edict of Nantes, in 1685. For years he had been quietly oppressing the Protestants, but within the liberal laws laid down by his grandfather. Then, in the period just preceding the move to Versailles, he began to think of ways of converting all of the Protestants. In 1681, Mme. de Maintenon rejoiced: "If God preserve the King there will not be one Huguenot left twenty years hence." Four years later the blow fell. His outspoken sister-in-law, Liselotte, Duchess of Orléans, explained acidly:

> The old trollop [Mme. de Maintenon] and Père La Chaise persuaded the King that all the sins he had committed with Montespan would be forgiven if he persecuted and expelled the Huguenots and by doing this he would get to Heaven . . .[9]

Accordingly the edict went out that "All temples of the . . . so-called reformed religion should be demolished forthwith" and any assembly for public worship by Protestants banned. Only this policy of annihilation would sate Louis' stringent desire for unity and order.

Louvois added an extra note of horror to Louis' Revocation policy with the brutal *dragonnades,* armed raids accompanied by torture, pillage and scorched-earth against Protestant dissenters in the provinces—such as Kosovo was to experience three centuries later. Languedoc in particular was made to suffer. Between 1657 and October 1685 more than 587 Protestant churches were demolished throughout France. Within a matter of months of the Revocation, France's Protestants had been reduced by three-quarters: most had become Catholics; some had emigrated; others had been sent to the galleys. Goods and property were confiscated, to further inhibit them from leaving the country. Protestants were excluded from public positions, and decent livelihoods. There was violence against them in the countryside, where they were obliged to go to mass and take communion; those spitting out the host were to be burned alive.

Some of the most prestigious among the Protestant nobility in Paris were now expedited to the Bastille by *lettre de cachet,* subject to a strict regime and freed only once they converted. Many died in prison and were interred without confession in the garden of the château. The zealots could boast that heresy had been "trampled underfoot in 1685." Among the Parisian Protestants were leading painters, sculptors, architects and court musicians as well as businessmen and public servants—France lost 400,000 of her finest subjects. It could indeed be rated the greatest mistake of the whole reign.[10]

Many of France's leaders in finance, industry and science fled the country after 1685. They included men like Christiaan Huygens—inventor of the pendulum clock and the first to derive the theory that the stars were in fact other suns—who returned to his native Holland. Silk-makers immigrated to England, glassmakers to Denmark, and 600 army officers departed to reinforce the ranks of France's enemies. At the battle of the Boyne, hundreds of French Huguenots fought in the ranks of William of Orange against the Irish Catholics. Encouraged by Frederick the Great, one important faction ended up in Prussia. By 1700 between a third and a half the population of Berlin was reckoned to be refugees from Louis' misguided religious strategy. Later, descendants of these Huguenot refugees would lead the cohorts invading France in three successive wars from 1870 onwards: men like General von François in the First World War, and Admiral Souchon, commander of the brilliant escape of the battle-cruiser *Goeben,* which would bring Turkey into the war on Germany's side, and in the Second World War *Luftwaffe* ace, Adolf Galland.

Further afield, the Revocation also hardened Protestant opinion abroad, with Benjamin Franklin recalling how, as a child, he had heard the preacher in Philadelphia's Old South Church inveigh against "that accursed man, persecutor of God's people, Louis the Fourteenth." The League of Augsburg, uniting as it did France's enemies against her, was but one consequence, while the loss of capital accompanying the waves of Huguenot émigrés was incalculable. Indeed, one could almost make the parallel that Louis' folly in driving out the Huguenots compared with the catastrophe Hitler wrought on Germany in depriving her of the Jewish intelligentsia, among them the scientists and physicists who would eventually design the atomic bomb to put the final lid on Nazi ambitions.

The Huguenots were not the only religious body to feel the scourge of royal bigotry. The Jansenists were a gloomy sect, founded by a Dutchman called Cornelius Jansenius (1585–1638), who had sought a return to the simplicity of the early Christians, with beliefs in free will and predestination reminiscent of Calvin's. In their austerity they often seemed holier than the Jesuits, and it was sometimes said that Louis hated the Jansenists even more than the Protestants. Among the eminent supporters of Jansenism was Blaise Pascal (1623–62), a frail genius who died when he was only thirty-nine. One of the stars in the firmament of the Roi Soleil, he postulated one of the key philosophical questions of the reign: "Is Christianity primarily a religion of reason or a religion of love?" But Pascal died before his great work, the *Apologie de la Religion Chrétienne,* could be finished.

As Louis fought his battles, and threw his energies and the state's resources into developing Versailles, so in the years 1689–97 military misadventure again exacerbated the plight of the poor. Then, in 1693, a poor harvest (compounded by inefficient and probably corrupt means of storing grain) made the nation hunger for peace. A new prayer, at once seditious and blasphemous, went the rounds:

> Our Father who art in Versailles, thy name is no longer hallowed; thy kingdom is diminished; thy will is no longer done on earth or on the waves. Give us our bread, which we totally lack . . . and deliver us from the Maintenon. Amen.[11]

Encapsulated concentrically around the person of the King, life went on at Versailles. Surely the politest, most courteous monarch there ever was, he lived among some 10,000 courtiers, virtually without a guard. For all the numbing grandeur of Versailles, the *ennui* must have been excruciating. Where other absolute rulers had secret police, or barbed wire, or a Berlin Wall, the secret weapon of the Roi Soleil and his Bourbon successors was boredom. To keep the French aristocracy at his fingertips was all part of Louis' essential apparatus of state, but in the long term it also proved the ruin of every element of local government in France.

At Versailles in the morning, the King worked with his ministers, three or four at most, to preserve secrecy. The Dauphin was kept out of everything; "Monsieur," the King's brother, was allowed in to deal with unimportant matters once a fortnight, while Philippe, who was to become regent, fared no better. The afternoon would be occupied with hunting, with masques and elaborate entertainments among the grottoes, or dallying in the groves populated by gods and goddesses of classical antiquity, or boating on the magnificent canals Le Nôtre had dug for him; except on Good Friday and Easter day when the royal family would spend the whole day in church. After supper would be some amusement, such as a ball or masquerade or concert—and the endless gambling complained of by Mme. de Sévigné, leading to the ruin and self-exile of many a courtier too anxious to cut a dash in front of his sovereign. Every event of the day was accompanied by music; the violins played during the *levé* and at lunch; hautbois, flutes and sackbuts accompanied his walks through the park; there were motets by Lully during chapel; at supper extracts would be played from his favourite operas; even at the *coucher* somebody would sing a new tune or cantata.

Just as Louis was seen every moment of the day, so he saw everybody and everything: "not one escaped him, not even those who hoped to remain unnoticed," recorded Saint-Simon. The prospects of "a man I never see" were dim indeed.

Following the marriage of the doted-on Marie-Adélaïde to his grandson, in 1697, the great ball of the reign took place in the Galerie des Glaces. The Roi Soleil's family life had never seemed sunnier. He was the most favoured, as well as the most powerful monarch on earth. In manners, style and the arts—in almost all things—other nations tried to model themselves on France. French furniture and French porcelain were to be seen everywhere in the houses of the rich all over Europe. Led by France, there was virtually a common European civilisation, which was French and aristocratic. French was, and remained, the international language of polite society. For Frederick the Great of Prussia, French became his language of choice, with orders to his own prime minister even written in it.

Then, for Louis, a terrible sequence of reversals began. The bad omens were there the very year of the move to Versailles with the death in labour of the Dauphine, as she gave birth to Louis' first grandson, the Duc de Bourgogne. Charmingly, the quacks prescribed that a sheep be flayed alive in her room, and the ailing princess wrapped in its skin; the ladies-in-waiting were horrified; the Dauphine died in agony anyway. Then, in 1701, queer old "Monsieur" died of a stroke, supposedly brought on by a row with his elder brother. "And so ended this year, 1701," wrote Saint-Simon, "and all the happiness of the King with it." Even Louis now seemed to weary of the polished regularity of court. Carrying with it the seeds of its own destruction, and a bill that would be paid for in 1789, for all its splendours, Versailles was to become a kind of forerunner of the horrible self-contained habitation or *unité* imposed on France by the Swiss Corbusier in the twentieth century. Mme. de Maintenon complained: "Symmetry, symmetry, if I stay much longer here I shall become paralytic. Not a door or a window will shut. . . ." Displeasure with the world she had helped create seems to have got her down to the extent of even inviting Ninon from Paris to reside at Versailles and liven things up—as a kind of seventeenth-century Pamela Harriman. Wisely, Ninon declined, for Paris once more had become more fun than Versailles; and even at the risk of permanent expulsion from paradise, more and more courtiers trickled off to the pleasures of a libertine city, as piety and ever more sober rules replaced the old, fun-loving regime of the younger Louis.

1702 brought the disastrous Wars of the Spanish Succession—something that Louis never wanted, but into which he was entrapped by the diplomatic follies of the past. "The Pyrenees are no more," Louis was supposed to have declared arrogantly. Europe, however, refusing to see a Bourbon prince on the throne of Spain, united against Louis. Marlborough marched to Blenheim and back, destroying French armies on every side as he went. In 1706, a total eclipse of the sun seemed like a portent for the Roi Soleil. The following year, Dutch scouts—full of vengeance for past injuries—pushed almost to Versailles. Living from hour to hour, the court prepared to evacuate to Chambord.

THE WINTER OF 1709 brought perhaps the worst cold ever recorded; in Paris, on 13 January, the thermometer fell below −21°F, and even sunny Provence registered temperatures of −16°F. Altogether France lost half of its livestock that winter; vines everywhere were killed. In Burgundy, children were reported living off boiled grass and roots; "Some even crop the fields like sheep." The Seine froze solid, the cold killing even Louis' confessor, Père La Chaise. Impoverished by war, for which he had melted down his gold plate yet again, Louis was unable to pay for the "King's bread" of past years that had sustained the poor of Paris—except by raising fresh taxes. On his way out hunting, the Dauphin found his way barred by ravenous women clamouring for food. Wolves again roamed the provinces. In Paris, 24,000 people died that winter. Mobs set off ominously for Versailles amid rumours that Mme. de Maintenon was buying up wheat. The chief of police, d'Argenson, feared a calamity: "I foresee that the fires will soon burn in this capital and I fear they will be difficult to extinguish."

Mme. de Maintenon could not lift Louis' depression. "Sometimes," she recorded, "he has a fit of crying that he cannot control, sometimes he is not well. He has no conversation." France's leading light had fallen into dark introspection, but his personal afflictions had hardly begun. In 1711, "Monseigneur" the Dauphin, kept in infuriating isolation at Marly, where he "stood in the corner whistling and tapping his snuffbox," caught smallpox and died. All Louis' hopes and affections now centred around his grandson, the new Dauphin, a serious young man of twenty-nine who reflected Louis' own capacity for hard work, and his twenty-five-year-old wife, Marie-Adélaïde of Savoy, whom Louis adored and whose charm and gaiety had brought new life to an ageing court. But, in January 1712, while Louis was still in mourning for his son, Marie-Adélaïde caught measles, and she died on 9 February. Ten days later, her husband succumbed to the same disease. In March—as the Allies were beginning to threaten Versailles—their five-year-old son, Louis, was gathered. Suspicions of poisoning arose against Philippe, the new Duc d'Orléans, a libertine known to read Rabelais during mass, whom the deaths brought close to the throne. Panic swept the court, though Louis kept his head, murmuring piously to Villars:

> Few have known what it is to lose, but I have lost in the space of a few weeks, a grandson, a granddaughter-in-law and their son. God punishes me, and I have deserved it. I shall suffer less in the next world.

At the end of the terrible year, 1712, the fall of France to the Allies was averted by Villars' miraculous eleventh-hour counter-stroke. But Louis would only briefly enjoy his country's liberation. On 13 August 1715, the King felt a stabbing pain in his left leg; ten days later, despite prescriptions of massive doses of asses' milk, it turned black. Gangrene had set in. Louis sent for his heir, his five-year-old great-grandson, and told him "Mignon, you are going to be a great King" and passed him this lapidary last testament:

> Try to remain at peace with your neighbours. I have loved war too much. Do not copy me in that, or in my over-spending . . . Lighten your people's burden as soon as possible, and do what I have had the misfortune not to do myself . . .

On 1 September 1715, the Roi Soleil was extinct, four days short of his seventy-seventh birthday, and having reigned for seventy-two years and a quarter. "His name cannot be uttered without respect, without linking it to an eternally memorable century," wrote Voltaire with a degree of homage rare for so sceptical a critic. Yet, as the great King was put to rest, Voltaire also could remember seeing little tents set up along the road to Saint-Denis, along which the funeral cortège would pass, where "people were drinking, singing and laughing." Perhaps more accurate was Albert Sorel's stricture: "He carried the principle of monarchy to its utmost limit and abused it—to the point of excess."[12]

Louis' long reign, the longest in French if not in European history, had begun with the brutal Frondes and the child-King's coming of age; in the 1660s and 1670s Louis and Colbert made energetic reforms amid Paris scandal; then the move to Versailles introduced, from 1682 on, the period of Louis' self-indulgence in affairs and foreign wars, followed by decline from the turn of the century until his death in 1715.

The old monarch had begun to seem immortal, imposing burdens on his nation without any expectation of redress, ruling by his will alone—the most absolute of absolute monarchs. Now the *grand siècle* was truly over. For France Louis had achieved a certain (but by no means universal) prosperity, stability and semblance of order; but now there were heavy bills that would shortly be due for payment.

# NINE

# Louis XV: Towards the Deluge

Mignon, you are going to be a great King. Do not copy me in my love
of building or in my love of warfare.

—*Louis XIV on his deathbed, August 1715*

ON THE DEATH OF LOUIS XIV, Mme. de Maintenon withdrew from Versailles, declaring that he had died "like a hero
and a saint." She herself followed four years later. At Versailles
the atmosphere of gloom-bound piety lingered on for a while, at least
until the new King, Louis XV (1715–74) would be old enough to take
over. It was a melancholic place (in many ways it still is), haunted by
phantoms and memories:

> Round and round the ghosts of beauty glide
> Haunting the places where their honour died.[1]

What glamour was left there had died with the old King. On the accession of the Regent, Philippe Duc d'Orléans, the court—and life itself—
moved back to Paris, after an exile of thirty-five years. Once again, it
became the true centre and soul of France. The Regent had been living
in Richelieu's Palais-Royal for many a year. It now became his official
residence.

Philippe was forty-three, but he looked older. Too many drunken
evenings had taken their toll. Under his Regency, and in part in reaction
against the rigid etiquette of Mme. de Maintenon's Versailles, France
entered perhaps the most dissolute period of its history. Mme. de Maintenon groaned: "I would prefer not to paint you a picture of our current

mores," as she commented on an orgy. Even the Regent's mother deplored how "Our state of general debauch is dreadful . . . youths of both sexes . . . conduct themselves like pigs and sows . . . Women . . . particularly those of our highest families . . . are worse than those in houses of ill-repute."[2] It was also a time of cruelty, where one drunken count could kill peasants for sport the way other men went hunting. Yet Philippe was also a man of great charm, and wit. He was voraciously well read, in literature as in philosophy, and was gifted with a remarkable memory. Though he was rumoured to have seduced his own daughter, to have poisoned the Dauphin, and even the King, he was in fact more compassionate and tolerant than most of his contemporaries. His principal handicap was that the Roi Soleil had permitted him to play no part in public life so he was totally lacking in political experience.

Nevertheless, the man with the daunting task of running the country in the wake of Louis XIV, the third in a line of three consecutive regents of France, proved himself in the arts, soldiery and diplomacy more than just a Rabelaisian profligate. He encouraged Watteau and the melancholy gaiety of the *fête galante.* He helped bring to an end Louis' wars that were ruining France; he opened the prisons and liberated the galley slaves—one of the most dreadful abuses left over from the Middle Ages, encouraged by Louis. In his efforts to educate the silent and reserved child-King, Louis XV, he did his best, with a light touch, saying: "But are you not the master? I am here only to explain, propose, receive your orders and execute them." Philippe could also claim advanced, and—to say the least—venturesome ideas on how to restore the stagnant economy; but here he came unstuck, with disastrous consequences that were to bring revolution closer.

He brought in John Law, an Edinburgh financier (and one of the few *anglo-saxons* to rate entry in *Le Petit Larousse*). Law introduced paper money, setting up in 1716 a "General Bank" to discount commercial paper, which in 1718 became the Royal Bank with the state as its sole shareholder. This was followed by an adventurous scheme to settle the wastes of Louisiana (named after Louis XIV; New Orleans was named after the Regent, Philippe). A wave of ill-conceived speculation swiftly spiralled out of control. Greed—or prescience—persuaded the Prince de Conti to arrive with three waggons, demanding gold in exchange for his 14 million shares. Nervous bourgeois speculators followed, swamping the bank with paper money and swiftly cleaning out the reserves; the full vulnerability of "Law's System" was exposed. By May 1720, an edict had slashed the value of paper shares and notes by half. Commented

Saint-Simon: "every rich man thought himself ruined without resource, and every poor man saw himself a beggar." With the collapse of Law's empire, the contagion even spread to London, where the "South Sea Bubble" was also shortly to burst.

In scenes not witnessed since the Frondes social discontent transformed into civil disorder, with murders and robberies rampant. In July, Law—recognised by the mob—narrowly escaped being lynched; one woman clutched the bridle of one of his horses, screaming "Bastard, if there were only four other women like me, you would be torn to pieces."[3] At one point, it looked as if the Regent himself was at risk as pamphlets proliferated, shrieking: "Save the King, kill the Tyrant . . ." Punishments were desperately meted out to stem the tide of revolt. The legendary bandit, "Cartouche," was finally cornered, having terrorised the wealthy quarters of Paris for many months. He was broken on the wheel, facing the dreadful death with remarkable composure, in front of an eager crowd of thousands gathered at the Place de Grève. Able-bodied vagabonds were sent off by the hundreds for transportation to the wilderness and disease-ridden swamps of Louisiana. A talisman of the times, Abbé Prévost's heroine Manon Lescaut ended up dying in the "burning sands."

Excoriated as "that miserable Englishman" (unfairly, as of course he was a Scot), Law resigned, retiring to die quietly in Venice nine years later, "a sorry beggar, timidly making excuses." But Law and his over-optimistic "System" had made the monarchy totter. The bourgeoisie, created and enriched by the Roi Soleil, had been ruined; worse, they had become dangerously disillusioned with the regime. A new and trustworthy Banque de France would not be established for another eighty years, and would need the genius of a Bonaparte. Then in 1723, drained out by his debaucheries and the Law catastrophe, Philippe died—in the arms of a mistress. A grisly story circulated that, at his post-mortem, one of his Great Danes jumped up and ate his heart. Had he lived longer, might Regent Philippe, debauched but enlightened, possibly have made young Louis XV move faster to modernise France?

LOUIS XV was then still an immature child of thirteen. Whereas his illustrious great-grandfather had been hardened by the Frondes, Louis XV was brought up to know only flattery and licentiousness, "a handsome young man, frail and gloomy, with the pretty face of a girl, unfeeling and cold." He succeeded in being both timid and violent. Where the

Roi Soleil sought the spotlight, Louis XV preferred privacy and was rarely seen by the public. Moving back to Versailles after the death of the Regent, he was to find himself, "forever caught in the web spun by his terrible ancestor,"[4] and cut off from his people. He found little diversion in literature, music or the arts—until Mme. de Pompadour came along. Nor did he seem to have any particular purpose in life—except the pursuit of pleasure and the maintenance of the status quo created by his great-grandfather. Government had become much more complicated, with ministers grown more independent and administration bogged down by a plethora of *intendants* across the country. Then, from the 1730s, there was a steady rise in prices to discomfort government.

At first, following Philippe, young Louis turned over the governance of France to Cardinal Fleury, described by the French historian Jules Michelet as "an agreeable nobody." When Fleury died, aged ninety-eight, in 1743, the King allowed himself—and France—to be ruled by his mistresses. In marriage, he affronted Spain by his change of intent, wedding the daughter of the Polish claimant, Maria Leszczinska. Without ever addressing more than a word or two to her, Louis gave her ten children in ten years. ("Always going to bed, always being brought to bed," sighed the unhappy Queen.) She bored Louis, and then closed her bedroom door to him when he was only thirty. Possessed of the true Bourbon temperament, he had affairs with four (de Nesle) sisters in a row. When the last of them died—poison was rumoured—Louis, out hunting, picked up a Mlle. Poisson. Of modest birth, but considerable character, she was promoted Marquise de Pompadour. Denigrated by Carlyle as that "highly rouged, unfortunate female of whom it is not proper to speak without necessity,"[5] Mlle. Poisson, too, appears to have become frigid after a while, keeping a hold on the King by supplying him with a succession of young girls—including, allegedly, her own daughter. The Parc-aux-Cerfs at Versailles—visited nightly by Louis for assignations arranged by Pompadour—gained an infamous reputation.

> Here lies one twenty years a maid,
> Fifteen a whore, and seven a procuress

was the epitaph the pamphleteers gave her when she died, aged forty-three and of natural causes, in 1764.

On account of her interference in high policy, her extravagance and her wanton influence on the King, Pompadour died unmourned, despised by the court as a bourgeoise, hated by the bourgeois of Paris as being in league with the tax-collecting monarchy. Nevertheless, France's cultural heritage owes more to her than it likes to admit. The Petit Trianon, in Paris the École Militaire and the Place de la Concorde, not to mention Sèvres porcelain, all owe something to Mlle. Poisson. She also bequeathed to the nation the Élysée Palace as a home for future Republican rulers of France. When she died her place was taken by another of low birth, a pretty prostitute called Jeanne Bécu, later Comtesse du Barry. She was, so Louis confided to that great expert on the art of philandery the Duc de Richelieu, "The only woman in France who can make me forget that I am in my sixties."[6]

Taking the lead from example at the top, the country's moral code continued much as it had under the Regency. It was no accident that the age produced both Choderlos de Laclos, author of *Liaisons Dangereuses,* shocking at the time it was printed, and the Marquis de Sade. Indeed, it seems that the writing of pornography by the aristocracy, particularly in Provence where de Sade hailed from, was a far from uncommon hobby. The King was conspicuously more lenient towards the sexual misdemeanours of noblemen than were the bourgeois parlements. A blind eye was turned to pederasty (still a capital offence) among the-great-and-the-good, while the press was barred from reporting aristocrats' misdemeanours. This was one good reason why, bar the occasional prison sentence, de Sade managed to emerge unscathed from the dreadful deeds he committed, and not only wrote about. Also, as a dedicated *voyeur* himself, the King seems to have derived pleasure from the reports on de Sade's doings from his police chief, Louis Marais. Thus it is hardly surprising that, from mid-century onwards, the French bourgeoisie became progressively enraged by licence allowed the errant nobility. With it, understandably, went a notable decline in the nation's affection for the monarch; from having been the *bien aimé* he found himself berated in the underground press as a "vile, imbecilic automaton," "father of thiefs and harlots."[7] Although his amorous exploits were no more excessive than those of his Bourbon ancestors Henri IV and Louis XIV, because of his ineffectiveness as a ruler they became unpalatable.

There was never to be a Mme. de Maintenon who could bring Louis XV in his maturer years to a sense of *gravitas.* The surface frivolity of the life and times of Louis XV are reflected in the dramas of Marivaux, perhaps specially trivial when compared with Molière, let alone the tragedies of Racine; while such serious talents as Voltaire, Rousseau, Montesquieu and the *encyclopédistes*—illustrious as they were—hardly lent support to a threatened dynasty. Painted by Pompadour's protégé, Boucher ("His lovers are shepherds, but incapable of watching a flock," said the critics), life at Versailles grew ever more feckless, pointless and removed from the real world. Indeed, the court there was composed notably of absentee landlords from estates that were falling into rack and ruin. Unlike their English counterparts, they never travelled or made the "grand tour," so their preoccupations became ever more insular—incestuously French and aristocratic. More than a diversion, at Versailles sex became the principal occupation; it was acceptable that when Princes of the Blood such as the Chartres dined out, they would ask for the use of their hostess's bed during the course of the meal. In contrast with Empress Maria Theresa's respected and austere court in Vienna, Louis' earned its reputation as the most corrupt in Europe—Mme. du Barry the symbol of the completeness of its corruption.

In Paris the tenor of life at court was embodied in the person of the wicked but brilliant Armand, Duc de Richelieu (1696–1788), Marshal of France and grand-nephew of the great cardinal. Adept equally at climbing in and out of bedroom windows, he married three times under three reigns and sired a child (illegitimate) in his eighties. Strolling round the Place Royale, the Duke was given to reminiscing happily that he had slept with the lady of every single household. Aged ninety-two, still *en plein vigueur,* His Grace chose prudently to die one year before the revolution.


FOR FRANCE, victories on the battlefield exonerate scandals; but Louis XV was a loser. Paying little heed to the last words of his predecessor, Louis likewise impoverished the country by his wars (though he hated battle). Plundering far into the eastern marches of Europe, Louis supported that new upstart, Frederick II (later "the Great") of Prussia, but then turned against him. France was then roundly defeated by an embattled Frederick at Rossbach, and Prussia gained at France's expense. Worse still, in the course of the bitter Seven Years' War (1756–63), France lost her empire in Canada (scathingly written off by Voltaire as "a few acres of snow"), the Mississippi territory and India. Britain gained hers. French historians accept that the Peace of Paris, signed in 1763, was one of the saddest in the nation's history. About the only territorial acquisition of Louis' reign was Corsica, where an important protagonist and sometime successor was waiting to be born.

At home, a dispute over regional taxation and the national deficit led Louis to abolish the parlements and establish new courts. Immense opposition was aroused, with many writers joining in; the King was accused of being a tyrant, in violation of the "natural rights" of the citizen. The Paris Parlement called out the mob to attack Louis' new courts.

BY THE 1750s Louis had already been forced to construct a *Route de la Révolte* whereby he could travel from Fontainebleau to Versailles, without traversing turbulent Paris. This foolish and costly King survived an assassination attempt by a half-mad serving-man, Robert François Damiens, in 1757. Only Louis appeared to be surprised: "Why try to kill me?" he asked, "I have done no one any harm." Damiens was put to death as cruelly as Henri IV's assassin, Ravaillac, a century-and-a-half earlier. His flesh was torn open by giant red-hot pincers and molten lead poured into the wounds, before he was pulled limb from limb by four horses. Even Voltaire approved of the punishment of the failed regicide, and neither torture nor the repugnant "wheel" was to be abolished in Paris until the eve of the revolution—so much for the "Age of Enlightenment."

In May 1774, regretted by no one and horribly disfigured, Louis was carried off by smallpox at Versailles. His burial was performed in secrecy at Saint-Denis, for fear of the cortège being attacked by angry Parisians. With remarkable similarity to the end of Louis XIV, both the Dauphin and his wife had predeceased the King. So it was Louis' grandson who inherited, as the nineteen-year-old Louis XVI (1774–92)—as popular as his predecessor had been unpopular, acclaimed with a fervour not seen since the days of Henri IV. Rather pathetically, he proclaimed, "I should like to be loved." He immediately felt compelled to abandon Louis XV's ill-conceived courts and reinstate the parlements—a serious admission on the part of the Crown. At least superficially, once again, the barometer looked set fair.

AT LEAST IN ONE RESPECT, eyes were distracted from the bad auguries on the ground to a spectacle in the air, where, in the last days of the *ancien régime,* was to be pioneered one of the modern world's greatest inventions: human flight. On 5 June 1783 the Montgolfier brothers sent up their first hot air balloon. They were watched by a huge crowd, including Benjamin Franklin recently arrived in Paris full of scientific knowledge and fresh revolutionary zeal, who was to remark to those doubting the value of balloons his famous: "Of what use is the new-born baby?" The Montgolfier balloon flew for twenty-five minutes at an altitude of 100 metres across an astounded Paris. (One of the two pilots, the intrepid de Rozier, was killed soon after while trying to cross the English Channel—a success that promised a life pension from Louis XVI.)

The city that the pioneering balloonist looked down upon had been changing dramatically since the beginning of the 1760s. Ten thousand new houses were erected, accompanied by an immense amount of demolition—as witness the superb records painted by Hubert Robert (1733–1808), the chronicler supreme of ruins. The old wooden houses encumbering bridges like the Pont Notre-Dame were pulled down. Architecture settled down into the elegant classicism developed under Louis XIV that was being copied throughout Europe. By far the most lasting architectural achievement of the century, bearing the stamp of Pompadour's influence, was the massive Place Louis XV. The ending of the War of the Austrian Succession in 1748 brought little on which France could congratulate herself, but, while in England Handel celebrated it by composing his great *Fireworks Music,* in Paris the King generously offered a large open site just west of the Tuileries Gardens for a statue in Louis XV's honour. No sooner was it was erected, showing Louis as a Roman emperor on horseback, than placards were attached to it damning the King's vices* and his indifference to the plight of the poor. It was to mark the site of the guillotine that would shortly remove the head of his grandson.

A THICKSET MAN with a puffy face not brimming over with the light of intelligence, and bulging, myopic eyes, Louis XVI comes across now as an honest blockhead. He resembled more the Saxon side of his mother's family than the Bourbon. (On seeing the unflattering portrait of him by Boze, Winston Churchill was to remark: "Now I understand why there was a French Revolution.") Louis was pious and chaste— though this gained him little credit from his uncharitable countrymen, whereas Louis XV had been condemned for precisely the opposite. Probably Louis was also partially impotent, his marriage to Marie-Antoinette not being consummated for several years. His Habsburg brother-in-law, Joseph, helpfully suggested "he ought to be whipped, to

---

*"Oh! la belle statue! Oh! le beau piédestal! Les Vertus sont à pied, le Vice est à cheval" proclaimed one, pinned on the neck of the horse.

make him ejaculate, as one whips donkeys." Unlike his predecessor, Louis was humanitarian by instinct, well meaning but lethargic. But, with a fear of wielding power that perhaps harked back to the humiliations he had suffered as a child at the court of his grandfather, he was indecisive; too indecisive to revive the authority of the monarchy. Louis would estrange public opinion by such gauche moves as banning Voltaire as well as Beaumarchais' hugely popular *Marriage of Figaro.*

Justly or unjustly, Marie-Antoinette will always be renowned for her bovine Habsburg extravagance; if she didn't actually say "let them eat cake," she might as well have done. Whatever good things she did accomplish, they would unflaggingly be annulled by the Frenchman's ingrained hatred of the Austrian—dating back to Charles Quint, and beyond. While Louis was generally more intelligent than history allows (foolish, but not stupid, he played a significant part in planning the naval war during the American War of Independence), Marie-Antoinette seems to have suffered more from her lack of formal education—but nor was she innately stupid. At their lavish wedding celebrations in May 1770 at the still incomplete Place Louis XV, a stray rocket ignited a depot of fireworks and in the ensuing fire 133 panicking onlookers were killed in the narrow defile of the Rue Royale. The superstitious populace viewed it as the most sinister of omens. Observing from Berlin, the parsimonious Frederick the Great wrote simply that such festivities must help drive France into financial ruin; seven years later he would predict of Louis XVI, whom he had come to despise and whose predecessor he had roundly defeated in the recent Seven Years' War, that mismanagement of his finances was such that revolution was inevitable.

Through no fault of hers, in 1785 Marie-Antoinette fell victim to a twenty-first-century-style scam, "The Affair of the Diamond Necklace," which provided the scurrilous contemporary press with long-running delight. A tale of great complexity, it involved an unscrupulous jeweller, Boehmer, with a ff2 million *bijou* to market; a crooked countess, Lamotte; a forged letter purporting to bear the Queen's signature; and a cardinal, Rohan, who found himself under arrest. The only innocent in the whole affair was the unfortunate Queen herself; yet it was the reputation of the poor, unpopular *autrichienne* (a crude play on words) that was never to recover.

At Versailles, Marie-Antoinette and her ladies cavorted, playing innocently at shepherdesses in her *hameau,* a phoney peasant hamlet

constructed in the park, while real countrymen—even the rural nobility—were struggling against hunger and impoverishment. Nevertheless,
as the *ancien régime* obliviously played out its final days, there were great
plans on the drawing board. Paris would be surrounded with a new
*grand boulevard:* there was to be a new Place Royale, all the houses clut-
tering the Louvre and the Tuileries were to be removed, the number of
bridges and public fountains was to be increased, the quays embellished.
(Ironically, almost all these projects were later to be carried out after the
revolution by Napoleon, or Haussmann.) In power was the most
reform-minded, humanitarian government of the century—yet it was to
be damned for its intrusiveness. Liberalism had become positively
respectable; yet, typically, it would be followed shortly by the introduction of far worse excesses than those which it sought to moderate.

LOOKS AND AUGURIES were against Louis XVI; so too were circumstances. Predominantly Louis was unlucky. Neither Louis XV nor he
was an especially malicious king (nor, for that matter, was the last of the
Romanovs, Tsar Nicholas II), and in ordinary times Louis XVI (as well
as Nicholas II) might well have survived. But these were not ordinary
times. Whereas under the first of the Bourbons, Henri IV, absolutism
seemed acceptable, under Louis XVI it was intolerable. The times were
out of joint for him. In Paris, serious riots in 1725 and 1750, accompanied by lynchings and displays of anti-clericalism, would come to seem
like a preamble to 1789. Right from the beginning, Louis' reign coincided with a prolonged period of economic stagnation. On the other
hand, by 1789 there was a widespread belief that a time of prosperity was
at hand, coupled to an era of universal felicity. The cost of the American
Revolution, supported ardently by men like the young Lafayette, both
tallied with the Enlightenment and hit at the traditional foe, England,
but it cost more than the country could bear; in addition to the financial
burden, the echoes set up by the attractive precedent of overthrowing a
monarchy were to return to Versailles—and be reinforced in Paris by
such highly articulate Republicans from the New World as Benjamin
Franklin and Thomas Jefferson. Meanwhile, since the days of the Roi
Soleil, the press had grown immeasurably in strength and virulence;
between 1745 and 1785 alone the number of periodicals had risen from
fifteen to eighty-two. The lifting of censorship, in 1788, created a sense
that every citizen had a right to say how the government should operate.

That right was reinforced by the remarkable *Encyclopédie* and its contributors. Read throughout France (and also immensely profitable), it had a span across all the literate classes which made it a kind of eighteenth-century website, bringing to the widest public the sceptical thinking of *philosophes* such as Rousseau, Voltaire and Diderot. Though as individuals they differed greatly from one another, their net impact shook all the assumptions and beliefs that lay at the foundations of French society. In a direct line from Descartes, the message of the *philosophes* was based on reason as opposed to faith; thus, by extension, they challenged the existing order and the divine right of kings, as well as providing a fountainhead for anti-clericalism. Though they were wedded to thought rather than action, and none played any part in public affairs, between 1750 and 1770 the influence of Enlightenment reasoning was throughout France profoundly discrediting to the *ancien régime* in all its facets. Their very volatility, however, made it hard for the *philosophes* to be held accountable; and, besides, Voltaire, Rousseau and Diderot were all gone well before the storm—which they had done much to blow up—burst on France.

Another powerful influence, though it is not easy to generalise, was the striking social role of French women before the revolution. From the days of a century previously, when a *grande courtesane* like Ninon de Lenclos could reject a royal summons to Versailles, the power and position of women of the upper and bourgeois classes had risen inexorably. In no other country was it as great. England's Joseph Addison was quite shocked to discover that they were "more *awaken'd* than is consistent either with virtue or discretion,"[8] while the Scottish philosopher David Hume was equally shocked to discover how France "gravely exalts those . . . whose inferiority and infirmities are absolutely incurable."

Among the working-class women of eighteenth-century France, reputation was based by and large on moral "purity." It was not so among men of the proletariat, nor of women of the upper echelons of society; yet, at both ends of the spectrum, the role of women as "opinion-makers," indeed as a branch of the media, was not to be underestimated. During the revolution, *mégères* and *tricoteuses* like Mme. Defarge were not simply products of the fertile imagination of Charles Dickens. Unsophisticated visitors from the infant United States, like young Gouverneur Morris, would be amazed at the "cut and thrust" of gossip they found in the salons of Mmes. Necker and de Staël—"the upper region of wits and graces,"[9] where absolutely nothing was sacred. He was impressed by the fierceness of the women, chiding Louis XVI for his "uncharacteristic chastity," and by the volatility of their ideals. "A Frenchman," Morris wrote perceptively, early on in his stay:

> loves his king as he loves his Mistress to madness, because he thinks it great and noble to be mad. He then abandons both the one and the other most ignobly because he cannot bear the continued Action of the Sentiment he has persuaded himself to feel.

For the past hundred years, ever since the Roi Soleil, the monarchy's splendid absolutism had entranced, overpowered and provoked the French people, catching them between helpless admiration and despair. Now Louis XVI was to suffer the end of the affair—and the recriminations. One wonders whether a Philippe-Auguste, a Henri IV, a Louis XIV or even a Bonaparte could have averted what befell him. Equally, it is amazing that the "deluge" hadn't burst on France a hundred years previously. With all the blithe unfairness of which Fate is capable, Louis XVI would pay for the wars and extravagances of both his predecessors, Louis XIV and Louis XV. So the sombre acceleration of events piled up, hastening the Bourbon caravan towards its final crash.

# The Great Revolution

Amid all these pleasures, we were drawing near to the month of May
1789, laughing and dancing our way to the precipice. Thinking people
were content to talk of abolishing all the abuses. France, they said, was
about to be re-born. The word 'revolution' was never uttered . . . Had
anyone dared to use it he would have been thought mad . . .

—Mémoires, *Mme. de La Tour du Pin*

NEVER HAD PEOPLE BEEN SO PLEASURE-SEEKING as in
the spring of 1789,"[1] wrote Mme. de La Tour du Pin, a woman
of the nobility closely associated with the court of Louis XVI.
"For the poor," she went on to admit, "the winter had been very hard,
but there was no concern for the misery of the people. There were races
at Vincennes, where the horses of the Duc d'Orléans* ran against those
of the Comte d'Artois."† It was after the last of these races (in April), she
added, "that we found ourselves in the midst of the first riot, the one
which destroyed the worthy Réveillon's wallpaper factory."

The previous summer had been disastrous for the harvests, while the
winter that followed had indeed been a particularly harsh one, where
cold, hunger and discontent all linked hands against the government.
Yet who could then have foretold what lay ahead for France, for Europe:
the most devastating cataclysm in the whole of Europe's past history;
and, indeed, its future until the coming of the First World War in 1914

---

*Later "Philippe-Égalité," the turncoat regicide, cousin of the King who himself
ended on the guillotine.

†Younger brother of Louis XVI, who later became the reactionary Charles X, last of
the Bourbons.

and Lenin in 1917? From the earthquake of the revolution (six years) through the tornado of Napoleon (another twenty) to the Restoration would embrace just the lifetime of one generation. A *roué* like the Marquis de Sade (1740–1814) could easily have been born into the indulgent embrace of the *ancien régime* of Louis XV, and live almost to see out Napoleon; while another *roué*, but also a great and supple statesman like Talleyrand (1754–1838) would survive to witness the restoration of the Bourbons—and the bourgeois triumph of Louis-Philippe. But what events they saw! What a generation!

BY 1786 FRANCE'S COSTLY FOREIGN POLICY, particularly her support for the American War of Independence, had saddled an already shaky economy with ponderous debts. Some radical fiscal reforms were clearly essential. A new finance minister, Loménie de Brienne, aged fifty-nine, former Archbishop of Toulouse and Marie-Antoinette's man (as opposed to the King's) replaced the unsuccessful Charles de Calonne. In August 1788, in an atmosphere of growing unrest among the nobles, Brienne agreed that there should be a crisis meeting of the Estates-General in order to examine the nation's *cahiers de doléances* (literally, "lists of grievances" drawn up by local government bodies). They had not met since 1614 under Louis XIII, their first meeting having been in 1302 under Philippe le Bel. Brienne's measures also failed to resuscitate the Treasury, now on the brink of bankruptcy, and he resigned—to be consoled with promotion to cardinal. In his place came Jacques Necker (1732–1804), a highly competent Swiss banker—and, surprisingly, a Protestant, the first to fill such a high post. In desperation the French Establishment sought him out for those solid Swiss Calvinist virtues.

The King had attempted to impose taxation, which was his prerogative, but had been overruled by both the Assembly of Notables (Nobles and Clergy) and the Parlement of Paris. He then abolished the Parlement and, the following January, the hard-pressed Necker, unable to cope with France's unprecedented national debt of 1 *billion* livres, persuaded him to convoke a meeting of the Estates-General that May. Though it seemed the situation had been momentarily defused, the state was simply bankrupt. There were acute food shortages, accompanied by steep rises in the price of flour and bread. The age-old spectre of famine rose up in the hard-hit provinces, and there were riots in many areas. Peasant complaints included the poll tax, salt tax, the tithe—and, not least, the exclusive rights of the nobility to hunt rabbits and game, which destroyed their crops.

When the Estates-General met at Versailles on 5 May 1789, the signs were unpromising. The King insisted on the venue, partly so it could be under his wing, but also—like so many of his forebears—because he loved hunting and did not fancy having to travel far afield from the forest; in addition, Paris was considered too inflammable. But the proximity of court life was humiliating for humbler delegates of the Commons. Moreover, it was Versailles that had manifestly cut the monarchy off from the country. The deputies of the Commons were required to be clad in sombre black and penned together in a special enclosure, while the Nobles and Clergy wore their most ostentatiously extravagant and gaudy robes. The sovereign himself "wore the robes of the Order of the Holy Ghost . . . richly embroidered and very thickly encrusted with diamonds," observed Mme. de La Tour du Pin, but he "was not dignified in appearance. He stood badly and walked with a waddle; his movements were abrupt and lacking in grace."[2] (One wonders, had he half the presence of *le grand Louis,* might he yet have carried it off?)

Despite fully sharing the prevailing sense of illusion, Louis "hoped that they were about to enter a Golden Age." An observer like young Gouverneur Morris, arriving hot from the recent revolution in America, equally noted it as a "hopeful political moment." At the inaugural procession of the Estates at Versailles, he was impressed how Louis was cheered enthusiastically (though the Queen not at all). Immediately, however, there were political problems with the constitution of the assembly. The Nobles numbered 285, the Clergy 308, and there were 621 for the "Third Estate," or Commons. The first two Estates (representing perhaps jointly half-a-million men) insisted on voting weighted by order of rank; the more numerous Commons, representing 25 million "common people" and having, over the feverish campaigning of the previous six months, come to recognise itself as a significant political force, demanded that voting should be by head. But there was no discussion about the crucial issues of national solvency for which the gathering had been called; meanwhile in the nation at large there was mounting discontent in both town and country.

Disenchanted, if not outraged, on 17 June the deputies of the Commons proclaimed it the "National Assembly." The King responded by locking them out, marching off at the head of the Nobles and Clergy. An alarming division had occurred, with the monarchy manifestly siding in defence of feudal privilege and against the people. "Never had a regime so speedily committed suicide," remarks André Maurois. The Commons promptly set up shop in a nearby covered tennis court, the famous Jeu de Paume—a scene historically depicted by David. Here the deputies swore a solemn oath, or *serment,* not to separate until France had a constitution "established on solid foundations." There was talk about a constitution based on English precedents, but few had any idea what this actually meant.

At their head emerged Honoré-Gabriel Riqueti, Marquis de Mirabeau, a *provençale* noble who had changed sides, the most feared and powerful orator of his day. A huge shambling bear of a man, with an enormous head and face ravaged by smallpox, Mirabeau claimed, "My ugliness likewise is a power." Like many ugly men through the ages, he had surprising success with women—and an appetite to match. Although he remarked with bitterness that "there is no one at the helm," he believed in a constitutional monarchy, and in moderation to the last. But, as a courtier came with royal orders to clear the Jeu de Paume, Mirabeau declared in resounding words: "Sir, go tell your master that we are here by the will of the people and that we shall leave here only at the point of the bayonet!" He remained an optimist almost to the end, persuading himself that, although history had "too often recounted the actions of nothing more than wild animals . . . now we are allowed to hope that we are beginning the history of man." This was, of course, to prove somewhat over-optimistic.

At this point the King still had both the power, and the legitimacy, to have his will carried out. It was still *reform,* not *revolution,* that the people of France wanted. Now, and at various subsequent points even after the storming of the Bastille, the cataclysm could have been avoided. History might have been different if Louis had asserted his authority with more conviction. But, indecisive as ever, wavering between his genuine humanitarian instincts and the Bourbon belief in the divine right of kings, and invariably choosing the wrong moment to act, he quailed. There was also something in him that seemed to gibe at a reform movement that he could not control. The aristocracy had lost its influence; the bourgeoisie now began to want something more than just reform—though what it did not quite know until the Jacobins led the way. On 11 July, the King sacked Necker, now regarded as the people's champion, blaming him for the civil unrest. With Necker went the last best hope of reform. Fearing national bankruptcy, the Bourse closed its doors. An empty exchequer and republican sentiment now combined.

RELENTLESSLY, EVENT FOLLOWED UPON DISASTROUS EVENT of what Thomas Carlyle categorised as the "bestial dawning of the Age of Reason." Inevitably, it was in turbulent Paris that the violence began. On 28 April the first shots in the overture to the revolution proper were fired in the wretched east end Faubourg Saint-Antoine—just where the final combats of the Frondes had taken place against young Louis XIV. Rumours ran round that a paper manufacturer called Réveillon (the very name, meaning a reawakening, had ominous undertones) was planning to cut his workers' wages. A symbol of conspicuous consumerism of the times, the "worthy Réveillon," as he was regarded by the bourgeoisie, was respected as a generous employer. It was he who had supplied the special paper for Pilâtre de Rozier's first Montgolfier balloon, and it was from his garden that de Rozier had taken off, in the crowning achievement of Louis XVI's reign. Réveillon's intentions appear to have been simply to lower wages in line with the drop in the price of bread, which had been fixed by the government so as to ease social pressures. But his workers saw it otherwise and rioted. As Mme. de La Tour recorded, the factory was looted and burnt out; troops intervened and opened fire, killing thirty or more. Réveillon fled for his life into the great fortress that loomed over the district, the Bastille.

The Paris authorities should have seen what was in the wind. As July began, however, all seemed quiet again in Paris. On the 13th, Mme. de La Tour sent her horses off from her house at Versailles to the country, via Paris—an indication that "we had not the slightest presentiment of what was to happen in Paris the next day."[3] Nevertheless, fierce anger had smouldered since the demise of Necker. Rioting mobs destroyed the tollgates. In quest of arms for the new civic Garde Nationale, created to counter an impending coup, they invaded city arsenals. Then, on the morning of 14 July the Invalides was targeted, and cannon and muskets taken. Attention was next turned on that most formidable arsenal of all: the Bastille.

Mme. de La Tour's first indication of the day's events came when her frightened concierge babbled: "They have fired the cannon of the Bastille. There has been a massacre and it is impossible to leave the city . . . the Gardes Françaises have risen with the people."[4] The outrageous Marquis de Sade, though he narrowly missed being a witness to events, seems to have played his part in stirring up the mob on returning to custody in the Bastille. According to the Governor, de Launay, he had

stood at his cell window, shouting "at the top of his lungs that the prisoners were being assassinated, their throats cut, and that they must be
rescued."[5] He had even used part of his "urinary equipment," a long
metal funnel, bellowing down it as a loudspeaker to get his message
across to the mob outside the Bastille. De Launay urged his minister
(successfully) to have de Sade transferred to the lunatic asylum at Charenton, where he would be "less of a threat to public order." But it was
too late.

On 14 July insurgents from the turbulent *faubourg* of Saint-Antoine
marched on the Bastille. In fact, it held no more than seven prisoners,
one of whom had spent twenty-three years there, and—blinded by the
sun—emerged into daylight wondering whether Louis XV was still on
the throne. But the ancient fortress was regarded as a symbol of royal
authority. De Launay only had a mixed bag of 110 troops, but thought
he was under attack. Ninety-eight in the crowd were killed by fire from
the Bastille; the mob went mad. The fortress was seized, the unfortunate
Governor de Launay killed and his head stuck on a pike—and the
Bastille demolished stone by stone.

The day before the storming of the Bastille, there had been a foretaste of these forces with the pointless sacking of the convent of Saint-
Lazare. Formerly a hospital for lepers, the convent had since become
renowned for its charity, but even the fruit trees in the convent orchard
were chopped down, while ferocious women—forebears of the *tricoteuses*—killed and made off with all the chickens in its poultry farm.
When the police arrived the following morning, they were just in time
to rescue two old priests about to be hanged from nearby lamp-posts,
while some of the mob had decapitated a marble statue of Saint Paul and
stuck the head on a pike, and were parading it through the streets. It was
an unpleasant harbinger of what revolution was about to bring.

After the seizure of the Bastille, Gouverneur Morris could still
observe with sardonic mildness that "this day's transactions will induce a
conviction that all is not perfectly quiet." Yet, a week later, having witnessed the cavalry pelted with stones on the Concorde, and two dignitaries hacked to death, he now saw a different face to the Paris mob:
"Gracious God what a People!"[6] A terrible wave of latent ferocity now
surged through the city, which would not finally be quelled until the
advent of Napoleon. All the impassioned hatreds that had been storing
up in Paris since the Roi Soleil exploded. Returning that afternoon from
his favourite pastime, *la chasse*, Louis XVI enquired, "Is this a rebellion?"
"No, Sire," came the reply. "It is a revolution."[7]

In the countryside, noble dwellings were sacked, feudal records destroyed, barns raided, tithes reclaimed. Feudal rights were abolished, with disastrous consequences for the incomes of good and bad landowners alike. On 26 August, the Declaration of the Rights of Man and of the Citizen, rapidly promulgated, became the foundation document of the revolution. Debates in quest of a constitution intensified, with Mirabeau playing a dominant part. With extraordinary speed, *les aristos* began to flee France—as many as 150,000, in three separate phases. They included many officers from the army; here was one very good reason why increasingly Louis could not depend on its loyalty, or efficacy.

ON 5 OCTOBER, an armed Paris mob, conspicuously led by a troop of enraged women, marched on Versailles. The previous day there was no bread in the bakeries of Paris; an angry crowd seized one unfortunate baker and hanged him on the spot. Virtually unopposed they now invaded both the Palace and the Assembly. As an unwilling witness, Mme. de La Tour du Pin watched the scene aghast as the mob surged into the sacred realm of the Roi Soleil. Feebly the royal Garde allowed itself be corralled, while one unfortunate soldier, abandoned by his fellows, was torn to pieces by the mob. The King attempted to escape, but the mob cut the traces of his horses and led them away.

In total humiliation the royal couple were now escorted back to Paris, accompanied by a jeering mob, carrying the bleeding heads of his murdered guards on pikes immediately in front of his carriage. There now entered on the scene the King's turncoat cousin, the Duc d'Orléans, darling of the mob on account of his liberal sympathies, and greeted with cries of "Long live our King d'Orléans!" Following the royal family's departure from Versailles—to be empty and untenanted for many a year—Mme. de La Tour du Pin recalled that "the only sound to be heard in the château was the fastening of doors and shutters which had not been closed since the time of Louis XIV."[8] Treated with utmost contempt, they were now herded back to the Tuileries. The following day, Louis under severe pressure agreed to reside in the capital henceforth. There they would remain as virtual prisoners of the newly formed Paris Commune for next three years.

Meanwhile the national debt, unchecked, had soared out of all control. In response to bankruptcy, on 3 November the Assembly decided to nationalise and sell off Church lands and property, potentially an immense source of wealth—and already a target under the assaults of the deist *philosophes*. As the revolutionaries realised just how affluent the Church was, so their ferocity, and hatred, against it mounted. Possibly the greatest casualty of the revolution, the Church lost all its power and autonomy; monasteries and convents were dissolved, tithes payable to the Church were abolished, and *Assignats* against its property were issued—scraps of paper that were as worthless as the "Continentals" that been used to finance George Washington's revolutionary armies a decade earlier. The Pope refused to recognise the Assembly's action, threatening excommunication. The Assembly retaliated by enforcing on all clergy a separatist oath of obedience to "the King, the Law and the Nation." Accordingly the Church of France found itself divided into "constitutionalists" and "dissidents," a division that would be perpetuated in the Republican structure of the nation. The Church was already divided between the very many decent, but often extremely poor parish priests, barely scraping a living, and the rich reprobates like the Bishop of Autun, Talleyrand, who brought it a bad name by their shameless flouting of their priestly vows, and generally sacrilegious behaviour.

With attacks on Church property proliferating in the provinces, gradually a state of open civil war took hold. In Paris, however, a strange normalcy persisted through 1790. Brightly coloured posters filled public places, hawking the promises of various political factions. The first anniversary of 14 July, called *Fête de la Fédération,* was a bright and cheerful affair (except, no doubt, for relatives of the murdered guardians of the Bastille). The tea parties continued, in salons where the gossips prattled away. Smart women wore "liberty" hats and "constitution" jewellery. Beaumarchais was still all the rage—although his *Figaro* remained banned by Louis XVI, on account of its assault on authority. Strange people popped out of the woodwork, in unexpected places; the Marquis de Sade, liberated from his asylum, became a republican—plain Citizen Louis Sade. Excoriating his beloved King as "a traitor, a rascal," he somehow found himself in charge of renaming streets in his elegant district of the *premier* (it must have afforded him particular pleasure to have Rue des Capucines renamed "Rue des Citoyennes Françaises"). He sat down to write *Justine* in his spare time, as a *travail alimentaire* or pot-boiler. Meanwhile, however, religious services continued to be well attended by the workers.

Following the huge financial losses suffered in 1789, Paris tradesmen were grievously affected by the disappearance of rich customers; sectors that flourished under the revolution were the doctors, scientists and schoolteachers—and, of course, the printing industry, working overtime to print pamphlets, tracts and windy speeches. Meanwhile, the work of the Constitutional Assembly lost none of its momentum; at that point it was still very much a body of the bourgeois, driven by Mirabeau. Ominously Mirabeau predicted, however: "When you undertake to run a revolution, the difficulty is not to make it go—it is to hold it in check."

As 1790 began, the perceptive Gouverneur Morris foresaw that the "new order of things cannot endure . . . the present set [of leaders] must wear out in the course of the year."[9] In November 1790, Edmund Burke published his *Reflections on the French Revolution*. Given that he had been regarded as a "friend" of the revolution, his book came as a tremendous shock in France—particularly his dire warning that "in the groves" of revolution "at the end of every vista you see nothing but the gallows." Thomas Paine, the Englishman turned passionate American revolutionary, responded to this claim in *The Rights of Man*: "Whom has the National Assembly brought to the scaffold? None." It was not a good prophecy. Meanwhile, the émigré nobles abroad, notably across the Rhine, were busily plotting and planning the imminent overthrow of the revolution. Nothing was to prove more disastrous for the French monarchy.

IN FEBRUARY 1791, the Assembly debated a law that would regulate the movement in and out of France of suspected émigrés, and give itself powers to declare them outlaws. For opposing it, in the name of liberty, as "barbaric," Mirabeau came under virulent personal attack which left him profoundly shaken. It was in fact, as Simon Schama notes,[10] "*the* turning point of the French Revolution" when it "licensed itself as a police state."

Just a month later, after spending a demanding night with two dancers from the opera, Mirabeau was struck with the most violent intestinal pains. On 2 April he announced calmly to his physician: "I will die today. When one has come to that, all one can do is be perfumed, crowned with flowers, enveloped in music and wait comfortably for the sleep from which one will never awake." To Talleyrand he prophesied: "I carry away with me the last shreds of the monarchy." He was shocked that he had achieved nothing except "that he had contributed only to a vast demolition." It was true; it would not be the last time that sexual excess affected the course of French history, but with Mirabeau there expired France's—and certainly the King's—last best hope. Mirabeau had urged him to move out of Versailles and Paris to a reliable centre like Rouen; to rally the loyal, and summon the Assembly there; but he beseeched him not to consider crossing a national frontier, for "a king, who is the only safeguard of his people, does not flee before his people."

Unfortunately, neither the King nor the Queen had trusted the physically unprepossessing Mirabeau. They put more faith in the aristocratic and dashing Lafayette who, still only thirty-two in 1789, had already helped bring revolution to the American colonies and chase out the British. Partly because of Lafayette's extreme vanity (Mirabeau called him a "clowning Caesar"), the two had never been able to collaborate; working together, they might well have been able to govern France. Thus, not entirely through his own fault Louis lost what was probably his last chance. With the approach of Easter in 1791, Louis and Marie-Antoinette set off from the Tuileries for Saint-Cloud, in order to avoid having to receive communion from a "constitutional" priest. But just as the mob had forced them from Versailles that October 1789, it now compelled their return to the Tuileries. Lafayette proved powerless to dispel the mob with his own National Guard, over whose loyalties he now had little control, and he resigned in humiliation.

WITH MIRABEAU AND LAFAYETTE GONE, and the temperature of protest outside the Tuileries rising daily, sheer despair gripped the King. He now decided to escape from Paris, to join the émigré and coalition armies in Brussels that were mobilising against France, hoping to be helped by his wife's Austrian relatives. Dressed as a lackey, he made a getaway on the night of 20 June 1791. It was organised with absurd incompetence by Count Fersen, allegedly the lover of Marie-Antoinette. Louis left behind him a proclamation that denounced all the concessions he had made since October 1789; with pathetic realism, he appended, "What remains to the King, except the empty sham of royalty?"

Just short of the border, the King's coach was recognised and stopped in the "miserable little town" of Varennes in the Argonne, only a few miles from where his supporters were to meet him and convey the royal family to safety. In his diary Louis noted, laconically: "Left Paris at midnight, arrived and arrested at Varennes-en-Argonne at eleven in the evening."[11] A posse of 6000 armed peasants and National Guardsmen escorted the royal family back to Paris. At the Tuileries that night the perplexed and frightened little Dauphin, aged six, had a nightmare of being pursued by wolves and tigers about to devour him. Alone the Duc de Provence, Louis' brother, the future Louis XVIII, managed to escape to Brussels, and thence to England. Varennes was the end of the line for Louis, though he would linger on as a prisoner in his own palace for over a year. To the Assembly, where ever more violent enemies of the monarchy replaced Mirabeau, by his attempted flight the King was seen as having gone to join the nation's foreign enemies; even more unforgivably, the enemies of the revolution.

Yet Louis was not the first French king to have taken flight from his adversaries; Louis XIV with his mother had done so, and had survived and returned. Had his descendant succeeded, the royal family would have been spared the guillotine, but would the revolution have taken a less bloody course? Hearing of the flight a few days later, Gouverneur Morris noted in his diary: "This will produce some considerable Consequences. If they get off safe a War is inevitable, and if retaken it will probably suspend for some time all monarchical government in France." That was something of an understatement.

FROM NOW ON THE PACE of France's descent into the revolutionary abyss accelerated. In the political struggle to replace Mirabeau and his moderates, the Assembly became increasingly polarised. One faction was succeeded by another that was yet more extreme; monarchist Feuillants gave way to the Girondins (among them Pierre-Victurnien Vergniaud, who, later to be guillotined, made his immortal remark about the revolution, like Saturn, devouring its own children). They in turn were swept aside by the radical Montagnards—seated in the highest section of the Chamber; then came the Jacobins, the Cordeliers—and ultimately the purveyors of the Terror. With ever-mounting radicalism, power had passed from the preponderantly conservative, and royalist, middle classes to the Parisians, notably to the *sans-culottes,* who wore their egalitarian, breechless garb as a sign of proletarian defiance.

On 14 September 1791, a powerless Louis signed a constitution which rode roughshod over many of the principles of liberty and equality (franchise, for instance, was limited; and there was public censorship). Its work complete, the Constitutional Assembly was replaced on 1 October by the even more radical Legislative Assembly, as fears grew that the European monarchies would shortly move to crush the revolution. Abandoning the initial prospect of a constitutional monarchy, it became progressively more bellicose, persuading itself that external war would solve all internal problems. France had been there before, under many a monarch.

In August 1791, the crowned heads of Austria and Prussia met at Pillnitz near Dresden, joined by the hardline Comte d'Artois and other leading émigrés, to discuss Marie-Antoinette's appeal for intervention by her kinsmen and fellow sovereigns. The declaration they produced was extremely cautious; but the firebrands in the Assembly perceived their collaboration to be a clear threat. More aggressive was the alliance's stance the following February, demanding that France restore the German territories of Alsace which *le grand Louis* had grabbed a hundred years earlier. On 20 April 1792, Louis was coerced into going to the Assembly and, with tears in his myopically peering eyes, declaring war on the Emperor of Austria—his wife's nephew.* It was accompanied with an ultimatum for the removal of the émigré forces mustering on the Rhine. In Paris there was ever-mounting rage and hatred against the *autrichienne,* Marie-Antoinette. The declaration of war marked the beginning of the Revolutionary Wars; these in turn would lead directly into the Napoleonic Wars.

TWO MONTHS LATER, let in by compliant National Guards, a hideous and enraged mob of evil-smelling *sans-culottes* invaded and pillaged the Tuileries. They carried with them a grisly doll hanging from a gibbet, labelled "Marie-Antoinette à la lanterne." They placed a revolutionary's red cap on the helpless King's head, forcing him to drink with them. Over a torrid summer the quality of life of the royal prisoner deteriorated markedly. In July, Prussia's Duke of Brunswick heaped fuel on the flames by threatening the "total destruction" of Paris if the royal family were to suffer "even the slightest violence." The Assembly proclaimed "la patrie en danger" on 11 July, but the initiative now shifted to the insurrectionary Paris Commune. Throughout Paris, tables decked with the tricolour were set up to recruit a surge of volunteers. Then, in a fiercely hot August, the Tuileries were attacked again, this time much more violently. Forewarned, the royal family took refuge under the shelter of the Assembly, in its adjacent quarters. The Swiss Guards bravely

---

*Her brother, the reformist, gentle Emperor Leopold, had recently died. More specifically, his successor declared war on France, not as Emperor, but as King of Hungary and Bohemia.

defended the Palace, but were massacred to a man, their bodies stripped and mutilated. The Tuileries itself was reduced to a shambles of blood and smashed furniture, with drunken insurgents wiping bloody hands on velvet mantles they found in the King's wardrobe. Some dressed themselves in the Queen's finery. Guards were even murdered in the chapel where they had sought sanctuary. Clearly the King was no longer safe under the roof of the Assembly, so the Paris Commune, assuming the prerogatives of guardianship, transferred the royal family to the sombre Temple, in the Marais on the north-east fringes of Paris. This confinement truly marked the end of Louis' reign.

Fresh revolutionary leaders, extremists like Danton, Marat and Robespierre, began to emerge in the panic that swept the capital, as serious reverses at Longwy and Verdun opened the road to Paris to the invading Austrians. These defeats led in turn to the most ferocious wave of promiscuous killings—the September Massacres in which more than 1200 inmates of the prisons of Paris, women and children included, were hacked to death. Even harmless prostitutes were caught up and butchered by the drunken mob, together with many priests. One of the most unspeakable atrocities was committed against the Princesse de Lamballe, Marie-Antoinette's First Lady of the Bedchamber and close confidante. Handed over to the mob by the tribunal, her body was ripped open and her entrails mounted on a pike, her head on another. The mob then paraded the head outside the window where Marie-Antoinette was under house arrest.

THE CITY SEEMED SEIZED by a mindless and uncontrollable lust for blood. The Legislative Assembly dissolved itself on 21 September, giving way before the new National Convention, elected by universal (male) suffrage. Its seemingly hopeless task was to save the revolution. But that same day came the miraculous news that the newly raised Revolutionary Army, under Generals Dumouriez and Kellermann, had inflicted a decisive defeat on the Prussians at Valmy, not 150 miles east of Paris. The cannonade that enveloped the enemy from the rear was even heard, some claimed, in the city. Goethe, who watched the battle at Valmy, reckoned that he was witnessing the "beginning of a new era in history." As the future of the revolution now seemed assured, so the bitter factions battled for leadership. None of the former members of the Assembly was permitted to take part in the new Convention: "A subject for contemplation that was sombre, lugubrious, frightening, but sublime," in the words of Victor Hugo. Inexperienced, there remained for it "only one great mistake to make," declared the moderate, Pierre Ma-louet, "and we did not fail to make it." It was the decision to execute the King.

On 18 January 1793 Louis XVI, under the common name of "Louis Capet," was condemned to death, with no right of appeal. He was taken to the guillotine on the Concorde on 21 January 1793, a few yards from the empty pedestal where the fallen statue of his grandfather had once stood. After a terrible period of imprisonment in Philippe le Bel's grim Conciergerie and a risible trial, Marie-Antoinette followed him to the scaffold on 16 October; 30,000 troops had to be deployed to keep order that day. Under mysterious circumstances never resolved, the little Dauphin, in effect Louis XVII, died in the Temple (possibly of tubercu-losis) two years later.

WITH THE DEATH OF THE KING, the revolution found itself fight-ing a war on two fronts—England joined in the First Coalition (the first of many) against France, and the Vendée in the south-west erupted in open revolt. There was also, in reality, a third front—the internecine struggle between the revolutionaries themselves, as mutual suspicions of treason led one after the other to the guillotine. For the next three years—the most violent of the revolution—all central authority more or less ceased to exist. A month after the Tribunal sent for Marie-Antoinette, the turncoat Duc d'Orléans, "Philippe-Égalité," himself was sentenced to death. And so it went on.

In the Vendée, loyalist, Catholic and counter-revolutionary forces rose up, and were crushed with great brutality—though resistance and repression was to continue into 1795. In March and April 1793, the dread Revolutionary Tribunal, under the frightening Fouquier-Tinville, with his pale lips and low forehead, and the Committee of Public Safety were introduced. In June a Revolutionary Army was dispatched to police the countryside, bringing with them portable guillotines. In hiding near Bordeaux, Mme. de La Tour du Pin recalled such brutal excesses as when a husband was guillotined, his wife lashed to a pillory facing the guillotine, with her two young sons on either side. "People's Representa-tives" under twenty-six-year-old Tallien arrived from Paris with orders to impose taxes on produce of every kind. The penalty for refusing, death; the result, "an immediate breakdown in the supply of goods." Many bakers refused and were executed. A harmless-sounding body called the

Bordeaux Association of Young Men was rounded up—all were executed en masse, for implication with the royalists. In the churches of Bordeaux an insensate destruction of church ornaments was carried out. Mme. de La Tour also recorded an anti-religious parade "preceded by some horrible creature impersonating the Goddess of Reason," and culminating with "an enormous pyre, which burned all that magnificent treasure." Grim penalties were meted out to the peasantry for hiding *aristos,* as the guillotine made its "patriotic tours." (Eventually, in March 1794, the height of the Terror, Mme. de La Tour managed to escape to Boston on a tiny boat, in the riskiest of sea-crossings. Her father was guillotined the following month.)

Probably the total number of killings carried out in the Vendée exceeded the victims of the guillotine in Paris (2800 to an estimated 14,000 for all the provinces). There was a similar "purging" of Lyons by Collot d'Herbois, at Toulon by Barras, and at Nantes by Carrier, and the anarchic, often repulsive, "dechristianisation" practised by the loathsome Fouché—himself an ex-priest, later to re-emerge as Napoleon's Chief of Police. At Toulon in 1793, Fouché had gloated to a colleague in Paris, "Tonight we will execute 1213 insurgents. *Adieu*—tears of joy flow from my eyes." During the massacres in Lyons he was alleged to have been seen carrying a pair of human ears dangling from either side of his hat.

In the war against the external foe, at first the revolutionary armies suffered serious defeats. Then, under the able direction of Lazare Carnot (whom even Napoleon was to rate "the organiser of victory"), the *levée en masse* turned things round—not the least spur to success being the threat of the guillotine for any general who lost a battle. It showed a remarkable aptitude for requisitioning, "living off the land," unrealised by the posher, conventional monarchist armies of the Coalition. The winter of 1793–94 saw the enemy forced to retreat beyond the frontiers of France. Morale soared. When the French arrived in Antwerp, and in Holland, they aroused serious suspicions in London of a revival of the expansionist policies of Louis XIV. Soon it would be Germany and Italy under threat. As with Trotsky's Russia in 1919, success at home urged them on to spread the message of revolution across Europe. What they achieved was to inseminate fears that bound together the First Coalition—funded as it was by "English Gold."

Nevertheless, through 1793, economic crisis and the psychoses bred by the early defeats led to agitation for yet more repressive measures. The young Girondin supporter Charlotte Corday stabbed Marat in his bath and went to the guillotine. Marat's assassination launched another wave of purges; the following month Robespierre, the fanatical "sea-green incorruptible," a misogynist who dared to wear silk breeches, possessed of the fearful certitude of a man who believes himself to have a mission, assumed supreme power. In September the *loi des suspects,* ordering the arrest of anyone suspected of "disloyalty" to the revolution, was passed. It marked the beginning of the true Terror. "That which constitutes a republic," declared Saint-Just, "is the destruction of everything which opposes it."

The Republic Calendar, introduced on 5 October 1793 (but antedated to 22 September) was yet one more attempt by the revolutionaries to break with the past, and with Christian tradition. Twelve months named after seasons (*Brumaire* instead of November, month of mists; *Germinal* instead of April, month for sowing seeds) each had thirty days, divided into three *décades*—or weeks of ten days. The only thing it achieved was confusion, and it was repealed by Napoleon in 1806.

October saw the trial and execution of the moderate Girondin leaders. In March 1794, the extremist Hébert and his supporters, followed by the remaining "moderates"—Danton, Fabre d'Églantine and Camille Desmoulins—followed in the tumbrils as the wave of executions soared. The Concorde reeked of blood as the ferocious *tricoteuses,* true *Parisiennes,* howled for more. The anti-religious cult of the Supreme Being was instituted, but gradually opposition to the monstrous barrister Robespierre was mounting. Some witnesses testified to an extraordinary calmness of Paris during the Terror: "There are days when we do not seem at war any more than in the midst of a revolution." The Tuileries gardens were well kept up, and elegant carriages still seen in the streets. But when Gouverneur Morris returned to America, he summed up to Washington his experiences before he left: "I saw misery and affliction every day and all around me without power to mitigate or means to relieve."[12]

Abruptly the anti-religious orgies of destruction ground to a halt, just in time to save Notre-Dame from total destruction, though many of its medieval saints had been decapitated or mutilated, as had occurred throughout France. In a complete turnabout, Robespierre declared atheism to be "counter-revolutionary," quoting Voltaire's "If God did not exist, we would have to invent him."

On 8 Thermidor in the Revolutionary Calendar, or 26 July 1794,

Robespierre delivered a rambling speech calling for the punishment of more unspecified traitors. A point had been reached when even the most extreme of the Jacobin revolutionaries sickened of Robespierre's obsession with counter-revolutionary corruption and conspiracy, and his peremptory denunciations of both personal and public enemies. Along with his murderous Jacobin followers, including Saint-Just, he was arrested and executed two days later. Tallien and Barras, who practised the Terror themselves, were hailed as its conquerors.

WITH THERMIDOR AND THE EXECUTION of Robespierre, the reign of terror reached its peak, and it subsided with extraordinary swiftness. Within a month the Convention had dismantled all its central institutions. November saw the closing down of the feared Club des Jacobins. The *Maximum* (price fixing and food controls), that ultimate bastion of revolutionary government, was abolished on 24 December; laws against emigration were relaxed; and, symbolically, Marat's body was removed from the Panthéon on 8 February 1795. Bribery became commonplace, as surviving Girondins crept out of hiding during the period known as *la réaction thermidorienne,* which lasted over the next fourteen months. Theatres staged anti-Jacobin plays; the salons returned. So too did some royalist elements; gilded youths appeared in Paris wearing the green collar of the Vendée, with their hair cut provocatively short *à la victime*—in emulation of those about to mount the scaffold; and there were the *incroyables* dandies sporting heavy sticks with which they beat surviving Jacobins, and scandalising the country with their profligate demeanour. Yet the Thermidor revolt was essentially of the *petit bourgeois,* the clerks, rather than of the nobles.

On 5 October 1795, there was a bloody uprising in Paris in protest against the continued existence of the Convention, which had proved itself a feeble and incompetent body. It had to be put down by a vigorous young general called Napoleon Bonaparte, who gave the citizens a "whiff of grapeshot." This was the first time that the army had taken action against Paris since 1789. That month capital punishment was abolished, and a general amnesty declared for "anti-revolutionary acts." The Place de la Révolution, which had seen so much blood flow, was renamed Place de la Concorde. But suffering was exacerbated by a severe winter, which was followed by another uprising on 1 April 1795, when the Convention was invaded by people shouting for bread, and a return to the more liberal constitution of year II. In the provinces there were outbreaks of royalist counter-terror (called "La Terreur Blanche"), in the Lyonnais, the Rhône valley and the south. A bicameral legislature was now introduced; the lower chamber (the Conseil des Cinq Cents) would initiate legislation, the upper (the Conseil des Anciens) would ratify or reject it. Executive power was vested in five directors of the Directoire, meant to protect the Republic from extremism. But they had little authority; that was soon shown to rest with the army.

With the removal of controls, the economy collapsed. The cost of living doubled; countless families died of cold. Speculation was rampant; fortunes were made and lost overnight. A class of new rich danced the Paris nights away, where only recently Madame Guillotine had provided the entertainment. The departure of Terror was replaced by corruption on a large scale, and runaway inflation. Shoes worth 5 livres in 1790 cost 200 in 1795, and 2000 in 1797. Politically, the country veered from left to right. A series of coups and counter-coups were instigated by the directors themselves—with Barras, the Directoire's most corrupt and dissolute figure, emerging as its leader. There were royalist plots, and one abortive attempt at a working-class uprising in Paris. Its leader, François-Émile Babeuf, was sentenced to death, but committed suicide in 1797; thirty of his "Babouviste" followers were executed.

AFTER ALL THE KILLING, the destruction of the national heritage, all the misery, the Great Revolution had got rid of the *ancien régime*— temporarily; but would what replaced the monarchy rule France any better? And the *aristos* were soon to return. Perhaps the *tricoteuses* had executed the wrong king, in the wrong century? And what had actually been achieved? *Liberté?* Royal tyranny was at an end, but real freedom had already begun to look illusory. Revolution had improved the lives of the peasants; but wrecked agriculture. *Égalité?* The under-classes of Paris, who thought the revolution was their affair, ended up little better off than before. Only the bourgeois prospered. In the army, *égalité*, certainly, would make Napoleon's rise possible and enable him to build up the most fearful military machine Europe had yet seen. *Fraternité?* But what did that really mean? Since the revolution the country had been riven by factionalism and civil strife. Did it not leave a terrible latent instinct for similar violence—to explode again in 1830, 1848, 1871 and 1944? What about education? Science? Literature? Few men of literary renown had emerged, and the revolution guillotined the greatest French poet of the eighteenth century, André de Chénier (1762–94), three days before the fall of Robespierre and the end of the Terror. Yet it had—in the heartland of the enemy—given birth to Wordsworth's *The Prelude* (though he was soon to reverse his glowing sentiments about "the attraction of a country in romance!"). Music? Well, it did inspire what is still arguably the world's greatest national anthem.

Did the revolution make the French happier? Questionable. More prosperous? No; prosperity in depth would only be achieved, late in the day, with the Industrial Revolution, after the defeat of Napoleon and kick-started by the victorious English. In the meantime, the fresh avalanche that Napoleon Bonaparte was about to bring down upon them left Frenchmen little time, or breath, to consider whether the Great Revolution had left them truly better off—or not.

ELEVEN

# The Age of Napoleon

Oh, French people, how frivolous you are! You show us the leash and
you prove that you need to be led . . .

—*Mme. de Sade, letter to Gaspar Gaufridy*

B ECAUSE OF HIS BRILLIANT YOUTH and early death, one
tends to forget that Napoleon was born—in 1769—under the
reign of Louis XV and started his military career under Louis
XVI. At the peak of all his military successes, at Tilsit in 1807, he was still
only thirty-seven and he saw final defeat at Waterloo in his mid-forties.
Yet, if he was a child of the *ancien régime,* he was also very much a product of the revolution. Commissioned as a second lieutenant at the age of
sixteen, from the harsh military academy of Brienne, he made his first
real mark on military affairs at the siege of Toulon in 1793. The key naval
base was then held by an English fleet under the command of Admiral
Hood; Napoleon, as a young artillery captain, produced a winning strategy for the ragged French revolutionary forces besieging it. He became a
hero in the ranks, promoted to the dizzy rank of *général de brigade* when
still only twenty-four.

His next opportunity came when, in Paris on sick leave during the
autumn of 1795, he was called in by Barras to forestall the revolt of *Treiz-
ième Vendémiaire.* Barras, grateful but also nervous at having Napoleon
too near the centre of power, then appointed him—at the age of twenty-
seven—Commander-in-Chief of the French Army of Italy.

Ever since 1792, France had been at war with the First Coalition of
her enemies, bent upon reversing the revolutionary tide that seemed to

threaten all Europe. Lack of adequate preparation and incompetence among the new leaders of the revolutionary French forces had been matched by differences of interest and lethargy among the Allies; the stiff forms of eighteenth-century warfare, unaltered since the days of Frederick the Great, had encountered a new revolutionary fervour. The British bungled a landing at Quiberon Bay, while Prussia abandoned the First Coalition the following year. But, over-extended and unhelped by the dithering and corrupt rule of the Directoire, France's new "Army of the Sambre-and-Meuse" experienced a series of defeats across the Rhine at the hands of the Austrians.

Napoleon's mission in Italy was to wrest the initiative from the Austrians, entrenched in the north. He found French forces unpaid, hungry, poorly equipped and on the verge of mutiny. Stendhal cites the example of three officers who owned but one pair of shoes, one pair of breeches and three shirts between them. By his extraordinary capacity to inspire, Napoleon transformed the forces under him within a matter of days, and over the next eighteen months led them—with minimal resources—to a series of victories culminating in the momentous battle of Rivoli. By October 1797, he had defeated seven armies, captured 160,000 prisoners and over 2000 cannon, and chased the Austrians to within 100 miles of Vienna, to force his beaten enemy to sign a peace with France, and definitively end the wars of the First Coalition.

His star was irresistibly in the ascendant as he returned in triumph to Paris. "You are the hero of all France," the Directoire told him. "From that moment," Napoleon wrote after the first Italian campaign, "I foresaw what I might be. Already I felt the earth flee from beneath me, as if I were being carried into the sky." For France—and for Europe—it signified that the war party had triumphed. Following Napoleon's Italian victories, at the Treaty of Campo Formio (17 October 1797), France gained the Cisalpine Republic—which was to germinate the modern Italy—together with Belgium and control of the left bank of the Rhine. Henceforth the Belgians were "as much French as the Normans, the Alsatians, the people of Languedoc or Burgundy."

But could England ever be persuaded to accept a French Belgium? Of her foes of the First Coalition, only England remained at war with France, but with no weapon to strike at her across the Channel; so England contented herself by extending her empire at the expense of both enemy and allies. After Campo Formio, however, in exchange for a durable peace, she too declared herself ready to accept France's "natural frontiers." At last, revolutionary France was offered the security for which she had fought so passionately over the previous five years; it looked like a good time to make peace with England.

Success, though, went to the weak head of the Directoire. Back in 1790, the Assembly had declared the noble ideal: "The French nation renounces the undertaking of any war with a view to making conquests, and it will never use its forces against the liberty of any people." Inflated by Napoleon's achievements, however, the Directoire now let itself be enticed into a war of expansion and enrichment. It is instructive that France's wars of aggrandisement began, not under the Consulate or the Empire, but under the revolutionary movement. The new hero was now put in command of the Army of England, charged with carrying the war across the Channel. But the previous year, 1796, General Hoche with 14,000 troops had made an abortive descent on Ireland, disrupted by storms, and Napoleon considered it "too chancy to risk *La Belle France* on the throw of a dice." Instead, he placed in the mind of the Directoire the daring idea of striking at British sea-power in the eastern Mediterranean—the key to England's empire and trade in the Orient.

With England's Pitt still under the misapprehension that he was heading for Ireland, Napoleon sailed for Egypt. With him he took as reading matter the Koran, to reinforce his hopes of setting the Muslim world afire against England—and also the *Campaigns of Julius Caesar.* (This and other similar works were being studied at the same time by an unknown young general then stationed in India, Arthur Wellesley, later Duke of Wellington. Had the Egyptian enterprise succeeded, the two arch-enemies might well have met and fought it out at a much earlier date than they did.) But Egypt was to prove a disastrous campaign. The French won repeatedly on land, notably at the battle of the Pyramids, but a junior English admiral, Horatio Nelson, swept the seas at Aboukir Bay and the Nile. Fighting moved up into Palestine and the Levant. In his massacre of prisoners at Jaffa, Napoleon revealed himself at his most ruthless and cruel. Meanwhile, this twenty-nine-year-old—a man of so many contradictions—had recently issued inspiring instructions for the creation of an Institute of Science and Art in occupied Cairo. It was typical that to accompany his military campaign Napoleon took with him Champollion, the Egyptologist. He lost the war in Egypt, but discovered the Rosetta Stone; though many looted treasures of antiquity went down with the French flagship, *l'Orient,* at Aboukir Bay, lost for ever in the sands of the Nile delta.

Although Napoleon himself seemed immune to the plague that decimated his men, the revolutionary General Kléber growled that he was "the kind of general who needed a monthly income of ten thousand men." Encouraged by British naval successes, in 1798 a Second Coalition was formed against the French, comprising England, Naples, Austria, Russia and Turkey. But Napoleon abandoned his battered army in the Middle East upon the news that at home the Directoire was in political trouble. Dodging Nelson's patrols, he landed secretly back at Fréjus on 9 October 1799. In Paris, he found the Directoire tottering. After a brief moment of historic indecision, when it was not certain whether his grenadiers would support him or arrest him, until Murat shouted "Vive la République!" and "Vive Bonaparte!," on 9 November (18 Brumaire in the Revolutionary Calendar) Napoleon effected a *coup d'état* that ended the rule of the Directoire. "Hypocrites, intriguers!" he castigated them, promising that he would "abdicate from power the instant the Republic is free from danger." Of course, he would not. The revolution was over; France had a new master.

AT FIRST, Napoleon made himself one of three Consuls (the others being Sieyès and Ducos, its two *illustres inconnus*). The terminology of Consul was significantly borrowed from ancient Rome, but Napoleon swiftly found an excuse to establish himself as First Consul, with a tenure of ten years and dictatorial powers greater than those of Louis XIV at the height of his glory. It was perfectly clear that "France had not been raped; she had yielded." Tactfully, the new master now dressed himself in civilian clothes to stress the fact that, rather than rule as a general, his priorities would be domestic.

The war, however, continued. Consolidated in power politically, Napoleon set off once more to chastise the Austrians in Italy. By transporting an army of 50,000 secretly over the 8000-foot Great Saint Bernard Pass, still covered in snow in the May of 1800, he struck the unwary enemy from the rear. June brought stunning victory at Marengo, a copy-book classic of manoeuvre combined with opportunism. The *coup de grâce* was administered by Moreau's victory at Hohenlinden in December. Although the following summer, General Abercromby's British expeditionary force was to expel Napoleon's abandoned Army of the Orient from Egypt, the Second Coalition had now collapsed in ruins.

Military supremacy belonged to Napoleon. In 1801 and 1802, the Austrians agreed to retreat from northern Italy, and a smarting England agreed to part with most of her recent colonial acquisitions. A grateful France confirmed Napoleon as Consul for life—in a plebiscite, by a huge majority of 3.5 million to 8000. For the first time in a decade, there was even a possibility of lasting peace among the battered European nations, but this was more of a hopeful desire than a realistic end. As Napoleon had written prophetically to his lieutenant and potential rival, Moreau, during the more ecstatic moments of 1800: "Greatness has its beauties, but only in retrospect and in the imagination."

ON NAPOLEON'S RETURN to Paris following his victory at Marengo, the city went wild. A dense crowd converged on the Tuileries where he and Josephine had installed themselves, and he had to show himself several times on the balcony "amid a tempest of cries of joy." According to the remarkable French historian Laborie,* "never since Henri IV, had a conqueror been so triumphally fêted, not even Condé, Turenne or Villars."[1]

The Marengo campaign would give Napoleon nearly five years of peace, the longest in his career, to devote to restoring and reforming the social fabric of France. There was much to be done; the country was bankrupt, but imbued with the singular urge to reinvent itself. As Balzac was to explain several decades later, "The overall longing for peace and tranquillity, that everyone felt after the violent upheavals, produced a total obliteration of the most sinister prior occurrences. History aged very quickly, its ageing accelerated by ever new and burning interest."[2] The last days of the Directoire, in reaction against the Terror, were probably among the most dissipated in the city's history. Suddenly the city appeared to discover, or rediscover, "a moneyed upper bourgeoisie clad in Greco-Roman clothing," and—for the women—very diaphanously transparent clothing at that. With it revolutionary morals had gone out of the window.

Returning to France in 1800 after seven years' self-exile, the writer Chateaubriand had been deeply shocked by the ravages that he found

---

*Laborie's eight-volume study, *Paris sous Napoléon,* was published between 1900 and 1913, and incomplete by the beginning of the First World War. Written a century after the events it describes, it reads with remarkable freshness and little prejudice. A mine of information for scholars of the period, in England it appears to have been little read; the set I borrowed out of London Library appears to have lain there dormant for the best part of a century, its pages still uncut. Finding it, I felt a little like the Prince in *La Belle au Bois Dormant.*

still left by the Revolution, particularly in its excesses of atheism: "the ruinous castles, the belfries empty of bells, the graveyards with never a cross and the headless statues of saints." At Saint-Denis, the resting place of French monarchs from time immemorial, tombs had been defaced, decapitated or totally destroyed, their royal contents sacrilegiously scattered. In Paris, though horribly vandalised, Notre-Dame had escaped by a whisker—scheduled for destruction, its stones were actually put up for auction. In Paris the great houses of the nobility and the bourgeoisie had been pillaged, with barely a courtyard gate still left on its hinges.

Although the massacres perpetrated on the royalist Vendée far exceeded the Terror in Paris,[3] apart from the destruction, human as well as physical, the mess left behind by the revolutionary Commune would have daunted any lesser man than Napoleon, but he wasted no time in pursuing a grand reform of French society, from the top to the bottom. He found religion in post-revolutionary France in a state of chaos, if not jeopardy. In some regions, "refractory priests" were still hiding out as outlaws, while in Paris each church, renamed "Temples of Concord," of "Hymen," etc., had its own cult. Under the Revolution and the Directoire, marriage had been a simple affair, the couples usually dispatched in batches at "decadal" temples to the accompaniment of derision from layabout onlookers. With divorce made equally simple, marriage became regarded as a short-term obligation. "What could be more immoral," declared a contemporary, "than to allow a man to change his wife like a coat, and a woman to change her husband like a hat?"[4] It was the ambition of Bonaparte, the good Corsican Catholic, to make the family once more the pivot of society, so the marriage tie was encouraged to regain its former significance. An exception was made for speedy marriages of soldiers on leave from the front (under almost everything Napoleon did, one could discover a pragmatic military relevance). Of course, Napoleon himself had numerous love affairs, but—true Mediterranean to the core—was loath to tolerate them in others.

NAPOLEON ALLOCATED some £4 million for the restoration of churches, and had the synagogues reopened. He was influenced less by architectural values than by an appreciation of the underlying importance of the Catholic Church when it came to winning over the French nation. In place of the Revolution's phobic anti-religious zeal in the last years of the old century came a marked religious revival. As ever sensitive to the popular mood, Napoleon healed the wounds that still divided

France with the brilliant gesture of a Concordat with Pope Pius VII. It was an integral part of his programme to enlist every element of French life behind him. For similar reasons he supported a liberal-minded emancipation of French Jews; stating at the siege of Acre, a hundred and fifty years before the State of Israel was declared, that Jewry had "the right to a political existence as much as any other nation." Speaking to ultra-Catholic Vendéean leaders when First Consul, he made his thinking abundantly clear: "I intend to re-establish religion, not for your sake but for mine."

The Concordat re-established the Roman Catholic Church as "the religion of the greater majority of Frenchmen"; but at the same time it clearly demarcated its powers. It removed the main grievances that had sustained civil war in the Vendée, and helped ease Napoleon into the sympathies of Catholics both at home and in other soon-to-be subject nations. Although rejected by Louis XVIII's government-in-exile, the Concordat was supported by most of the returning aristocracy, including Chateaubriand who found a Paris where "the émigré was returning and talking peaceably with the murderers of his nearest and dearest."

On Easter Day 1802, Napoleon sealed his diplomatic coup of the Concordat with a grand *Te Deum* sung at Notre-Dame, where he was received under the portico by the recently nominated archbishop. Cynics noted that, of those present, only two defrocked priests, Talleyrand and Fouché, knew properly how to genuflect. Others wondered if all military guards were there solely to "prevent God the Father from being burgled!" But Napoleon presented himself as the champion of old France, a hero-leader who would restore its values and repair the depredations of Robespierre. The fall of the Terror and its replacement by the inept and corrupt Directoire left a vacuum that was moral, military and political—and into it Napoleon slid easily. From St. Helena he would admit: "I had but one goal: to reunite all, reconcile all, have all hatreds forgotten, bring everyone together, gather together so many divergent elements and compose them anew in one whole: one France and one *patrie*."

IN MARCH 1802, Napoleon concluded the Peace of Amiens with England. What the English uncharitably dubbed "the peace which passeth all understanding" heralded for both France and Napoleon a halcyon period. English tourists, and two-thirds of the House of Lords poured across the Channel in their tens of thousands to spend willingly and savour the abandoned joys of post-Directoire Paris. Tickets could be purchased at Charing Cross for £5.

It was during this fleeting period of peace that Napoleon, acting with the same speed and remarkable concentration of energy that characterised his military operations, established the majority of the civil reforms that were to provide France with a new constitution, set her finances in order and produce a durable modern political and social structure for France.

After coming to terms with the Church, Napoleon abolished the savage Law of Hostages, which had made the illegal return of émigrés punishable by death. In 1802, he proclaimed a general amnesty, mindful again of gaining the support of the monarchists for his future plans of continental conquest. Within a year over 40,000 families returned. The titles of *Madame* and *Mademoiselle* once more replaced the appellation of *citoyenne,* with all its fearful associations. The revolutionary calendar disappeared in favour of the old Gregorian Calendar, so that "18 Brumaire, An VIII" once more became 9 November 1799; and traditional festivals like Christmas and Easter returned.

In May 1802, Napoleon instituted the new award of the Légion d'Honneur—a new society, he reasoned, needed a new elite, an aristocracy not of birth, but of merit. Boundless in his own ambition, Napoleon derided it in others, remarking cynically of the Légion: "it is by such baubles that one leads men by the nose!" Yet under the Empire no fewer than 48,000 *rubans rouges* were distributed, denoting the Légion. The cynics may have derided the institution as "hanging by a thread," nevertheless it would continue to be a source of power and influence for even Republican regimes long after Napoleon's demise.

THOSE BRIEF TWO YEARS of the Peace of Amiens, in retrospect, certainly seem like one of the nation's Golden Ages—comparable to the advent of Henri IV, or Louis XIV after the Frondes. For Napoleon and Josephine personally it would rate as the "happiest time of their lives." They had their idyllic retreat at Malmaison, an hour's drive out of Paris (about the same now). And they had each other; in the longest time they would spend together. At Malmaison also Napoleon had a better chance of keeping the voracious sexual appetite of the hot-blooded Creole under control; she could even keep a reasonable tab on his passing infidelities. Anyway, she loved it; Malmaison was Josephine's "creation and her paradise."*

In the country at large Napoleon's rule seemed unshakeably established, with the constitution of 1802 leading all wires back to his one pair of hands. He had the authority of a monarch, but there was still no arrangement for the succession. Already in December 1800, the fact that the First Consul might be less than immortal had been suggested when, on his way to the opera, he had narrowly escaped the explosion of a powerful mine in the Rue Niçaise which killed several bystanders. Then, at the beginning of 1804, two further plots were uncovered; one led by a Vendée royalist from Brittany called Georges Cadoudal, the other by two generals, Pichegru and Moreau. Cadoudal (with whom the British government had rashly connived) was swiftly picked up by that master counter-spy, Fouché. Cadoudal's involvement in the Rue Niçaise bomb was revealed, and he was executed on 25 June 1804. Pichegru died in prison, garrotted by his own neckerchief; while Moreau, as the popular hero of the battle of Hohenlinden, was permitted to disappear into exile, thereby removing one of the few potential rivals to Napoleon.

The Cadoudal plot provided Napoleon with just the excuse he needed to present himself with an imperial crown, thereby ensuring the hereditary succession of the Napoleon dynasty; but it was also to lead to his most deplorable miscalculation, the murder of the Duc d'Enghien. A fairly distant, and disinterested potential claimant to the Bourbon throne, d'Enghien was an attractive young man of thirty-two who made occasional secret visits to the German state of Baden, in the pursuit of love. On one such visit he was kidnapped on Napoleon's orders, and brought to France (along with his inseparable dog).† After an arbitrary trial on charges of conspiracy, he was summarily shot, in the fortress of Vincennes. Totally innocent, d'Enghien was even unaware that any conspiracy against the First Consul existed. The shots rang around Europe; in the famous phrase attributed (wrongly) to Talleyrand, whose own hands were far from clean, the deed was "worse than a crime, it was a blunder." Certainly no other single act did Napoleon more harm, showing as it did what pointless evil this glamorous hero was also capable of. Combined with his forthcoming coronation, the greatest *spectacle*

---

*So it remains today, though (as of 2002) the roses seem neglected, and some disrepair hangs over Malmaison. Its shutters removed (why?), the frontage looks bleak, reflecting the general air of sadness.

†The faithful dog in fact somehow survived, to become adopted by King Gustavus IV of Sweden; on its collar read the inscription "I belong to the unhappy Duc d'Enghien."

Napoleonic Paris was ever to see, the two events would provoke a Third Coalition against France. "We have achieved more than we intended," declared the royalist conspirator Georges Cadoudal, with acid humour as he courageously faced the scaffold in June 1804. "We came to give France a king; we have given her an emperor."


EACH OF NAPOLEON'S STREAM of important reforms between 1799 and 1804 incremented his personal power. Though heir to the revolution, Napoleon was however in no way himself a revolutionary, rather a reformer and a moderniser prepared to graft innovations on to the stock of both the *ancien régime* and the few sensible benefits bequeathed by the revolution. In February 1800, the various departments were placed under the charge of prefects, the following year the metric system was introduced, and in 1802 a new national police force was raised. France was to become more tightly centralised than ever it had been even under the Roi Soleil. Prior to Napoleon, the country had been bedevilled by the existence of 360 separate local codes; he now set about the immense task of unifying them into one set.

By 1804 the *Code Civil* (later, and better, known as the *Code Napoléon*) was voted through the legislature. Though comprising over 2000 articles it took only four years to complete. It remains Napoleon's most solid and enduring achievement, and is still largely operative today—not only within the EU. Regulating virtually every function of life, the *Code* insisted on the equal division of property among sons, which in fact did more than the revolution to fragment the big estates. Reflecting Napoleon's own very Corsican disbelief in feminine equality, heavy emphasis was laid on the authority of the male, removing many of the contractual rights that women had enjoyed under the *ancien régime.* The *père de famille* was granted almost dictatorial rights over the family, including the right to imprison his child for a month, while illegitimates were barred from inheritance. Wives were forbidden to give, sell or mortgage property and could acquire it only with their husband's written consent. In this respect Frenchwomen were better off under Louis XVI, or even Louis XIV.

The Civil Code, which became law in 1804, was followed by the Codes of Civil Procedure, of Commercial Law, of Criminal Procedure and the Penal Code. All embodied the key achievements of the revolution—national unity and the equality of citizens—and were to survive as the basis for most civil law throughout the modern world. Napoleon may be accused of being an opportunist, but he carried with him from Corsica no burden of class distinction or privilege, which was to help him immeasurably in founding his own elite regardless of whether they were former aristocrats, revolutionaries or of the humblest proletarian stock. In this sense, he did succeed in uniting France—to his own advantage. Of the three democratic institutions nominally governing France, under the Consulate the Tribunate could discuss proposed legislation, but not vote on it; in the Legislative Body it was voted on but not discussed; while the Senate came to have no powers at all.

UNDER THE *ANCIEN RÉGIME* education in France had resided largely in the hands of village priests and religious orders. Napoleon's views on education were simply stated, essentially traditionalist, and certainly non-revolutionary. At a session of the Council of State in 1804–5, he declared:

> the only good education we have met with is that of the ecclesiastical bodies . . . An *Ignoranti* friar knows enough to tell a working man that this life is but a passage. If you take faith away from the people you end up producing highway robbers.[5]

In 1795, the Directoire had introduced a new secular system on to which stem, accepting the best and rejecting the worst, Napoleon grafted, in 1802, one of the most favoured and enduring of all his reforms—the *lycées,* or state secondary schools. Principles were applied similar to those by which Napoleon had obtained uniformity in his artillery pieces, with education organised as for the training of an army. In all France's secondary schools, for instance, it could be reckoned that the same Latin passage was being translated at the same hour. Pupils would be summoned to recitations by drum-roll—and remarkably, a century later the drums were still rolling in unison across the country.

The system provided a steady flow of military and administrative cadres essential to the Napoleonic war machine. At the same time, the high-grade École Polytechnique, founded by the Convention in 1794, was transformed into a military college for gunners and engineers, and state funds were allocated to the École Normale Supérieure, likewise initiated by the Convention and still today the breeding ground of a particular genre of French intellectual leadership. For all the talk about *égalité,* it was all extensively elitist; by the last year of Empire there were still only thirty-six *lycées* with 9000 pupils in all France, and most of them came from the middle and upper classes.

Paris's Sorbonne University swiftly felt the new broom. Under the revolution, the great university, founded by Abelard and expanded by Richelieu, had received rough treatment from the revolutionaries on account of its clerical orientations. Closed down, the Sorbonne remained empty until Napoleon took a hand in 1806. Then he established the Académie de Paris, the Faculté des Lettres, des Sciences et de Théologie in its buildings. Revitalised, the Sorbonne thrived anew.

Typical of Napoleon's fervent intervention in cultural matters that went *pari passu* with military campaigning was his "living encyclopaedia" of scientists, geographers, orientalists, chemists, zoologists and artists, 160 strong. They included Monge, the great mathematician, and Champollion, the Egyptologist, whom Napoleon had taken with him on the expedition to Egypt. Equally typical had been his tireless touring of provincial France, during the Peace of Amiens, to encourage the manufacturers of cities like Lyons, Rouen, Elbeuf and Le Havre, as had been the many occasions when he presided in person over meetings of the Conseil d'État to work out the new Civil Code.

By the end of 1804, Napoleon had concentrated every aspect of power within his own hands. Now his immediate goal could be the imperial crown, and those guarantees of succession it would carry with it.

THE CORONATION of 2 December, a day of intense cold in Paris, was an extraordinary mixture of *spectacle* and farce. There was a most brisk sale of rosaries in Paris—one operator made ff40,000 that January alone; while the police estimated that some 2 million persons were present in the capital for the event. Acting with a grandeur befitting the status that he had already acquired in Europe, and in consequence of the Concordat, Napoleon had managed to bully the Pope, Pius VII, to come to Paris to officiate in person and bestow the imperial crown on him at Notre-Dame. Upon his arrival Napoleon alternately cajoled and threatened the frail old man, weary from his long journey. Napoleon's relations with the Pope would always be paradoxical; he would despoil him of Vatican treasures, intern him, and get himself excommunicated, yet remain the official master of France's clergy.

The whole façade of Notre-Dame had been clad with a cardboard Gothic exterior for the occasion, provoking the comment from a wit that "so much work has been done that God Himself would lose his bearings!" As he ascended the steps to an immense throne, Napoleon is said to have murmured to his brother: "Joseph, if only our father could see us now!" Napoleon elected to place the imperial crown on his own head, as Josephine knelt before him in obeisance. There were moments of dissonance in this scene of high majesty. Between the altar and the throne, an altercation broke out between Josephine and her jealous Bonaparte sisters-in-law carrying her train. The *mauvaises langues,* too, whispered that the imperial coach was over-the-top; that in the attire he had chosen, the Emperor, his short, plump body encased in a bejewelled costume inspired by the huge frame of François I, ludicrously resembled the King of Diamonds. Returning to the Tuileries, now no longer Bonaparte but henceforth Napoleon I, the Emperor encountered an unfortunate omen. The weighty crown toppled off the coach.

In a state of *post coitum triste,* the new Emperor gloomed to his secretary the following day: "I have come too late; men are too enlightened; there is nothing great left to do." This was not, however, a view generally shared by the denizens of a Paris bemused by the "bread and circuses" feat *par excellence,* or by European leaders alarmed by this extraordinary fantasia of power and sheer machismo. There were critics, too: in Vienna, when Beethoven learnt that Napoleon had proclaimed himself emperor, in a rage he scratched out his name from the dedication of the *Eroica.* Napoleon, he is said to have exclaimed, was "nothing more than an ordinary mortal"; he would, Beethoven predicted, "trample on all human rights . . . [and] become a tyrant." It was a fair prediction.

AS NAPOLEON now had vested himself in the pomp and circumstance of power comparable only to that of the Roman Caesars, of Charlemagne and of the Holy Roman Emperors, he stood at his zenith both physically and intellectually. Still only thirty-five, "Le Petit Caporal" or "Le Tondu," as the army called him affectionately, was beginning to show just a few signs of thickening; his cheeks were fuller, the waistband of his breeches tighter, his complexion sallower. Already he had been cuckolded by Josephine (and vice versa). Even at Malmaison he preferred to live in the martial simplicity of the camp. He was no gourmet; fifteen minutes, he always said, was enough for any meal—and about the same for making love. He condemned sexual love as "harmful to society and to the individual happiness of men," and was known to have derided it as merely "an exchange of perspirations"; yet he was incapable himself of avoiding both its entanglements and torments of jealousy.

There was hardly a woman in his entourage he did not attempt to seduce, including wives of his generals, and he could be relentless when rebuffed. He was attracted by the certainties of mathematics and sciences of the reason, while mistrusting anything to do with human passions; yet he could never quite escape from being a child of the Romantic Movement himself. He was bred on the egalitarian ideals of the revolution, but was to found a new aristocracy and a new despotism of his own. "The terror he inspires is inconceivable," wrote his enemy Mme. de Staël. "One has the impression of an impetuous wind blowing about one's ears when one is near that man."

As for his relationships with his soldiers, perhaps the single most remarkable feature was the total dedication he was able to exact; the *grognards* would march to Moscow and back for him—and then, once again, pick up their muskets during the Hundred Days. There were manifest rewards; it being no exaggeration to say that every soldier of the Grande Armée marched with a marshal's baton in his knapsack. Only two of twenty-six Napoleonic marshals had noble antecedents (the Revolution, partly, had seen to that) and by the time of Austerlitz in 1805 half of the officer corps had risen from the ranks. The flamboyant cavalry genius, Murat, was the twelfth son of a humble Cahors innkeeper; Ney, "the bravest of the brave," was the son of a cooper; Masséna, one of Napoleon's finest marshals, was the orphaned son of a grocer who had gone to sea as a cabin-boy; Bernadotte rose from the ranks to become, eventually, King of Sweden; Lefebvre, whose wife was a washer-woman who proudly looked and played the part, had also risen from the ranks. They were young, insofar as Bonaparte reckoned that no commander had any gumption left by the time he was forty-five.[6] And the same considerations applied throughout his civil administration.

At the other end of the social scale, there were also great (and often scandalous) opportunities for self-enrichment. Typical of both the regime and the man, Talleyrand was permitted to make a fortune by buying up bonds, knowing of the stipulations of a treaty that these would subsequently be honoured. There was hardly ever a worse case of "insider-trading." Meanwhile, by 1804 the bourgeoisie owned approximately twice as much land in parts of northern France as it had done in 1789.

Napoleon had thus contrived to gain successively the loyalties of most elements of French life: the Catholics, the bureaucracy, the peasantry and the bourgeoisie. With the old aristocracy his policy of reconciliation had been less successful, and it had continued to keep a mistrustful distance—at least until Napoleon's staggering successes began to have a look of permanence; much in the same way that the German upper classes were to react to Corporal Hitler. So Napoleon created his own Empire nobility of 1000 barons, 400 counts, 32 dukes and 3 princes (not to mention a handful of kings from his own family). "The Government," he declared in one of his earliest proclamations, "neither wants, nor recognises parties any more, seeing in France only Frenchmen."[7]

INDISPENSABLE TO NAPOLEON in all matters were two ex-priests; Joseph Fouché, thoroughly odious, unscrupulous but eminently efficient police chief, and the notorious Charles Maurice de Talleyrand de Périgord. Fouché started life in the Church; typically, although he had ruthlessly suppressed a revolt against Robespierre in Lyons, when Thermidor arrived Fouché acted with equal zeal against Robespierre and the Jacobins. Under the Directoire he had worked as a spy for Barras in Holland. Operating always like a mole, underground, Fouché was made Napoleon's dreaded Chief of Police after Brumaire, and stayed there for the next decade. In 1810, Napoleon sacked him for holding secret peace talks with the British. After the retreat from Moscow in 1812, Napoleon, no longer trusting him to remain behind in Paris working behind his back, dispatched Fouché first to Prussia, then as ruler of Illyria. But Fouché was reinstated as police chief at the beginning of the Hundred Days. Napoleon saw him and his ubiquitous intelligence service as "living in everybody's boots"; Fouché was essential to him in both his rise and maintenance of power.

Fouché and Talleyrand, the greatest and the wiliest diplomat and politician of them all, were forever coupled by Chateaubriand's devastating remark, as the two entered the room, arm in arm, at the time of the Restoration: "A vision of Vice supported by Crime." One Scottish peer thought Talleyrand was "the most disgusting individual I ever saw. His complexion is that of a corpse considerably advanced in corruption."[8] When death finally overtook him, Louis-Philippe's reaction to the news was: "But there is no judging from appearances with Talleyrand!"

Talleyrand had escaped the Terror by fleeing to America as a royalist exile. There, working in a Philadelphia bookshop, his patron, Saint-Méry, as a sideline to books had introduced contraceptives to the grateful Americans. In his two years in America, Talleyrand took on board the useful lesson that the young United States remained at heart still more English than not; therefore, in the event of renewed war with England, France would have to lean over backwards to prevent America from falling into the enemy camp.

It was against the background of such sensible advice that Bonaparte was persuaded to transact the Louisiana Purchase, thereby presenting Washington with the best bargain—at $15 million—in US history and roughly doubling the size of the nation. Talleyrand was appointed Minister of Foreign Affairs by the Directoire on his return from America in 1797, aged forty-three. In the well-chosen words of his biographer, Duff Cooper, the difference between Talleyrand and Fouché was that for the former "politics meant the settlement of dynastic or international problems discussed in a ball-room or across the dinner-table; for Fouché the same word meant street-corner assassination, planned by masked conspirators in dark cellars."[9]

FOR ALL NAPOLEON'S ACCRETION of power by 1805, alas for imperial grand design in the words of Winston Churchill "the tourist season was short." The Peace of Amiens was to turn out to be little more than a brief unnatural truce which both sides sought to vitiate, while laying the blame on the other. Soon France and England were at war again. Already in the year preceding his coronation, Napoleon had been massing barges on the Channel coast with the intention of invading that implacable, relentless enemy—Pitt the Younger's England. Admiral Villeneuve and the French Navy were sent doubling off to the West Indies in an attempt to lure the Royal Navy away from the Channel. However, beaten to the trick by a vigilant Nelson, Villeneuve let Napoleon down. So, at the end of August 1805, he switched plans with precipitate speed, left the Camp of Boulogne, and marched eastwards.

There the Austrians and Russians, backed by a hesitant Prussia, were combining forces to attack; but with incredible speed Napoleon struck out across Europe to forestall them. At every turn he outwitted and outfought the dazed Allies with their cumbersome armies. Morale in the Grande Armée was never higher: but the risks for it, heavily outnumbered and far from its bases, were enormous. First he defeated the Austrians at Ulm; at Austerlitz on 2 December, Napoleon, however, carried off his finest victory, one of the greatest in the history of warfare. From there he would head north, still further into the dangerous depths of Europe, to crush the recalcitrant Prussians at Jena and Auerstädt the following year.

But, as with most dictators, these triumphs would only demand the next; as Wellington once remarked of him, Napoleon was like a cannon-ball—he had to keep in motion, as the moment he ceased it was all over. The quest for *la gloire* led him into Poland, in pursuit of the not-quite-defeated Russians, masters in the art of fighting withdrawals—and into the arms of Marie Walewska in Warsaw. The campaigns of 1805–7, Napoleon's most triumphant, ended with the bloody battles of Eylau and Friedland in distant East Prussia. Had he but realised it, those two battles were harbingers of the future; the "glory days" were over.

What looked like a decisive, definitive conclusion came with the Peace of Tilsit, signed on the raft midstream on the River Niemen, the very frontier of Russia, between Napoleon and all the rulers of continental Europe, whose armies he had defeated one after the other. It was indeed a historic, head-turning moment. Yet one nation was absent, and uncowed—England. The month before Napoleon had trounced his land-borne enemies at Austerlitz, so unseen far to his rear Nelson and his "distant, storm-beaten ships, upon which the Grand Army never looked"[10] were winning at Trafalgar the sea battle that eventually would lead to the destruction of all Napoleon's imperial hopes.

DOMESTICALLY, THE DISASTER at Trafalgar was obscured by the sequences of news from eastern Europe. In fact, the victories of the Grande Armée had come only just in time to halt, and reverse, a major disaster at home.

The French economic and financial system had still not recovered from the Revolution. The wheels of commerce turned but they were still shaky. Under the Directoire, taxes had been restructured and—for almost the first time—actually collected with remarkable efficiency. The Banque de France was established in 1800, and granted total control over the national debt and the issue of paper money. Industrial prosperity was stimulated by ubiquitous government intervention, and various innovations of social welfare were encouraged, though along largely paternalistic lines. Nevertheless, trade unions were ruthlessly stamped on as "Jacobin" institutions, or as diseases exported by the insidious British. Unemployment was kept at a low level, but labour was hard and the hours long. In summer, builders worked from 6 a.m. to 7 p.m.; the life expectancy of bakers was under fifty, and until 1813 children under ten were still employed in the mines. From 1803 onwards every working man had to carry a registration book stamped by his employer, without which he was treated as a vagabond. When it came to litigation it was always the employer's word that was accepted. In rural France, the average peasant was not much affected by either the Consulate or the Empire. The great roads built by Napoleon radiated out towards frontiers with distinct military purposes, and did little to bring the countryside into contact with the modern world.

At least, both peasant and urban working classes seem to have been better fed than they were before 1789, partly thanks to strict government controls placed on corn exports and price levels. Then, in 1805, the French economy plummeted. A poor harvest made bread prices soar, the budget was in deficit and huge manufacturing stocks piled up. There was serious unemployment, which recruitment for the Grande Armée only partially sopped up. That autumn, just as Napoleon stood on the threshold of his greatest military successes, Paris was rocked by the collapse of the Banque Récamier. The bank suspended withdrawals, resulting in a sequence of bankruptcies and industries brought to a standstill.

The shock at the Banque Récamier failure was immense; the bank was a rocklike institution, the elderly Jacques Récamier a tower of respectability. Indeed, it was almost certainly only by the success of Napoleon's triumphs on distant battlefields that Paris escaped serious disorders. After Austerlitz, miraculously the economy appeared to recover with government bonds rising dizzily from 45 to 66 per cent. The winter of 1806–7 continued with difficulty and hardship as the English naval blockade hit not only Paris but cities as far away as Lyons. Then, on 7 July 1807, cannon thundering out from the Invalides announced the triumphal peace that Napoleon had imposed at Tilsit. Once again the stock exchange rose dramatically—but artificially.

Emulating Louis XIV after the Peace of Nijmegen in 1678, the Emperor bestowed upon himself the title "le Grand" following Tilsit. Indeed, he gazed down on an empire that stretched from the Pyrenees to the Niemen, ruled over either by puppet sovereigns or by members of his own clan—an empire greater than anything achieved by Louis XIV, greater (at least, in appearance) even than the world of Charlemagne. Ruling a France intoxicated with glory, after Tilsit the Emperor was no longer in a mood to listen to anybody. He closed down the Tribunate. Talleyrand resigned, to offer his services, questionably, to Napoleon's enemy, the Tsar. He was replaced by the docile Minister of the Interior, Champagny. Thus Napoleon became surrounded by sycophants, a sure sign of the corruption of power.

The Peace of Tilsit seemed to give him endless options, but would the peace last, any more than the Peace of Amiens had? Seldom had peace terms been harsher; the defeated nations would not accept them for ever. Older Frenchmen wondered where it would all end. Talleyrand's intuition dictated that general war was going to begin again, and he wished no part in it; sure enough, within barely a year, Napoleon had got himself involved in Iberia, where eventually the "Spanish Ulcer" would prove his undoing.

MEANWHILE, from his far-flung army HQs in eastern Europe, Napoleon had never ceased to bombard the administration in Paris with plans for his civil innovations, managing amazingly to run his empire of 70 million people hands-on, involving himself in almost every fact of life. He had sent off no fewer than 300 bullying, chivvying and commanding letters in the spring of 1807 alone. It was as a dictator that France now began to see him, and no one could say "no" to his plethora of edicts. Censorship was introduced. In Paris, the number of newspapers was reduced from over seventy to thirteen, and the number of theatres alike shrank to eight. The once lively press became uninformative and unchallenging. From the programmes of Talma's Comédie-Française to the operation of the fountains of Paris, from the rebuilding of the city to the reorganisation of the German states, there was absolutely no aspect of life in which Napoleon would not intervene— sometimes with brilliant, but often with disastrous results. From Tilsit, after settling the destiny of Europe, he sent a warning note to Champagny, then his Minister of the Interior, "*Monsieur le Ministre,* peace has been made with the foreigners; now I am going to make war on your offices." He was swift to carry out his threat, sweeping away the inefficient city administration of Paris that he had inherited from the Directoire, and presiding over the new administrative bodies himself.

Under equally sweeping plans for making Paris "the most beautiful city that could ever exist," Napoleon cleared away the old medieval huddle of buildings around the Louvre to create the majestic Rue de Rivoli (named, of course, after a famous victory). The Louvre he turned into the Musée Napoléon, under Vivant Denon, the genius who had accompanied him to Egypt. Together they filled it with artefacts looted from Italy and other conquered territories. To mark his victories he built the Vendôme Column, out of melted down Austrian cannon captured at Austerlitz, and the Carrousel Arch topped with the magnificent horses plundered from Venice. He reburied the grateful dead of Paris out at leafy Père Lachaise Cemetery; but, among numerous projects he was unable to complete was the great Arc de Triomphe. Perhaps it was fortunate for Paris that Wellington cut Napoleon short before he could achieve some of his more dramatic ambitions:[11] on St. Helena, he declared that "If only the Heavens had granted me another twenty years and some leisure, you would have looked in vain for the Old Paris; you would not have been able to see the slightest trace of it."[12]

ONE OF THE PERENNIAL DISCUSSIONS of the novels of Jane Austen is how she could have lived through all the Napoleonic era, have written so much, but mentioned virtually nothing about the brutal war going on all round. It becomes perhaps somewhat less remarkable when one considers equally how little life in France and particularly the bourgeois enclaves were affected by the war—until the Allies arrived on the doorstep in 1814. What is far more significant is how few writers of distinction were thrown up in France at all during the periods of the revolution, the Consulate and the Empire. Yet this was a time when, across the Channel, England was enjoying one of its greatest ages of literature, dominated not only by Jane Austen but also by the poetic forces of Wordsworth, Keats, Shelley, Byron and Coleridge. It was also a time when Schiller, Goethe and Kleist produced their greatest works in Germany. Yet, not a single French play of any value dates from the Napoleonic period. For true poetic talent comparable to the great contemporary Romantics of England, one has to reach out for a master of prose, Chateaubriand. Together with Chateaubriand, the other founder of the French Romantic tradition, Germaine de Staël, spent most of her working life under the Empire abroad in exile. Disenchanted, she soon found that her France had become "a garrison where military discipline and boredom rule." She was forced into exile in Switzerland in 1803, again in 1806, and—definitively—after the seizure of her highly critical *De l'Allemagne,* in 1810. With some courage, she would repeatedly endeavour to return, but would repeatedly be expelled. It was also this atmosphere and its essential lack of liberties which, once their gaze had penetrated the shiny surface of Napoleonic France, gradually disenchanted the liberal visitors from England during the Peace of Amiens, making them think themselves perhaps better off after all in their own backward but libertarian society.

Suspicious as he was of any kind of intellectual and artistic ferment, if Napoleon's relations with great literary figures of the time like Mme.

de Staël and Chateaubriand were strained, his dealings with the scientific intelligentsia were much more serene—and deserving of praise. One of his ministers of the interior, Jean-Antoine Chaptal, was also a scientist, authorised by Napoleon to endeavour to synthesise politics with industry. Among scientists who benefited under the Empire were Louis XVI's mathematician and astronomer, Joseph-Louis Lagrange, who in his old age was brought back from Berlin, given an important position in the Académie des Sciences and made senator and Count of the Empire, and Claude-Louis Berthollet, discoverer of the use of chlorine for bleaching, also one of the founders of the Polytechnique. Napoleon helped him to set up a laboratory in Arceuil as an important semi-official centre of scientific research. When circumstances of war made it possible, British scientists like Humphry Davy and John Dalton from the Royal Society derived considerable benefit from the work of their counterparts in France. Robert Fulton, too, the brilliant American inventor of the first submarine prototype, was encouraged by Napoleon. Altogether, under the Empire science in all its ramifications was accorded the highest privileges and priorities, and made enormous strides.

Yet, for all these advances in science and technology—where Napoleon's interests clearly lay—in the world of the imaginative arts imperial France remains something of a cultural desert. Napoleon seemed unable to inspire in that miraculous manner in which he could repeatedly call forth remarkable military deeds, or even great administrative achievements. Great music of the epoch was left to foreigners abroad, like Ludwig van Beethoven. In furniture design, the decorative arts did flourish under the Empire, but there was little painting of distinction. The elegance of the eighteenth century, the exquisite draftsmanship of Watteau, Fragonard, Greuze and Hubert Robert, all designed to lift the spirits—where had that all gone? France could mourn its passing, but there would be little to celebrate until the advent of Delacroix and Géricault with the Restoration. Most of the best French talent, like Ingres—disappointed by cool Parisian reactions to his work—drained off to Italy. Thus the field was largely left open to Jacques-Louis David (1748–1825), the historical painter turned Romantic, court painter to Louis XVI, who disowned the court to become the "Raphael of the *sans-culottes.*" Backed by the Emperor, David came to exercise a semi-dictatorship over contemporary French art. Under David—shamelessly ambitious, and greedy—it became "imperial, pompous and allegorical." There was his pupil and protégé, François Gérard, the portraitist commissioned by Bonaparte to decorate Malmaison—and to paint the famous battle triumph of Austerlitz; there was Baron Antoine-Jean Gros, another pupil of David, and equally employed in the glorification of the regime with his massive canvas of Eylau;* and there was Pierre-Paul Prud'hon, famed for his commissioned portraits of Napoleon and Josephine. But few others.

It was following the Austerlitz campaign that massive paintings of Napoleonic victories began to be commissioned. Artists were paid handsomely: for nine big paintings, David received ff12,000 each; and ff6000 for seven smaller ones. His huge painting of *The Sabines* had already brought in ff72,000, which enabled him to buy a farm in Brie; he then tried to double his profit by reselling the same painting to the Emperor for a further ff72,000. Napoleon, however, angrily riposted with a brusque "Adjourned." Under pressure from Denon, Napoleon haggled over the payment of the famous coronation picture—from ff100,000 down to ff30,000; so, in protest, David painted himself into the scene. Eventually by his importuning, David killed the goose that laid the golden egg, finding himself replaced as court portraitist by the famous Italian sculptor Antonio Canova. Welcomed fulsomely by Napoleon— "Here is the capital of the arts; you must stay here"—Canova nevertheless sought every possible excuse to return to Rome.

DESPITE THE ALARM which Napoleon's dynamism, and the legacy that he had inherited, continued to arouse among his neighbours, Napoleon's positive cultural impact was probably greater abroad than at home. The Great Revolution had shaken the whole European dynastic system so fundamentally that beyond France's frontiers there was also barely a nation whose institutions had not been affected. In Poland in 1794, Kościuszko, sparked by what he had experienced in America and observed in France, had launched an abortive insurrection against the Russian oppressor. In Prussia, where intellectuals like Kant and Hegel, Goethe and Schiller were sharply divided by the revolution, Silesian peasants in 1792 had refused to pay their tithes to their Junker landlords; in Piedmont, Italian peasants had rioted for land reform. In England, radical agitation had spread through liberal "Corresponding Soci-

---

*Depressed in his later years after the fall of the Empire, he drowned himself in 1835.

eties"—although perhaps a more influential phenomenon was the religious revival (especially within the Nonconformist Churches) provoked by outrage at the excesses of French atheism.

To many thinkers and writers in foreign lands at the time, Napoleon—at least initially, and perhaps superficially—appeared as a hero of the Romantic Movement. At home in France, the movement would fail to bloom until late in the nineteenth century. Even in hostile England, where he found sympathy among liberal Whigs, to whom the ideals of the revolution of 1789 appealed, there were chords to be struck among the Romantics. Writing far from the realities of war, attitudes towards Napoleon among British *litterati* tended to be highly personalised, and depictions of him often idealised. Some of the poets were also very young; Keats was not born till the year Napoleon fired off his "whiff of grapeshot"; Shelley, the year the monarchy fell; while Byron was still at Harrow (where he proudly displayed a bust of Napoleon in his room) when the Grande Armée was encamped at Boulogne. Only Wordsworth (b. 1770) and Coleridge (b. 1772) were relatively more mature.

In the early days, at least, Napoleon appealed as embracing the "human rights" expectations of the revolution—or as an embodiment of the hero "in an age in which the artist was increasingly seen as heroic," observes Simon Bainbridge in his excellent book, *Napoleon and English Romanticism.* Keats would damn Napoleon for having done "more harm to the Life of Liberty than anyone else could have done"; yet was not beyond adopting him as a symbol. Shelley would rate him as a hero, then as "Tyrant of the World" (while still at school), and finally damn him for the war in Spain, "where ruin ploughs her gory way." With high subjectivity, Byron tended to swing with every prevailing wind, seeing in Napoleon something of his own self-willed, isolated heroes (at least until he invaded Spain); while Wordsworth became increasingly vehement in his detestation of Napoleon as the wars against him progressed— shocked, particularly, by Napoleon's cruelty to the simple country-dwellers of the countries he invaded. In 1804, he was writing how the French had

> . . . become oppressors in their turn,
> Frenchmen had changed a war of self defence
> For one of conquest, losing sight of all
> Which they had struggled for.

Perhaps surprisingly, however, it was in the lands invaded by Napoleon that his star burned brightest. Saxony's Goethe, as late as 1811, was writing:

> What centuries have dimly meditated
> His mind surveys in brightest clarity;
> All that is petty has evaporated,
> Here nothing is of weight save earth and sea.

Nowhere was Napoleon's influence stronger than among the *litterati* of invaded Germany. Hegel was said to have stood with bareheaded reverence in the street, even when the French soldiery stole his possessions; to him Napoleon represented the "Embodiment of the Absolute Ideal."

IN THE PROVINCES of France, Napoleonic life was more prosaic. In a nation of 33 million no city apart from Paris and Lyons had a population of more than 100,000. Heavily centralised under the Roi Soleil and before, under Napoleon France came to assume an even more lopsided aspect. Edicts and propaganda rallied the nation yet, even two generations after Napoleon, for half of its citizens French would remain a foreign language. Travel and communication were still so laborious that communities were kept apart, their inhabitants forced to live an isolated life, as if in a chemical retort. An existence of unrelieved tedium as suffered by Mme. Bovary in her mid-century Normandy village was probably even more the norm at the time of Napoleon several decades earlier. But the plight of the ruined nobles, who had survived the revolution living in the countryside, making the best of a dull existence in the small plot of land still remaining to them, was particularly dreary. Hospitality was perhaps their one and only luxury; there would be no butler, but still a cook. How much worse was it for those lower down the social scale?

Denizens of Paris were contemptuous of what they found in the provinces; to Stendhal, Dijon and Rouen was each one "an execrable hole, inferior even to Grenoble"—though he confessed a certain indulgence for Marseilles where he had had a few jolly love affairs. After attending a ball in Moulins in 1805, Julie Talma complained: "I don't think you would find such a senseless *canaille* [rabble] anywhere but here." Nevertheless, she noted how the theatre was an important focal

point; by 1813 the provinces could boast no fewer than 128 regular theatres—despite the high fees demanded by visiting stars from Paris.

When time, and campaigns, permitted Napoleon would make frequent visits to the provinces, and indeed a new era of closer oversight
and involvement had begun with the nomination of prefects by the
Consulate, instead of as perks doled out among local grandees. As in
Paris, there was substantial reconstruction of old cities such as Lyons and
Cherbourg—canals were dug, marshes drained and bridges thrown over
rivers. The peasant population and the middle classes felt the benefit of
all this, but war and the collapse of the Empire was to bring a premature
end to all such new development.


AT ERFURT IN 1808, Napoleon had been rather more successful in
charming Goethe than Tsar Alexander II, still aggrieved by the defeats of
the preceding years, and humiliated by Tilsit. For Napoleon things had
begun to go sour since Tilsit the previous year, as the British naval blockade bit ever harder at home, with sugar (from the cut-off West Indies)
becoming almost a luxury of the past. In his attempt to break the stranglehold, Napoleon allowed himself to become embroiled in his greatest
strategic folly to date. He would chase Sir John Moore all the way across
Spain, killing him and expelling his "contemptible little army" from
Corunna, and all but expel Wellington from the Iberian Peninsula.* He
made his inept brother King of Spain, his brother-in-law Murat King of
Naples, and so on; the conquest of Europe might seem complete, yet on
her thrones were only relatives, cronies or time-servers.

Like Hitler in the mountains of Yugoslavia in the Second World War,
in Spain Napoleon would be defeated by guerrilla warfare and the same
brutal living-off-the-country which he himself had invented. Eventually
the "Spanish Ulcer" cost him a quarter of a million men, soldiers the
Grande Armée could well have used in Russia in 1812. Provoked by this
disarray, Austria rose up to strike again in 1809; Napoleon won once
more, but Wagram was his last victory—and a costly one at that. At the
same time as he was endeavouring to conquer all Europe, he was arous-

---

*It is worth noting that, before 1808, few British soldiers had fought on the European
continent. (At Waterloo, only 35,000 of Wellington's troops would be English, the other
43,000 German and Dutch.) Thus it could be said that Napoleon himself gave Wellington the opportunity to open a vital "Second Front" in Portugal and Spain.

ing just that popular nationalism which had made the revolutionary France he himself had inherited so formidable in the first place.

NAPOLEON HAD RETURNED to Paris from Spain in January 1809 to find morale there disquietingly low. The stock exchange was nose-diving, once more. Ever desperate to ensure the permanence of his dynasty, Napoleon had decided to divorce Josephine, since she had proved unable to present him with an heir. Now the superstitious groaned; even the Emperor had admitted that the popular Empress was his guiding "star." To replace her, Napoleon contracted a marriage with the daughter of his recently defeated enemy, the Emperor of Austria, the nubile nineteen-year-old Archduchess Marie-Louise. Riding out to meet her cortège at Compiègne, the impatient Emperor, making sure of his deal in the best Mediterranean tradition, bedded her then and there, without waiting for the elaborate state wedding that was to follow. The following year an imperial heir was indeed produced: Napoleon II, the unhappy and short-lived "l'Aiglon." His father named him King of Rome, possibly in cynical remembrance of the defunct Holy Roman Empire that he had liquidated after Austerlitz. Yet France would never bestow upon his mother, the new empress, an Austrian princess, any-thing like the affection it had felt for the beautiful and elegant Josephine. Too many recalled the hated *autrichienne,* Marie-Antoinette.

Meanwhile, only a few years after the crisis precipitated by the Banque Récamier collapse, France was hit by another. The causes lay in the chaotic legacy of the Revolution, the flaws within the imperial sys-tem itself, but, most immediately, in the ever tightening grip of the British trade embargo and the impact it had on European commerce as a whole. England, too, was feeling the pinch by 1808; business prospects were gloomy, with mounds of unsold manufacturing goods piling up at the docks. Her economy, however, was rich enough and sound enough to take the strain; France's was not. Within days of rejoicing at the birth of his heir, on 24 March 1811 Napoleon was presented with some unpleasant home truths. Despite constantly raising the level of taxation, the national deficit was ff50 million. He was forced to pass an Imperial Decree cancelling the arrears of pay owed to the soldiers who had died for him, and thereby—in effect—cheating even the dead. There were intermediaries selling goods they never possessed, without paying, and without delivering. Speculation was rife in illegal goods run through the blockade. Even some of the generals were involved; Dupont, for instance, was supposed to have lost ff800,000 in 1810, in the collapse of a business. In the spring of 1811, a major consignment of contraband muslins and other fabrics were seized in the Rue Le Peletier, in the elegant centre of Paris.

IN JUNE 1812, driven over the brink by the double-dealing of his ally, Tsar Alexander, with the English arch-enemy, Napoleon recrossed the Niemen to invade Russia and teach the Tsar a lesson. It was within twenty-four hours of the date that would be chosen by Hitler, 22 June 1941—with equally disastrous consequences.

With his eyes solely on Russia, Napoleon failed to turn to his advantage that most foolish of all England's wars, the War of 1812 against the USA. At home, to the renewed financial crisis was added the *Disette,* or famine, of 1811–12. Initially the harvest of 1811 promised to be excellent; then repeated thunderstorms caused damage. By the beginning of 1812 the price of flour and bread was beginning to spiral. With the bakers of Rouen charging four times the price of 1803, there were riots in the provinces—with less trouble in the cities only because of the black market and Fouché's ubiquitous secret police. On 3 May, Napoleon held an emergency meeting at Saint-Cloud—right on the eve of his departure for Russia. Reserves of grain had all but run out. In January 1813, the grain "reserve" made its last distribution of flour to the bakers—ending a duration of more than fourteen months; then a very abundant harvest that summer finally brought relief. If it shook the faith of France that the modern nation should face starvation while its great leader was away campaigning, that faith was tested further by the sombre news of defeat coming from Germany.

TO TALLEYRAND, out of office and under a cloud, news of Napoleon's defeat at Borodino, on the way to Moscow, in September 1812 marked "the beginning of the end," and he felt "the end itself could not be far distant." Though it had been swiftly crushed by Savary's secret police, while Napoleon was away in Moscow there had been a warning in the shape of an abortive rising by one of his disaffected generals. By the spring of 1813 the vengeful Russians, pursuing Napoleon, had entered Prussian territory, threatening the German states still allied to him. Marie Walewska's Poland disappeared once again into the Tsarist maw, while the defeated Germans saw their opportunity to launch into a war of liberation, known as the Battle of the Nations. Napoleon had brought it on himself, by sweeping away—in 1806—the old political structure of the German states, and—in 1807—by his foolishly harsh treatment of proud Prussia. It had left her territorially truncated, and made her the leader in the eventual uprising against him. Added to this was the Grande Armée's brutal policy of living off the land (copied from the revolutionary *levée en masse,* and perfected by Napoleon) in the German territories they marched through, whether allies or conquered. This heedless pillaging would feed a German nationalism that would return to plague future generations of French, and Europeans.

Despite the disaster of 1812 in Russia, Napoleon was able once more to raise a new army 700,000 strong. But, in the summer of 1813, for the first time he found himself having to confront simultaneously the armies of Russia, Austria and Prussia. In the south-west there was Wellington, grinding forward relentlessly towards the Pyrenees. In October, Napoleon suffered a decisive defeat at Leipzig, the bloodiest battle of them all, where a total of nearly 100,000 men fell. The triumphant Allies closed in remorselessly on France itself—for the first time since 1793. The following spring Napoleon fought one of his most brilliant campaigns, rallying his tattered forces with the rousing cry of "La patrie en danger!" But by March he was cornered in Paris, and sought refuge at Fontainebleau. Empress Marie-Louise abandoned him, returning home to Vienna with the crown diamonds, worth some 18 million francs—something in return for all the Habsburgs had suffered. As she took Napoleon's son with her too, the little King of Rome, heir to it all and for whom so much had been sacrificed, screamed: "I don't want to go away!" Behind them Paris was to experience all the horrors of occupation.

RUSSIAN TROOPS entered through the east of the city, on their third assault carrying the fortified redoubt which brave students of the Polytechnique had run up among the tombs of Père Lachaise. On 30 March the city came under the first cannon-fire: "Only the roar of the cannon and the sight of peasants who had fled to the suburbs with their families, belongings and domestic animals, overcame the general disbelief,"[13] wrote one observer, incredulous that things should have come to this, that *la ville lumière* could actually be subjected to the fate Napoleon had meted out to other European capitals. Wounded men dragged themselves towards hospitals, unaided by the Parisian populace. Lunatics were driven out of asylums by the army to make way for the hordes of wounded. Refugees from the country hurried in pell mell with their cows, their sheep and their scanty baggage, cursing the severity of Napoleon's conscription. Close on their heels came the Prussian cavalry and Russian infantry—"like a merciless dark tide of green uniforms and bright plumes," on a day of superb weather. They were said to know only two words of French, "Brûler Paris." Yet somehow defeat went hand in hand with a sense of deliverance for the Parisians. In a sudden change of mood, cries were heard of "À bas le Corse . . . Vive notre libèrateur." Orders by Napoleon to blow up the main Paris powder store were fortunately disobeyed.

Cossacks clattered down the Champs-Élysées, and then encamped there—the first time since the Hundred Years' War that an invading foreign army had entered the proud city. "*Mon Dieu!* Not Cossacks in the Rue Racine!" exclaimed Mme. de Staël from the safety of her Swiss retreat at Coppet. Their behaviour was far from immaculate—but, after what Moscow had suffered, it was surprising that it was not far worse.

On 6 April Napoleon abdicated, having ill-advisedly refused Allied terms which might have allowed France to retain the frontiers of 1793. On the 28th he was dispatched aboard HMS *Undaunted* for Elba, the Allies thereby (in the words of André Maurois) "bestowing on Caesar the kingdom of Sancho Panza." Europe breathed a sigh of relief, though it was a temporary exile that would last less than a year. Many Parisians turned out to welcome the return of an obese Louis XVIII, his court transported in imperial carriages hastily painted over with Bourbon colours, passing corpses of soldiers being buried in indecent haste. A fortnight after Empress Marie-Louise's precipitate departure, the Comte d'Artois, future Charles X, was sleeping in the Tuileries. *Parisiennes* were reported to be showing "a very agreeable and polite restraint" towards the Allied troops. The Tsar arrived, acclaimed at the opera—when accompanied by King Louis and the indestructible Talleyrand—by cheers of "Vive Alexandre!" that resounded for over half an hour. Austria's Prince Metternich, arriving to make a peace treaty, was greeted with similar enthusiasm; and, once again, curious English tourists flooded into Paris. Yet, within a matter of months Paris had become so unsafe that even the Tuileries were kept lit up all night, the main problem being the swarms of unemployed and penniless veterans of the Grande Armée dumped by the new regime.

Disillusion with the new/old regime followed with astonishing rapidity; vicious caricatures of Louis' obesity appeared as he proved Talleyrand's adage about the Bourbons having "learnt nothing, and forgotten nothing." The economy sagged, and inflation took over. Some 12,000 ex-officers on half-pay took to meeting in cafés, to lament the "good old days" of the Empire and to conspire for the Emperor's return. Fretting on his tiny prison "empire" of Elba, Napoleon learned that Louis was refusing to pay his pension, and that there was talk about transferring him to a more remote island. One day his unfortunate "guardian" on Elba, Colonel Sir Neil Campbell, was visiting his mistress in Florence, and Napoleon slipped away aboard a French brig, *L'Inconstant*. On 1 March, accompanied by a thousand men, he landed in the Golfe Juan near Cannes, and began marching swiftly upon Paris, collecting supporters as he went in the most remarkable fashion. In Paris a shaky King Louis told an aide: "It is revolution once more" and prepared one more hasty getaway.

THERE NOW BEGAN the miraculous Hundred Days, "the episode in his adventurer's life which came nearest to pure adventure story," in the words of Napoleon's critical contemporary biographer, Correlli Barnett. A brief daily report on his progress was provided by the government newspaper, *Le Moniteur Universel,* calling initially on Frenchmen of goodwill to resist, with the words: "The ogre has left his den." Swiftly, as Napoleon moved upwards from Grenoble, gathering generals and loyal *grognards* as he went: "The Emperor has arrived at Fontainebleau." And, finally, "His Imperial and Royal Majesty yesterday made his entry into his Tuileries Palace amid his faithful subjects."

When the "ogre" reached Paris, against all calculations, there took place yet another astonishing volte-face which amazed even Napoleon himself. "They let me come back just as easily as they let the others go!" he exclaimed. In the Tuileries Palace, seamstresses who had been busy unpicking the Napoleonic bees from the carpets, and replacing them with hastily sewn fleurs-de-lys, started putting them back as the portly King left his kingdom for the second time in a year.

AS THE ALLIES BEGAN TO MASS in Belgium, at remarkable speed and with a view to marching once again on Paris, Napoleon's former staff (except for the several generals who, wanting no more Napoleonic adventures, had defected) "calmly and quietly" resumed their duties. It was as if he had returned from "only a short journey," commented Alexandre Laborde, then serving on the Paris National Guard. On a forebodingly cold day in May, Napoleon reviewed his swiftly reconstituted new armies on the Champs de Mars. It must have seemed, to Parisians, like a long hundred days as Napoleon then set off to meet his fate at Waterloo.

As the Iron Duke famously admitted, "it was the nearest-run thing you ever saw"—a miracle that, with all the circumstances against him and so short a time to whip together another army, Napoleon did as well as he did on the field of Mont Saint-Jean. Some of his best marshals, such as Berthier, Marmont, Oudinot, Davout and Murat, were no longer at hand. Instead there was the brave but unreliable Ney, and the freshly promoted Grouchy. The deluging rain made it hard for Napoleon to wheel his cannon into position, and sodden ground swallowed up their deadly ricochet effect. Nevertheless, on 16 June he struck a devastating blow at the main body of Blücher's army at Ligny, which recoiled backwards, only 25 miles south of Brussels. He exchanged hard knocks with Wellington's forces at Quatre Bras, the first time the two had actually fought each other. Wellington withdrew, while Napoleon made the mistake of giving him a respite in which to prepare a defensive position on the reverse slopes of Mont Saint-Jean. The decisive day of the 18th was almost certainly lost to Napoleon by Blücher's courageous decision to obey his ally's appeal—to reinforce Wellington at a critical moment instead of falling away from him. Inspecting his sodden troops on the night of the 17th/18th, Napoleon declared, "We shall sleep in Brussels tonight." But his "star" had finally deserted him. Less than twenty-four hours later, the Imperial Guard had made its last heroic charge and had broken on the "thin red line" of the British Brigade of Guards. Some 40,000 soldiers and 10,000 horses lay dead and dying on the battlefield, as Napoleon abandoned his army in the field for the third and last time, and hastened back to Paris.

In the immediate aftermath of the great battle, false rumours about victory percolated through to Paris. Then came the tattered relics of the once proud Grande Armée with their true eye-witness accounts of what had happened. The Place Vendôme was covered with wounded soldiers lying on straw. They received little care from a populace apprehensive at what was to come. France had become simply too inured to the horrors of war. Paris prepared for siege, but it was only a gesture. Then entered the conquerors, this time an enraged Blücher leaving a "desolate path" of destruction all the way from Waterloo to Paris. Determined to wipe out

TOP: Flight to Varennes. The arrest of Louis XVI and his family at Varennes, 21 June, 1791. Le Sueur Brothers, eighteenth century.

ABOVE LEFT: Execution of Louis XVI, 21 January, 1793.

ABOVE RIGHT: A deputy of the convention. Portrait of Jean-Baptiste Milhaud by Jacques Louis David, 1793.

Portrait of Napoleon I in his coronation robes, by Anne Louis Girodet-Trioson, 1804.

TOP: *The Distribution of the Eagle Standards*, 5 December, 1804 (detail), by Jacques Louis David, 1808–10.
ABOVE: *The Battle of Wagram*, 6 July, 1809, by Emile Jean Horace Vernet, 1836.

TOP: Last moments of Napoleonic glory. Russian POWs paraded in Paris after the Battle of Montmirail, 17 February, 1814. Pen and ink and watercolours on paper by Etienne Jean Delecluze.

RIGHT: Spirit of the Age of Enrichissez-Vous. Portrait of Madame Moitessiers, by Jean Auguste Dominique Ingres, 1856.

TOP: Members of the Commune at the Hotel de Ville in Paris and field officers deliberating, 1871.

RIGHT: Emperor Louis-Napoleon Bonaparte and his son, Prince Napoleon Eugene Louis Jean Joseph Bonaparte, who was killed with the British Army during the Zulu wars. French School, nineteenth century.

LEFT: The Second Empire. A poster, designed by Jules Cheret, advertising Jacques Offenbach's operetta, *La Vie Parisienne*, 1886.

BELOW: France restored: the Belle Epoque at the Moulin Rouge.

Haussmann builds Avenue de l'Opéra, 1858–78. Photograph by Charles Marville.

# Le Petit Journal

Le Petit Journal
CHAQUE JOUR 5 CENTIMES
Le Supplément illustré
CHAQUE SEMAINE 5 CENTIMES

## SUPPLÉMENT ILLUSTRÉ
Huit pages : CINQ centimes

ABONNEMENTS
TROIS MOIS   SIX MOIS
PARIS ............ 1 fr.    2 fr.    8
DÉPARTEMENTS 1 fr.    2 fr.    4
ÉTRANGER ...... 1 50    2 50    5

Sixième année

DIMANCHE 13 JANVIER 1895

Num

Dreyfus disgraced. *The Traitor: The Degradation of Alfred Dreyfus*,
cover of *Le Petit Journal*, 13 January, 1895. Engraving by Henri Meyer.

the dreadful slight to Prussians at Jena, he intended to destroy Napoleon's eponymous bridge; only Wellington forestalled him by posting British sentries to guard it (British forces controlled the right bank, Prussians the left). At one moment in the occupation, Prussian cannon were actually trained on the Tuileries Palace.

On the 22nd, Napoleon bade farewell to a loyal Marie Walewska and abdicated a second time. He then headed for Rochefort, in a final delusion that his implacable enemy at Waterloo might either grant him asylum in some comfortable country house in England, or else let him follow other "asylum seekers" to the USA, to Boston or New York. But they had other plans for the man who had wrecked the peace of Europe over the past twenty years, and on 15 July 1815 he was taken aboard HMS *Bellerophon* for Saint Helena—"the ugliest and most dismal rock conceivable," in the opinion of a British surgeon accompanying him.[14] (Incongruously, British sailors cheered him as he boarded ship.) On the other hand, had he been a surrendering enemy in 1945, he would almost certainly have shared the fate of Ney before the firing squad. Certainly compared with the Russian rape of conquered Berlin that year, the depredations of the Allies in Paris were extremely restrained. But these were more civilised times; warfare of the nineteenth century was a gentler and more humane affair than the genocidal struggles of the twentieth.

The same might well be said of the peace that was about to be imposed on a prostrate France by the Congress of Vienna.

# T W E L V E

# *Restoration and Revolt*

If you have not lived through 1815, you do not know
what hatred is . . .

—*André Maurois*

R EACTIONS TO THE ULTIMATE DEFEAT at Waterloo varied
across France, and across social strata. Pierre Fontaine,
Napoleon's official architect and one who had thus spent many
hours with him replanning Paris, noted three days after Waterloo how,
abandoning his army once more in defeat, "He came back to Paris like a
fugitive, thinking only of his person . . . the magic is gone. We can no
longer regard him as someone extraordinary . . ."[1] Or, in the words of
Metternich the previous year, excessively optimistic though they may
have seemed at the time: "People speak of him as if he had ruled in the
fourteenth century . . . All the eagles have disappeared . . ."

The twenty-five years of Revolution and Empire combined seem to
stretch like a great bridge across the history of the world. Beyond it, can
one truly say that this was where the "Modern Age" began? A Briton, triumphing in the reflected glory of Waterloo, might well ask, too, how
did a defeated Frenchman feel in June 1815? He would have gone
through two-and-a-half decades of hell and uncertainty; revolution,
endless stress, deprivation and terror. There had followed a few years of
hope and optimism, indeed joy, as it seemed that Napoleon was bringing in a New Order that worked, and overthrowing one after another
the reactionary old royal Houses of Europe, with their dedication to old-
fashioned, out-dated principles and ideas. There had been those ten halcyon years too, from Rivoli to Tilsit, irresistibly heady infusions of *la*

*gloire* when Napoleon had brought home victory after dazzling victory. Then had come the terrible years of 1812, 1813, 1814—and finally terminal defeat at Waterloo. There was, though, mitigating relief in some royalist quarters that here was peace at last; but to the historic-minded Frenchman, it had to signify the end of the *défi anglais,* going back to 1214, to the battle of Bouvines when Philippe-Auguste had first drawn a line under English hegemony over France. Now—what had been lost, and what preserved? At least, under the terms offered by the Congress of Vienna, *les goddamns* were still removed from the heartlands of *la patrie*—Calais, Aquitaine; the "hexagon" was largely preserved; her overseas empire was lost, otherwise the territory of France was much as Louis XIV had left it.

Occupation costs in 1815 had amounted to ten times what had been exacted the previous year, before the Hundred Days. They reflected the Allies' anger at having been led by the nose into war by Napoleon once again, and at the fresh casualties they had suffered to achieve final victory. In this light, the terms which Metternich, Castlereagh and Talleyrand, the professional survivor, between them cooked up at the Congress of Vienna seem generous if compared with what Napoleon had dictated to France's defeated foes at Tilsit. And, compared with the terms that Bismarck's Prussia would demand from a defeated France in 1871, followed by the harsh retribution of Versailles in 1919, this was surely an eighteenth-century peace rather than one of the twentieth. Nor for all his sins had Napoleon been a Hitler—no "war criminal," in the contemporary meaning of the term, or practiser of genocide.

Defeat, yes; but over the hundred years it lasted the *Pax Britannica* which followed Waterloo proved not unbeneficial to France. The country could grow prosperous, carve out a new empire for herself in North Africa and Indo-China, and even build up a powerful new army—anything as long as it did not upset Westminster's notion of the balance of power, the Royal Navy, or the trade patterns of Britain's race of shopkeepers. In fact, without the umbrella of *Pax Britannica,* would Hugo and Balzac, Flaubert and Zola, not to mention Manet, Monet and Renoir, have found that peculiarly fertile ground that was nineteenth-century France? A speculation not guaranteed to be universally popular in France—but one only has to recall the cultural desert that existed over the turbulent twenty-five years of the Revolution and Napoleon.

After Trafalgar, there would be no nation that could present Britain with a naval challenge, in an age when sea-power determined the international order. By and large philosophic Frenchmen accepted this.

Nevertheless, nevertheless . . . After all those years of *la gloire* fulfilled by the Roi Soleil and the little man in grey, for such a proud people was it not understandable that some resentment at defeat, a hankering after new military adventures, would linger dormant to erupt destructively —self-destructively—every once in a while? This would prove much of the essential backdrop to French history in the nineteenth century— from Algiers to Balaclava to Sedan to Fashoda. It was, after all, a somewhat shameful world in which a patriotic young Frenchman found himself in 1815.

So, WITH THE CONGRESS OF VIENNA, after twenty years of war peace came finally to Europe. England withdrew to her island and empire to prosper in a hundred years, not of solitude, but of peaceable hegemony. The fallen tyrant, the ogre, the disturber of Europe's equilibrium, was definitively mew'd up on dank, wind-blown and termite-ridden Longwood where he would die—possibly of arsenic poisoning, some continue to think—in 1821. But for France, and Paris in particular, there would be little real tranquillity in the short term. The country was financially, morally and physically in ruins. More insidiously still, the issues of the Great Revolution had never been properly resolved.

Little more than three decades were to pass between Waterloo and the next major upheaval in Paris, in 1848, which would bring the end of the French monarchy. During those three decades, there would be two more major revolts in Paris, and after each one the proletariat, the poor and the revolutionaries of the Faubourg Saint-Antoine would feel that the bourgeois had cheated them out of their birthright, the gains of insurrection, as they had after the Great Revolution itself. It was a sense of being cheated comparable to what the same strata felt in post-Soviet Russia, where it was the ex-apparatchiks who were seen, deplorably, to make off with the fruits of revolt. Nevertheless, there were elements in the Restoration that a British historian like Richard Cobb, one of the greatest experts on nineteenth-century France, could find to justify it as "the happiest period in the violent and intransigent history of modern France."

As NAPOLEON'S EMPIRE UNRAVELLED, and France slowly came back to life, the peace treaty finally signed in November 1815 preserved most of France's traditional frontiers—except for the new, neutral Belgium, Savoy handed over to Sardinia, and the German-speaking Saar to Prussia (which signified the beginning of a Teutonic presence on the left bank of the Rhine). With the return of Louis XVIII, France was also allowed to return, politically, to a *status quo ante*. As reparations she was required to pay ff700 million in gold, eventually whittled down to ff265 million. The Allies withdrew from Paris swiftly, and the Duke of Wellington—always the gentleman—insisted on paying the going market price for Pauline Borghese's sumptuous house on the Faubourg Saint-Honoré, which was to become the site of the new British Embassy. Said Metternich: "We could have destroyed France . . . we preferred a state of things which does not leave cause for well-founded discontent." But he predicted (as of June 1814): "it will happen of this peace as of all human beings. It will be found too harsh in France and too soft beyond their frontiers."[2]

Much more difficult to be made good by France were the losses in dead from the wars of the past twenty years, with estimates ranging from 430,000 to 2,600,000—almost certainly well over 1 million—for France alone, out of a total population of 33 million. As it used to be taught in British schools, "the French were a race of tall men before Napoleon."

So, *EN PRINCIPE*, the Age of Napoleon ended. But of course it did not—the age, the legend, continued long after Napoleon's own lonely death on Saint Helena in 1821. "If I happen to be killed," Napoleon had declared in grim prophecy in 1814, "my inheritance will not devolve upon the King of Rome. As matters stand only a Bourbon can succeed me." He was remarkably accurate. The heir Napoleon had so ardently sought would never succeed him; instead he spent the sad remainder of his short life as a virtual prisoner of his Austrian grandfather, with his mother in Vienna.

On 6 July, King Louis XVIII (1814–24) made his formal re-entry into the capital which had twice thrown him out ("Louis deux-fois-neuf" the wags called him). That day Chateaubriand—returning from his post as secretary at the embassy in Rome with Louis—witnessed those adept time-servers, Talleyrand and Fouché, welcome him at Saint-Denis, arm in arm. Wellington—amazed by the wild cheering—wondered whether it could possibly be the same Parisians who had also cheered Napoleon, and then himself in such rapid succession? Such caprice was hardly a sure foundation for France's return to legitimacy, to the *ancien régime*.

From his years of British exile Louis brought a (brief) bout of anglophilia with him. Byron and Walter Scott became household names. There were even hopes that Britain might become the political model for France's future; but this was not to be. Stendhal found a society "profoundly ill at ease with itself."[3] Typical of the confusion of loyalties inherited by the new regime was the varied fortune of the statue of Napoleon atop the Vendôme Column—melted down and replaced by a giant fleur-de-lys in 1818, restored by Louis-Philippe in 1833 with a *bicorne* hat which displeased the Emperor's nephew, Napoleon III, replaced with a copy of the original statue, before the Commune revolutionaries of 1871 brought the whole column tumbling down, to be finally restored in 1875 by Republican President MacMahon with the present-day figure crowned in Caesarean laurels.

Rashly the King announced his intention to spend half the year at Versailles, putting the clock back and thereby displeasing Paris. He invoked a passion for commemoration and expiation for the victims of the revolution—notably of his late brother and sister-in-law. There was the Chapelle Expiaitoire on the Rue Napoléon (renamed, with fine irony, Rue de la Paix) on the exact site where Louis XVI and Marie-Antoinette had originally been buried, and numerous memorial gardens. Swiftly Louis and his right-wing Catholic coterie tried to bring back much of the authoritarianism that had led his brother to the guillotine. "If these gentlemen [the Liberals] had full freedom," he complained, "they would end by purging me as well." Louis XVIII was already far too old and jaded to keep in check those *tricoteurs des salons*.

1815 AND 1816 WERE NOT GOOD YEARS for France. There was hunger and deprivation, and over parts of the countryside a "White Terror," comparable to the purge that was to follow the Liberation of 1944, held sway. Bands of royalist carpetbaggers looted and settled old scores. In Nîmes, Protestant women were beaten because of their religion. Marshal Ney—"bravest of the brave"—was executed by way of example. But others, like Marmont and Soult, survived to find places of honour and importance under the new regime; one of the least deserving, Bernadotte, was to become King of Sweden, no less.

With nothing like what Germany and Japan were subjected to in 1945—no "de-Napoleonisation" imposed by victorious Allies determined to raze an evil system and start again—French society swiftly repaired itself. Hardly had the Place Vendôme been cleared of the wounded from Waterloo than chic women were showing off their finest silks there. Government stocks began to take off, and visiting tourists found "brilliant society" milling about in the Tuileries Gardens. France retained the remarkable system, the *Code,* which it had inherited from Napoleon. There was one important exception: divorce, permitted briefly under the revolution and Napoleon, was banned once more, with the ascendance of the moralistic bourgeoisie.

But the Restoration was a bitterly divided society, with secret societies and ultra-Catholic groupings vying against each other, and—all the time—the Bonapartists glowering in the background. To have presided over, and healed, all the disarray left behind in 1815 France would have required an Henri IV, but Louis XVIII was "partly an old woman, partly a capon, partly a son of France, and partly a peasant." He was homosexual and therefore without a son. So obese and dropsy-ridden that eventually he had to be lifted in and out of his carriage, he would die after only ten years on the throne. The politician-historian Guizot saw him as "a moderate of the Old Regime and an eighteenth-century free thinker," but in his baggage train Louis brought with him a coterie of reactionary émigrés or "Ultras," which gave rise to the famous epithet about the Bourbons having "learnt nothing and forgotten nothing."

The Pavillon de Marsan in Paris became the headquarters of reaction where the future Charles X's sons, their wives, courtesans and bodyguards all talked treason twenty-four hours a day. Plotting away against the regime too was the Charbonnerie, a secret society based on an Italian prototype; while Louis' brother and heir, Charles Duc d'Artois— "an émigré to the fingertips and a submissive bigot," in Guizot's eyes—also conspired against him. When in February 1820 Louis' nephew, the young Duc de Berry, was assassinated by a fanatic called Louvel out of "hatred for the Bourbons," there was little public outcry. But the murder was used by the Ultras to press for a less liberal regime; for instance, one new law "on sacrilege" made theft of church vessels subject to the same penalty as patricide—the hand to be severed, and the head sliced off.

In 1824, Louis, old, infirm and half-blind, died. His younger brother, the dashing, ultra-conservative Duc d'Artois, succeeded him as Charles X (1824–30). Characteristically, Charles made his state entry into Paris on horseback, displaying with panache his fine figure, instead of in a carriage as every monarch had since Louis XIV—and from the west, the direction of Versailles. He was greeted with an enthusiasm that would not be long-lived; he thought, disastrously, that "the only good way of governing France is that of Bonaparte."

THOUGH THERE WERE NO MORE of the grand imperial projects initiated (and left incomplete) by Napoleon, French cities embarked on energetic building schemes. Pointedly, however, they were mostly orientated towards luxurious properties for the triumphant bourgeois—to the exclusion of the urban poor, who emerged from the turmoil precipitated in their name worse off than ever. The greatest building boom since the reign of Louis XV embodied the new ethos of *enrichissez-vous*. The population of the capital had risen to 715,000; by mid-century it would reach over a million, still crammed into a web of narrow, ill-paved and filthy streets.

Its growth rate of 86 per cent was, however, massively eclipsed by that of London at 136 per cent, which became double the size of Paris. For Chateaubriand, returning from exile, the Thames with its thousands of ships moored in the world's largest port "surpasses all images of power." Imported cotton goods as well as spices, silks and saltpetre poured in from the East Indian empire, while manufactured goods poured out through Liverpool to the ever-expanding US economy. The relative growth of the two capitals reflects how, amid the revolution and the Napoleonic Wars, the Industrial Revolution had bypassed and then come late to France. In comparison, by the first half of the eighteenth century England's canals and inland navigation were already becoming an imposing network. From the reign of Queen Anne, Britain's ironmakers had been using coal-coke for the smelting of iron, in place of wood-charcoal. In 1767, while courtiers in powdered wigs were decorously walking the corridors of Versailles, the "spinning jenny" had been invented in England, presaging the introduction of the wool factories; two years later Arkwright patented the water-frame and James Watt his steam engine, marking the birth date of mechanical power in cotton and engineering. In 1779, the third of the Abraham Darbys completed the world's first iron bridge. British patents issued in the quarter of a century following 1769 were more numerous than those issued in the previous century and a half. The Industrial Revolution in Britain was under way, only given extra impetus by the challenge of Napoleon—France had to catch up rapidly.

As the steam age began, the fastest transport in France was by mailcoach, carrying only four passengers in some discomfort from Paris to Bordeaux in forty-five hours, Lyons in forty-seven. In 1837, however, an ambitious decision, unique in Europe, was taken to link Paris by rail with all the frontiers. The railways spread outwards, with lines to Orléans and Rouen both opened in 1843; it was soon possible to reach Calais from Paris in nine hours. Balzac, perennially in debt but always the optimist and speculator, predicted (in a letter to his lover Mme. Hanska of 3 April 1848) what the railway would do for Paris:

> In six to seven years the remaining 1400 metres I own will be worth 300,000 to 400,000 francs . . . The reason is the train station for Versailles, Saint-Germain, Rouen, and Le Havre lines which is located between the future neighbourhood of Monceaux and that of Tivoli . . .[4]

Alas for Balzac, dead within two years, he was not to benefit from this gamble; but, in an epoch where self-enrichment had become a be-all and end-all, many others would.

A more significant symbol of French commercial growth was the rise of the Paris house of Rothschild, become the richest bankers in Europe, which had first arrived from Frankfurt via nineteen-year-old James in 1811. Discriminatory laws disappeared in 1818, marking the rapid growth of the Jewish banking community in France, which played an increasingly important role in the financing of government loans. In Louis-Philippe's reign the Rothschilds intervened frequently to avoid fresh warfare between France and Austria. Their famous carrier pigeons were able to bring vital political and commercial news far more swiftly than the diplomats could.

More modern technologies brought other benefits. Advances in medicine were reflected in increasing longevity (for the better-off); men like Victor Hugo, Thiers and that veteran of revolutions, Lafayette, all lived into their eighties or late seventies. Then there were inventors like Jacques Daguerre with the novelty of his pivoted "Diorama"—and, in 1838, the first photographs, or *daguerréotypes*. The first horse-drawn omnibus made its clip-clopping appearance on the clogged streets of Paris. And there was gas lighting, which, though a French invention (by Philippe Lebon in 1799), was first pioneered in London.

THE QUESTIONABLE BLANDISHMENTS of city life enticed more and more hopefuls to head for the boom-town by cart or train, but the vigorous expansion was not matched by any advance in health, hygiene or social welfare. By comparison with Paris (even though the drains of

Windsor would kill off Prince Albert), London was a sweet-smelling city. The Paris sewers still served mainly as street drains, discharging directly into the Seine. Cesspools still had to be emptied periodically. In 1832, Paris would be stricken with a major cholera epidemic. The Opéra-Comique was turned into an emergency hospital; the hard-line Prime Minister, Casimir Périer, died of it. Nevertheless, in September 1837, an optimistic Balzac could write to Mme. Hanska,

> In ten years we shall be clean, we shall no longer talk of the mud of Paris, and then we shall be so magnificent that Paris will truly be seen as a lady of the world, the first among queens, wreathed in walls.[5]

But no, in 1849 there was yet another plague of cholera, claiming over 19,000 victims. It was, of course, once again the urban poor who suffered most.

As the Restoration took root, so much of the positive social gains achieved during the revolution and under Napoleon evaporated. Gradually the gaps between classes widened. During the early days of the Restoration, there were reckoned (by Eugène Sue) to be 30,000 thieves in Paris, their numbers swollen by thousands of impoverished and discontented ex-officers of the Grande Armée, then the fresh influx from the provinces, creating a soaring underclass. Thus was it surprising that repeated uprisings between 1830 and 1871 would overthrow three successive rulers and their dynasties, and end by destroying much of the city?[6]

ONE OF THE MOST REMARKABLE FEATURES in all the history of France is how, following two crushing nineteenth-century military disasters—Waterloo in 1815, and the capitulation to Prussia and the Commune of 1871—each time there was an extraordinary blossoming in the gentler and more enduring works of humanity. It was almost as if they came in direct response to catastrophe on the military plane. Following 1871, it would be the burst of liberating colour and joy that was Impressionism; in 1815, it was the unique flowering of the great French novel, once the great dead hand of Napoleonic censorship was lifted from the arts. Whereas in 1813, only 3749 books had been published throughout the Empire, already by 1825, 7605 were being published in France alone. While some like Alfred de Musset condemned the new-found freedom of the press as "one of the blackest sewers of our civilisation," the number of journals multiplied; between 1830 and 1849, subscribers soared from 60,000 to 200,000. Swiftly Paris had become once more the literary capital of Europe, as France discovered Romanticism. Founders of *Romantisme,* the literature of revolt, artistic as well as political— Germaine de Staël (living just long enough to rejoice in the final fall of Napoleon), Chateaubriand, Stendhal and the poetic geniuses of Lamartine and Vigny—were followed closely by giants like Balzac (1799–1850) and later Hugo (1802–85). Both described *les petits gens* of the city, the meanness and unfairness of life in the back streets in such incomparable classics as *Père Goriot* and *Les Misérables.* Both took it upon themselves, virtually for the first time, to publicise what it was like to be really poor, in debt, pursued by the police, struggling to stay above water. Hugo, however—son of a Napoleonic general, royalist turned radical republican in disgust with the Second Empire, self-imposed exile, posturing, fulminating—in *Les Misérables* (which was written three decades after the events it describes) seems to be motivated as much by political as humanitarian outrage;* whereas Balzac's *Père Goriot* (1834–35) is the more directly concerned with immediate social inequalities.

Balzac never ceased to be obsessed by Restoration Paris. To him it was a monster; it resembled a volcano in permanent eruption, where "everything smokes, everything burns, everything seethes," or

> a vast field, ceaselessly swept by a store of interests beneath which there eddy hosts of men and women like standing corn which death reaps more busily than elsewhere, but which springs up again as thick as ever; folk whose contorted twisted features exude through every pore, the thoughts, the longings, the poisons of which their brains are full; they are not faces, but masks; masks of weakness, masks of strength, masks of wretchedness, masks of joy, masks of hypocrisy; all of them worn and wary, all graven with the ineffaceable marks of breathless greed . . .[7]

Here Père Goriot, a once prosperous merchant, survives in the most abject poverty in Mme. Vauquer's squalid boarding house on the present-day Rue Tournefort, between the Latin Quarter and the glum working-class Faubourg Saint-Marceau. His insatiable, heartless daughters live with their venal, titled husbands off Goriot's dwindling capital. Although, with the close proximity of the rich and the poor that defined

---

*I am expressing a highly personal prejudice.

Paris, they live within walking distance of Maison Vauquer, neither can be bothered to visit the dying old man, are embarrassed to have him seen in their chic homes in the Chaussée d'Antin and Rue Saint-Lazare, with their halls of marble mosaic. They are too busy even to attend his pauper's funeral at Père Lachaise. The mortal sin of the besotted old father, a truly Dostoyevskyan figure ("What am I? A wretched corpse whose soul is where my daughters are?"), is his over-devotion in a callous society.

Seen through the eyes of the naive young provincial Rastignac, in contemporary Paris: "success is everything, it is the key to power."

The very stink of powerlessness, in the Paris of the poor, the stale cabbage and untuned plumbing, its hollow-cheeked, pale and sallow denizens, seeps out from *Père Goriot* with Balzac's description of the *quartier* where "Pension Vauquer" sits:

> that illustrious valley of flaking plasterwork and gutters black with mud; a valley full of suffering that is real, and of joy that is often false, where life is so hectic that it takes something quite extraordinary to produce feelings that last. One can however occasionally encounter sorrows to which the concentration of vice and virtue imparts a solemn grandeur . . . the houses are gloomy, the walls like a prison . . . washed in that shade of yellow which so demeans all the houses in Paris . . .[8]

The corruption extends to Parisian women:

> If their husbands can't afford their wild extravagance, they sell themselves. If they can't sell themselves, they would rip open their own mothers to find some way to shine. They will go to any lengths. That is well known, well known!

Remarkably, less than two decades into the Restoration, Balzac identified a theme that was to be repeated throughout his vast work, that "wealth is virtue." Dumas père would echo it in the *Count of Monte Cristo,* portraying a society where everything—whether social standing, or revenge—can be bought at a price.

ON A MORE CHEERING NOTE, for the put-upon city-dweller there was always the theatre—now returned to its old unfettered, unbridled rowdiness of pre-revolutionary days. In 1817, the Comédie-Française, where Mlle. Mars, alias Anne Boutet, resumed its great tradition, provided a reminder of the uninhibited days of Louis XIV when Ultras and Leftists came to serious blows over a political lampoon. Thereafter theatre managers insisted that canes, umbrellas and other weapons be deposited at the door, giving birth to the present-day theatre cloakroom.

In February 1830 the Comédie-Française was the scene of another noisy battle, fought out by "Romantics" at the first night of Hugo's drama *Hernani*. In the expensive stalls sat the traditionalists, determined to dismiss the play and with it the pretensions of the new school; above, in "the Gods" were hordes of Hugo's young fans—led by Théophile Gautier in the cherry-coloured satin doublet that he made famous. The Hugo claque so out-clapped and out-shouted the traditionalists below that the success of the play and the future of Hugo and the *Romantistes* was assured. Up on the un-chic Boulevard du Temple, the Théâtre des Funambules ("tightrope-walkers"), founded in 1816, established enormous popularity with its performances of mime, vaudeville and melodrama, playing to even noisier audiences, and with an always more financially precarious company. Here the great, tragic clown Jean Deburau held sway as the lovelorn and pathetic Pierrot—ever hopeful, but always disappointed.

The comic opera, called the Italien from the eponymous adjacent boulevard, home of the new "Romantic" music, also thrived. Rossini, living in Paris from 1824 to 1836, was appointed director in an epoch when concert-goers could hear Frédéric Chopin and Franz Liszt perform their works. By the early 1830s, Paris reckoned to have replaced Vienna as the European capital of music. Yet it was not all gold; returning to Paris, Hector Berlioz, his magical *Symphonie Fantastique,* written (for his Irish paramour) while he was not yet thirty, with its lilting Romanticism but sombre reminders of the guillotine that seemed to typify the age, went unacknowledged. He died crushed by the critics at the apogee of the Second Empire, where lesser musicians like Offenbach carried off the laurels.

"LA FRANCE S'ENNUIT," declared the Romantic poet Lamartine in January 1839, redefining that age-old national affliction that was to be repeated everywhere the further the passage of time removed France from Napoleon. For neither the first nor the last time, a French regime sought to divert dissatisfaction at home with a foreign adventure. Once it was Italy, now it was Algeria. In 1827, the Dey of Algiers lost his temper with the French Consul, Deval, struck him in the face with a fly-whisk, and called him a "wicked, faithless, idol-worshipping rascal." Here was a perfect pretext for the unpopular government of Charles X. Though they took three years in winding up to avenge the shocking insult, in June 1830 a French expeditionary force landed on a beach at Sidi Ferruch, 27 miles west of Algiers. At a grand ball on the eve of the expedition, which lasted till 6 a.m., a guest had observed to the Duc d'Orléans (the future Louis-Philippe) that it was "a truly Neapolitan fête; we are dancing on a volcano." Britain growled, then did nothing and the Algerian annexation swiftly yielded some satisfying diversions for the mother country; there were glamorous silk cloths, reaching even to provincial Rouen to help assuage the desperate *ennui* of poor Emma Bovary; in Paris there was the cancan, the bizarre and shocking new dance first seen in the cholera year of 1832, and said to be based on something discovered in barbaric Algeria. It would be under the liberal regime of Louis-Philippe, rather than Charles X, that the often brutal "pacification" of Algeria would take place. But the "adventure" would not suffice to preserve the thrones of either. Acquiring the world's tenth biggest nation would in fact grant Charles X only a few months more on the throne.

Most Frenchmen found the restored monarchy quite endurable, but Paris was as ever more politicised and less acquiescent. There the reactionary Charles X had become progressively more unpopular, especially since he expressed his intent to bin the reconciliatory and liberal Charter, to which the Bourbon monarchy had pledged itself on returning to power. "We must lock the Bourbons up in the Charter; so hemmed in, they will explode," declared a brilliant young anti-monarchist journalist, Adolphe Thiers. Indeed, had Charles X been prepared to respect the Charter, possibly the monarchy could have taken fresh root between 1815 and 1830. But by the summer of 1830, as in 1811, there were soaring bread prices, wage cuts and unemployment; some 64,000 Parisians had no stable employment, making them dependent on either charity or crime. Foreigners were horrified to discover four-year-olds working long hours in the mills. Soup kitchens appeared on the streets, as they had in the early years of the Great Revolution. The warning signals were out, but no one noticed them.

In June, Charles dissolved the Chamber of Deputies, in order to hold the fresh elections that would enable him to do away with the liberal Charter and suspended freedom of the press. On 26 July—a stiflingly hot day in the city—a demonstration broke out with a dense crowd in the gardens of the Palais-Royal. They were driven away by the police, and by midnight the calm suggested that the authorities were in control. Charles X, relaxing out at Saint-Cloud, put Napoleon's veteran commander, Marshal Marmont, in charge. It was a foolish choice; many Parisians remembered him as the man who had surrendered the city to the enemy in 1814. On the 27th once again the crowds were out on the streets, this time setting up barricades near the Rue Saint-Honoré and around the Bourse.

That day a young woman had been shot down in the Rue Saint-Honoré with a bullet in the forehead, and a butcher's boy carried the corpse into the Place des Victoires. The sight aroused the crowd with calls for vengeance. During the night of the 27th/28th barricades were run up in the eastern districts, the traditional haunts of revolution. Trees were felled and workers from Saint-Antoine plundered gunsmiths for weapons, as they had done in 1789, and seized the arsenal. On the morning of the 28th, demonstrators peacefully occupied the Hôtel de Ville, unfurling the *tricolore* flag from its towers, and fraternised with the rebels. Elsewhere, on the Place de Grève and the Rue Saint-Antoine, there was now a full-scale insurrection. At a serious disadvantage fighting in the narrow streets, Marmont could only order a withdrawal from the inner city. Nevertheless, the fighting continued savagely on the 29th. Its centre moved westwards to the Louvre. Swiss guards fled in panic up the Champs-Élysées as the mob entered and sacked the Tuileries, getting hopelessly drunk in its cellars. The Archbishop's palace was also occupied, its furniture and rare books hurled into the Seine.

By the afternoon of the 29th, the insurgents found themselves in control of the whole city, bewildered by the totality of their success. Taking advantage, liberal deputies under Thiers called for the abdication of Charles X. They rejected the call of the left for a republic (under the probable presidency of seventy-three-year-old Lafayette, still going strong after his third revolution), on the grounds of national unity. Instead they nominated Louis-Philippe, Duc d'Orléans, to assume the throne. In vain, Charles attempted to save the dynasty by putting forward his grandson, the Duke of Bordeaux, as Henri V. Constitutional monarchy held no charms for the last of the Bourbons; "I would rather hew wood than be a king like the King of England!" he declared, turning to the ever-at-hand Talleyrand: "I see no middle way between the throne and the scaffold." To this the old cynic, who had seen it all, murmured: "Your Majesty forgets the post-chaise!"[9] Charles took Talleyrand's advice, and the post-chaise—to hew wood in England. "Still another government," was Chateaubriand's acid comment, "hurling itself down from the towers of Notre-Dame." In Italy and partitioned Poland there were risings in emulation of the events in Paris.

A new breed of politic leaders was growing up, who were neither of the nobility nor of the *haute bourgeoisie*. The public had no high opinion of the Assembly (when did they?), holding it to be "A great bazaar where everyone barters his conscience for a job," but from the ranks of mediocrity—the Richelieus and the Decazes—two stand out: the Protestant François-Pierre-Guillaume Guizot (1787–1874) and Adolphe Thiers (1797–1877), the owl-like revolutionary deputy with his famous quiff of hair like the stalk of a fruit. Guizot would declare proudly in his memoirs: "I am one of those whom the élan of 1789 raised up, and who will never consent to descend again." Both were journalists and distinguished historians (professions which—unique to France—were to prove to be as suitable backgrounds for politics as any other), and with conspicuously long lives (eighty-seven and eighty respectively) which would span prodigious events. Thiers, son of a modest family from Marseilles and endowed with "furious energy," in his early years as Prime Minister under Louis-Philippe would complete Napoleonic projects like the Arc de Triomphe, crown the Concorde with an Egyptian obelisk, and build the great ring of forts to protect Paris from an enemy which (then) seemed too remote to identify. In his later years he would brutally crush the left-wing insurgents of the Commune, and—as its first President—establish the Third Republic firmly in France.

IN PARIS, following what came to be known as the *Trois Glorieuses* after the three days of uprising, the insurgents licked their wounds. They had lost 1800 dead and some 4500 wounded, most of whom were under thirty-five, while the royalists had suffered about a thousand casualties. But it was, once more, the bourgeoisie who had won this latest revolution.

Epitomising the bourgeois class, at fifty-seven Louis-Philippe (1830–48) was the great-great-grandson of the free-living regent to Louis XV, and his acceptability to both sides in 1830 stemmed partly from the fact that his father had been the regicide, "Philippe Égalité," though his duplicity had not saved his neck during the Terror. Even his own wife, the good Queen Amélie, regarded him a usurper, but few could doubt the good intentions of Louis-Philippe, who always tried to be all things to all sides—surviving as Lieutenant-General of the Kingdom under both Charles X and the Commune of Paris. It was symbolic that the last King of France accepted the crown not at Rheims but in the Palais Bourbon, as the politically elected choice of "the people."

Shorn of the monarchy's inherited mystique and the authority of Louis XIV or Napoleon, the "People's King," the "Citizen King," the "Grocer King" or the "Bricklayer King," reigned presidentially, but had little more power than a British constitutional monarch.

Louis-Philippe played the role well. He lived in the Palais-Royal— where his ancestor, the Regent, had once resided—without the pomp and circumstance of Versailles. He addressed workmen as "my friends" and the National Guard as "my comrades," and liked to stroll through the streets with a green umbrella under his arm, shaking hands promiscuously; at the least enticement, he would appear on the balcony, obligingly brandishing the *tricolore,* and lustily singing the "Marseillaise." Heinrich Heine was somewhat shocked to learn that the King had two pairs of gloves for the occasion, one for shaking hands

> with every spice merchant and partisan . . . he wore a special dirty glove for that purpose, which he always took off and exchanged for a cleaner kid glove when he kept more elevated company and went to see the old aristocrats, his banker-ministers . . .[10]

If he evoked the British "champagne socialist" of our day, Louis-Philippe's Queen Marie-Amélie, with her clutch of ten children (of whom eight survived), was the very quintessence of bourgeois virtue.

At first the bourgeois rejoiced in their new monarch, and the peace and prosperity he signalled. Delightedly they took up Guizot's exhortation of "enrichissez-vous!" (though it was widely misinterpreted; in truth a rider was attached: "but leave politics to me"). The humdrum royal family seemed rather incidental, for, as de Tocqueville perceived, and the populace soon detected, Louis-Philippe was moved by "no flaming passions, no ruinous weaknesses, no striking vices . . . he hardly appreciated literature or art, but he passionately loved industry." The bourgeoisie and the labouring classes hardly needed an exhortation to industry. Soon there would be few occasions when Louis-Philippe would not be savagely criticised by the newly emergent Parisian press, or derided with merciless cruelty by caricaturists like the new young genius, Honoré Daumier (1808–79), lampooning his pear-shaped features.

Within a year there was a serious revolt in Lyons, and fresh trouble on the streets of Paris. In February 1831 riots broke out and the Archbishop's palace was sacked; in October there were more riots over Louis-Philippe's proposal to drop the death penalty. In June half of Paris was taken over by some two thousand young insurgents, of whom one in ten were killed by cannon-fire amid cries of "Down with Louis-Philippe!" and "He'll die on the scaffold like his father!" In April 1834 further riots brought about a shocking butchery by nervous troops of innocent civilians in the Rue Transnonain—to be fixed for ever in Parisian minds by Daumier's cartoon of a slain man lying at the foot of his bed in nothing but nightcap and shirt.

The following year, on the anniversary of the *Trois Glorieuses,* a Republican terrorist called Fieschi fired a remarkable infernal machine, consisting of twenty-five musket barrels, lashed together like organ tubes, at Louis-Philippe's cortège as it rode slowly up the Boulevard du Temple. The Minister of War, Napoleon I's veteran Marshal Mortier, dropped with a bullet through the head; thirteen others died, including a fourteen-year-old girl, and twenty-two were wounded. The King's horse was also hit, but he himself was untouched, returning courageously to review the troops for two hours that afternoon, and declaring "It's me who is driving the coach!" Wounded by his own device, Fieschi (whose colleagues tried to cover their tracks by ensuring that Fieschi also died in the explosion) went to the guillotine. He was the first French would-be regicide to be spared torture.

THE KING'S COURAGE under fire gained him a respite. In 1840, he sought new favour from his increasingly vocal Bonapartist opponents by having the dead Emperor Napoleon brought back to France and reinterred under the imposing dome of the Invalides. As disenchantment with successive Restoration regimes had grown, so, also, did an inflated image of Napoleon. Writers like Hugo did much to help cultivate it.* Many hearts still beat for him across France, and between August and December 1830, no fewer than fourteen glorifying plays were performed in Paris. But no one did more to refocus Napoleon in French minds and legend than Louis-Philippe by returning him to Paris, fulfilling

*Though later in his life Hugo was to become a passionate opponent of his nephew, Napoleon III.

Napoleon's desire to be buried "on the banks of the Seine, midst the French people whom I love so well."

To compensate for the drabness of his own regime, Louis-Philippe arranged a rousing Napoleonic extravaganza. On top of the Arc de Triomphe—which Napoleon had left to Louis-Philippe to complete—was erected a massive plaster statue of the Emperor, decked out in his coronation robes, and flanked by statues representing War and Peace. From the Champs-Élysées to the Concorde and over the Seine to the Invalides there were gilded Napoleonic eagles and flags and boards bearing the details of Napoleon's victories. Balconies along the route were rented out for up to ff3000. Shortly after midday, the cortège, with the coffin borne in a huge coach drawn by sixteen horses clad in cloth of gold, reached the Invalides. Victor Hugo, letting himself go, wrote: "An immense murmur enveloped this apparition . . ." It was "as if the chariot were trailing the acclamation of the entire city, as a torch trails its smoke."[11] There were cries, not heard for many a year, of "Vive l'Empereur!" and "À bas les Anglais!" The dramatic ceremony aroused that latent militaristic and sentimental nostalgia.

For all the good Louis-Philippe's protestations that war was a "terrible scourge," it was hardly coincidental that the fictional but legendary figure of Monsieur Chauvin, hating foreigners and Algerians alike, was born under his reign. A new nationalism was beginning to take root. There was increasing talk about avenging Waterloo, while the great nineteenth-century historian Jules Michelet, perpetuating his own ardently nationalist image of France, urged that schoolchildren be taught to venerate his notion of *la patrie*; he exemplified the period. In 1840, Heinrich Heine would express the glum fear that "Deprived of all republican qualities, the French are by nature Bonapartist. They like war for the sake of war."[12] Meanwhile, among Heine's still disunited countrymen a new national consciousness was also beginning to form across the Rhine.

LIKE THAT OF 1968, 120 years later, the year 1848 was one of revolt and revolution across Europe. Old political structures collapsed like the walls of Jericho. Given the paucity of communications, the simultaneous shockwave of revolution was remarkable. "There was," wrote Philip Guedalla, "a sound of breaking glass in every continental capital west of the Russian frontier."[13] In Vienna even the seemingly immortal Metternich—who had given Europe its past three decades of peace—was deposed. For Britain alone revolution was to prove—literally—a damp squib, when, in April, a demonstration of half-a-million Chartists mustering on the South Bank of the Thames to march on Parliament was headed off by a combination of the "Iron Duke's" wily strategy and London rain. Prince Albert was able to sigh, comfortably from within the tranquil walls of Windsor Castle: "we had our revolution yesterday, and it ended in rain." By the end of 1848, except for Britain, there were to be dictators in almost every country of Europe. Writing to Brussels, Queen Amélie admitted, "I do not know where I am any more." The world had truly moved on its axis.

It had all begun in Paris. Public anger towards the regime had begun to crystallise the previous year with the shocking, and brutal, murder in high society of the Duchess de Praslin, by her husband—who was having an affair with the governess. There was widespread disgust that the Duke, using his title, was able to cheat the guillotine—though he had the good taste to poison himself in prison. The case simply exemplified the inequalities still endemic in France. Her population was much larger, yet had less than a quarter of the total number of voters in Britain; while a visiting Karl Marx was shocked by the misery of the proletariat that he had found in Paris, and developed his philosophy of revolution accordingly. For many, the dominant bourgeoisie had become, as de Tocqueville explained it, "a small aristocracy, corrupt and vulgar, by which it seemed shameful to let oneself be ruled." Somewhat inappropriately, given the prelude of poor harvests in 1846–47, on 22 February a mass banquet was planned by the Opposition to lend expression to Parisian discontent at the government's resistance to reform. But it was abruptly cancelled, and the following afternoon word was received from the Minister of the Interior that there was already fighting in the city. There were shouts of "Down with Guizot!," who, as successively Louis-Philippe's Minister of Foreign Affairs and Prime Minister, had been the virtual ruler of France for the past eight years. A highly reluctant Thiers was seized and carried shoulder-high by demonstrators. Barricades began to appear on the Rue de Rivoli. More ominously there were cries of "Vive la Réforme!" and "Down with Guizot!" even from the respectable ranks of the National Guard.

Near the elegant Boulevard des Capucines, the progress of "a decidedly villainous-looking mob," singing revolutionary songs, was blocked by the loyally royalist 14th Battalion of the line. One of the rioters thrust his torch into the face of its commanding officer and a trigger-happy sergeant shot him dead. It was a single shot that changed the course of French history. On hearing it, the other nervous soldiers fired a ragged volley into the crowd. A hundred or more people "were laid low, stretched out, or rolling over another, shrieking and groaning." News of the shooting spread instantaneously, and an outraged mob headed for the Tuileries.

After jettisoning Guizot, Louis-Philippe had been advised by Thiers to retire to Saint-Cloud and assemble a force for retaking Paris. The King refused; instead he called up the unpopular Marshal Bugeaud, pacifier of Algeria, to take over command; then ordered him to cease fire. The National Guard went over to the insurgents, and, as the sound of firing reached the Tuileries, on 24 February the King abdicated in favour of his son, the Comte de Paris. He who had once declared bravely, "It's me who is driving the coach!," now left in one, just like his predecessor, for exile in England. He and Queen Amélie escaped hurriedly through a side door in the Tuileries terrace. With Louis-Philippe, the last King of France, departed the thousand-year-old French monarchy.

Hardly had the King and Queen left than the mob invaded the Tuileries, just as they had done in the last days of Louis XVI. Though some looters were shot on the spot, women and children dressed themselves up in valuable tapestries; sofas and armchairs were flung out of the windows; portraits of the King were ripped to pieces; even Voltaire's bust was hurled down into the courtyard. The throne was carried in triumph through Paris, and set on fire at the foot of the July Column, amid a great crowd. The Palais-Royal was sacked and gutted, and a republic proclaimed, as workers flocked to the Hôtel de Ville.

With 350 dead over the three days, it was the least bloody uprising of the century. Says de Tocqueville: "this time a regime was not overthrown, it was simply allowed to fall." In truth, the monarchy had expired for "lack of panache." The good King had afforded France some of the happiest years in her history, but in the memorable words of a French historian, "the French do not live on happiness."[14] In its place came freedom of the press, freedom of assembly, and the right of every Parisian to join the National Guard. In April, France's first national election with universal male suffrage was held; it put her in advance of both Britain and the US. In St. Petersburg, a thoroughly alarmed Tsar shouted: "Gentlemen, saddle your horses; France is a republic!" No less than 84 per cent of 9,395,035 men eligible voted. In fact, the election represented a massive vote against radical Paris by the conservative rest of France.

IN PARIS the coming of the Second Republic was greeted with "a carnival-like exuberance, according to Gustave Flaubert's sympathetic recollection. But the mood changed as reality replaced fantasy. Unemployment spiralled to the previously unheard-of total of 180,000. The proletariat realised, more swiftly than in 1789, that they had emerged more abjectly poor, but now more concentrated and more aware of their own strength. These were conditions that remained highly favourable to revolt. This time, however, the government was ready for trouble; General Louis-Eugène Cavaignac, Minister of War and another successful "pacifier" in Algeria, had for some time been drawing up a battle plan and was now invested with almost dictatorial powers. In response to riots on 23 June, within twenty-four hours he brought in 30,000 regular troops by train from outside the city, as the rebels constructed barricades.

The next day Cavaignac attacked, deploying his artillery without compunction. The rebels fought back sullenly, without leaders and almost without hope, but the battle continued for three days as the provinces crushed Paris. When—most courageously—he tried to intervene, the Archbishop of Paris, Monseigneur Affre, was mortally wounded. Killed, too, were no fewer than five of Cavaignac's generals as well as hundreds of many unarmed civilians—at least the official number of 914 among the government troops, and 1435 for the insurgents. A police commissioner counted fifteen large furniture vans piled high with corpses; many were "shot while escaping," or summarily executed in the quarries of Montmartre or the Buttes-Chaumont in eastern Paris. The Rue Blanche reeked with rotting cadavers from those hastily interred in the Montmartre cemetery. Thousands were arrested and transported to the colonies, or Algeria, without trial. The details of 11,616 Parisians captured after the "June Days" were listed in the official records, while Flaubert provides a grim picture of one of the dungeons: "Nine hundred men were there, crowded together in filth pell-mell, black with powder and clotted blood, shivering in fever and shouting in frenzy. Those who died were left to lie with the others." When it was all over, bourgeois and dandies from the western *arrondissements* came out—in relief—to inspect the havoc.

June 1848 had unleashed the most sanguinary fighting that had ever been seen to date on the streets of Paris, including that of 1789, but the scenario of a republic butchering its own supporters in a way that no French monarchy or empire could rival would be repeated—with even more hideous consequences—twenty-three years later under the Commune of Paris. The June Days had only created a new embittered generation.

THE SECOND REPUBLIC LIMPED ON with the military in charge. There were elections for the presidency. In them a dark horse in the shape of Louis-Napoleon Bonaparte, nephew of Napoleon I, emerged from exile to win three-quarters of the total votes from a middle class and provinces dismayed by recent events. Louis-Napoleon collected 5½ million votes to Cavaignac's 1½ million, while the socialist candidate polled only 370,000 and the poet Lamartine fewer than 8000. He is, remarked Thiers scathingly in private of Louis-Napoleon, "A *crétin* whom we will manage."[15] With almost insouciant speed, life resumed its normal tempo, as was observed by the journalist Alphonse Karr, coining the immortal phrase in July 1848: "Plus ça change, plus c'est la même chose!"[16]

# THIRTEEN

## Empire and Siege

*. . . the Empire was like those unfortunate women who wear
a silk dress but under it have a dirty slip, stockings with holes,
and a torn camisole.*

—Lettres Parisiennes, *Emile Zola*

*They had in them that little flame which never dies.*

—*Jean Renoir, on the Communards*

FOR THE BEST PART OF TWO YEARS, the new President of
the Second French Republic trod warily, and kept his counsel.
Then, on the evening of 1 December 1851, he received guests at
the Élysée, the new presidential palace on the Faubourg Saint-Honoré.
He behaved with great calm, betraying no emotion, but tomorrow was
the anniversary both of Austerlitz and of his uncle's coronation as
emperor. After the last guest had left, he opened a file labelled *Rubi-
con*—obsessed, like Napoleon I, by the memory of Caesar. At dawn,
under pretext of monarchist threats, his troops occupied key positions in
the capital.

In contrast to the revolts of 1848, fewer than 400 were killed; one was
a courageous deputy, Dr. Jean-Baptiste Baudin, who gained immortality
by rashly climbing atop a barricade, proclaiming, "See how a man dies
for twenty-five francs a day!" (The daily wage of a Republican deputy.)
He was promptly felled by three bullets. A further 26,000 "enemies of
the regime" were arrested.

A brief period of terror stunned Paris, and on 20 December a
plebiscite confirmed the latest Bonapartist coup by a huge majority of

nearly 7,500,000 to 650,000. Louis-Napoleon now declared himself emperor, as Napoleon III (1852–70).* A *Te Deum* was sung in Notre-Dame. The following December an unctuous deputation from the (conservative) Corps Législatif came to salute him with the words: "No royal forehead will ever have worn a more legitimate or more popular crown."

AGED FORTY-THREE AT THE TIME of the 1851 coup, Louis-Napoleon had twice failed to overthrow Louis-Philippe. While in exile in England he enrolled as a special constable during the London troubles; there he had studied carefully how an authoritarian figure like the Duke of Wellington could bring to heel a great city, and outflank the revolutionaries. In his outward appearance, France's new ruler possessed little presence. One who met him while in exile found "a short, thickish, vulgar-looking man without the slightest resemblance to his imperial uncle or any intelligence in his countenance," while those who saw him in his full glory enthroned, like his uncle, were disappointed to find a man with dull eyes, a long moustache and faintly absurd *impérial* goatee beard—the delight of caricaturists like Daumier who immortalised him as Ratapoil, a broken-down Don Quixote. To George Sand, who was swiftly disgusted by the bourgeois rapacity alongside so much misery that came to stigmatise his rule, he was "a sleepwalker." It was a view later upheld by his conqueror, Otto von Bismarck, who saw him as "really a kindly man of feeling, even sentimental; but neither his intelligence nor his information is much to speak of . . . and he lives in a world full of all sorts of fantastic ideas."

To the perplexity of his biographers, seldom has so controversial a character held the sceptre of such power in Europe. It is hard to name an opposite not contained in him; outrageous audacity and personal courage wrestled with timidity; astuteness with almost incredible fallibility; seductive charm with the reverse; downright reaction with progressiveness and humanity ahead of their age. Machiavelli jousted with Don Quixote, and the arbiter was Hamlet. Kindly writers dubbed him "the Well-intentioned," but unfortunately most of his schemes were destined to end in dangerous failure because of his erratic character. "One must never rush things" was his favourite maxim; but this was something which in fact he never ceased doing. Above all, he pledged his peo-

*Napoleon II, the tragic one-and-only son of Bonaparte and Marie-Louise, died of TB, aged only twenty-two, in Vienna, a virtual prisoner of his Austrian grandfather.

ple that "the Empire means peace," but he gave them their most disastrous war.

Although his political legitimacy was questionable, he was a man of diverse interests and talents, his reading during the years of imprisonment having made him much better educated than most of his peers. Taking up chemistry, he had written a serious treatise on sugar, while a pamphlet on unemployment gained him a burst of popularity with the labouring classes. As early as 1835, his *Manuel d'Artillerie* had impressed military men; and he suggested a form of conscription similar to that in Prussia, which—if adopted—might have helped France match her adversary in 1870. That catastrophe still might have been averted had he not been confronted with two of the most adroit and dangerous statesmen of the nineteenth century, Cavour and Bismarck.

LOUIS-NAPOLEON'S SECOND EMPIRE pledged France to a return to the old Bonapartist ethos of authoritarian order, in contradistinction to the anarchic chaos of the short-lived Second Republic—yet it would end its days in a failed attempt to regain liberalism. To the envious world outside, it represented the acme of gaiety and frivolity, the music of Offenbach and the rediscovery of a joyous world in the splashes of Impressionist colour; it represented sexual liberation—yet, on its underside, decay and venereal disease. It would irreparably sweep aside much of what remained precious in the ancient capital. For the bourgeoisie and the new rich, like Daudet's Nabob, there would be an increment to the prosperity consolidated under Louis-Philippe; for the poor, however, it would signify no improvement in the misery of life—on the contrary. In foreign affairs, it would offer self-determination for "nationalities" abroad; but it would end with a friendless France in military collapse— her proud capital starved, bombarded, humiliated and, finally, incendiarised by her own citizens.

Louis-Napoleon's authoritarian regime valued prosperity over liberty. A Daumier cartoon of 1851 depicts two simple Parisians remarking: "*Ce bon Monsieur Ratapoil* promises that after they have signed his petition skylarks will fall down from the sky already roasted!"[1] In the early years of the Second Empire (admittedly cashing in on the groundwork laid by Louis-Philippe) he had been strikingly successful, and prosperity had become an acceptable substitute for some basic freedoms among the majority of Frenchmen. Industrial production doubled and within only ten years foreign trade did the same. Gold poured in from new mines in

California and South Africa. The Bourse re-established itself as the biggest money market on the continent. Mighty banking concerns like the Crédit Lyonnais and the Crédit Foncier were established, the latter especially designed to underwrite Louis-Napoleon's vast building programme. In Paris there sprang up huge emporia which to women like Denise, Emile Zola's provincial heroine in *Au Bonheur des Dames,* were modern wonders of the world: "Here, exposed to the street, right on the sidewalk, was a veritable landslide of cheap goods; the entrance was a temptation, with bargains that enticed passing customers."

The railway network increased from virtually nothing in 1840 to 11,000 miles by 1870. Telegraph lines radiated out all over the country, and shipbuilding expanded as never before. Fortunes and reputations bubbled and burst as speculation raged: "It's a contagious frenzy. Nowhere is one safe from it—nowhere."\* The contagion spread to the summit of the Establishment, with even the Emperor's most esteemed adviser, the Duc de Morny, heavily tainted; while de Morny was Ambassador to St. Petersburg, Bismarck recalled that he had used the diplomatic bag to send trainloads of valuables back to France duty-free, which were later auctioned and reputedly brought him a profit of some 800,000 roubles.

Yet out of this cauldron a new wealthy bourgeoisie had arisen, installing itself in the châteaux from which its forebears had driven the aristocrats. Just as ostentatious but determined not to be displaced in its turn, the bourgeoisie was the chief political mainstay of the regime, with which it flourished hand in glove, but with little mutual affection. France's population at the census of 1866 had grown up to 37.5 million, but the most remarkable feature was the immense growth of the big cities, especially Paris, as a result of industrialisation. In the twenty years between 1831 and 1851, Paris alone grew from 786,000 to 1,053,000, and it would reach 1,825,300 by 1866.

If only Louis-Napoleon could have stopped at expanding France's economic frontiers.

IT WAS PARIS, however, which reflected possibly the single most important measure enacted under the Second Empire, certainly its one truly ineffaceable landmark. "I want to be a second Augustus," declared

---

\*"C'est une frénésie, une contagion,
   Nul n'en est à l'abri, dans nulle région."

Louis-Napoleon even before coming to power, "because Augustus made Rome a city of marble." One of the first measures enacted by him after the coup of 1851 was for all future work connected with the transformation of Paris to be sanctioned by decree. From then on he would pursue the city's reconstruction with almost maniacal fervour. As an urban developer Louis-Napoleon ranks with Henri IV, leaving behind him far more than his uncle. The Paris of today is essentially that of Napoleon III—and Baron Haussmann. Georges-Eugène Haussmann (1809–91) had no training in architecture, but—a Protestant Alsatian with German in his genes—was a highly efficient, single-minded planner chosen principally "as a demolition artist." (To Richard Cobb, who deplored his works, he was "the Alsatian Attila.") In a city still with no mayor, his powers were untrammelled and reinforced by Louis-Napoleon's dictatorial decrees, enabling him to expropriate whole streets for development.

The extension of Napoleon I's Rue de Rivoli so pushed up the value of property bordering the development that the city was able to finance part of its costs virtually for nothing. Finally, too, the slums between the Louvre and the Tuileries were cleared. The Hôtel de Ville was besieged—for once—not by insurgents, but by battalion-size teams of masons and carpenters stirring up mud, dust and rubble.

On her state visit to Paris in 1855, Queen Victoria expressed boundless admiration for what had already been achieved: "Everything is so truly regal, so large, so grand, so comprehensive it makes me jealous that our great country and particularly our great metropolis should have nothing of the same kind of show!" French critics then and now, however, question the merits of Haussmann's new Paris. The conservative Goncourts said it made them think of "some American Babylon of the future." In the rough surgical language of Haussmann himself: "We ripped open the belly of old Paris, the neighbourhood of revolt and barricades, and cut a large opening through the almost impenetrable maze of alleys, piece by piece, and put in cross streets whose continuations terminated the work."[2] At a stroke of the Baron's quill pen, whole medieval *quartiers* that had resisted Henri IV, Louis XV, the revolution and Napoleon I were now swept away. The most radical impact was felt in the heart of Paris, in the Île de la Cité. Around Notre-Dame, great boulevards cut through the labyrinthine alleys of the old city, straight as a die like the Roman roads first bestowed on ancient Lutetia. The longest, Rue La Fayette, ran for 5 kilometres without a single kink, and remains one of the city's main arteries.

Achieving (at a cost of ff2 million) that which the long line of rulers dating back to Philippe-Auguste never had, he completed the Louvre. Continuing the long line of galleries along the Rue de Rivoli, and finishing those initiated by Louis XIV along the Seine, Louis-Napoleon turned the Louvre into the greatest palace in the world, larger even than Philip II's sombre vast pile of the Escorial. Westwards from its massive outstretched arms, and past the Tuileries Palace, with unprecedented speed Paris began to extend with beautiful regularity far beyond the Champs-Élysées. For Haussmann, however, architectural aesthetics had been only one of several priorities. It was evident what excellent fields of fire Haussmann's long, straight streets afforded, what opportunities to turn the flank of a barricade, of "cutting through the habitual storm-centres." Paris now seemed "as strategically ordered as any battlefield." In fact, and with what force will be seen later in the hideously destructive Communard revolution of 1871, he defeated his own purpose.

For Haussmann, ameliorating the life of the poor was a secondary priority. Indeed, the prices in the newly developed *quartiers* drove poorer residents eastwards and outwards, from the charmed city of the boulevards to crowded ghettos where a resentful sub-class, of which one in every sixteen was living off public charity, struggled to exist. Far from "piercing" the traditional trouble-centres, Haussmann had merely created new more marginalised and volatile districts, where in the latter days of the Empire no policeman would dare appear alone.

THE RECEIVED VIEW that has been handed down of Louis-Napoleon's Second Empire seldom pays due attention to the plight of the Parisian poor; yet it was that which, in the long run, was to destroy it. The image tends to be one of Offenbach and gaiety; of cancans and *grandes horizontales*; of glittering balls and lax morals. As Philip Mansel records in his excellent *Paris Between Empires, 1814–1852,* Louis-Napoleon once maintained that "his true friends were to be found in cottages, not in gilded salons."[3] Nevertheless, it was the "gilded salons" that set the tone, and—just as social mores in England followed the example of the sovereign—so Second Empire society eagerly followed the wandering paths of its pleasure-loving Emperor. The *haut monde* endeavoured to recapture the paradise of Louis XV. In the Forest of Fontainebleau courtesans went hunting with their lovers, attired in the plumed hats and lace of that period. The upper crust delightedly sought escape from the bourgeois virtuousness of Louis-Philippe's regime.

A curious film of hypocrisy slicked over the surface of the Second

Empire; Flaubert was prosecuted in 1857 for offending public morals with *Madame Bovary*, Manet was subjected to most virulent press attacks for the "immorality" of his *Olympia* and the *Déjeuner sur l'herbe*; and women smoking in the Tuileries Gardens were as liable to arrest as were young men bathing without a top at Trouville. According to Paris police records, during one month in 1866, 2344 wives left their husbands, and 4427 husbands left their wives; there were some 5000 prostitutes registered at the Préfecture, and another 30,000 "freelances." Sexual gallantry was the contemporary obsession. Underneath all the glitter there was corruption, with Renoir once lamenting that—because he alone of his friends like Maupassant, Goncourt, Baudelaire and Manet had not caught syphilis—he could not be a true genius. Zola's prostitute, Nana, was an icon of the Second Empire, and its motto the rhetorical question from Offenbach's *La Belle Hélène*:

> Tell me, Venus, what pleasure do you find
> In robbing me thus of my virtue?

What life behind the brilliance of the Second Empire was actually like for the majority has seldom been more vividly described than by the Goncourts. Jules Goncourt's former mistress, a midwife called Maria, had gone to deliver a child at the upper end of Paris's new Boulevard Magenta; there she found

> a room where the planks that form the walls are coming apart and the floor is full of holes, through which rats are constantly appearing . . . The man, a costermonger, who has known better days, dead-drunk during his wife's labour. The woman, as drunk as her husband, lying on a straw mattress and being plied with drink by a friend of hers, an old army canteen attendant who developed a thirst in twenty-five years' campaigning and spends all her pension on liquor. And during the delivery in this shanty, the wretched shanty of civilisation, an organ-grinder's monkey, imitating and parodying the cries and angry oaths of the shrew in the throes of childbirth, piddling through a crack in the roof on to the snoring husband's back.[4]

Hogarth could scarcely have done better.

As much as anyone else Louis-Napoleon was aware of the problem, and the dangers. He told Cobden ominously, "It is very difficult in

France to make reforms. We make revolutions in France, not reforms."
The proceeds of industrialisation were prodigious, but did little to
soften the life of workers; typified by the fact that between 1852 and 1870
the wages of a miner in the Anzin collieries increased by a mere 30 per
cent, while the company's dividends tripled. Though wages increased,
almost nowhere had they kept up with inflation in the cost of living.
Food alone could account for 60 per cent of earnings, which left very little over for the other good things in life. Bourgeois chroniclers of the
period claimed that the workers of Paris had little taste for meat; the
truth was that they simply could not afford it, and it was no coincidence
that in 1866 butchers first sold cheap horsemeat, thereby introducing a
taste which, within four short years, would be forced upon a much
wider clientele. Indebtedness was general, and workers seemed to spend
half their lives at the pawnbrokers of the *mont-de-piété,* where the family
mattress was the standard pledge. According to Prefect Haussmann
himself, in 1862 over half the population lived "in poverty bordering on
destitution." For the ff3.81 which (in 1863) was the average wage, the
Parisian worker was required to labour eleven long hours a day. Bad as
the conditions of Victorian England were, a visiting apprentice like
Edwin Child would note how much harder life was in Paris, with his
own day beginning at 5 a.m.

Louis-Napoleon wanted sincerely to improve the lot of the working
man. Herein lay the source of perhaps the saddest paradox of his reign.
It was the sector for which he strove hardest, yet when the crunch came,
the working class provided his most violent enemies. He set up institutions of maternal welfare, societies of mutual assistance, the establishment of workers' cities, and homes for injured workers; also projected
were shorter working hours and health legislation; the loathsome prison
hulks were abolished and the right to strike was granted. The Emperor's
personal contribution to charitable works was considerable, and in his
efforts to ingratiate himself with the workers he even decreed that,
instead of being named after his mother, Reine Hortense, a new boulevard over the covered-in Saint-Martin canal should be given the name of
a worker, Richard Lenoir. Many of Louis-Napoleon's more progressive
ideas, however, were frustrated by the greed of the new bourgeoisie and
the conservatism of the provinces, facts which did not escape the notice
of the *classes laborieuses.*

Behind the frustrations of the Parisian proletariat lay the dangerous
legacy of three bloody uprisings within the past century, the Great Revolution of 1789, the July Days of 1830 and the June uprising of 1848,

from the benefits of which they felt swindled. Only three ingredients were required to spark insurrection again: weapons, organisation and a moment's relaxation of the police state. By 1870–1, all three would be in place to explode with the most appalling consequences.

BEFORE THAT, Louis-Napoleon would throw one last party, what was to prove the finale of his "bread-and-circuses" regime, Paris' Great Exposition of 1867. The heart of it stood on the Champs de Mars, where Napoleon I had reviewed his troops before heading for Waterloo, and close to where the Eiffel Tower stands today. It was, quite simply, the biggest show of the age. There "art elbowed industry," wrote Théophile Gautier, "white statues stood next to black machines, paintings hung side by side with rich fabrics from the Orient." The pavilion was divided into seven regions, each representing a branch of human endeavour, where the various nations of the world exhibited their most recent achievements. It was the year that Lister introduced antisepsis, and Nobel invented dynamite; and a German-Jewish professor published a fateful book called *Das Kapital.*

Just recovering from its civil war, the USA had sent a complete field service or "ambulance," as it was then called, representing the peak of military medicine of the day. But the crowds passed it by, bestowing more attention upon a patent new piece of American furniture, described as a "rocking chair." Britain sent locomotives and imposing bits of heavy machinery, as well as a mass of Victoriana that attempted (with limited success, Parisians thought) to combine comfort with elegance. But from Bismarck's Prussia came an immense 50-ton gun exhibited by Herr Krupp of Essen, who had started life as a manufacturer of railway wheels. It was the biggest artillery-piece the world had ever seen, and for this—tactfully—it was awarded a prize. French military men eyed Herr Krupp's prize exhibit with more attention than they might have done, had that nation of droll professors and beer-swilling bombasts not astonished Europe by trouncing Austria, in a staggeringly short campaign, the previous year. For the moment, however, the world was all smiles, and more appropriate to the mood of the moment was Louis-Napoleon's own contribution of a statue of a robust nude reclining upon a lion—entitled *Peace.*

The beautiful and the frivolous formed a major part of France's exhibits, and illustrious visitors poured into Paris from every corner of the globe; among them England's Prince of Wales, smiling appreciatively on the pleasure city he relished. There was the King of Prussia and—above all—the Tsar of All the Russias. He was the real guest of honour because Louis-Napoleon ardently desired an alliance with him against the perceptibly growing threat of Prussia. Only Emperor Franz-Josef of Austria, and his brother, unhappy Maximilian, trapped in Mexico on Louis-Napoleon's foolish expedition there, were conspicuously absent.

One evening, the Emperor attended the premiere of Offenbach's *La Grande Duchesse de Gérolstein,* staged in honour of his royal guests. With the immortal Hortense Schneider playing the lead role, *La Grande Duchesse* depicted an amorous grand duchess of a joke German principality, embarking on a pointless war because its chancellor, Baron Puck, needed a diversion. Its forces were led by a silly German general called Boum, as incapable as he was fearless, who invigorated himself with the smell of gunpowder by periodically firing his pistol into the air. The farce, tallying so closely with Europe's private view of the ridiculous Teutons, was too obvious to be missed. When the Tsar came to see it, his box was said to have rocked with unroyal laughter. Between gusts of mirth, members of the French court peeped over at Bismarck's expression, half in malice, half in apprehension, wondering if the joke had gone too far. But nobody appeared to be laughing harder than the Iron Chancellor himself; was he enjoying some very secret joke of his own?

Few nights passed without one of the magnificent balls in which the Second Empire so excelled. At the sparkling embassies they waltzed till dawn to the latest Strauss number, "The Blue Danube." At the Tuileries, where the Empress gave a ball in honour of her Russian guests, Strauss himself led the orchestra. The gardens had been rendered more enchanting by cordons of that new invention, electric light, which made the extravagant uniforms and jewels glitter and flash. When could this *féerique* dream of a Thousand-and-One-Nights ever end, and what would replace it?

Then, suddenly, the party turned nasty. On the way back from the great military review at Longchamp, a twenty-two-year-old Polish patriot called Berezowski leaped out of the crowd and fired a pistol at the Tsar. He missed, but the white gloves of the Tsarevich were spotted with blood from a wounded horse. Louis-Napoleon was distraught; "Sir," he said gallantly, "we have been under fire together; now we are brothers-in-arms." The Tsar, shaken by this preview of the dreadful death in store for him, was icy. In one second all Louis-Napoleon's dreams for an accord with Russia had been shattered. Soon there was more bad news.

On 19 June, Emperor Maximilian I, abandoned by his French protectors to the mercy of the Mexican nationalists, was shot at Querétaro. All celebrations were at once cancelled, for with the death of Maximilian died the hopes of the Bonapartes' last foreign adventure. Manet immediately produced a huge painting of the tragedy, but was forbidden to hang it in his gallery, on the grounds that it might be construed as a criticism of imperial policy. And there were predictions of a bad harvest in France, portending a rise in food prices—and news from Algeria of cholera and famine. At the end of August, Baudelaire, paralysed by syphilis, died aged forty-six in a madhouse; two months later, workers began the dreary task of dismantling the Great Exposition.

"It was too lovely!" was Gautier's nostalgic reflection on the Second Empire in sadder days three years later. Meanwhile, the sounds of revelry lingered on. The masked balls continued; in 1869, the last would be held, with Empress Eugénie magnificently, but ominously, attired as Marie-Antoinette. The historian, with his potent instrument of hindsight, might wish that Louis-Napoleon could have concentrated his energies on the "bread and circuses" of 1867. Instead, foreign adventures would leave him with no friends and allies just when, suddenly, he most needed them. In Italy, in an echo of French policy from Charles VIII down to Napoleon I, his meddling cost the support of the Church without winning the friendship of the King or Cavour. The ill-advised "policy of nationalities" courageously backed Polish independence, but earned the hostility of the Tsar. The rash endeavour to found a new empire in Mexico, ending with the execution of Maximilian, cost the allegiance of his brother, the Emperor of Austria, while causing frowns in America and Britain.

Suddenly there was a powerful Prussia, and Bismarck bent on trouble, facing an isolated France.

At home, under pressure of public dissatisfaction, in 1869 Louis-Napoleon was forced to permit elections. Victory for the liberal candidates brought in the "Liberal Empire"—against the better judgement of the hard-liners. As de Tocqueville observes, the most dangerous moment for a dictatorship is when it begins to release the brake. So it was to prove for Louis-Napoleon. The Emperor himself was a tired and sick man, with a large stone growing in his bladder. The Tuileries was beset by nervousness. The writer, and friend of the regime, Prosper Mérimée, described the atmosphere as "like that aroused by Mozart's music when the Commendatore is about to appear." His name might be reread as Otto von Bismarck.

By contrast that June, the newly appointed British Foreign Secretary, Lord Granville, gazed out with satisfaction on the world scene from London and claimed—with reason—that he could not discern "a cloud in the sky." He could never recall "so great a lull in foreign affairs." In Paris, Napoleon III's Prime Minister, Émile Ollivier, echoed Granville by declaring—less convincingly—that "at no period has the maintenance of peace seemed better assured." It was the kind of summer, not unlike those fateful summers of 1914 and 1939, when tempers frayed. At the beginning of July 1870, a small cloud passed across the sun—but it seemed only a very small cloud. For the past two years the throne of Spain had been vacant, following the deposing of the unsatisfactory Queen Isabella. One of the possible candidates was a German princeling, Leopold of Hohenzollern-Sigmaringen. The idea of the Hohenzollern candidacy had originated in Spain, but when Bismarck pressed the case, Paris rose up in alarm at the thought of German princes on the Pyrenean frontier as well as the Rhine. This was the kind of hegemony that Louis XIV himself had sought to impose on Europe.

Disconcerted by inflammatory articles in the French press, Bismarck withdrew the Hohenzollern candidacy. But in Paris hotheads called for Prussia to be humbled for her presumption. None was pushing harder than the Empress, while Louis-Napoleon's heavy-handed Foreign Secretary, the Duc de Gramont, held a personal grudge against Bismarck for having once described him (not unreasonably) as "the stupidest man in Europe." Gramont now began to adopt a plaintive, hectoring tone towards Prussia. He sent the French Ambassador in Berlin, Count Vincent Benedetti, to badger the King at Bad Ems, where he was taking the waters. Benedetti was received with greatest courtesy by King Wilhelm, who had no desire (any more than his fellow German rulers) for war, observing that the unification of Germany would be "the task of my grandson,"* not his.

Bismarck had a different vision. He was in no way prepared to wait two generations, and calculated that a war with France would provide the essential mortar required to cement the loose German federation into a unified nation—dominated, of course, by his native Prussia. But the *casus belli* would have to be most carefully selected, to cast France as

---

*Who, in fact, would be Kaiser Wilhelm II, leading a united Germany into the First World War against France.

the initiating party in the eyes of Europe—and particularly of Prussia's German allies. As he once remarked, "A statesman has not to make history, but if ever in the events around him he hears the sweep of the mantle of God, then he must jump up and catch at its hem." With France now bent on scoring diplomatic victories, Bismarck saw his chance. Irritated by Benedetti at Bad Ems, the benign old King refused to guarantee that the Hohenzollern candidacy would never arise again, declining a request for a further audience. A telegram giving an account of the interview was duly dispatched to Bismarck in Berlin. Bismarck heard "the mantle of God"; he sharpened the tone of the dispatch before passing it to the Berlin press—and the world.

Even with Bismarck's editing, the famous Ems Telegram hardly seemed to constitute a *casus belli*. But Bismarck was well attuned to the mood in Paris. Frenzied crowds surged through the streets shouting, "À Berlin!" In one of the rashest claims in all military history, the French commander, Marshal Leboeuf, encouraged the hawks with his foolish declaration that the army was "ready down to the last gaiter-button." (Wits remarked that this was largely true, as there were no gaiters in stock anyway!) For one bright day, on 14 July, the peace party in the French government, moderates like Adolphe Thiers, had precariously gained the upper hand, and the Emperor himself urged Leboeuf to delay summoning up the reserves. Thiers observed glumly that, in France's foreign policy, there was not one mistake that remained to be made. But on receipt of Bismarck's telegram on 15 July, urged on by his Empress and Gramont, fired by the ever-shriller Paris press, Napoleon III declared war. In a state of exhilaration, the hawks recalled Napoleon's successes beyond the Rhine. But, through Bismarck's cunning, she found herself at once branded as a frivolous aggressor with neither friend nor ally. In England, Mr. Gladstone made it perfectly plain that Britain would only intervene "to take arms against either French or German violation of Belgium's neutrality." Said the *Illustrated London News*: "The Liberal Empire goes to war on a mere point of etiquette," and this was precisely how opinion, in America as in Europe, saw the new conflict. France was blundering into war "with the greatest military power that Europe had yet seen, in a bad cause, with her army unready and without allies."[5]

In sharpest contrast, the Prussian military machine was superbly prepared, superbly equipped and led, and well tested in battle. Within eighteen days of mobilisation, Bismarck and his German allies were able to field an unheard-of force of 1,183,000 men. The German organisation man, scourge of Europe over the next seventy-five years, had arrived. It was led by an imposing triumvirate of Bismarck, Field Marshal von Moltke and Roon, the Minister of War. They had been tested in war against Austria at Sadowa in 1866, while the French army commander Bazaine (who would later find himself locked up in Metz with his army) was an ex-ranker who had never commanded more than 25,000, and that only on manoeuvres. While Prussia could depend on a vast mass of well-trained reservists, when Marshal Niel, the French Minister of War, had asked for ff14 million for his Garde Mobile he had got ff5 million. Zola would understandably later write of a "Germany ready, better commanded, better armed, sublimated by a great charge of patriotism; France frightened, delivered into disorder . . . having neither the leaders nor the men, nor the necessary arms."[6] The laughter about General Boum and *La Grande Duchesse de Gérolstein* at the Great Exhibition of three years previously was suddenly muted; instead, Herr Krupp's terrifying great cannon seemed more pertinent. Scenes of dismal chaos accompanied French mobilisation: "Have arrived at Belfort," telegraphed one desperate general. "Can't find my brigade. Can't find the divisional commander. What shall I do? Don't know where my regiments are."

It did not bode well. Over the first six weeks of war, in swiftest succession there followed for France disaster after military disaster in the frontier provinces. The Prussian Chief of Staff, Field Marshal Helmut von Moltke, rapidly appreciated that the French Army would be divided by the line of the Vosges mountains, and deployed his forces so that they could concentrate with overwhelming superiority against either half, and defeat it in detail. It was taking a leaf out of the book of Napoleon I, who could not have done it better. The first blow fell at daybreak on 4 August, when men of General Abel Douay's division of MacMahon's army were caught breakfasting at Wissembourg in Alsace, in eastern France. The French fought heroically against superior numbers, but became demoralised when their general was killed by a shell. The main blow fell two days later at Woerth, when MacMahon, deceived as to the numbers that the Prussians could bring against him, allowed himself to be brought to battle by the Prussian Crown Prince, with twice as many infantry as himself. That same day, the other half of the French forces, optimistically labelled "The Army of the Rhine," and under command of the Emperor himself, suffered an equally crushing defeat at Spicheren to the left of the Vosges. For the Prussians they were costly battles—3000 to 4000 French at Spicheren, about 11,000 each at Woerth (substantially less than in a Napoleonic battle)—but they were clear-cut successes.

After Spicheren and Woerth, the French never again left the defensive. A long, disheartening retreat began. On the 12th, Louis-Napoleon handed over command to Marshal Bazaine. Following a sequence of disastrous orders and counter-orders, Bazaine fell back on the fortress of Verdun. But after all the French vacillations and changes of plan, he found his route cut off by Uhlan cavalry of Moltke's fast-moving Second Army near the village of Gravelotte, in the middle of the Woëvre Plain. On 16 August, a desperate battle-of-encounter took place. Here the Prussians and their other German allies were outnumbered, and only saved by Bazaine's excessive caution. Moltke had two days in which to bring up the whole strength of his combined First and Second Armies— 188,332 Germans supported by 732 guns, against 112,800 Frenchmen with only 520 guns, tired and somewhat demoralised. Watched by General Sheridan of American Civil War fame, on the 18th Moltke inflicted a decisive defeat on Bazaine at Saint-Privat. The 20,000 casualties he suffered, to 13,000 French, attested to the heroism with which Bazaine's men had fought; but, out-generalled, they now flooded back eastwards into Metz, where they remained isolated and under siege for the next two-and-a-half months.

In Paris news of the first defeats had caused the defeat of Louis-Napoleon's liberal Premier, Ollivier, by General Cousin-Montauban, Comte de Palikao, a right-winger. Abandoning all its previous pretences of pacifism, the left now relentlessly assailed the government for its military failures. Meanwhile, at the front, on 30 August, the Prussian Third Army, executing a grand right-wheel, caught up with MacMahon, trapping him inside the small citadel town of Sedan. It was the birthplace of the great Turenne, hammer of the Germans under Louis XIV—but also destined to be the scene of a second dreadful French disaster, in May 1940. In the forthright words of one of the French corps commanders, General Ducrot: "We're in a chamber-pot, and they'll shit on us."

There were rations in Sedan sufficient only for a few days. The situation was hopeless. On 1 September, a sick and defeated Napoleon III, rouged to hide his pallor, surrendered to King Wilhelm of Prussia at the head of his army. He handed him a brief note, dignified but tragic: "Not having been able to die among my troops, I am left with no alternative but to surrender my sword into the hands of Your Majesty. I am Your Majesty's good brother." Bismarck replied harshly, describing France as a nation full of envy and jealousy, and added, "We must have territory, fortresses and frontiers which will shelter us from an attack on her part." This hardly spoke of the prospect of a generous peace, in the style of the Congress of Vienna.

TWO DAYS LATER Paris received the news of the Emperor's capitulation in Sedan. "What a sight," recorded Goncourt:

> the news of MacMahon's defeat and the capture of the Emperor spreading from group to group! Who can describe the consternation written on every face . . . Then there is the menacing roar of the crowd, in which stupefaction has begun to give place to anger . . .*

Very soon it was mixed with some delight, too—even in some bourgeois *quartiers*—for Louis-Napoleon and his Second Empire were gone for good. Like her two predecessors in the Tuileries, Empress Eugénie fled to England through a palace side door, leaving pathetic signs of an unintended departure: a toy sword half-drawn on a bed, empty jewel cases strewn on the floor, and on a table some bits of bread and a half-devoured egg.

In the time-honoured sequence of French revolutions, the mob quickly set about effacing all traces of the fallen regime. Just as, at the onset of the Hundred Days, the fleurs-de-lys had been unpicked from the Tuileries carpets and replaced with Napoleonic bees, so now all the Ns and imperial eagles were chiselled and ripped off the public buildings, and busts of the deposed Emperor pulled down. At the main entrance of the Tuileries, later in the afternoon of 4 September, Edmond Goncourt saw scribbled in chalk the words "Property of the People."

It was a sparklingly sunny day, no blood had been shed, and all Paris now turned out in its Sunday best to celebrate the most joyous revolution it had ever had. George Sand, now aged sixty-six, rejoiced: "This is the third awakening; and it is beautiful beyond fancy . . . Hail to thee, Republic! Thou art in worthy hands, and a great people will march under thy banner after a bloody expiation." Everyone seemed united by an irrational optimism. The new sixteen-year-old wife of Paul Verlaine (her marriage postponed by conscription) voiced the widely shared mys-

---

*Edmond was now writing alone, his beloved brother, Jules, having died painfully— of syphilis—earlier in the summer.

tique of La République, asking, "Now that we have her, all is saved—
that's so, isn't it? It will be like in . . ." "Like in '92, she wanted to say,"
explained Verlaine. "They won't dare to come now that we have her,"
declared a workman, echoing Mme. Verlaine.

Not all writers agreed. In September 1870, ten days before he died,
that great patriot, supporter of the Empire and friend of the Empress,
Prosper Mérimée, wrote in grief to Mme. de Beaulain: "I bleed today
from the wounds of these imbecile Frenchmen, I weep for their humiliations and however unpleasant and absurd they are, I still love them."[7]

On the street it was automatically assumed that—now the mediocre
Emperor and his bellicose regime were gone—the Prussians would
return home. The Parisians could not see the solid German phalanxes
advancing ever closer, or hear the German press at home shrieking for
the destruction of "the modern Babylon." A bitter four-month siege lay
ahead, waged on the Parisian side with varying degrees of incompetence,
until late January 1871. At the Hôtel de Ville, the government set up to
succeed the Emperor consisted of moderate republicans—men like
Favre, Ferry, Gambetta, Picard, Crémieux and Arago. Thiers declined
office, but remained a powerful influence, while the post of President
was handed to General Trochu, the lethargic and uninspiring Governor
of Paris.

More dangerous, on the extreme left professional revolutionaries like
Blanqui and Delescluze, and firebrands like Pyat and Flourens, fulmi-
nated in the Red "Clubs" and gained military influence within the
National Guard. A constant threat to the organised government, for
them the invading Prussians equalled imperialism, which, triumphant,
would bring back the hated Emperor. Under this left-wing pressure,
with some reluctance Trochu and his team were pushed into continuing
the war. It was with an extraordinary degree of traditional arrogant self-
assurance that Paris did so virtually without consulting the rest of
France; once again she had decided on the country's behalf. This would
be almost the last time.

As Paris settled down to siege, some 170,000 territorial *Mobiles*
from the provinces reinforced the National Guard, which expanded
with indecent rapidity from 24,000 at the outbreak of war eventually to
number some 350,000. It was to prove more a liability—and a most
dangerous one—in the course of the siege. But the surest defence Paris
had were the ring of forts constructed (with foresight?) by Thiers in

1840. It meant that any investing army would be forced to occupy a contiguous front of approximately 50 miles against a possible break-out—and this might require every spare soldier of even Moltke's vast army. Meanwhile some 12,000 labourers set to work to reinforcing weak spots with improvised earthworks, and laying land-mines. As in days of Henri IV's siege, foodstuffs from all the surrounding countryside streamed in. In the Bois de Boulogne alone, there were herded an estimated 250,000 sheep and 40,000 oxen, while an army of foresters began cutting down the fine old trees in the Bois for fuel in the winter ahead. It seemed that, this time, in contrast to 1590, there was no way Paris could be starved into submission.

On 20 September, Uhlan cavalry from the two Prussian armies linked arms near Versailles, which surrendered without a shot. For the first time since Henri IV's investment of Paris the city was encircled, and besieged; in fact, it was the first full-scale siege of a capital in modern history. Out in the provinces—far from capitulating—France's surviving forces now took their orders from a provisional government in Tours; and under its command new armies were preparing for the day when, in concert with the Paris garrison breaking out, they could seize the occupying Prussians in a deadly vice. Gustave Flaubert, enlisted as a lieutenant in his local Garde Nationale in Rouen, was writing (with some optimism) to his niece of "armies being forged": "in a fortnight there will be perhaps a million men around Paris," and to Maxime du Camp on the day the Prussians completed the encirclement of Paris: "I guarantee that within a fortnight all France will rise. Near Mantes a peasant has strangled a Prussian and torn him apart with his teeth."

Now that Paris—the holy capital—was menaced by the enemy, there did seem to be a new, tough mood of resistance at large in France. The question was, who was going to exploit and canalise this will to fight; and how would these operations between Paris and Tours be coordinated with the city now totally cut off? What was needed was a kind of Winston Churchill. But was there such a man among France's new leaders—and, even if there was, how could he be got out of Paris?

A possible answer to the second question was sent, literally, from above. A patriotic Frenchwoman living in Prussian-occupied Versailles, on first seeing a balloon rise out of the besieged city, exclaimed, in the hearing of W. H. Russell of *The Times*: "Paris reduced to that! Oh good God! Have pity on us!" Yet it was the balloons of Paris that were to constitute probably the most illustrious, courageous and inventive episode of the siege. Today, the Siege of Paris usually evokes principally two images: the eating of cats and rats, and balloons. If the first represents the degradation and misery to which a modern civilisation can be reduced, the second shows the soaring imagination and resourcefulness that can be inspired by adversity. Often taking off into the night with primitive machines and no Houston Ground Control for back-up, the bravery of the balloonists of Paris surely compares to that of the early astronauts.

Seven balloons had been located around Paris, though most of them were in disrepair. One, the *Neptune,* was sufficiently patched up to be wafted out of Paris on 23 September. Its intrepid pilot, Durouf, landed safely at Evreux beyond the enemy's reach with 103 kilograms of dispatches, after a three-hour flight. Four other balloons took off in quick succession, with none of their crews being shot down or captured, or even coming to grief.

Manufactured in the deserted Gare d'Orléans, and the Gare du Nord, the balloons were constructed simply of varnished cotton because silk was unobtainable, and filled with highly explosive coal gas, which made them exceptionally vulnerable to Prussian sharp-shooters. Capable of unpredictable motion in all three dimensions, none of which was controllable, in inexperienced hands the balloons had an unpleasant habit of shooting suddenly up to 6000 feet, then falling back again almost to ground level. Altogether some sixty-five manned balloons left Paris during the siege. They carried 164 passengers, 381 pigeons, 5 dogs and nearly 11 tons of official dispatches, including approximately two-and-a-half million letters. Only five fell into enemy hands and only two balloonists died. The news they exported of Paris's continued resistance did much to kindle hope in the provinces. But above all, the knowledge that the city was not entirely cut off from the outside world, the ability to communicate, however haphazardly, with relatives there, and to learn that other French forces were still resisting the enemy somewhere in the provinces, went far towards maintaining Parisian morale. Whatever its fate, Paris could point—with pride—to the epic of the balloons as having been its "finest hour."

Despite all efforts, it only ever proved possible to balloon out of Paris, and not back in. Hence the government in Tours resorted to the humble carrier-pigeon, bearing messages reduced to a minute size, printed on feathery collodion membranes, and dispatched back to the capital. One pigeon could carry up to 40,000 dispatches, equivalent to the contents of a complete book. Unfortunately, their flights were unreliable. During the siege, 302 pigeons were sent off, of which fifty-nine actually reached Paris. The remainder were taken by birds of prey, died of cold and hunger, or ended in Prussian pies. As a counter-measure, the Prussians imported falcons; to which one of the many Parisian "inventors" suggested that pigeons be equipped with whistles, to frighten off the predators!

THE TROCHU GOVERNMENT decided to balloon a new plenipotentiary to the Provisional Government at Tours. Few volunteers came forward—except Léon Gambetta. As Minister of the Interior, Gambetta seemed to be an obvious choice when it came to organising a *levée en masse* in the provinces, though his more remarkable attributes were not then apparent. He was only thirty-two, the son of an Italian grocer living in Cahors, but a careless bohemian life had prematurely aged him so that his beard and his mass of unkempt black hair was streaked with grey. However, he had already established himself as one of the great orators of France, with "authority even in his laugh," and all that he seemed to lack was military experience. Gambetta having arrived safely in Tours, he set about vigorously organising the Army of the Loire to continue the fight.

As far as Paris was concerned, given the vagaries of pigeon post, Gambetta's intentions remained unclear. Nevertheless, Trochu decided to launch a major sortie from Paris, across the Marne to the south-east. It was very late in the day—and a couple of counter-strokes had previously failed to break through the Prussians' ring of iron. The date for the "Great Sortie" was fixed for 29 November, and it was to break the siege in coordination with an offensive by Gambetta's forces outside. But not until the 24th, only five days before D-Day, was the vital intelligence to Gambetta dispatched—aboard the *Ville d'Orléans*. The thirty-third balloon to leave Paris, it carried a crew of two: Rolier, the pilot, and Béziers. Because Prussian anti-balloon measures now made daylight flights so risky, the *Ville d'Orléans* took off under cover of darkness, shortly before midnight. After a record-breaking journey, it in fact landed in Norway—having had to jettison the crucial dispatches for Tours. Miraculously, these were eventually recovered from the sea, but they reached Tours too late for Gambetta to coordinate his forces with Trochu. In consequence, the supreme effort to break the Prussian stranglehold collapsed.

Trochu's defeated forces reeled back into Paris. Morale plummeted, then the indiscriminate bombardment by Prussian heavy guns began.

INSIDE PARIS, as the siege ground on, anger on the left was steadily mounting. There was a very real sense that nothing was being done—just "spin" from the Hôtel de Ville. It seemed that Trochu would rather do a "deal" with the Prussians than face a Dantonesque war *à outrance*—and which risked the physical destruction of Paris. Another bourgeois swindle at their expense in the offing! At the end of October, after news of Marshal Bazaine's surrender at Metz, angry "Reds" broke into the Hôtel de Ville. There had been farcical and humiliating scenes as the swashbuckling Gustave Flourens, magnificently booted and spurred and wielding a massive Turkish scimitar, leapt on to the table, kicking over inkwells on a level with President Trochu's nose. Order was only restored by loyal troops quickly reaching the Hôtel de Ville via a secret subterranean passage from the nearby Napoleon Barracks, built by its namesake for just such an eventuality.

"The sufferings of Paris during the siege?" Edmond Goncourt wrote in his diary for 7 January 1871, from the comfort of his house in the semi-detached village of Auteuil: "A joke for two months. In the third month the joke went sour. Now nobody finds it funny any more, and we are moving fast towards starvation." Among Goncourt's circle, Gautier lamented that he had to wear braces for the first time, "his abdomen no longer supporting his trousers."[8] They were luckier than most, but by early October even bourgeois Paris had begun to eat horsemeat. To a *belle* who (exceptionally) had refused to dine with him, a frustrated Victor Hugo wrote:

> I would have offered you a meal beyond compare:
> I would have killed Pegasus and had him cooked,
> So as to serve you with a horse's wing.

As belts were tightened, so many a champion of the turf ended its days in the casserole; among them were the two trotting horses presented by the Tsar to Louis-Napoleon at the time of the Great Exhibition, originally valued at ff56,000, now bought by a butcher for ff800.

From the desperate shortages of mid-November onwards originated the exotic menus with which the siege is immortally coupled. Most of the animals from the Jardin d'Acclimatation disappeared; even its pride, two young elephants called Castor and Pollux, were dispatched after several disgracefully inept attempts with explosive bullets. The lions and tigers survived; as did the monkeys, protected apparently by the exaggerated Darwinian instincts of the Parisians, and the hippopotamus from the Jardin des Plantes, for whose vast live-weight no butcher could afford the reserve price of ff80,000. Otherwise no animal was exempt. The signs "Feline and Canine Butchers" made their debut. At first the idea of slaughtering pets for human consumption provoked indignation in dog-loving Paris. But necessity bred familiarity, and by mid-December Henry Labouchère, the "Besieged Resident" of the London *Daily News,* was reporting in a matter-of-fact way, "I had a slice of spaniel the other day" (though it made him "feel like a cannibal"). Next it was the turn of the rats. Together with the carrier-pigeon, the rat was to become the most fabled animal of the siege of Paris, and from December on a good rat-hunt was one of the principal activities of the National Guard, although the number actually consumed was relatively few. The elaborate sauces required to make a rodent palatable meant that rats were essentially a rich man's dish; hence the famous menus of the Jockey Club, featuring such delicacies as *salmi de rats* and "rat pie."

Despite the quite sensible entreaties of the left wing, no measures were taken to establish proper control of food distribution. Meanwhile Labouchère noted that "in the expensive cafés of the Boulevards, feasts worthy of Lucullus are still served." The situation altered little as the months passed. More reprehensible were the speculators who sat on foodstuffs until prices seemed sufficiently attractive. Beetroots bought in October at 2 centimes a piece later sold for ff1.75. It was more profitable to sell "under the counter"; so, hour after hour the wretched housewives waited, often leaving empty-handed, with hatred in their hearts equally for the *petit bourgeois* as represented by the heartless butcher and for the rich bourgeois who could afford to buy without queuing. Curiously enough, there was never any shortage of wine or alcohol. In the poorer districts of Paris drunkenness was never more widespread, nor more wretched. While the women of proletarian Paris queued and hungered, the men got drunk on the barricades—all the while fuming against the government.

On 22 December, Trochu signalled to Tours warning that Paris would have no food left by 20 January. Cold now added to the miseries of hunger, with the Seine freezing over in the bitterest winter in living memory. In a move aimed at ending the siege at the end of December, Bismarck and Moltke now added a new component of horror: the escalated bombardment of the civilian population. The shells—from monster cannon like the one Herr Krupp had shown off at Expo '67—fell at a rate of 300–400 a day, at random and with no attempt to single out military targets. It marked a beginning of the German technique of war by *Schrecklichkeit*. But, once the initial fear of the unknown had passed, in a manner comparable to the London Blitz of 1940, or the Allied bombing of Berlin, indignation was replaced by a remarkable indifference.

THE PRUSSIAN COURT had ensconced itself at Versailles early in the siege. Inside the great staterooms where the Roi Soleil and Mme. de Maintenon had paraded less than two centuries previously, German wounded lay in cots dominated by the rows of vast patriotic canvases, endlessly proclaiming past French victories over their countrymen. Court-painters were rushed to Versailles to record at top speed an historic event, one that was to have far more significant consequences for European history than the disembowelling of innocent children in Paris by the terror-weapons of the new warfare. By 18 January the scene was set in the Galerie des Glaces, where only so few years previously Queen Victoria had danced with Louis-Napoleon amid all the splendours of the Second Empire at its zenith. King Wilhelm I had himself proclaimed emperor of a Germany united over the corpse of a defunct French Empire. At 12 o'clock, recorded Russell of *The Times*:

> The boom of a gun far away rolls above the voices in the Court hailing the Emperor King. Then there is a hush of expectation, and then rich and sonorous rise the massive strains of the chorale chanted by the men of regimental bands assembled in a choir, as the King, bearing his helmet in his hand, and dressed in full uniform as a German General stalked slowly up the long gallery, and bowing to the clergy in front of the temporary altar opposite him, halted and dressed himself right and front, and then twirling his heavy moustache with his disengaged hand, surveyed the scene at each side of him.[9]

This pleasing scene, multiplied in the great mirrors, may have been less colourful than that of 4 December 1804, in Notre-Dame, but it was none the less dramatic—and consequential. As the heavy figure of Bismarck, clad in the blue tunic and great boots of a Prussian *cuirassier* and holding his *Pickelhaube* by its spike, stepped forward to proclaim the

German Empire, he was in effect triumphing over Louis XIV and everything he had stood for.

After a short while, and loud huzzahs, it was all over; the silhouette of the new Germany passed boldly across the mirrors, the footsteps died away and the great mirrors were left waiting in an empty gallery—for another historic scene nearly half a century later. In besieged Paris, Goncourt spoke for many Frenchmen when he mourned prophetically: "That really marks the end of the greatness of France." A special bitterness was injected into Franco-German relations for the next three-quarters of a century. Though it might hardly be seen at the time, the event also marked the beginning of the end of the greatness of Britain.

ABOUT THE SAME TIME as the scene in the Galerie des Glaces, Trochu made one last, hopeless attempt to break the Prussian stranglehold. It was the turn of the National Guard, which had been so loud in its condemnation of the Hôtel de Ville's ineptitude and apathy. They attacked at Buzenval to the west of Paris, with half-trained troops debilitated by hunger and cold; predictably, the result was a massacre. In fury, the left launched yet another assault on the Hôtel de Ville, on 22 January. "Civil war was a few yards away," wrote Jules Favre, in retrospect. His government at the end of its tether, Trochu sent an emissary to Bismarck, asking for an armistice.

The peace negotiations were painful, the Prussian terms brutal. France lost Alsace and Lorraine, two of her fairest and richest provinces, and was required to pay a crippling indemnity of ff5 billion—the equivalent of £200 million in contemporary money—or more than seven times the total reparations demanded by the Allies in 1815 after twenty years of war, in which French armies had devastated half the continent. Most hurtful to the pride of the defeated nation was Bismarck's insistence on a triumphal march along the Champs-Élysées. The Prussian occupation lasted just twenty-four hours, but the insult lingered on.

The city was united in rage; patriotic Paris would have none of the treaty of shame; republican Paris would have none of the new assembly created in the provinces; would not tolerate the government's move to Versailles, just vacated by the Prussians. Food supplies came rushing in, largely from Britain. Yet it was rash of Jules Ferry, on 5 March 1871, confidently to telegraph from Paris to his colleague, Jules Simon, in the tranquillity of Bordeaux, "The city is entirely calm. The danger has passed . . ." It had not; far from it.

THIERS SUCCEEDED TROCHU as president of a new council. Capitulation to Bismarck now convinced the belligerent Left of Paris that Thiers and the new Republican Assembly were doing a deal with the enemy to restore the old imperial regime. The ingredients which were to spark off the Russian Revolution in 1917—military humiliation, suppressed revolutionary fervour and deprivation—were all there. Missing only were the weapons. As the siege ended, Trochu's commanders had established safely up at Montmartre a guarded artillery park of some 200 cannon. Most of the guns bore National Guard numbers, and had been "bought" by public subscription during the siege. Thus the left-wingers of the Guard were persuaded they were the rightful owners. At the end of February, detachments of the Guard seized the guns. Efforts by loyal troops to regain them in March were not only repulsed but ended in the brutal lynching of two elderly generals—shot in a courtyard of Montmartre's Rue des Rosiers, amid scenes reminiscent of 1789; this despite the efforts of the mayor, a young Georges Clemenceau, who would later rise to fame as the uncompromising leader of France in bringing victory in the First World War.

The Montmartre guns shifted the whole balance of power, causing Thiers to move the army out of Paris to Versailles—just as he had recommended Louis-Philippe should have done in 1848. The revolutionaries set up a rival regime, called the *Commune de Paris,* inside the Hôtel de Ville. Had the Communards promptly marched on Versailles, with their 200 cannon, they could almost certainly have defeated an army that had been largely disarmed by the Prussians. Karl Marx, who later made his name from his work on the Commune, claimed this to have been a cardinal error (the other, its reluctance to seize the Bank of France): "the defensive," he wrote, "is the death of every armed rising; it is lost before it measures itself with its enemies." This was an error that his future pupil, Lenin, born the previous year at Simbirsk, would not repeat when his time came. Mutual atrocities widened the gulf between Paris and Versailles. The Commune ordered the taking of hostages, beginning with no less a person than the Archbishop of Paris, Monseigneur Darboy.

THE COMMUNE was certainly anti-religious, "Red" and left-wing, but it was not strictly speaking "Communist," having in fact pre-dated Marx to 1789. Then it had been improvised simply to assume responsibility for administering Paris. With the extremists taking over in 1792 it was transformed into the "Revolutionary Commune," which forced the Assembly to dethrone Louis XVI. By default, led by the violent Danton, it then found itself for a time the real government of France. The almost miraculous success with which it had then chased the foreign royalist invaders from French soil during the Revolution now, in 1871, helped to provide it with an all-powerful, though somewhat mystical appeal for all manner of social, political and philosophical grievances against the "Establishment." In its ranks there were the veterans of the barricades of 1848 and 1851—and even 1830. There were revolutionary feminists like Louise Michel, and there were history's homeless Poles, like Dombrowski and Wroblewski, redoubtable fighters in the cause of abstract freedom: "They were, above all, *des candides.* Never can leadership of a political movement have been so naive, so incoherent, and so incompetent,"[10] as Richard Cobb says. Except for the horrible Communard police chief, Raoul Rigault, "most were innocents who were not built for the scale of such tragic events."

The Commune was overloaded, indeed overwhelmed, by personalities, ideologies and interests. By the end of April 1871, the Versaillais troops, reinforced from the provinces, were beginning to close in, their guns already shelling central Paris in a second bombardment—just as indiscriminate towards the civil population as Moltke's had been. The Communards had still failed to establish any effective chain of command: everybody gave orders, few obeyed them. Meanwhile, Thiers' generals had spotted that the Achilles' heel of the Communard defences lay at the Point du Jour, the extreme south-western tip of the city, close to where the Seine flows out towards Sèvres. It was here that they would try to break in.

In a city riddled with spy mania and accusations of conspiracy, twenty-six-year-old Louis Rossel, son of a Scottish mother, a colonel of the engineers during the first siege, now found himself in charge of the Communard forces. He was by far their most efficient soldier, who should have been put in charge back in March. Now he ordered the immediate construction of barricades behind the city ramparts, like those constructed by Thiers himself in the 1840s, as a second line of defence. But it was to little avail. When ordering an attack, Rossel found his battalion commanders had evaporated. On 8 May he resigned in disgust.

Regardless of the imminent military menace from Versailles, the Communards went from folly to irrelevant folly. Thiers' private house was spitefully demolished. In the Place Vendôme the great column erected by Napoleon I to celebrate the victories of 1805 was brought crashing in a final, futile gesture of contempt for the fallen Empire. Then, on the sunny summer evening of Sunday, 21 May 1871, the Commune held a grandiose concert in the resplendent Tuileries Palace. No fewer than 1500 musicians were engaged to take part. While the Communards enjoyed the party, just outside the walls troops belonging to the legitimate government of Adolphe Thiers were entering the besieged city from Versailles, unchallenged. Close to the Point du Jour gate, they had spotted a white flag. Waving it was a civil engineer named Ducatel, who felt no love for the Commune and who had happened quite by chance to stroll near the battlements on his afternoon promenade. He was astonished to perceive that, around the Point du Jour, which had been heavily pounded by Thiers' cannon over the past few days, there was not a defender to be seen. By dawn the next day, Marshal MacMahon, Napoleon III's old commander, had already poured thousands of troops through five gaping breaches in the walls. With a belated sense of purpose the Communards rushed up the barricades that should have been completed weeks earlier.

On the Left Bank, they fought at Montparnasse Station until ammunition ran out; then their withdrawal was covered by a single defender, who kept up a steady fire into the station from a one-man stronghold inside a newspaper kiosk. Haussmann's layout of the new Paris, with the provision of diagonal intersections for outflanking revolutionaries' barricades, now worked in favour of the government forces. Nevertheless, about their only advance on the Monday afternoon had been to capture the garden of the British Embassy on the Faubourg Saint-Honoré. In scattered little packets, the Communards were beginning to fight as never before—the fight of despair.

THE DAWN OF TUESDAY THE 23RD broke on another ravishing May day, and with an assault on the bastion of Montmartre from two directions. Up there, about the only Communard detachment that showed spirit was a squad of twenty-five from the Women's Battalion, headed by the redoubtable Louise Michel, the *vierge rouge,* who had orders to blow up the entire Butte Montmartre if necessary. Now began the "expiation" for which Thiers had called. Some forty-nine captured Communards were collected at random and summarily shot in the Rue des Rosiers, scene of the lynching of the two generals back in March. All through the 23rd, Paul-Antoine Brunel and his men had continued to hold out with the utmost tenacity at the barricades in the Rue Royale and the Place de la Concorde. Turning movements from the direction of the Opéra were threatening their rear, and now rifle-fire from sharp-shooters on top of the high buildings along the Rue Royale mowed them down behind the barricades. Swiftly Brunel—justifying the nick-name of "The Burner" that he had gained during the first siege—ordered the firing of these buildings.

That night, away in the darkness, Parisians saw the red glow of a great fire. Inside the Tuileries Palace, where only two days previously the last of the famous concerts had taken place, barrel after barrel of gun-powder had been piled. With a tremendous roar the central dome hous-ing the Salle des Maréchaux disappeared.

By the following night, the Tuileries, a large part of the Palais-Royal, the Palais de Justice, the Préfecture de Police, the Légion d'Honneur and the Conseil d'État had been set on fire. Whole sections of streets like the Rue de Lille and much of the Rue de Rivoli were ablaze; so was the Min-istry of Finance, housed in one wing of the Louvre, threatening the priceless treasures in the museum itself. At Notre-Dame, which had escaped destruction by so narrow a margin during the Great Revolution, National Guards built up a large "brazier" from chairs and pews. They were just forestalled in time; but, evacuated by the desperate Commune, the superb medieval building of the Hôtel de Ville, the focus of so much Parisian history from Philippe-Auguste onwards, was also consigned to the flames.

Now there entered into the limelight *Les pétroleuses;* whether by leg-end or fact, these were fearful maenads from some infernal region, women who allegedly crept about the city, flinging Molotov cocktails into basement windows belonging to the bourgeoisie. That night, too, the Communards committed their most infamous crime: the execution, in an alley outside the prison of La Roquette, of the hostage Archbishop of Paris. Retribution was not long delayed in catching up with Raoul Rigault, the Communard Chief of Police responsible. The next day Rigault was seized on the Left Bank, at lodgings he shared under an assumed name with an actress. Shot in the head, for two days his body lay in the gutter, partly stripped by women of the district and kicked and spat upon by passers-by.

On the evening of Thursday the 25th, as Commune resistance was beginning to crumble, its last leader, Charles Delescluze—dressed as always like an 1848 revolutionary, in a top hat, polished boots, black trousers and frock coat, a red sash around his waist and leaning heavily on a cane—set off towards an abandoned barricade. He was seen slowly to clamber to the top; then pitch forward on his face.

Friday 26 May was a day of savage killings on both sides, in which the battle became a ruthless mopping-up operation. Goncourt was moved to pity by the sight of the Communard prisoners:

> The men had been split up into lines of seven or eight and tied to each other with string that cut into their wrists. They were just as they had been captured, most of them without hats or caps, and with their hair plastered down on their foreheads and faces by the fine rain that had been falling ever since this morning. There were men of the people there who had made themselves head coverings out of blue check handkerchiefs. Others, drenched to the skin by the rain, were carrying a hunk of bread.

One of the Versailles generals, the dashing Marquis de Gallifet, now secured for himself a reputation for ferocity that Paris would never forget. "I am Gallifet," he told prisoners. "You people of Montmartre may think me cruel, but I am even crueller than you can imagine." Twirling his moustachios, with his mistress on his arm, pointing out who should die and who should live, he is described as "making caustic jests as he did so." Thiers' regulars were also approaching the last of the Commune's remaining strongholds: the vast cemetery of Père Lachaise that Napoleon I had laid out. There the last Communard defenders, firing from the cover of its elaborate family mausoleums, had to be winkled out gravestone by gravestone. Fifteen miles outside Paris, Alphonse Daudet recalled hearing the last rumbling of the cannon, which reminded him of:

> a great ship in distress . . . I felt that the Commune, about to go down, was firing its last distress rockets. At every minute I could see the wreck heave up, the breach in it grew bigger, and then inside I could see the men of the Hôtel de Ville clinging to their

stage, and continuing to decree amid all the din of the wind and the tempest.

The next morning, 28 May, Thiers' army moved in for the kill. It was Whit Sunday. Within a few hours, there was only one Communard barricade left, on the Rue Ramponneau, where an unknown lone defender held off the attackers with a cool and deadly aim; having fired off his last cartridge, he strolled calmly away and disappeared. At La Roquette the unburied corpse of the murdered Archbishop had been discovered. That Whitsun morning the Versailles troops marched 147 of the captured Communards out to Père Lachaise and shot them against a wall of the cemetery. Over two days, inside La Roquette and Mazas prisons, over 2000 Commune prisoners were shot.

THE LAST GREAT SIEGE of Paris was at an end. France was sick of the slaughter. "Let us kill no more, even murderers and incendiaries!" the *Paris-Journal* implored on 2 June. "Let us kill no more!" The number of lives lost during *la semaine sanglante* was probably between 20,000 and 25,000—far more than the blood-letting of the Terror of 1793 in Paris. The orgy of killing represented, to some extent, a savage but deliberate settling of accounts that dated back to 1789. Among the surviving Communards deported to insalubrious colonies for long sentences, Louise Michel eventually returned to France; still a violent anarchist, she was arrested several times more before having to flee to London, where she died in 1905—exultant at the news of revolution in Russia. "Burner" Brunel, though badly wounded, escaped from Paris (and a death sentence) and four years later found employment teaching French at the Royal Naval College, Dartmouth, until he died in 1904. Among his pupils, incongruously, was the future King George V.

At the end of the hostilities in May 1871, Paris presented a terrible sight. Théophile Gautier, returning to a city whose silence oppressed him, was appalled by the familiar Rue de Lille, on the Left Bank, where his fellow author Prosper Mérimée had once lived: "it seemed to be deserted throughout its length, like a street of Pompeii." Of Mérimée's old house, nothing remained but the walls; his famous library was in ashes.

A silence of death reigned over these ruins; in the necropolises of Thebes or in the shafts of the Pyramids it was no more profound.

No clatter of vehicles, no shouts of children, not even the song of a bird . . . an incurable sadness invaded our souls . . .

Yet more of the city had survived than people could imagine. The *Vénus de Milo* was lifted reverently from the storage "coffin" within the incendiarised Préfecture de Police, where she had been preserved since before the first siege. As she returned to the Louvre, it seemed like a symbol of the return of life to Paris herself. Almost like a sign of regeneration, too, Georges Rouault, the painter, had been born in a cellar while the last fighting raged just overhead. Worth, the couturier, bought up part of the wreckage of the Tuileries to construct sham ruins in his garden, and the work of rebuilding Paris was under way almost immediately when the fighting ended. That summer omnibuses and carriages were plying the streets again, *bateaux-mouches* bustling up and down the Seine. Even the enterprising Thomas Cook was sending hordes of English tourists to goggle at the "ruins" of Paris. But, as a reminder of the horrors of the recent past, some noticed Parisians for a long time preferring to walk in the road rather than on the pavements—to avoid any suspicion that they might be *pétroleuses* intent on popping their incendiary packets through basement windows.

As an epitaph to those terrible days of May 1871, "they were madmen," said painter Auguste Renoir, who himself had narrowly escaped death at Communard hands; "but they had in them that little flame which never dies."

# FOURTEEN

# *The* Belle Epoque *and the Road to War*

The ceding of Alsace-Lorraine is nothing but war to
perpetuity under the mask of peace . . .

—*Edgar Quinet*

You are weary of this old world at last.

—*Guilliame Apollinaire*

WITH THE CRUSHING of the Communards and, coupled
with it, the destruction of much of central Paris, for the
first time since 1789 the capital recedes from the front of
the stage, as France strides forward. The opportunities of peacetime are
met with a formidable regenerative surge in industry, as well as in the
pursuit of leisure. After sketching dead Communards at the barricades,
Manet was back at Boulogne painting *La Partie de Croquet.* Renoir and
Degas came back to find studios; Monet and Pissarro returned from
refuge in dank and foggy London. Suddenly, as if in reaction against the
grim drabness and the sombre horrors of the Siege and the Commune,
the Impressionists burst forth into a new, passionate, glorious blaze of
colour, redolent with the love of simple, ordinary existence. They would
be immortalising with new life places like Courbevoie, Asnières and
Gennevilliers, once front-line names during the two sieges, pleasant
riverside villages which, in the coming century, would be swallowed up
in new suburbs peopled by the modern workforce of prodigious French
industry. Seurat would be painting his masterpiece of summer reveries
on *La Grande Jatte,* the sand bar in the Seine which only so recently had
seen Trochu's Garde Nationale charge across the river in its last, hopeless

attempt to break the Prussian ring round Paris. It almost seemed to mirror the resurgence of French literature that had followed the cataclysm of 1815. Out of the ruins, the Hôtel de Ville was rebuilt with remarkable speed, a faithful image of its old, medieval self, and a symbol of resurrection. Napoleon I took his place once more atop a resurrected Vendôme Column.

EUROPE'S BANKERS were amazed to see the first half billion of the ff5 billion in reparations that France had to pay Germany handed over just one month after the collapse of the Commune. The rest followed with a rapidity none would have predicted; as early as September 1873 the crushing bill had been paid off, and the last German soldier removed from French soil. By 1875 the budget showed a comfortable surplus; saving deposits were up 27 per cent; coal production up 60 per cent; and iron 26 per cent; a further 18,000 kilometres of railway track had been built, and foreign trade expanded by 21 per cent. In 1872, the new Republican Assembly passed the first of the laws designed to restore the efficiency of her humiliated army; and with it went a new spirit. Accompanying it also went a vocal urge for revenge which alarmed British residents; they had not suffered a humiliating defeat that had seen two of their fairest provinces handed over to the enemy. Throughout the next forty-three years, as the statue of the city of Strasbourg on the Concorde remained shrouded in black, Frenchmen would ponder in silence Deputy Edgar Quinet's remark at the time of the debate on Bismarck's peace terms: "the ceding of Alsace-Lorraine is nothing but war to perpetuity under the mask of peace."*

This was approximately what Thiers had warned greedy Bismarck at the time. As long as Prussian soldiers stood guard the wrong side of Metz, less than 200 miles by straight, flat road from the capital, Frenchmen would grieve and dream dangerously of *la revanche*—the dream that was "never spoken, but never forgotten." It may have been hardly apparent at the time in smugly prosperous mid-Victorian Britain, where Mr. Gladstone was about to give way to Disraeli, a Britain currently preoccupied with domestic debates on reform, women's rights and Ireland, but otherwise at peace with the world. Yet the settlement in the Hall of Mirrors spelled the beginning of the end of *Pax Britannica*—though it

---

*Quinet, a distinguished historian, and idealistic patriot, was also rated as an expert on Germany.

might free-wheel for a few decades yet. Louis-Napoleon's ill-conceived war and its disastrous consequences had fundamentally disturbed that illusive structure, created by Metternich, the European balance of power.

THE FUNERAL OF THE OLD TITAN of literature, Victor Hugo, in May 1885 at the Panthéon (just restored to its revolutionary usage as a mausoleum for *grands hommes*) was a tremendous affair barely exceeded by the reinterment of Napoleon four decades previously. But did Hugo—master of bombastic silliness during the siege—quite deserve to lie among the best and greatest in the land? What about Balzac, Molière, Racine? The spectacle only tended to remind Frenchmen of how, under the dull respectability of the Third Republic, the nation needed a hero. It was not to be the Bourbon "pretender," the Comte de Chambord, grandson of Charles X, who affected to call himself Henri V, but wrecked what slender chances there existed for a new monarchist Restoration by stalwartly refusing to accept the *tricolore*—or the principles for which the revolution had been fought. (Once again the Bourbons showed they had learned nothing; nevertheless the royalist "Legitimists" continued long—well into the twentieth century—to be a factor in French politics.) Adolphe Thiers, the old veteran of so many political battles, he who had crushed the Paris Commune, was defeated by a conservative coalition in 1873, and died four years later; Gambetta died shortly after retiring from office, in 1882, aged only forty-four; and with him also went much of the colour and romantic flavour of French politics. Nevertheless, both had lived long enough to see the new Third Republic established on sound, if not exciting, foundations.

The new Constitutional Law of 1875 which founded France's Third Republic was passed by a margin of only one vote. The system—resembling more closely that of the USA than any of the European monarchies—deliberately did not encourage strong or colourful leaders. The nation felt it had had enough of those for the time being. The President was to be elected, for a period of seven years, by a joint session of the Chamber of Deputies and the Senate. He had the right to dissolve the Chamber, with the consent of the Senate; but otherwise he had no power of veto, and in effect played the role of a constitutional monarch. The Senate, sitting in Marie de' Medici's resplendent Luxembourg, was to be elected indirectly by colleges formed by the municipalities; thus, in the view of Gambetta, it was to become "the grand council of the communes of France." Only the deputies of the Chamber were to be elected by direct vote. Every precaution was taken to prevent the possibility of another Louis-Napoleon effecting a *coup d'état* by means of a popular plebiscite.

IN CONSEQUENCE, instead of being ruled by flamboyant titans like Gambetta, for the next few decades France would find respectable mediocrities like the triplicate of Juleses—Ferry, Simon and Grévy. Yet, as the British Ambassador observed in 1886, in a caustic dispatch: "The Republic here has lasted sixteen years and that is about the time which it takes to make the French tired of a form of government."[1] The very next year there followed the *affaire Boulanger.* In a momentary outburst of jingoism, it looked alarmingly as if France might have found the new hero, the star she sought, in the shape of General Georges Boulanger. The dashing fifty-year-old Minister of War was the epitome of the general on a white horse—except that his was black. When he appeared, martially magnificent, at the 14 July review at Longchamps—though no more than a simple soldier not over-burdened with brains, who had comported himself with bravery during the lost war—spectators went mad with delight. Songs were heard in the street that evoked the bloody summer of 1870: *Regardez-le là bas! Il nous sourit et passe: Il vient de délivrer le Lorraine et l'Alsace! "Look at him! He smiles at us and moves on: He is going to liberate Lorraine and Alsace!"* In Berlin, Bismarck's finger crooked round the trigger. In the Chamber, Boulanger was greeted with less gravity, when the Premier, Charles Floquet, jeered: "At your age, Sir, Napoleon was dead!" Fortunately for the peace of Europe, the inflammatory Boulanger lost the political initiative and, three years later, committed suicide upon the grave of his mistress, the evocatively named Mme. de Bonnemains. In the words of Clemenceau's savage epitaph, he died "as he had lived, like a subaltern." The episode said something about the fragility of the Third Republic, the underlying simmer of Bonapartism—even without a Bonaparte.

A quite different political crisis exploded in 1892. Ferdinand de Lesseps, the brilliant engineer and hero who had dug the Suez Canal, underestimated the costs of digging a similar canal across the Isthmus of Panama. To muzzle criticism, the Panama Company had paid money to newspapers and "bought" votes in the Chamber. In 1892, the right-wing press—notably a wildly anti-Semitic paper, *La Libre Parole,* saw a political weapon and broadcast the scandal. Baron Reinach, an eminent Jew who had acted as intermediary between the company and government deputies, was driven to commit suicide. In the ensuing investigations, only one politician was found guilty, but the mud bespattered a whole generation of French politicians. Even Clemenceau was compromised and had to spend long years in the wilderness—when France most needed his leadership.

In the middle of the Panama scandal, the anarchist outrages, an irrational wave of terrorism which struck throughout the western world, reached Paris. In the twenty years leading up to 1914, six heads of state were assassinated, culminating with Empress Elisabeth of Austria (1898), King Umberto of Italy (1900) and US President McKinley in 1901. Describing the pointlessness of the anarchist cause, Barbara Tuchman writes that, of their victims, "not one could qualify as a tyrant. Their deaths were the gestures of desperate or deluded men to call attention to the Anarchist idea . . ."[2] The first ruler to die, in 1881, was Tsar Alexander II; here his Narodniki assassins struck the wrong target, since of all the Russian autocrats he did most to liberate the serfs, and his death was followed by a campaign of savage repression. In Paris the anarchist scourge began with the bombings of houses of public figures by one Ravachol (alias François Claudius Königstein); then a bomb was deposited, to coincide with a miners' strike in November 1892, in the mine company's office on the Avenue de l'Opéra. It exploded as an unfortunate agent was carrying it into the nearby police station, blowing up him and five others. The following December, thirty-two-year-old Auguste Vaillant exploded a bomb inside the Chamber of Deputies; it was intended to be a non-lethal protest, but wounded several deputies and led Vaillant to the guillotine. The week after his execution, another bomb exploded indiscriminately in the Café Terminus of Gare Saint-Lazare, killing one and maiming twenty. The culprit, Émile Henry, also proved to be the perpetrator of the bomb in the Avenue de l'Opéra, and was duly guillotined. Then, a month after Henry's execution, in May 1894, the anarchists *en revanche* claimed their most eminent French victim when President Sadi Carnot was stabbed to death in Dijon by a young Italian worker.

Suddenly, however, the wave of anarchist outrages, which was beginning to hold Paris in a grip of terror, ebbed as swiftly as it had begun. Meanwhile, in the backstreets and Bohemia, Ravachol briefly became something of a hero; a verb, *ravacholer,* meaning to "wipe out an enemy," became current, while a song called "La Ravachole" was sung to the tune of "La Carmagnole," with the refrain of

It will come, it will come
Every bourgeois will have his bomb.[3]

But if Ravachol's death had any lasting significance, it came in 1895, a year after the last assassination attempt, when Paris workers responded by creating the Confédération Générale de Travail (CGT)—the first time since the Commune that the prostrate city proletariat dared raise its head to take collective action. From those militant beginnings the trade union movement would become integral to the workings of the French state.

ON 6 JANUARY 1895, on the parade ground of the École Militaire, a French army officer had his epaulettes ceremoniously ripped off his shoulders in disgrace. It was the beginning of one of the most unpalatable, and destructive, episodes in all French history. For more than a decade, the Dreyfus Affair, or simply *l'affaire*, focused the passions and attention of the entire country, averting its eyes from the clouds that were now mounting over the eastern horizon. At this distance, and for an *anglo-saxon* reader, it is often difficult to appreciate the bitterness generated by *l'affaire*, where even the highest in the land were involved. In the army, where *l'affaire* had its origins, divisions were magnified and particularly disastrous. Broadly, the cleavage fell between the conservative, traditionalist, partly monarchist and largely Catholic, caste of the army and the new republican, progressive and often anti-clerical elements of post-1870.

The whole sordid story has been told and retold so often that few can be totally unfamiliar with it: Dreyfus was a thirty-five-year-old French artillery captain, of a moderately prosperous Jewish family, but born in the Alsace seized by Germany when Dreyfus was still a child. Like many Alsatian Jews, the Dreyfuses fled westwards, to escape Prussianism and likely conscription into the Germany Army. The swelling numbers of Jews gave rise in Paris particularly to an increase in anti-Semitism, fanned by allegations emerging from the Panama scandal.[4] Though he seemed never to have been comfortable among his fellow officers, and lacking in charisma, Dreyfus was passionately attached to Alsace and France, and it was his dedication to *la revanche* that led him to join the army. In October 1894, he was confronted by a fellow officer, on the orders of the chief of the French General Staff, with a *bordereau*—a memorandum—filched by a cleaner from the wastepaper basket of the

German military attaché. It was alleged to have been written in Dreyfus' hand and contained some low-grade intelligence about the latest French cannon. Dreyfus protested to the end of his life that it was a forgery. No one at the time believed him, and after a mockery of a trial he was subjected to that humiliation on the parade ground; then deported to Devil's Island for the rest of his life.

Terrible years went by before Colonel Picquart, an intelligence officer on the French General Staff, discovered that the *bordereau* was in fact a forgery. The real spy was revealed to be a captain of Hungarian descent called Esterhazy, an unsavoury man of many mistresses and many debts. Despite the powerful evidence he brought the French General Staff, Picquart himself was given a jail sentence. The waters were further muddied by a new forgery inserted into the Dreyfus file by Picquart's successor at the head of French intelligence, Colonel Henry. Eventually this forgery too was exposed, and Henry committed suicide (on 31 August 1898). Esterhazy fled to England, where he died under an assumed name many years later. Because of the French military establishment's determination to hush up the scandal (at the retrial of Dreyfus in Rennes staff officers even rattled their swords to drown out the voice of the appellant's lawyer), still more years went by; then Émile Zola entered the lists. Up till then the brutal realism of Zola's novels had generally aroused criticism, if not disgust, but now he suddenly seized on a cause far transcending just the squalor of proletarian Paris. He espoused it with utmost passion and vigour, to write one of the most powerful pieces of journalism of all time—"J'accuse!" It whipped up such powerful public emotion as to make a retrial unavoidable—though Zola, too, went to prison for his pains.

"J'accuse!," an open letter to the President of the Republic, forced to the surface all manner of latent prejudices—not least the anti-Semitism that had lurked since the days of Philippe le Bel. It forced people to take sides; Dreyfus symbolised either the eternal Jewish traitor—or the denial of justice. *L'affaire* now became, in the words of Léon Blum, a future prime minister and a Jew himself, then in his twenties, "A human crisis, less extended and less prolonged in time but no less violent than the French Revolution." It "would have divided the angels themselves," wrote the Comte de Vogüé, representing the opposite side to Blum. Zola himself was subjected to a barrage of insults and excrement; at his own trial for libel in 1898, the screaming crowds shouting "Death to Zola!" and "Death to the Jews!" sounded (to Zola) alarmingly "as if they were waiting for someone to throw them meat." Mobs broke the windows of *L'Aurore,* the newspaper that had published "J'Accuse!" At cafés "Nationalists" and "Revisionists" sat at different tables on opposite sides of the terraces; salons became polarised; Marcel Proust's father refused to speak to him for a week because of his support for Zola; Monet and Degas did not speak for years; the author, Pierre Louÿs, and Léon Blum never saw each other again, while many other former friends passed each other in silence.

Divisions reached to the highest in the land; Clemenceau fought a duel with Édouard Drumont, author of the fiercely anti-Semitic *La France Juive*; and six out of seven Ministers of Defence resigned in the course of *l'affaire.* A bizarre twist was added in 1899 when President of the Republic Félix Faure was in his presidential office as various supplicants awaited his pleasure in the anteroom. Suddenly the shrieks of a woman in pain were heard; rushing into the Salon Jaune, equivalent of the White House's Oval Office, orderlies were confronted with the spectacle of a stark naked President. Dead of a heart attack, his hand was clenched with the fixity of *rigor mortis* in the hair of a lusty redhead, in equal *déshabille.* (Some visitors to Père Lachaise Cemetery feel Faure's tomb there is more deserving of the inscription accorded to soldiers killed on the battlefield—*Mort en Brave.*) As Faure was an anti-Dreyfusard, his sudden death was a blow to their cause; some even fantasised that he had in fact been poisoned. At Faure's funeral, an ultra-nationalist, Paul Déroulède, tried to mount a coup, but it was a lamentable failure. A few months later Faure's successor, newly elected pro-Dreyfus President Loubet, had his top hat cleft on Auteuil race course by the heavy cane of an anti-Dreyfusard baron.

For at least three of the twelve years that *l'affaire* dragged on, the French political scene was dominated by it. *L'affaire* coincided with the publication in France of the first effectively anti-military novels—yet the most lethal impact was on the French Army, still recovering from its debacle of 1870–71. When Dreyfus was finally rehabilitated, in July 1906 after four-and-a-half years on Devil's Island, it fell deeper into disrepute than Boulanger had already guided it. None of this went unnoticed in Kaiser Wilhelm's Germany, as internal conflict appeared to absorb all France's energies.

*L'AFFAIRE* HELPED OBSCURE ADVANCES, material and technological, as well as political and social, that were being made by France during the last decades of the nineteenth century. Replacing gas-light, there was electricity (thanks to the "Wizard of Menlo Park," Mr. Edison). There was the gramophone; there was the telephone (already functioning, in Paris, about as efficiently as it would for much of the next century), of which Goncourt observed, in 1882, that it was "the very latest thing, this leave-taking which cuts out all possibility of argument." There were horseless carriages, and in 1894 the first automobile race took place from Paris to Rouen, 78 miles. In 1885, Louis Pasteur discovered a vaccine cure for rabies. In 1895, Louis Lumière showed the first moving pictures.* Rail networks proliferated and became faster—and there were more train crashes. But, given what it had had to put up with over the past six centuries, perhaps the greatest technological advance was Paris' new sewer system.

The capital itself was becoming full of the new wonders of the world—not least, inescapable from the eye wherever you went, the Tour Eiffel. It was constructed for the 1889 Exposition to mark the hundredth anniversary of the revolution, a commemoration as well as an act of reconciliation; to hail France's recovery and its spectacular entry into an industrialised world. Using 2½ million rivets, 300 steeplejacks working only 7000 tons of steel, at a modest cost of ff7.8 million, exerting a deadweight pressure per square inch no more than that of a man seated in a chair, the tower was not intended to last for more than twenty years. In 1909, it was only saved from being dismantled by the fact that its huge aerial antennae had become essential to the new development of radio. Many eminent Frenchmen hated it—"a monstrous construction," "a hollow candlestick," "metal asparagus," or—worse—a "solitary riddled *suppositoire*." "Douanier" Rousseau was one of the first artists to break ranks and treat it as a respectable subject for the canvas. By the time of its centenary in 1989, visitors equivalent to almost four times the 1889 population had climbed up the Eiffel Tower (or, more likely, had taken the lift).†

---

*There remains some controversy as to whether he or Thomas Edison could properly claim to be the father of the moving picture. Edison's "Kinetograph," patented in 1894, was an immobile studio affair weighing 1000 lb; Lumière's *cinématographe,* hand-cranked and weighing less than 20 lb, could reasonably claim to be the first commercially viable projector.

†A nice, typically Parisian, anecdote concerns the lifts under the German occupation of 1940. When the *Wehrmacht* took possession of the tower, a piece of foreign machinery essential to running the lifts was found missing, and could not be replaced; so the Germans had to walk up all through the war; then—with the Liberation in 1944—the missing piece was mysteriously rediscovered.

THE TOWER MAY HAVE DOMINATED the 1889 Exposition, but at its feet had been constructed a remarkable, temporary city in which the central theme was France's new colonial empire. Providing in part a distraction for minds and hearts from France's territorial losses at home, like the old British Empire France's new one had been collected also more or less in a "fit of absent-mindedness." There had been, in 1885, a bitter confrontation between Clemenceau, whose obsession was—and would ever remain—east of the Rhine, and Jules Ferry eager to make indigenous piracy in the Gulf of Tonkin a pretext for creating a French colony there. He and the other proponents of the Tonkin Expedition became national heroes. Soon the rest of Indo-China—Cochin-China, Annam (latter-day Vietnam), Cambodia and Laos joined Tonkin in the colonial basket. Great empire-builders like Lyautey and Gallieni served their apprenticeship in *Indo-chine*. Meanwhile, in West and Saharan Africa, explorers like de Brazza and Faidherbe carved out a French empire, contiguous with French Algeria, that reached from the River Niger to Lake Chad and the sources of the Nile. To the north-west the kingdoms of Morocco and Tunisia became "protectorates," forming, with Algeria, one huge block from the Mediterranean to the Atlantic. In the east of the African continent, France acquired Madagascar and Djibouti, and in the far Pacific, territories rich in strategic minerals, like New Caledonia.

Towards the end of the century, more of the map of Africa had become shaded green even than the pink of imperial Britain. As British imperialists dreamed of a Cape-to-Cairo railroad running through those all-pink possessions, and French explorers and colonialists sought to cut across Africa horizontally, there was bound to be a collision. In 1898, it came when an expedition under Major Marchand, having crossed Africa, ran into a far stronger force, under General Kitchener, at a small village called Fashoda in the Sudan. London demanded the withdrawal of Marchand, and there was a violent flare-up of nationalism in Paris. The fleets of both countries were actually mobilised; and it was the last time since Waterloo—and up to the present day—that Britain and France, those "dear enemies," came close to war with each other. An ugly situation was brilliantly defused by Foreign Minister Théophile Delcassé—recognising that Britain required a free hand in Egypt and the troublesome Sudan; France in turbulent Morocco. His classic diplomacy was to lead to the epoch-making Entente Cordiale just a few years after Fashoda.

TERRITORIAL EXPANSION across Asia and Africa ran parallel with the rise in prosperity during the Third Republic in the 1880s, 1890s and right through to the outbreak of war in 1914, enjoyed by a larger number of Frenchmen than at any other time in their history. Alternately dubbed *la belle époque,* "banquet years" or "miraculous years," it seemed like a period that would, or should, continue for ever. This age of repeated excitement, fear combined with optimistic expectation, produced a kind of dawn of the consumer society in what one author dubbed the *nivellement des jouissances* ("levelling of pleasures").[5] Cutting right across France, both socially and geographically, life was wonderfully, unmistakably good. *La vie douce* could barely convey all it meant—though the Germans' envious expression of "content as a God in France" perhaps came closest.

But the soaring prices of living accommodation in the capital accounted for one of the most important migrations in its history. Artists moved from the Left Bank's Latin Quarter, from Montparnasse to Montmartre. In almost every way Montmartre suited them better. The narrow irregular streets and low houses of what until recently had been a detached village, with windmills, vineyards and gardens, put on the map by the balloons of Paris flying from it during the siege, provided an exhilarating contrast to Haussmann's monumental, orderly and alienating Paris, with all its stress and dizzy whirl. An earlier generation led by Berlioz and writers like Murger, Nerval and Heine was replaced by Pissarro, Cézanne, Monet, Renoir and Toulouse-Lautrec, in turn replaced by Van Gogh, Picasso, Braque, Matisse and Dufy, with the millennium year of 1900 acting as a kind of watershed. There in this sleepy village the artists, and their favourite models like Jeanne Avril, "La Goulue" and Valentin-le-Désossé brought immortal fame to cafés and *bals musettes* such as the Moulin Rouge, the Moulin de la Galette and the Lapin Agile (variously known as the "Lapin à Gill" or "La peint A. Gill"). Montmartre became something of a year-long carnival, where anyone abandoning bourgeois respectability could submerge his identity for a few hours, disappearing into an alluring milieu of bohemians, prostitutes and criminals. For the artists it represented cheap and congenial living—with plenty of motifs to paint all round them. Slowly arising above them was the sugary white cupola of the Sacré Coeur—the monument to reconciliation after the blood-letting of the Commune, loathed by some but painted by many others, eventually to become as integral a part of the Paris skyline as its opposing pinnacle, the Eiffel Tower.

Never had there been so much for so many. It was an epoch of soaring ideas and creativity. The bicycle and *le football* introduced new pleasures; the Orient Express and *wagons-lits* (sleepers) brought new and wider worlds within range of Parisians. As Paris assumed once more her God-given eminence as the world's centre of culture and pleasure, with every passing year it seemed increasingly impossible that the humiliation of 1870, let alone the Commune, had ever happened. National pride was further inflated by Blériot's feat of hopping across the Channel in an aeroplane.

In the provinces, improved communications and the spread of prosperity had wrought an unparalleled homogeneity to a country where only so recently French was the native tongue of only one in five Frenchmen. It was a period of unprecedented European prosperity (enjoyed even by poor backward Russia), where French peasants, too, were better clothed and fed than they ever had been; there was an abundance of good bread; consumption of wine and potatoes had increased by 50 per cent in the second half of the nineteenth century; consumption of meat, beer and cider by 100 per cent. By 1913 a nexus of communications, such as roads, books, the press, posts and the telephone, had welded together a unified sense of nationhood. After the British, French financiers were the bankers of the world. By 1913, she was producing 45,000 automobiles a year, making her the world leader. Between 1875 and 1913 a massive increase in state expenditure of ff68 million per annum signified a proportionately huge increase in social services.

Yet, in the vital measure of commerce, France had slipped to third place in the world after Britain and Germany. Even more worrying was the shift in their relative levels of population, hugely to France's disadvantage. Between 1800 and 1900 France's had increased by only 45 per cent, that of the new, vigorous German Empire by 250 per cent (between 1816 and 1900). In the Expo of 1900, in contrast to that first great Expo of Louis-Napoleon almost half a century previously, the German exhibit comprised powerful dynamos churning out electricity to light the fair's innumerable illuminations; while it was left to the host nation to show off her latest military weapon, a long-range gun by Schneider-Creusot. German experts were not impressed. Otherwise—

once again—the French emphasis lay on proud displays of colonial progress, with replicas of Angkor Wat; and, even more emphatically, on the new role of woman and femininity in French society.

THE GATES TO THE EXPO itself were, symbolically, dominated by a vast female figure entitled *La Parisienne.* That figure was appropriately suggestive of just how far at least sophisticated Frenchwomen had come in the Brave New Age (and there were now many more sophisticated women, even in the provinces, since Emma Bovary). As Edith Wharton, embarking on a new life in the Rue de Varenne in 1906, observed, with a touch of envy: "as soon as a woman has personality, social circumstances permit her to make it felt."[6] There were women lawyers and women tennis players; there was Marie Laurencin with her soft pastel colours, perhaps the first woman to paint wholly as a woman; there was Marie Curie, the only woman to win the Nobel Prize twice, sharing both work and love in a rarely idyllic marriage with Pierre, until he was killed in a senseless street accident, run over by a horse-drawn waggon. And there was Colette, unhappily wed to the rascally Willy, who grabbed all the credit for her "Claudine" novels. (She revenged herself in the arms of other women.) In the 1890s, the discovery of the poems of Sappho, coupled with Pierre Louÿs' *Songs of Bilitis* (one of the great literary hoaxes of the time), demonstrated that lesbianism had been respectable in classical times.

Then there was Henriette Caillaux, standing up for her husband by shooting down his tormentor, the editor of *Figaro,* Gaston Calmette, in his own office on the eve of the First World War, declaring as she fired four out of six shots into him: "There's no more justice in France. It was the only thing to do." She was acquitted. And there was Sarah Bernhardt, with her multitude of unhappy love affairs, awarded the Légion d'Honneur (like Dreyfus)—though not for acting, because an independent actress was still not considered a "respectable" profession in France.

In 1904, women's working hours were reduced from eleven to ten hours; in 1907, a married woman was granted sole right to her earnings; in 1910, she was allowed eight weeks' unpaid maternity leave; and in 1913, a minimum salary was established for women working at home. Curiously, there was less pressure than in England to get the vote. Although it was a French word, in pre-1914 France the *suffragette* carried little weight. There were perhaps better ways to influence the political scene. With all these changes inevitably came a dramatic change in dress. Women had to be physically mobile, to be able to clamber into a bus, or get into the new Métro, or into a *teuf-teuf.* The cumbersome bustle disappeared; instead, between 1900 and 1908 the "Swan Bend" look took over, based on a tight corset, prominent bust and behind. Long tight-fitting skirts with leg-of-mutton sleeves entered the Paris scene. And with the new fashions also came new, daring dances—like the cakewalk and the tango.

To FRANCE AND HER WELL-WISHERS, as well as the Benthamite optimists, Expo 1900 seemed to herald a new century of infinite human progress, without boundaries. But linking the exhibition grounds on both sides of the Seine, the resplendent new Pont Alexandre III, "peerless in all the world" in the eyes of contemporaries, had its cornerstone laid by the ill-fated President Félix Faure and young Tsar Nicholas II, in honour of the latter's tyrannical father. To the Kaiser and the nervy sabre-rattlers of Berlin, it represented the provocative Franco-Russian alliance of 1894, engineered by Delcassé, which in turn equalled the encirclement of Germany, Berlin's anxiety of both past and future. Amid all the razzmatazz, one manifestation they would certainly not have missed that summer was the sombre procession of men in black velvet suits, carrying flags draped in black crêpe through the Concorde, as they did every 14 July. Before the stone female figure of Strasbourg they made emotive speeches, followed by several minutes' silence, then moved off chanting, "You will not have Alsace and Lorraine!"

During the *belle époque* the national press increased immeasurably its outspokenness—often amounting to scurrility. Opening in 1886, one new review, *La Vogue,* lasted only nine months but in that time had managed to collect a circulation of 15,000. This expansion was good news for writers and artists, assured of a receptacle for their writings and of critiques for their *oeuvres*—but at the same time cut-throat competition led to a pursuit of sensation and virulence in foreign affairs, fuelling the flames of populist nationalism. The consequences were too horribly predictable, as memories of the actual horrors of war faded with every passing year.

THE YEARS 1900–1914 offered much for journalists to sink their teeth into in the political arena. First of all, the triumph of the Dreyfusards signalled a swing-back reaction to militant anti-clericalism, ever lurking in the undergrowth since 1789. *L'affaire* brought to the fore the radicals, with the right (which was seen closely to embrace both the Church and the army) as the enemy. Following on its heels came an episode which, to English minds, smacked of Henry VIII in the twentieth century. In 1902, Émile Combes, a sixty-seven-year-old anti-clerical politician (who had started life studying for the priesthood, then become disenchanted), came to power in Paris determined to complete the separation of Church and state in France. That had already been begun in 1880 by Jules Ferry, who controversially suppressed religious education in state schools. Possessed of all the prejudices of the small-town provincial, Combes now legislated further against "unauthorised" religious orders; even religious processions were stopped. Nunneries and monasteries were expropriated and pillaged. The army was finally called in to effect the expropriations, thereby confronting its officers with a grave issue of conscience.

The newly appointed anti-clerical General André abused his power deplorably. Officers were set to spying on each other; the Grand Orient Lodge of the Free Masons was used as an intelligence service to establish dossiers on their religious persuasions; promotion became more a matter of an officer's political views, and particularly to which church, and how often, he went on Sundays. Only dossiers labelled "Corinth" gained promotion; those marked "Carthage" did not. An able officer like Foch, whose brother was a Jesuit, would always be at a disadvantage. It was no coincidence that in 1911 the office of the new Chief of the General Staff fell to a general who ostentatiously ate meat on Good Friday, rather than demonstrated any outstanding military ability.

*L'affaire,* Combes and André were followed by the most intense bout of socialist-led anti-militarism that France had experienced since 1870. All politicians alike distrusted the General Staff. In 1905, a new Act reduced the size of the army by 75,000. The new Kaiser with his bellicose moustaches, a mass of Adlerian complexes attributable to his withered arm, and his all-powerful general staff, needed only to wait.

IN FRANCE that first decade and a half of the new century before the deluge was still one of relentless optimism—and of contentment. Her capital continued to be the centre of modern art. The immortal Cézanne died senselessly of hypothermia after being caught in a storm in 1906, aged sixty-seven, but close on the heels of his great legacy came the "Nabis" (derived from the Jewish word for prophet) movement of Sérusier, Bonnard and Vuillard (and influenced by the early Pont Aven Gauguin). Then there was the scandalising new group, led by Matisse, who proudly assumed the pejorative nickname of "Fauves." Entering this world of flamboyant colour at the Salon d'Automne of 1905, a critic exclaimed that it was "Donatello au milieu des fauves"—(Donatello in the wild beasts' den). Matisse, son of a grain-dealer from Flanders, Dufy, Vlaminck and Van Dongen were all northerners seeking refuge from the greyness of the north in the exuberant colours of the south, influenced by a Picasso just emerging from his exquisite, colourfully wistful Rose Period.

In marked contrast to the Paris of a century previously, in which Napoleon had contrived to whittle down the number of theatres to a small handful, there were once again some forty-odd. Theatre life was as lively, and disputatious, as it ever had been. In 1905, there was another dramatic efflorescence in Paris. At the summit, Sarah Bernhardt reigned sublime. In 1900, she had managed to squeeze her fifty-five-year-old frame into a tight-fitting corseted uniform to appear as Rostand's tragic twenty-year-old hero in *L'Aiglon*; despite the absurdity of the casting, Paris loved every minute of its four hours.

In those "Banquet Years," opera and ballet audiences were as excitable as ever, with the arrival in 1908 from Russia of Diaghilev's Ballet providing one of the major events on the cultural scene of pre-war Paris, as well as a second important spin-off from the fateful alliance sealed in 1894. The year 1913 was to bring Stravinsky, *The Rite of Spring*—and more sensation. But, more in tune with the happier mood of the *belle époque* was the comic theatre of Georges Feydeau, that dashing figure of the boulevards. Speed, the speed of the era of electricity, telephone and motor car, was the essence of Feydeau's hilarious farces. He drew on rich material from his own life, and his favourite prop was the bed, with people in it, hidden under it or behind it; his central figure, the cuckolded husband. By 1913 Paris already boasted thirty-seven cinemas; one of them, the Pathé, near the Invalides, ran to an orchestra of sixty and claimed to have the world's largest screen. There was more leisure time to dispense with since the working day had been shortened from twelve to ten hours; and the *petit bourgeois* was, for once, satisfied with his modest income.

France's technical successes continued to proliferate: by 1907 there were 4000 *teufs-teufs* clogging up the centre of Paris, and despoiling the tranquillity of the centuries. Great Routes Nationales were being built by latter-day Bonapartes to rush them and their owners to all parts of France. In 1902, France pioneered the famous Paris-Vienna race—won by Renault at a speed faster than the Arlberg express. The ambitious Paris-Peking race, sponsored by *Le Matin,* followed in 1907; maddeningly it was won by an Italian prince.

The Republic, writes André Maurois, "was still Athenian"; it had "no reason to be envious of Louis XIV's France, or of the France of the Renaissance; never had the country had a greater renown or a more justifiable prestige." All this nostalgia would be summed up in 1913 with the appearance of the first instalment of Proust's monumental *À la Recherche du Temps Perdu.* Yet, if ever there was a sign of the fragility, and hubris, of human endeavours, the previous year, 1912, was the year that the unsinkable *Titanic* sank. And, in Europe there was the rumble, though seemingly distant, of wars in the Balkans.

The nations of Europe hastened to take sides like children at school in readiness for a contest. On the western side, most of the picking of teams has taken place in Paris. First, since Delcassé's "defensive" Franco-Russian pact, all things Russian had grown increasingly popular—from Diaghilev to Stravinsky. In England, the death of both Queen Victoria (mother-in-law of the Kaiser) and Lord Salisbury, whose policy had done much to seek greater friendliness with the Germanic powers, brought a change of line. A new Germany, lacking the steady hand of Bismarck (sacked by young Kaiser Wilhelm II), became alarmed at potential enemies combining to West and East, and lined up Austria, Bulgaria and later Turkey. Then, in 1903, the francophile Edward VII came over to charm a city still piqued by the imperial humiliation of Fashoda, alienated by the unpopular Boer War and instinctively anti-England; the following year the Entente Cordiale, so unnatural though it may have seemed to many a Frenchman and *anglo-saxon,* was signed. When fun-loving Edward died, Paris was draped in black, and cabdrivers tied crêpe bows on their whips.

In 1905, and again in 1911, the Kaiser blundered into Morocco, stretching nerves in the Chancelleries of Europe, inciting instant crisis and providing grist to the mill of Paris' fervid, Hun-eating nationalist press. The Entente Cordiale, once a diplomatic *politesse,* became an alliance-in-waiting as Britain bristled at the challenge of the Kaiser's swiftly expanding navy. In 1906, the peace-minded Liberal Sir Edward Grey was moved to sanction "military conversations" with the "old enemy" across the Channel. In the Sorbonne, German experts like Charles Andler and Romain Rolland, striving for peace with kindred spirits across the Rhine, were progressively outgunned by the *Écho de Paris,* where Maurice Barrès damned Andler as a "humanitarian anarchist," ready to "betray" Alsace-Lorraine. One of Europe's best hopes of peace was the Socialist leader Jean Jaurès, son of a road-mender from the Tarn. He bitterly opposed France's pact with a reactionary, feudal and unstable Russia, but hoped to defeat jingoism with an accord between French and German socialists never to make war on each other. He was convinced that, in the unspeakable event of war, German socialists would tear up the railway lines rather than allow their brothers to go to war.

Events defeated him; the spirit of the *belle époque* gave way to deep distrust of Germany and her intentions. Three days before the outbreak of war, Jaurès himself was shot down in a Paris café by a deranged young zealot, Raoul Villain. There was a sudden last-minute rally to the army, fanned by the jingoist press; in 1912, the restoration of military service to three years, hitherto vigorously opposed, was greeted with remarkable enthusiasm. The eighteen-year-old Prince of Wales, future Edward VII, received a welcome that would have amazed his disapproving mother Queen Victoria—even though there were powerful sections of opinion among the Liberals at home, dead against any commitment to France. In Paris—as opposed to the calmer provinces—war fever mounted. Even some sensible writers began to feel that war was not only thinkable, but perhaps actually desirable, in preference to the continuing tension—like a thunderstorm clearing away oppressively sultry weather. Declared Abel Bonnard, in the *Figaro*: "War refashions everything anew . . . We must embrace it in all its savage poetry." Visiting the France he loved in spring 1914 after a prolonged absence, the Austrian writer Stefan Zweig expressed deepest alarm at "how deeply the poison of the propaganda of hate must have advanced through the years."[7]

# FIFTEEN

# The Great War and Versailles

Mourir pour la patrie, c'est le sort le plus beau.
(To die for the Fatherland is the most beautiful fate.)

—*French 1914 slogan*

ON 3 AUGUST 1914, Frenchmen found themselves at war again. Happily unable to see what lay ahead, they would optimistically call it the "Great War," the "War to end all Wars." Historians of the next generation would recognise it merely as the "First World War," but their successors might well come to see it more realistically as simply the first act in a second "Thirty Years' War."

At a sudden end was the age of prosperity and unlimited promise which all Europe had begun to enjoy—and in which even poor medieval Russia was beginning to participate. Europe was about to descend into a new Dark Age whose shadows stretched unforeseeably far into the future. For the next four years, it was to seem as if War itself had become the sole arbiter in the world, with human leaders—so proud and powerful in the world of 1900—reduced to impotence in the face of a force infinitely greater than anything they had, or could have, foreseen, or been taught to handle. On both sides there were many—and not just among the Kaiser's entourage in Berlin, or the sword-rattling *revanchistes* in Paris—who greeted the fall into conflict almost with relief, such had been the stresses and strains of holding back from it in preceding years.

André Gide hastened back to Paris by the last available civilian train; as it went by, he heard a railwayman shout: "All aboard for Berlin! And what fun we'll have there!" Three days into the war he anticipated adventure of a higher level: "The wonderful behaviour of the Government, of everyone, and of all France . . . leaves room for every hope. One foresees the beginning of a new era: the United States of Europe bound by a treaty limiting their armaments."[1] Naturally, as to most Frenchmen now, the *sine qua non* of such a rosy future had to be—above all—the rightful return of Alsace-Lorraine. Marcel Proust, however, right to the end, refused to believe in the prospect of war; it would be simply "too frightful," he thought; he was much more concerned in finding a Paris publisher for his very long novel, *À la Recherche du Temps Perdu*. His chronic asthma disqualified him from military service. In the provinces, reactions to the coming of war were distinctly more sombre, and more sober.

Among those to rally to the colours at the first opportunity were many members of the Dreyfus family. Alfred's son, Pierre, fought in the first battles of 1914 as a corporal, then through Verdun and fifty-four days on the Somme, was gassed, promoted five times and ended the war a captain with the Croix de Guerre and Palm; nephew Émile died of wounds in 1915, awarded the Légion d'Honneur on his deathbed; his niece's husband, Ado Reinach, was reported missing in August, his body never found. By the war's end all but four soldiers from the Dreyfus and Reinach families had disappeared. It was a common story made exceptional by the patriotism of a Jewish clan which had suffered so much at the hands of the army. Alfred himself, despite being too old for the army aged fifty-five, repeatedly requested to be sent to the front and was finally permitted to take part as a gunner in the disastrous Nivelle Offensive of 1917.

There was little repetition of the wild, clamouring cries of "À Berlin!" in that July of forty-four years previously. On 28 July 1914, the British Ambassador, Lord Bertie, recorded in his diary: "There is much nervous excitement, but no popular demonstrations for war . . ."[2] Parisians, he noted, hoped that Britain would be the "deciding factor" in keeping Germany out of the war. He told Foreign Secretary Grey that if Britain should "declare herself *solidaire* with France and Russia there will be no war." But, with much pro-neutralist opposition at home, Grey and the Asquith government dithered, sending no clear-cut message to the Kaiser. In execution of the Schlieffen Plan, mobilising a huge force of 1,300,000 men (out of a massive total of 3,120,000 heading east and west in 11,000 trains), Germany marched into and through Belgium. On 4 August war became general.

IN THE LAST MONTHS before the avalanche, and of his life, the great Jaurès had piously hoped that, in the event of war breaking out, his fellow German socialists would rip up the railway lines leading to the front. But his assassination put paid to such dreams. On the eve of war, socialists carrying placards proclaiming "Guerre à la Guerre!" gave the cabinet fearful visions of working-class riots and civil strife, but the scenes were brief. In fact, when Germany and France mobilised, socialists on both sides marched with everyone else. Jaurès was buried on the day a general war was declared, and his dreams were interred with him. Remarkably, a patriotic "Union Sacrée" coalition was formed to prosecute the war, and all politicians, even the left-wing pacifists, backed it. Across the country an atmosphere of quiet, rather businesslike resolve prevailed. Raymond Poincaré, a staunch *revanchiste* from Lorraine who would never allow himself to forget his childhood memories of *Pickelhaube* occupying his homeland, had been elected president, and the country was whole-heartedly behind him. The press, thoroughly brainwashed by its own Russophile outpourings of the past years, continued to deceive the public with imaginative accounts of the Tsar's steam-roller crushing the enemy in the East.

THIS TIME, in some respects at least, the French Army was genuinely, superbly ready. In fact, it was perhaps a little too ready. Morale had climbed. The proportion of defectors on mobilisation, predicted to be 13 per cent, was in fact less than 1.5 per cent; but an exaggerated notion pervaded the army of 1914 that the *Furia Francese,* the *élan vital* of the revolutionary and Napoleonic armies, would somehow suffice to repel and defeat the attacking Germans. This seemed quite justified according to the "positivist" philosophy of Henri Bergson, then all the rage in France. In the crucial pre-war years there had been far too little pragmatic study at the École Militaire, so it was hardly surprising that in 1913–14 300 books on war were published in Germany, to only fifty in France. "You talk to us of heavy artillery. Thank God, we have none. The strength of the French Army is in the lightness of its guns,"[3] the General Staff told the deputies in 1909. Thus, by August 1914, the whole French Army possessed only 300 heavy guns; the Germans 3500. The French military planners were not over-impressed by the new, deadly machine-gun, either. In

1910, General Foch, then Commandant of the Staff College, was among those who had reckoned on a brief, brutal conflict of a matter of weeks. Meanwhile, so that the enemy should see them clearly and be terror-struck by the *furia* of their onslaught, the infantry went to war in the red *képis* and blue pantaloons of the Second Empire, despising the Germans for converting to the less martial though more practical *feldgrau*.

France's Commander-in-Chief was General Joseph (his middle name, conspicuously, was "Césaire") Joffre, son of a humble cooper, one of a family of eleven and, like Foch, a Pyrenean. He was an elderly offi-cer with an immense belly and an extraordinary capacity for calm (that rather un-French characteristic), which was his single greatest asset. Under him, the French forces were committed to Plan XVII. This pre-scribed that, on the outbreak of war, four out of her five armies, totalling 800,000 men, were to charge forward—predictably—towards the lost territories, objective the Rhine. Well informed of all this, the Germans wedded themselves to their Schlieffen Plan.* Swinging down through neutral Belgium (the *casus belli* for Britain entering the war on France's side) it comprised a vast right hook which would sweep around behind Paris, and then pin the French armies that were attacking eastwards up against the Swiss frontier. Under this blueprint (drawn up some years before the war), France would be knocked out in one mighty blow, before Russia could join in. Speed was essential, and there would be no room for any mistakes. Likened to the action of a revolving door, under Plan XVII the French Army would in fact add momentum to the door's rotation, thereby doing just what Schlieffen wanted. Fortunately for France, unfortunately for Germany, his successor, Moltke—nephew of the military genius who crushed France in 1870, but there the resem-blance ceased—tampered with the masterplan, weakening both the cru-cial right wing and the covering force facing the Russians. This would play a vital role in the battle of the Marne that was to follow.

All along the frontier the French infantrymen in their bright uni-forms, carrying heavy packs and long, unwieldy bayonets, broke into the double behind their white-gloved officers. Many sang the "Marseillaise." In the August heat, sometimes the heavily encumbered French attacked from a distance of nearly half a mile from the enemy. Their courage was supreme; but never had machine-gunners had such a heyday. The French stubblefields became transformed into carpets of red and blue. Splendid cavalrymen in glittering breastplates from the age of Murat

---

*Under which 3,120,000 Germans were transported to the front in 11,000 trains.

hurled their horses hopelessly at the guns that were slaughtering the infantry. It was horrible, and horribly predictable.

FOR THE FIRST TERRIFYING WEEKS of August it looked as if the Schlieffen Plan was going to work. German outriders reached and captured the racing stables at Chantilly, just 25 miles north-east of Paris; one cavalry detachment claimed it could see the Eiffel Tower. Railway stations to the west and south were besieged with Parisians wanting to get out before the enemy arrived. The Minister of Defence rushed to the Élysée to demand that Poincaré appoint a military governor of Paris—a role that had been filled by the flaccid General Trochu in the last siege of Paris.

General Joseph Gallieni was to prove an unlikely national hero. He was sixty-five, retired from active service and already afflicted by the prostate cancer that would kill him in two years' time. As a twenty-one-year-old second lieutenant he had fought—and been captured—at Sedan in 1870. He was a quiet intellectual, who carried himself like an officer on parade. Tall and spare with a pince-nez (like Dreyfus) and a bushy grey moustache, he resembled no other French general of the epoch. Of the Commander-in-Chief, Joffre, he complained: "How fat and heavy he is; he will hardly last out his three years!" Gallieni insisted he be given a covering force of three active army corps; but for the best part of two crucial weeks he was left "Commander of the Armies of Paris" without an army. Pessimistically, he warned Poincaré that ministers were "no longer safe in the capital." On the night of 2 September, almost the anniversary of the 1870 debacle at Sedan, the government left by train for Bordeaux. A bitter parody of the "Marseillaise" made the rounds of Paris:

> Aux gares, citoyens!
> Montez dans les wagons!

as the city prepared itself for a siege more hopeless than in 1870—or total destruction from the giant German 420 mm "Big Berthas" that had already reduced the Belgian forts to rubble.

MEANWHILE, A MIRACLE WAS IN THE OFFING which would evoke to devout Parisians the intervention of Saint Geneviève in turning back the Hunnish invaders in the fifth century. French Intelligence had acquired a haversack taken off the body of a German cavalry officer attached to General von Kluck's First Army. In it was a bloodstained map showing lines of advance swinging south-eastwards, *away* from the capital. Joffre had been prepared to sacrifice Paris, but now he and Gallieni immediately realised the significance of the move: as von Kluck's army was on the right flank of the massive German wheeling movement, it meant that its sweep was no longer going to envelop Paris, but was to swing to the east to trap the French against the Swiss frontier. Even better, this in effect denoted the collapse of the whole German strategy, initiated by Moltke's tampering with the masterplan. In the east, unexpectedly, the Russians had been able to mount a powerful offensive that had taken most of East Prussia before Hindenburg and Ludendorff, Germany's most successful team in the war, had been able to smash it at Tannenberg. In the meantime, and in alarm at the Russian success, a timorous Moltke had dispatched eastwards divisions from von Kluck's vital right flank in France. With forces already removed to reinforce the centre, von Kluck simply had insufficient men to carry out the great wheel west of Paris, while keeping in step with von Bülow's Second Army on his left.

Gallieni swiftly realised, "They offer us their flank!"[4] He pressed the normally ponderous Joffre into turning the whole elephantine army around and launching an immediate combined offensive. Gallieni would unleash General Maunoury's newly formed Sixth Army to attack out of Paris, into von Kluck's exposed flank. The Sixth Army units had only just arrived, exhausted, after long forced marches. The whole of the six armies under Joffre's command—including General French's small but heroic British Expeditionary Force—were also tired out after a month of retreats, dispiriting defeats and horrendous casualties. But the German Army was just as exhausted; in the coming battle many German prisoners were actually taken asleep, unable to move another step.

After a passionate appeal to General French to turn the retreating British forces about, Joffre from his makeshift Grand Quartier Général (GQG) near the battle-front issued the critical order: "We are going to fight on the Marne."[5] The first blow of the Allied counter-offensive came from Paris on the 6th, with 60,000 of General Maunoury's troops who had barely detrained rushed to the front. The civilian response was phenomenal: 600 of the little red Renault taxis, so familiar to tourists, plied back and forth to the Ourcq battlefield only 35 miles distant. Each carrying five soldiers, they made the round trip twice in the day, rushing up crucial reinforcements. The "Taxis of the Marne" in the apt words of Barbara Tuchman, did indeed constitute "the last gallantry of 1914, the last crusade of the old world."

The immediate, tactical effect of Maunoury's attack was to force von Kluck to swing his flank westwards to meet the threat. As a result, a critical gap 30 miles wide opened up between his left and von Bülow's Second Army. Into this gap marched French's tired BEF and the French Fifth Army. To their right, in command of a newly formed Ninth Army, the fiery General Foch, whose aggression had already proved an expensive liability, now came into his own with his famous order: "My centre is yielding, my right is falling back, situation excellent. I am attacking!" But it was the brave adventurism of Gallieni and the city he commanded which turned defeat into victory. After three days of battle, on 9 September von Bülow ordered his army to fall back over the Marne. Two days later the retreat became general.

Sadly, the exhausted and slow-moving Allies could not press their advantage to roll up the whole enemy front. Now it congealed into a line of static trench warfare reaching from the Channel to the Swiss frontier. But the "Miracle of the Marne" provided battered France with an immeasurable psychological victory. Germany had in fact lost the war, though it would take another four—or thirty—years to persuade her of this. But at what a cost for France: in the two weeks that the terrible Battle of the Frontiers lasted, she had lost over 300,000 men killed, wounded and missing, and 4778 officers—representing no less than one-tenth of her total officer strength. By the end of the first five months of the war in killed alone the French Army had lost 300,000 men (or nearly a fifth more than Britain's total dead in the whole of the Second World War). Because of the efficacy of the censors, the country did not realise the full extent of these losses for a long time. France had also lost the important cities of Lille, Valenciennes, Arras, Amiens, Cambrai, Laon and Soissons, as well as Rheims—where all the kings of France from Clovis to Louis XIV had been crowned—abandoned as an open city on 3 September. Nearly 12 per cent of all her territory, comprising 16.3 per cent of her manufacturing capacity and 20.4 per cent of the wheat crop, was now in enemy hands—as was, still, Alsace-Lorraine; while nearly 900,000 hungry and destitute refugees had been added to the hungry mouths France had to feed.

Nevertheless the country was saved—in one of those amazing recoveries that recur in her history. The government returned amid a mood of contrition, almost of smugness. A young Jean Cocteau would be employed contributing, for a little literary review, drawings of Belgian children who had, supposedly, had their right hands cut off by German soldiery. As more reports of German atrocities came in from the occupied territories, there was a growing sense that "France equalled Civilisation, Germany, Barbarism."

OUT OF THE VICTORY of the Marne, Joffre emerged as immeasurably the most powerful figure on the whole Allied side. It might be said that the war was very nearly lost with him, but—with his unshakeable nerves—it would almost certainly have been lost without him. Isolated in its palace at Chantilly, Joffre's GQG lived in an atmosphere of backstabbing intrigue reminiscent of the court of Louis XIV at Versailles. Throughout 1915 they pursued the simple-minded, but murderously wasteful, strategy of what Joffre called *grignotage,* or nibbling away at the enemy—which has also been described as "trying to bite through a steel door with badly fitting false teeth." It was the least successful year of the whole war for Allied arms; and never again would the prospects seem so bright for the Central Powers as at its close.

In France a whole war industry was set up to improve the morale of the soldier at the front. Not allowed leave until March 1915, his need for female company was synthesised by an institution called "Marraines de Guerre" ("Godmothers of War"). It began as a scheme for women to adopt an unknown soldier, keeping him supplied with woollen comforters, and it grew into a powerful propaganda instrument. Sometimes frightened soldiers would be prompted into action by fear more of their *marraine's* contempt than of their lieutenant's revolver. For the majority, the *marraine* was simply an unseen, unknown Beatrice who wrote her soldier beautiful letters telling him to be brave and die well; the happy minority sometimes also found her willing to share her bed with him on leave. One sergeant, who collected forty-four *marraines,* eventually found that his leaves were never long enough to keep them all contented, and so deserted.

Now that he was acquainted all too intimately with the realities of war, the French front-line soldier became progressively irritated, then angered by the propagandists' *bourrage de crâne* (brainwashing), which flowed out like lava from the capital. These were the writers and newspapermen, paid hacks of the propaganda machine and tools of "Anastasie," the censor, who from their comfortable offices in Paris wrote of the nobility of war in the terms of Déroulède; of the brave boys dying beautifully *pour la patrie.* Forerunners of what today would be called the arti-sans of "spin," they published accounts of the piling up of "mounds of German dead" at each attack at Verdun—to the accompaniment of "negligible" French losses. They published photographs of the teenaged *grands mutilés* with such captions as "A Soldier Who Has Lost Both Feet, Yet Walks Fairly Well With Clever Substitutes," or "A Soldier Who Has Lost Both Hands, Yet Can Handle a Cigarette and Salute as Before."* Nothing enraged the men submitted to the unimaginable suffering of Verdun, and its hecatombs of French lives lost there, more than nau-seous effusions like these. At the front their officers would often go to extraordinary lengths to obtain copies of *Le Journal de Genève,* for a rea-sonably accurate *rapportage* of the war. The propagandists gave the com-mon soldier a new nickname, the *poilu,* or "hairy-one"—the epitome of the tough soldier, coupled with the slogan: "To die for the Fatherland is the most beautiful fate" in an often-played military hymn. The *poilu,* however, had a rather different view: "The most beautiful fate is to live a long time and to be happy. Why lie?" wrote soldier and former professor Paul Cazin in the spring of 1915. The *bourrage*—largely directed at the civilian population—liked to depict the *poilu* as a perpetually cheerful bloke, as per Maurice Barrès when the spring offensives foundered in April 1915: "They are all gay hearted! They are having fun!"

By the end of the first year of war, Paris journalists were offered fewer reports of the laughing *poilu,* though the motif of singing, jovial soldiers persisted. There were exuberant propaganda posters captioned "On les aura!" But with the bitter life-and-death struggle at Verdun that lasted through 1916, these were replaced by the new, defiant slogan of "Ils ne passeront pas!" In February 1917, only months before the French armies mutinied, the cover of *La Vie Parisienne* deludedly depicted a jaunty infantryman, striding off to the front, pipe in mouth and mongrel at his heel, with all his needs strapped to his vast pack—including a coffee grinder and a girl in knickers.

But a new language grew up at the front, much of its vocabulary derived from the slang of Parisian workers, and their own songs. About the same time that some disaffected men were chanting the "Interna-tionale," "Quand Madelon" had become both a military march and a

*On the other side, the Germans also suffered (though, because of the greater imagi-nativeness of the French writers, perhaps not quite to the same extent); typical of German *bourrage de crâne* were the reports at the beginning of the war that French shells did not explode and their bullets tended to go clean through their victims without causing exces-sive damage.

sentimental hit, which embroidered the theme of the *marraine,* the Dantesque unreachable and impeccable heroine:

> Nous en rêvons la nuit, nous y pensons le jour,
> Ce n'est que Madelon, mais pour nous, c'est l'amour . . .
> ("We dream of her at night, we think of her by day,
> It's only Madelon, but—for us—it's love . . .")

Even before the war ended, the composer—Louis Bousquet—wrote a successor hit, "Le Mariage de Madelon," where the eponymous heroine marries a corporal and produces a lusty son.

Contrary to popular belief, the *poilu* on leave disliked the bawdy entertainment offered in the Paris music halls—unless it was witty. He had his own bitter songs about the *embusqués,* the draft-dodgers, whom he hated almost more than the *Boches.* For the *Boches,* he reserved a respect that the Paris press did not, or was not allowed to, share. About the highest insult was "gueule de civil" (mug of a civilian). While patriots in Paris continued to hope for the bold offensive and sudden knock-out, the *poilu* had the simpler ambition of survival. Entering a second year of war, "acceptance" was really the operative word. Those who in 1914 had groused about conditions had by now either vanished or submitted.

AT THE END OF 1915 Haig and Joffre drew up a plan for the next year, whereby in the summer the French would attack with forty divisions on a 25-mile front south of the Somme, the British with some twenty-five divisions along the 15 miles to the north. It would also coincide with a Russian offensive on the eastern front.

But the enemy was to strike first, at Verdun. On 21 February 1916 the Germans attacked. Between the Marne and Ludendorff's last-gasp assault in March 1918, it was the only time they would assume the offensive on the Western Front. It had supposedly a limited objective; not to capture Verdun, but to "bleed white" the French Army by forcing it to fight for the linchpin of her defences, the strongest fortress on earth— supposedly. Caught horribly unprepared, having denuded the forts of most of their guns, the French Army would suffer over 400,000 casualties; the attacking Germans, supported by an unprecedented weight of artillery on a front only 15 miles across, were to lose almost as many. General Philippe Pétain would be brought in to restore a disastrous situation. He managed to persuade the badly shaken troops: "You went into the assault singing the 'Marseillaise'; it was magnificent. But the next time you will not need to sing the 'Marseillaise.' There will be a sufficient number of guns to ensure your attack's success."

In the ten months that it lasted, the battle of Verdun was to gain the grim repute as the worst battle of all time; certainly it was the longest. Another gigantic German miscalculation, it would end in one of the most glorious victories in France's history; yet its cost would lead her down the road to defeat a generation later. 1916 was also, for Britain, the year of the Somme, the year when her new armies came of age in that terrible bloodletting on whose first day alone 60,000 young Britons and Empire troops would fall. The hero of the Marne, Gallieni, would retire and die; Joffre would be sacked—and so would his German opposite number, the chilly Falkenhayn, who had launched Verdun. Russia would launch its last offensive before succumbing to revolution.

IN CONTRAST TO GERMANY, where the Royal Navy's blockade was biting hard by 1916, the French civilian population behind the lines suffered fewer deprivations. (The exception was, of course, in the occupied areas of the north-east; but even there life on the whole was more bearable than it was in Occupied France under the Nazis in the 1940s.) The worst scarcity was in coal since the German capture of the Lille area. For all the agricultural losses, food rationing never became a serious matter.

On his infrequent leaves, the *permissionaire* from the horrendous butchery at Verdun naturally gravitated towards Paris. Though a mere 150 miles away, it was indeed like entering another world. Sometimes the front-line *poilu* wondered whether the capital knew about the war at all and viewed its dazzling scenes with mixed feelings. By the time of Verdun, combatants on both sides equally had begun to sense a certain alienation for the "rear" and the civilian population. It was "them" and "us." In Henri Barbusse's great war novel, *Le Feu*, published already that year, 1916, one of the characters comments bitterly while on leave: "We are divided into two foreign countries. The front, over there, where there is too much misery, and the rear, here, where there is too much contentment." In Remarque's German classic, *All Quiet on the Western Front*, the same sentiment is echoed by his protagonist complaining while home on leave: "They are different men here, men I cannot properly understand, whom I envy and despise."[6] After a spell in the line soldiers, whether French or German, felt as if they belonged to some exclusive, isolated monastic order whose grim rites were simply beyond the comprehension of the laymen behind the lines. With only a few sous pay in their pocket, pleasure—or even simply relief—would often be hard to find.

DESPITE HER TERRIBLE LOSSES and her suffering, France—like Germany—still displayed a remarkable solidarity in the pursuance of the war. From 1914 onwards this had been propped up by the staunch bulwark of the Union Sacrée. Its spirit was reminiscent of that which (temporarily) levelled the social barricades in Britain during the 1940 Blitz. For a nation of radicals and independents such as France, creation of the Union Sacrée, whereby men of all political hues submerged their feuds in the interests of national unity, had been one of the miracles of all time. There was that anti-militarist, socialist and crypto-anarchist, Anatole France, who attempted to enlist, aged seventy, and then resumed his seat among the conservatives of the Académie, which he had abandoned shortly after the Dreyfus affair; and there was that eater of clerics, Clemenceau, observed kissing an *abbé* on both cheeks.

Another source of great strength in the war effort were the women of France. To them the war had brought an emancipatory revolution. At the outbreak of war, almost to a woman they had rushed off to become nurses, fill the administrative gaps left by the men, work in the munitions factories. The soldiers grumbled on returning home to find their wives turned yellow by picric acid, but they had little redress. As the Frenchwomen who had not lost a husband, lover or brother became fewer and fewer, their initial excitement was replaced by a formidable dedication. Most of them had become *marraines* to one or more soldiers, according them benefits ranging merely from parcels of food to the highest a woman can offer a man. No other section of the French community was shoring up the will to war more substantially than the women; and perhaps symbolic of the whole spirit of 1916 was the divine Sarah Bernhardt, one leg now amputated, stumping the boards with a wooden leg. Here was France herself, mutilated but undaunted.

AS THE REVERSES AND CASUALTIES PROGRESSED, however, the distortions and corruption that war breeds were readily detectable. The *embusqués,* who had somehow dodged the war and the call-up, and the profiteers who had already amassed sizeable fortunes rapidly enriched the restaurateurs and the jewellers, who had never known business to be better. Even the humblest worker in a war plant was earning

100 sous a day, compared with the *poilu's* 5 sous. As a result, inflation was gaining speed; by the end of 1916, the cost-of-living index had reached 135 ( July 1914 = 100). There was a vigorous black market. Agriculture had been disrupted by the number of peasants called to the colours, and eventually some had had to be returned to the fields; the great Renault motor works was closed down, all but for a small shop making stretchers (motor vehicles evidently being considered a luxury). But somehow the economy functioned under what was derisively known as the "Système D" (a derivation from the verb *se débrouiller,* meaning literally "to muddle through").

JUNE 1916 had seen the climax at Verdun, with the Germans stopped within sight of the city; it also marked a turning point in the First World War. Fort Douaumont was finally being retaken in the bitter cold of December, marking the end of the ten-month-long battle. It was the only significant strategic defeat inflicted on the Germans since the "Miracle of the Marne"; but at an almost suicidal cost. Too many *poilus* from Verdun had spent their *permissions* in Paris to keep it quiet. A serious malaise afflicted "those in the know" about the state of morale in the army. But, nevertheless, here now was a brave new general, Nivelle, replacing the exhausted "Papa" Joffre, who had a new "formula," heralding a much-talked-about new offensive.

Alas, Nivelle's new formula led only to new disasters. Far too much talked about, it permitted Hindenburg to dig in and prepare for it. On 16 April 1917, the French infantry—exhilarated by all they had been promised—poured out of their trenches. By the following day, they had suffered something like 120,000 casualties. The Medical Services, seldom brilliant (in one hospital there were reported to be only four thermometers for 3500 beds), were overwhelmed. Nivelle persisted with his offensive—but he had lost the belief of the army. The kind of incidents that had occurred sporadically at Verdun multiplied. Macabre, sheeplike bleating was heard among regiments sent up to the line. Men on leave sang revolutionary songs imported from Russia. They beat up military police and uncoupled engines to prevent trains leaving for the front. Interceding officers—including at least one general—were set upon. On 3 May mutiny broke out. The 21st Division—which had gone through some of the worst fighting at Verdun the previous year— refused to go into battle. The ringleaders were summarily shot or consigned to Devil's Island. But unit after unit followed the 21st, and over

20,000 men deserted. Regiments elected councils to speak for them, ominously like the Soviets that had already seized power in the Russian Army. One regiment attempted to reach the Schneider–Creusot arms plant, with the apparent intention of blowing it up. By June the mutinies had spread to half the French Army; at one point there was not a single reliable division standing between the Germans at Soissons and Paris. There were mass strikes in Toulouse and the Loire.

Astonishingly, the mutiny was not picked up by German Intelligence until order had been restored by the new chief, General Philippe Pétain, the "Hero of Verdun." Even Lloyd George and General Haig were little better informed than Hindenburg. Almost to the end of the twentieth century, details of the French mutinies remained veiled, their secrets lying inside the *Services Historiques de l'Armée,* within the recesses of the sombre Château de Vincennes. Certainly many brave men were shot summarily, though from time to time accounts seeped out of how whole units were marched to quiet sectors of the front and then deliberately *haché* by their own artillery. Such was the fate of the wretched Russian Division in France, which news of revolution had reduced to a state of utter and contagious rebellion.

COUPLED WITH THESE DRACONIAN MEASURES, Pétain—nick-named "le Médécin de l'Armée"—assured the men that he would never again permit their lives to be squandered in vain, instead: "We must wait for the Americans and the tanks." And so it would be. But the French Army would never quite recover; indeed, it would not have done by 1940. As one veteran observed, "They [the leaders] have broken the heart of the French soldier" and later, prophetically, "What kind of a nation will they make of us tomorrow, these exhausted creatures, emptied of blood, emptied of thought, crushed by superhuman fatigue?"[7] Henceforth much of the fighting on the Western Front would devolve on Haig's British Army, and the new fresh "doughboys" of Pershing's American Expeditionary Force just beginning to arrive in France. But they would only be ready for the final battles.

Behind the lines throughout this grim period of 1917, there abounded rumours that had previously been submerged of profiteering, conspiracy and treason, espionage and defeatism. Political leaders like Caillaux were contemplating a compromise peace; more sinister were the activities of the traitors who earned millions of francs from German sources for their work of demoralisation, and the out-and-out defeatists, ranged around the *Bonnet Rouge* newspaper. Their leader, a former Minister of the Interior called Malvy, was sentenced to five years' banishment, and the glamorous spy Mata Hari (possibly innocent, certainly insignificant) shot. The first great air-raids on Paris were carried out by heavy "Gotha" four-engined bombers. Once again, as in 1870 and in the London Blitz of 1940, this indiscriminate attack on the civil population proved counter-productive. Politically, however, the situation was dire. The miraculous Union Sacrée collapsed, as the Socialists withdrew their support.

There was one hope left: Clemenceau. As Poincaré pointed out in 1914, Clemenceau was "capable of upsetting everything! The day will perhaps come when I shall add: Now that everything seems to be lost, he alone is capable of saving everything." The stormy petrel of French politics for over forty years, already a grown man and Mayor of Montmartre during the Siege and the Commune, leader of the Radicals, and now an old man of seventy-six, he was in himself a kind of one-man committee of public safety. From now on the war would be waged relentlessly, and ruthlessly. In the inimitable words of Winston Churchill: "The last desperate stroke had to be played. France had resolved to unbar the cage and let her tiger loose upon all foes, beyond the trenches or in her midst." The Jacobin returned to the governance of France. At the front, when the soldiers spied Clemenceau's old felt hat, the stubbornness of this old man inspired them—as Churchill was to do for Britain in 1940.

WITH THE ARRIVAL OF CLEMENCEAU, together with Pétain and—later—Foch redeemed, and now Pershing and his doughboys, everything began to change. It was as well for the Alliance that there was a Clemenceau ready to take up the fight, for 1918 was to bring the most dangerous months of the war since 1914. German forces liberated from the East by the post-revolutionary collapse of Russia enabled Ludendorff in March 1918 to launch a massive offensive aimed directly at Paris. Astutely, he struck on the hinge of the French and British Armies, tearing a great hole in the British front through which his troops poured to the very gates of Amiens, and—eventually—to Château-Thierry, 54 miles from Paris. Then, on 24 March 1918, explosions suddenly occurring in the middle of Paris, with no aircraft in the sky, were reckoned to be coming from a super-long-range gun, firing from inside the German lines. Nothing like this had ever been heard of before, or deemed possible outside the world of Jules Verne; once again, the genius of Herr Krupp had contributed a new novelty to civilisation.

Each shell carried only a small explosive charge, but—like the V2 rockets that struck terror into London from the end of 1944—what was so frightening about the "Paris Gun"* was that its projectiles exploded without any warning, and quite indiscriminately. Clearly the Germans hoped that, coupled with the Ludendorff offensive, the continued bombardment would break the French will to resist. Most wickedly, it was aimed at the Louvre, but happily not a single shot hit this huge target. The greatest casualties it could exact came on Good Friday, 29 March, when a shell struck the church of Saint-Gervais during mass. Seventy-five were killed and ninety injured, though many died later of their injuries. Once again, as in August 1914, people began to flee out of Paris. In fact, Herr Krupp's barrels wore out faster than Parisian nerves. One of the two monsters blew up, wiping out seventeen of its crew. It would not affect the course of the war, but would certainly harden the peace terms.

By July 1918 the offensive power of Ludendorff's armies was spent. With a regenerated Foch declaring "tout le monde à la bataille" and supported by fresh American troops, the Allied counterstrokes hammered forward all along the line. On 8 August, Haig's British Army inflicted what Ludendorff admitted was "the black day of the German Army." By early autumn the German line had been rolled back, out of France, out of the territory they had held for the past four years—some of it, for nearly fifty years.


AT II A.M. ON II NOVEMBER 1918, all the guns ceased firing. A dense crowd congregated around the Chamber of Deputies in Paris where Clemenceau was expected to speak. Inside, as the cannon continued to fire outside, the seventy-seven-year-old "Tiger" with the white walrus moustache, architect of victory, rose trembling and declaimed: "Let us pay homage to our great dead, who have given us this victory!"[8] Countless women dressed in mourning joined the crowds, which grew and grew as peasants poured in from the countryside, and soldiers returned from the front. There were warm displays of inter-Allied amity; but they would barely see out the signing of the peace treaty.

When the celebrants of Armistice Day in Paris paused to consider

---

*Popularly, it was misnamed "Big Bertha," like the weapons that smashed the forts at Liège and Verdun; but those in fact were short-range mortars, while the "Paris Gun" was an extremely long (112-feet) barrelled rifle. Germans called it either the *Pariser* Gun or *Langer Max.*

costs in the grey light of the following day, they counted 1.4 million Frenchmen killed in action, the largest proportion of any of the combatant nations; on top of that came the civilian dead and victims of the flu epidemic that took 40 million lives across the globe—together leading to a loss of 7 per cent of what France's population would otherwise have totalled. Thus it was perhaps hardly surprising that the post–Armistice Day cry across the breadth of France was "Plus jamais ça!" "My work is finished," observed an exhausted but triumphant Marshal Foch to Clemenceau, on Armistice Day; but "your work is beginning." It was the understatement of the epoch.

FOR THE NEXT SIX MONTHS, as VIPs and delegates for the forthcoming peace conference began to swarm in, Paris once again became the centre of the world's affairs. The Hôtel Crillon was found to be too small for the Americans' 1300-strong delegation, so Maxim's round the corner in the Rue Royale was annexed to it. The British delegation, which had numbered fourteen in 1815 had risen to 400. News of the German collapse had been greeted with headlines in *Le Matin* of "Revenge for Sedan, 1870" and "The Hour of Punishment," and diplomats arriving for the peace conference were greeted by posters of "Let Germany Pay First," with deputies proposing that the Germans be made to pay for the entire cost of the war.

The serious work of drafting the treaty began in January—and, pointedly, with a meeting of the "Ten" in the French Foreign Minister's private office in the Quai d'Orsay; pointedly, because from beginning to end it was the French who would endeavour to direct and manipulate the negotiations. "I never wanted to hold the conference in his bloody capital," Lloyd George complained later of his wartime ally, and—though in the gentler language of the American campus—Woodrow Wilson would come to share roughly the same opinion. Lloyd George and Wilson's powerful adviser, Colonel House, would have preferred to stage the vital conference in a neutral city, like Geneva: "but the old man wept and protested so much that we gave way." Anyway, where else? After all, it was France that had suffered most from the war, and had the greatest call for punishment of the enemy. And it was punishment that was the order of the day.

The talks dragged on from week to week, month to month; meanwhile, Parisian goodwill towards their former allies understandably evaporated. The new invaders were seen to commandeer scarce food and accommodation, and the best women. Young Harold Nicolson on the British Foreign Officer team, "gathered a vivid impression of the growing hatred of the French for the Americans. The latter have without doubt annoyed the Parisians."[9] As delegates would spend their weekends off making tourist trips to the lunar landscapes of the Somme battlefields, a bitter new song, "Qui a gagné la guerre?" began to make the rounds.

THE DISCOURAGINGLY SWIFT TURNAROUND in Franco-American relations was not entirely surprising when one recalls how the most prominent figure of the moment was Thomas Woodrow Wilson. The French felt that this ascetic, unworldly professor from a stern Presbyterian background never really understood them. He did indeed seem curiously out of place. Only eight years after emerging from the obscurity of a New Jersey campus, Wilson had, as seen by his colleague, Herbert Hoover, "reached the zenith of intellectual and spiritual leadership of the whole world never hitherto known in history."[10] His capacity for inconsistency, and for turning on his friends and allies, had however been renowned long before he was picked to run for president; his capacity for suspicion was also unrivalled, but he could not bear plain speaking on the part of others. His remedy for the world's problems was simple: "the only cure for the ills of democracy is more democracy." A tendency to lecture was not well received by either Clemenceau or Lloyd George, who both had a view that their nations too had been involved in a war to make the world safe for democracy. "Talking to Wilson is something like talking to Jesus Christ," complained Clemenceau; while Lloyd George thought of him as being like "a missionary to rescue the heathen Europeans, with his 'little sermonettes.' " When it came to imposing the sweeping aphorisms of his "Fourteen Points," Wilson the academic swiftly realised that it was rather easier to impart than to apply instruction. He was certainly no Talleyrand; nor was there any thought of inviting the Germans, as the Congress of Vienna had invited the defeated French in 1814–15, to attend the peace conference before the terms had been drawn up.

The inequalities that war had imposed upon the peacemakers were potently apparent. France had the biggest army in the world, but no money; the USA had the money, but no military force; Britain possessed only some of each. While Germany was quite intact, in France there lay the shattered skeletons of towns across the northern countryside and 1.4 million French dead. France's public debt had increased from ff33.5 billion in 1913 to over ff219 billion in 1919, and she owed ff33 million abroad. Did her allies not understand? France needed to be more than repaid for her loss. She had to have lasting security, with frontiers in the ethnically German Rhineland, such as Louis le Grand and Napoleon had sought. In 1919, the French Army—still enduring terrible conditions—was rumoured to be once more on the verge of mutiny. Some British, so disciplined during the war, did in fact mutiny. In the East, the Soviet Russians were moving in on Poland, and the Germans—racked with the threat of civil war, Spartacist and Bolshevik revolution—were preparing for war again on their eastern marches.

By March on his return to the conference Lloyd George was sick, and tired, his shock of Welsh hair turned white. To Churchill, old Clemenceau seemed "grim, rugged, snow white." Shortly after the talks had begun in February, he had narrowly missed an assassination attempt when a young man stepped out of a *pissoire* and emptied his pistol into Clemenceau's car, hitting him near a lung, with the declaration: "I am a Frenchman and an anarchist." Maynard Keynes viewed the principals and their negotiations unflatteringly:

> Clemenceau, aesthetically the noblest; the President [Woodrow Wilson], morally the most admirable; Lloyd George, intellectually the subtlest. Out of their disparities and weaknesses the Treaty was born, child of the least worthy attributes of each of its parents, without nobility, without morality and without intellect . . .

By April none of the delegates meeting at the Quai d'Orsay were happy people. In France's desperate pursuit of security at any price, Clemenceau—the man of 1871—had failed to gain for her a permanent frontier on the Rhine (instead he got a fifteen-year tenancy, which Adolf Hitler would promptly supersede), or annexation of the coal-rich Saar (though, throughout its entire history, the German-speaking Saar had only been French for eighteen years). Wilson told Clemenceau: "You base your claim on what took place 104 years ago. We cannot readjust Europe on the basis of conditions that existed in such a remote period." Wilson, however, was thwarted in most of his lofty ideals; a hostile Congress at home would renege on them, then he succumbed to the illness that would eventually claim him. The Italians—troublesome throughout the peace conference—felt cheated of the Allied wartime promises, which had been offered out of all proportion to Italy's modest military contribution, and opened the door to Mussolini. The British, fed up with arguing and with their allies, just wanted to get back across the Channel as quickly as possible.

FINALLY, AND AT THE LAST MINUTE, the peace treaty was ready. The scene shifted from the Quai d'Orsay to Versailles. Why Versailles? Clemenceau, with his bitter recollections as Mayor of Montmartre in 1871, claimed that—if the Germans were to appear in force in Paris—there could be riot and revolution as per the Commune. Also, all the administrative machinery of the Allied Supreme War Council had been out there since 1919. But of far greater significance was the pleasing historical congruence of making the enemy sign at the scene of his triumph, and France's humiliation, forty-eight years earlier. On 28 April the German delegation set off from Berlin to receive the treaty that was to be imposed on them, headed by Count von Brockdorff-Rantzau from the Foreign Office. As they reached the battlefields of northern France, the French train driver—determined that the Germans should have the clearest view of the devastation the war had caused, slowed it down to 10 miles an hour. On arrival, a French colonel formally conducted them to the Hôtel des Reservoirs; by no accident selected because, in 1871, it was where the dejected French peace commission had resided while suing for peace with Bismarck. They found the building surrounded by barbed wire. Although there were French troops lounging in the courtyard, the Germans were made to carry their own baggage and seek their own rooms.

In the Trianon Palace Hotel, located on the edge of the park of Versailles, at three on the afternoon of 7 May, a hot afternoon and the first real day of summer, there was a shout by the *huissiers* announcing "Messieurs les délégués allemands!" Then the Germans received the Allied peace terms. As soon as they were seated, looking grimly isolated amid an assemblage of more than 200 dignitaries, Clemenceau as president of the peace conference began without ceremony. "Gentlemen, plenipotentiaries of the German Empire," he declared, standing up:

> this can be neither the time nor the place for superfluous words . . . The hour has struck for the weighty settlement of our account. You have asked us for peace. We are disposed to give it to you. The volume which the secretary general of the conference will shortly hand to you will tell you the conditions we have fixed . . .
> I am compelled to add that this second Peace of Versailles has

been too dearly bought by the peoples represented here for us not to be unanimously resolved to secure by every means in our power all the legitimate satisfactions which are our due.[11]

The Germans would be allowed just fifteen days in which to send "written observations" to the Allies; then they would be informed of the date upon which the finalised treaty would be signed.

Brockdorff-Rantzau, emaciated, ashen-faced and trembling, looked distinctly unwell and responded sitting down—possibly because he feared his legs might give way, though this apparent discourtesy to Clemenceau was taken by some (including Lloyd George) as proof that the Germans were as arrogant and unrepentant as ever. "We know the intensity of the hatred which meets us," said Brockdorff-Rantzau frostily,

and we have heard the victors' passionate demand that as vanquished we shall be made to pay and as the guilty we shall be punished. The demand is made that we shall acknowledge that we alone are guilty of having caused the war. Such a confession in my mouth would be a lie.[12]

That night when they read the terms set out in the lengthy document, with its 440 separate articles and 75,000 words, the German delegates were rendered speechless. The reparations alone would ruin the country, while most of her coal mines, Germany's principal economic asset, had been distributed among the Poles and the French. For the first time they began to speak of a *Diktat*; no German government could possibly accept it. After all, had they not signed an armistice rather than a capitulation?

Reactions among some of the Allied delegates echoed their sentiments. Wilson was recorded as commenting: "If I were a German, I think I should never sign it." Young William C. Bullitt, who would return as US Ambassador to deal with the fallout of Versailles two decades later, resigned from the American delegation; in his note of resignation he declared forthrightly that he was "going to lie on the sands of the Riviera and watch the world go to hell." Lloyd George recalled the prophetic fears he had expressed earlier in the conference:

You may strip Germany of her colonies, reduce her armaments to a mere police force and her navy to that of a fifth-rate power; all the same in the end if she feels that she has been unjustly treated in the peace of 1919 she will find means of exacting retribution on her conquerors.[13]

But the die was cast; Germany had to sign. As Brockdorff-Rantzau and his dejected team left for Berlin, rocks were thrown at their cars by jeering members of the Ligue des Patriotes; some of the Germans cut with broken glass. Scheidemann's government resigned; the German High Seas Fleet scuppered itself in Scapa Flow. Foch ordered remobilisation of the French Army, and a new war seemed likely to break out. Then the Germans, under their new Chancellor, Gustav Bauer, crumbled, as the Allies poised to march on Berlin.

On 28 June, a Saturday, the great hall in the palace was ready for the occasion it had been awaiting since Bismarck's triumphant Prussians had desecrated it by daring to crown an enemy emperor there. The Gardes Meubles storerooms of Paris had been ransacked for Savonnerie carpets to restore the deserted rooms to their old imposing grandeur. Instead of Uhlans with spiked helmets, this time the avenue up to the château was lined with French cavalry—the pennants of their lances fluttering red and white in the sun. Never, "since the Grand Siècle," thought Harold Nicolson, "has Versailles been more ostentatious or more embossed."[14] It made him feel "civilian and grubby"—and extremely unhappy. (What the German delegates felt can best be imagined.) In the centre of the Galerie des Glaces, a horse-shoe table had been set up for the plenipotentiaries; in front of it, "like a guillotine," a small table for the signatures. Clemenceau, still presiding, seated himself beneath the scroll of the heavy ceiling which reads: "Le Roi Gouverne Par Lui-même." The heat was oppressive. Out of the silence, with a "harshly penetrating" voice, Clemenceau called out: "Faites entrer les Allemands!"

Once more the huge mirrors had Germans reflected in them; this time, in place of the triumphant, uniformed princes and grandees of Prussia, they were two very ordinary little men in frock-coats, Dr. Müller and Dr. Bell, "isolated and pitiful." Both deathly pale, to the watchful Nicolson they did

not appear as representatives of a brutal militarism. The one is thin and pink eye-lidded: the second fiddle in a Brunswick orchestra. The other is moon-faced and suffering: a *privat dozent* [unpaid junior university lecturer]. It is all most painful . . .[15]

In front of 200 pairs of anxious eyes, the Germans signed first of all. With this done, the other plenipotentiaries lined up to append their signatures. Amid a hum of relaxed conversation, Dr. Müller and Dr. Bell walked to a corner of the great gallery, to sit in comfortable obscurity between Japan and Uruguay. A Bolivian delegate came over and asked for their autographs. From outside there was a crash of guns, announcing to Paris that the "Second Treaty of Versailles"—as Clemenceau dubbed it—had been signed. "La séance est levée," rasped Clemenceau—not a word more or less.

"Well, little girl, it is finished, and, as no one is satisfied, it makes me hope we have made a just peace; but it is all in the laps of the gods," commented Woodrow Wilson to his wife.[16] Whatever pity might have been felt for the two German delegates that day, historians would reflect that—had the Kaiser and Ludendorff won—the punishment for Britain and France would clearly have been no less harsh; the Treaty of Brest-Litovsk imposed on a prostrate Russia demonstrated that. To tidy, and unforgetting, French minds, Versailles 1919 may have represented a full circle from 1871; but it would soon prove to be only a half-circle. In a prophecy of deadly accuracy, Foch declared: "This is not peace, but a truce for twenty years." "The next time," he warned, with deadly accuracy, "the Germans will make no mistake. They will break through into northern France and seize the Channel ports as a base of operations against England."

The circle would be completed twenty-one summers later, with Hitler's little jig performed outside the *wagon-lits* coach at Compiègne, the same where Foch signed the armistice of 1918; his feet dancing on the Versailles *Diktat*. Surely even arrogant old Louis, looking down from the ceilings of the palace he built, with its dedicatory inscription of "À Toutes les Gloires de la France," would have recognised what misery his successors and their discordant, increasingly reluctant allies were laying in store for themselves that June day of 1919? And, if only Louis-Napoleon had not been quite so proudly foolish in 1870 . . . wrote Winston Churchill in *The World Crisis*: "Victory was to be bought so dear as to be almost indistinguishable from defeat." France had selected the stage for the final act in the tragedy entitled *Revenge* with an unsurpassable sense of theatre. As Churchill also remarked at that time, "the hatred of France for Germany was something more than human." It was hardly a promising basis for the peace that was to end all wars.

# SIXTEEN

# *Years of Illusion*

Victory was to be bought so dear as to be almost
indistinguishable from defeat.

—The World Crisis, *Winston Churchill*

O N   T H E   N I G H T before the great celebration of 14 July 1919,
100,000 spectators had already taken up positions along the
Champs-Élysées, their tone one of restrained jubilation tempered by the presence of so many women still clad in mourning for a
loved one. The janitors and charwomen had barely finished sweeping
away the debris of diplomacy from Versailles' great Hall of Mirrors, but
peace was now a fact. The signature of the treaty had swiftly become
eclipsed by the imminence of this other, tangibly more magnificent
occasion—the day of the Victory Parade; to many Frenchmen, never
could there be an occasion more fitting of *le jour de gloire* acclaimed by
the "Marseillaise" than this first *quatorze* since Alsace-Lorraine had
returned to the fold from its forty-eight years of bondage.

As the dawn came up, down at the Porte-Maillot the massed Allied
contingents could be seen forming up behind their leaders, greeted by
members of the Municipal Council, who, like the *aediles* of antiquity,
were opening the city to the conquering armies. At 7:45, a car arrived at
the Étoile bringing Clemenceau. Occasionally shooting fierce glances to
right and left, the old "Tiger" shambled slowly up to the official stand.
Accompanied by France's two glorious marshals, Joffre and Foch, President Poincaré laid a wreath at the Arc de Triomphe. The marshals then
drove off to take up their positions at the head of the parade. At the
Porte-Maillot, a captain took out his watch and gave the order heard at

so many lethal dawns during the preceding four years: "Avancez!" Trumpets sounded those peculiarly Gallic, almost querulously high-pitched notes, and approaching the Arc de Triomphe was soon heard the music of the regimental bands playing out the stirring strains of "Vous n'aurez pas l'Alsace et la Lorraine!"

Now, for the first time since Bismarck's Prussians had paraded through it, marching men appeared under the sacred arch. But those who led the way in this historic moment were not Foch or Pétain; not the cavalry, or any Allied detachment, but three young men, unspeakably maimed by war, still in uniform, wheeled along in chairs by their nurses. Immediately behind them came a large contingent of more *grands mutilés*. Officers and simple *poilus,* all mixed together, many already in mufti, marched—or hobbled—without precedence or semblance of military order, twelve abreast. Many bore on their chests France's most coveted decoration, the Médaille Militaire. The blind— some accorded the privilege of being ensign-bearers—were led by those who had lost a leg or an arm; men with their destroyed faces mercifully hidden behind bandages; men with no hands; men with their complexions still tinted green from the effects of chlorine gas; men with mad eyes staring out from beneath skullcaps that concealed some appalling head injury. Some were famous heroes, easily recognised by the crowd; among them, identifiable by his immense stature, limped Sergeant André Maginot, already a well-known figure in the National Assembly, who had lost a leg at Verdun.

With a painful, halting pace the column moved down the Champs-Élysées. For a moment the spectacle of the broken men was met with a nervous silence. Then, as they passed a stand filled with 150 young Alsatian girls in national costumes, flowers rained down upon them: "an immense cry, which seemed to spring from the very entrails of the race, arose from the vast crowd, a cry which was both a salute and a pledge."[1] No one who watched the *mutilés* pass could be unaware of what they represented: the many thousands more, hopelessly mauled, lodged in hospitals across the country which they would never leave; the hundreds of thousands of other war casualties, only relatively more fortunate. Here was the price France had paid, the true price of glory. No combatant nation, except little Serbia, had suffered a higher mortality rate; higher than Russia, higher than Germany or her allies. It was a fact brutally brought home on this luminous day of victory celebrations. A squadron of magnificent Republican Guards then rode through the Arc de Triomphe, accompanied by a thunderous military fanfare, preceding the victorious marshals, Joffre and Foch, and Pétain, then wave upon wave of marching *poilus* and Allied contingents.

REVELLERS DANCED THAT NIGHT AWAY in the streets of a dazzlingly illuminated city. Yet the morning-after the greatest uncertainty had not been dispelled: what had the peace to offer the people of France? From the great *défilé* of the *quatorze* one army had been missing, one without whose aid the "Miracle of the Marne" could never have happened and without whose seemingly bottomless reserves of men there would not have been any victory celebrations at all: Russia, rent by revolution and civil war, and forgotten by her allies. For battered France, however, she sent a spectre to the feast; it was called Communism. For any Parisian who read the small print in the newspapers, it was apparent. On the very day of the signature of the peace treaty a fortnight before, Communists had brought about a Métro and bus strike, paralysing the city. That spring, inflation and the growing restiveness of the workers had led to *la vie chère* instead of *la vie douce* becoming the main topic of conversation in many a French household. The government was being tough with these left-wing demonstrators, but its toughness had only embittered the atmosphere.

A political constellation of the far left—Communists, Internationalists and extreme Socialists—had boycotted the victory celebrations. The recent war, in their eyes, had been but a criminal affair between the capitalist classes. The workers in millions had died in it, but pointlessly without a universal revolution, bringing the overthrow of the existing order, as had happened in Lenin's Russia. Therefore there was no cause at all for rejoicing. Instead, the extremists had decided to stage their own show. Together with some disabled ex-servicemen demonstrating against wartime profiteers, about a hundred people gathered near the Place de la Trinité. As a macabre demonstration against militarism, they had intended to roll several of the *mutilés* in their invalid carriages in front of Foch's horse as he rode past the Opéra. They were forestalled by the police, re-formed on the exterior boulevards and marched through the east end of Paris to pay tribute to the Communard martyrs enshrined at Père Lachaise Cemetery. There was a scuffle at the cemetery, and some twenty arrests were made. The next day, Marcel Cachin, editor of *L'Humanité*, blazed against the Victory Parade:

Bitterness! Disgust! I have recognised the crowd. It is not the crowd that took the Bastille and sang for the first time of liberty in the streets. It is not the crowd that religiously followed the bier of Zola or Jaurès . . . It is the brutish elemental crowd which does not change, which slavishly acclaims Caesar and Boulanger, which yells at the vanquished, which chooses indifferently its heroes among boxers, gladiators and captains.[2]

With most lured away by the greater attraction of the Victory Parade that day, the small turnout of Cachin's supporters was deceptively unrepresentative of the intrinsic, let alone the potential strength of the new left in France. For in none other of the victorious nations had Russia's October Revolution evoked stronger sympathies than among the workers of Paris—the home of revolution itself. It struck powerful chords with the ancient and deep-rooted revolutionary mystique of 1793 and 1848, but above all with the Commune of 1871, the brutal repression of which remained stamped in the minds of the French left wing and whose failure Lenin had used as a textbook to perfect his own revolution. The foundation in March 1919 of the Third International in Moscow raised radical hearts in France, while it was no accident that among the interventionist forces in Russia it was the French at Odessa who had raised the flag of mutiny. The bourgeois, property-owning classes closed their ranks accordingly.

In Washington, where the Senate was beginning its deliberations on the peace treaty, rumours were emerging that President Wilson might yet have difficulty in persuading the American Congress to ratify the instrument that was to guarantee France's security. With political parties polarised between extremes of right and left, and fickle, self-destructive splinter groupings in between, French politics now embarked on what de Gaulle would one day scathingly designate "this absurd ballet." In place of the "Banquet Years" or "Miraculous Years," writers about these times would seek less acclamatory titles such as the "Locust Years," the "Years of Illusion," the "Hollow Years" or the "Crazy Years."

In January 1920, Paul Deschanel had been elected President of the Republic, in succession to Poincaré. Like a symptom of the national malady, the new president was soon worrying his entourage by his increasingly erratic behaviour; on one occasion after a delegation of schoolgirls had presented him with a bouquet, he tossed the flowers back at them one by one. Then, early in the hours of a day in May, he was found in his immaculate pyjamas, wandering along a railway track 70 miles from Paris, on the route to Lyons. Allegedly he had fallen out of a *wagon-lit* on his way to an engagement in Roanne—miraculously unscathed, bar a few grazes. In the best French way in which the deviations of politicians are kept quiet, the episode was hushed up, though *chansonniers* swiftly set it to verse

> Il n'a pas oublié son pyjama
> C'est épatant, mais c'est comme ça.[3]

A short while after recovering from his nocturnal foray, Deschanel walked out of a state meeting at Rambouillet—and straight into the lake, fully clothed. That September, after less than a year in office, he was quietly removed to an institution. His sad tenancy at the Élysée said something about the pressures henceforth to be imposed on France's political leaders, as well as perhaps symbolising the 1920s as *les années folles*.

IN ECONOMIC TERMS it was indeed a haggard France that faced the dawn of victory in July 1919. Yet, showing the same extraordinary recuperative capacity that had amazed the world in 1871, she repaired her shattered industries, and got her raddled fields back under plough far quicker than any foreign observer could have imagined. It was to the financial structure that lasting damage had been done. To pay for the war, France had issued a flood of paper money. By the armistice, the franc had lost nearly two-thirds of its value. This was only a beginning; whereas it then exchanged at 26 francs to the pound sterling, already by the time of the Victory Parade it had depreciated to 51 francs to the pound. By the middle of 1926 its value had sunk to 220. Fanned by the new virulence of the revolutionary left, the French workers' justifiable demands for higher wages to offset this inflation gave the spiral an extra spin. Additional millions had to be spent in funding the pensions of the legions of ex-servicemen—notably the *mutilés*.

The Budget of 1919 had been postponed more than seven months, during which time further vast loans had been launched, so that when finally agreed it showed an enormous deficit of ff27,000 million. Nobody viewed this too tragically; automatically, it was assumed, the

Allies would be accommodating, and generous. When America would not help out, France fell back on the happy illusion that "the *Boche* will pay." But Germany could not, would not pay; and the Allies would not make her. After all, as they were frequently reminded from Berlin, November 1918 had brought only an armistice, *not* a capitulation. And had Frenchmen forgotten already how the harsh settlement imposed by Prussia in 1871 had kept alight France's own fire of revenge for the best part of half a century? The post-war Minister of Finance, Louis-Lucien Klotz (according to Clemenceau "the only Jew who knows nothing about money"), made it clear that he expected France's budgetary deficits to be redeemed by German reparations, but in 1923 Germany defaulted on her payments. France occupied the Ruhr to force her to pay. Down in Bavaria an angry unknown Austrian ex-corporal acquired his first national publicity. On being forced (unbacked by England) to pull back out of the Ruhr, the illusion of France's power in the post-war world received its first serious shock.

Although the return of Raymond Poincaré in 1926 brought France an almost miraculous three-year period of quasi-stability (as well as prosperity), in the seventeen months after his retirement in 1929 another five governments came and went. In Paris, by the mid-1920s prices had doubled several times since 1914. While Britain and America were already emerging from the tunnel of the world slump, France was still in economic stasis; between 1928 and 1934, her industrial production dropped by 17 per cent; between 1929 and 1936, average incomes fell by 30 per cent; and by the end of 1935 over 800,000 were unemployed. Thus the nation's financial dilemma extended into the 1930s, bringing down government after government and rendering impossible any consistent foreign policy or reconciliation with Germany. It bedevilled the Third Republic throughout the remainder of its existence, and finally hamstrung it when the necessity to rearm confronted France with desperate urgency.

BY THE "HOLLOW YEARS" of the 1930s, France had a maturing population of just over 40 million. Between 1900 and 1939 it had grown by little more than a million, and that was largely due to immigration. At the same time Germany, once again, had increased hers—by 36 per cent. Two-thirds of France's population lived in the towns and cities; just before the turn of the century (1890) the figure had been exactly the reverse, with two-thirds living on the land. The explanation for this dramatic swing lay partly in the devastating losses suffered among the sons of the peasantry in 1914–18, partly also in the universal drift towards city jobs and amenities. Paris remained, as always, the principal magnet.

There was one important faction of society which found life there wonderfully good—and *bon marché*: the expatriates, and particularly Americans. In 1921, foreign residents of Paris comprised one in twenty of the population; ten years later the figure had almost doubled, while it also accounted for a quarter of all those arrested by the police. Oscar Wilde's Mrs. Allonby observed that when good Americans die they go to Paris; but after 1919 even not-so-good Americans took off there in droves. The allure was at least partly negative; Paris offered an escape from the restrictive, false Puritan world that Prohibition under the Volstead Act had imposed on young Americans returning from the war; in Paris, by contrast, one was left free to lead one's private life, to swim—or sink.

Many young Americans had sampled the delights of Paris when serving as Pershing's doughboys during the war, and wanted to come back for more. Gertrude Stein was already there; among the other notables were John Dos Passos, e. e. cummings, Stephen Vincent Benét, Archibald MacLeish, Louis Bromfield, Philip Barry, Robert Benchley and Dorothy Parker—not to mention F. Scott Fitzgerald and Ernest Hemingway, and, of course, the irresistible Josephine Baker. There was Sylvia Beach, famed founder of Shakespeare and Co., the English bookshop and gathering point near the Odéon—and brave publisher of Joyce's *Ulysses* and *My Life and Loves* by Frank Harris. By 1927, there were known to be 15,000 Americans in Paris—but the real figure was estimated to be much more like 40,000. It was Stein who dubbed her countrymen "the lost generation." Then came the crash of 1929. Many had to join the queue at the American Embassy for emergency funds to return home. The waves closed over their heads, just as the cold Seine closed over the *chiens écrasés,* as suicides were coldly dubbed by the Sûreté—the tragic failures of those crossed-in-love, the *amputées de coeur.*

A KIND OF FALSE CHEER reigned through much of the 1920s and 1930s in France. In the music halls, Maurice Chevalier, the self-proclaimed ace French lover, epitomised the jaunty optimism of the era with his 1921 theme-song: "Dans la vie, faut pas s'en faire" (In life you mustn't worry). Art was one form of escapism; born of the war, Dadaism was (fortunately) short-lived but demonstrative of the move away from the happy realities of the Impressionists; in the late 1920s it was succeeded by Surrealism, the declared "enemy of reason." Pointedly it began in a wartime hospital for shell-shocked *poilus,* where poets André Breton and Louis Aragon, both in their early twenties, had met as medical orderlies. Equally pointed, both founders of the new movement started life in the Communist Party. Surrealism stressed the priority of sexual freedom removed from religious constraints, and liberation of the unconscious. Symbolic, too, was the spectacle of Braque returning from the war with a turban of bandages covering his head wound. It was the horror of trenches which made many like them recoil from the traditional world that had taken them on the road to Verdun, embracing instead an idealist fantasy—just at the time, ironically, when Lenin and Stalin were perpetrating their own worst excesses in southern Russia.

In literature, Dadaism and Surrealism in art were matched by the *fantaisiste,* fairy-tale world of Cocteau and Giraudoux. Another postwar literary form emphasised the humour of cuckoldry; it was escapism especially designed for the middle-aged male, known as *le démon de midi*; or, by way of compensation for their female opposite numbers, best-sellers like Raymond Radiguet's brilliant novel, *Le Diable au corps* (1923), featuring an early "Mrs. Robinson" figure. But of far more profound significance for French literature in the late 1920s was the spate of anti-war literature that swept Europe, telling of its horror and wastefulness, combined with the cynical callousness and sheer incompetence of the war leaders. In Germany, Hitler had been swift to stifle such books as Remarque's *All Quiet on the Western Front,* but in France it had become a top best-seller, challenged only by the terrifying novel of Henri Barbusse, *Le Feu* (first published 1916, winning the Prix Goncourt and selling 300,000 by the war's end). For France's Verdun generation, and for their juniors, *Le Feu* related a nightmare the re-enactment of which must be avoided at all costs. Wielding enormous intellectual influence were various anti-war associations formed by such giants of France's literary left wing as André Gide, Paul Éluard, Louis Aragon and Romain Rolland. Barbusse was the torch-bearer; when he died in 1935, more than 300,000 followed his coffin to Père Lachaise Cemetery in Paris.

In 1930s France, the passion for romantic travel, powerful in the twenties, gave way to an equal fascination in the personal "heroic quest" of the agonising man-of-action, adventurers such as Saint-Exupéry and Malraux. But where exactly should one place Céline's picaresque journey through the First World War (where he was wounded and decorated), *Voyage au bout de la nuit* (1932) with all its relentless, defeatist pessimism, which, nevertheless, made him an instant best-seller?

For all its philosophy of "engagement," possibly no form of literature demonstrated a greater revolt from reality than the existentialism of young Jean-Paul Sartre and his fellow hot-house inmates of the Café Flore in the latter 1930s. Sartre's mistress, Simone de Beauvoir, furnishes a revealing chronicle of the attitude of French left-wing intellectuals. The autumn of 1929 had made her feel she was living in a new "Golden Age": "Peace seemed finally assured; the expansion of the German Nazi party was a mere fringe phenomenon, without any serious significance . . . It would not be long before colonialism folded up."[4] Of Hitler's coming to power in 1933, she writes: "like everyone else on the French left, we watched these developments quite calmly." She records, almost *en passant,* Einstein's flight from Germany; nevertheless, "there was no threat to peace; the only danger was the panic that the right was attempting to spread in France, with the aim of dragging us into war."

In their film-going, their own brand of escapism led Sartre and Beauvoir to skip Jean Renoir's classic anti-war film *La Grande Illusion,* by preference seeking out such American farces as *My Man Godfrey,* and *Mr. Deeds Goes to Town.* Despite having given birth to the cinema, France got off to a slow start in the inter-war period. Of 430 films opening in Paris in 1934, less than a quarter were French and few survive. A spectacular exception was Abel Gance's eight-hour silent epic, *Napoléon,* of 1926—possibly the most outstanding silent film ever made. Renoir's *La Grande Illusion,* rather than being just anti-war and reflecting the political divisions of the Popular Front era, says almost more about the internal class distinctions that divide men—an aristocrat, a banker, a mechanic or a Jew—and the transcendence in comradeship that war can achieve. Its impact was such that, when the French prisoners of war sang the "Marseillaise" in one moving scene, Parisian audiences—regardless of political hue—also rose to their feet to sing. Star of *La Grande Illusion* was Jean Gabin, the current heart-throb of the French screen, who frequently took the role of the "little man" struggling against a hostile society. Then in 1939—appearing almost on the eve of war—came *La Règle du jeu,* pitilessly depicting the middle classes as selfish and destructive. When first shown, *La Règle* provoked riots, and it was banned successively in wartime France by both the Daladier and Vichy regimes.

IN 1933, ADOLF HITLER, product of the bitterness over Versailles and its consequences for Germany, came to power. So often in history when the unpleasantness of reality induces emotional confusion, societies are tempted to bury themselves in imaginary pleasures and distractions. With his instinctive genius, Hitler knew well how to play on all French fears and desires for escapism, accompanying each new foreign adventure with barrages of peace propaganda.

Frenchmen could sleep all the more comfortably at night behind the notional safety of their impenetrable and invincible defences. Collectively, the French General Staff and successive governments concluded from the early disasters of 1914, and the costly defence of Verdun, that the only way to assure survival in a future war was to dig an immense, impenetrable concrete barrier in the east of the country. Hence came the costly, but technically superb Maginot Line—named after the then Minister of Defence, the one-legged hero of Verdun, former sergeant André Maginot. The project had the support of the defensive-minded Marshal Pétain, following the death of Foch, France's most influential soldier. The concept was fine; except that all great walls offer a standing invitation to go over, under or around them. The Maginot Line was to cost so immense a chunk of France's declining defence budget that it was impossible to continue it all the way from Sedan to the Channel, and there was not enough money left to provide the mobile forces needed to counter a possible breakthrough. These were ardently called for—but in vain—by a young military thinker called Colonel Charles de Gaulle. In 1930s France, military call-up was beginning to suffer acutely from the effect of the drop in births during the First World War. In Hitler's Germany, the 1915 class could produce 464,000 effectives; in France, only 184,000—a ratio that would continue right the way through to the Second World War.

UPON THE FUTILE THIRD REPUBLIC POLITICS there burst a miasma of corruption cases. The first big shock came in 1928 with the arrest of Klotz, the former Minister of Finance about whom Clemenceau had been so scathing, on charges of issuing dud cheques. Then there was Serge Stavisky, a seductive young man of Ukrainian-Jewish extraction, who for all his enviable connections had come under official scrutiny. The police found his body in a house in Chamonix—conveniently perhaps for Prime Minister Camille Chautemps, whose own brother-in-law was the prosecutor who had mysteriously failed to bring him to justice. Overnight Stavisky became the best-known name since Dreyfus—costing further public trust in the government and arousing renewed anti-Semitism.

On 27 January 1934, the Chautemps government fell—after an inning of just two months and four days. From mid-1932 up to the outbreak of war in 1939, France's score of governments would total nineteen, including eleven different premiers. Thus, France lacked any continuity in the direction of her affairs, her leaders regarded with increasing contempt. A favourite insult hurled from Parisian taxis became "Espèce de député." On 6 February, 1934, a group of right-wing nationalist factions, sickened by France's retreat from *grandeur* since 1919, as by the corrupt ineptitude of her politicians, and fearful of the rising strength of the new "Bolshevik" left, united to march on the Assembly.

Just when, across the Rhine, Adolf Hitler was consolidating himself in power, this day marked the beginning of what approximated to civil war in France. On the right wing were "leagues" such as the Camelots du Roi, shock troops of the monarchist, Catholic, anti-Semitic *Action Française* journal of Charles Maurras,[5] which had influenced the furore around Stavisky. There were the violently anti-Communist Jeunesses Patriotes, and Solidarité Française created by funds from the perfumery fortune of François Coty, its members wearing a paramilitary uniform of black beret and blue shirt and with a motto of "La France aux Français!" The most articulate of the leagues was the Croix de Feu led by Colonel Casimir de la Rocque, and dedicated to the purgation of the Third Republic. "Honesty" and "Order" were its twin battle cries, and, though it was not fascist like some other leagues, it shared their admiration for the vigour that Mussolini had instilled into Italian youth. As the scandals multiplied, so the Croix de Feu adopted a more blatantly anti-republican attitude. The patrician colonel himself was certainly no rabble-rouser like Hitler. His voice was too high, his diction too elaborate, for mass appeal; just too genteel. Nevertheless, to the left, Colonel de la Rocque epitomised everything that it loathed and feared in fascism.

On the morning of the 6th, *Action Française* printed with the most provocative headlines: "the thieves are barricading themselves in their cave. Against this abject regime, everyone in front of the Chamber of Deputies this evening." At about 6 p.m., the first push—with a number of *grands mutilés* veterans placed conspicuously to the fore—attempted to force through police barriers drawn up on the Pont de la Concorde.

They hurled bottles, stones and sections of lead piping at the police, and when the mounted police charged, the hocks of their horses were slashed with razors tied to sticks. Inside the Chamber, the new government, headed by Édouard Daladier, was still struggling to get a vote of confidence. By 7:30, warnings by the police had not dispersed the crowd, and they opened fire. It was not until midnight that the deputies could conclude they were safe. Had Daladier not taken precautions to have the Chamber guarded, there might well have been a repetition of the scenes of February 1848 on the Paris streets.

Out of some 40,000 demonstrators, sixteen had been killed and at least 655 were known to be wounded; well over a thousand policemen received injuries. The next day Colonel de la Rocque proclaimed from his secret battle headquarters: "The Croix de Feu has surrounded the Chamber and forced the deputies to flee." It was a gross exaggeration; but the Communists now also took up cudgels against the government. One eye-witness actually saw a Camelot du Roi and a Communist jointly pulling down a lamp-post—just about the last occasion in time of peace that the two extremes of French political life would be able to find common cause. In the heated atmosphere, Daladier resigned. It was the first time since 1871 that a Paris mob had brought about the fall of a French government. Ex-President Gaston Doumergue, aged seventy, formed a "National Government," but in a patriotic gesture to the right wing made his contemporary, Marshal Pétain, the "Hero of Verdun," Minister of National Defence.

The entire left thought in terror that it saw the imminence of a right-wing *coup d'état,* with Colonel de la Rocque primed for the role of Louis-Napoleon—or Benito Mussolini. On the morning of 9 February, the communist *L'Humanité* called a mass meeting in the Place de la République, to demand the dissolution of both the Chamber and its ephemeral right-wing allies. That night near the République, two rival columns approached each other, one of Communists, the other of Jeunesses Socialistes, representing the two principal left-wing parties. The two had hardly been on speaking terms since their schism of 1920–21. At first it looked as if there would be conflict. However, amid cries of "We're not clashing, we're fraternising . . . we're all here to defend the Republic," the heads of the two columns mingled and clasped hands, then marched together. The whole left swung behind a general strike. "United as at the front!" had been on the lips of Colonel de la Rocque's *anciens combattants* on 6 February, "Unity of action!" the slogan of the heirs to the Commune three days later.

These developments did nothing for national unity. That July, Blum the Socialist leader and Thorez the Communist signed a pact; by October *L'Humanité* was beginning to talk about a "Front Populaire contre le Fascisme." Meanwhile, France's economic plight was lending further cohesive force to left-wing solidarity. The plight of many French workers and their families was genuinely appalling.*

ON 14 JULY 1935, de la Rocque's Croix de Feu marched with smart military precision down the Champs-Élysées. But the day belonged to the left, demonstrating at the other end of Paris. Down from Belleville and the Faubourg Saint-Antoine they flooded to the Place de la Bastille; probably over half a million strong. Beneath great red banners proclaiming "Paix, Pain, Liberté!," the Front Populaire was officially launched. That afternoon Daladier, the Radical-Socialist former prime minister whose downfall the Communists had helped bring about the previous year, marched with them; arm in arm, like blood brothers, went Blum and Thorez, Herriot and Barbusse and Duclos. At their congress that October, the French Radicals too decided to throw in their lot. On 3 May 1936, France went to the polls and the Front Populaire was swept into power. Formerly with only 10 seats, the Communists now emerged with no fewer than 72; the Socialists, gaining another 49 seats, became the strongest party and accordingly it fell to Léon Blum to form a government. The left had scored its greatest triumph since 1871; but how, with the clouds growing more and more sombre beyond the Rhine, was it going to exploit this victory?

Buoyed up with the exhilaration of victory, and now united, French workers declared they would strike unless Blum gave them what they demanded, at once. Three weeks after his election, the Lavalette factory in north-west Paris and the Nieuport aircraft works at Issy in the southwest—building aircraft urgently needed by the French Air Force—were paralysed by sit-in strikes. Friends outside provided them with food, cigarettes and bedding, and they settled down for the night, arguing and playing cards or *boules*. Alcohol was banned, but the general tone was of insouciant levity. Day by day the bizarre situation renewed itself, the factory owners being told that if they attempted to break the strike, their

---

*On my first trip abroad as a child before the war, I still remember being struck by the skinny-legged, ricket-ridden and emaciated children by the railway track as the train approached the Gare du Nord.

plants would be burnt down. Gradually the unions assumed formal control. Eventually affecting 12,000 enterprises, strikes smoothly took over the Farman aircraft works and the factories of Citroën, Renault, Gnome et Rhône, and Simca—all vital to the French armaments industry. Sunday promenaders headed out to the factories to gaze at the workers laughing and entertaining themselves among the dead machinery.

Blum began hastily to prepare reforming legislation as prices on the Bourse plunged, and money was taken abroad. Blum was now the focus of opprobrium, including anti-Semitic emotions reawoken by Stavisky—sloganised as "rather Hitler than Blum"—only exacerbated by the influx of thousands of Austro-German Jewish refugees. Then at 1 a.m. on 8 June 1936, Blum signed the famous "Matignon Agreement." Under what was undoubtedly their greatest ever single advance in French industrial relations, the workers were guaranteed compulsory collective bargaining and annual paid holidays, a forty-hour week, and an immediate general rise in wages of 7 to 15 per cent. Yet still the strikes continued, until on the 11th Thorez was forced to intervene by telling his Communist supporters: "You must know when to end a strike!" That 14 July—at what was both the high point and the swansong of the Front— the entire left celebrated, linking arms once again around the Bastille— after almost a century-and-a-half, at last delivered to the proletariat.

INTO THE WARM CAMARADERIE of France's socialist triumph and her perennial game of legislative musical chairs, there burst the malignant, irreconcilable figure of Hitler. In March 1936, he marched into the demilitarised Rhineland, in gross breach of Versailles. His as yet still feeble *Wehrmacht* had orders to withdraw immediately in the event of any French reaction. But reaction came there none. France looked towards Britain. London, however, was preoccupied with Italy and Abyssinia; besides had not their wartime ally declared, just two years previously, that "France will henceforth guarantee her security by her own means?"*—thereby killing the Disarmament Conference. In any case, a large portion of Britons now agreed with Lord Lothian's historic comment about the Germans "only going into their own back garden." In

---

*As A. J. P. Taylor remarked of the Barthou declaration of 17 April 1934, "the French had fired the starting pistol for the arms race. Characteristically they then failed to run it." Three decades later the Anglo-Saxons were to find parallels in de Gaulle's withdrawal from NATO, when he declared that henceforth France felt strong enough to dispense with its benefits.

the opinion of Paul Reynaud, had France acted alone, Britain would have been bound to back her up. Rebuffed, Hitler might well have been uprooted by a German opposition that still had teeth. Increasingly, with hindsight, historians now see the Rhineland—not Munich two years later—to have been the point where the Battle in the West was won by Hitler, lost by France. But, for all her crushing military superiority then, France did nothing. It was Blum who declared "not a penny, not a man for Berlin."

INSTEAD, THE "MATIGNON AGREEMENT," so Simone de Beauvoir recorded, "filled us with joy"—a thoroughly escapist pleasure. Thanks to fifteen days of paid holidays and the forty-hour week, "couples on tandem bicycles could now be seen pedalling out of Paris every Saturday morning; they came back on Sunday evening with bunches of flowers and foliage tied to their handlebars." "Leisure! Leisure!" one newspaper rejoiced. Arcadian photographs appeared of workers thronging the beaches, picnicking and camping in the hitherto unfrequented countryside. A mass following grew for sports, notably football and cycling; between 1936 and 1938, the number of bicycles rose from 7 to 9 million. As the sporting pages of *Paris-Soir* made it overnight the journalistic success story of the decade, the Tour de France acquired a new popularity. For the long under-paid and under-privileged, it looked like Paradise gained. But could France afford it, with Hitler about to move on Austria and Czechoslovakia, and rearming at terrifying speed? Movingly, Léon Blum remarked: "I had the feeling, in spite of everything, of having brought a lull, a vista, into their dark difficult lives . . . we had given them hope."

Yet the truth was that it had rendered the future of France as a whole more hopeless, as the French military and industry continued to stagnate. By 1938, French industrial production had sunk an estimated 25 per cent below the 1930 figure; in Germany it had risen 30 per cent. Incredibly, the Conseil Supérieur de la Guerre (CSG) met but thirteen times during the four critical years of 1935–39, and was apparently never once consulted about tactical operations of major units. These were the years when damage was done to the French Army which it became too late to remedy (and, incidentally, despite the blame heaped on him subsequently, they were the years when Pétain's influence had been totally removed). When the Berlin-based American correspondent, William L. Shirer, visited Paris in October 1938, he found it a frightful place, completely surrendered to defeatism with no inkling of what has happened to *France* . . . Even the waiters, taxi-drivers, who used to be sound, are gushing about how wonderful it is that war has been avoided, that it would have been a crime, that they fought in one war and that was enough.

That would, he thought, "be okay if the Germans, who also fought in one war, felt the same way, but they don't."[6]

BY 1939 FOREIGN CRISES were effecting all sorts of contradictions in Paris. After Hitler had completed his devouring of Czechoslovakia, in March Britain gave Poland a guarantee of her national integrity. After Mussolini had grabbed Albania, France joined Chamberlain in extending similar guarantees to Romania and Greece; but the Quai d'Orsay under the defeatist and dislikeable Georges Bonnet threatened to take the *Nouvelle Revue Française* to court the moment it attacked either Hitler or Mussolini. In May the pro-German pacifist Marcel Déat (who would come into his own the following year) published a powerful article entitled "Do We Have to Die for Danzig?"—and with it *mourir pour Danzig* entered the Parisian vernacular. The 150th anniversary of the Great Revolution came and went with minimum fuss; certainly gazes were discreetly averted from the menaced *Liberté* and *Égalité* of the Bohemians or Poles. There was much more interest in the thirty-second Tour de France—though boycotted by German and Italian riders.

Then came the last 14 July celebration, an echo full of the splendid panoply of a past age; Foreign Legionnaires, Senegalese, cuirassiers in shining breastplates—and a detachment of British grenadiers in red tunics and bearskins to reassure Frenchmen as to the reality of the entente—all under a drenching rain. Proclaimed by Premier Daladier to be a "fête of national unity," in fact it was a day of rival marches and counter-marches. Instantly 3 million Frenchmen took off to the mountains and beaches on paid holidays; with them many took the new best-seller from America—*Autant en emporte le vent* (*Gone With the Wind*)—for their holiday reading. President Lebrun retired to his home in Lorraine; Premier Daladier reclined on the yacht of a friend in the Mediterranean; Finance Minister Paul Reynaud sailed off to Corsica. Even the Communist leaders departed insouciantly—Thorez to the Mediterranean, and Duclos to the Pyrenees, as *L'Humanité* continued to call for a pact with Moscow. One politician with his eye on the ball did visit the Maginot Line—but it was not a Frenchman, it was Winston Churchill. How radically concerns had changed since that *jour de gloire* of just twenty years previously! Where were the alliances Delcassé had worked so hard to build? In the East, Soviet Russia was an enigma; America had returned to isolation; and the force Britain could offer in case of war was relatively even weaker than the "Old Contemptibles" she had sent in 1914. And France was riven with political faction, demoralised and trying to forget the losses of 1914–18.

ON 23 AUGUST news of the Ribbentrop-Molotov Pact brought the sojourn to a chilling end. Reservists only recently released following the Munich mobilisation were recalled, but as Paul Reynaud remarked, "The Allies had lost the game." On 1 September, as *Je Suis Partout* ran a headline "À BAS LA GUERRE, VIVE LA FRANCE!" Hitler invaded Poland; two days later France and Britain declared war on Germany. This time, in a reversal of 1914 France reacted six hours behind her allies. Sartre began a letter to Simone de Beauvoir, "Folly has triumphed"; more appositely Anatole de Monzie wrote in his diary: "France at war does not believe in the war." That said it all. The odds facing her were colossal. Looking back from the vantage point of 1940, Joseph Goebbels observed:

> In 1933 a French premier ought to have said (and if I had been the French premier I would have said it): "The new Reich Chancellor is the man who wrote *Mein Kampf,* which says this and that. This man cannot be tolerated in our vicinity. Either he disappears or we march!" But they didn't do it. They left us alone and let us slip through the risky zone, and we were able to sail around all dangerous reefs. *And when we were done, and well armed, better than they, then they started the war!*[7]

Though containing some distortion of the historic facts, the basic truth here is hardly to be denied. The new German blitzkrieg smashed the valiant Poles in three weeks—without any intervention from General Gamelin's French Army. There was the expected chaos as mobilisation took place; but the Bourse held fast; cheerfully optimistic slogans of "We will be Victorious because We are the Strongest" appeared everywhere. And there was, of course, the invincible Maginot Line to keep the *Boches* at bay this time. Gamelin set up his GQG at Vincennes, on the eastern outskirts of Paris, in order to be as closely in touch with his political masters as possible. This was the reverse of what Joffre had done, and it meant, equally, that Gamelin was even more out of touch with the front than Joffre had been. All other comparisons are invidious; Gamelin lacked his power, his calm strength of will, his ability—and his forces. On paper, these forces were not all that disparate to the Germans; France in fact had more tanks, and some were better, but they were deployed in an antique fashion throughout the army, instead of concentrated into powerful *Panzer* divisions, such as Colonel de Gaulle had called for. And of course both she and her British ally were fatally weak in the air. Much of that could be attributed to the idle workshops in the heady days of the Front Populaire.

FRANCE'S INVOLVEMENT in the Second World War falls into roughly four phases: Phase I, the "Phoney War" from the declaration of 1939 to the capitulation of June 1940; Phase II, the Occupation up to the Allied landings in North Africa of November 1942; Phase III, from "Torch" to "Overlord," 6 June 1944; and, finally, Phase IV, Liberation, 1944 to May 1945. As if by some bizarre natural law governing the climate in years that preface a cataclysm, such as 1914 and 1870, seldom was there a more sparkling spring than that of 1940. Parisians lingered in the trottoir cafés, listening to the strains of "J'attendrai" and thinking wistfully of last year's paid vacations. A visiting American journalist, Clare Boothe, went into raptures at how

> chestnuts burst into leaf on the lovely avenues of Paris, sunlight danced off the opalescent grey buildings, and the gold and grey sunsets, glimpsed through the soaring Arc de Triomphe at the end of the long splendid vista of the Champs-Élysées, brought a catch of pain and pleasure in your throat. Paris was Paris in April![8]

There were art shows in the Grand Palais, racing had resumed at Auteuil (it had been suspended on the outbreak of war), and soccer matches took place between Tommies and *poilus* in the suburbs. "The shop windows of van Cleef and Arpels and Mauboussin and Cartier sparkled with great jewels in the sunlight," Clare Boothe recalled. "And lots of people bought them." The Ritz, as usual, was "crowded with lovely ladies wearing simple dresses or the smart uniforms of the Union des Femmes de France service."

With Hitler apparently hesitant to attack the mighty Maginot Line, much of the fears of the previous winter had dissipated, to be replaced by the dread malady of *l'ennui*—particularly insidious within the dank casemates of the Line. The *poilus* of 1940 (according to Jean-Paul Sartre, who was one) took to looting vacated Alsatian farmhouses instead. Morale at the front during the *drôle de guerre* (Phoney War) was low—though quite unaffected among those in Paris. The Academy was to be found peaceably working away on its eternal dictionary:

> The definition of the word *aile* led to a passage of arms between Abel Bonnard and Georges Duhamel. The previous edition had called a wing "a muscle." "It's perfectly ridiculous," said Bonnard. "A wing is a limb.

"On the contrary," said Dr. Duhamel, "a wing is a muscle. What you eat in the wing of a chicken is the muscle, no more and no less."

And so the argument continued. Could anything, one might have wondered, could anything alter the basic facts of French life? Underneath this veneer of "business as usual," reality however was all too evident to a discerning future prime minister, Pierre Mendès-France. Returning on leave from Syria at the beginning of May, he was shocked at what he found:

> Everyone, civilian and military, thought only of organising his personal life as well as possible in order to get through this seemingly indefinite period without too much risk, loss or discomfort . . . One heard only of recreation for the army, sport for the army, art and music for the army, theatrical shows for the army and so on.[9]

Meanwhile the limp Daladier, ill-named the "Bull of Vaucluse," had been replaced by Paul Reynaud—a diminutive figure whose courage belied his stature—and in England Chamberlain was about to be replaced by Churchill. But both were to prove too late to save France. The real war had begun.

# SEVENTEEN

# *The Darkest Years*

They only call me in in disasters.

—*Pétain at Bordeaux, 1940*

O N 10 MAY 1940, Hitler struck in the West. With forty-five divisions von Rundstedt attacked through Belgium and Holland. Under the Schlieffen Plan of 1914, the German thrust had started in north Belgium, without breaching Dutch neutrality, and then wheeled southwards. The *Sichelschnitt*\* Plan of 1940 struck immediately to the south, through the supposedly "impenetrable" Ardennes, followed by a hook north-west to the Channel ports, encircling the elite of the French and British forces that had moved eastwards to help Belgium. By 13 May Hitler's General Guderian had broken out across the River Meuse at Sedan, north of where the Maginot Line ended. Two days later, scattering piecemeal French armoured counter-attacks, the *Panzers* ripped a hole 60 miles wide in the French defences, and poured in, apparently in the general direction of Paris. The force with which von Rundstedt speared France had in effect a steel tip but a soft wooden shaft; the tip formed by the few elite *Panzer* and motorised divisions— the shaft made up of the mass of second-rate infantry divisions, often still dependent on horse and cart. France possessed no concentrated and determined armoured force (such as de Gaulle in France and Liddell Hart in England had urged), capable of slicing into this soft section of the German Army. As the sides stood in May 1940, under *Sichelschnitt*

---

\*Literally, "the cut of a sickle."

the Germans marched to one of the most outstanding blueprints for victory in the history of war.[1]

The Dutch capitulated on the 14th, the Belgians two weeks later. Amid an atmosphere of incredulity mixed with panic, the Reynaud government discussed leaving Paris, as in 1914; then Reynaud's resolve hardened, declaring that it "ought to remain in Paris, no matter how intense the bombing might be." On the 16th, Winston Churchill, Prime Minister for less than a week, flew to Paris for a meeting in the Quai d'Orsay, that same building where less than twenty years previously the victorious Allies had drafted the peace treaty for the defeated Germans to sign. Present were Reynaud, Daladier (now Reynaud's Minister of National Defence) and the French Commander-in-Chief, General Maurice Gamelin. "Everybody was standing," Churchill recalled in his memoirs.

> At no time did we sit down around a table. Utter dejection was written on every face. In front of Gamelin on a student's easel was a map, about two yards square, with a black line purporting to show the Allied front. In this line there was drawn a small but sinister bulge at Sedan . . .

Churchill asked Gamelin: "Where is the strategic reserve?" then:

> breaking into French, which I used indifferently (in every sense): "*où est la masse de manoeuvre?*"
> General Gamelin turned to me and, with a shake of the head and a shrug, said: "*Aucune.*"
> There was another long pause. Outside in the garden of the Quai d'Orsay clouds of smoke arose from large bonfires, and I saw from the window venerable officials pushing wheelbarrows of archives on to them.

It would be impossible to have any more graphic sign of defeat and collapse than Churchill's picture of the air outside filled with whirling scraps of charred paper—state secrets and battle plans reduced to the same ash as meaningless inter-departmental memos.

It seemed like 1914 all over again; but this time there was no Governor Gallieni in Paris; and the French Army was not the army of 1914. Churchill returned to London with the grim realisation of what the future would hold. Reynaud, a lone voice of resistance, spoke that night on the radio, admitting to the French public that the Germans had managed to create "a broad pocket, south of the Meuse," but "We filled in plenty in 1918, as those of you who fought in the last war will not have forgotten!" However, the city went from maelstrom to mausoleum in a matter of days, with two-thirds of its residents departing in every manner of transport. Ilya Ehrenburg, who stayed on as a correspondent of Hitler's Russian ally, was moved to compassion while, as he watched, "An old man laboriously pushed a handcart loaded with pillows on which huddled a small girl and a little dog that howled piteously." In contrast, a recently promoted brigadier-general, de Gaulle, related how in the course of an arduous journey through the night, attempting to reach his newly formed 4th Armoured Division, he passed a long stationary line of refugees:

> Suddenly a convoy of luxurious, white-tyred American cars came sweeping along the road, with militia men on the running-boards and motorcyclists surrounding the procession; it was the Corps Diplomatique on its way to the châteaux of Touraine.

One of the great beauties of *Sichelschnitt* as a plan was that it left the Allies in the dark as to whether the *Panzers* were heading for Paris, or for the Channel, until it was far too late. On 20 May, after a series of staggering advances, the Germans reached the Channel, bypassing Paris but cutting the Allied armies in two. Reynaud, at last sacking Gamelin, called in the two old soldiers of the First World War: Pétain, aged eighty-four, to be Deputy Premier, and Weygand, seventy-three, who had never held battle command, to succeed Gamelin. Both were committed anti-parliamentarians, and committed defeatists.

Weygand attempted one ill-coordinated riposte to slice through the narrow "Panzer Corridor," then soon made it plain that there should be only "one last battle," for the sake of the army's honour, before France should sue for a separate peace. Within a week of his arrival, Weygand was dangling before the cabinet's eyes the spectre of a Red coup, of a new Commune taking over in Paris; a prospect that seemed to afflict him more than surrender to Hitler. Momentarily, Hitler lost his nerve before Dunkirk and issued his controversial "halt-order," which was to save the British Expeditionary Force. The "Miracle of Dunkirk" came to pass; 337,000 men—including 110,000 French—were evacuated by the Royal

Navy and the "little boats." But the campaign then became largely a matter of marching for the Germans, a pursuit down the highways of France. Then, on 11 June, Weygand decided to declare Paris an "open city." Unlike Warsaw it would capitulate without a struggle—and be preserved for posterity.

The brilliant six-week blitzkrieg had cost the Germans no more than 27,074 in killed—only marginally more than Britain's dead on that one first catastrophic day of the Somme in July 1916. Contrary to the received image, the French Army—or at least its effective units—had fought bravely: it lost in killed alone 100,000 men, roughly equal to the rate of casualties at Verdun in 1916. But 1 million prisoners of war had been taken, and they would remain in miserable conditions, sometimes exploited as slave labourers, in Germany for the next five years.

Disobeying civilian authority, Weygand refused "to leave the soil of France even if put in irons," should the government decide to continue the war in Africa or elsewhere, and refused to carry out Premier Reynaud's proposal that France seek only a military capitulation. "For twenty-three years I have followed closely the work of the politicians," he declared acidly, "and I am thoroughly aware of all their responsibilities in the current drama." On 16 June, Reynaud stepped down in favour of Pétain, who, within hours, was approaching the Germans for an armistice; six days later it was signed in the railway coach at Rethondes where Foch had received the defeated Germans in November 1918. Two days later, in another act of indiscipline (for which he was condemned to death *in absentia*), the lanky forty-nine-year-old brigadier-general, Charles de Gaulle, unfurled in London the standard of the Cross of Lorraine, of defiance and revolt against Pétain and the armistice.

For the next four years France and her army would be split between Vichy and Free France; two governments, each of them headed by a soldier. De Gaulle was dubbed by Winston Churchill, with his deep sense of history, "the Constable of France," who brought with him the honour of an undefeatable nation. Nevertheless, the post-1940 split imposed agonising dilemmas of loyalty—which Anglo-Saxon armies had fortunately been spared, since Cromwell, or the American Civil War. As an indication of the dimensions of this *crise de conscience,* one small group of French officers, including several from the old nobility, were unable to accept the legitimacy of either Pétain or de Gaulle. Instead they took themselves to the Soviet Union, where they formed the Normandie-

Niemen Air Squadron. It fought with utmost courage and dreadful losses on the Russian front for the rest of the war.*

The terms of the armistice imposed by Hitler were draconian. France was divided into an Occupied and an Unoccupied zone. Occupied France included Paris and the whole Channel and Atlantic seaboard, from which Hitler planned his "Sea Lion" invasion of Britain, and—later—he installed huge bases for U-boats which would all but strangle Britain's convoy lifeline. The rump, including the Mediterranean coast and France's overseas empire, was administered by Pétain's regime from Vichy—a damp, glum spa best known for its evil-smelling waters. It was greatly to Weygand's credit, however, that the French Army, as permitted under the armistice, was reconstituted, and the mainstream of its traditions kept alive. He also succeeded in barring the Germans from French North Africa, where the 120,000-strong core of the new "Armistice Army" was safely maintained—although he was to become one of the principal post-Liberation whipping-boys of the Gaullists. In North Africa were officers like de Lattre de Tassigny, now a general, whose division had been one of the few to acquit itself with distinction in May 1940—and would again in the Liberation of 1944.

FRANCE NOW DISAPPEARS into what became known as the "Dark Years"—the darkest and longest fifty months of her long existence. Neither the Tsar's entry into Paris in 1815, nor the Prussians in 1871, would approach the humiliation that she would suffer between 1940 and 1944, when the light of the *ville lumière* would be extinguished. Even with the euphoric moment of *La Libération* in August 1944, the darkness would not end; out of the pit there would follow the bitter *épuration* or purge, the savaging of one Frenchman, or one group of Frenchmen, by another—a merciless civil conflict that would add thousands more victims to the huge figure of war casualties. Worse, it would leave wounds still unhealed after two generations. Then, the ending of this *épuration* would be followed by another decade of deprivation and reconstruction of a shattered country, internal political wrangling far more debilitating even than that of the Third Republic, and murderous and costly colonial wars.

*At the war's end, each of the tiny number of survivors was given the freedom of the Soviet Union and his own private Yak plane; one of the few recorded instances of Soviet recognition of Allied assistance in the Second World War.

THE STORY OF THE OCCUPATION is so unredeemingly terrible that an Anglo-Saxon historian is confronted with great difficulties. How, anyway, can we Anglo-Saxons begin to comprehend the pressures and stresses imposed on both collaborators and members of the Resistance—we who, thank God, were never occupied? In writing the official biography of Harold Macmillan, when the subject of de Gaulle's rejection of Britain's entry into the EEC came up, I remember being profoundly shocked to hear him remark, "If Hitler had danced in London, I would never have had any difficulty with de Gaulle." At the time I thought it the most cynical remark I ever heard Macmillan make—then I realised its underlying truth. After all, what most sets us in Britain apart from other European nations: we alone were never conquered by a foreign army. But does our ignorance, our lack of experience entitle us to pass condemnation? I often wonder, which of us would have been collaborators, the Cêlines, the Drieu la Rochelles, the Brasillachs—or even a Sartre or a Cocteau? Or which of us would have joined the *maquis* in the Welsh mountains? What option would a South Kensington or Islington mother choose—watching her children slowly starve? What *might* we have done—especially in those early days of no hope, when Germany seemed certain to emerge triumphant? Smugly we think Drancy and the deportations could not happen here.

Standpoints of criticism are so very different. What many Frenchmen today hold against former President Mitterrand is not that, in his twenties, he was in some way involved in the deportation of Jews, but that the truth was *caché* all those years. Before consigning them to the lowest circle of *collabo* hell, it is worth remembering that men like Céline and Darnand had all fought heroically in the First World War, before that pacificism which it generated led them to take the wrong turning of collaborating with the Nazi oppressor. Even Pierre Laval at his post-war trial proved to be a man of great courage as he faced the inevitable death sentence. Events were just too big for them—including the old Marshal, at the head of it all in Vichy.

THE PRINCIPAL VICTIM—as well as the arena—of the Nazi Occupation was, of course, Paris.[2] What was so particularly shattering for Paris, and it was to set the tone for the whole ensuing four years of Occupation, was the sheer speed of the German takeover. One day

Parisians were swapping bargains at the stamp market on the Champs-Élysées; the next moment the refugees from eastern France were straggling in; then it seemed—just like at the Marne in 1914—the invading hordes were turning away and leaving Paris in peace. But, no! Just as their blueprint for 1940 intended, suddenly the Germans were there, marching across the Concorde. Here was the end of a centuries-old tradition: Paris the "fortress" had become the "open city." As the Germans came in, the Prefect of Police, Roger Langeron, reckoned that three-quarters of the pre-war population fled. The fashionable western *arrondissements* were all but empty. Three weeks later some 300,000 returned, forced by destitution and pressure from the Germans. Exhaustion shows in photographs of a working-class family trudging home on foot, wheeling an exhausted grandmother in a child's pram. Some could not face the future; like the eminent neuro-surgeon, who, having seen the Germans arrive on the Champs-Élysées, injected himself with strychnine.

Under strict orders, the first Germans to arrive behaved well—*sehr korrekt*. In the Métro members of the *Wehrmacht* ostentatiously gave up their seats to women and old people. The widely disseminated slogan was "Have confidence in the German soldier." Initially, the German Army made every attempt to woo the Parisians. Every day brass bands played in the Tuileries; the *Glockenspiel* topped with clusters of tiny bells, with its echoes of the sentimental rusticity of pre-war Bavaria or Austria. It all helped lend the naive Parisian a simplistic illusion that the Occupation was going to mean "Mozart in Paris." In their smart *feldgrau* the occupiers looked like serious soldiers compared with their own demoralised beaten rabble. There were sharp comparisons made, too, with the Tommies who had sailed off and left France at Dunkirk—and with Woodrow Wilson's Americans, who let France down so badly in 1919, and were not lifting a finger to help her now. Within the month would come the unspeakable news of the Royal Navy sinking the French fleet, without warning and killing 1300 French sailors, at Mers-el-Kebir. It was a deed for which an agonised Churchill took personal responsibility, fearful that—afloat under its Vichy commanders—the fleet might fall into Hitler's hands, and tip the whole balance of the war in the Mediterranean.

ON HIS WAY HOME from having danced his little jig of revenge outside the surrender *wagon-lit* in the clearing at Compiègne, on Sunday 23 June, Adolf Hitler himself paid a surprise visit to a prostrate Paris. In less than three hours he managed to "do" the whole city. Like a peculiar day-tripper, he was photographed on the deserted steps of the Trocadéro—with the Eiffel Tower in the background. He took in the Louvre, the Sainte-Chapelle and Notre-Dame, condemned Sacré Coeur as "appalling," and angrily ordered the destruction of the statue of First World War General Mangin behind Les Invalides. It reminded him of the French occupation of the Ruhr in the 1920s.

The oppressive reality of the German occupation very soon became apparent. There would be a strict curfew from 9 p.m. to 5 a.m. each night. Loudspeakers warned the inhabitants: "The German High Command will tolerate no act of hostility towards the occupation troops. Every aggression, every sabotage will be punished by death." That first winter, as rationing was imposed, the conquerors pillaged the rich granaries of Occupied France.

Part of the trauma of defeat derived from the astonishing speed and Teutonic efficiency with which the new German administration established itself, even while the battle outside Paris still continued. Had Hitler mounted Operation Sea Lion with similar dispatch, Britain would surely never have survived the grim summer of 1940. Almost overnight there appeared outside the Opéra a maze of signs directing to various military sections, HQs, units, hospitals, "kinos," hotels, recreation centres and every other kind of *Wehrmacht* function. As the war moved on, by summer 1944 there was even a helpful arrow pointing "To the Normandy front." The grand Hôtel Crillon on the Concorde (named after Henri IV's brave lieutenant) was requisitioned to house the sinister *Sicherheitsdienst* (security service); the *Luftwaffe*—directed by Goering's eye for luxury—occupied Marie de' Medici's Luxembourg; for their officers' club the *Luftwaffe* also occupied the choice address on the Faubourg Saint-Honoré which later became the American Residence. Supreme insult, the Chamber of Deputies in the Palais Bourbon—where Daladier had stood up and declared war on Germany just nine months previously—now decked with swastikas, was requisitioned for the offices of the Kommandant of *Gross Paris.* The Gestapo moved into 74 Avenue Foch, where, as the Resistance developed, neighbours would be kept awake at night by the screams emanating from the interrogation rooms.

THROUGHOUT THE OCCUPATION one of the most influential of all the Nazi organs was the post of German Ambassador, held by Otto Abetz. Only thirty-seven in 1940, Abetz was by his own lights a genuine francophile—married to a Frenchwoman—who had spent much time in pre-war France. He had been a keen member of the Comité France-Allemagne, which aimed at Franco-German friendship but was in fact a Nazi front organisation. A skilled persuader, Abetz convinced Hitler that France, if treated considerately, might swiftly accept a subordinate place in the "New Order." His job in Paris was to work on "elements receptive to conditioning public opinion favourably"—and he was immeasurably successful. Around him Abetz collected a powerful support team of Francophone Germans. Among them was an unusual figure called Ernst Jünger, who had won the highest German decoration in 1918 and whose book, *The Storm of Steel,* was one of the most remarkable on the First World War to come out of Germany. As a *sympathique* writer he ranged widely through the salons of Occupied Paris, and wrote perceptively in his Parisian diaries[3]—though the reality of the suffering of the Jews seems largely to have passed by this curiously detached, dehumanised spectator. Illustrative of how fashionable society reacted to the more *sortable* among the former enemy is Baron Élie de Rothschild's account of the parties given at his town mansion on the Avenue de Marigny while occupied by a *Luftwaffe* general. On returning from prison camp, Rothschild observed to the old family butler, Félix, that the house must have been very quiet during the war; the butler replied:

> "On the contrary, Monsieur Élie. There were receptions every evening."
> "But . . . who came?"
> "The same people, Monsieur Élie. The same as before the war."[4]

Least considerable, and generally unheeded, was the "Embassy" of Pétain's regime in Vichy, capital of Unoccupied France. Set up in style at the Matignon, residence of prime ministers of France, the Vichy Embassy had derisory powers and little influence, and kept Vichy eminently ill-informed as to what was happening in Paris. Although Abetz adroitly always showed it a smiling face, under Laval's policy of total collaboration it earned the contempt of the German military.

Under the mantle of Abetz, censorship in the shape of the "Bernhard List" proscribed 150 books to be removed from the libraries. Also under way was the requisitioning of Jewish houses in Paris and the works of art contained in them, as well as in Jewish-owned galleries. The Jeu de

Paume became a huge depot for pillaged works of art on their way to Germany. It was Vivant Denon in reverse. By the end of the war it was estimated that some 20,000 works of art followed this route to Germany. Perhaps between 500 and 600 paintings deemed "unfit for sale" were burned in the Louvre courtyard—including works by "decadents" like Miró. Many more were destroyed in air-raids, or never recovered; that so many were located and returned safety was greatly due to the courage and tenacity of the *conservatrice* at the Jeu de Paume, Rose Valland, who managed to keep a discreet inventory of every item that passed out of the building.

WHILE THE GERMAN MILITARY instinctively inclined towards dealing with the right, Abetz's preference was for collaborators of the left, notably among the pre-war pacificists and those committed to the belief that Versailles had given Germany a raw deal. From the first, his wide network of French contacts included writers like Fernand de Brinon, Drieu la Rochelle and Jean Luchaire, editor of *Le Matin*, which reappeared in the earliest days of the Occupation. Abetz and Luchaire were reckoned to have an almost symbiotic relationship. Equally dedicated to the success of Germany, Jacques Doriot—originally a metalworker—had started on the Politburo of the Communist Party, then swung right to form the Fascist Parti Populaire Français (PPF). Also from the left, Marcel Déat had at one time been violently anti-war and regarded as Blum's successor in the Socialist Party. Now his Rassemblement National Populaire (RNP) appealed largely to the middle aged and middle class. Among the most ardently anti-Semitic of the *collabos* was the apocalyptic Céline, so obsessed by death and destruction. He declared to Ernst Jünger (who seems to have been taken aback by his vehemence), "how surprised he was, in fact stupefied, that we soldiers are not shooting, handing over, exterminating the Jews."[5] This from a prize-winning French author.

Then there was Robert Brasillach, released as a prisoner of war to take over editorship of the splenetic, extreme right-wing *Je Suis Partout*, which rose to have an astonishing circulation of 300,000. Brasillach later explained himself (in 1944) in clearest terms:

> The German genius and I had an affair . . . whether one likes it or not, we lived together. Whatever their outlook, during these years

the French have all more or less been to bed with Germany, and whatever quarrels there were, the memory is sweet.

Could anything be less ambiguous? All these *grands collaborateurs* acted in the certain belief that Hitler was going to win (which, in summer 1940, looked a fair bet). They would pay a heavy price. Next came the French Communists, sullenly committed by Stalin's pact of the previous August to supporting the Germans. Until Hitler turned round and savaged the Soviet Union the following year, *L'Humanité* was allowed to thrive. Typical was a headline of 14 July: "It is particularly comforting, in these times of misfortune, to see numerous Paris workers striking up friendliness with German soldiers . . . Bravo, comrades, *continuez.* . . ."

While at the other end of the social scale, those with most to lose took the Germans into their salons, lower down the staircase of collaboration came the massed ranks of the *petit bourgeoisie,* the merchants, artisans and grocers, *bistrotiers* and *restaurateurs*—the majority of Frenchmen dependent on "business as usual." Most often their relationship with the occupiers, in the shop and in the street, would be one of wary correctness. Isaiah Berlin once offered a useful definition on the propriety of collaboration with an enemy: "You have to 'get on' with them; but you don't have to be *cosy.*" Many in the Occupied Zone—not just the ideologically committed—were distinctly "cosy" with the former enemy. Already by October 1943, 85,000 illegitimate children had been fathered by Germans in France, which French writers considered to be "only the tip of the iceberg." But, apart from the eminent ladies, like Coco Chanel and Arletty, who lustily acquired German officer lovers, the ordinary *collabo horizontale* perhaps deserves more sympathy now than she found at the time. With 2 million French males sequestered in Germany, perhaps these relations were no more than "a minor victory for human nature." Many of the occupying *Wehrmacht* were attractive and well behaved; but, most of all, as wartime conditions became harsher, sleeping with a German might be the only way a woman could keep her children from starvation.

Harder to understand were the professional compromises made by artists and intellectuals. To be published at all, writers and journalists had to perform the Faustian commitment of submitting their work for approval. As of September 1940, the association of French publishers signed an agreement with Abetz amounting to "self-censorship"; in exchange for suppressing works by Jews and "subversives" the publishers were granted a margin of discretion in deciding what to publish and what to censor. During the Occupation the number of publications actually grew, so that in 1943 France led the world with 9348 titles—compared with Britain's 6705 and even the USA's 8320. Well-known authors published under the occupation included Cocteau, Simenon, Saint-Exupéry, Camus, de Beauvoir and Sartre. "Politically," Beauvoir complained (in *La Force de l'âge*), "we found ourselves reduced to a position of impotence." But she and Sartre spent their time either gossiping at the Café Flore or bicycling in the countryside—apparently undisturbed by war or occupiers—while also freely publishing their works. Sartre's first play, *Les Mouches,* was staged in 1943 at the Théâtre de la Cité (formerly the Sarah Bernhardt) and highly praised by the drama critic of the German *Pariser Zeitung*; while in June 1944, as the Allies were landing in Normandy, his best-known play, *Huis Clos,* with its famous line "hell is other people," opened in Paris. Sartre meanwhile joined the Comité National d'Écrivains, acidly described by David Pryce-Jones as being "less interested in resistance than in drawing up lists of other writers and journalists whom they would proscribe and silence after the war."

Perhaps closer to the norm was Colette, who during the Occupation fell back on a philosophy of "le sage repliement sur soi"—translatable, in less poetical terms, as lying low. A close French friend of mine who later joined de Gaulle, and married a heroic member of the Resistance, deported to Ravensbrück, commented to me on what it had been like to be twenty-three years old, in paralytically boring Vichy: "You didn't listen to the news, you didn't read newspapers; you wondered where your next meal would come from—and who you would date. You just got on with life."[6] Almost certainly the same priorities would have ordained life in the Occupied Zone.


FOR THE INHABITANTS of Occupied France, particularly the Parisians, the winter of 1940–41 was one of a "constant hunt for fuel and food," remembered as the worst of the war—possibly because the populace was so ill-accustomed to real hardship. Just as in 1870–71, for the poor with no purchasing power, the food shortage hit hardest. On a wage of perhaps ff1000 a month, how could one survive when potatoes cost ff20 a kilo, and butter ff150–200? Unemployment reached a total of over 1.1 million. As in the worst years of Napoleon, in-between men made considerable fortunes profiteering on scarce commodities; leather fixed at ff9 a kilo would cost ff70 by the time it reached its ultimate (German) purchaser. An operator called Szkolnikoff managed to make off with an estimated ff2 billion in real estate deals. With communications still interrupted there was a scarcity of fuel for heating, and no petrol for civilians. Strange-looking *vélo-taxis,* rustic bicycle rickshaws, often seen propelled by an emaciated woman with two strapping Germans and their girlfriends in a cartlike trailer, made an appearance on the streets.

APART FROM THE POOR, there was one particular section of the French left more dispossessed and persecuted than any other. Within the briefest interval of the Occupation establishing itself, Jews were forbidden to stand in food queues. By 27 September 1940, the German authorities had put in place the first ordinances proscribing the Jews in France, the jaws of the deadly trap that would close around them; Vichy followed suit with its own statute a week later, defining what constituted a Jew. Of approximately 300,000 Jews in France, a quarter were of foreign origin, notably those who had fled from the Nazis and other anti-Semitic regimes in central Europe during the 1930s. What was remarkable, and in some ways incomprehensible, was that all but a few thousand of the Jews in Paris went docilely to register. One of the first to do so was a frail old man of eighty-two, a non-practising Jew, an *académicien* and Nobel Prize winner—the famous philosopher Henri Bergson. Only three months later (mercifully) Bergson died, leaving these last brave words: "I would have converted, had I not foreseen the formidable wave of anti-Semitism that was about to engulf the world."

Property and business premises were requisitioned. Pettily, Jews were also not allowed to use public telephones. Jewish professors were forced to resign from the Sorbonne—as being hostile to the German Reich. As Jewish writers and artists were censored into obscurity, in September 1941 an anti-Semitic exhibition was mounted in the Palais Berlitz entitled *Le Juif et la France.* Over 200,000 visited without exciting protest, criticism or demonstration. Then came the enforced wearing of the yellow star; the odious stigma of the East European ghetto under Hitler. Parisian reactions to it were mixed; generally it was "better not discussed," though there were a few disgusted Parisian Gentiles who actually volunteered to wear the yellow star themselves. The collaborationist press vigorously supported the Nazi measures, with *Au Pilori* publishing an article, on 8 November 1942, that declared: "The Jewish question must be resolved immediately by the arrest and deportation of *all* Jews without exception."

On 27 March 1942, the first of the deportations to Auschwitz took place; out of 1148, nineteen survived. Starting with the non-French Jews,* the victims were systematically swept up into bleak temporary camps either at Drancy, a suburb close to Le Bourget, or inside the "Vél d'Hiv," the huge cycling stadium in the 15th *arrondissement*. Even Ernst Jünger was moved, watching the *grande rafle* of 16–17 July 1942:

> a large number of Jews were arrested here in order to be deported—first of all the parents were separated from their children, so that their crying could be heard in the streets. Not for a single moment can I forget how I am surrounded by wretched people, human beings in the depth of torment.[7]

Of the French role, damningly a native writer like Jean-Paul Cointet declares: "The enterprise would have been impossible to carry out without the assistance of the French administration."[8] Although one-third of those deported were French citizens, the French police, and—later—the *milice* aiding the Gestapo would act with shocking brutality.[†] Equally shocking was the frequency of *délations*—or denunciations of Jews in hiding.

The family of Alfred Dreyfus was affected like many others. Alfred's granddaughter, Madeleine, who joined a Resistance group in the southwest in her early twenties, was arrested and shipped to Auschwitz, where she died—weighing 70 lb—in January 1944; his nephew, René, one of the most decorated of the family in the First World War, also never returned from Auschwitz. Nor did Rachel Dreyfus Schil's sixty-three-year-old son Julien, denounced by his concierge in the 16th *arrondissement* and deported to Auschwitz by the Gestapo—readily assisted by the French police. Another related Parisian Jewish family was that of Nissim Camondo, once known as the "Rothschilds of the East," who had moved to Paris from Turkey under Louis-Napoleon, establishing themselves in the notably Sephardic area of the Parc Monceau. Of the next generation, Isaac Camondo, a passionate lover of music, helped finance

---

*In the *rafles* of July 1942, 12,884 foreign Jews were rounded up, of whom three-quarters were women and children.

†An enthusiastic and key participant was René Bousquet, *secrétaire général* of the police, who somehow managed to emerge untainted from the post-war *épurations* until finally his past caught up with him in the 1990s.

TOP LEFT: Pétain: the hero of Verdun.

TOP RIGHT: French Generals of World War I, de Castelnau (left), Joffre (centre) and Pau (right).

ABOVE: What World War I did to France; French propaganda photograph at a base hospital. Original caption, as printed by the *New York Times* in 1916, reads: "A Soldier Who Has Lost Both Feet, Yet Walks Fairly Well With Clever Substitutes."

The failed peace conference at the Quai d'Orsay, 1919 (centre, left to right: Woodrow Wilson, Clemenceau and Lloyd George). Painting by Sir William Orpen.

# BULLETIN
# DADA

SALON DES INDÉPENDANTS

GRAND PALAIS DES CHAMPS-ÉLYSÉES

(Avenue d'Antin)

Jeudi le 5 Février à 4 h. 1/2

Matinée

MOUVEMENT DADA

FRANCIS PICABIA

manifeste lu par 10 personnes

GEORGES RIBEMONT-DESSAIGNES

manifeste lu par 9 personnes

ANDRÉ BRETON

manifeste lu par 8 personnes

PAUL DERMÉE

manifeste lu par 7 personnes

PAUL ELUARD

manifeste lu par 6 personnes

LOUIS ARAGON

manifeste lu par 5 personnes

TRISTAN TZARA

manifeste lu par 4 personnes et un journaliste

N° 6

Prix : 2 fr

écrire
à
tristan
tzara
32,
Avenue
Charles
Floquet
Paris
(VII°)

Mouvement Dada le 5 février 1920

MATINÉE DU

toutes les femmes sont déco-
rées de la Légion d'honneur.
Les hommes portent cet
insigne à leur boutonnière.
Francis Picabia le loustic.

Peace: Dada, a short-lived craze. Front cover of *Bulletin Dada No. 6*, February 1920. Colour lithograph by Marcel Duchamp.

LEFT: "Le Front Populaire Contre la Misère, le Fascime, la Guerre, pour le pain, la paix, la liberté," cover of a brochure, 1936. Colour lithograph, French School, twentieth century.

BELOW: "Le Front Populaire"; For and Against. Protest against the Popular Front, from *Le Pèlerin* magazine, 11 October, 1936. Colour lithograph by Eugene Damblans.

ABOVE: War again. Chic Parisiennes carrying gas masks during the phoney war, 1939–40.

RIGHT: Art under the Occupation: Pierre Reverdy, Pablo Picasso, Jean Cocteau and Brassaï (Gyula Halasz).

LEFT: France defeated: Hitler in Paris, Summer, 1940.

BELOW: Vichy: *Appeal of Marshal Philippe Pétain*, 1941. Coloured engraving, French School, twentieth century.

TOP: Liberation, 1945.
Churchill and de Gaulle at the
Arc de Triomphe.

RIGHT: Parisian students take
to the streets, 1968. President de
Gaulle and Premier Pompidou,
*Sunday Express* cartoon by
Cummings.

LEFT: Francois
Mitterrand and
Helmut Kohl, Verdun,
1986.

BELOW: Funeral of
François Mitterrand,
his mistress and their
daughter.

the Théâtre des Champs-Élysées, famed for introducing Stravinsky and Diaghilev. His cousin, Moïse Camondo, built a magnificent house at 63 Rue de Monceau; tragically his only son, Nissim, was shot down in 1917 as a young lieutenant in the French Air Force. Moïse never recovered, selling his share in the family business and turning the house into one of the most remarkable small museums in Paris, named after his son, Nissim. His daughter, Béatrice, converted to Catholicism; nevertheless she, her husband Léon Reinach, and her children, Fanny and Bertrand, were all shipped off to Auschwitz. All died there in 1943; the family was extinguished, the French authorities doing nothing to save them. In a melancholy house full of ghosts, the photograph of a young boy in a big floppy cap, Bertrand, looks out at you reproachfully. Meanwhile a foreign Jew like Gertrude Stein was fortunate to sit out the war, unmolested, down at Culoz in the south-west.

A total of 75,721 Jews, possibly more unrecorded, were deported; only 3000 survived. The shame remained.


IN THE WORLD OUTSIDE, the war continued. Surprisingly, Britain had survived the Blitz, and in Egypt had severely mauled the Italian Army. Churchill was defiant; de Gaulle was at his side, gradually rallying the Free French, who now began to seem like a serious force, even retaking from Vichy some of the French colonies in Africa. It was not done without bloodshed. In 1940, an operation to take Dakar, incompetently and insecurely organised by the Free French, was repelled by Vichy forces; a successful effort to take over Syria and the Lebanon also met with heavy resistance, with fewer than one in six of the French troops there opting to join de Gaulle. More distinguished were the heroic march from Chad by General Leclerc (his real name, Philippe de Hauteclocque) to join the Allied armies across the Sahara, and General Koenig's brave defence of Bir Hakeim in Libya in 1942.

Inside France, under the British-run Special Operations Executive (SOE) an incipient Resistance movement was already raising its head. That first bitter winter of deprivation had shown the Nazis at their harsh worst. In December the first execution took place, of a harmless Parisian engineer called Jacques Bonsergent, involved in a minor scuffle with a drunk German soldier leaving a brasserie—in no way an act of resistance, or terrorism. Thrown into the prison of Cherche Midi, he was sentenced to death and executed at Vincennes on Christmas Eve. Then, in June 1941 an earthshaking event occurred which, as well as changing the course of the war, profoundly affected French attitudes to it. Hitler invaded Russia. Frenchmen with a sense of history recalled the horrors of 1812, and where that had led Napoleon and the Grande Armée. Most immediately, the powerful French Communist Party, from being an ally of Hitler, became a bitter enemy. Automatically the *maquis* and the Free French of the Interior (FFI), backed and supplied by the SOE from London, began to form a potent arm of resistance at the back of the *Wehrmacht.*

The first real *réseau,* or resistance network, was formed among ethnologists in the Trocadéro's Musée de l'Homme. One of them was a remarkable woman called Germaine Tillion who, among other deeds, helped British prisoners of war to escape after Dunkirk. Inexperienced, imprudent and betrayed, the *réseau* was tracked down before it could become much more effective than courageously producing an underground newspaper, *Résistance.* Between January and March 1941 arrests were carried out one by one, totalling eighteen. The following February, seven of the ethnologists were executed at Mont-Valérien; the remainder were deported. Tillion was the only one of the four leaders to survive Gestapo torture and three years in the appalling women's concentration camp of Ravensbrück, for which she was awarded the Croix de Guerre, *avec palme,* and the Légion d'Honneur.

The incredible courage and dedication required to set up and maintain a *réseau* in Paris, the dangers and difficulties involved, are hard for us to imagine so many years later. Paris was not the *maquis* or the *massif central,* where members of the Resistance had at least some prospects of escape and regrouping. With no transportation, in Paris they had to rely almost exclusively on the Métro, always watched by the enemy. Under permanent surveillance and the ever-present fear of *délation* by vigilant neighbours, constantly having to change their abode, and racked by hunger and fatigue, the agents lived a frightening and exhausting life of clandestinity. Radio operators with their primitive and heavy equipment were readily tracked down by sophisticated German radio direction-finding vans. Typical among the radio operators was the heroic Indian princess, Noor Inayat Khan, sent in by the SOE and caught and executed in 1944. There were many, many others like her. The Resistance found itself progressively caught between on the one hand the German security service and Gestapo, and on the other, the French police. They soon came to realise that there was little difference between being arrested by the Germans, and by their own people. In the estimate of one expert, David Schoenbrun: "Practically everyone in the resistance was eventually arrested by the French police or the German gestapo. Some escaped and carried on, but the majority suffered torture, deportation, concentration camps and death."[9]

Following the invasion of Russia came, in April 1942, the creation of the Communist-dominated Francs-Tireurs et Partisans (FTP), which added a new ruthlessness to the savage cycle of acts of assassination and sabotage against the German and Vichy French authorities, followed by the execution of innocent and uninvolved hostages taken at random by the Nazis. It was, however, a serious—and denigrating—distortion of history to suggest, as did the controversial post-war film *Le Chagrin et la Pitié* (1971),* that all the serious resistance was carried out by the Communists, and that the rest tended to be gay eccentrics.

On 21 August 1941, Pierre Fabien shot a German naval officer at the Barbès Métro station in Paris' 18th *arrondissement,* heralding a long series of such killings. A week later there was an assassination attempt at Versailles against Laval and Déat at the launch of the Légion des Volontaires Français (LVF)—poor fools enlisted to fight alongside the *Wehrmacht* in Russia, photographed departing for the East in trains with graffiti that proclaimed their abiding obsession, "Mort aux Juifs," painted on the sides of the train doors. Given the odium attached to seeing Frenchmen clad in *Boche* uniforms, the news of the attempt provoked "a lively satisfaction in Parisian opinion," according to J-P. Cointet.[10] After each such act the executions enacted in reprisal were often of those swept up out on the streets after the curfew. The Germans blamed everything on the Communists, hundreds of whom were executed at Mont-Valérien, in the hopes that Parisians would become sickened by the killings. In Tulle in south-east France, on 9 June 1942, ninety-nine inhabitants were hanged by the SS, following an ill-prepared attack on a German garrison by the *maquis.* One witness thought that they were "laying out or repairing telephone or electricity lines. All the ladders . . ." He could not believe the sight of the bodies when he saw them dangling: "I asked myself if I was the victim of a hallucination."

In spring 1943, the capture, torture and murder of the mysterious Jean Moulin[†] struck a shattering blow to de Gaulle's Resistance move-

---

*On recent English language release as *The Sorrow and the Pity.* For a long time it was banned in France.

[†]Still to this day there are questions as to whether Moulin was betrayed by his fellow *résistants,* or by the Communists; and indeed whether he himself may have been turned.

ment, after which the focus moved from Lyons to Paris. The cycle of killings and reprisals stepped up, with one in three of those being deported to the death camps by the end of the war being women. In the aftermath of Liberation the Communists made vastly inflated claims as to the number of their own martyrs. As Galtier-Boissière noted caustically, out of the 29,000 Frenchmen and -women executed during the Occupation, no less than 75,000 were claimed to have been Communist.[11]

In November 1942, the British and Americans landed in French North Africa. The defending Vichy troops there faced a dilemma: "They might obey standing orders to resist any and all invaders; they might do nothing until clearer orders from higher authority had been received; or they might issue orders on their own authority contrary to standing orders to resist." Typical was the reaction of one junior officer among the Vichy "defenders":[12] "I received two contradictory orders at ten minutes' interval; one from my major, to rally with my section to the disembarking American troops; the other from my colonel, to resist to the bitter end." Escaping a ten-year prison sentence for indiscipline, de Lattre de Tassigny fled to join the French forces in North Africa, thence to become France's top soldier at the Liberation. The Germans invaded unoccupied Vichy France; and, Allied preparations began for the invasion of the country under Generals Eisenhower and Montgomery.

As this prospect grew closer, so—naturally—did the numbers of the Resistance swell; the latest joining becoming sarcastically known as *résistants de la dernière minute,* or *naphtalines* insofar as they had only just taken their uniforms out of mothballs. At the same time the two rival groups, Communist and Gaullist, planned their post-victory agendas for takeover in France. The spiral of anti-German violence, followed by more and more brutal reprisals, continued. Darnand's *milice* increasingly took over the odious work of repression and deportation from the Germans, as every spare soldier was now required on the Eastern Front. With everything to lose, including notably their heads, the leading French *collabos* became entrenched diehards. Philippe Henriot, a Vichy journalist and leading *milicien,* declared in one of his broadcasts: "It is no longer enough to speak of civil war; the truth is that the manhunting season is now open." Ten days after his own murder in June 1944 came the cold-blooded return killing of the imprisoned Georges Mandel, the Jew who had been one of the most courageous of Paul Reynaud's ministers in 1940. Even Pétain, from his isolation in Vichy, was sparked to complain to Laval of the "sinister action," where "proofs of collusion between the *milice* and the German police are daily provided . . . French prisoners are denounced and handed over to the German police."

Relations between occupier and occupied worsened as, after 1943, the Germans made it plain that all they now wanted from France was labour and resources, rather than her willing support. By the end of the war, the systematic plundering of France had resulted in the stripping of 50 per cent of her iron output, 99 per cent of cement, 92 per cent of lorry production and 76 per cent of locomotives—not to mention the proportion of industry used for building and repairing German armour, etc. Around 646,000 French forced labourers had been transported to Germany, 60,000 civilians sent to concentration camps, and more than 75,000 made victims of the Holocaust.

As D-Day 1944 approached, Paris burned with impatience. Charles Braibant grumbled gloomily in October 1943, "It has taken twenty days to liberate Corsica, our one and only insular departement . . . At this speed, how many Frenchmen will have died of hunger or cold by the time our ninety departements are liberated?" In the run-up to Operation Overlord, the ruthless Allied Transportation Plan, to sever *Wehrmacht* communications with Normandy by day and night bombing, brought suffering and heavy casualties to the inhabitants of northern France. When even the area round Montmartre in Paris was heavily bombed in April 1944, the eighty-eight-year-old Marshal Pétain made his one and only visit to the capital to console the wounded. But in unliberated France the grim execution of *résistants* and hostages went on apace. There were atrocities like Oradour where villagers were herded into the church and burned alive. In the Vercors, the impregnable mountain stronghold near Grenoble, the SS landed in gliders purporting to be Allied, and wiped out the entire Resistance force, as well as hundreds of innocent civilians. Among the Nazi force, and committing some of the worst atrocities, was a division of Cossacks—whose forced repatriation to the Soviets was subsequently to provoke a furore in post-war England.

On 6 June 1944, in a reversal of that invasion of nine centuries previously, five Allied (US, Canadian and British) divisions, backed by 8000 bombers, 284 warships and 4000 landing craft, swarmed ashore in Normandy. A little more than two months later, they had broken out and

smashed the German armies. As defeat grew closer, so the desperate bru-
talities by the occupiers multiplied. Hitler from his bunker in East Prussia determined that Paris should go down with him and his Thousand
Year Reich. Specific orders for destruction were sent to the German
Commandant, General von Choltitz. He was deeply reluctant, but still
an obedient Prussian officer, and following the failed bomb plot against
Hitler on 20 July, he was fearful for his own skin and the safety of his
family.

IT WAS A QUESTION of whether the Allies could reach Paris before
von Choltitz and his SS underlings were compelled to begin pressing the
plungers. Eisenhower's original plan following the breakout from Normandy in early August was to bypass Paris and head full speed for Germany. It was a crucial matter of time, and petrol—Montgomery's and
Patton's columns being severely limited by supplies, all of which still had
to come ashore over the beaches of Normandy.* Repeatedly de Gaulle
beseeched Eisenhower to detach a column to liberate Paris—at first in
vain. It was not just the destruction of Paris that de Gaulle feared; like
Weygand in June 1940 and Adolphe Thiers seventy years previously, he
was alarmed at the prospect of the Communists establishing a Red
Commune in a destroyed city. His own FFI were outmatched by the
Communists, who now numbered the best organised, and often the
most courageous troops inside Paris. In the minds of all the French proponents as Liberation approached was the fate of Warsaw, only a matter
of weeks before. General Bor-Komorowski's heroic Poles had risen in
anticipation of the arrival of their Russian liberators but halted on the
wrong side of the Vistula; the Red Army did not arrive before Warsaw
had been viciously and systematically destroyed and 166,000 Poles
slaughtered.

On 13 August Parisians heard the first sounds of distant gunfire to the
west. Within a matter of days, a spontaneous uprising began in the
city—beyond the control of either de Gaulle's headquarters in London,
or the approaching Allies. In command of the Communist forces was a
thirty-six-year-old firebrand, "Colonel Rol." Alarmingly, he declared
"Paris is worth 200,000 dead"; a view that was echoed by one of his
commanders, Roger Villon, who exclaimed when it seemed Notre-

---

*It was subsequently reckoned that two crucial weeks on the advance to the Rhine
were lost by the Allies through the diversion to liberate Paris.

Dame was facing destruction: "So what if Paris is destroyed . . . Better Paris be destroyed like Warsaw than that she live another 1940 . . ."[13]

On the 15th the Communists brought the Paris railway workers out on strike. For the first time during the whole period of German occupation the Métro stopped; electricity and gas failed; the cinemas closed— though, bizarrely, the theatres went on performing to the very last moment, by candlelight. Just as during the Commune in 1871, euphoric young Parisians set to erecting hundreds of barricades—though they would hardly be a match for a Panther tank. Under constant pressure from Hitler in his East Prussian "Wolf's Lair" (one of the Führer's last communications being the famous exhortation, "Is Paris burning?"), methodically von Choltitz set about preparing the demolition charges in buildings like the Opéra and the Luxembourg. Trucks carrying naval torpedoes containing tons of explosive set off round the city. Redoubts, backed by twenty anti-tank guns, were set up round key points like the École Militaire, the Palais Bourbon, the Ministry of the Marine and the Quai d'Orsay. Already the Grand Palais had been largely gutted by fire from fighting around it. When Rol's men trapped four truckloads of German soldiers in the tangle of streets and alleys between the Seine and the Boulevard Saint-Germain, they used Molotov cocktails to turn them into human torches. This killing of men under his command under-standably infuriated von Choltitz, who now prepared to blow up the Madeleine and the Opéra "in one stroke."

On the 19th the police went out on strike, allowing the Préfecture on the Île de la Cité to be taken over by the FFI, who turned it into a fortress. For the first time since 1940, Parisians saw the *tricolore* float above it. For the next five days the Préfecture held out as a focus of resist-ance as the Germans attacked it with every arm in their arsenal. From his HQ across the river in the Marais, de Gaulle's representative, Alexan-dre Parodi, watched in alarm as Rol unleashed his premature uprising. Urgently he radioed de Gaulle to persuade Eisenhower to send troops. Finally de Gaulle's entreaties won. With a superb sense of diplomatic imperatives, Eisenhower ordered General Bradley to dispatch the French Second Armoured Division, under his subordinate, General Leclerc, to head full speed for Paris. Bradley was to have a back-up of units from the veteran US Fourth Division following close alongside Leclerc—just in case. De Gaulle had meanwhile arrived at the recently liberated Château de Rambouillet, some 35 miles south-west of Paris. According to an aide, as he awaited Leclerc, he took down from the library bookshelves a copy of Molière to steady his nerves. To Leclerc he gave the order to move—and: "Go fast. We cannot have another Com-mune." De Gaulle took leave of Leclerc with some envy, musing to himself, "How lucky you are" and contemplating that, particularly in this very special context, "in war, the luck of generals is the honour of governments."[14]

General Bradley now learned, to his extreme annoyance, that Leclerc was already under way and planning to swing eastwards so as to enter Paris from the south, through the Porte d'Orléans—the same route that Napoleon had followed in 1814 at the beginning of the Hundred Days, but contrary to the line of march laid down by Bradley's US 12th Army Group HQ. French history books would henceforth be able to relate how Paris had been liberated by French forces, with a little Allied assis-tance. Nevertheless, the move on Paris was to prove barely in time. Inside the city Raoul Nordling, an inspired Swedish consul, managed to arrange a brief ceasefire with von Choltitz which almost certainly saved the men beleaguered in the Préfecture.

UNDER THE CEASEFIRE the German occupiers began to pull out, accompanied by truckloads of loot; one officer was even seen trying to tear down the curtains at the Majestic and stuff them into his suitcase—to "make a dress later." On the Rue Lafayette, Galtier-Boissière watched as there sped by "monocled generals, coming from the sumptuous hotels in the *quartier* of the Étoile inside shining torpedoes, accompanied by elegantly dressed blondes who seemed on their way to some *à la mode* beach."[15] With them also left the leading *collabos*—heading for an uncertain future in Germany. Most of them were unrepentant and filled with illusions born of despair at the realisation of German defeat. From D-Day onwards, Marcel Déat had been assuring his cohorts: "The Nor-mandy enterprise is developing very favourably for the Axis" (17 June) and "The route to Paris has been barred" (7 August). Ten days later he made his own precipitate departure from Paris. (He died in refuge in Italy in 1955.)

"You could feel that everything was at an end," wrote Robert Brasil-lach in his journal, almost with a note of elegy:[16]

You could measure the catastrophe inch by inch, and yet the weather was marvelous, the women were delicious, and you caught your breath at the most magical sights—the Seine, the

Louvre, Notre-Dame—the whole while wondering whatever would become of it all.

In parts of Paris bitter fighting was already under way, but the imperturbable fishermen with their long *cannes* still fished unprofitably in the Seine, and daily Brasillach continued to take himself off to the Bibliothèque Nationale to work on his Greek anthology. Finally he too went to ground in a Parisian garret, giving himself up when he heard that his mother had been arrested in his stead. Céline, together with his wife and cat, joined others piled into German trucks and evacuated to join Pétain and Laval—scooped up from the luxury of the Matignon—and other *grands collabos* in semi-house arrest at Sigmaringen on the Danube. There they sat out the remaining eight months of the war miserably, treated with contempt by their Nazi "liberators," waiting for the Allies and their inevitable fate. With their departure *Je Suis Partout* was rechristened by Parisian wits: *Je Suis Parti.*

As fast as the German SS under von Choltitz mined buildings, the *fifis* (nickname of the FFI) cut the wires. At long last on 24 August, just as the defenders were running out of food and ammunition, a plane under heavy fire from German tanks dropped a message on the Préfecture: "Hang on, we are arriving." Moving from their base around Rambouillet, and sweeping aside desultory resistance, Leclerc's armour entered Paris. In command of the French spearhead were American Sherman tanks, all bearing the names of famous French victories of 1914–18—*Marne, Verdun, Douaumont* and *Mort-Homme.* One American major with the US Fourth Division, recalled: "fifteen solid miles of cheering, deliriously happy people waiting to shake your hand, to kiss you, to shower you with food and wine."[17] The welcome threatened to slow the advance more than the German 88s. No less emotional was the welcome of Resistance prisoners freed from the death cells of Fresnes Prison.

Arriving on the Concorde after a brisk firefight, *Douaumont* heroically rammed and knocked out a lethal Panther. (Perhaps appropriately it was *Verdun* that led the capture of the École Militaire.) A short while later, just outside von Choltitz's HQ, *Mort-Homme* was destroyed. Inside, von Choltitz had received one more signal from *Wehrmacht* GHQ with the imperative question: "Demolitions started?" He calmly finished his lunch, listened to the church bells outside proclaiming the arrival of the Allies, instructed his orderly to pack for prisoner-of-war camp, and surrendered. Despite all he had tried to do to stave off Hitler's intentions to raze Paris, von Choltitz only narrowly escaped being lynched by Colonel Rol's soldiers, enjoying better fortune than many Germans taken that day.

By the end of fighting on 27 August, the battle for Paris had cost Leclerc 71 killed and 225 wounded—in addition to approximately 990 FFI killed and some 600 civilians. Nevertheless, that night US war correspondent Ernie Pyle recorded "the loveliest, brightest story of our time."

ON 25 AUGUST, after pacing impatiently up and down the great terrace at Rambouillet, Charles de Gaulle set forth for Paris, "simultaneously gripped by emotion and filled with serenity." At the Palais Bourbon to accept the German garrison's surrender, de Gaulle expressed disapproval that Colonel Rol's name should appear on the surrender document, alongside Leclerc's. Then he went to "reoccupy" his old office at the Ministry of War in Rue Saint-Dominique, where he found nothing had changed since he and Paul Reynaud had left together on the night of 10 June 1940. Reaching the Hôtel de Ville, on foot, de Gaulle declared he would only receive the various representatives of the Resistance in a government building—although it was Communist cohorts who had in fact done most of the fighting during Liberation week. Nobody in London or Washington had planned to see de Gaulle installed and functioning like this for some time. Yet there he was, digging in, and—as one senior US diplomat recognised—"nothing short of force was going to budge him out." At the Hôtel de Ville, de Gaulle told the euphoric members of his entourage austerely: "The enemy is shaken, but he is not beaten . . . more than ever our national unity is a necessity . . . War, unity, *grandeur*—that is my programme."

The war was still on; the *grandeur* was there all right—but was the unity? Georges Bidault, political President of the Conseil National de la Règsistance (CNR), invited de Gaulle to "step on to the balcony and solemnly proclaim the Republic before the people here assembled." De Gaulle brusquely refused, declaring unambiguously, "The Republic has never ceased to exist . . . I myself am President of the Government of the Republic. Why should I proclaim it now?" Then he did go to the window and made a brief speech to the throbbing mass of people that now crammed the Place below, but engaging the whole city and nation at his feet:

> Paris! Paris outraged! Paris shattered! Paris martyrised! But Paris *liberated*. Liberated by herself, liberated by her people, in concurrence with the armies of France, with the support and concourse of the whole of France, of fighting France, the only France, the true France, eternal France.[18]

Mention of any Allied involvement in these great events was judiciously withheld, while many outside the Hôtel de Ville that day had doubtless been there only four months previously to acclaim Marshal Pétain. Now the crowd began to chant rhythmically "De Gaulle, de Gaulle, de Gaulle." As he left, one of the Communists on the CNR was heard to remark, "We've been had." So, for that matter, had the General's allies; and on that day was sealed the bid for independence and Gaullist preeminence that would be the source of Anglo-Saxon headaches in years to come.

26 AUGUST was Charles de Gaulle's greatest day: the day he had been waiting for since that forlorn date of 18 June 1940—possibly, indeed, the day for which Fate had been preparing him since he fell wounded and a captive at Verdun in February 1916. Arguments about legitimacy, as well as *who* liberated Paris, and harsh years of austerity and recuperation might lie ahead; nevertheless, as the authors of *Is Paris Burning?* suitably remark of that day in August 1944, "rarely in history had it been given to a man to live a moment of triumph as dizzy and exalting."[19] Wearing as always his uniform and *képi* of a simple brigadier-general, recognisable above all the crowds, his only decorations the Cross of Lorraine and the red-and-blue badge of the Free French, de Gaulle made his historic and solemn *promenade* up the Champs-Élysées. It had all the appearance of spontaneity, yet de Gaulle must have conceived it long before. He laid a simple wreath of red gladioli at the tomb of the Unknown Soldier at the Étoile, relit the eternal flame, then began the walk down the avenue which had been laid out by previous French rulers for just such a purpose. All the way down to the Concorde rooftops and windows were crowded with cheering thousands, in a day of perfect sunshine. The

lofty, towering, haughty, unsmiling figure dominated all around him; at his side, or rather an appropriate step behind, came the diminutive Bidault—almost skipping to keep up—followed by all the other Gaullist political notables who would resume trading under the flag of the Fourth Republic—and Generals Koenig, Juin and Leclerc, who had led the Free French on the long route march from Africa and defeat. Behind came a mêlée of those who only so recently had been fighting to liberate Paris, intermingled with the less admirable *naphtalines* and *résistants de la dernière minute*. It was an uneven mass; de Gaulle had specifically wanted to avoid anything resembling a formal military parade. Lining the streets between the Étoile stood the battle-worn troops of Leclerc's division; this in itself was yet another source of antagonism with the American High Command—for Leclerc had been ordered to rejoin the march towards Germany, but de Gaulle had countermanded the order with the cool response: "I loaned you Leclerc . . . I can perfectly well borrow him back for a few moments." Pointedly, none of the American troops of the US Fourth Division now in Paris were invited to participate; their day would come.

At each step down the 2 kilometres of the Champs-Élysées a particular vision of France and her past unfolded itself in de Gaulle's mind:

> It seemed to me that the glories of the past were associated with today's . . . On his pedestal, Clemenceau, whom I hailed in passing, looked as if he were springing up to march beside us. The chestnut trees in the Champs-Élysées that L'Aiglon, in prison, dreamed about and which had seen for so many, many years the grace and prestige of France displayed beneath them, offered themselves now as joyous grandstands to thousands of spectators. The Tuileries, which framed the majesty of state under two emperors and two monarchs; the Place de la Concorde and the Place du Carrousel, which had observed the frenzies of revolutionary enthusiasm and the reviews of conquering regiments; the streets and the bridges named after battles won; on the other bank of the Seine, Les Invalides, its dome still sparkling with the splendour of Le Roi Soleil, the tombs of Turenne, of Napoleon, of Foch; and the Institute, honoured by so many illustrious minds—these were the benevolent witnesses of the human stream that flowed between them . . .
>
> History, gathered in these stones and in these squares, seemed to be smiling down on us . . .[20]

Even though Paris also remembered its terrible days, when—four times within two lifetimes—the Champs-Élysées had had "to submit to the outrage of invaders parading in time to their own odious fanfares."

For the historian-warrior, there also came warnings that day: "Quite near me," de Gaulle was reminded, "Henri IV fell victim to fanatical hatred." His "stroll" down the Champs-Élysées was also an extraordinarily courageous, if not foolhardy undertaking. Between him and von Choltitz's withdrawing forces were only one US regiment and a combat team of Leclerc's division. Heavy fighting continued in the northern districts through the 27th; the city had not yet been cleared of enemy snipers, and there were many trigger-happy members of the FFI still at large—as was soon to be witnessed. But this extraordinary man, on this extraordinary day, "believed in the fortune of France"—as he had never ceased to do. As the procession debouched into the Concorde, shots rang out. Many of the crowd threw themselves down for cover, but de Gaulle walked straight on. An American sergeant, who admitted hiding behind his jeep and "felt ashamed," watched de Gaulle keep on moving, standing "very straight, standing tall for his country."

Towards 4:30 in the afternoon, the entourage reached Notre-Dame for a solemn *Te Deum*. Once more mysterious shots rang out, their provenance still a mystery to this day, though de Gaulle firmly blamed the Communists. Among the congregation, which included Edith Piaf and Yves Montand, was Malcolm Muggeridge, then a British Intelligence officer who had reached Paris late the previous night:

> The effect was fantastic. The huge congregation who had all been standing suddenly fell flat on their faces . . . There was a single exception; one solitary figure, like a lonely giant. It was, of course, de Gaulle. Thenceforth, that was how I always saw him—towering and alone; the rest, prostrate.[21]

From that day Muggeridge noted how,

> Wherever de Gaulle appeared, he was the government, and recognised as such. Witnessing this performance I realised that it was not just his political acumen, and the undoubted charisma of his weird angular disposition, which made him the unquestioned master of the situation. Rather, he had some second sense arising out of his complete confidence in himself and his destiny, which guided his steps.

The shooting confirmed de Gaulle in his intention to disarm and bring under military discipline the FFI as soon as possible; to stand down the CNR, and to assume "the legitimate power" himself.

After 26 August 1944, remarked an American journalist: "de Gaulle had France in the palm of his hand."[22] With a modicum of hindsight a historian today might also say that it was just as well. For all the huffing and puffing in Washington and London at de Gaulle's self-promotion, his prompt intervention in August 1944 probably saved France from the type of murderous revolution that overtook Greece on liberation later that same year. He forestalled a Communist takeover in Paris which could have seen a repeat of the Commune of 1871; it proved that he knew his French history better than the political advisers of the Allied High Commission, let alone Roosevelt's in Washington.

That night, as Paris indulged in her reclaimed freedom, Hitler carried out a last act of futile vengeance. The commander of *Luftflotte 3,* who had earlier offered his services to von Choltitz, launched from Le Bourget a valedictory raid of a 150 planes on the east of the city. It was the heaviest air-raid Paris experienced during the entire war; in the celebrations, not a single anti-aircraft gun responded. Nearly a thousand Parisians were wounded, 214 killed—and the Halles aux Vins largely destroyed. As de Gaulle watched the bombing from his old office in the Ministry of War, almost echoing Clemenceau in 1919, he sighed to an aide: "They think that because Paris is liberated, the war is over. *Eh bien,* there you see—the war goes on. The hardest days are ahead. Our work has just begun."[23]

# EIGHTEEN

# *After the Liberation*

The Fourth French Republic was arguably the most successful
of all French republics, except that it failed.

—The First Indochina War, *R. E. M. Irving*

Algeria is France.

—*François Mitterrand, 1954*

THOSE THREE HEADY DAYS 24–26 August 1944 in Paris were
followed, alas, by a period in which the French inflicted upon
themselves wounds almost as painful as those they had suffered
under the Occupation itself. Even before the last Germans left the *épurations* began in which vengeance, and the settling of personal scores,
was often inextricably mixed with justice. The first victims, understandably, were the German troops themselves, often lynched or stood up
against a wall as they emerged from their strongholds with hands raised.
Then came the alleged *collabos*. What particularly struck Allied eye-
witnesses was the brutality with which women were treated. The shaving
of heads, seen all over France, was perhaps the last indignity. Jean
Cocteau records being shocked by the sight of one woman, "completely
naked," on the Avenue de la Grande Armée: "they tore at her, they
pushed her, they pulled her, they spat in her face. Her head had been
shaven. She was covered in bruises and carried around her neck a plac-
ard: 'I had my husband shot.' "

Writers, journalists, actors and artists were among the first to be
affected—while industrialists who had worked for the Germans,
strangely enough, seemed to escape. Many individuals were held with-

out charges or documentation until in September de Gaulle finally intervened. He appointed an inspector of prisons and internment camps, gradually punishing excesses, but nevertheless the *épurations* continued. Once again *délation* played its role as neighbour denounced neighbour. All crimes and evils were, of course, heaped on the head of Vichy and the old Marshal, currently awaiting his fate in Sigmaringen. The beautiful Arletty, who had just made *Les Enfants du Paradis,* deprived of her *Luftwaffe* lover and suite in the Ritz, was arrested in September. What was held against her was not so much that she had slept with a German senior officer, but that she had dined with him at the Ritz when other Parisians were hungry. Occasionally the accused bit back with spirit; to wit one *horizontale* who declared unashamedly, "mon cul est international, mais mon coeur est toujours français!"; or, as the mother of one seventeen-year-old complained: "Why ever cut off her hair for it? . . . She's just as willing to go to bed with the Americans!"[1]

Allied soldiers, too, were shocked by the head shaving. Malcolm Muggeridge, still working with MI6 in Paris, was struck by the "horrifying callousness, arrogance and brutality" of the young members of the FFI who invited him to join them on one of their nightly vigilante sweeps. Muggeridge adds acidly, of the exaggerated protestations of *bonne foi* during the Occupation, that he "scarcely ever met a Frenchman who had not, at some point or other in the war, had at least one RAF pilot hidden in his attic . . . I often reflected, our Air Force would have been so huge that we should have won the war before it began."[2] The *épurations* stuck in his mind as "one of the more squalid episodes in France's history."

When in 1945 the surviving deportees began to trickle back from German concentration camps, their appalling condition aroused another acute wave of anti-*collabo* feelings. After newsfilms had been shown of the horrors of liberated Belsen, two gaols were stormed and collaborators taken out and lynched. The trials of the *grands collabos* ground on through 1945 and 1946. Brasillach was shot, despite a plea from fellow writers for clemency; he was spurned by Sartre and de Beauvoir but supported by the noble Camus, who—unlike the former—had taken up arms with the Resistance, and begged for "justice without hatred." The public figures brought back from Sigmaringen as well as gangsters like Bonny and Lafont were all executed. Doriot was killed in 1945 when his car was strafed by Allied aircraft. Céline, fleeing to Denmark, somehow escaped the firing squad, getting away (in 1950) with a sentence of one year in prison that would have been unimaginably light five years previously.

In the summer of 1945, in the Palais de Justice, began the trials of the leaders of Vichy, Pétain and Laval. To foreign observers, it seemed like a trial of Vichy itself, as the French, denied access to anything that could be described as a newspaper during the Occupation, learned of its realities for the first time. Feelings towards Pétain palpably tilted as the iniquities committed in the name of Vichy came to light. The old hero of Verdun, fallen into such disgrace, refused to speak in his own defence. The only time when his face—according to an American journalist present—took on "a marble mask of shame" was when the prosecution revealed the deportation of 120,000 Jews, of whom only 1500 returned. The trial ended in August, the day after the end of war, with the Marshal disappearing for life into the fortress prison of the Île d' Yeu. He died there, aged ninety-five, six years later. A more disgraceful farce was the show-trial, beginning in October, of the hated Pierre Laval. It reminded some of "a cross between an *auto-da-fé* and a tribunal during the Paris terror."[3] Screaming back at his prosecutors, Laval dominated the court, comporting himself with formidable courage up to the very moment when, barely resuscitated from taking cyanide, he died lashed to a chair before a firing squad at Fresnes Prison.

A murmur of low-voice sympathy for the two leaders betrayed the depressing reality that the Resistance had represented but a small minority, compared with the "silent and massive acquiescence" of the rest of France. This despite 30,000 Frenchmen killed by the Germans and the *milice* during the Occupation. The real number of those killed afterwards in the course of the *épurations* has never actually been verified; it varies from a high of 105,000 for all France down to a recent estimate of only 9000 summary executions, mostly carried out before the Allied Normandy landings, plus 767 death sentences carried out after lawful trials. This would make the *épuration* in France more "moderate" than in Belgium, Holland, Norway and Denmark. The jury is still out. However, in Paris alone there were 100,000 arrests. In lieu of prison a quarter of all defendants were sentenced to the newly coined penalty of "National Indignity." In the measured opinion of the authors of *Paris after the Liberation*, Antony Beevor and Artemis Cooper, "the *épuration* was both too harsh and too weak. The failure to pursue some of the greatest criminals, particularly those responsible for the deportation of the Jews . . . created greater trouble in years to come." Trials went on until the end of 1948; though, at the time of writing, the shameful secrets continue to come out—to wit the trials in the 1990s of Papon and Bousquet, who somehow not only managed to escape the net but rose to high estate in France subsequently.

AFTER THE LIBERATION OF PARIS, the *Wehrmacht* had retreated back across the Rhine, leading the over-optimistic to recall 1918 and to assume that collapse would follow in short order. But in December 1944 von Rundstedt struck back hard in the Ardennes. When the Americans recoiled westwards, briefly it looked to the French as if there might be a replay of 1940. News emerged that Eisenhower was locked into his head-quarters by over-zealous security, fearful of a German Fifth Column attack, and rumours spread of a major breakthrough with Strasbourg retaken. Once more the overloaded refugee cars made their appearance on the roads. There followed the harshest winter since 1940—and so soon after the euphoria of August. Gas and coal shortages meant that there was neither heating nor even cooking. For a family of three, a week's ration came to half a pound of meat, three-fifths of a pound of butter. The irrepressible *chansonniers* produced a song entitled "Sans beurre et sans brioches"—a pun on the *brave* Bayard, "le chevalier sans peur et sans reproche."[4] By the end of 1945, even wine was rationed to one litre per adult per month, and it was not finally unrationed till mid-1948. Even then some of it was watered down—or what French wits call "baptised."

Largely through US military racketeers, the black market assumed giant proportions; sometimes even the trucks disappeared into its void along with the food they brought, threatening the Allied advance into Germany. There was nothing black-market cigarettes could not buy. To François Mauriac, government efforts against black markets resembled those of "the child Saint Augustine saw on a beach who wanted to empty the sea with a shell."[5] Intelligently, the government gave up, in contrast to the law-abiding British who put their faith, not in their own enter-prise, but in the austere queue mentality of socialism.

Unlike the aftermath of other national catastrophes that had laid France low, her recovery was agonisingly slow and halting. Bridges, roads, railways, industries had been destroyed by war. The Germans had taken out crops and farms, two-thirds of the country's trucks and rail-way rolling-stock, and over 1½ million buildings were destroyed. Among her neighbours, even Britain was hardly better off; for the best part of five years the continent's only source of relief was America. There were still 800,000 French skilled factory workers serving as slave labour in Germany, another million or more in the prisoner-of-war camps, plus the deportees. Altogether there were estimated to be 4 million more women than men in France as the war ended—many in mourning. Shop windows were empty. Newspapers were reduced to a sheet or two. Over the course of 1946 even the cost of being ill and dying rose by over 40 per cent. There was officially no petrol—except for doctors and taxi drivers. Ancient cars ran, flatulent, crepitating and farting, either with great gas bags lashed to their roofs, or with coke burners hanging off the back—these were my first recollections of the France I discovered as a young soldier in 1947.

OF VICTORY THERE WAS HARDLY A SIGN. Morally, four years of Occupation had left behind it a universal torpor. VE-Day came and went with modulated elation. As one tired, middle-aged veteran remarked with weary cynicism: "that great world insomnia which is war has come to an end once again." Such enthusiasm as there was at the ending of the war in Europe was greatly tempered by the return of 300 women from Ravensbrück, met by General de Gaulle—who wept. Eleven had died en route from East Germany; too much suffering showed in the survivors' faces and bodies. Compensation of a pitiful ff1000 per returnee seemed derisory. Many were disgusted by what they discovered of a return to self-centred pre-war ways, of national life beginning already to suffer from party political wrangles.

Bourgeois former Vichyite *préfets* and politicians smugly congratulated themselves on "victory," and grumbles of revolution continued from among the Communists, who felt de Gaulle had cheated them. As the "hot" war moved, almost without break or seam, into the "Cold War" the situation grew tenser. With VE-Day the Communist Party was convinced that it would soon be swept into power. Its boss, Maurice Thorez, who had spent the war conveniently in Moscow, having deserted from the French Army in 1939, declared menacingly, "We are in favour of revolution, tomorrow . . . We are not going to help the capitalist regime to reform itself."[6] It set the scene for the Fourth Republic. Mme. de Gaulle momentarily expected a Russian para drop on her at home in Colombey-les-Deux-Églises. It all tended to prove just how right de Gaulle had been—and the Allies wrong—to have taken over in August 1944. He had indeed saved France from the fate that Greece, plunged into civil war, suffered after her liberation from the Germans.

In October 1946, a referendum duly killed off the Third Republic, after seventy-six turbulent years. A contemporary press cartoon showed a pitiful "Marianne," on being brought baskets of votes on her deathbed, wailing "and not one love letter in the lot." Whereas the Third Republic had started off life so rich that, even after the depredations of the Franco-Prussian War, it easily paid off its debt to the enemy, the Fourth Republic was so poor that it had to begin by borrowing from her American ally. In the view of one (female) observer, it was a bit like "a woman with three hands, two left and one right"—the two left hands being constituted by the Socialists and the alarmingly powerful Communist Party, the right by the Catholic, moderate conservative Mouvement Républican Populaire (MRP). In the running conflict between these elements, governments came and went, twenty of them between 1945 and 1954; M. Pleven succeeded M. Queuille, who then replaced M. Pleven, who in turn pushed out M. Queuille—all in the space of thirteen months. When asked by an American senator what happens when French governments "run out of horses," President Auriol replied, "We go back to the original ones!" Thus were the old hacks of the Third constantly recycled. For the next decade and a half, "this absurd ballet," as de Gaulle called it, would render government by political democracy all but impossible in France.[7]

WHEN DE GAULLE ASSUMED THE REINS in August 1944, his view—stated with sublime modesty—was that "I was France, the State, the Government . . . that moreover was why, finally, everyone obeyed me." And—like Louis XIV and Napoleon I—he was determined there should be no rivalry to the central authority of the state. But when he found that he would not, in fact, be "obeyed" by the returning players from the Third Republic and that the authority of the government would constantly be challenged, in January 1946 (on the anniversary of Louis XVI's execution) he pulled out, into a retirement that he said was "like Longwood." When asked what he intended to do, he replied, laconically: "J'attends!" Before embarking on the long wait, which would last twelve years, he left a stern New Year's Day warning: "I predict you will bitterly regret having taken the road you have taken." France would regret. At the Palais Bourbon the Fourth Republic lurched on, from crisis to crisis. Unpopular Premier André Marie, who survived just one month in the summer of 1948, owing to his pious name, had his brief regime rudely christened "the government of the Immaculate

Deception." Certainly there was little enough political virginity in the Fourth Republic; a few years later I well remember graffiti painted up on walls within clear sight of the Assembly: "À bas les dé-putains!"*

FOOD SHORTAGES CONTINUED for at least another two years after the war, hand in hand with a sense of gloom—and a bitterly anti-German feeling, much more so than in Britain.[†] There was constant fear of a Communist, Soviet-backed takeover. 1947 was a year of paralysing strikes with, at one point, 3 million workers out across the country. Then, suddenly, a reversal occurred when in December Communist miners in the north derailed a train, killing sixteen people. On every street corner in the capital, armed police guarded against further atrocities, as the arrival of the news caused universal revulsion. The derailment of the Paris-Tourcoing express caused a significant turnaround of political sentiment. "We have had a brush with civil war and, given the possibility of Soviet intervention, with war itself."[8] So President Vincent Auriol wrote in the last pages of his diary for that year, but "despite that France has begun her recovery."

The following year, the creation of NATO brought military security to France; Marshall Aid brought the beginnings of new prosperity. Despite the burgeoning post-war graffiti of "Ami, go home," the Minister of Finance had the good nature to confess in Paris that a "great lifting of the heart goes from us towards the generous American people and towards its leaders." Rationing had ended; there were traffic jams in Paris, and the first influx of American tourists since 1929; the franc was soaring, the dollar—overloaded by its generosity—sinking. Nevertheless, endless strikes continued to paralyse the French economy. At first they had an economic and social background; then demonstrations were sparked (by the Communists) against NATO, then on the more universally unpopular issue of German rearmament, from 1953; from 1955 onwards it was the Algerian War. Many work stoppages were politically motivated by the Communists, who already in 1946 began pressing for an immediate wage increase of 25 per cent—others sparked off by incredibly trivial causes. One such was the strike of August 1953, set off by two postmen who inadvertently did a Watergate on an incomplete draft of a government economic initiative, which, they thought, specifi-

---

*"Putain," meaning "whore."
[†]Mysteriously, by the end of the century attitudes would be roughly reversed.

cally omitted postmen. They brought out all the postal workers, followed in sympathy by 4 million Frenchmen, and the country was at a standstill.

Ingeniously, year after year, the farmers and the middle classes, as well as the very rich, somehow avoided paying taxes with impunity. Inflation ran wild, resulting in a regular devaluation of the franc. In 1951 alone (so Edgar Faure, premier for just two months, told the Assembly), France's cost of living rose 39 per cent. By 1953 prices stood at twenty-three times their pre-war levels. While United States industrial production had doubled since 1929, Britain's had risen by 54 per cent and war-shattered Germany's by 53 per cent, France's had expanded by a mere 8 per cent. Everything conspired to lower morale: an alarming number of Frenchmen sought refuge in alcoholism, and this in turn slashed at productivity. For several decades the French economy made practically no headway.

BRITONS COULD WATCH PIOUSLY, but outside the popular gaze some outstanding civil servants, products of France's admirable Polytechnique and École Nationale d'Administration, were laying remarkable long-term economic and industrial plans. (Under Attlee's Socialists and Churchill's Conservatives, no such similar providential thinking was in process in London—alas.) Already in December 1945, at the Hôtel Bristol, Jean Monnet and a small staff of brilliant men were at work contemplating what was to become, eventually, the Schumann Coal and Steel Pool, the forerunner of the EEC and the European Union. For the first time in 150 years, France was offering actually to help the Germans re-create their basic industries in conjunction with France's, so as to provide a new foundation for peace and prosperity in Europe. In June 1950 there was a first meeting, at the Quai d'Orsay's historic Salon de l'Horloge in Paris, of the European "Six"—a six from which Britain was markedly absent. The meeting of the Six raised little excitement at the time, eclipsed as it was by the fall of yet another French government and by the Communist invasion of South Korea.

DURING ALL THE SEVENTY-SIX YEARS of the now-defunct Third Republic, France had had the German *défi* to contend with; now, no longer a great power, in addition to her own internal problems, she had to face Stalin's empire menacing from Eastern Europe just a few hundred miles beyond her frontier with prostrate Germany, the demands of her British and American allies, and, it seemed likely one day, a phoenix-like Germany rearmed to meet the Soviet threat. More immediately, an exhausted France found herself fighting to hold the imperial prize of Indo-China in a war waged single-mindedly by that one-time assistant-cook from the Ritz who had attended the peace conference of 1919, and had seen the mighty colonial powers in disarray there—Ho Chi Minh. Here began what soon came to be known as France's *sale guerre*—and which, of course, would lead in a direct line to America's long involvement in Vietnam. For France it was to mean that, between 1939 and 1962, the French Army would enjoy no more than a few weeks of true peace. In the eight years that it dragged on, the running sore of the Indo-China War cost France more than the total she received in Marshall Aid, an annual 10 per cent of the national budget; was to swallow up an entire class of Saint Cyr officers every three years; and—by the time it ended—was to account for thousands more casualties than the USA lost in Korea. As Raymond Aron noted: "In order to maintain herself in Indo-China, France committed more military strength than had been needed to establish herself there."

The same could be said later with equal truth of Algeria. As a result, France, uniquely among the western powers, expanded rather than reduced the size of her army in the immediate post-war years. From 1945 to 1947, the numbers of the French combined services fell rapidly from 1.2 million to 490,000; but from there it rose steadily back to the 1.2 million figure by 1957. The human and economic costs made the *sale guerre* progressively more difficult to justify. It was unwinnable—but, to politicians in the comfort of the Palais Bourbon in Paris—unlosable. De Gaulle remarked that "the determination to win the war alternated with the desire to make peace without any one being able to decide between the two."

Whatever the motives of the politicians in hanging on to Indo-China, France's restored army discovered a special mission for itself there. Alsace-Lorraine had long been regained, Hitler was destroyed and Germany flattened, and the European Defence Community was neither a popular nor a particularly romantic conception. The enemy (partly a hangover from Vichy and the pre-1939 traditions, but also suddenly become infinitely—and genuinely—more menacing) was now Soviet Communism. In the jungles and paddy fields of Indo-China, gradually France's battle-hardened colonels came to convince themselves that they were defending a bastion of western civilisation against Communism.

There was also an element of *la gloire* involved, as François Mitterrand wrote in 1957:

> When the war in Indo-China broke out, France was able to believe that the 1940 defeat was nothing more than a lost battle, and that the armistice of 1945 was going to restore its power at the same time as its glory.

By May 1953, 65 per cent of a French poll declared itself for ending the war: but still the politicians ordered its soldiers to go on fighting. Following in a direct line from the 1930s, from Weygand and the Vichy Army, the officers of Indo-China blamed the politicians for all that went wrong, in this particularly unpleasant war of ambushes by unseen guerrillas. "Now we know that a French army, on no matter what territory it fights, will always be stabbed in the back," wrote one veteran with characteristic bitterness. "We have to examine a form of warfare that is new in its conceptions and new in its practices. This is the form of warfare we call 'revolutionary war,' " wrote another thoughtful philosopher-soldier, General Lionel-Martin Chassin, in 1954:

> It is time for the Army to cease being the *grande muette* . . .* What can the Western nations do to avoid the accomplishment of Mao's plan for world conquest? We must oppose a struggle based on subversion with the same weapons, oppose faith with faith, propaganda with propaganda, and an insidious and powerful ideology with a superior one capable of winning the hearts of men.

If they despised the politicians, France's young "revolutionary" colonels educated in Indo-China also had little higher opinion of their old school generals. Perhaps rightly. At the end of 1953, the French High Command planted its main striking force in an isolated, Verdun-like position called Dien Bien Phu. General Giap took up the gauntlet, and after a fifty-six-day siege that cost the heroic French defenders 3,000 lives, Dien Bien Phu surrendered in May 1954. That was the end; a humiliating withdrawal followed. But the French Army quit Indo-China with a bad conscience gnawing at them over what they considered a base betrayal of the Catholic population there. Having turned its French Army pupils into superb warriors, the *sale guerre* had, moreover,

*Equivalent, roughly, to the "silent majority."

also made them highly political animals, which was to have serious consequences for democracy in France during the forthcoming Algerian War.

With the collapse of the Laniel government, catastrophe in Indo-China brought to power one of the ablest and most honest politicians of the Fourth Republic, a brilliant dark-horse, a Sephardic Jew with the face of a pessimistic matador, Pierre Mendès-France. He promised he would have France out of the war in thirty-three days. He was as good as his word. In the face of huge opposition, with the usual unpleasant undertones of anti-Semitism on the right, Mendès-France was able to extricate France, handing on the baton to the USA. The period of peace, the first France had known since September 1939, was to last just five months and twenty-three days. Within half a year of Dien Bien Phu, encouraged by France's defeat there, concerted revolt broke out in Algeria.[9]

There were already uprisings to force France out of Tunisia and Morocco; however, established back in 1848 as an integral part of metropolitan France, as much as Languedoc or the Dordogne, Algeria was no mere colony, but the diamond in France's imperial diadem. It had a million French *pieds noirs** colonials settled there—many of them for several generations—in a sea of 9 million indigenous Muslim Algerians. Demographically, the Algerian birth-rate was exploding; economically, the gulf between Algerian and *pieds noirs* expectations was widening. Thus, when the revolt began in November 1954, Mendès-France declared, "Ici, c'est la France!" while his Minister of the Interior, a good Socialist called François Mitterrand, took an even more hawkish line: "The only possible declaration is war . . . for Algeria is France." However, a secondary answer to why France hung on to Algeria was the French Army, which was to make a troth out of *Algérie Française.*

A combination of the political dispute surrounding the war and Mendès' unpopular attempts to wean Normandy schoolchildren from calvados on to milk—shocking meddling in an unalterable tradition—brought him down. The Algerian FLN (National Liberation Front) had inadequate equipment to fight more than a series of guerrilla actions; the French had insufficient troops to be everywhere in this vast territory.

---

*The nickname came perhaps because metropolitan Frenchmen scornfully considered their feet to have been burned black by too much sun.

So in 1956, Guy Mollet, another French Socialist, took the dramatic step of sending half a million conscripts to Algeria. The most notable effect this had was to spread popular awareness about the war to metropolitan France; much as the escalation of the USA's commitment in Vietnam did in America. Meanwhile the FLN, with consummate skill in canvassing support within the Afro-Asian Third World, in the USA and at the UN, succeeded in internationalising what France determinedly maintained was an internal dispute. The savage war struggled on for a further six years, destroying the Fourth Republic, nearly achieving a military takeover in France, and bringing back de Gaulle as the only possible saviour.

Among the troops who fought them, first the *sale guerre* in Indo-China then Algeria led to a sense of alienation from civil society not unlike that between the front and the rear in 1914–18. "You don't know these people," wrote an officer of the colonial paras from Indo-China in 1953. "You have nothing to do with them [the metropolitan bourgeois], it's another universe."[10] In retrospect, he no longer thought of his "period in Indo China, but of his period in France." Things made more sense in the war; there he felt at home, and elsewhere he was "abroad." Transposed to Algeria, it was an alienation that would rebound to hit de Gaulle—and metropolitan France—hard in the 1960s. And, as young conscripts came to be sent to Algeria, so it became increasingly difficult for domestic opinion to stand aloof from the conflict.

DESPITE THE WARS, by 1954 the French economy had put on growth. Industrial production had reached a level 50 per cent higher than it had been in 1939. During the 1950s there was also a gradual revival of commercial property values in France's cities, but—with rents still frozen since 1914—little post-war development of offices or apartment blocks. Paris continued to remain largely as Haussmann had left it a century previously. For a new architectural impetus it had to await de Gaulle who, despite his traditionalist bent of mind, could also grasp the need for modernisation. The outstanding architectural monuments to the Fourth Republic were two great curved complexes of monotone concrete and windows, the roughly constructed UNESCO Building on the edge of the Bois (completed in 1959) and the ORTF broadcasting centre (completed between 1956 and 1963) on the Right Bank of the Seine, supposedly designed to resemble a gigantic electro-magnet. Also laid down under the Fourth was the immense Palais des Congrès project at the Porte Maillot, which seemed to reflect socialism's passion for huge popular get-togethers, offering a cavernous theatre with over 3000 seats. Conditioning all city planning, as well as being its worst enemy, was the automobile. For years the city was heaved up as vast car parks, sometimes seven storeys deep, were burrowed under the Concorde, the Place Vendôme and almost everywhere else.

THE END OF THE WAR and the removal of the dead hand of Vichy led to an immense hunger for ideas, restricted initially only by shortage of paper. The new writing based itself in Saint-Germain-des-Prés, and more specifically the bar of the Café Flore—which happened to be convenient to the residence of the great guru of Existentialism, the new religion of *café au lait* socialism, Jean-Paul Sartre and his consort, Simone de Beauvoir. In 1940, Sartre had been taken prisoner of war in the Maginot Line, escaping back home the following year. Sartre and his plays thrived under the Occupation; then, like many, he had claimed a marginal role with the Resistance. Though he ended the war dedicatedly in the Communist camp, his Moscow allies shocked his coterie by rating him "a jackal with a pen"—which was perhaps not an unfair description. Holding forth with a torrent of sophistry in the smoke-filled rooms of the Flore, he never lacked a captive audience of students, many of them American, who hung on his every word. Whether they understood them or not was immaterial. I recall being taken to meet the master by a left-wing playwright of Russian extraction, Arthur Adamov, who had written a play about the Commune. Smelling like a goat, he rather set the tone. If ever there was a philosopher guilty of the sin Socrates was accused of, being a false corrupter of youth, Sartre seemed to be it. His notions of liberty of the individual were totally distorted; it took Albert Camus to put a finger on the Existentialists' fundamental contradiction—justifying a system that was totally opposed to the responsibility of the individual. In the post-war atmosphere of libertarian Paris, youth gratefully reached out to Sartre for a welcome excuse selfishly to abandon all moral prescripts of responsibility, sexually in particular. (Within this context, the advent of the pill was to remove much of the significance of Sartre.)

De Beauvoir, sometimes known as *la grande sartreuse,* like a prim governess with her hair austerely tied back, was ever the better writer, breaking new feminist ground with her *Le Deuxième Sexe,* and providing valuable material for contemporary historians with her various books of memoirs, and her criticism of the Algerian War in *La Force des choses* (1963). Her major work of fiction, *Les Mandarins* (1954), was a seminal work drawing one to study contemporary France. But it also portrayed, in its more ridiculous light, the self-satisfied and elitist intellectual left, who moved in a very narrow physical and social circle, bicycling through France in the aftermath of Hiroshima, and seriously discussing—puff, puff, pedal, pedal—whether it would be preferable to be nuked by the friendly Russians or the abhorrent Americans. Out of all this vapid theorising, Camus alone emerges with stature; a short time later he broke with Sartre and de Beauvoir over the brutality of the Soviet system; the Sartres followed in disgust after the Soviet crushing of Hungary in 1956; but the damage, the new *trahison des clercs,* to a whole generation of western youth had already been done. During the Algerian War the Sartres joined the powerful group of antis; rightly, they exposed the horrors of torture committed by the French Army there, but eventually came close to justifying FLN terrorism.

A literary event almost as meaningful as the sophistry of Sartre came, in 1947, when his friend Jean Genet punched a critic of *Le Figaro* for being rude about his play, *Les Bonnes.* Among the other new writers of the 1950s whose books about the past war deeply shocked Parisians were Jean Dutourd, first of all with his flaying attack on the nastiness of the *petits collabos* in *Au bon beurre* (1952), and then, three years later, with *Les Taxis de la Marne,* which exalted heroism at the same time as it excoriated the debility of the "men of '40." A few months after the publication of *Au bon beurre,* Parisian theatre-goers were agog with excitement at the first night of Samuel Beckett's *En Attendant Godot*—even if many missed its cheerless message. Highly contemporary, but much more entertaining was Raymond Queneau's irreverent best-seller of 1959, *Zazie dans le métro,* set against the backdrop of a Métro strike that was symptomatic of Paris of the era, with a horribly knowing child from the provinces, precociously aware of transvestism, lesbians, paedophilia and child prostitution—her one desire to travel on the Métro.

In an intensely hot August of 1954 the revered Colette died and was given a public funeral in the Cour d'Honneur of the Palais-Royal, paid for by the state—the highest posthumous honour attainable, and the first time it was ever accorded a woman. "What a beautiful life I've had," she was recorded as remarking towards the end. "It's a pity I didn't notice it sooner."[11] During her interment at Père Lachaise, one of the most violent storms of the century broke out. Colette would have enjoyed it, thought her biographer, Judith Thurman. As Colette left the scene, so almost simultaneously a new nineteen-year-old female writer arose to fill the gap—and take France by storm—Françoise Sagan, who was both a product of, and a reaction against, the Existentialist wave. Of *Bonjour Tristesse,* her first novel, which swept Paris, François Mauriac praised its literary merit but described her as "a charming little monster." She was a true child of the new France of the 1950s. In her romantic novels, which combined the jet-set life with vigorous support for left-wing causes, the themes of casual sexuality—somewhat in advance of the times—were all fairly similar. In *Bonjour Tristesse* it is a manipulative adolescent; in *Aimez-vous Brahms?* played poignantly in the film by Ingrid Bergman in one of her most brilliant—and favourite—roles, an attractive woman trembling on the brink of forty falls for a much younger man (Anthony Perkins).

As literature, the exquisite writings of Camus—full of human feeling that totally eluded Sartre—will surely outlive him, even cut short as they were by his tragic and untimely death in a car accident in 1960, aged only forty-seven. He was one of the outstanding journalists of the 1950s and 1960s, founding *Combat* as a Resistance organ during the war, to continue long afterwards as a national paper—with his rallying cry that it was required of his generation to "être à la hauteur de son désespoir" ("rise up to the level of its despair"). There was also the vigorous young figure of Jean-Jacques Servan-Schreiber, launching *L'Express*. Known popularly just as J-J S-S, Servan-Schreiber headed the attack on French policy in Algeria, exposing the worst excesses of torture. After Algeria he went on to attack the foe of American universal power, in *Le Défi américain*.

IN THE WORLD OF PAINTING Picasso, forgiven—like others—his wartime career, went from strength to inventive strength (and from mistress to mistress), turning his hand to sculpture, fashioning marvellous bulls out of bits of old bicycles, broken urns and baskets. In 1949, he re-established both his pre-eminence and the claim of Paris once more to be the global art forum at an exhibition of sixty-four recent canvases; at the same time there was a retrospective of ninety works by Léger at the Musée d'Art Moderne. Five years later another major exhibition, held at the Communist Maison de la Pensée Française, ended prematurely in the face of a writ issued by the daughter of the great Tsarist art collector of pre-1917, Sergei Choukine, to regain "stolen family property" in the shape of thirty-seven canvases grabbed by the Soviets, which had been condemned as decadent, bourgeois art and had disappeared into the cellars of Moscow and Leningrad. The writ failed; but Picasso, in his new passionate attachment to the Soviets, was put on the spot. (When Khrushchev gradually relaxed things, both Picasso's and Matisse's "lost" works were allowed to reappear at an exhibition that made Paris gasp.) As Picasso cornered the market, so other fabled contemporaries left it. In 1954, Derain died, knocked off his bicycle aged seventy-four; a court order had recently prohibited him from "reworking" any of his old paintings, his estranged wife fearing that he might diminish their alimony value on his death. Matisse followed, in November, at eighty-four, before he could see again his masterpieces of five decades previously still buried away in the cellars of the Hermitage. He was followed, in 1955, by Léger, his funeral held under the auspices of the Communist Party, of which he, like Picasso, was a member, and by Utrillo—tragically alcoholic since the age of ten, he was much overrated as an original artist, but his canvases of a grey Montmartre still command serious prices.

One of the most popular, and unusual, exhibitions of the early postwar era was held in the Salon International de la Police, displaying counterfeits of paintings—in the wake of the exposure of the famous Dutch forger, Van Meegeren. Prices soared, and continued to soar, in the sale rooms, with true works by Juan Gris—who had tried, often successfully, to sell them at £5 a piece in his lifetime—reaching up to ff6 million by the end of 1947.

IN ONE BRANCH OF THE ARTS Paris had always led the world, and did again just as soon as wartime restrictions lifted—*haute couture*. Just to reclaim its ascendancy, and declare *nous voici* to the world, the industry put on a most remarkable exhibition even before the fighting ended, in the Louvre's Pavillon de Marsan at the end of March 1945, masterminded by Robert Ricci (son of Nina), Lucien Lelong, Christian Bérard, Dior, Patou, Carven and other great names in the industry. February 1947 saw a newcomer, Christian Dior, put on his first post-war show in the Avenue Montaigne. The crush was so great that some Parisians even tried to get through the top of the house with ladders. It was that night that the "New Look," with its tightened waists and ample skirts, was born; and Parisian *haute couture* was once more back on its rightful throne, never to be deposed. Dior was followed by Givenchy, Balmain, Balenciaga, Courrèges and Saint-Laurent.

BESET BY THE UNENDING ALGERIAN WAR, by the merry-go-round of collapsing governments that seemed finally to have run out of talent, and by perennial strikes, the Fourth Republic stumbled on—accompanied by the habitual run of diverse hazards and disasters. In 1952, the French suffered their worst bout of foot-and-mouth since 1939; unlike their slaughter-minded neighbours across the Channel they vaccinated the cattle—and forgot about it. In 1954, there was an epidemic of flying saucers—nicknamed *Les Churchills,* for no very clear reason, except that one resembled a cigar. The autumn of 1956 brought the deep humiliation of Suez—in French eyes, not loyally supported by the British, marking a caesura of distrust of her *anglo-saxon* allies that was never quite to be repaired. In France emotions ran far higher over Soviet intervention in Hungary than over Suez—in contrast to London, where Suez dominated the scene. Coincidental with the disastrous Suez operation, by a daring *coup de main* in mid-air, of highly dubious legality and without the sanction of the French government, French army intelligence hijacked Ben Bella and the entire external leadership of the FLN. It was another indication of how desperate the need was to find a solution to the Algerian situation. But the war went on. In 1957, through resorting to the toughest measures (notably torture), General Massu's elite paras won what looked like a clear-cut military victory in the famous "battle of Algiers," breaking up the whole FLN network in the city. But in April 1958, following one economic crisis after another, Premier Gaillard fell, leaving France without a government in the most dangerous power vacuum since 1945. The war had already toppled five governments, and was about to bring down the Fourth Republic itself.

As a final indictment on the decay of political institutions, there came the nine-day phenomenon of Pierre Poujade, a thirty-five-year-old shopkeeper from the Lot. A powerful, macho, populist rabble-rouser, who appealed to his audience by performing a kind of striptease on the platform, hurling off his jacket, pullover and finally his shirt as he warmed to his subject, Poujade created a grassroots political party out of the discontent of France's small shopkeepers. Called unambiguously the Union de Défense des Commerçants et Artisans (UDCA), it had unpleasantly thuggish and anti-Semitic tendencies, but swept into the Assembly on a wave of *petit bourgeois* discontent. Poujade urged his *com-*

*merçant* supporters to strike rather than pay taxes and amazed himself by picking up 2½ million votes, alongside Communist gains. The elections of January 1956 saw the worst defeat for the conventional parties of the centre since the Republic first saw the light of day. Within the year the Poujadists in the Assembly, an undistinguished lot, began to disintegrate; but Poujadism remained—in the English as well as the French vocabulary.

FOR A DOZEN YEARS since his abrupt departure from politics in 1946, de Gaulle had remained in the wilderness, fretting at Colombey-les-Deux-Églises, more and more sickened at having to witness, impotent, men of the circus of the Fourth Republic seemingly dedicated to reducing France to a third-rate power, with fifth-rate pretensions. Then, just as it was the Second World War that brought de Gaulle to the forefront in 1940, and again in 1944, so it was the disastrous Algerian War that brought him back again in May 1958. His Second Coming, if one can risk blasphemy, was precipitated by a crisis in Algiers, after all the false incarnations of the Fourth Republic had proved powerless to bring peace. Tempers had been rising among the forces in Algiers since the beginning of 1958, and the last straw had come with the killing in Tunisia of three captured French soldiers, on charges of torture, rape and murder. Exasperated, the army staged a coup, beginning on 13 May with the seizure of the Gouvernement-Général building where resided the organs of civil authority. The redoubtable General Massu formed a Committee of Public Safety—sinister sounding name to any of their countrymen with a sense of history. It was the first time since June 1940 that the French military had intervened directly in national politics. A series of plots and counterplots, in Corsica and on the mainland as well as in Algeria, thrust forward an apparently reluctant de Gaulle, aged sixty-seven. De Gaulle played hard to get, calculating sagely that to acquire a modicum of legitimacy he should step forward only when a clear majority of Frenchmen seemed to want him. Over several anxious days, Paris braced itself for a possible landing of the French paras from Algeria, tough and hard-fighting men sick of the insipid principles of civilian politicians.

The army putsch in Algiers provoked rumour and confusion. Never since the bloody clashes of February 1934 had circumstances so favoured a seizure of power by the mob. On 17 May, seventy American tourists refused to leave their plane at Orly for fear of being caught up in a revolution. A week later paras from Algiers staged a bloodless takeover, and the focus of attention moved to Paris, where events now became largely a matter of constitutional haggling and a race against time before General Massu's paras would come floating down from the skies. Police reservists (those who could be reckoned loyal) were mobilised. Trade union leaders were briefed to halt all trains in the event of a landing—with some absurdity; as someone sagely pointed out, "the paras don't often go by train!" There was dangerous talk about arming the Communists, who claimed to be able to get 10,000 militants out on the streets at a moment's notice. In Paris at the time, I recall it vividly as a period of extraordinary anxiety and tension, when the country seemed to tremble on the brink of civil war and anarchy. Cars flew up and down the Champs-Élysées sounding their horns, the drivers shouting "Vive de Gaulle!"; nevertheless, despite the crisis, on that warm Whit Sunday holiday of 25 May, a record number of cars still headed insouciantly out of Paris for the countryside.

Finally, on 28 May, two weeks after the Algiers putsch, Premier Pflimlin resigned; de Gaulle, returning late to his hotel, told the concierge, "Albert, j'ai gagné!" The left reacted violently, with a giant demonstration of perhaps half a million winding its way from the Place de la Nation to the Place de la République—though not nearly as violently as some feared. President Coty intervened; de Gaulle agreed to form a government.

On 1 June, he presented himself to the Assembly, and was accepted. The Communist deputies thumped their desks and shouted, "Le fascisme ne passera pas!" But 30 per cent of Communist electors deserted the party. Bizarrely, industrialists and big business also opposed de Gaulle initially—on the grounds that he stood for change. Otherwise his accession was a cause of relief, for here was a leader with purpose. As he left the Assembly and got into his car, de Gaulle seemed to be completely unaware of the rain that was sheeting down on him. In September he held a referendum to put a new constitution, containing strong powers for the president, to the nation. Sartre voiced the left's opposition to "King Charles XI," declaring, "I do not believe in God, but if in this plebiscite I had the duty of choosing between Him and the present incumbent, I would vote for God; he is more modest." Nevertheless, de Gaulle won by a sweeping majority. After all the uncertainties of the last days of the Fourth Republic, and the real fears of May, the new authority and majesty ushered in by him had an immediate, and galvanising effect on the nation. On his first official visit to Paris in June, Britain's Prime Minister, Harold Macmillan, noted already how the large crowds

> all seemed very relaxed and in a most friendly mood . . . I have never seen a French crowd cheer in such a friendly way . . . everyone is confident that the General's policy will succeed. No one knows what it will be—all the same it commands general confidence.[12]

# The General's Republic

Well, my dear country, my old country, here we are together, once
again, facing a harsh test . . .

—*de Gaulle, January 1960*

To de Gaulle, from his Grateful Country: Once and for All, MERCI!

—Canard Enchaîné, *on the ending of the Algerian War, 1962*

I N JANUARY 1959 the following year, shortly after his sixty-ninth
birthday, de Gaulle became president; his only, laconic words to his
predecessor, "Au revoir, Monsieur Coty," seemed like a calculated
snub to the Fourth Republic and the contempt in which he held it and
its participants. The Fifth Republic, and the new Gaullist era, had
begun. France's allies felt encouraged.

With de Gaulle authority moved back from Algiers and its rebellious
factions to Paris. So too did the direction of the war, which at the same
time hit the world stage as a dominant issue. There it would remain,
long after the war itself ended, as a paradigm for anti-colonialists and
revolutionaries from Cuba to Palestine, to the African National Congress in South Africa, and as a textbook to western staff colleges studying
the lessons of terrorism.

Promptly in June 1958, de Gaulle flew to Algeria where he stunned
the *pieds noirs* with his "I have understood you" speech—though it soon
became apparent that he had understood them not in quite the way they
had hoped. Whereas, to the French Army and the *pieds noirs,* Algeria
was everything, to de Gaulle it was only one factor in his overall ambition: the resurrection of the greater glory of France—and it was on no

account to get in the way of that. In September 1959, de Gaulle offered the Algerians the fateful words of "self-determination," a compromise that fell short of the hopes of all sides. Soon disillusion was renewed as it became apparent that even Charles de Gaulle had no simple formula for ending the war. With uncharacteristic indecision, de Gaulle let eighteen months run through his hands, and his attempts to achieve a ceasefire with the FLN were rejected with a crushing snub. Meanwhile the *ultras* among the *pieds noirs* of Algiers were becoming steadily more violent in their opposition, now, to de Gaulle.

On 24 January 1960, there was a fresh eruption in Algiers. Well-armed *ultras* started building barricades; gendarmes were brought in to clear them and firing broke out, killing twenty-four and wounding two hundred among the unfortunate gendarmes caught in a deadly crossfire. For France it was the ugliest moment in the five-year-old war to date; Frenchmen were killing Frenchmen for the first time. What was almost worse, some of the elite para units showed signs of fraternising with the *pieds noirs* behind the barricades. Like Thiers during the Commune of 1871, de Gaulle now realised how brittle an instrument the army was. As "Barricades Week" dragged on, there was a sense in France that, once again, revolution and civil war were a very real possibility. Then on the evening of the 29th, the weather took a friendly hand; in Algiers the skies opened on the overheated citizenry. That same night de Gaulle appeared on national television, dressed—with deliberate effect—in his uniform with two stars, familiar to so many in the army who could recall 1940 and the historic promenade through Paris in August 1944. It was as a soldier as well as head of state that he ordered the army in Algeria to obey him, and not to side with the insurrection: "Finally, I speak to France. Well, my dear country, my old country, here we are together, once again, facing a harsh test."[1] Though saying nothing new, it was one of his finest speeches, a performance of hypnotic wizardry. De Gaulle's appeal won; under an icy rain in Algiers the would-be insurgents broke up and went off home.

1960 was, nevertheless, to be a year of little comfort to de Gaulle, bringing less support and fresh enemies, as it brought the FLN new allies, both in the outside world and within France herself. More and more articles were appearing in the national press by young national servicemen returning from Algeria shocked by the "immoral acts" in which they had been forced to participate, had seen, or heard about. Out of all this inflammation of liberal sentiment there emerged in September a powerful "Manifesto of the 121," which incited French conscripts to

desert. The 121 signatories were all celebrities, including Sartre, de Beauvoir, Françoise Sagan and Simone Signoret. At the same time the "Jean-
son Network" physically aided the underground work of the FLN in
France, running funds for it and helping FLN terrorists in hiding.

OVER EASTER 1961, there were plastic bombs in Paris killing six and
wounding fifty; a bomb in the men's room of the Bourse injured thirty.
Then, in April, came the gravest challenge to de Gaulle that the Algerian
War was to bring. In Algiers four disaffected senior generals raised the
standard of revolt in the name of *Algérie Française*—headed by a much
respected airman, General Maurice Challe,* and the highly political and
wily principal in the 1958 coup, known as "the Mandarin"—General
Raoul Salan. Challe had come closer than any other commander-in-
chief to winning the war on the ground; but in doing so he felt that he
had—in the name of de Gaulle—traduced undertakings to the loyal
Muslim levies, called *Harkis,* that France would never abandon them. A
man of highest principles, he considered honour left him no alternative
but revolt.

On the night of 21 April, de Gaulle and his new Minister for Algerian
Affairs, Louis Joxe, attended a performance in Paris of *Britannicus,*
Racine's play about treason at court during the early rule of Nero—a
favourite of de Gaulle's and from which he could quote whole verses.
Later that night Joxe heard the first news of the putsch and—breaching
a strict standing order—telephoned the Élysée to rouse de Gaulle. With
immediate sangfroid, as usual, de Gaulle simply enquired:

> "What are you going to do, then, Joxe?"
> "I suppose go to Algeria, somehow."
> "*Bien . . .*"[2]

Joxe flew off courageously into the unknown, in an attempt to win over
wavering commanders in the field.

At the first meeting of cabinet ministers the next day, de Gaulle
talked contemptuously about the possibility of a coup by "this army
which, politically, always deludes itself." To his *chef de cabinet* he
remarked with a gesture of weary cynicism,

*Who became a friend of the author, on his release from prison, in the 1970s.

If they want to land in France, they will land. That's up to them. There won't be much to stop them. What will happen? Oh, it's not difficult to guess: these are men of narrow vision; they will very soon be faced with problems that will be beyond them.

De Gaulle's premier, Michel Debré, issued somewhat hysterical instructions for "citizens" to go to any airfields where paras might be dropping, and "convince the misled soldiers of their grave error." Possibly the true hero of that day of utter stupefaction in Paris was Roger Frey, de Gaulle's Minister of the Interior. Acting with speed and vigour, he swooped to arrest a general and several other conspirators *in flagrante,* thereby nipping in the bud a serious attempt to march on the capital. To this end some 1800 lightly equipped paras actually had been waiting in the Forest of Orléans, and another 400 in the Forest of Rambouillet. Joining up with tank units from Rambouillet, they were to move in three columns on Paris, seizing the Élysée and other key points of the administration. But the venture had a strongly amateurish note about it, with some of the waiting putschists apparently unaware even of the codeword "Arnat" (a simple elision of Armée and Nationale). Once they were rendered leaderless by their general's arrest, no orders came through until a detachment of gendarmes appeared in the forest and gave a brusque order to disperse, with which the powerful body of paras sheepishly complied.

On Sunday, 23 April, Paris presented an extraordinary spectacle under the warming spring sunshine. I was awaiting a permit to go to Algeria, which was promptly frozen in consequence of the putsch; instead I watched elderly Sherman tanks of Second World War vintage rumble out from retirement and take up positions outside the Assembly and other government buildings. Some broke down and had to be towed across the Concorde. Compared with the modernity of equipment in Algeria, it was painfully plain that—as de Gaulle had remarked—there was not "much to stop them" should Challe's paras make a determined bid to land in France. All air movement round the city was halted; buses and trains stopped running, and even the cinemas closed down. Only the cafés remained open for business, and they were crammed with Parisians discussing the latest turn in the crisis.

Then, at eight o'clock that night, all France clustered round the television as de Gaulle again addressed the shaken, anxious nation in his brigadier's uniform. Dark circles round his eyes visibly filled with pain as he spoke of his beloved army in revolt. Scathingly he dismissed the rebel leaders as a " 'little clutch' of generals in retirement." But here was "the nation defied, our strength shaken, our international prestige debased, our position and our role in Africa compromised. And by whom? *Hélas! Hélas! Hélas!* By men whose duty, honour and *raison d'être* it was to serve and to obey." Striking the table with his fist to reinforce his words, he enjoined: "In the name of France, I order that all means, I repeat all means, be employed to block the road everywhere to those men . . . I forbid every Frenchman, and above all every soldier, to execute any of their orders." No excuses or extenuating circumstances whatever for disobeying this order would be accepted. Finally, he ended with one of his most impassioned, personal appeals: "*Françaises, Français!* Look where France risks going, in contrast to what she was about to become. *Françaises, Français! Aidez-moi!*" Janet Flanner was one who rated the speech de Gaulle's "greatest speaking performance of his career": "When he cried three times '*Hélas! Hélas! Hélas!*' it was the male voice of French tragedy, more moving, because anguished by reality, than any stage voice in *Britannicus.*"

In what became known as the "Battle of the Transistors," an important essay in the power to influence via modern communications, all across Algeria French conscripts listened to de Gaulle's speech—and heeded him. The vast majority refused to go along with their rebellious colonels and generals, and the 1961 putsch was over. The elite Foreign Legion paras, the power behind the revolt, dynamited their barracks in Zeralda and marched out defiantly singing Piaf's "Je ne regrette rien." Challe surrendered to French justice. He received a maximum sentence of fifteen years' imprisonment, and loss of his rank, decorations and pensions—ruined by a reluctant commitment to "save the honour of the army." Salan disappeared into hiding in Algiers, to emerge as titular head of the Organisation Armée Secrète (OAS) which would spread indiscriminate and senseless terror across Algeria, and soon import it to Paris. But the divisions and weaknesses that the Challe revolt had displayed within the French Army meant that any prospect of *Algérie Française* was now dead. De Gaulle was forced to negotiate with the FLN rebels—and not on his terms, even though France, the very same week as the putsch, had shown her muscle by exploding a first atomic bomb at Reganne deep in the Algerian Sahara. In May 1961, the first talks took place at Evian on Lake Geneva; by July they had failed, with the FLN holding out for total capitulation by de Gaulle.

DURING THE COURSE of the Algerian War, over thirty separate attempts were made on de Gaulle's life. On 8 September 1961, a disaffected young colonel, a would-be Stauffenberg, Jean-Marie Bastien-Thiry, executed the most spectacular to date, exploding a huge mine of explosive and napalm at Pont-sur-Seine as de Gaulle's Citroën passed on his way home to Colombey-les-Deux-Églises. Supplied from old Resistance stock, the explosive had deteriorated and evidently failed to detonate properly; de Gaulle's chauffeur, handling the slewing car with exceptional skill, drove through the sheet of flame, somehow managing to keep on the road. Over the six months, culminating in February 1962, that the main OAS offensive in France lasted, it would only tilt French sympathies towards de Gaulle's acceptance of a precipitate withdrawal from Algeria.

Even without the OAS, an atmosphere of violence between the police and the domestic Algerian community had been progressively alienating liberal opinion. In this brutal little sideshow, no fewer than sixteen police were killed and forty-five wounded, most of them during the months of August and September 1961. Inevitably, the police reacted with parallel brutality; in mid-October, some 25,000 Algerian workers from the poor suburbs (undoubtedly activated by the FLN) launched an unarmed demonstration against the harsh curfew and repressive measures imposed on them by the government. It was broken up by the police with a disproportionate violence that was shocking to French public opinion. There were rumours that "dozens of Algerians were thrown into the Seine and others were found hanged in the woods." As the truth began to come out over three decades later, during the trial of arch-wartime collaborator Maurice Papon, the true figures appear to have numbered close to 200 fatalities. At the same time the deadly device of torture used by the French Army in Algeria, the *gégène* (a dynamo used to administer shocks to sensitive parts of the body) made its ugly appearance on the Parisian scene, and by January 1962 *France-Soir* was lamenting that there was "something wrong with justice" when indicted torturers repeatedly escaped sentence.

Compared with the indiscriminate, murderous mayhem that would be imposed on London by the IRA, the bombings that hit Paris would never approximate. As heartless killers, the OAS were rank amateurs. Walls were covered with graffiti by night; fairly ineffectual bombs were placed to damage property, while avoiding any possible injury to life or limb. In December it was the turn of the newspapers; *France-Soir* was bombed, provoking little more than an editorial demanding that "the

French population has a right to be protected"; the editor-in-chief of *Le Figaro* was *plastiqué* twice. The black-and-white flag of the OAS was impudently hoisted three times in a single day from the Gothic pinnacles of the Hôtel de Ville. On 4 January 1962, the OAS machine-gunned French Communist Party headquarters in the Place Kossuth. Later in January another thirteen bombings celebrated the second anniversary of "Barricades Week." Among them, on 22 January, was a bomb set off in the Quai d'Orsay, which killed one employee and wounded twelve others, the most lethal incident so far. Plans captured by the Paris police enabled them to forestall, just in time, attempts to dynamite the Eiffel Tower and to explode another series of forty-eight bombs. But otherwise, as in Algiers, the metropolitan police showed an extraordinary lethargy in arresting any of the terrorist leaders.

BY NOW THE FRENCH PUBLIC was becoming thoroughly fed up with the OAS, and it would require but one more outrage for something to snap. It now occurred. On the morning of 7 February 1962, among ten other bombings that day, an OAS commando set out to bomb the Boulogne-sur-Seine home of André Malraux, de Gaulle's Minister of Culture. Malraux lived upstairs, and anyway was absent that day. The *plastique* was detonated on the ground floor, close to where a four-year-old child, Delphine Renard, was playing with her dolls. It drove splinters of glass from the windows into her face, blinding her in one eye and painfully disfiguring her. A week later a silent and solemn procession, estimated at half a million strong and emotive of the commune, marched to Père Lachaise Cemetery. Nothing like it had been seen in Paris since the bloody days of February 1934; some reckoned it to be the biggest street turnout since the Liberation. *Algérie Française* was all but dead—killed by the OAS.

The organisation's leader, Salan, was captured in Algeria in April 1962. However the last—and most nearly successful—attempt against de Gaulle took place in August at the Petit Clamart, just outside Paris. An OAS band equipped with machine-guns and led once again by Bastien-Thiry ambushed the President's car, with Mme. de Gaulle in the back. The bullets passed behind his head and in front of the head of his wife. Never losing his composure, de Gaulle the soldier criticised the would-be assassins as "bad shots." Equally unperturbed, Mme. de Gaulle remarked: "for my son-in-law, it would have been sad, but for the General and myself, it would have been a fine ending."[3] Bastien-Thiry was caught and shot, the first senior French officer to pass before a firing squad in many years. His death, and the last attempt to remove de Gaulle, were all to no avail. The second Evian talks had already concluded, with de Gaulle giving the FLN every concession—including the recently discovered Algerian oil which France had fought so hard to keep. The *tricolore* was finally lowered in Algeria. Amid tragic scenes, 1 million *pieds noirs* left the land and the homes that had belonged to many of them for three generations. It was a sell-out, but also a miracle, owing almost entirely to the remarkable boom in the economy, that France was able to assimilate, virtually overnight, so enormous an increment in her population. In independent Algeria, after brief intermissions of hope, killings between Algerians would continue to the present day. In France the fiercely satirical, generally heartless *Canard Enchaîné* took Parisians by surprise by printing in boldest caption: "To de Gaulle, from his Grateful Country: Once and for All, MERCI!"

YEARS LATER HAROLD MACMILLAN, Prime Minister at the time, remarked that whenever he had talked to de Gaulle "behind him I always saw the shadow of Algeria."[4] Typical of the man and the times, before the trial of the renegade Salan ended, it was eclipsed in the Paris press by *rapportage* of de Gaulle's Élysée press conference on the European Common Market. Closing the European door to *les anglo-saxons* and pulling France out of NATO now assumed top priority for de Gaulle.

Political reform followed political reform, referendum upon referendum—until the French electorate tired of having to troop to the polls yet again. In fact, there were few fronts on which de Gaulle was not attacking with vigour and dedication in his first six plenipotential months. First and foremost there was the new constitution, involving a mountainous work of drafting and consultation. "I considered it necessary," declared de Gaulle, "for the government to derive not from parliament, in other words from the parties, but, over and above them, from a leader directly mandated by the nation as a whole and empowered to choose, to decide and to act."[5] Henceforth the president would be elected by universal suffrage; the executive would emerge immeasurably strengthened, with many of the weaknesses that had been the undoing of the Third and Fourth Republics purged from the body politic. Well before the triumphant result of the constitutional referendum it was abundantly clear that henceforth France was now going to be ruled.

For the first time in nearly a hundred years, certainly for the first time under either the Third or Fourth Republic, France had a president vested with authority. Under the immense personal prestige of de Gaulle, a new national unity began to emerge. The debilitative wrangling of the parties was a thing of the past—so was any kind of political corruption. For the next few years France enjoyed a unique degree of stability, unique since the heyday of Louis-Napoleon. Critics might grumble at de Gaulle's authoritarianism, that he was "Charles XI" or a new Bonaparte—but he was never a self-serving despot nor a would-be dictator. In his mystical "certain idea of France," if there was any visible affinity, it was with Louis XIV, with his overriding pursuit of one thing: *La grandeur de la France.*

De Gaulle began to travel ever more widely, to remind the outside world of the sound of France's "voice." As he challenged the mighty dollar, it was a sound not always harmonious to the ears of her friends. The new year of peace, 1963, began with de Gaulle's exclusion of Britain from entry into the EEC, with some brutality towards his loyal wartime colleague, Harold Macmillan. To Macmillan, wounded several times in the First World War, the Germans would ever remain a subject of distrust, if not dislike; de Gaulle, equally wounded in that war, and taken prisoner of war at Verdun in 1916, viewed the present differently—possibly with a more profoundly philosophic interpretation of history. No sooner had he dealt this blow to his old ally Macmillan (who had in fact done much to defend de Gaulle from the wrath of Churchill and Roosevelt) than de Gaulle was off to Germany, declaring "Long live Franco-German friendship!" and wooing a receptive Dr. Adenauer, like him a product of the Catholic world of pre-1914.*

In 1966, de Gaulle completed the break with NATO, explaining that France did not want to be drawn into any war not to her own liking. (From their Paris HQ the departure ceremony of the fourteen NATO nations took place with admirable good humour, British Army bands playing "Charlie Is My Darling"—as witty a musical rebuke as possible to the deliberately absent President de Gaulle.) He embarked France upon her own go-it-alone, nuclear *force de frappe*—its missiles aimed no longer at the Communist danger, but, in a muzzily menacing fashion, in all directions. He recognised Mao's Peking, and in 1966 visited Khrushchev's Soviet Union—to the consternation of the *anglo-saxons.*

---

*Would de Gaulle, one wonders, have been so assiduous in wooing Adenauer had he been able to foresee German reunification, three decades later?

*The Times* observed that suddenly he seemed to be "the only active revolutionary in Europe." And France was at last "free to look at France."


DE GAULLE WAS ABLE TO WRITE in his memoirs, "France's revival was in full flower. She had been threatened by civil war; bankruptcy had stared her in the face; the world had forgotten her voice. Now she was out of danger."[6] Indeed, so it seemed. Life began to resume its course with customary celerity. The Brittany farmers embarked upon an "artichoke war," to the discomfort of Parisians. Academicians began to fret about the incursions of *franglais* in the Assembly. The title of the new Vadim-Bardot film, *Le Repos du guerrier* (*The Warrior's Rest*), seemed to set the tone. Already in 1962 France's gross national product was rising by 6.8 per cent in the year. The politician Debré was replaced at the Matignon by the banker Pompidou.

Shed of the burden of Algeria, France's economy at last began to show a blossoming from the thoughtful planting done in the latter years of the maligned Fourth Republic and the first four years of Gaullism. Similar initiatives in London would receive a cold shower of scepticism. Things were markedly different from the days of the Third Republic when France's economic teaching was mocked by the British and Germans as backward. By 1964 a state visit from the President of Togoland revealed that in relative terms France was spending three times more of her GNP on the underdeveloped countries than the USA. Entering its seventh year, in 1965, the Fifth Republic showed its sudden miraculous fiscal prosperity with official reserves reaching $5 billion—unequalled in all Europe except for the mighty Bundesbank. Colour television came in—at a high cost per set. On 15 June 1964 the last French troops pulled out of Algeria, but the technical modernisation dreamed of by de Gaulle was already well under way.

Nevertheless, in the white heat of France's sudden turnaround to prosperity, the old shadows were not entirely banished. The serpent of Communism was still very much alive and wriggling in its opposition to de Gaulle and his *dirigiste* handling of the economy. In 1967, Paris was paralysed by what the media recorded as the greatest strike by the greatest number of strikers that France had ever known. Accompanied by slogans of "Down with Pompidou!" and "No Government by Decree!," it was not a strike for wages, but a purely political strike for purely political reasons. Around 150,000 workers paraded for three hours from the

Bastille to the République. As one foreign correspondent observed, "only the sun and the moon continued their movements."

NAPOLEON I NEVER FACED such disruption, and nor would de Gaulle let it deflect him from his grand conception of the nation—his "certaine idée de la France." Like Napoleon, de Gaulle looked forward to a day when a magnificent new Paris might become the wonder, if not the formal capital of Europe. It was still overcrowded—with 143 people per acre compared with 43 in London. By 1962 population figures reached 7 million for greater Paris, though the central city had declined slightly in the twentieth century to 2.7 million. With his ultimate lofty objective in mind, de Gaulle made the inspired choice of appointing André Malraux as his Minister of Culture, which post he held until 1969—charged with taking Paris in hand. Under this remarkable man, eleven years younger than de Gaulle—writer and artist, philosopher, aesthete and man of action, fighter with the Republicans in Spain, convert from Communism, scourge of both left and right, and member of the Resistance, whose life resembled a novel that might have been written by Malraux—the stones of Paris came to life again. It was Malraux who was responsible for the *blanchissage* (whitening) of Paris, digging out the lower floor of the Louvre's Cour Carrée and returning it to its pristine glory, and restoring the Marais, with the Place des Vosges, dilapidated almost to the point of total destruction, as its *pièce de résistance.*

This *blanchissage* of Paris totally transformed much of the capital. So did works begun on the remarkable RER express underground system, capable of whisking Parisians on silent rubber wheels from Saint-Germain to the Étoile in four minutes during the rush hour, at 60 m.p.h., to become the envy of London's wretched urban travellers. Less felicitous, at least in the view of this writer, were architectural scandals like the Tour Montparnasse (started in 1969, but not finished until 1973), the greatest urban project since Haussmann, and designed to be the highest skyscraper in all Europe, menacing the ascendancy of the Eiffel Tower and the Invalides. Then came Richard Rogers' Centre Pompidou, the unhappy child of the first international competition ever held in Paris, and which looked as if it might not still be standing by the millennium (alas, it was, just). There was the great and windy complex out at La Défense (where the last battle of the siege of 1870–71 was fought and lost) and various other high-rise developments ringing Paris and

threatening its historic skyline. Swallowing up ancient woodland like
the Forêt de Sénart, Paris built itself into the twentieth century. One
horrible dormitory complex of 300,000 new flats was built in the form
of a wriggling snake, nearly half a mile long.

UNDER MALRAUX'S GENIUS many great art retrospectives were held
in the 1960s: but by 1964 he was left grumbling that, whereas a few years
ago some 3000 people every evening sat at home watching television,
now it was 3 million. "You can put unimportant things on the screen,"
he observed gloomily. "Make no mistake about it, modern civilisation is
in the process of putting its immense resources at the service of what
used to be called the Devil." Earlier in 1964 another powerful grumble
was heard about French culture, on a theme close to the General's heart.
Paris bookshops were filled with a wittily written book on a most serious
subject by a professor of literature at the Sorbonne, René Étiemble:
*Parlez-vous franglais?* It slated the insidious creeping into the sacred language of such barbaric usage as *le week-end, le booking, le snack* and *le
quick* (pronounced *queek*)—and *un baby Scotch sur les rocks.* Not without reason, the learned professor deplored that

> Since the Liberation, our blood has become much diluted . . . the
> vocabulary of the young generation that will be twenty years old
> in 1972 is already one-fourth composed of American words. At 20
> these young people will not be able to read Molière, let alone
> Marcel Proust.

Apart from resolving the sex of the automobile, what was the Académie
doing? Soon the fear of *franglais* was followed up by the opening of a
new American-style "drugstore" in Saint-Germain, right opposite
Sartre's fortress at the Flore.

In 1963, within a few hours of her friend, Jean Cocteau, Edith Piaf
died—the tiny sparrow figure in the plain black dress, who had done so
much to cloak a glum Paris in the 1940s with the warm light of "La Vie
en Rose," going on to enchant the wide world beyond her Montmartre
with "Milord" and the paras' favourite, her tragic, autobiographic, "Je
ne regrette rien":

> Farewell to love with its tremolo.
> I start again at zéro . . .

All France grieved. Forty thousand turned up to accompany her to her simple grave in Père Lachaise. Meanwhile women in Paris's oldest profession, who had always found a sympathetic friend in Piaf, were suffering a hard time under de Gaulle, doubtless influenced by his sternly moral wife "Tante Yvonne." Determined to clean up Paris, he reactivated a draconian 330-year-old law that threatened, with the forfeiture of his property, any landlord who allowed prostitutes to work in his premises. Business was stricken. On another level conventional morality was under siege by François Mitterrand, in opposition. He seized on France's archaic attitudes to family planning and contraception, long a taboo subject, making them political issues. With joy the Paris gossip columnists leaped on the young pro-pill generation, jeering at its Catholic opponents as *les lapinistes,* or rabbit clan, devoted to a culture of excessive fertility.

BY THE MID-1960S, despite all the material benefits that his regime had brought about, what de Gaulle dubbed the "snarlers and grousers" were soon raising their voices in anticipation of the end of the Fifth Republic and an electoral replacement of the solitary ruler in the Élysée. Could it be that he had served his purpose? That once again in its history France, Paris, *s'ennuyait?* As he once acidly remarked, "How can you govern a country that has 246 varieties of cheese!" The presidential elections of 1965 ended with de Gaulle gaining only 44 per cent of the vote. Humiliatingly for him, there had to be a second ballot. Ten-and-a-half million votes had gone to the new star on the now united left, François Mitterrand, who had suddenly proved himself a most effective orator. Janet Flanner of the *New Yorker* compared the results to "a famous public fountain losing its soaring strength"; but she was being premature when she claimed that "the extraordinary Fifth Republic of General de Gaulle ended when he failed to be reelected its President"[7] on that first election.

The sparkling period of economic expansion had run out of steam; Frenchmen began to hoard gold once more. The next political blow to de Gaulle came at the beginning of 1967 when his protégé, the brilliant young *énarque* economist, Valéry Giscard d'Estaing, launched a new splinter Gaullist Party. It had considerable success in the parliamentary elections, which reduced de Gaulle's majority to a dangerously small margin of just one seat. Still the barometer looked set fair; at his twice-yearly press conference in the Élysée in November 1966, de Gaulle was able to declare: "We have nothing dramatic to say today. In contrast to the past, France right now is not living in any drama."[8]

There was a certain smug unspoken comparison to Lyndon B. Johnson's America, crippled as it was by the ongoing nightmare of Vietnam. The press conference at the same time the following year, November 1967, provoked *Le Figaro* to voice the unmentionable with a witty cartoon captioned "What would I do if I didn't have me . . . ?" When one correspondent had dared enquire about "après Gaullisme," the seventy-seven-year-old President had replied with considerable verve, "Everything always has an end, and everyone eventually comes to a finish, though for the moment that is not the case." "*Après de Gaulle* might begin tonight, or in six months, or even a year," he continued. "However, if I wanted to make some people laugh and others groan, I could say that it might just as likely go on as it is now for ten years, or even fifteen. But, frankly, I don't think so." Correspondents present laughed nervously at this display of hubris, as de Gaulle went on to offend in turn the United States, the Queen of England, the non-French Canadians of her Commonwealth, the British Labour government in again refusing English entry into the Common Market, Israel and world Jewry, and President Johnson and his hawks by reference to the "odious" Vietnam War. Nor could his words have greatly pleased the Chinese or the Russian Communists. His performance was viewed as a remarkable *tour de force* for a seventy-seven-year-old with no identifiable problems on the horizon himself.

But what a shock lay in store within only a few brief months, at the coming of 1968. A kind of universal madness sets its stamp on the year—surely one of the most troublesome and nasty, yet exciting, of the post-war era. It was the year of violent student revolt, and of assassination. It determined the defeat of America in Vietnam and a fall in Paris. It also displayed the fissures that were to bring the whole Soviet monolith toppling more than two decades later. Some caught up in it likened 1968 to that other year of revolution, 1848, when old political structures across Europe had collapsed like the walls of Jericho—not least in Paris, where the events of February 1848 had brought down that easygoing, liberal king, Louis-Philippe. In Britain the year began with Malcolm Muggeridge resigning as rector of Edinburgh University over plans to offer the pill free to students. In America, Dr. Benjamin Spock of nursery fame was indicted for anti-draft activities, while in Russia writer Alexander Ginsburg was gaoled for "slandering the state." Such events were indications of what 1968 held in store.

On 31 January, the peace talks that were shortly to begin in Paris were pre-empted in South Vietnam by the Viet Cong seizing advantage of the traditional New Year's Tet celebrations to launch a major coordinated series of attacks on South Vietnamese cities. US forces were thoroughly taken by surprise, and briefly it looked as if the Viet Cong had won. Nevertheless the US forces reacted with vigour, inflicting a clear-cut defeat on the Communists. But America was stunned by the announcement that President Johnson, worn down by Vietnam and anti-war protest, would not be a candidate in the 1970 presidential elections. French watching their new colour televisions cheered as Jean-Claude Killy won three golds in the Winter Olympics, and—in Prague—as a heady "Prague Spring" broke out when Alexander Dubček stunned the world by relaxing press censorship and arresting the Chief of Police. For a few rapturous weeks it looked as if Czechoslovakia would regain the freedom it had lost twenty years previously.

In Paris anti-Americanism was bolstered by noisy Vietnam demonstrations—and given an extra spin by the horrendous news of the assassination of Martin Luther King, in Memphis, Tennessee. About the same time, in Germany, a left-wing student called Rudi Dutschke was shot in the head by a gunman claiming to emulate the King killing. Dutschke survived, but the shooting triggered off student riots across Germany. In France, de Gaulle's Premier Pompidou was able to declare comfortably that there was "no opposition capable of overthrowing us, much less capable of replacing us."

Then the Sorbonne exploded.

IT ALL BEGAN, back in February, at Nanterre, a new and particularly drab suburban campus surrounded by mud, combining the worst features of American and French universities. Its graffiti-plastered concrete still seemed to belong more to backward, revolution-torn Bolivia than to Gaullist Paris in the second half of the twentieth century. Founded as an overflow for the overwhelmed Sorbonne, Nanterre already had over 12,000 students in inadequate accommodation, with only 240 professors and assistant professors. There was a lack of warm food, and canteen queues could last an hour and a half; hence there was plenty of time for revolutionary chat. As a subject, sociology (described by some French intellectuals as affording "certificates in anarchy")[9] predominated, under left-wing professors on whom the mantle of Herbert Marcuse rested heavily. Most of the students, however, came (by car) from the essentially bourgeois *arrondissements* of western Paris. Shades of 1848! To be exiled there, instead of going to the Sorbonne, must have felt like being a noble exiled from the court of Louis XIV. On graduation they were faced with either no jobs, or dreary ones. Thus it was not unnatural that, if student revolt were to break out in Paris, it should be at Nanterre.

Many at Nanterre were bored bourgeois youth—boys come to establish themselves in the same building as girls who, like protagonists in a Sagan novel, were also bored. Equally shocking to less liberated spirits were graffiti proclaiming "merde au bonheur." Recalling by comparison the real deprivations of the war and yet how happy Paris had been in 1944, an *académicien* like Maurice Druon found such sentiments in an age of stable prosperity quite "devastating"; for "Youth had never been more free, but never complained so much about being oppressed."[10] What to do? Helpfully the Gaullist Minister of Education told the Nanterre students to take a cold bath. On 4 May, Nanterre was placed in suspension.

Revolt was carried from Nanterre to the Sorbonne by a red-headed firebrand, Danny Cohn-Bendit, who was not even French, but the son of affluent German Jews. The date coincided with the opening of the Vietnam peace conference, and it so happened the tenth anniversary of de Gaulle coming to power—a moment for ten years of accumulated grievance to light up with student discontent.

THE SORBONNE appeared to have changed little since the age of Napoleon—if not the Middle Ages. The place was neglected—not only physically dingy and sad, but with little attention paid to the task of education. As Raymond Aron recalled:

> The best students continued to take exams and their degrees without ever setting foot in the Sorbonne. The others were left to themselves, except for the help provided by the assistant. The professor, for the most part, did nothing but deliver lectures. My weekly schedule consisted of three hours . . .[11]

By 1968 the Sorbonne had become obscenely overcrowded: with 130,000 students it totalled more than Oxford and Cambridge together—more than the total population of Paris at the time of its founder, Abelard. Aron recalled one colleague who had published nothing in twenty years, and who "had accomplished the considerable feat of having virtually no students at his lectures." It was by no means unusual for a professor to start the year with 150 students in his lectures, and end up with none. Every professor was "supreme master of his Chair below God." There was a complete absence of any obligation or sanction.

In sum, with dreadful overcrowding in lecture halls, *Mandarinisme* on the part of the teachers, the absence of any form of pre-selection, over-centralisation, bureaucratism, the fossilisation of the syllabus, and the tyranny of endless examinations, the Paris students of May 1968 had a case. Thus, at the Sorbonne in May 1968, Daniel Cohn-Bendit and his *enragés* from Nanterre found the most inflammable material. Egged on by their own professors, they then widened their target from establishing student power to turning a university revolt into a social and political revolution.


ON THE AFTERNOON OF FRIDAY, 4 May, the head of the Sorbonne, Rector Jean Roche, called in the Paris police. It was an act that violated the sanctuary of the university, maintained over many centuries, and an unpardonable academic error. The next day the police in their *paniers à salade* moved in, closing the Sorbonne and arresting 596 students. Predictably, the traditionally brutal CRS detachments over-reacted, causing many hundred casualties. Fortunately there were no deaths; given the heat already generated on the Left Bank streets it is hard to imagine how far insurgent violence might have gone had only a few young students been mown down by CRS bullets. The students took to the streets, and occupied the Sorbonne buildings, brought in a piano, played and sang through the night and slept in the empty classrooms. Around the university and the "Boul' Mich" they set to digging up the cube-shaped *pavé,* sawing down ancient plane trees and dragging up burnt-out cars to construct barricades—just as their ancestors had done in the past century. What caught all foreign journalists by surprise in the early days of *les évènements* was the remarkable spontaneity, the atmosphere of exultation and wild euphoria, evocative of the early halcyon days of the Commune. To the deep disgust of academics like Aron and Druon, in the initial euphoria there were numerous cases of professors supporting the students, chemistry teachers showing them how to make a Molotov cocktail.

What had started as a student protest edged towards full-scale political revolution, aimed at nothing less than the overthrow of the de Gaulle government. New slogans appeared—and not just on the Left Bank adjacent to the Sorbonne: "Ten years, that's enough!" "De Gaulle to the museum!" and "De Gaulle to the stake!"

By mid-May, 3 million workers had come out on strike, a week later numbers had risen to 10 million. With garbage piling up in the streets, no petrol in the pumps and food running short, the Banque de France itself went out; as well as the engravers at the Mint, so banknotes were also running short. The Pompidou government had at least prevented "Robespierre" Cohn-Bendit returning from Germany, where he had gone on a visit.

The greatest turn of fortune for a beleaguered regime came, however, when students tried to spread the revolt to the big Renault works at Bil-lancourt. Striking workers occupied the plant (as they had done in 1936), but would not join forces and fulfil the Marxist dream of workers and students marching hand in hand. The workers' aloofness came partly on account of the bourgeois origins of the striking students—*les fils à papa,* as they scathingly dubbed them. The schism was palpably more between generations than classes, between youth and its elders.

Taking advantage of the revolt, the *pègres*—those of the under-world—began to join in. Property and shops became at risk. People who had at first supported the revolt now became increasingly alienated by its anarchic, nihilist face. Returning from America during the third week of *les évènements,* Raymond Aron was forced to ask himself, "Am I still in France, or Cuba . . . or in some weird country? Can this country which is gripped by collective madness, really be France?"[12]

DE GAULLE AND POMPIDOU returned from their leisurely travels in the east to a swiftly worsening crisis. But still the government did virtu-ally nothing to reverse the slide into chaos. Paris was alive with rumours, but the most disturbing—in the last turbulent week of May—was that de Gaulle had bolted. It looked like a repeat of what he had done in 1946, when in his disgust with French party politics he had retreated to Colombey-les-Deux-Églises. The truth was that, in what seemed like panic, and without telling his prime minister, on Wednesday 29 May de Gaulle did fly mysteriously out of Paris, eastwards. For a moment, Pom-pidou believed he was following in the footsteps of Louis-Philippe. In fact he had headed to Baden-Baden, to get the support of General Massu and the French Army in Germany; but he had indeed departed in deep pessimism and evidently told Massu, "I have had it up to here. I can't stand it any more and I am leaving." Massu urged him not to; minutes later de Gaulle admitted that he had "had this moment of weakness; because I am too old, and I must go." "I cannot fight against apathy, against the desire of a whole people to let itself break apart." However, the ever-dependable Massu assured de Gaulle that the army would remain loyal. The deal was that de Gaulle would amnesty distinguished soldiers like Challe and Salan, currently languishing in gaol for their roles in the 1961 putsch—to rehabilitate the army's repute.

The following day de Gaulle returned—deeply unpopular though he had become, walking tall once more—to broadcast the last powerful appeal of his career. A tremendous rallying cry, it came only just in time. Using crude barrack-room language, he dismissed the students as *chie-en-lits* (shit-abeds), while in uncompromising terms he accused the Communists of seeking "an international autocracy." As Raymond Aron saw it,

> One fighting speech from an old man of 78, and the people of France rediscovered the sense of reality, petrol pumps and holidays. We still have to come to understand this episode of French history—a history rich in strange episodes.

It was to be the last time the master of language and persuasion would be able to deploy the old magic. But it worked. That very same evening the Champs-Élysées filled with 100,000 pro-Gaullist counter-demonstrators, a sea of blue-white-red *tricolores* protesting against the red of anarchy and Communism, assembled with a spontaneity as remarkable as that with which *les évènements* had broken out in the first place.

France's most breathlessly frightening month since the war was over. It now had to count the cost.

THE BILLS FOR PARIS' MONTH OF MADNESS were soon coming in—ff150 million, over £13 million or $30 million. By the following year the total bill would come to something more like $2–3 billion—resulting, in the words of Georges Pompidou, in a "slow haemorrhage" in the nation's finances. Devaluation of the franc became unavoidable. The first item was for the relaying in the streets around the Boul' Mich' of a million stone paving blocks, prised up by the students to construct barricades. After a century-and-a-half of insurrections and barricades, the city fathers finally decided to tar over the *pavé*. The workers were placated by a huge wage boost of 10–14 per cent. But the invisible, long-term cost to Paris of 1968 was greater still: the international art market began to abandon its traditional home for London and New York.

For the Sorbonne—an ancient institution in disarray—a new law was hurriedly adopted. Thereby the old university of 130,000, proven impossible to administer, was broken up into thirteen successors each of a maximum of 20,000 members. But the revolting students did not get the participation in university governance for which they had clamoured. The elite École Normale Supérieure, the Polytechnique and the École Nationale d'Administration remained largely untouched. For at least a year, students at the Sorbonne learned nothing at all; then they went back to their studies—the fun was over.

THE NEW YEAR OF 1969 opened as if nothing had happened in Paris the previous May. Spring brought yet another referendum, the fifth of the Fifth Republic. This time it was a much discussed scheme to modernise and streamline the paralysing centralisation of the country on Paris, which dated back to Louis XIV and beyond, and to reorganise the Senate. It was not a major issue, but a thoroughly sensible measure, part of de Gaulle's programme for France "marrying her age." As with past referendums, it demanded simply a "Yes" or a "No" at the polls, framed as a choice "between progress and upheaval." But France was bored with going to the polls, with de Gaulle and his measures. *La France s'ennuit.*

On 10 April, de Gaulle gave a television interview in which he abruptly declared that, if the referendum failed, he ought not continue as chief of state. The challenge was there. The bill ran to several thousand words long; many voters never received their copy. On a poor turnout the referendum was lost by a narrow margin of 47–53 per cent. Immediately, de Gaulle packed up and departed from the Élysée, pausing only to shake hands with Colonel Laurent, commander of his palace military guard, and to issue the tersest of communiqués to an ungrateful people: "I am ceasing to exercise my functions as President of the Republic. This decision takes effect from midnight tonight."[13] There was no constitutional reason whatsoever for him to resign; but over the past months he had been expressing disillusion to his intimates: "What's the point of all that I am doing? . . . nothing has any importance . . ."[14] Was he seeking an excuse to go? It seemed almost like Samson pulling down the columns at Gaza. After over a decade in residence, only one small van sufficed to remove all the baggage of the General and his wife.

The Republic survived, dedicating itself to improving law and order, and the pursuit of economic and technical efficiency. De Gaulle's departure was in no way followed by the chaos he had so often predicted. This in itself seemed almost like one more sign of disrespect from an ungrateful populace, who had turned on this ageing general just as they had turned on Pétain, Louis-Napoleon, Louis-Phillippe and Charles X before him. De Gaulle took himself off to storm-battered western Ireland, to contemplate. The following year he died at Colombey-les-Deux-Églises—*dans son village et son chagrin.* "France is a widow," declared the new president.

It was indeed the end of an epoch—an epoch which, through the person of de Gaulle, stretched back to the wars in Algeria and Indo-China, and to the Second World War, the Occupation, Liberation and *épuration,* and beyond to the turbulent, depressing 1930s and even to the First World War, where he himself had fallen wounded on the hideous field of Verdun and was made a German prisoner of war. It marked the end of the most personal experiment in modern government that France has known since Napoleon Bonaparte had grasped the crown imperial to place it on his own head in Notre-Dame.

On de Gaulle's departure the inevitable parallels were also drawn to Saint Louis and Philippe-Auguste; but he had given his country a strong regime without ever falling for the institutional brutality of fascism—whatever his foes on the left might say. He had, it could be claimed, saved the country of which he cherished that romantic, mystical "certain idea," once, twice, three times and more. He had changed the intangible map of Europe, and France's position on it. Then, on the turn of a poll, he lost faith. Yet, in the Fifth Republic which he had created, he had left much on which the future could build. For one thing, by some curious kind of osmosis his successors living in the grandeur of the Élysée Palace would all acquire the presidential profile that had been stamped on the coinage by the lofty General—even a man affecting to be so much of the people as François Mitterrand.

# TWENTY

# Another New Start:
# Pompidou to Mitterrand

*. . . Mitterrand as an individual incarnated the French people in all their shades of opinion, rules, certainties and misjudgements.*

—*from M. Maclean,* The Mitterrand Years—Legacy and Evaluation

L IKE MANY OTHER FRENCH LEADERS in the past, "le grand Charles" left office largely unregretted. In the elections of June 1969, Georges Pompidou easily defeated his Socialist opponents. As he moved seamlessly into the Élysée, Gaullism carried on: "Le Roi est mort; vive le Roi!" Until de Gaulle brought him out of merchant banking to replace Debré in 1962, Pompidou had never been in politics. Born in 1911 of robust peasant stock in the Cantal, inheriting all its virtues, a plump, bonhomous, easygoing figure, he hated upheavals such as May 1968. He had been a schoolmaster until the Liberation, teaching at the Lycée Henri IV throughout the Occupation (he once reprimanded a pupil for taking down a portrait of Pétain). The mythology and pretensions of the Gaullist barons of the Resistance irritated him. After the Liberation, rising to be a director of Rothschilds, he found it a career that opened his eyes to what he called the "industrial imperative" for modernising France. For his prime minister, he selected Jacques Chaban-Delmas, a much-decorated Gaullist baron who had risen to the rank of brigadier-general aged twenty-nine, and had been Mayor of Bordeaux since 1947.

Derided in the latter years of the Gaullist regime as de Gaulle's "poodle," but out of favour with de Gaulle, who operated ruthlessly behind

his back, Pompidou had nevertheless struggled on. Now Gaullist policies were faithfully followed under Pompidou: tweaking the tail of
"Uncle Sam," Pompidou pursued France's goal of national independence between the two superpowers, and equally the Gaullist dream of a
third force "super-power" Europe of 250 million people (led, of course,
by France). The large part of French exports—notably arms—continued going to the Arab world (not least Iraq); Pompidou visited the
Soviet Union three times, while Brezhnev came to France twice. But his
Soviet policy got nowhere, whereas in a trip to Chicago in 1970 Pompidou was booed by a pro-Israeli demonstration, prompting Mme. Pompidou to return immediately to France, and blighting Franco-US
relations. The only deviation from Gaullist foreign policy was to permit,
under heavy pressure from the zealous pro-European Edward Heath,
Britain at last to enter the *marché commun,* in 1973.

In September 1970, Chaban launched his American-style "New Society," creating widespread interest but annoying Pompidou with its challenge to presidential policy. Two years later, under a cloud of tax evasion
charges, Chaban was sacked. Otherwise, on the domestic front, dedicated to practical reform, Pompidou's "industrial imperative" achieved
the greatest successes of his period. If the well-favoured Pompidou
resembled anyone, it would have to be Louis-Philippe's François Guizot.
Pompidou oversaw the culmination of what came to be known as the
"Thirty Glorious Years." These were years of unparalleled growth and
prosperity, when—between 1946 and 1975—France's population had
risen by 12 million, equalling growth over the previous century and a
half. To borrow Prime Minister Harold Macmillan's oft-miscontrued
remark, France had "never had it so good." The figures proved it:
between 1960 and 1973 gross domestic product increased at an unprecedented annual rate of 5.8 per cent; between 1968 and 1973 France (now
the fourth largest exporter in the world) doubled her exports, achieving
the highest industrial growth rate in Europe. With living standards up
by 25 per cent, France left Great Britain trailing, was now neck and neck
with Germany, and had reached a level of technology achieved by the
USA and Japan. In almost all sections of society, prosperity was now so
visible that it gave an immense boost to the morale of ordinary Frenchmen and -women. Abroad, for perhaps the first time, France's "techno-
structure" was widely envied. Those French with a sense of history could
see that, beyond Pompidou's input, it might have had something to do
with de Gaulle's mystical resurrection of the *grandeur de la France.*

Consumerism took off. In 1964, only one in four French houses had a fridge; more than double that by 1972. Television, especially new colour television, made a huge impact; households with television rose from a wealthy minority of 13 per cent in 1960 to 80 per cent in 1974. It had become modern-day France's equivalent of running water on every floor—or Henri IV's historic ambition of a "chicken in every pot." On 21 July 1969, 10 million viewers watched the US landing on the moon—with the result that Électricité de France had to switch on emergency power. Prosperity also revealed itself tangibly in the style of life. "Panty girdles" were replaced by panties *tout court,* while young men took to parading in open-neck shirts, *le pull-over* and suede "desert-boots." The most powerful invasion of all, from the USA, came with the arrival of the blue jean, although the practical idea for denim had come centuries back "de Nîmes." This was not the only loosening up in the pant depart-ment: in domestic life, surveys showed that, while in 1969, 17 per cent of couples had lived together before marriage, by 1974 this figure had risen to 37 per cent; while the increase in the rate of premarital conception had jumped from one child in five to one in four.

As of 1954, 58.6 per cent of the French lived in urban, or suburban, areas. By 1975, this figure had risen to 72.8 per cent; a staggering rate of increase of almost 2 per cent a year. A building "frenzy" gripped the country—not all of it by any means felicitous. Infamous high-rise sub-urbs, anathema to many, continued to girdle Paris, creating a new kind of slum that would have challenged a Haussmann; while in its very cen-tre there shot up the barbaric Tour Montparnasse, "crushing the city" with its 210 metres. As mentioned previously, to link the new *banlieues* with the centre came the most brilliant, but formidably expensive, mod-ern express rail system, the RER, envy of all Europe—certainly of peren-nially gummed-up London. Then there was the La Défense complex, dominating the view from the Concorde to the Arc de Triomphe, a great wind-tunnel, an arch commemorating no triumph in either battle or peace. The name of Pompidou was to be attached to only one (singu-larly unfortunate) building. A devotee of modern art, he will be forever associated with the appalling British-designed Centre Pompidou, built on the site of the former Halles. In 1990, a poll conducted among Parisians ranked it as the first monument they wished to see pulled down.

On 2 April 1974, stricken by cancer, which he had bravely struggled to conceal for over two years, Pompidou died in office. At the same time, France plunged into economic crisis, sparked off by soaring oil prices that had followed the Yom Kippur War (Pompidou had given clear support to the Egyptians, thereby increasing disfavour in Washington). So the era of conspicuous prosperity, the Thirty Glorious Years, expired with Pompidou.

THE UNSCHEDULED ELECTION caused by Pompidou's untimely death brought in Valéry Giscard d'Estaing, who had enraged de Gaulle in 1962 by founding a splinter party of independent republicans. A young man in a hurry to leap-frog Chaban, thus had he put himself forward clearly as a potential candidate for the presidency, with strong backing from private sector banks as well as senior civil servants. The 1974 election was a near-run thing. Against Mitterrand's threat of a newly united left, Giscard nipped home with a mere 50.8 per cent of the vote.

Grandson of a member of Vichy's National Council, Giscard (he allegedly added the "d'Estaing") joined the French Army just in time for the invasion of Germany in December 1944. He married well, into the Schneider steel fortune, and became de Gaulle's Minister of Finance at the youthful age of thirty-five, serving from 1962 to 1966, and again under Pompidou in 1969–74. As lean and ascetic as his predecessor was plump and comfortable, Giscard was a typical product of the elitist *hautes écoles.* He endeavoured to "demystify" the presidency by wearing a city plain suit instead of formal dress, and was wont to use the back door of the Élysée—notably on nocturnal trysts. But when it came to his pet subject, the economy, his arrogance knew (and continues to know) no bounds. I remember well an occasion, at a weekend in his country house, when his voice rose to a high pitch of indignation discussing his opposite number, Margaret Thatcher: "Why, *cette Thatcher, cette dame*—she even lectures to me, *moi:* on *economics!*"

He himself tended to talk down to the electorate much as a professor from the *grandes écoles* would have lectured his students. Vain and authoritarian, to some *anglo-saxons* he evoked Louis XIV. He interfered constantly with the daily running of affairs of the government, not only its composition. Giscard was in theory superbly equipped to deal with the economic problems he found; economics was, after all, his forte. But, because of the bad hand passed him by the oil price riggers of Arabia post-1973, in fact nothing went right. Giscard's economic "Stabilisation Plan" failed; unemployment, negligible in the 1960s, soared to 1 million in 1975.*

---

*But it would be 3.4 million by end of 1993.

In foreign affairs, he managed to infuriate the Americans by welcoming Ayatollah Khomeini in October 1978, and then went on, in the best Gaullist tradition, to refuse to boycott the 1980 Moscow Olympics following the Soviet invasion of Afghanistan—and to sign an arms deal with Nicaragua. In Africa, he supported the hyper-corrupt leader of Zaire, Mobutu; while even more extraordinary was his patronage of Bokassa, handing him ff4 million for his Napoleonic-style coronation as emperor. Under him French troops had a disastrous involvement in Rwanda, finally withdrawing in disorder and failure in 1994.

At home, various architectural *projets* were launched during Giscard's presidency—but none was to bear his name. Perhaps his chief epitaph was the extension of women's rights, including the right to abortion. Giscard ended his term under a cloud of scandal concerning diamonds given him by the undesirable Bokassa. Never one to admit defeat, however, he went on to lend his expertise in economics—at high price—to the international lecture circuit, then to re-emerge in old age as father of the controversial EU "constitution."

WITH THE END OF GISCARD'S TERM of office, in 1981, there also came to a close the Gaullist Fifth Republic. In the national elections of May-June of that year, François Mitterrand and his coalition of Socialists and Communists, the recently formed Union pour la Démocratie Française (UDF), boosted by the scandals that had beset the last days of Giscard, swept the board in a truly historic victory. They won with 51.75 per cent of the votes to Giscard's 48.25 per cent. Under Mitterrand, the first Socialist president to be elected by universal suffrage, France would reach the very brink of the twenty-first century; his two-term span of fourteen years would exceed that of any twentieth-century French president including de Gaulle, and would also last longer than Napoleon's term as emperor, while the changes it brought would compare to those occurring under the long-serving great sovereigns of the past, like Louis XIV. These were French leaders to whom this remarkable politician would be compared, in different ways.

The 1981 results were greeted with delirium across France. It was Mitterrand's third attempt on the presidency. He was already sixty-four. Pompidou's triumph in 1969 had seen the left in a disastrous predicament; but Mitterrand had come close to winning in 1974. This time, with consummate political skill, he had woven together a new Front Populaire of the two Socialist Parties and the Communists under its new secretary-general, Georges Marchais. The once mighty French Communist Party (PCF) had seen its share of the vote steadily decline, in tandem with the popularity of its icon, the Soviet Union. It had remained disastrously loyal—through Stalinism, Hungary, Prague, the revelations of Solzhenitsyn, and now Afghanistan and the menace to Poland's Solidarity. The PCF's continuing decline was swiftly to allay fears of the Communist tail wagging the Socialist dog. As an enticement, the party was offered four ministers in Mitterrand's first government, but these would dwindle away along with its national support.

Mitterrand's personal achievement in welding together his winning alliance was remarkable not least because he had done so using the mechanics of the Gaullist Fifth Republic. His victory represented the culmination of an extraordinary political odyssey. He was a man full of fascinating contradictions. Born in Jarnac but with roots in the Morvan, a poor rural area in the *massif central,* and a church-going Catholic, as a dreamy young student in 1934 Mitterrand had joined Colonel de la Rocque's semi-fascist Croix de Feu. In 1939 he was called up, only to be wounded and taken prisoner in the debacle of 1940—significantly, close to the First World War battlefield of Verdun. That, the grimly symbolic name, was a factor that would never cease to preoccupy and haunt him.* The war also brought an abrupt and sad end to a passionate first love affair. In prisoner-of-war camp, Mitterrand gained a reputation as an intellectual, giving a lecture on *Lady Chatterley's Lover.* Somehow, in December 1941, he managed to escape, making his way back to Unoccupied France. There he joined the Vichy government, concerned notably with the plight of prisoners of war. Though he viewed the complexities of Vichy as "bedlam," Mitterrand's admiration for Pétain, primarily as the "Hero of Verdun," was—and remained—eternal; he was photographed with Pétain and received Vichy's Francisque medal—facts that were savagely held against him at the close of his life. He always steadfastly maintained: "I have nothing to be ashamed of."

In June 1942 (like many other Vichyites), he joined the Resistance, still in his mid-twenties. By December the following year he had become important enough (despite his youth) to merit an audience with de Gaulle—and to order the assassination of a leading collaborator with the Gestapo. Explaining the transition years later, Mitterrand declared, baldly: "I became a *résistant* without any agonising." Mitterrand seems

---

*By a most curious coincidence, Captain de Gaulle had also been wounded and taken prisoner at Verdun—in 1916, the year Mitterrand was born.

to have had a good record in the Resistance; he was high on the Gestapo list, and more than once narrowly escaped arrest. It was here that he met and married Danielle. At the same time, among the varied and controversial friends he collected over the years was the dubious René Bousquet, and the writer Marguerite Duras, who herself had a curious relationship with a Gestapo chief.

To us *anglo-saxons* Mitterrand's "reinvention" of himself during the war may seem hard to accept. How could one be anti-Nazi and pro-Vichy? Join the Resistance, and yet continue to be a diehard supporter of Pétain? But then, as we have seen, not all Frenchmen supported either Pétain or de Gaulle; the Resistance was a river that had many tributaries. The wartime enigma of Mitterrand is the essential conundrum of a whole generation of Frenchmen born in the First World War, adult in the Second World War and assuming power and responsibility in the post-1945 world. It is one that enfolds the whole story of wartime France, and is what makes Mitterrand so fascinating a personality, so central to this, or any, history of France.

Out of the war, and his experience with the internecine squabbles of the Resistance and its unpatriotic attachment to Moscow, Mitterrand emerged distrustful of the PCF, and a staunch anti-Communist. He admired American achievements but—with de Gaulle—mistrusted *anglo-saxon* "hegemonism." In 1971, he visited Allende's Chile and was so open in his admiration of Latin America's first elected Marxist president in his defiance of "*Yanqui* imperialism" that there were those who thought that Mitterrand in power would emulate the *compañero Presidente.* They misjudged their man. Though no longer an active Catholic, he would make an annual pilgrimage to his favourite shrine at Vézelay.

When the Algerian War exploded on France in November, as Minister of the Interior under Mendès-France his display of sturdy nationalism "The only possible declaration was war . . . for Algeria is France"[1] was to blow back on Mitterrand in later years. As the Algerian War grew increasingly unpopular with the French electorate, subsequently he endeavoured to make himself appear as a left-wing hero against *Algérie Française.* But if he had one unwavering, fixed star during the post-war years it was Europeanism, frequently stating his conviction—based on his own wartime experiences—that "only European integration could replace European wars."

In October 1959 Mitterrand's access to power was seriously impeded by an extraordinary episode that smacked more of an Alain Delon gangster film than respectable political life. In the "Observatory Affair," as it came to be known, Mitterrand claimed to have been narrowly missed in a machine-gunning attempt on his life. At the same time there were threats against his family. Out of the "affair" Mitterrand gained much publicity, and sympathetic support; until one of those involved, a shady figure called Pesquet, came forward to claim that the whole affair had been faked with his aid. An indictment against Mitterrand was eventually dropped, but the slur remained—indicating a shadowy side to his character.

During his long, prolonged, twenty-three years out of power in the Gaullist era, Mitterrand showed exceptional patience. An unshamed intellectual (something which, in France, was never marked against a politician), he developed a remarkable command of the language, with a cutting sense of humour. Yet he never came over as an inspiring leader. At only 5 feet 7 inches, not much taller than Napoleon, he was seen to compare poorly with a towering de Gaulle, the stately Pompidou and the cultivated patrician loftiness of a Giscard—not to mention Ronald Reagan's lofty height, or the towering Helmut Kohl. When I met Mitterrand, in the "wilderness year" of 1973, at his house in Paris' chic Rue de Bièvre, he struck me as being not noticeably Socialist, more a product of the affluent bourgeoisie, and not obviously electable; in fact I wrote him off as one of yesterday's men. (On this last assessment I was proved totally wrong, eight years later.)

Nevertheless, as with so much of Mitterrand, his affinity with true Socialism was, to put it mildly, enigmatic. When he finally succeeded Mendès-France as leader in the 1970s, he made it immediately plain that he would sup with the Devil and make an electoral alliance with the Communists. The high-principled Mendès had always refused this, recalling how, in the 1930s, the then powerful Communist Party (PCF) had boasted that within the Front Populaire they would "pluck the Socialist chicken." Contemptuous of the ability of the PC leaders, Mitterrand would soon firmly put the boot on the other foot. Scathingly, de Gaulle remarked of Mitterrand at the time of the 1965 elections that he "only had one thing going for him: ambition." But it was this ambition that—endeavouring to appear as a man of the "real left"—would make Mitterrand and the alliance he cobbled together with the Communists electable in 1981. It became clear that he regarded the Socialist Party not as a vessel of holy doctrine, but rather as a weapon for securing a shift in political power that would bring the left to government. (Could similarities be drawn here with Tony Blair and Britain's "New Labour"?) For all these reasons he was, not unfairly, nicknamed "the Florentine," "the

Medici" or "Machiavelli." *Les évènements* of May 1968, revealing as they did serious chinks in the Gaullist armour, gave Mitterrand his first opening, but it would take him another thirteen years to attain power; even then he did not look an obvious winner.

WITH ALL THE ZEAL OF NEWLY EMPOWERED SOCIALISM, Mitterrand's first government (including those four Communist ministers—much to the alarm of the French bourgeoisie, and Washington) set forth at a tremendous clip. Capital punishment was abolished, the most radical drive on decentralisation since the revolution was initiated, and widespread nationalisation of banks and major companies, as well as punitive taxes on wealth, were introduced. The most ambitious reform of terms of employment, the "Auroux Laws," were promulgated—including a thirty-nine-hour week (though a further reduction to thirty-five hours was aimed at) and "workplace councils." Economic planning came to the fore. On every aspect of the cultural scene, sweeping new measures were promoted under live-wire minister Jack Lang. Though, in opposition, Mitterrand had fought long and hard against the constitution of de Gaulle's Fifth Republic, once in office he did nothing to amend it; rather he used the powers it provided to further his own purposes, showing himself resolutely set against all serious constitutional change. Thus imbued with the most wide-ranging authority of any western democracy, as one historian put it, "France became an enormous laboratory in which every aspect of national life came under the microscope."[2]

The Socialist honeymoon of this leader who didn't truly believe in Socialism lasted no more than a year and a half. Facts of life of the economy brought his dreams crashing. A massive balance of payments crisis, and a run on the franc, forced three consecutive, and panicky, devaluations of the currency between 1981 and 1983 (and two again in 1986–87). In March 1983 Mitterrand was forced to perform a radical U-turn, the most dramatic in all France's post-war economic history, adopting a policy of economic *rigueur*—or austerity. It indicated that he had singularly failed to deliver his mandate of two years previously, and now he was abandoning most of the political programme. No lesser politician than Mitterrand could have got away with it, and yet continued to claim that he was "working for Socialism." The Auroux Laws were seen to have caused France to lose out on the global upturn of the 1980s; by 1986 unemployment had soared to 2.5 million, or 12.5 per cent. An estimated

5 million Frenchmen awoke to find themselves "socially excluded," as the gap between rich and poor was not narrowed but actually widened. Was this Socialism? The U-turn put a marker down on Mitterrand's greatest policy failure; though, by adopting unsocialist Keynesian principles, he managed to check, and reverse, inflation. Meanwhile, in 1984, he was forced to accept another reversal—on his programme of educational reform. There were steel industry closures, accompanied by massive demonstrations, and banking debacles. Even mighty Renault was shut down—and under a Socialist regime—while nationalisation schemes were shelved, accompanied by massive sackings of heads of public sector enterprises.

Between 1975 and 1989, the number of French industrial workers declined markedly; growth in terms of GDP fell from 3.3 per cent in the years 1976–80 to only 1 per cent by 1996. (Nevertheless, despite these economic travails, during Mitterrand's first term France still managed to overtake Britain's industrial performance under Thatcher.) The dramatic flight of agricultural workers from the land—falling from 20 per cent of France's working population in 1962 to 10 per cent in 1975, and only 5 per cent by 1990—marked a decimation among the small farmers of traditional society. At the same time, an advanced nuclear power programme took over the majority of French electricity generation, and the trade in arms thrived—notably the Mirages and Exocet missiles that helped Argentina in the Falklands War against Britain.

In January 1984 Mitterrand told France categorically: "The French are beginning to understand: it is the firm that creates wealth, it is the firm that creates employment." Later that year Laurent Fabius replaced Mauroy as prime minister, on a platform of *moderniser et rassembler.* There were no Communists in Fabius' ministry. The growing weakness of the PCF might have encouraged Mitterrand; on the other hand, that January, too, a new threat to the supremacy of the Socialists had arisen with the launch of the Green Party—followed soon thereafter by Le Pen and his National Front. In July 1985 there was an event involving the Greens that was to bring censure down on the Mitterrand government both at home and abroad. A small boat manned by Greens called *Rainbow Warrior* appeared in the South Pacific, intent to sabotage French nuclear tests. It was blown up while in harbour in New Zealand by a mysterious frogman—killing a member of the crew. Eventually the deed was pinned down to the long hand of the French Intelligence Services, over-extending themselves as they so often had during the Algerian War. Nominal sentences were handed out, but swiftly commuted.

Aside from this "little local difficulty," Mitterrand's handling of foreign affairs was generally far more adroit and successful than his performance on the domestic scene. Though just as nationalist-minded as de Gaulle, he was much more supple. Little of his approach bore much connection with traditional French Socialist policy. In the Middle East he switched traditional support for the Arabs to display greater friendliness towards Israel. Turning a blind eye to the bombing of Iraq's nuclear installation in 1981, he paid the first visit of any French president to Tel Aviv the following year; although, in his private cosmogony, the slaughter of Verdun may have ranked closer than the Holocaust—at least in the eyes of one of his biographers, Ronald Tiersky.

He was much more of an "Atlanticist" than de Gaulle had ever been, showing greater affinity towards NATO. With America he had a love-hate relationship, once declaring "I like the Americans, but not their policy . . . My relations with the American ambassadors in Paris always had a touch of trouble." (True: Reagan's ruggedly right-wing, but francophone Ambassador in Paris, Evan Galbraith, was pointedly not awarded the statutory Légion d'Honneur on his departure, having instead to await its bestowal from Chirac.) Mitterrand got on surprisingly well with Reagan personally, though he fell into dispute over four major issues: the sale of arms to Nicaragua was one, the US invasion of Grenada a second. He refused to support US measures against the Soviet Union, following the suppression of Poland's Solidarity,* and was equally resistant to US pressure to stymie the building of the gas pipeline from Siberia to western Europe.† At the same time Mitterrand staunchly backed US deployment in West Germany of intermediate-range missiles (passionately opposed by the left in Britain), and pressed the Germans to accede, too.

To the rising generation, Marxism was coming to be regarded now as a positive evil; it was held to be responsible for the Terror under Stalin as 1789 had led to Robespierre in 1793. To some extent Mitterrand shared de Gaulle's expressed philosophy: "Communism will pass, but Russia is eternal." Yet even the reforming, benign Gorbachev was viewed with far greater suspicion by Mitterrand—and France as a whole—than by the British or Americans.

---

*In December 1981, Foreign Minister Claude Cheysson generated bitter protests when he stated that the arrest of Solidarity activists in Poland was a purely internal affair.

†US reckoning, as of the 1980s, was that—by suddenly cutting it off—the Kremlin could hold the whole of Europe in fee. The pipeline is now a major asset for Europe's energy-hungry markets.

If Mitterrand, however, had any overriding conviction, any *grand projet* in foreign affairs, and enduring over both his terms of office, it was the goal of an indissolubly integrated Europe. To him the symbol that would never leave him was Verdun, and all that it meant to more than one generation of Frenchmen. It was on this battlefield that for most solemn moments of the renewed Franco-German entente Mitterrand would come to stand silently hand in hand with (and dwarfed by) Chancellor Helmut Kohl. For him Germany was the all-important keystone to the future of Europe—as it had been for de Gaulle, though to a lesser extent. He recalled how "the good German" of the inter-war era, Gustav Stresemann, had recognised that "fear of seeing Germany rise again paralyses the will of French politicians and prevents them from thinking objectively." As early as 1982–83 he had seen the importance of the single market and single currency—not least to help stabilise France's own volatile currency. In getting the West Germans to bind themselves to these projects, Mitterrand was particularly aware of "time's winged chariot," appreciating that Helmut Kohl might well be the last German chancellor with whom it would be possible to build Europe. Such intimate and delicate negotiations fell conveniently within the "reserved domain" which de Gaulle's constitution had handed his Socialist successor—and he was progressively aware of his own mortality.

In 1986, following defeat in the legislative elections and the decline in popularity resulting from the accumulated failure of his domestic policies, Mitterrand was forced to accept Jacques Chirac, his conservative opponent, as his prime minister. It was a first experiment, unique to the Fifth Republic so far, of *cohabitation.* And it worked—even though the two fell out over privatisation (Mitterrand found it impossible to realise his electoral pledge of "ni privatisation ni nationalisation"). In the spring of 1988, Mitterrand was reelected for a second seven-year term, with a reduced but still comfortable majority. Considering the record, it seemed a remarkable achievement. He was now able to replace Chirac with a party faithful, Michel Rocard, and concentrate on his continental design in foreign policy. In the meantime, major international events were taking place. In November 1989, the Berlin Wall fell, followed inevitably by the reunification of East and West Germany. Mitterrand—affected by all the residual misgivings of a twentieth-century Frenchman—was hesitant, though not so vocally as Margaret Thatcher.

Close as Mitterrand's love-affair with Kohl was, remarkably it seems

not to have soured his relationship with "the Iron Lady," Margaret
Thatcher, however far she was from sharing his passion for Kohl and the
Germans. Far apart as their political philosophies may have been, there
always remained a curious sympathy between the two. Not only in
remarks to me personally, but also from observations by British diplomats in attendance, it was clear that she had a soft spot for him, and—
on a personal level—was not altogether immune to his legendary charm
for the opposite sex. Briefly, after the Berlin Wall came tumbling down
in November 1989, they shared the same visceral unhappiness about
German reunification, the classic French view being represented by
François Mauriac's famous witticism that he loved Germany so much
that he was always "delighted there were two of them." Nevertheless
Mitterrand went on to press through the historical Maastricht Treaty,
binding France irrevocably to an integrated Europe—and to a reunited,
powerful Germany. (Not everyone noted that the crucial vote occurred
on the 200th anniversary of the defeat of the Prussian Army by French
revolutionaries.)

In 1990, the first Gulf War broke out. A divided French government
joined the coalition, though it caused the resignation of the Foreign Secretary, Jean-Pierre Chevènement. The French contingent, though much
trumpeted on the media, in fact played but a minor role in the campaign—revealing, uncomfortably, how far France had fallen back in
terms of military technology over the thirty years of her isolation from
NATO. Similar weaknesses were compounded when Yugoslavia
exploded into horrendous civil war. A large proportion in France
instinctively supported the Serbs, but militarily she was impotent to
exert much of an influence. The same debility arose in the old-style ex-
colonial intervention in Africa at the time of the Rwanda massacres.

Prior to the 1974 elections, which brought the first prospect of a
Socialist/Communist-dominated administration, there were ugly rum-
bles in the army, which was unwilling to trust national security to a government with pro-Soviet sympathies. But in fact, when Mitterrand
finally came to power in 1981, neither did the army "move," nor was
there even a notable number of officer resignations. In the event, the
French armed forces got on well with Mitterrand's Minister of Defence,
Charles Hernu, and Mitterrand accepted unequivocally the nuclear
strike force, vigorously attacked by the left when out of power.*

---

*In noting the contrast in protests against nuclear weaponry inside France compared
with, for instance, Britain and West Germany in the early 1980s, it has been suggested that

In 1986, Mitterrand had resolutely refused Reagan's request to use French over-fly rights for the punitive bombing of Libya, much to US aggravation. This did not, however, do much to palliate French relations with the Arab world. As immigration from North Africa surged, so race relations deteriorated—fanned by the leader of the National Front, Le Pen. In 1994, the Algerian War once again crossed the Mediterranean to plague France, when a plane was hijacked by the GIA Islamic fundamentalists. A preview of the events of 9/11, the objective was to fly it into the Eiffel Tower; fortunately it was thwarted by France's newly created anti-terrorist unit—which had been much aided by exchange of information with the British, in their experience of dealing with IRA bombers.

IF THERE WAS ONE ASPECT common to both Mitterrand's terms of office in which failure said something about the state of France and Mitterrand's own weaknesses, it has to be the advancement of women. All through the Fifth Republic it had proved singularly difficult to find electable women deputies. When asked about creating a minister for women's affairs, de Gaulle had retorted in a scathing display of old-fashioned male chauvinism: "A ministry? Why not an under-secretaryship of state for knitting?"[3] Even in the latter part of the twentieth century, French husbands could exert a power of veto over their wives working. Only 10 per cent of those admitted to the scientific *grandes écoles* were women; it was not till 1980 that the first woman was allowed to become an *Immortelle* and admitted to the Académie (Marguerite Yourcenar); the first woman stockbroker was not appointed till 1985. There was deep shock when, in 1971, 343 women (including Simone de Beauvoir, Françoise Sagan and Catherine Deneuve) signed a manifesto demanding free and legal abortions, and confessing that they had all had abortions at one time or another. In politics, in the seventies there had only been 33 women deputies out of a total of 586, whereas by 1993 the picture revealed no more than 35 out of 577—the lowest proportion of any European country except for Greece. Equally, during the Mitterrand years the maximum number of women ministers never exceeded eight, of which four were only juniors. If this seems extraordinary for a Socialist regime, supposedly more attuned to the call of femi-

an explanation could be found in the fact that, under the independent *force de frappe,* France has her own "finger on the button," and not that of the US High Command.

nism than the traditional right, it is even more extraordinary for a society where—from the time of Louis XIV and before—women have traditionally wielded so powerful an indirect influence on public affairs.

Under pressure to make amends, in May 1991 Mitterrand appointed France's first woman prime minister, Edith Cresson, in replacement of Rocard. He immediately came under ferocious criticism, it being widely accepted that Cresson had been one of his (numerous) mistresses. Cresson proved an almost unqualified disaster, her principal claim to fame being her, purportedly knowledgeable, assertion that the majority of English males were homosexual. A hint of the political forces aligned against her within the government may be found in an egregious remark made by the macho Corsican, a future Minister of the Interior, Charles Pasqua: "She cannot succeed and her failure will discredit women for a long time." In the event, Cresson lasted less than one unhappy year, to be replaced by Pierre Bérégovoy in April 1992. (He committed suicide, under taint of corruption, the following year.)

BY TRADITION, *les intellos* (intellectuals) constitute a more respected part of French life than they do in Anglo-Saxon countries. Watched over and nurtured by the Académie, they are a source of pride, rather than of mistrust or disdain, as often seems the norm north of the Channel. Thus it was of particular concern that, with the departure of de Gaulle and the towering figure of André Malraux (d. 1976), a kind of caesura was inscribed. Many of the towering grandees departed, and were replaced by few. Sartre died in 1980, aged only seventy-five; his consort, Simone de Beauvoir, in 1986; Raymond Aron in 1983; the philosopher Michel Foucault (of AIDS, aged only fifty-eight) in 1984; Roland Barthes, the literary critic, in 1980 (aged only sixty-five); Fernand Braudel, the great historian of the Mediterranean, in 1985. Who has followed them? Where are the *intellos* today? Commenting with some acerbity, a contemporary British historian, Robert Gildea, picks out the popular Bernard-Henri Lévy as a prototype of the new *intello,*

> with his romantic coiffure and Yves Saint-Laurent silk shirts, marrying the glamorous film star Arielle Dombasle before the cameras in 1993, no longer describing himself as a philosopher but as a writer, and quintessentially a media personality, lovingly exposed to every medium.[4]

In the "postmodern" environment, Gildea goes on to find Adidas to be rated of "equal value to Apollinaire."

The heart of the problem is, of course, the behemoth of television and its progressive dumbing down, which has stricken France in the last half of the twentieth century just as it has Britain and America, though it was longer in putting down its roots in France. In 1964, the average person saw 57 minutes of television a day; already by 1970 this had risen to 115 minutes. As one result, newspapers and magazines suffered; the circulation of *Paris-Match,* for instance, plummeted from 1,800,000 in 1958 to 800,000 over the same period. By 1988 *Le Monde*—France's leading serious newspaper—had a circulation of no more than 387,000, and it was estimated that one-half of the "reading public" never read anything but television magazines. On the brighter side, however, Malraux could reckon that "More people would see a Racine play one night on television than had seen it in the theatre across all the intervening centuries."[5]

As the century ended, there were still nearly 200 million francophones across the globe, and every government in Paris would spend millions of francs energetically protecting France's traditional *mission civilatrice*—indeed, far more energetically than either Britain or the USA attempts to project its culture. As always, the gloriously beautiful French language continued to be officially watched over and nurtured. For long the spokesman at the barricades would be the marvellously mellifluous *sécretaire perpetuelle de l'Académie Française,* Maurice Druon, who contributed an entertaining, but instructive, regular column in *Le Figaro* on "le Bon Français." Nevertheless, by the close of the glum twentieth century, it was beginning to look like a losing battle as such abominations as *le mixed grill, le aftershave, le self-made-man, le zapping* and *le drugstore* became accepted into the language, despite all the efforts of the *beaux sabreurs* of the Académie.

The situation was equally discouraging in the world of film. Even in the ten years 1979–89 the share of the market for French-made films fell from 50 to 34 per cent, displaced by Hollywood, and the French government sought the assistance of the European Commission to get cultural products exempted from free trade agreements in 1993. Similarly with pop music—between 1973 and 1988 numbers of those who attended a pop concert doubled. Nearly all the most popular, as well as the most innovative, music has been Anglo-American—projected into France by radio and MTV. France, however, could boast her own Johnny Halliday as well as the traditional strength of the French *chanson,* with its roots going back to the medieval *jongleurs.*

When André Malraux left the scene in 1969, he had much to be proud of. Apart from the monumental cleaning of Paris and the restoration of the Marais, he had compiled a general inventory of all the artistic riches of France, restored the Chagall ceiling of the Paris Opéra, and achieved the (highly controversial) safe loan of the *Mona Lisa* to New York and the *Vénus de Milo* to Tokyo. There was hardly any corner of the French cultural scene that did not bear his mark; above all, he liked to claim his mission had been to "make accessible to the greatest number of French people the greatest works of humanity, beginning with those of France." On entering the Élysée, Mitterrand, the committed *intello,* dedicated much of his considerable energies to furthering the goals of Malraux, appointing a workaholic called Jack Lang to take over the role of plenipotentiary Minister of Culture, and doubling the state budget. For his massive *grands projets* of building he came to be nicknamed "Mitterramses." Like his great predecessors, from Louis XIV to the two Napoleons, he showed a "somewhat exhibitionistic desire to live on in stone." (It may be interesting to note that de Gaulle was the one president who did not build monuments.) Declaring to his cabinet that "there can be no great policy for France without a great architect," Mitterrand expounded the notion (deriding the unfinished projects of his predecessor, Giscard) that periods of impoverished architecture also correspond with bouts of political debility.

He took the greatest personal interest, even down to choosing the colour of the seats of the new Bastille People's Opéra. "I am attracted by pure geometrical forms," he admitted—the result being the Pei pyramid in the courtyard of the Louvre; controversial at the time but perhaps the most successful of his *grands projets.* The Bastille Opéra was much less successful: tiles regularly fell off its lamentable exterior, as the scenery collapsed inside, and its bad record of strikes provoked wits to compare it unfavourably with the *Titanic*—"at least the ship's orchestra played on!" Three directors gave notice in as many years. Equally disastrous was the hideous modern brutalism of the Arab Institute and new Finance Ministry at Bercy, across the Seine, and—above all—the unappealing new Bibliothèque Nationale, which, for years, simply did not work. In 1994, Mitterrand had the option of closing down the dread and already decaying Centre Pompidou, but decided instead to shore it up—at a cost of something like ffr billion. Rather better, in almost every sense, was the brilliant conversion of the Gare d'Orsay into the new Musée d'Orsay. Nor were the provinces left out, with the creation of a new School of Dance at Marseilles.

Working with a huge budget that would turn his British opposite number green with envy, Jack Lang, described as a "cultural revolutionary," spent fortunes on subsidies for "heritage films." France turned out masterpieces like Pagnol's *Jean de Florette* and *Manon des Sources.* Zola's *Germinal* was the most expensive film ever made in France; nevertheless, it was eclipsed at the box office by *Jurassic Park,* and Lang was roundly criticised for "vulgarising and fossilising literature." Lang sent free videotapes to schools, but was attacked for foisting "official, state-sponsored culture on a mass audience whose own popular tastes are ignored." For all the vast expenditure, the "heritage film" project proved a failure. The tide of *le défi américain* was not stemmed.

Turning to broadcasting, become a jungle of free enterprise since de Gaulle's authoritarian ORTF state monopoly had been demolished, Lang and Mitterrand imposed regulatory conditions with strict rules that applied to ownership as well as content. The new technology of cable and satellite was exorbitantly expensive—and did not work. A new highbrow European cultural channel, which became a joint Franco-German venture called ARTE, was a success, and this was followed—in 1994—by a new educational channel, La Cinquième. It too ran into enormous problems—but at least it was a serious effort to counter "dumbing down," while the British media were heading Gadarene-like in the opposite direction. At the same time, legislation hung on nobly to French privacy laws, protecting public and political figures from media investigation—again in contrast to England. It would take the advent of Chirac to lower the barriers, and the tone of French television.

Busy everywhere, Lang created "Zeniths," popular music halls capable of seating 7000 people, in most major cities. (Wealthy Lyons, curiously, found it could not afford one.) But the vast majority of the French stayed away; in what was an unprecedented "cultural revolution," by 1988 the improvement in public participation was at most an anticipated 3 per cent. Lang's interventions sometimes seemed inconsistent; he would denounce *anglo-saxon* music, ostentatiously refusing to open the festival of American film at Deauville in 1981; yet Sylvester Stallone would receive a decoration for services to art, and in 1993 the inauguration of Euro Disney at the very gates of Paris would seem to have opened the floodgates to American culture at its lowest denominator.

In his public patronage of the arts, Lang's tentacles reached out to writers, too. I well remember leading, in the 1980s, a British delegation of writers and publishers to Fontevraux, burial ground of the Anglo-French Plantagenets, to discuss literature—and specifically what could be done about improving exchanges between the two languages. Exhilarating promises of rich *bourses* for translators came from the French side; nothing materialised. Out of all the expenditure of the Mitterrand-Lang "Cultural Revolution," which lasted until Lang's departure in 1993, no novel was produced in France to compare with Michel Tournier's classic, *Le Roi des Aulnes,* published back in 1970; and did that even sell more than the one million copies that William Boyd achieved in translations from the English? The field of history/biography threw up a few outstanding authors, such as Emmanuel Le Roy Ladurie (*Montaillou,* 1975), and Georges Duby, the medievalist (who sadly died in 1996). As memories of the Occupation receded, there was a spate of introvertive studies of Vichy (viz. Eric Conan and Henry Rousso, *Vichy: Vu Passé qui ne passe pas,* of 1994), and numerous inquests into the mysterious death of Jean Moulin—but few to compare with the American R. O. Paxton. There were some outstanding biographies, such as Jean Lacouture's massive (and heavy-going) works on de Gaulle and Mitterrand. But how few, how pathetically few, compared with the outpouring of history and biography of distinction in the English language over the same period. But then history, over the ages, has seldom been a French forte.

Ask any British publisher attending the Frankfurt Book Fair; they wring their hands at the lack of French titles worthy of translation. What a pathetic return for massive state sponsorship over the past five decades. France has some 3000 literary prizes to offer—but where is the literature? When did she last produce a truly great playwright, novelist, poet, painter or architect of world stature? "There is no Molière or Racine, no Corneille, not even a Le Nôtre," complained the British *Spectator*'s resident *intello,* Paul Johnson. (On the other hand, a Frenchman might riposte, where in Britain are the Shakespeares and Jane Austens?)

Meanwhile, in the world of higher education, which should be producing future leaders of French culture, despite the post-1968 shake-up, a recent survey revealed that only three French institutions could rank among the world's fifty "high-performance" universities. Do courses at the Sorbonne still teach the edict of the literary critic of "structuralism" and "post-structuralism," Roland Barthes: that you don't need to know anything about the life and times of Racine to be able to comprehend his work? On a brighter note, however, at lower levels British educationalists continue to look with some envy at the French secondary school system. The universality of the Napoleonic legacy still applies; there are none of the distortions of the British system of expensive independent schools at one end, and rotten comprehensives at the other. For one thing, there is no such thing as an Eton or a Winchester. In selection for higher education, it is elitism, the elitism of talent, that rules—regardless of social or financial status.*

At least it could be said that Jack Lang did try to arrest the decline in French culture. When Lang departed in 1993, about the best his successor could do in the constant war against the invasion of *franglais* was, rather pathetically, to introduce a law prohibiting the use of English words where good French equivalents existed, enforceable by hefty fines. (Hitler tried something similar with German in the 1930s, and made himself a laughingstock.) Two years later this was followed by a law to allot French songs 40 per cent of the time devoted to popular music on the air. Nevertheless, even the Académie in the most recent edition of its famous dictionary sold the pass to allow 6000 new words into the language, including *le cover-girl, le bestseller* and *le blue jeans.* Yet, in common parlance, there still remained such controversial horrors as "je fais un *booking* pour le *week-end,* avec un *supermodel* anglais (sans *name-dropping*) dans un *twin-set*—si je trouve mon *babysitter,* sans *stress . . .*" Meanwhile the teaching of French abroad dwindles. Given another half-century, will French have become a semi-fossilised language like Welsh or Gaelic, as *intellos* like Maurice Druon fear?

SOME TIME EARLY ON IN HIS FIRST TERM, probably even before the end of 1981, Mitterrand discovered that he had cancer of the prostate. It seems nothing short of miraculous that his doctors, plus his own extraordinary willpower, managed to keep him alive for another fifteen years. Equally remarkable was the fact that his illness was kept secret from the world until well on in his second term—something that would be inconceivable in an Anglo-Saxon democracy, or with the intrusive media of today. To Mitterrand it was simply "None of the public's business." The illness could also account for the urgency with which he pressed to conclude Maastricht and his indissoluble bond with Kohl's Germany. Equally, as the cancer took hold—accompanied by a great

*On a point of some relevance to the de Gaulle-Adenauer and Mitterrand-Kohl entente of the past half-century, a recent survey showed that at many French secondary schools German, not English, was chosen as a second language.

deal of pain—so progressively things went wrong during the latter years of his second term.

Mitterrand's physical decline grew apparent from 1992 onwards, at the same time as disastrous losses in the legislative elections of 1993 brought to office an opposition prime minister, Balladur, leaving Mitterrand bereft of significant political power. Then his past—Vichy—came back to plague him. As Montaigne once observed, "Fortune appears sometimes purposely to wait for the last year of our lives in order to show us that she can overthrow in one moment what she has taken long years to build." First there were the trials, fifty years after the event, of men like Barbie, Touvier, Papon and Bousquet, indicted for terrible crimes during the Occupation, who had somehow slipped through the net of *épuration*. Barbie, the Gestapo "butcher of Lyons" and the only German, was brought to trial in 1987 and sentenced to life imprisonment. Touvier, eventually found guilty of crimes against humanity, was the first Frenchman to be thus condemned; he also received a life sentence. Papon, resurrected as police chief in Paris, was found additionally responsible for the deaths of some 200 Algerian demonstrators in 1961. Bousquet, organiser of the Vél d'Hiv round-up of Jews from wartime Paris, was later assassinated at his Paris flat in 1993, in mysterious circumstances.

Bousquet's wartime connection and continued post-war friendship with Mitterrand was more than just an embarrassment. At the time of the Touvier trial Mitterrand declared, "You cannot live the whole time on memories and grudges." Not all of France agreed with him, but he was nothing if not courageous in consistently sticking up for Pétain and laying wreaths on his grave. Then, in 1994, a bombshell hit France in the shape of a book, *Une Jeunesse Française; François Mitterrand, 1934–1947,* written by professor and journalist Pierre Péan, evidently with Mitterrand's full collaboration. Was it the deathbed confession of an old, mortally ill man? All France was shocked to see, on their television screens, a sick and weak, aged President of the Republic, replying with a faltering voice to penetrating questions about what had become almost a taboo subject—Vichy. He did not lie, but nor did he tell the whole truth. What shocked, however, was not so much the facts revealed, many details of which were already in the public domain, but that the President should have kept quiet about them for so long. Emphatically he declared that he had "nothing to be ashamed of," but it was somehow as if he were holding a mirror, unflattering and highly unpleasant, up to an entire generation of Frenchmen. The whole unhappy story of Vichy, occupation and collaboration, in all its complexity, was once more resurrected.

Would it ever be put to rest? Perhaps only with the death of Mitterrand—or that whole generation, born in the First World War and growing to maturity in the terrible 1940s.

IN MAY 1995, Mitterrand ceded the presidency to his rival, Jacques Chirac. Six months later, on 8 January 1996, in his seventy-ninth year, he finally lost the struggle against cancer. Like de Gaulle, laid to rest at Colombey-les-Deux-Églises, Mitterrand was buried quietly and privately. Alongside his wife of sixty years, Danielle, in solemn mourning there also stood his long-term mistress and their teenage daughter, Mazarine. The existence of his "other family"—known but not talked about—had only been acknowledged two years previously; it was, in effect, the last mystery of this hugely enigmatic figure. Again, it seems extraordinary that it should have taken so long for the media to uncover—perhaps a testament in itself to France's long-held belief that the private life of a public figure is his or her affair alone, and not a matter of public interest.

The funeral of Mitterrand, and with it the revelation of the existence of Mazarine and his "other" family, sparked off once more in the outside world reflections on that unique institution, the French mistress. Harking back to the Middle Ages, great ladies of France, wrote André Maurois, "had a lover when at the same time they had a husband; here were the beginnings of a long tradition."[6] In tandem with it came the mystique of the mistress, a long tradition semi-accepted at many levels of French life. The first definition contained in Larousse gives "person who commands, governs, exercises an authority." Precisely. From earliest days, from Mme. de Maintenon to Pompadour, to Paul Reynaud's Hélène de Portes in 1940, the *maîtresse* of the man-in-power in France has wielded all these powers—often banefully, and far in excess of simply being a lover. She is her man's spy, his sounding box, his confidante, his confessor and his adviser; he trusts her. She fills a role quite distinct from that in any other country, Latin or Anglo-Saxon. Why? A lifelong expert in such matters, Taki of the *Spectator,* comments:

For starters . . . In France, people have always treated sexual conduct as being outside the scope of moral judgment, not so in puritanical Albion . . . Whether the mistress loves the Frenchman is immaterial. She needs him, and he in turn communicates his ideas to her. *C'est tout!* The Frenchman informs his mistress of his power, and discusses it with her . . . The mistress, in fact, is more associated with the thoughts of the man, than the *cinq à sept* quickies she is usually associated with by the popular press. Oh, yes, I almost forgot. Mistresses in France do not go public, no matter what price is dangled in front of them . . .

The French mistress is, as Mitterrand's official, extra-curricular consort was, by definition totally discreet—and quite indispensable. Also, like the high walls that traditionally protect the Parisian bourgeois from prying eyes, privacy of the individual had long been a priority of French life.

HISTORICALLY, THE END OF THE MITTERRAND ERA really came, not with his leaving the Élysée, but with his death in 1996. With him also passed a half-century of French history, one of the most vexing and complex in all its past 2000 years. Mitterrand was to some extent the embodiment of that complexity and—at least from the viewpoint of an outsider—was more representative of France, certainly in its darker side, even than de Gaulle, whose eventful tenure of office he had exceeded. Like Flaubert's Emma Bovary, he could say, with some justification, "I am you." One of Mitterrand's own favourite observations was "Il faut donner du temps au temps." The same might be said of his own career; it is too early to judge. Because of his Machiavellian suppleness (some would call it deviousness), many of even his own Socialist supporters would not rank him with Jaurès or Blum; yet he was more successful than either. He brought the left into meaningful power in France, just as Blair with his "New Labour" did in Britain.

He failed to realise the Socialist egalitarian dreams for which he was elected in 1981; but he triumphantly managed to break the monolithic power of the Communist Party, which had dogged French politics since 1918. Despite failing to resolve France's economic woes—5 million "have-nots" in 1995—he left a France stronger and more competitive in world markets than he had found her. Undoubtedly he displayed some serious errors of judgement, especially in his waning years, such as the appointment of Edith Cresson; but his outstanding achievement has to lie in the integration of Europe, with Kohl's suddenly expanded Germany. Over his fourteen years in office, he came to personify the Presidency as much as any of his predecessors—perhaps even as fully as de Gaulle; certainly he became more a President of all the French than was the latter. (In a curious way, Mitterrand's profile even came to resemble the famous death mask of Napoleon.) In the opinion of the biographer of both de Gaulle and Mitterrand, Jean Lacouture, it could be said he "seemed the most French of all the French of his time."

On balance, can François Mitterrand be denied the rank of a great French statesman? Certainly few have evoked more public discussion.

THE REST IS NOT, AS THEY SAY, HISTORY, but current events. Mitterrand once declared how he saw that "the role of France is to retain its rank." As his successor, Jacques Chirac, took her into the twenty-first century, the third millennium since her remarkable story began, many of France's problems continued to be familiar, and seemingly endemic: unemployment and labour unrest, demands for higher wages for shorter working hours, too many students pursuing places in outdated universities, the social demands of an ever-ageing population, corruption tainting even the highest political circles, and serious differences with the *anglo-saxons,* for instance over war in Iraq. More than ever before the question is whether, in the new world order of American Empire—or what the French call *hyperpuissance* and a dramatically weightier Germany, France can reasonably maintain this rank—or at least preserve the precious identity that France and the French have so assiduously sought to promote, and preserve, over all past centuries. Are her resources up to her determination to remain a great culture, and a world power? When all is considered, perhaps Rudyard Kipling judged France aright back in 1913:

> Broke to every known mischance, lifted over all
> By the light sane joy of life, the buckler of the Gaul;
> Furious in luxury, merciless in toil,
> Terrible with strength that draws from her tireless soil;
> Strictest judge of her own worth, gentlest of man's mind,
> First to follow Truth and last to leave old Truths behind—
> France, beloved of every soul that loves its fellow-kind![7]

# SOURCE NOTES

### ONE  Beginnings: Caesar to the Capetians

1. Druon, *The History of Paris*, 28.
2. Druon, ibid., 36.
3. Druon, ibid., 70.
4. Maurois, 55.
5. Eco, 5.
6. Eco, 8.

### TWO  A Golden Age: Abelard to Philippe-Auguste

1. Gilson, 74, 76, 124.
2. Bjerken, M. P., *Medieval Paris,* Princeton, 1973, 61.
3. Druon, 84.
4. Peter of Blois, q. Trevelyan, 141.
5. Lavisse, Tome III, Vol I, 72.
6. Paien Gatineau, q. Lavisse, 280.
7. Lavisse, ibid., 101.
8. Lavisse, ibid., 109.
9. Lavisse, ibid., 121.
10. Lavisse, ibid., 148.
11. Lavisse, ibid., 158.
12. Evans, 231.
13. Maurois, 57.
14. Le Breton.
15. Lavisse, ibid., 191.
16. Lavisse, ibid., 192.
17. Lavisse, ibid., 195.
18. Le Breton, 175.
19. Trevelyan, 168.
20. Lavisse, ibid., 202.

### THREE  Middle Ages: "Saint-Louis" to Philippe le Bel

1. Baldwin, pp. 107, 185–6.
2. Rashdall, 335.
3. Toynbee, A., *Cities of Destiny,* London, 1967, 192.
4. Bjerken, M. P., 105.
5. Holmes, 81.
6. Holmes, 40, 57.
7. Holmes, 103.
8. Holmes, 163.
9. Maurois, 75.
10. Maurois, 105.
11. Lavisse, Tome III, Vol I, 279.
12. Druon, 95.
13. Castries, 78.
14. Lavisse, ibid., 30.
15. Maurois, 63.
16. Laffont, 45.
17. Lavisse, ibid., 121.
18. Jordan, 214.
19. Boussard, 154.
20. Lavisse, ibid., 183.
21. Lavisse, ibid., 192.
22. Lavisse, ibid., 199.
23. Druon, *The Accursed Kings,* Vol 3, 49; Vol 6, 87, 327.

FOUR　The Second "100 Years' War":
France Survives and Joins the Renaissance

1. Druon, *The Strangled Queen,* 11.
2. Trevelyan, 225.
3. Maurois, 96.
4. Maurois, 97.
5. Kendall, 197.
6. Commynes, q. Kendall.
7. Kendall, 290.
8. Maurois, 136.
9. Maurois, 142–3.
10. Castries, 156.


FIVE　Henri II's Succession: The Wars of Religion

1. *The Rise of The Dutch Republic,* I, New York, 1856, v.
2. See Sutherland.
3. Maurois, 164.
4. Garrisson, 153.
5. Garrisson, 153.
6. Lavisse, Tome VI, Vol I, 33–4, 318.
7. See Franklin, *Journal.*
8. Franklin, ibid., 159.
9. Garrisson, 159.
10. Garrisson, 160.
11. Greengrass, 65.


SIX　Henri IV: Good Sense and Good Taste

1. Garrisson, 169.
2. Wolfe, 151.
3. Lavisse, 388.
4. Maurois, 170.
5. Henri IV, 6 August, 1590; Franklin, 202–5.
6. Berthault, from Ehrlich, 211–12.
7. Ehrlich, B., *Paris on the Seine,* London, 1962, 93.
8. Sutcliffe, 23.
9. Greengrass, 253.
10. Greengrass, 148.
11. Lavisse, Tome VI, Vol II, 129.


SEVEN　Louis XIII: Richelieu to the Fronde

1. Maurois, 175.
2. Ranum, 195.
3. Gallienne, R. Le, *From a Paris Garret,* London, 1943, 42.
4. Maurois, 191.
5. Johnson, 78.
6. Olivier d'Ormesson, in 1641.
7. Voltaire, 27.
8. Voltaire, 32.
9. Voltaire, 37.
10. Voltaire, 33.
11. Voltaire, 49.


EIGHT　The Age of Louis XIV

1. Voltaire, 51.
2. Sévigné, 31.
3. Sévigné, 240.
4. Sévigné, 240–1.

5. Nuspe, research notes 22–3.
6. Saint-Simon, 145.
7. From Cronin, 148.
8. Trout, A., *City on the Seine; Paris in the Time of Richelieu and Louis XIV,* London, 1966, 177.
9. *Complete Letters of the Duchess of Orléans,* London, 1843, 171.
10. Maurois, 220.
11. Maurois, 224.
12. Albert Sorel, q. Church, 63.

## NINE  Louis XV: Towards the Deluge

1. Pope, *Rape of the Lock.*
2. Du Plessix Gray, 30.
3. Du Plessix Gray, 270.
4. Mitford, 8.
5. Mitford, frontispiece.
6. Laver, 68.
7. Du Plessix Gray, 46.
8. Samia, I. S., q. Du Plessix Gray, 141.
9. Brookhiser, 104, 107, 126.

## TEN  The Great Revolution

1. De La Tour du Pin, 103.
2. De La Tour du Pin, 105.
3. De La Tour du Pin, 108.
4. De La Tour du Pin, 110.
5. Duplessix Gray, 292–3.
6. Davenport, 158–9.
7. Maurois, 273.
8. De La Tour du Pin, 136.
9. Brookhiser, 121–2.
10. Schama, 540.
11. Fraser, A., *Marie Antoinette,* London, 2001, 323.
12. Brookhiser, 144.

## ELEVEN  The Age of Napoleon

1. Lanzac de Laborie, I, 95–6, 100.
2. Balzac, *Une Ténébreuse Affaire* [*La Comédie Humaine*].
3. In Paris, 2498 total; 1119 on the Concorde alone.
4. Robiquet 141.
5. Baring, M., *Have You Anything to Declare,* 198.
6. By comparison, it is worth noting how Allied commanders of the Second World War, like Montgomery, Eisenhower, Bradley and Patton, were all well into their fifties.
7. *Le Figaro,* 64.
8. Cooper, Duff, *Tallyrand,* New York, 1932, 272.
9. Cooper, ibid., 123.
10. Admiral Mahan.
11. Horne, A., *The Age of Napoleon,* London, 2004.
12. Las Cases, II, 120.
13. De Broglie, 252.
14. Barnett, 211.

## TWELVE   Restoration and Revolt

1. Mansel, 81.
2. Mansel, 27.
3. Keates, 247.
4. Willms, 227.
5. Balzac, *Lettres à Mme Hanska*, I, 534.
6. See Horne, A., *The Fall of Paris: The Siege and the Commune 1870–71*, London, 1965.
7. From *Fille aux Yeux d'Or*.
8. *Père Goriot*, 1–3.
9. Laver, 174.
10. Willms, 200.
11. Hugo, 180–4.
12. Mansel, 369.
13. Guedalla, 54.
14. Maurois, 380.
15. Maurois, 393.
16. Mansel, 413.


## THIRTEEN   Empire and Siege

1. Daumier exhibition, Paris, 1999.
2. Haussmann, 54.
3. Mansel, 425.
4. Horne, A., *The Fall of Paris: The Siege and the Commune 1870–71*, London, 1965, 25–6.
5. Howard, 57.
6. See Horne, A., *The Fall of Paris: The Siege and the Commune 1870–71*, London, 1965; *The Terrible Year; the Paris Commune 1871*, London, 1971, 2004.
7. Mansel, 429.
8. Horne, A., *The Fall of Paris: The Siege and the Commune 1870–71*, London, 1965, 176.
9. Horne, A., *The Fall of Paris: The Siege and the Commune 1870–71*, London, 1965, 218.
10. Cobb, 128–31.


## FOURTEEN   The *Belle Epoque* and the Road to War

1. Horne, A., *Price of Glory*, 6.
2. Tuchman, *Proud Tower*, 63.
3. Tuchman, ibid., 80.
4. The Reinach and Dreyfus families were interrelated.
5. Willms, 335.
6. Wharton, 117.
7. From Cronin, *Paris on the Eve*, 419.


## FIFTEEN   The Great War and Versailles

1. Gide, *Journal*, 6.9.1914.
2. Bertie I, 3–9.
3. Horne, *Price of Glory*, 13.
4. Tuchman, *The Guns of August*, 400.
5. Poincaré, III, p. 136.
6. See Horne, A., *Price of Glory*, 190.
7. Horne, A., *Price of Glory*, 340.
8. Dallas, 174.
9. Dallas, 348.
10. Watt, 4.
11. Hankey, 153.
12. Watt, 410.
13. Lloyd George, 267.
14. Nicolson, 366.
15. Nicolson, 367–8.
16. MacMillan, 497.

## SIXTEEN  Years of Illusion

1. See Horne, A., *To Lose a Battle*, 37.
2. Horne, A., *To Lose a Battle*, 55.
3. Wiser, W., *The Crazy Years: Paris in the Twenties*, London, 1938, 11.
4. Horne, A., *To Lose a Battle*, 87.
5. In 1945, Maurras was sentenced to life imprisonment as a collaborator.
6. Berlin, *Diary*, 125.
7. Johnson, P., *Modern Times: The World from the Twenties to the Eighties*, New York, 1983.
8. Quoted Horne, *To Lose a Battle*, 235.
9. Horne, A., *To Lose a Battle*, 236.

## SEVENTEEN  The Darkest Years

1. It was to be replayed by Israelis in 1973—with almost equal success.
2. See Horne, A., *Seven Ages of Paris*, Chapter 19.
3. *Premier journal parisien*, Paris, 1980.
4. Beevor and Cooper, 253.
5. Jünger, 72.
6. F. Huré, 4.4.01.
7. Jünger, 136.
8. Cointet, 232.
9. Schoenbrun, 76.
10. Cointet, 207–8.
11. Beevor, 255.
12. R. Paxton, 344, 422.
13. Collins, 173.
14. Collins, 216.
15. Galtier-Boissière, 253.
16. *Journal d'un Homme Occupé*, q. Pryce-Jones, 197.
17. Collins, 272.
18. De Gaulle, 308.
19. Collins, 334.
20. De Gaulle, 313–14.
21. Muggeridge, 211–12.
22. Collins, 336.
23. Collins, 342.

## EIGHTEEN  After the Liberation

1. Beevor, 88, 92.
2. Muggeridge, 219–24.
3. Beevor, 192.
4. Giles, 17.
5. Mauriac, *Journal*, q. Beevor, 116.
6. Elgey, 32.
7. De Gaulle, II, Auriol, 13.
8. Auriol, V., *Journal du Septennat*, 1947–1954, 529.
9. See Horne, A., *A Savage War of Peace* and *The French Army in Politics*, *1870–1970*.
10. Gorce, 391.
11. Thurman, 500.
12. MacMillan, H., *Diaries*, 29–30 June 1958, London 2003.

## NINETEEN  The General's Republic

1. Horne, *A Savage War of Peace*, 369.
2. Conversation with the author, 1973.
3. Q. Dulong, 63.
4. To the author, 1979.

5. See Horne, A., *A Savage War of Peace*, 312.
6. De Gaulle, *Memoirs of Hope*, p. 305.
7. Flanner, 88–91.
8. Flanner, 138.
9. Druon, *L'Avenir en désarroi*, 76.

10. Druon, 40.
11. Aron, *Memoirs*, 232.
12. Aron, *The Elusive Revolution*, 15.
13. Dulong, 229.
14. Dulong, 238.

TWENTY    Another New Start: Pompidou to Mitterrand

1. See Horne, A., *The French Army and Politics*, 78.
2. Serge Berstein; q. Maclean, 54.
3. Gildea, 120.

4. Gildea, 157.
5. Gildea, 160–1.
6. Maurois, 75.
7. Kipling, *France at War*, London, 1915.

# BIBLIOGRAPHY

A full bibliography of the History of France would, of course, run into thousands of pages. Below I have just tried to list sources that I have consulted for this book.

Amouroux, H., *La Grande Histoire des Français sous l'Occupation,* vols viii & ix, Paris, 1988–91
Ardagh, J., *The New French Revolution,* New York, 1968
Aron, R., *The Elusive Revolution: Anatomy of a Student Revolt,* New York, 1969
———. *Histoire de la Libération de la France,* Paris, 1959
———. *Histoire de Vichy,* Paris, 1954
———. *Memoirs,* New York, 1990
Ashley, M., *Louis XIV and the Greatness of France,* London, 1946
Babelon, J.-P., *Nouvelles Histoires de Paris,* Paris, 1986
Baldick, R. (ed.), *Pages from the Goncourt Journal,* London, 1962
Baldwin, J. W., *The Government of Philip Augustus: Foundations of French Royal Power in the Middle Ages,* Berkeley, 1986
Baldwin, J. W. (eds. Robert L. Benson and Giles Constable), *Masters at Paris from 1179 to 1215: A Social Perspective in Renaissance and Renewal in the Twelfth Century,* Cambridge, Mass., 1982
Balzac, H. de, *La Comédie Humaine* (12 vols), Paris, 1976–81
Baudot, F., *Mémoire du Style Empire,* Paris, 1990
Beauvoir, S. de, *La Force de l'Âge,* Paris, 1967
Beevor, A., and A. Cooper, *Paris after the Liberation,* London, 1994
Berstein, S., and J.-P. Rioux, *The Pompidou Years, 1969–1974,* Paris, 2000
Bertie, Lord, *Diaries 1914–18* (2 vols), London, 1924
Boglie, A.-C.-L.-V. duc de, *Souvenirs, 1785–1870,* Paris, 1886
Boothe, C., *European Spring,* London, 1941
Brasillach, R., *Journal d'un Homme Occupé* (6 vols), Paris, 1964
Bredin, Jean-Denis, *The Affair: The Case of Alfred Dreyfus,* New York, 1986
Briggs, A., *Fins de Siècle: How Centuries End, 1400–2000,* London, 1996
Briggs, R., *Early Modern France, 1560–1715,* Oxford, 1977
Brookhiser, R., *Gentleman Revolutionary—Gouverneur Morris,* New York, 2003
Bruce, E., *Napoleon and Josephine: An Improbable Marriage,* London, 1995
Burns, Michael, *Dreyfus: A Family Affair, 1789–1945,* London, 1992
Bury, J. P. T., *France 1914–1940,* London, 1949
Castelnau, J.-T. de, *Le Paris de Louis XIII,* Paris, 1928
Castries, Duc de, *The Lives of the Kings and Queens of France,* London, 1979
Champion, P., *Paris au Temps des Guerres de Religion,* Paris, 1938

Chaptal, J.-A.-C., *Mes Souvenirs sur Napoléon,* Paris, 1893

Chastenet, J., *Une Époque de Contestation: La Monarchie Bourgeoise (1830–48),* Paris, 1976

Chateaubriand, F. R., *Mémoires d'Outre-Tombe* (3 vols), Paris, 1951

Church, W. F. (ed.), *The Greatness of Louis XIV: Myth and Reality?* London, 1959

Clemenceau, G., *Discours de Guerre,* Paris, 1968

Cobb, R., *French and Germans, Germans and French,* London, 1983

———. *Promenades,* London, 1980

Cohen, E., *Ninon de Lenclos,* London, 1971

Collins, L., and D. Lapierre, *Is Paris Burning?,* London, 1965

Courteault, H., *La Fronde à Paris,* Paris, 1930

Courtin, R., *De la Clandestinité au Pouvoir: Journal Parisian, Août-Septembre 1944,* Paris, 1994

Cronin, V., *Louis XIV,* London, 1964

———. *Paris: City of Light, 1919–1939,* London, 1994

———. *Paris on the Eve, 1900–1914,* London, 1989

Coward, D., *A History of French Literature: From Chanson de Geste to Cinema,* Oxford, 2002

Dallas, G., *1918: War and Peace,* London, 2000

Davies, N., *Europe,* London, 1996

Diefendorf, B., *Beneath the Cross,* Oxford, 1991

Dos Passos, J., *1919,* New York, 1932

———. *Mr. Wilson's War,* London, 1963

Druon, Maurice, *L'Avenir en Désarroi,* Paris, 1968

———. *The Accursed Kings* (6 vols), London, 1956–61

———. *The History of Paris from Caesar to St. Louis,* London, 1969

Dulong, C., *La Vie Quotidienne à l'Élysée au temps de Charles de Gaulle,* Paris, 1974

Dupeux, G., *French Society 1789–1970,* London, 1976

Duffy, E., *Saints and Sinners: A History of the Popes,* London, 1997

Eco, U., *Art and Beauty in the Middle Ages,* Milan, 1986/New Haven, 1986

Elgey, G., *Histoire de la IVe République,* vol 1, Paris, 1965

Evans, J. (ed.), *The Flowering of the Middle Ages,* London, 1966

Evenson, N., *Paris: A Century of Change, 1878–1978,* Yale, 1979

Fabre-Luce, A., *Les Cent Premiers Jours de Giscard,* Paris, 1974

Fenby, J., *France on the Brink,* London, 1998

Flanner, J., *Paris Journal, 1944–1965,* New York, 1965

———. *Paris Was Yesterday,* New York, 1972

Flaubert, G., *L'Éducation Sentimentale,* Paris, 1864

Franklin, A., *Journal du Siège de Paris en 1590,* Paris, 1876

———. *La Vie Privée d'Autrefois,* Paris, 1973

Frieda, L., *Catherine de Medici,* London, 2003

Fuller, J. F. C., *The Decisive Battles of the Western World* (vol II), London, 1957

Gallieni, General, *Mémoires; Défense de Paris, 25 Août–11 Septembre, 1914,* Paris, 1920

Galtier-Boissière, *Journal,* Paris, 1944

Garrioch, D., *The Making of Revolutionary Paris,* Berkeley, Calif., 2002

Garrisson, J., *Henry IV,* Paris, 1984

———. *L'Édit de Nantes et sa Révocation: Histoire d'une Intolérance,* Paris, 1985

———. *Marguerite de Valois,* Paris, 1994

Gaulle, C. de, *Mémoires de Guerre,* Paris, 1956

———. *Memoirs of Hope,* London, 1971

Geremek, B., *The Margins of Society in Late Medieval Paris,* New York, 1987

Gildea, R., *France since 1945,* Oxford, 1995

Giles, F., *The Locust Years: The Story of the Fourth French Republic, 1946–1958,* London, 1991

Gillet, L., *Correspondence avec Romain Rolland,* Paris, 1949

Gilson, E., *Héloise and Abelard,* Michigan, 1960

Giscard d'Estaing, V., *Le Pouvoir et la Vie,* Paris, 1988

Goncourt, E., and J. de (ed. R. Ricatte), *Journal. Mémoires de la Vie Littéraire* (4 vols), Paris, 1958

Gorce, P. de la, *The French Army: A Military-Political History,* London, 1963

Gray, F. du Plessix, *At Home with the Marquis de Sade,* New York, 1998

Grayson, C. T., *Woodrow Wilson: An Intimate Memoir,* New York, 1960

Greengrass, M., *France in the Age of Henri IV,* New York, 1984

Guedalla, P., *The Hundred Years,* London, 1936

Guéhenno, J., *Journal des Années Noirés, 1940–1944,* Paris, 1947

Hallam, E. M., and J. E. Everard, *Capetian France,* Harlow, 2001

Hankey, M., *The Supreme Control at the Paris Peace Conference, 1919: A Commentary,* London, 1963

Haussmann, G.-E., *Mémoires* (3 vols), Paris, 1894

Heine, H., *Französische Zustände,* in *Sämtliche Schriften,* Munich, 1975

Holmes, U. T., *Daily Living in the Twelfth Century—Based on the Observations of Alexander Neckam in London and Paris,* Madison, Wis., 1952

Hoover, H., *The Ordeal of Woodrow Wilson,* New York, 1958

Horne, A., *The Age of Napoleon,* London, 2004

———. *The Fall of Paris: The Siege and the Commune, 1870–71,* London, 1965

———. *The French Army and Politics, 1870–1970,* London, 1984

———. *How Far from Austerlitz? Napoleon 1805–1815,* London, 1996

———. *The Price of Glory: Verdun 1916,* London, 1962

———. *A Savage War of Peace: Algeria, 1954–1962,* London, 1977

———. *Seven Ages of Paris,* London, 2002

———. *The Terrible Year: The Paris Commune 1871,* London, 1971, 2004

———. *To Lose a Battle:* France, 1940; London, 1969

Howard, M., *The Franco-Prussian War,* London, 1961

Howarth, T. E. B., *Citizen-King,* London, 1961

Jack, B. E., *George Sand,* London, 1999

Jackson, J., *France: The Dark Years, 1940–1944,* Oxford, 2001

Jackson, J. H., *Clemenceau and the Third Republic,* London, 1946

Jaurès, Jean, *Histoire Socialiste de la Révolution Francaise, 1789–1900* (vol 6 for Napoleon), Paris 1901

Johnson, D., *A Concise History of France,* London, 1971

Jordan, W. C., *The French Monarchy and the Jews,* Philadelphia, 1989

Jünger, E.: *Strahlungen,* Tübingen, 1949

Kendall, P. M., *Louis XI,* London, 1971

Keates, J., *Stendhal,* London, 1994

Kipling, R., *France at War,* London, 1915

Lacouture, J., *De Gaulle: Le politique, 1944–1959* (vol 2), Paris, 1985

Lanzac de Laborie, Léon de, *Paris sous Napoléon,* Paris, 1900–1913

Las Casas, E. de, *Le Mémorial de Sainte-Hélène,* Paris, 1951

Lavedan, E., *Nouvelle Histoire de Paris: Histoire de l'Urbanisme à Paris,* Paris, 1975

Laver, J., *The Age of Illusion, Manners and Morals, 1750–1848,* London, 1972

Lavisse, E., *Histoire de France depuis les Origines jusqu'à la Révolution* (9 vols), Paris, 1901–11

Le Breton, G., *Gesta Philippi Augusti* (2 vols), Paris, 1882–5

Lewn, Gwynne and C. Lucas (ed.), *Beyond the Terror: Essays in French Regional and Social History, 1794–1815,* Cambridge, 1983

Liddell Hart, B. H., *History of the World War, 1914–1918,* London, 1934

Lloyd George, D., *Memoirs of the Peace Conference,* New Haven, 1939

Lough, John, *An Introduction to Seventeenth Century France,* London, 1954

Maclean, M., *The Mitterrand Years: Legacy and Evaluation,* London, 1998

MacMillan, M., *Peacemakers: The Paris Peace Conference of 1919 and Its Attempt to End War,* London, 2001

Magne, Émile, *La Vie Quotidienne au temps de Louis XIII,* Paris, 1964

Mansel, P., *Paris Between Empires, 1814–1852,* London, 2001

Mauriac, F., *Journal* (5 vols), Paris, 1953

Maurois, A., *History of France,* Paris, 1949

May, G., *Stendhal and the Age of Napoleon,* New York, 1977

McPhee, P., *A Social History of France 1789–1914,* London, 1992

Mendès-France, P., *The Pursuit of Freedom,* London, 1956

Mercier, S. de, *Paris Pendant la Révolution 1789–1798,* Paris, 1962

Michelet, J., *Histoire de France* (17 vols), Paris, 1901–11

Mitford, Nancy, *Madame de Pompadour,* London, 1954

———. *The Sun King,* London, 1966

Mongrédien, G., *La Vie Quotidienne sous Louis XIV,* Paris, 1948

———. *Louis XIV,* Paris, 1948

———. *Madame de Montespan et L'Affaire des Poisons,* Paris, 1953

Monzie, A. de, *Ci-Devant,* Paris, 1942

Morris, Gouveneur (ed. B. C. Davenport) *A Diary of the French Revolution,* London, 1939)

Muggeridge, M., *Chronicles of Wasted Time: The Infernal Grove,* London, 1973

Murphy, R., *Diplomat among Warriors,* London, 1964

Nicolson, H., *Peacemaking, 1919,* London, 1933

Ousby, I., *Occupation: The Ordeal of France, 1940–1944,* London, 1997

*Oxford Book of French Verse,* Oxford, 1907/1957

Painter, G., *Marcel Proust: A Biography,* London, 1989

Paxton, R. O., *Vichy France: Old Guard and New Order,* New York, 1982

Péan, P., *Une Jeunesse Française,* Paris, 1994

Pevitt, C., *Philippe Duc d'Orléans: Regent of France,* New York, 1997

Peyrefitte, Alain, *The Trouble with France,* New York, 1981

Poincaré, R., *Memoirs* (4 vols), London, 1926

Pompidou, G., *Pour Rétablir une Vérité,* Paris, 1982

Powicke, F. M., *The Thirteenth Century, 1216–1307,* Oxford, 1962

Rabelais, F., *Pantagruel,* Paris, 1534–64

Radice, B. (ed.), *The Letters of Abelard and Heloise,* London, 1974

Ragache, G., and J.-R., *La Vie Quotidienne des Écrivains et des Artistes sous l'Occupation, 1940–1944,* Paris, 1988

Ranum, O., *Paris in the Age of Absolutism,* New York, 1968

Reichardt, J. F., *Vertrauten Briefe aus Paris, Geschrieben in den Jahren 1802 und 1803,* Hamburg, 1804

Rémusat, C. de, *Mémoires de ma Vie,* Paris, 1958

Retz, Cardinal (tr. by P. Dovall), *Memoirs,* Dublin, 1777

Rioux, J.-P., *The Fourth Republic* (tr. Godfrey Rogers), *1944–1958,* London, 1987

———. *La France d'un Siècle à l'Autre, 1914–2000* (dictionnaire critique), Paris, 1999

Robiquet, J., *Daily Life in France under Napoleon,* London, 1962

Saint-Simon, Duc de, *Memoirs* (8 vols), Paris, 1983–88

Schama, S., *Citizens: A Chronicle of the French Revolution,* London, 1989

Schoenbrun, D., *Soldiers of the Night,* New York, 1980

Seignobos, C. (tr. C. A. Phillips), *A History of the French People,* Paris, 1933

Sévigné, Madame de (Bibliothèque de la Pléiade), *Lettres,* Paris, 1953–57

Seward, Desmond, *The Bourbon Kings of France,* London, 1976

Shattuck, Roger, *The Banquet Years,* London, 1955

Shennan, J. H., *France before the Revolution,* London, 1983

Shirer, W. L., *Berlin Diary,* Paris, 1942

Sparrow, E., *Secret Service: British Agents in France, 1792–1815,* London, 1999

Sutcliffe, A., *Paris: An Architectural History,* New Haven, 1993

Sutherland, N. M., *The Massacre of St. Bartholomew and the European Conflict, 1559–1572,* London, 1973

Tapié, V.-L., *France in the Age of Louis XIII and Richelieu,* Cambridge, 1984

Thiers, A., *Histoire du Consulat et de l'Empire,* Paris, 1932

Thompson, J. W., *The Wars of Religion in France, 1559–1576,* New York, 1958

Thurman, J., *Secrets of the Flesh: A Life of Colette,* New York, 1999

Tilly, C., *The Contentious French,* Cambridge, 1968

Tocqueville, A. de, *L'Ancien Régime,* Oxford, 1925

Tombs, Robert, *The War Against Paris, 1871,* Cambridge, 1981

Tour du Pin, Madame de La (ed. and tr. F. Harcourt), *Memoirs,* London, 1970

Trevelyan, G. M., *History of England,* London, 1926

Tuchman, B., *August 1914,* London, 1962

———. *A Distant Mirror: The Calamitous 14th Century,* New York, 1978

———. *The Proud Tower,* London, 1996

Vidal-Nacquet, P., *Torture: Cancer of Democracy,* London, 1963

Voltaire, F. M. A., *The Age of Louis XIV,* London, 1752

Watt, R. M., *The Kings Depart,* New York, 1968

Wawro, G., *The Franco-Prussian War: The German Conquest of France in 1870–1871,* New York, 2003

Weber, E., *Peasants into Frenchmen,* London, 1977

Weber, E., *The Hollow Years: France in the 1030s,* London, 1995

Wedgwood, C. V., *Richelieu and the French Monarchy,* London, 1949

Wharton, E., *French Ways and Their Meaning,* New York, 1919

White, E., *Proust,* London, 1999

Willms, J. (tr. E. L. Kanes), *Paris: Capital of Europe from the Revolution to the Belle Epoque,* New York, 1997

Wolfe, M., *Piety and Political Allegiance: The Duc de Nevers and the Protestant Henri IV, 1589–1593,* London, 1988

Wood, J. B., *The King's Army: Warfare, Soldiers and Society during the Wars of Religion in France, 1562–1576,* Oxford, 1996

Zeldin, T., *France, 1848–1945* (2 vols), Oxford, 1973, 1977

Ziegler, P., *The Black Death,* London, 1969

Zola, É., *Une Page d'Amour; les Rongon-Macquart* (5 vols), Paris, 1960

# INDEX

# ALSO BY ALISTAIR HORNE

*"Knowledgeable and colorful, written with gusto and love. . . .
[An] ambitious and skillful narrative that covers the history
of Paris with considerable brio and fervor."*
—Los Angeles Times Book Review

## SEVEN AGES OF PARIS

In this luminous portrait of Paris, celebrated historian
Alistair Horne gives us the history, culture, disasters, and
triumphs of one of the world's truly great cities. From the
rise of Philippe Auguste through the reigns of Henry IV and
Louis XIV (who abandoned Paris for Versailles); Napoleon's
rise and fall; Baron Haussmann's rebuilding of Paris (at the
cost of much of the medieval city); the Belle Epoque and the
Great War that brought it to an end; the Nazi Occupation,
the Liberation, and the postwar period dominated by de
Gaulle—Horne brings the city's highs and lows, savagery
and sophistication, and heroes and villains splendidly to
life. With a keen eye for the telling anecdote and pivotal
moment, he portrays an array of vivid incidents to show us
how Paris endures through each age, is altered but always
emerges more brilliant and beautiful than ever. *Seven Ages
of Paris* is a great historian's tribute to a city he loves and
has spent a lifetime learning to know.

History/1-4000-3446-9

VINTAGE BOOKS
Available at your local bookstore, or call toll-free to order:
1-800-793-2665 (credit cards only).